Athans: His luck finally

By DAVID AGNEW
Staff Writer

It didn't start out to be one of George Athans' better days.

The 23-year-old native of Kelowna, B.C., fell on his first pass and only managed a dismal ninth-place finish in the trick event at yesterday's $14,300 Belvedere King Size International professional water ski tournament on Long Pond, Centre Island.

He didn't fare much better in the slalom, rounding only two and one half buoys at 32 off, compared to four buoys at

Athans soared an unofficial 172 feet to capture the jumping title and the overall title with 3,366 points.

Athans collected $1,500 for each of his title wins, plus $100 for the ninth and sixth placings in trick.

The jump is u... the figures and re... jump are re... tournament offic... through a compu... then has to be... World Water S... approval, a proce... at le...

'had a chance in the jump. After the first two jumps (162 and 163 feet) I knew I had to come up with a big one.

"It felt good. You get that second lift in the air and I

was disallowed. Grimditch had a third in the slalom and finished seventh in the tricks for a sixth-place placing overall.

Bruce Cockburn of

most important event. If I jumped one foot farther, I would have won the overall and $750 more," he said.

. . .

King Clancy gets the nod as best Leaf this season

The King is in excellent company.

winner of the special slalom, finished second in 1:20.53. She was followed by teammate nadians Nancy Greene and Anne Hegytvelt who won Olympic and world champion-

Jom in 1:30.59 mi... took a poor 37th place... "I cannot explain... I had just passed the... and I was thinking

By winning, Miss Clifford joined the ranks of sister-Ca...

Figure skater Petra Burka voted top female athlete

Petra Burka, 19-year-old figure skating star, is Canada's top female athlete for the sec...

place votes, almost three times as many as the rest of the candidates combined. She

award with 212 points to 186 for second-place Nancy Mc-Cre...

Mrs. Ellen Burka, who coached her daughter to th...

As Everyone Knows

It's Lionel Conacher

As Greatest Athlete

Now it's official. Lionel Conacher Longboat, the late Six Nations is Canada's outstanding all-round serve Indian who burned up male athlete of the half century. marathon routes of Canada and

Jump victory in New York sweetest: Day

Elaine spins another record

MEXICO CITY — Tonight Elaine Tanner goes for the world record in the 100-metre backstroke — and Canada's first medal of the 19th Olympiad.

Yesterday morning she tied her own Olympic record of 1.07.6 which she set last week as lead-off swimmer of the Canadian relay team. This was ...

MEXICO 68

CHARLES McGREGOR

SPORTS EDITOR

an awful lot of competition here — Kay Hall of rome's T-shirt which carried the slogan "You can

to heap on the broad shoulders of a Winnipeg high school girl.

But it's about time O Canada was played here. And it's about time the Maple Leaf was raised so people here can see what it looks like.

Canada's other medal hope, Ralph Hutton, easily won his qualifying

But the day belonged to a young Mexican swimmer by the name of Felipe Munoz, surprise winner of the gold medal in the men's 200-metre breaststroke.

Munoz, trailing world record holder Vladimir Kosinsky of Russia in the last leg, was spurred on by the deafening cheers

Gold medal for Nancy

MONTREAL — (CP) — Maurice (Rocket) Richard, the man who scored more goals and gave hockey fans more thrills than any other player in history, has finally reti...

Speak English he... years" in last night: "For

Training camp's especially tough on players who may not make it

THE GLOBE AND MAIL, TUESDAY, JUNE 9, 1970 **33**

Grand jury rules Sawchuk death accident

TORONTO DAILY STAR, Mon., Dec. 1, 1969 **14**

Toronto bowler wins masters title in Tokyo

The internal injuries Sawchuk received apparently were caused by his being hit extremely solidly. His abdominal muscles, after more than 20 years of stretching and pulling and crouching, were highly developed.

Cahn said there was no substantiation of published re-

ports by Miss Sasso that Sawchuk had been spitting blood for two weeks before the misadventure.

Stewart, who will be 38 next month, left immediately after his half hour of testimony for his home in Barrie. He did not appear as shaken as he did last Friday, when he was interrogated by Cahn.

TOKYO (CP)—Graydon (Blondie) Robinson of Toronto gave his wife a spectacular anniversary present yesterday — the World Bowling Cup.

The Robinsons who today...

He won the Toronto city singles in 1966 and 1969 and was Canadian all-star champion twice. He qualified for the Tokyo event by beating seven other Canadians in a Montreal match...

Longden's Amazing Saddle Career Embraces 31 Years

Betsy keeps Nancy Greene's giant slalom title in Ca...

The Rocket Steps Into Retirement

Rain Cancels ...n Concert

The Toronto Sun, Monday

Canada's Sporting Heroes

by S. F. WISE & DOUGLAS FISHER
for CANADA'S SPORTS HALL OF FAME

GENERAL PUBLISHING COMPANY
LIMITED
Don Mills, Ontario

The Sports Hall of Fame would like to thank
the Department of Health and Welfare,
Ottawa and the Ontario Department of Education for the financial assistance and encouragement which made this book possible.

First published in 1974 by
General Publishing Company Limited,
30 Lesmill Road, Don Mills, Ontario

DESIGN/KEN RODMELL

PICTURE RESEARCH/M. H. (LEFTY) REID

ISBN 0-7737-0036-1
Printed in Canada

In 1968 Prime Minister Trudeau appointed W. Harold Rea head of the "Task Force on Sports for Canadians". The warm reception given to the Task Force report on its publication in May 1969 made its author a popular choice for chairman of the Sports Hall of Fame. The directors of the Sports Hall of Fame would like to pay special tribute to Harold Rea for his enthusiastic leadership during the past five years. The authors and directors are also grateful for Harold Rea's vital and continuing contribution to this book.

Contents

Introduction

In 1970 Harold Rea, chairman of the board of Canada's Sports Hall of Fame, asked us to write a book based on the achievements of the members of the hall.

The Sports Hall of Fame shares a building with the Hockey Hall of Fame at the Canadian National Exhibition in Toronto. Both halls attract thousands of visitors to the displays of medals, trophies, photographs, equipment and other sporting artifacts. The high point of the year comes at exhibition time, when the Sports Hall of Fame formally inducts new members.

Selection of athletes for the hall began in 1955. Automatic admission is accorded to Canadian athletes who have won gold medals at the Olympics or have won genuine world championships. Other members are chosen annually by a selection committee of sportswriters from nominations made by interested Canadians. By July 1973 there were 177 members from more than forty types of sport. Among the 177 were 146 men, 28 women, and – somewhat anomalously – a ship (the *Bluenose*), a powerboat (*Miss Supertest*) and the great Canadian-bred racehorse, Northern Dancer.

What Harold Rea wanted from us was a series of accurate biographical accounts of the members of the Sports Hall of Fame, sufficiently detailed to provide the interested reader with as much information about careers and achievements as space would allow. Harold Rea and his board believe in competitive sport and the striving for excellence essential to it as good in themselves and as important contributors to individual and social health. The qualities to be found among members of the Hall of Fame – high skill, dedication, perseverance, sportsmanship – make them worthy of honour and emulation.

Our views on such matters are not dissimilar, though we arrived at them by a somewhat different roads. Both of us were rather indifferent but enthusiastic athletes, and sport has retained its interest for us long after we became short of wind and long in the tooth. In addition, we have long shared the view that any account of the Canadian experience that leaves out our sporting past is an inadequate description of the life of the people. Soon after we graduated in history from the University of Toronto we began publishing occasional pieces on sports history, most of them in the *Canadian Forum*. Working with Harold Rea, Nancy Greene and Dr. Jacques Des Ruisseaux in the preparation of the report of the Task Force on Sport for Canadians in 1969 gave us an opportunity to introduce a certain historical perspective.

But writing the task force report, a policy-oriented document, was straightforward compared to the problems presented by a book on the members of the Sports Hall of Fame. We believed that it was necessary not only to compile a series of biographies, but also to attempt to fit these athletic lives into a larger picture, in order to provide a sense of the continuity – and the diversity – of Canadian sports history, and to show, however inadequately, how this history was part of the general social history of our country. We have tried to do this by grouping the biographies into sections of like interest, and by providing both general introductory chapters and briefer historical prefaces to each biographical section. But there were difficulties, and we are only too aware that in many respects, quite apart from the usual problems of space, our ambitions outran our performance.

The fact that hockey, football and lacrosse have their own halls of fame, and as a result have few representatives in the sports hall, created an obvious problem. These games have been so central to Canadian sports history, and have had so great an influence upon other sports, that we simply could not pass them by. The introduction to the chapter on team games, therefore, is an attempt to provide an overview of the history of these three sports, and to indicate their importance.

Most people directly engaged in sport have little sense of history; their concern, quite properly, is with the "now" of sport. Those who study and write about the past have commonly ignored sports as a theme. Only a decade ago, one of our most well-known historians published the first important social history of Canada in which sport got some two and one-half pages. Until very recently, Canadian historians have been chiefly concerned with such matters as political development, religious history, federal-provincial relationships, and the history of large-scale economic enterprise: all important matters, but also subjects which touch the lives of the mass of the population only infrequently or indirectly.

Of course, Canadian academic historians are an élite writing about the activities of other élites, and in their attitude towards sport they reflect not only a traditional academic prejudice but also the values of our society's directing groups. The concern of these groups has been with government and commerce, and with that form of culture characterized by small audiences and large subsidies. Mistrust of athletics and hermetically embalmed "culture" are both survivals of our puritanical past. Perhaps if Egerton Ryerson, when he laid the foundations for Ontario's school system in the 1850s, and provided the model for schools systems elsewhere in the country, had been less impressed with Prussian exercise drill and more taken with the "games days" and general participation of the English schools, we might earlier have developed a more balanced and civilized view of the good relationship between mind and body. Pioneer earnestness dies hard, however, and so the attitude remains that games and sports are at best frivolous and unrewarding diversions, and at worst the preoccupations of the light-minded, the unstable and the socially inferior, tinctured with rowdyism, violence and gambling.

As we have already suggested, those involved in Canadian sport (with some exceptions) have not been historically minded. There are a variety of reasons for this, but the most important lies in the nature of sport itself. The past and its heroes are soon lost to the collective memory. Why? Partly it is because sports have a seasonal rhythm of competition, and as a new season begins, the achievements of even the immediate past rapidly recede. Moreover, the unfolding story of sport is chronicled in the daily press and, more recently, in the even more ephemeral media of radio and television. The path back scarcely interests the sportswriter or commentator: his concern is with today, next week, this season. As well, there is the jealous relationship between each generation of athletes and its audience, between those for whom the talents of a Howie Morenz, a Maurice Richard, a Bobby Orr admit of no valid comparison. This immensely personal equation between the great athlete and his audience has been repeated many times over since organized sport and trained athletes began to emerge in Montreal in the 1870s.

Athletic careers are short. The athlete's cycle of apprenticeship, emergence, maturity and stardom, and eclipse is brief. Twenty years at the top is extraordinary; ten years is unusual; the norm is shorter. So, with certain variations within sports, the parade of victors changes swiftly, and within two such generations, most of those who have passed before have been forgotten. This process has been accentuated by the twentieth century's liberal invention of new games and the proliferation of competitive sports. It has also been assisted by the way in which most of our leading sports have become inextricably linked with the American sporting scene, and with the immense flood of information by which the North American professional sports business advertises itself. Inevitably, and perhaps irreversibly, our ideas of what is excellent in sport have become tributary to American standards, a further aspect of the well-established Canadian inferiority complex.

All this is a rather long way of saying that the sources for the writing of the social history of Canadian sport are limited. Canadian historians are only beginning to develop a critical history of our society's past. As for sport itself, the bulk of material useful for a discovery of its history is buried in the files of daily newspapers and periodicals. Some pioneering work in the exploitation of this material has been done within the physical education faculties at a number of Canadian universities, but usually in a form that is not generally available to the interested public.

It is still too soon, therefore, to make the kinds of connections between sports and the general patterns of evolving Canadian life we had hoped to do. We are also conscious that this book, resting as much of it does on evidence taken from the newspaper and periodical press of the last one hundred years, probably contains a number of mistakes in fact. Both we and the Sports Hall of Fame would welcome, for the purpose of future editions, information from readers who can set us straight.

We have tried, within the limitations of our sources, to assess the evidence critically. In one area, however, we have been quite uncritical. We believe that Canadians, far from being the dour, safe, temperate and unimaginative folk who populate so much of our historical writing, have been, in terms of their life in sport, marvellously inventive, daring, and successful, and in a word, joyous. For giving us the chance to exploit this innocent prejudice, we are grateful to the board of the Sports Hall of Fame.

We also have to thank those many athletes and sports administrators, or their relatives and friends who, though too numerous to name, provided invaluable assistance and needed corrections of what we had written. We wish to thank specifically Tom West, Dana Johnson, and Diane Mew, each of whom did much of the research work for the project and aided us with drafts of some biographies. Staff members at the Library of Parliament, the National Library, and the Public Archives were helpful and patient. "Lefty" Reid, the curator of the Sports Hall of Fame, was most cooperative in providing material and good advice.

S.F. WISE
DOUGLAS FISHER
Ottawa August 1974

Prologue

It is the early evening hours of 28 September 1972 and Canada is collectively transfixed in front of a TV set. The eighth and final hockey game in the Team Canada – USSR series is in its last minute and the game *and* the series is tied.

Impossible!

Canada, the country that invented hockey more than one century ago actually *tied* by the Russians who have been playing the game for only twenty-five years? Impossible? More: an affront to the national honour.

Now, with thirty-four seconds left to play, Paul Henderson swoops from the left corner, gathers in a Phil Esposito pass, fakes once and drives the winning goal into the net behind the remarkable little Russian, Vladislav Tretiak. Canada heaves a sigh; pride has been bent and bruised but not broken.

That episode in the Team Canada – USSR series was more than a last-minute salvage of national pride. It was, among other things, a clear sign that a sport, spawned and nurtured on the frozen lakes and rivers of Canada, could no longer be considered an uniquely Canadian fief. Hockey had matured, had become truly international. To the hockey honour roll of such names as Esposito, Dryden and Cournoyer had to be added names such as Kharlamov, Yakushev and Tretiak.

The series might also have reminded Canadians that hockey was neither the first sport to have been invented in this country, nor the first to have been given to the world by Canadians. For a nation of relatively few people, scattered across an immense land, Canada has had a rich athletic history, and has produced a remarkably large number of international champions.

This book is about that history, and those champions.

CANADA
"WHOM WE LOVE AND PRIZE"
Tennyson

Genesis

Chapter 1

Sports in Canada flowered in the second half of the nineteenth century. The newspapers, magazines, sporting annuals and photographs of the time, testified to the joyful preoccupation of Canadians with play and competition. This athletic explosion, remarkable though it was, was not a sudden break with the past. Behind every game – even those Canadians thought they had invented – was already a tradition and a history immeasurably old.

Before everything else, of course, comes the universal fact of play. Play is the foundation on which all athletic events are built. In play a child learns to run, jump, dodge and throw – all basic physical skills. And in play with other children, the child learns the social control or "rules" which organize play into games. There is a large difference between the simple games that children play and athletic encounters of some considerable complexity but there is direct connection between the two.

We know that ancient cultures – Egypt and China, for example – produced athletic contests which we may choose to call sports. It is, however, with the ancient Greeks that our Western tradition of sports begins.

The early Greeks treasured athletic prowess beyond all other virtues; when one young Olympic champion, Diagoras of Rhodes, was crowned with the symbolic wreath of olive leaves, he was advised by a friend, "Die, Diagoras, for you have nothing short of divinity to desire."

The Greek preoccupation with athletic superiority had a military base. War often broke out between jealous city-states and, in those days, it was largely a hand-to-hand affair.

Canadians have played at sports from their early beginnings to present day. *Left,* **a montage of the activities of the late 1800s in Canada.**

A warrior trained his muscles and his reflexes as an athlete in order to survive in combat. The close relationship between war and athletics can be seen in the sports the warrior engaged in. In addition to the chariot race, the Homeric Greeks competed in foot races, wrestling, boxing, and throwing the javelin and the discus. All events, except the last, had a direct military application.

Organized athletics had an extraordinary continuity in Greece. The first Olympic Games were played at least as early as 776 BC and names of the winners of various events were recorded for almost every series of games until they were abandoned in 393 AD. (The modern Olympics were inaugurated in 1896, appropriately enough in Athens.) Just as remarkable is the fact that the rules governing the Olympiad competitions remained in effect, unchanged, for more than a thousand years.

The Olympic Games were for men only, another reflection of their military significance. The athletes competed in the nude. (The Greek word *gymnastic* meant "exercises performed while naked.") Similarly, the spectators were exclusively men although an exception was made for the priestess of Demeter.

There were no weight classes in boxing and wrestling and, as a result, these sports were dominated by big, agile men. Boxers wore thin gloves, more to protect the wearer's hands then his opponent's face. There were no rounds, a bout lasting until one contestant raised his hand in defeat or collapsed into unconsciousness. Wrestling, possibly the most popular Greek sport, was a rugged affair with all manner of holds permitted that are barred today. The *pankration* (from *pan,* all, and *kratos,* strength) was a combination of no-holds-barred wrestling and bare-knuckled boxing. The Greeks considered the *pankration* less civilized

1

than wrestling because it involved grovelling on the ground, one of the few things banned in straight wrestling. At one Olympics, a practitioner of *pankration* named Arrhachion was strangled while breaking the toes of his opponent; his opponent accepted defeat at the same moment Arrhachion died. His corpse was crowned with the olive wreath.

There is no direct link between the Greek athletic achievement and the sports of today. The Romans, with their fondness for gladiatorial contests and other bloody forms of mass entertainment, corrupted the Greek tradition beyond recovery. Not until modern times did organized sports with widely accepted rules reappear. Their beginnings can be traced in medieval Europe.

By the Middle Ages, social class decided what games one played. The chief social types were the knight, the priest, and the peasant, and, with certain exceptions, each class played different games. The medieval knight, the key figure in war and manorial society, played chiefly at forms of mock warfare from which lesser folk were excluded. Jousts and tournaments fought with blunted weapons, though staged as entertainments for the great, were nevertheless real training for war. But long after the armoured knight had ceased to be an effective soldier on the battlefield, the courtly and aristocratic entertainment of the tournament continued throughout most of Western Europe as a kind of noble ceremony, not dying out until the seventeenth century. As a gentlemanly pursuit, it was followed by fencing, and the bloody "sport" of duelling was practised until relatively modern times.

In England, the typical feudal array of armoured, mounted knights was supplemented by the free peasant with his longbow. So important did the archers prove to English kings in their wars with Scotland and France that laws were passed to ensure that on holidays, commoners practised archery at the butts instead of engaging in sports less useful to the state. In 1365 Edward III ordered that on such days the citizens of London were to practise archery, not "the hurling of stones, loggats and quoits, handball, football or other vain games of no value," on pain of imprisonment. Preaching before Henry VIII, Bishop Hugh Latimer declared that archery was "a gift of God" to England, "whereby He hath given victories against our enemies." He deplored the tendency of men to shun it for idle pastimes. Both laws and exhortations were useless; the days of Robin Hood would never return.

Unlike the martial games played by laymen, the sport associated with the priesthood of the Middle Ages was, oddly enough, tennis. It was not the tennis of today, but its ancestor, known as court or "real" tennis. This game was played indoors on a court resembling a cathedral cloister. The resemblance was no accident, for it was precisely in such a place that the first mention of the game occurs. The game was played with a ball and nets and the ball was struck with the hand, not a racket, hence its name, *jeu de paume*. On Easter Day, 1287, at Nevers, it is recorded that "the Canon of St. Cyr joined with the bishops in believing that their dignity would not suffer by a little volleying of a tennis ball."

Tennis, not horseracing, then became the sport of kings. Specially-built courts and expensive balls and rackets (which came into use in the early sixteenth century), as well as punitive legislation, confined the game to the upper classes. As early as 1292, there were thirteen tennis professionals in Paris and by 1400 there was a Guild of Tennis Masters which set the rules of play and enjoyed a monopoly over equipment manufacture. Henry VIII had his own tennis pro, Anthony Ansley, and Henry built the court at Hampton Court which is still in use. Charles II spent as much time on the court as Henry did; he usually played for two hours every morning and kept careful account of the weight he sweated off.

Folk games have a much less well-recorded history than such royal sports as tennis. Throughout medieval Europe a wide variety of ball games existed, some played with clubs or sticks, some merely using the hand or foot. All kinds of balls were used, but even more varied were the ways in which different ball games were played; each community played the game according to its own ancient pattern. All ball games tended to be violent, and all were connected to events or seasons which suggests that in their oldest form they may have been fertility rites. In many villages, weddings were followed by ball games, usually between married and single men, and frequently the participants were naked. Footraces between naked contestants were also a feature of rustic weddings. In Derbyshire in England, in the middle of the seventeenth century, such a race was reported on a winter's day when "two antagonists, stark naked, runn a foot race for two or three miles with many hundred spectators." A wedding race of the same kind was reported in Yorkshire as late as 1851.

In England, football was the most widespread of the folk ball games. Apparently women sometimes played a version of it; Sir Philip Sidney wrote of a village woman, "with skirts tucked very high, with girls at football plays." Usually, however, it was a man's game and was played once a year, on Shrove Tuesday, probably as a survival of a pagan spring festival. In medieval times the annual football match, played with the inflated bladder of an animal, was a kind of wild brawl, an occasion for evening old scores and a legal outlet for repressed violence. One of the classic indictments of football's violence and turbulence was that of a Puritan preacher, Philip Stubbes, in his *Anatomie of Abuses,* published during the reign of Elizabeth I:

> Football playing may rather be called a friendly kind of fight, than a play or recreation; a bloody and murdering practice, than a fellowly sport or pastime. . . . Sometimes their necks are broken, sometimes their backs, sometimes their legs, sometimes their arms, sometimes one part thrust out of joint, sometimes another, sometime their noses gush out with blood, sometimes their eyes start out. . . . They have sleights to meet one betwixt two, to dash him against the heart with their elbows, to hit him under the short ribs with their gripped fists . . . And hereof groweth envy . . . hatred . . . and sometimes fighting, brawling, contention, quarrel picking, murder, homicide and great effusion of blood.

In Cornwall "hurling" was the game. It bore no resemblance to the Irish game of the same name, but was a little like modern rugger, with fifteen to thirty men a side. The object was to carry the ball through goals set about one hundred yards part. The ball carrier could defend himself by punching a tackler in the chest, but nowhere else; if tackled, he could pass the ball behind him.

At Easter, the English engaged in such sports as running, jumping and throwing, while May Day was the occasion for wrestling. Each locality had its favourite style. Cornishmen "hugged" to secure a fall; in Devon, kicking and tripping were allowed; in Norfolk, "loose" wrestling was the norm – the wrestlers took hold of each other's clothing at the beginning of a match. Sir Thomas Parkyns, an eighteenth century admirer of wrestling who wrote whimsically of its attractions, also perpetuated his love of wrestling on his tomb: his stone effigy is in the first position of the Cornish hug.

Folk sports were rough and boisterous, but so was the society that produced them. The English loved bull or bear baiting and cockfighting. Such entertainments were patronized by the great and a number of English kings maintained masters of the bears. A sixteenth century German visitor to London described the pit in which such events occurred: The bear or bull was chained to a pole, and giant bulldogs were set loose to worry it. "It sometimes happens that the dogs are killed on the spot; fresh ones are immediately supplied . . ."

But the English enjoyed less brutal sports as well. Bowling or "bowls" was almost a national sport. Every schoolchild is familiar with the story of Sir Francis Drake refusing to leave his game at Plymouth even as the Spanish Armada was sailing up the English Channel intent on the destruction of the English fleet.

Bowling began as a game of the upper classes. Repeatedly laws were passed to prevent the lower classes from playing the game. In 1541, for instance, an ordinance was passed which forbade labourers, artisans, apprentices and servants from bowling except as a treat at Christmas, and then only "in their master's house or in their master's presence." In 1674 Charles Cotton commented in his *The Compleat Gamester* that "a bowling green or bowling alley is a place where three things are thrown away besides the bowls, viz., time, money and curses . . . " By this time the authorities had long given up the effort to curb the Englishman's love of bowling; every country inn had its green.

It was in the England of the sixteenth and seventeenth centuries that there first arose two conflicting views of the place of sports and physical exercise in everyday life, differing viewpoints that still influence us. The earlier of the two arose from the Renaissance ideal of the education of the whole man, and looked back to the emphasis on athletics in Greek education. In this view physical exercise was important in itself because efficiency in sports led to success in war. Moreover, physical accomplishment was part of the equipment of the gentleman; it was important to play with grace and style. This aristocratic concept of athletic activities was first enunciated in the sixteenth century by the Italian author, Conte Baldassare Castiglione, in *The Courtier.* "The noble art of tennis [Castiglione wrote] shows off the disposition of the body, the quickness and litheness of every member [through which] a good name is to be won, especially with the crowd." The creed was echoed by the English scholar, Roger Ascham, who wrote in his sixteenth century discourse, *The Schoolmaster*:

> To ride comely, to run fair at the tilt . . . to run, to leap, to wrestle, to swim, to dance comely, to sing and play of instruments cunningly, to hawk, to play at tennis and all pastimes generally . . . which be fit exercise for war or some pleasant pastime for peace, [are] very necessary for a courtly gentleman to use.

A conflicting view arose from the protestant reformation. The English Puritans and the Scottish Calvinists rejected sports and physical recreation as idle diversions from the true path of righteousness. Men who indulged risked their immortal souls and led others astray. The body was merely the soul's lodging; undue emphasis upon it – given the weaknesses of the flesh – led inevitably to sin and vice. The best thing for the body was work, not play. "Diligent labour mortifieth the flesh [the reformers believed] and keepeth under its luxurious inclinations, and subdueth pride and lust and brutish sensuality which is cherished by an idle life." The puritan mentality was to be responsible for the English-Canadian Sunday, an institution that robbed the urban working classes of their recreational opportunities while scarcely touching the lives of the wealthy whose recreations could take place beyond the reach of city blue laws. When, in the nineteenth century, the Canadian puritan grudgingly acknowledged that some form of physical exercise was desirable for public schoolchildren, the species adopted was soul-deadening "PT." At the same time Canadian private schools, offspring of the aristocratic tradition, permitted their students the joys of sports and games.

The Puritans believed in humiliating the body, not glorifying it. Still, they recognized that a healthy body was essential to a prosperous life, one of many goals that every Puritan hoped to attain. Thus, the Puritans' ideal of physical exercise tended to such individual pursuits as brisk walks and solitary, but strenuous, swims. When the Puritan compulsion towards salvation in the afterlife, combined with its drive for success in this, was applied to the field of sports, it produced a powerful incentive for stern training and victory at almost any price.

These clashing outlooks made sports a political issue (alongside the great matters of religion and the constitution) that divided Royalists from Roundheads in the quarrels that culminated in the English civil war. James I valued sports; he told his son: "I think exercises of the body most commendable to be used by a young prince, in such honest games or pastimes as may further ability and maintain health . . . I grant it to be most requisite for a king to exercise his engine, which surely with idleness will rust and become blunt." He practised what he preached. He established Newmarket as the centre of English horseracing, introduced into his adopted country the Scottish game of golf, and imported the first Arabian horse into England for breeding stock. In answer to Puritan magistrates and preachers who tried to curb folk games, especially on Sundays, James issued in 1618 a declaration on sports (known as the *Book of Sports*). It laid down that "no lawful recreation" should be prevented, since his subjects had no freedom for play except on Sundays, and to deprive them of sports would make them unfit for military service, "when we or our successors shall have occasion to use them." The Puritans got short-lived revenge during the Commonwealth period and cracked down hard on all forms of sports. But restoration of the monarchy in 1660 restored sports to the English social scene.

Sports emerged with a broadened base of support – the nobility shared with the monarchy in the patronage of games. Aristocratic patronage was prompted by more than mere love of athletic endeavour – it was primarily love of gambling, a pursuit to which most sports

were admirably suited. Professionalism followed hard on the development of sports gambling. A nobleman's servants might also be his wrestlers, boxers or jockeys. By the eighteenth century the British nobility had taken over horseracing as its private preserve – although the rank and file participated in the wagering. Many sports benefited from the patronage of noblemen who made it their purpose to cultivate and advance the game – the Marquis of Queensberry, noble patron of boxing, is the most obvious example.

The close association of sports and gambling brought with it a curious side effect: the rules of various games became more elaborate, more codified, less open to dispute. The reason was not hard to find: gamblers – especially *noble* gamblers – did not like to lose their money on disputed contests. Thus the "fair play" we value so highly in athletic contests was initially prompted by the gamblers' desire to avoid disputations.

Folk sports such as football were changing also but for other reasons. The rule of the Puritans had eliminated from the English calendar many of the old feast and saints' days, and the games once associated with them declined. The decline of the folk sporting pattern was also connected to the beginnings of industrialism, which set off migration from country to city, and disciplined workers to long hours and regular work periods. Yet just when it seemed that football would die out, it was taken up by schools like Eton and Harrow, Rugby and Shrewsbury. In other words, the sport moved from its lower-class origins to the training schools of the middle and upper classes. Each school played its own brand of football, no less violently than English villagers had. Out of the variants of football played by the schools came, by the middle of the nineteenth century, both soccer and rugby football. The modern Canadian game of football is an offshoot from this ancient family tree.

Cricket also became an organized sport in these years. The original version of cricket – and of baseball too – was a 600-year-old game called stoolball. Joseph Strutt, in his *Sports and Pastimes of the People of England* (1801), described the game in this way:

> A certain number of stools are set up in circular form, and at a distance from each other. Every one of them is occupied by a player. When the ball is struck, which is done with the hand, they are every one of them obliged to alter his situation, running in succession from stool to stool. If he who threw the ball can regain it in time to strike any one of the players, before he reaches the stool to which he is running, he take his place.

This game was taken to colonial America by the early settlers. One of its earliest forms was called baseball, even in England. The Reverend

Cricket was one of the games played by original settlers in Canada. Note the curve of the bat, not unlike the stick used to play hockey.

Thomas Wilson spoke disapprovingly in 1700 of having seen "morris-dancing, cudgel-playing, baseball and cricketts, and many other sports on the Lord's Day." A children's book published in London in 1744 called *The Little Pretty Pocket-Book,* described baseball as a game with a pitcher and a batter and with three bases marked by posts.

Cricket began in Sussex as a game the shepherds played, a wicket substituting for the stool or stump previously used in ball games. In the seventeenth century cricket was taken up by the gentry of the same region. By the early eighteenth century, the game was moving to other parts of the country – the first recorded county match was between Sussex and Kent in 1709. Noble families like the Sackvilles became patrons of cricket, and divisions appeared between "gentlemen" and "players" – that is, the noblemen's servants who were, in fact, professionals. Thomas Lord, backed by a duke and an earl, opened his famous cricket ground in London in the late eighteenth century; the Marylebone Cricket Club (MCC), founded in 1788, made Lord's its home. The MCC rules became the recognized rules wherever cricket was played, whether in Britain or the colonies.

The rise of such sports as horseracing, cricket and football, and the gradual establishment of rules to control them, was the great eighteenth century contribution to the development of modern sport. But in that era, foxhunting was the English country gentleman's chief enthusiasm.

The hunt for food is as old as mankind; as a sport for the nobility it soon became a form of recreation surrounded by pomp and ritual. By early modern times kings and their courtiers had decimated the great ox and boar, so the mild-mannered hare became the object of the hunt. Then it came time for the fox to be the unwilling victim. Fox hounds were bred for speed and stamina in coursing with the fox over the fields and hedgerows of the countryside. In a later day Oscar Wilde was to categorize the sport as "the unspeakable in pursuit of the uneatable," and even during the eighteenth century the sport was not without its critics. To Englishmen transplanted to the colonies, however, foxhunting was one of the marks of a gentleman. Socially aspiring colonials began their own awkward versions of this English pastime over the farmlands of British America. In colonies like Virginia where rural upper classes emerged, foxhunting was carried on very much in the English manner; George Washington's diary shows that he rode to hounds fifteen times in January and February 1769.

Colonial America received many other English sports as well. The Puritan founders of Massachusetts Bay and Connecticut banned most sports from the outset, but not everyone could be a saint. Governor Bradford was shocked to find a group of newcomers on Christmas Day, 1621, openly playing "stoolball and such-like sports" in the streets of Plymouth. If New England had its blue laws, Virginia and other southern colonies had their class lines. A tailor was fined in Virginia in 1674 for arranging a horserace with a gentleman, "it being contrary to law for a labourer to make a race, being a sport for gentlemen." Governor Sir

5

Francis Nicholson established prizes in 1691 "to be shott for, wrasttled, played at back-swords and run for sudden horse and foott . . . the better sort of Virginians only, who are batchelors."

Canada's Indian peoples played a great variety of games. Games of ball were common to many tribes; one of them, baggataway, was a violent and spectacular sport. The fur trader, Alexander Henry, gave a description of the game he saw played at Michilimackinac in the 1760s:

> Baggataway, called by the Canadians *le jeu de la crosse*, is played with a bat and ball. The bat is about four feet in length, curved, and terminating in a sort of racket. Two posts are planted in the ground, at a considerable distance from each other, as much as a mile or more. Each party has its post, and the game consists in throwing the ball up to the post of the adversary. The ball, at the beginning, is placed in the middle of the course, and each party endeavours as well to throw the ball out of the direction of its own post, as into that of the adversary's.

Another fur trader, the Nor'wester Daniel Harmon, who travelled across the Prairies and into the Rockies in the years after 1800, found that "every tribe has amusements peculiar to itself, but some plays are common to all, who reside on the east side of the Rocky Mountains." The Assiniboines and other plains Indians spent "much of their time about their horses, and are fond of trying their speed." Among all the plains tribes "the young men often amuse themselves, in the summer season, by a game of ball." Swimming and footraces were normal for Indian children and Indian youths universally practised the bow and arrow, so necessary in hunting and in war. As Harmon said, "Their youth from the age of four or five to that of eighteen or twenty years, pass nearly half of their time in shooting arrows at a mark, and to render this employment more interesting, they always have something at stake." As a result "they become at length the best marksmen, perhaps, in the world."

The first Canadians to be exposed to Indian culture were the settlers of New France and Acadia. They brought with them the amusements and sports of France, their mother country, but very quickly adapted themselves to the new environment. Especially adaptable were the *coureurs de bois,* the incredibly hardy men whose labours with snowshoe, pack and canoe supported the fur trade and the spread of French empire in North America. Governor Frontenac was astonished by the physical endurance and toughness of the Canadians. "Unless one had witnessed it [he wrote] one could not believe the exhaustion of those men, dragging the boats, most of them having been in the water a great deal of the time up to their arm-

Tulloch-Chich-Ko ("he who drinks the juice of the stone"), a celebrated Indian lacrosse player of the nineteenth century.

pits and balancing on rocks so sharp that some of them had legs and feet running with blood, yet their gaiety was undiminished and as soon as they got back to camp some of them began to jump about, to perform gymnastics and all manner of games."

Much of the history of physical sport in French Canada has merged into myth. In the days before sports became organized, before rules were laid down and before a records-keeping sports bureaucracy appeared, the figure of the athlete was transmuted into a folk hero, and his feats, passed on by word of mouth, became the stuff of popular myth. Canada has had its share of such semi-legendary figures, but nowhere has there been a richer folk tradition than French Canada – with the exception possibly of Cape Breton with its strong Highland men. This tradition reveals much about the French-Canadian attitude towards sport. This numerically small group of people, mainly rural until the twentieth century and largely excluded by social position, economics and the facts of power from the gentlemanly games of the English élite, concentrated its attention upon feats of endurance and strength. While French Canadians were eventually to take a prominent place in such sports as lacrosse and hockey, it was in such sports as weightlifting, boxing and similar feats of strength and endurance that they first shone.

It was natural that it should be so. Most French Canadians until recent times were trappers, farmers and lumbermen, and their sports were extensions of the physical qualities these occupations demanded. When E. Z. Massicote published in 1909 his *Athletes Canadien-Français,* he concentrated upon strongmen and rough and tumble fighters. Massicote recited tales of the legendary Grenon, "the Hercules of the North," whose massive strength had amazed and cowed Wolfe's redcoats, and of Joseph Montferrand, trapper and lumberman, who at eighteen defeated the best boxers in the English garrison at Montreal and "le champion de la marine anglaise" in a seventeen-second bout on Queen's Quay at Quebec. The most renowned strongman (before Louis Cyr) was Claude Grenache, a farmer and blacksmith who is supposed to have given directions by lifting and pointing his plough. Grenache, known in the United States as the Canadian Samson, was a touring professional who gave exhibitions of strength until his death in 1862 while serving with the Union forces during the American civil war.

Throughout the stories of Massicote and other French-Canadian writers run two themes: veneration for strength, muscularity and amazing feats of power and endurance; and a strong nationalism. The typical hero is calm, dignified, and slow to anger, but once roused, he terrifies the bullies and braggarts – usually les Anglais – by his stormy wrath and immense strength, and thus demonstrates the virtues and hardihood of his own people.

Almost from the outset of British rule in 1763 French Canadians took readily to at least one English sport – partly because they already knew a good deal about it. That sport was horseracing, brought by the members of the British governing class to Quebec, to Nova Scotia and later to the loyalist provinces of New Brunswick and Upper Canada. The military of the garrisons gave the lead, though the races were invariably under the patronage of the local governor and his little court of officials. The Quebec *Gazette* of 5 July 1764 warned that any dogs found "on the race ground . . . will be put to death"; the entry suggests that the first race meet preceded that date. Frederick Tolfrey, attached to the Quebec garrison, was an enthusiastic hunter, fisherman, carriole driver and rackets player. He was proudest of his ability as an amateur jockey, and helped found the Quebec Garrison Racing Club in 1817. The Governor-General, the Duke of Richmond, became patron of the new club, and soon the officers were importing racehorses from the US, a grandstand was built, and crowds from the town thronged to the meets. Surrounding the sport was the lavish social display of the governor-general's circle: "the magnificent gold plate and racing cups of the noble duke astonished the Canadians not a little whenever any large state parties were given, and to which the

natives on these occasions were invited."

In the 1820s French Canadians became actively involved in racing, although well before that time they must have been among the spectators at garrison meets. By 1829, interest was so great that special boat trips were laid on to bring Montrealers to Quebec for the races, and the Montreal newspaper *la Minerve* held its presses in order to bring its readers the latest results. The first active involvement of the Canadiens was out-and-out nationalistic. Meets organized at Montreal and LaPrairie restricted entries to Canadian-bred horses, in order to disqualify the imported thoroughbreds raced by the British military. To churchmen, indulgence in games of any kind, except to maintain health and spirits, was an error, and led to sensuality, vanity, idleness and avarice. Newspaper editors thundered against the drinking, swearing, scuffling and gambling they saw as the chief feature of horseracing.

But by the 1850s, the people of Quebec had clearly rejected the attempt of their élite to guide them in the right path. Regular race meetings were held in forty towns and villages throughout the province, the chief centres being Montreal, Quebec, St. Hyacinthe, Ste. Rose, and Trois Rivières. Some meets, especially trotting races, were run and patronized almost entirely by French Canadians; in most, the two language groups collaborated.

Horseracing got an early start in other colonies too. Digby, Nova Scotia, had a racecourse as early as 1787, probably started by the loyalists, who were more easy-going in their attitudes than the strait-laced Yankees who had settled the colony before the revolution. It would be surprising if the garrison at Halifax, founded in 1749, had not raced its mounts long before this. In Upper Canada, the Queen's Rangers organized race meets in the early 1790s at the little capital of Niagara-on-the-Lake; purses of ten and twenty guineas were competed for, "best two of three heats over a mile of ground." The second capital, York, had a racecourse on what became Toronto Island before 1812; Kingston, too, had early racing and in each town it was the garrison and "the better sort of people" who participated.

Trotting races were also popular in rural Upper Canada. As in French Canada, "trots" were often held during the winter months on the ice of lakes and rivers. The Streetsville *Review* (in a fair sample of early sportswriting prose) reported that a trotting meet on the Credit River had attracted more than "500 bipeds [and that] a temporary hostel erected on the congealed element was liberally patronized by the company."

The many bees and barn-raisings, so much a part of pioneer life, were times when

Upper Canadians could forget the hard task of wresting an existence from their bush farms, and turn to the sports and games of their forefathers. Major Samuel Strickland described a mowing and cradling bee in Darlington township in 1825; thirty-five men cut hay and rye the whole day, and in the evening, when the crops were in, "there was time for gymnastics, trials of strength, running and jumping, and other popular pastimes as throwing the hammer and putting the stone."

Wrestling and boxing, frontier style, were both popular in Upper Canada. Dr. William Caniff, writing in 1869 of the pioneer life he had known, welcomed the fact that boxing, once general, was now "confined to those of a brutish disposition," since "it is only the lowest who find amusement in engaging in or witnessing pugilistic encounters." These genteel sentiments were not shared by an early historian who described a wrestling tournament between the champions of the Bay of Quinte townships of Marysburgh and Adolphustown:

> The hour was fixed, and a nearby field was selected where hundreds were on hand "to see fair play," and help decide which township had the best men. Samuel Dorland, afterwards a colonel in the militia and a leading official in the Methodist Church, was an expert wrestler, and used to boast, even in his old days, that he seldom if ever met a man who could lay him on his back. He soon had his man down. Samuel Casey, who afterwards became a leading militia officer and a prominent justice of the peace, was one of the strongest men in the township, but not an expert wrestler. He was so powerful in the legs that his opponent, with all his skill, could not trip him up, and at last got thrown down himself. Paul Trumpour . . . was not so skilled in athletics but he was a man of immense strength. He got his arms well fixed around his man and gave him such terrible "bear hugs" that the poor fellow soon cried out "enough" to save his ribs from getting crushed in, and that settled it.

There was as much diversity in the games Canadians played, and in the way they played them, as there was in their social and ethnic origins. The population base of the colonies was French and American; the great waves of English, Irish and Scottish immigration did not begin until after 1815. Whatever their origins, most settlers did not have much time for sports and other amusements. Most men and women lived out their lives in their own communities, whether in the fishing villages of the Atlantic colonies, or the seigneuries of the St. Lawrence valley, on the backwoods farms of Upper Canada, or around the trading posts of the Hudson's Bay Company in the West. When time permitted, they played the games known to them but certainly not in any organized way. Sport at this stage reinforced localism, rather than bridged it.

Class lines also cut across the sports played by early Canadians. Cricket was the

Toronto Public Library

game of the colonial upper class and of those who aspired to it. Its beginnings everywhere in British North America can be traced to the officers of the military garrisons; it was played in the private schools and by members of the "compacts" and little social élites to be found in every colonial capital. Upper Canada College, the "prepare-a-Tory" school founded by Sir John Colborne in 1830, played cricket from the start, often against "the gentlemen of Toronto." Thus, in 1836, the Upper Canada College cricket team played a Toronto eleven comprised of men with close associations with the Family Compact as well as Sir Francis Bond

Head, lieutenant-governor of the province.

Canadian cricket had scarcely emerged in an organized fashion when it became involved in an international relationship with American cricketers. The relationship began through a misunderstanding: in August 1840, a team from the St. George's Cricket Club of New York turned up in Toronto, expecting to play the Toronto Cricket Club. The Americans had been victimized by a practical joker – no match was planned. An informal match took place instead, followed by further friendly matches over the next couple of years. Then, on 24-5 September 1844, the first international cricket

Little excuse was needed for festive occasions. Canadians decked out in their finery for the "celebration of the Royal Wedding Day on the ice of Burlington Bay, Lake Ontario, Canada West."

match in the history of the game was held – not between England and Australia, but between elevens from Canada and the United States. Some 5,000 spectators watched as the Canadians won. In the years to come the series alternated between the two countries. Though there have been several long hiatuses, there seems little doubt that this almost unknown interna-

9

tional series is the oldest of its kind in the world.

Though the emergence of an international series was precocious, there is no doubt that in Canada at least a firm base for it had developed by the 1850s. In 1858 the St. Catharines Cricket Club published *The Canadian Cricketer's Guide,* with full directions for playing "the truly British game." The guide listed eighty-one matches that had been played chiefly in Canada West (Ontario) the previous season, of which the editors had received accounts. Of these, fifty-two were intertown games, a remarkable total, indicating that the participants had both the money to travel and the leisure to take part in this time-consuming game. In addition, on 19-21 August 1857, Canada beat the US in an international match held at Toronto. The Canada eleven of 1858 included cricketers from Toronto, Montreal, St. Catharines, London, Brockville, Kingston and Cobourg. The guide listed fifty-six clubs in Canada West, some of them of recent foundation, others going back to the 1830s.

Cricket's claim to be Canada's favourite pastime did not survive the 1850s, and even in that decade it had a rival. If cricket got off to a good start because of its social base, curling had a powerful ethnic foundation. Large Scottish communities were to be found in every British North American colony, and of all the British immigrants, the Scots were the most tightly knit. The ancient Highland tradition of the "gathering" brought them together for track and field sports as well as piping and dancing. One of the earliest gatherings was held by the Caledonian Club of Prince Edward Island in 1838; the Caledonian Society of Cape Breton organized Highland games at Sydney in 1848. Montreal's Caledonian Society got started in 1856, and similar organizations were formed in Ontario not long after. But important though these societies were in stimulating athletics in Canada, curling was the first Scottish sporting gift to the country.

Curling began informally among the Scottish merchants of Quebec and Montreal before 1800. The first club was that of Montreal (later the Royal Montreal), formed when twenty Scots met at Gillis's Coffee House on 22 January 1807 to lay down the rules. Clubs were organized in Quebec and Kingston in 1820, and later in New Brunswick and Nova Scotia. James Bicket, the secretary of the Toronto Curling Club, which was operating in 1836, published in 1840 a little book called *The Canadian Curler's Manual,* which contained a history of the game, its rules, a glossary of terms, the constitution of the Toronto club, and a short account of curling in Canada. The Mont-

Curling, informally initiated before 1800 by Scottish merchants of Quebec and Montreal, had become extremely popular in Canada by the turn of the twentieth century, as illustrated in this photo taken in 1905.

Unlike today, when curling is almost exclusively an indoor game, the sport in its formative years was played outdoors on ponds, sloughs, rivers or bays – wherever a group of interested sportsmen could clear a patch of ice of sufficient size.

real and Quebec clubs began intercity bonspiels in the 1830s; the fact that they used bell-shaped irons as curling stones, while Upper Canadian rinks used local stone or hardwood blocks loaded with lead, lessened the chance for interprovincial competition, but by 1840 there were bonspiels between Upper Canadian clubs. Not until 1859, on Toronto Bay, was anything approaching a provincial bonspiel held; while 1865 seems to have been the date of the first international bonspiel when, on Lake Erie near Black Rock, Canadian and American curlers met, twenty-seven rinks a side. Well before this time, curling clubs had sprung up throughout western Upper Canada, and the game had

begun to attract non-Scots. In 1840, Bicket had been sure that curling was to become "a favourite" in Canada, not only because it suited the climate, and got men out of "the enfeebling influence of confinement to our close and heated winter houses," but also because it brought out those sterling moral qualities prized by every upright Scot. Perhaps this is why some of the most active promoters of the game were Presbyterian ministers, though their presence does not seem to have made for austerity. When the Quebec and Montreal clubs held a bonspiel at Trois Rivières in 1835, they could find neither haggis nor good whiskey in the town, and so made do with nine turkeys washed down with champagne.

Curling, horseracing and cricket had a headstart as organized sports in Canada in the years before Confederation. The great creative age of Canadian sport, however, had not yet dawned; we must look to the city of Montreal for its beginnings.

11

Chapter 2

On 28 and 29 August 1844 Montrealers took part in what for them was a pleasurable entertainment, but in terms of the history of sport was also an epoch-making event. The city was holding its first "Olympic Games," consisting (according to the Montreal *Gazette*), of rifle-shooting, vaulting, leaping, hammer throwing and cricket ball, climbing the pole, pedestrianism, quoiting, putting the shot, a steeplechase over four-foot hurdles and "other athletic exercises." Neither in Britain nor in the United States had anything quite like these games yet been held. Toronto, a few years earlier, had held a number of field days; so had some American cities. But in their size, organization, variety, and social and cultural diversity Montreal's Olympics were unique; on the basis of them Montreal has a strong claim to be considered one of the birthplaces of modern organized sport.

Among the "other exercises" were two lacrosse matches: a game between Indian teams, and one which pitted Indians against whites. Though the whites gave them a good struggle, the Indians proved masters of the game, which the *Gazette* described as "much resembling the game in Scotland termed 'shinty.' " Indians also played a prominent part in other events; the mile, for example, was won by the Iroquois Tarisonkwan in 4:52 minutes. In fact, however, the games drew upon all components of the Montreal community, from Scottish soldiers serving with the garrison to "some of the most eminent citizens of Montreal."

The impetus for the games had come from a group of gentlemen who, the previous year, had formed themselves into the Olympic

Winter carnivals were a major event early in Montreal's sporting life. *Opposite:* **scenes from the winter carnival of 1885.**

Club. In a petition to Governor-General Sir Charles Metcalfe, seeking his patronage, they described themselves as having been "stimulated by a desire to introduce and cultivate a taste for Athletic Games and Gymnastic Exercises in this City," even though, as they conceded, "the great importance of such an undertaking [was] by no means universally felt in the community." The support given the petitioners both by Metcalfe and the city corporation was substantial and without precedent; it was an indication not only of their own status in the community but also of the place sport was to hold in Montreal life.

Montreal's vanguard role in the history of organized sport has never been fully appreciated. In five creative decades from 1840 to 1890 Montrealers – or rather, a fairly small, energetic group of Montrealers – gave us and the world the organized team games of lacrosse and ice hockey; they were involved at the beginnings of both Canadian and American football; the idea of a winter carnival, with snowshoeing, tobogganing, figure and speed skating was theirs; they pioneered what were to become international curling bonspiels, as well as national rifle matches and international rifle teams; they established both the first multi-purpose athletic and social club in Canada and the first national amateur sports union; they founded a gymnasium as early as 1843, and supported it and our first outstanding teacher of physical education, Frederic K. S. Barnjum, for many decades.

Not only did Montrealers build a complex sport culture in their own city, but they exported it with missionary zeal. They took their enthusiasms, their games, their rules, their organization to Ontario and from there to the rest of Canada. Two of their finest sons, James Naismith and Tait Mackenzie, were the most outstanding of the many Montrealers who spread the gospel in the United States. Montrealers took lacrosse to the US, Britain, and the Antipodes, and their winter carnival was both a magnet and a model for imitators throughout Canada and northern US.

That Montreal should have been, in so many ways, the leader in the development of organized sport in Canada was no accident. Precisely how the economic life and social structure of a community affect the kinds of sports and recreations the community favours is a large and complicated question. But there can be no doubt that the experience, talent and resources that Montreal possessed in business, trade, the professions and government had a direct impact upon the development of sports in the city.

By the beginning of the nineteenth century Montreal was already the commercial metropolis of Canada. Its position on the St. Lawrence made it a prime gateway to the heartland of North America, New York's rival, and the key to what historian Donald G. Creighton has termed "the commercial empire of the St. Lawrence." Beginning as the transshipment point for goods coming from Europe and the West Indies, it became the headquarters of the enterprising firms which pushed Canada's vast fur trade to the Pacific and Arctic Oceans. The town turned out to be the principal shipper and supplier to the growing agricultural settlements of Upper Canada, launched banking and shipping, and vigorously pushed the construction of canals on the St. Lawrence River. Its merchants, financiers and entrepreneurs (many of them Scots, or sons of Scots who had amassed their wealth in the fur trade) were men of continental and imperial vision, who sought constantly to buttress the natural advantages of Montreal and to pull the vast North American hinterland into the city's orbit. By the 1840s and 1850s they were shifting their interests from canals to railways, seeking to extend their reach east to the Maritimes, south to Portland, west to Toronto – and later, with the great Canadian Pacific project, to the Pacific Ocean itself.

It was this same prosperous, dynamic group which supplied the impetus for the incubation of Canadian organized sport. The men who comprised the group were not numerous, but Montreal's business, professional and entrepreneurial élite had energy, some leisure, considerable wealth and an awakening interest in many forms of physical recreation. Though older cities such as Halifax had wealthy mer-

Victoria skating rink was the most popular gathering place in Montreal in the winter, either for a regular night out (*above*) **or the numerous festive carnivals** (*below*).

14

cantile élites, and Montreal's thrusting new rival, Toronto, was beginning to generate strong metropolitan drives of its own, nowhere in British North America was there a ruling group so confident and practiced in the professions, trade, shipping, merchandising and the employment of large numbers of workers in substantial enterprises. The Montreal élite was as sophisticated and self-reliant most of the time as its counterparts in Boston and New York. There was Sir George Simpson, governor of the Hudson's Bay Company, operating his trading empire from Lachine. There were the Molsons with their breweries and steamboats; the Torrances and McGills, powers behind the Bank of

Montreal; and other prominent business families like the Redpaths, McCords, Stephens, Claxtons, Youngs, and Rosses. To Montreal in the 1850s came Sir William Dawson to make something of McGill University. And until the 1860s there was the British garrison. The affection of its officers for many forms of sport, including horseracing, hunting, cricket, football, and marksmanship, gave sport a respectability and stimulated Montrealers to competition.

In short, mid-century Montreal was a lively, diverse and increasingly self-confident community. Its daily press, both French and English, provided good coverage of world events and commercial news, but was sprightliest in its treatment of local news. The same strong interest in community affairs was expressed in a variety of ways, from the healthy support given to churches and charities or to the fledgling YMCA (it was Montrealers who led in promoting the YMCA cause in North America), to the backing of such civic projects as new sewerage, water and streetcar systems, to the building in 1862 of the Victoria Rink, "the largest and best in the world" (as one local newspaper boasted). The rink's roof rose 52 feet above an ice surface of 200 by 80 feet. It held 2,000 spectators plus a band; for night skating gas jets lit the ice surface brilliantly.

Even in the agonizing year of 1837, when Montreal was wracked with acute political crisis that culminated in rebellion, sporting and recreational news formed a kind of counterpoint to the darker tidings in the Montreal press. On 10 January the Montreal *Transcript* reported an outing by the Tandem Club: "Saturday last there was a very full meeting. We counted seven equippages, well turned-out, and the drivers were not shy of exhibiting the scarlet uniform of the club. We were much pleased to see them drive around Place d'Armes . . . " Four days later the same paper carried news of a curling match between the Quebec and Montreal clubs at Trois Rivières, won by Quebec. "The ice was so bad, and led in so many directions, that the result, in great measure, depended on chance. The stones of the Montreal club are round and keen and those of the Quebec somewhat flat, so that the slightest bias carried the former out of the proper course."

These two activities – the genteel outing of the Tandem Club and the curling bonspiel – signify a dualism that has been present ever since in Canadian sport. The Tandem Club was the Montreal Hunt Club bundled up in winter clothes; the sports its members favoured – summer and winter – were those practised by the upper orders and characterized by exclusive attitudes. Curling however, though originally the exclusive preserve of the Scots, was a more democratic game, expansionist in nature. The Scots were not without a national pride and a conviction of their own superiority but unlike those – predominantly of English origin – who favoured the hunt and cricket, the Scots did not display any feelings of social or ethnic exclusiveness.

Flanking the entrance to the Montreal Amateur Athletic Association clubhouse on Peel Street are two images, set in stained glass, of a snowshoer and a lacrosse player. Though Montrealers play many sports, these two were pivotal in crystallizing the modern structure of organized, competitive sport. That neither sport is prominent today must not detract from the seminal importance of both. Fortunately,

there are full records for both – because their followers enthusiastically promoted their virtues in the press and in pamphlets, articles and books. Thus in 1882 Hugh Wylie Becket published *The Montreal Snow Shoe Club: Its History and Record with a Synopsis of Racing Events of Other Clubs Through the Dominion from 1840 to the Present Time,* a bulky, jumbled compendium of newspaper stories, club records and the author's good-humoured commentary, together with dozens of the poems and songs that over the years had enlivened the literary evenings, the dinners and the carnivals of Montreal's snowshoers.

Becket, who in 1882 was vice-president of the Montreal Snow Shoe Club, was the archetype of the nineteenth century Montreal sportsman. His father, John C. Becket, had come to Montreal from Scotland in 1832, and founded the city's printing industry. As well, the elder Becket operated a stationery and bookstore, was a long-time president of the St. Andrew's Society, the founder of the first Oddfellows Lodge in Montreal and a leading Presbyterian layman. From this overwhelmingly respectable past came Hugh Wylie Becket: also beyond reproach and an athlete as well. He first appears in the Montreal sporting record in 1868 as a sprinter and hurdler on snowshoes; the same year he became the Montreal Lacrosse Club's premier goalkeeper, earning himself the nickname "Stonewall."

According to Becket, the Montreal Snow Shoe Club began modestly in 1840 with twelve members who went on country tramps every Saturday afternoon in winter. "On their return, after a ten- or twelve-mile walk, they repaired to a famous café on St. James Street . . . whose hospitable board afforded every luxury relished by the jolly crew . . . " So many enthusiasts were turning up for the tramps by 1843 that the club formally organized itself, and elected Colonel Charles Oakes Ermatinger, a former fur-trading partner in the North West Company, as its first president. Other members included Judge C. J. Coursol, a future Montreal mayor and MP, and Edward Goff Penney, later chief political writer and proprietor of the Montreal *Herald,* and a senator. Though the club was heavily weighted with the élite, it included as well such members as Edward Lamontagne and Nicholas Hughes, the two best non-Indian snowshoers of their time. Neither man, in terms of education or station, was at the level of other club members – Hughes, for example, was a clerk for the garrison's quartermaster. Yet Hughes was the athletic hero and acknowledged leader of the club until his death. Though he died in 1884, club members paid an annual visit to the grave of "Evergreen" Hughes in Côte des Neiges cemetery on the club's "Veterans Night" until the

16

1930s – a fifty-year tradition.

It was also in 1843 that the first snowshoe races were organized by the club. Over a four-mile course laid out on the St. Pierre racetrack, club members tried their skill against the Indians. Ingenuity won: a sharp freeze after a mild spell left the track a sheet of ice, and the Métis Nor'Wester, Deroche, fitting spikes to his shoes, left the field behind. Hughes was second followed, says Becket, by five Indians "rather disgusted no doubt with the advance civilization had made." "Thus [Becket wrote] were the first races on shoes won in Canada under our auspices. We have no records of any other and may take the credit to ourselves of instituting the national sport of snowshoeing." The pattern thus set became the model for the annual Caledonian Games which began in 1855, and for the annual track and field meets of the Montreal Lacrosse Club, which got underway in the 1860s. Indeed, the snowshoe club supplied many of the officials – patrons, stewards, timers and starters – who ran the summer games. At this stage, while playing a creative role in stimulating other organized sports, snowshoeing was still close to its social and economic roots.

The Indian, Ignace, who won the four-mile race in 1856 in a time of 31 minutes, was "one of those selected by Sir George Simpson . . . on account of his great muscular power and strength of endurance, to accompany the last expedition in search of the remains of Sir John Franklin and his crew; consequently he was so well accustomed to run and walk on snowshoes that the four mile-run was . . . but a mere pastime."

Snowshoeing's chief appeal, in the Confederation era, remained recreational and convivial, but its growing popularity was accompanied by a more earnest athleticism. With some disquiet, a Montreal Snow Shoe Club member observed in 1860 that "one straight heat seemed to be the favourite way of testing the merits of competitors in the 'old time' races, and the hope still lingers fondly with some of us that those days may return when we can leave our office stools to compete, with some chance of success, instead of resorting to the laborious system of training which now threatens to bring our gentlemanly sports to the level of professionalism." This complaint was connected with the appearance of new shoeshoe clubs launched by younger men (often ex-members of the Montreal club) who were more interested in racing than in tramping. The Aurora Club, founded in the late 1850s, was the first of them, and it was followed later by such clubs as the Dominion and the Alexandra. Out of these came notable snowshoe athletes (though still very much of the Montreal élite), men such as Hartland MacDougall, D. R. McCord, C. Peers Davidson and P. S. Ross. Yet snowshoeing was still the recreational face of the Montreal business community. A verse of 1863, alluding to the completion of the great Victoria bridge, shows the Montreal club's pride in its members' leadership:

> Our mighty bridge of Canada now spans St. Lawrence tide,
> Well is it named 'Victoria,' our honour and our pride,
> More lasting monument of worth, no other land can show,
> It was tho't of first out snowshoeing a long time ago.

By the late 1860s snowshoeing was enjoying mass popularity. Not only were the Irish (the

Montreal Snow Shoe Club began modestly with twelve members in 1840 but by the 1870s there were hundreds *(below)* **taking ten and twelve-mile tramps through the countryside.**

Emerald Club) and the French Canadians (le Canadien) becoming involved, but the sport was spreading beyond Montreal. Meets were held almost every weekend. Entrants, including professionals, began to appear from Cornwall, Brockville, Ottawa and Toronto. The finest of all Iroquois snowshoers and runners, the legendary Keroniare, dominated racing for a decade. Expatriate Montrealers launched clubs at Fort William, Winnipeg and St. Paul, Minnesota. By the early 1880s, the parent Montreal club boasted nearly 500 members, there were more than thirty other clubs in the city, and dozens more were scattered across Canada and the northern United States. Snowshoeing had become a major focus of the city's social, recreational and athletic life. Concerts and masques staged by the clubs played to packed houses, proceeds going for the maintenance of club rooms and worthy charities. Beginning in the early 1870s, partly because of the enthusiasm of Lord Dufferin, the governor-general, the custom grew of throngs of Montrealers tramping over Mount Royal by torchlight. At one such gathering, in 1873, Dufferin addressed the snowshoers assembled in his honour:

> In studying the characteristics of Canada, I have been impressed by the devotion of the people to manly sports and exercise. The importance of these can hardly be overrated. They contribute in a great measure to the vitality of a nation's temper and independence of the national spirit. Perhaps no people can boast of a greater variety of sports than Canada in snowshoeing, tobogganing, skating and lacrosse, the last of which is the gayest, liveliest, and manliest of games.

Lacrosse was snowshoeing's summer face, drawing its support from the same level of Montreal society. More than any other man, Dr. W. George Beers, "the father of lacrosse," was responsible for organizing and popularizing the game. He was Canada's first prolific sporting journalist, an excellent athlete, an uninhibited patriot, a ready and effective orator, a songwriter and poet, the founder and editor of Canada's first dental journal and the dean of the first dentistry school in Quebec. His was the creative mind and the driving force behind the first national sporting federation.

Beers was born in 1843, and educated at Phillips School and Lower Canada College. He began to play lacrosse at six, and at seventeen was a goalkeeper in a great match played in honour of Edward Prince of Wales during his visit to Montreal to open the Victoria bridge. The Montreal Lacrosse Club had been organized in 1856, featuring such players as Redpath, Coffin, Christie and Blackwood. Some changes had already been made in the Indian game, but it was young Beers who first laid down the basic rules in a pamphlet published in 1860, in which the size of the field was fixed, the size and nature of the goals specified, the number of players, the names of positions, the definition of illegal play and the duration of a match – all defined and codified. Through letters to the newspapers and a series of articles in the popular American sporting magazine, *Spirit of the Times,* Beers began to popularize lacrosse, believing that the refinements he had made in it were "as much superior to the original as civilization is to barbarism."

His master stroke came in 1867, when he organized at Kingston the founding convention of the Canadian National Lacrosse Association, with representatives present from twenty-nine clubs from Quebec and Ontario. He had seen that if lacrosse was to grow, and especially if it was to surpass such rivals as soccer, rugby and baseball, there had to be thorough preparation. Strong leadership and patronage were vital; so was an appeal based upon the essentially Canadian nature of the game. The rules had to be clear and simple; there had to be an organization beyond the merely local, providing system and continuity through elective officers, regular meetings, and the chance for clubs at all levels and regions to participate. Finally, to spread the game, there had to be a manual of instruction for would-be players, coaches and organizers.

To Beers, Ontario was crucial; he doubted that the English-speaking enclaves in Quebec City, Sherbrooke and the Eastern Townships were sufficient to carry the game. The Montreal Lacrosse Club had taken teams to Ottawa and Cornwall to put on demonstration matches in the early 1860s; Beers knew that the game had to be spread west to Kingston, Peterborough, Toronto, Hamilton and into populous Southwestern Ontario. Thus the formation of the National Lacrosse Association on 26 September 1867 was a personal triumph for Beers.

He followed this organizational victory with an important and influential book, *Lacrosse: the National Game of Canada,* published in 1869. His object was to convince the reader that lacrosse was easy to learn and a pleasure to play: "The aim of lacrosse is so evident and simple that a child looker-on can intuitively understand it. It has no elaborate nomenclature to make it puzzling, its science and beauty need but eyes for discovery." The equipment was cheap; the game had "no barroom associations"; above all, there was "no beastly snobbishness about it." Unlike cricket, there was no need for marquees, special fields, expensive balls, pads and shoes. The game was immediately exciting for spectators, and for players, demanding as well in terms of skills and physical condition. "Canadians love hard work [Beers wrote, and lacrosse was] real hard work," just like rowing, snowshoeing and tobogganing. Because of this, the game was the very thing to train Canada's young manhood: "It knocks timidity and nervousness out of a young man, training him to temperance, confidence and pluck; teaches him to govern his temper if he has too much, or rouses it healthily if he has too little."

Beers's campaign for the game that he, more than anyone, had developed and organized was immediately successful. In 1867 two of the finest lacrosse teams of all time were formed – the Shamrocks of Montreal and the Torontos – and strong intercity competition began. The Shamrocks were testimony to Beers's declaration that there was no upper-class snobbishness about the game: they represented Montreal's Irish community and demonstrated the fact that lacrosse was becoming a game for all social classes to play.

George Beers was not content with having been the architect of organized lacrosse in Canada. In 1876 he took a lacrosse team to Britain. While it toured the isles (and played before the queen), Beers trumpeted the glories of the game to the press. So unceasingly did he identify lacrosse as Canada's national game that by the time of his death in 1900 a myth had grown that the game had been so declared by act of parliament. Although this was not true, Beers's work had made it so in fact if not in law.

George Beers was also one of the leading figures in the formation of the Montreal Amateur Athletic Association, a landmark event in Canadian sporting history. As we have seen, the membership of the Montreal Snow Shoe Club and the Lacrosse Club overlapped. In 1877 the two bodies joined in the renting of year-round club rooms. They attempted to acquire a Montreal gymnasium and were successful in 1881 under a Quebec act incorporating them as the Montreal Amateur Athletic Association (MAAA). They were joined in the venture by the Montreal Bicycle Club, formed in 1878; shortly after, the Tuque Bleue Toboggan Club and the Montreal Football Club became affiliated as well.

The confluence of all these strong, active sporting groups into one association was undoubtedly the most important single development in the history of Canadian sport. An excellent gymnasium, swimming pool, track and field facilities, football field, outdoor rinks, toboggan slides, reading rooms, billiards and bowling facilities were all quickly produced. Soon hockey, chess and cricket clubs came in under the MAAA umbrella, as well as drama, music and debating.

The MAAA was Canada's first substantial sporting and social club, with a membership of thousands, fielding teams and athletes across virtually the whole range of sporting ac-

Montreal Shamrocks, one of the finest lacrosse teams of all time, won many championships. *Below:* Shamrocks' 1899-1900 world champions.

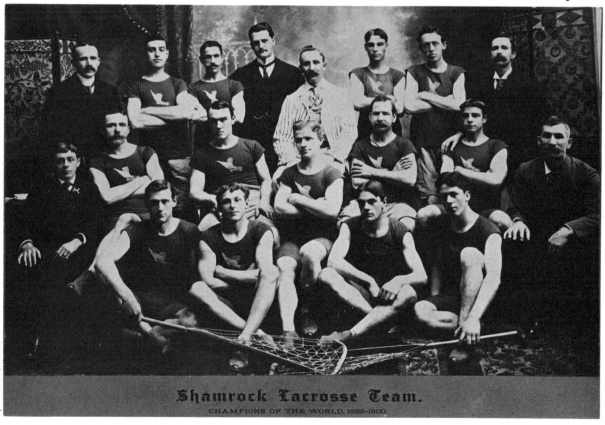

Shamrock Lacrosse Team.
CHAMPIONS OF THE WORLD, 1899-1900

19

Montreal Amateur Athletic Association was the umbrella organization for all organized sport in that city, including the bicycle club *(above).*

tivities; for example, the membership for skating alone in the winter of 1890 was 3,400. From its membership came the leaders and officers for sporting organizations being developed nationally. Through its energies and organizational expertise were formed the Canadian Wheelmen's Association, the Canadian Hockey Association, and the Canadian Rugby Football Association. When the first modern Olympics were held, it was natural that the MAAA should be the chief Canadian sponsor. Ever since these early days, the Canadian Olympic Association has been led largely by Montrealers.

McGill University has assiduously fostered the notion that it was primarily responsible for Montreal's remarkable progress in sport. *Old McGill,* the university's annual, stated in 1912 that "for the first record of athletic activity we must turn to the colleges and especially to McGill. This applies particularly to football and hockey, both of which received almost their first impulse at our university." Though there is no doubt whatever about McGill's important role in the rise of rugby football, for the rest it is clear that it was the

non-academic community that took the lead. Lacrosse was never popular at the university; McGill followed the general civic pattern in snowshoeing, tobogganing, skating, and rifle shooting. McGill's prime contribution to the Montreal sporting scene was its promotion of intercollegiate sports, especially with New England schools. As early as 1873 a McGill law student, D. E. Bowie, won the first major US intercollegiate track championship in a distance race. From the first football match with Harvard in 1874 to the creation of the Canadian Intercollegiate Athletic Union in 1898, the Scarlet and White's teams and athletes were to be found in meets and matches in the United States. A McGill engineering professor named McLeod made the first attempt to time races accurately and in partial seconds by electricity.

The place of the French Canadians in the Montreal sporting scene is more difficult to determine. At the dawn of organized sport in Montreal, there were two separate worlds: that of the English-speaking élite, and that of everyone else. By Confederation, the Catholic Irish were moving in to begin the democratization of sport, but not until later did the French-speaking population begin to share the new sporting interests of the English. Donald Guay, director of the *Groupe de Recherche sur l'Histoire de l'Activite Physique* at Quebec, has found through analysis of French-language newspapers from 1820 to 1900 that horseracing seems to have been the most popular sport. Far behind come rowing, hunting, snowshoeing, skating, baseball, lacrosse and fishing. French Canadians were particularly slow to take up team games. There seems to have been little encouragement for them – or indeed for athletics in general – from the parish organization of the church; what stimulus there was was purely secular, and came from the successes of the Irish in defeating the socially and economically superior English and Scots at their own games. By the 1880s and 1890s French-Canadian clubs specializing in a variety of sports were beginning to appear.

In 1899 a much more ambitious venture was undertaken: the formation of *la Société Canadienne pour l'avancement du Sport,* with Montreal's Mayor Préfontaine as honorary president, Governor-General Lord Minto as patron, and an executive composed of business and professional men from the French-speaking community. The organization aimed to establish a "golden book of honour" for outstanding athletes, a sporting archives and library, and a scientific approach to the problems of training and coaching. Despite the backing of M. H. U. Dandurand, the promoter of Queens-Parc, a complex for lacrosse, cycling, and horseracing, the society petered out in a year or so. The failure of the French-speaking élite to emulate the MAAA was scarcely significant. In the decade before the first world war young French Canadians were taking up sport as they never had before. Snowshoeing, now waning among the English, surged forward among the Canadiens. In the cities, baseball, lacrosse and hockey were attracting thousands of French-Canadian youngsters. Hesitantly, the church and the classical colleges followed behind. Not until the 1920s, in its *Semaines Sociales du Canada,* did the church begin to formulate a Catholic approach to leisure, recreation and sport, and to take some account of the successful American model, the Catholic Youth Organization.

No account of Montreal as the cradle of Canadian sport would be adequate without mention of a man whose methods and influence touched the lives of many for more than a generation. In the early 1850s a young Englishman, Frederick S. Barnjum, settled in the city and established a gymnasium. He had been trained by the Oxford educator, Archibald MacLaren, the man who had synthesized the British passion for sports with the Scandinavian stress upon formal gymnastics. It was Barnjum, more than anyone else, who made the English-speaking community of Montreal conscious of the value of physical fitness. For many

years he taught Montreal high school and McGill students, as well as classes of younger boys and girls. A serious and high-minded man, he deeply believed in the social and moral virtues of physical education, and that life and learning, without exercise, were out of balance. In a public lecture on 11 January 1867, he criticized the current educational establishment for its failure to cultivate "the bodily powers." Physical exercise was left to "the benevolent care of chance" and to individual inclination. The body, however, was meant to be "a fitting helpmate to the indwelling mind"; only through cultivation of both could "noble specimens of our race" be produced. Too often young men sacrificed their health to their studies, and "having gained high academic honours, have found but a laurel wreath to deck their funeral bier."

Barnjum was particularly vehement about the taboos surrounding physical exercise for women:

> What shall we say of girls who, by the conventional rules of society, are debarred from taking more than the semblance of exercise. They have not the same opportunity for romping as boys. Poor little missie must walk home in the most genteel manner possible, perhaps indulging in a softened laugh with some companion her arms carefully hugged to her sides, motion of the lower extremities only being permitted, added to which her poor little body is in all probability forced in by one of those instruments of death called corsets, binding up the naughty muscles that are begging and praying to be let loose and have an opportunity of strengthening themselves, and the young lady is considered to be in a *highly satisfactory condition* if she is pale and weak; but no matter, it is the natural thing for girls to be weak . . . I do not hestitate to say that any young lady placed under the care of an intelligent, well-educated teacher, cannot fail to attain a degree of health which otherwise she never would have dreamed of.

Barnjum had a direct influence upon two of the most important figures in the history of physical education. When James Naismith came from Almonte, Ontario, to McGill in 1883, he fell immediately under Barnjum's spell, and the next year won a medal for all-round gymnastic proficiency. In 1885 Tait Mackenzie followed in Naismith's footsteps. He described Barnjum as "an English gentleman, a lover of horses and all forms of sport, and an inspiring teacher." Barnjum's methods might seem a little authoritarian today:

> He believed in promotion for merit, [Mackenzie wrote later] and when the class lined up before the bridge ladder, over which we went in procession, our hands grasping the sides or rungs, and progressing by steps or jumps backward and forward, he was accustomed to take the meritorious student by the arm and place him high in the line. At the end of the exercises the first ten were numbered, and next class day they lined up in that order and had to fight for their place each day. The pride of making the first ten was sufficient reward for the ambitious beginner.

Frederick S. Barnjum deeply believed in the social and moral virtues of physical education and it was in his gymnasium that many Montrealers kept themselves fit.

When Barnjum died in 1889, it was Naismith and Mackenzie who took over the gymnastic classes at the university. For both of them, it was the beginning of their work in physical education. Naismith was to go on to the YMCA training college at Springfield, Massachusetts, and then into physical education at the University of Kansas. Mackenzie became the first holder of the chair in physical education at the University of Pennsylvania, from which he exerted a profound influence on the development of physical education in North America, as well as being the chief architect of the physical and recreational programs for both the Canadian and American forces during the first world war. His artistic talent and his medical training took him into drawing, then sculpture. Ultimately, he became one of the most popular and well-commissioned sculptors of his times, famed for his depictions of athletes.

Well before Barnjum died, some Montrealers were beginning to wonder whether he, the MAAA, the monster carnivals and the city's other numerous sporting organizations might have been *too* successful. In its absorption with athletics had not Montreal taken "a retrograde step towards a primitive condition of civilization?" asked Dr. Wesley Mills, a noted McGill physiologist, in 1884. Could such a city "still make progress in art, science, literature and morals worthy of the wealthiest and largest city in the dominion of Canada?"

It is unlikely that any Montrealers listened too attentively to Dr. Mills. The Montreal *Gazette,* in an editorial of 17 November 1884, showed the degree to which sport had captured the uncritical approval of the city's citizens.

> The success of Canadians during the present year in international contests requiring the exercise of muscle, skill and pluck may well be a subject of national pride. In at least four departments of outdoor sports the championship of the continent has been won by Canadians. Our own city has McTaggart, the champion cross-country runner; in Thompson, the champion all-round athlete; in Laing, the champion sculler; and in the Shamrocks, the champion lacrosse team. Toronto prides herself on the possession of the champion four-oared and double scull crews, while all Canada may claim the credit of the picked twelve in the international cricket match at Philadelphia. . . . The list of honours is not exhausted but it is ample enough to establish a claim of supremacy for this country in athletic exercises. Considering the comparative smallness of our population, the absence of wealthy classes from whom young men of leisure and means can be drawn, and the relative disadvantages under which our youth labour in preparation for many classes of sport, the successes achieved are not a little remarkable.

Selecting a few facts from a larger whole may distort the overall picture; by highlighting the sports of snowshoeing and lacrosse we may have left the impression that Montreal was barren of other sports. Far from it. The Montreal Caledonian Games were the forerunner of track and field events. Throughout the nineteenth century Montreal was host to regular billiard and chess competitions of high calibre. Fencing, gymnastics, wrestling and boxing had their supporters and their organized clubs. If Montreal fell short at all it was in quality and enthusiasm for aquatic sports; Toronto and the other towns along Lake Ontario held a firm grip on watersports. Still, Montreal *did* have its annual regatta. It was the earliest Canadian community to have both swim clubs and swimming races.

Cricket never lost all of its devotees and throughout the seventies and eighties there were active baseball clubs, particularly in the working-class neighbourhoods. Until the late 1880s Montreal seemed to have an edge on Toronto in equestrian terms – thoroughbred and trotting races, in shows and judging. In winter sports, in particular, Montrealers exploited their snow and ice rather than hibernate indoors.

A social critic may make the challenge about Montreal sport and the MAAA, as we present it, that it all seemed to have been very "upper crust." What kind of model could the MAAA be to the thousands in the city who could not afford the ten dollar annual membership or who did not have the energy and time because of long hours of work? Clearly, the MAAA was not an all-inclusive organization. It was essentially the club – sporting and social – for what we would today label the prosperous middle classes. The answer has to be that the MAAA was not rigidly exclusive; its membership was rather broadly based. More important it was an institutional example in a moderately open society. Its leaders and its captains and coaches had an eye cocked for a good athlete and made him welcome. The other values of the MAAA came from the imitation it engendered.

The marvel of the Montreal Snow Shoe Club and the Montreal Lacrosse Club, the dual progenitors of the MAAA, was not in their membership strength nor even in their direct leadership in these two sports. The wonder was in the encouragement these models provided to dozens and dozens of other snowshoe and lacrosse clubs, first in Montreal, then beyond as Montrealers went West and East.

Rivalry and victory is at the heart of sport. The Irish of Montreal did not organize the Emerald Snow Shoe Club or the magnificently successful Shamrock Lacrosse Club because they were excluded from the MAAA. They just wanted to do it better. They itched to tackle the old established clubs and beat them. Such competitiveness leap-frogged out from Montreal. Just as Toronto was to discover later, when it became the town whose teams everybody else most enjoyed defeating, much of the zest for intercity competition that flowered in the 1870s in lacrosse, snowshoeing, football and rowing came from the challenge of licking the "superior" Montrealers.

The roster of membership of the Montreal Snow Shoe Club and later the MAAA reads like a commercial and professional *Who's Who* of the city. The exclusiveness of the "best" people was to grow in sport, not so much through the MAAA but through fads and enthusiasms as Montreal society became more sophisticated and there were greater extremes of wealth. The Montreal Hunt Club, the early golf and tennis clubs, the ever-costlier pursuits of yachting and rowing gradually drew off more and more of the most affluent Montrealers from the simpler, more rugged pursuits. The switch in interests was most noticeable when the much more expensive automobile swept away the mass involvement in bicycling in the late nineties.

Montreal, of course, always suffered as a centre for sporting development from its lack of a broad hinterland of farms and towns of English-speaking people. Toronto – even Hamilton and London – were eventually better, brighter stars in a sporting firmament of villages, towns, and small cities set in a broad countryside with mounting affluence and common interests. By 1885 one could say of the MAAA that it was a magnificent crystallization of Montreal sporting innovation and leadership. But by the same year it is clear enough that the weight of sporting participation and competition in Canada had swung west to Toronto and its tributary towns and cities.

All too often the picture of nineteenth century life in Canada as presented by modern authors, is one of a gloomy, stoical, rather puritanical people. A society without fun and games! This was not really the Montreal we have written about. No matter how chancey life was at that time, no matter that the fifty- and sixty-hour working week imposed harsh deprivations on the working man, this was a community in which large numbers of people were not intimidated by the brutal winters or recurring depressions. A vibrant, sports-conscious people, Montrealers enjoyed themselves. No one can determine exactly either the active participation or the numbers of the followers who watched and cheered during these decades. But the evidence from the daily press on the number of clubs and fans, plus the variety of sports, shows that there were relatively more adult athletes and players in Montreal and almost as many spectators as there are today.

Montreal Hunt Club (*below*), **became a commercial and professional** *Who's Who* **of the city by the 1880s as sport became more sophisticated.**

Notman Photographic Archives, McCord Museum

Chapter 3

It is impossible to understand and impossible to record a history of Canadian sport outside the context of team games. For one thing, until this present generation it was entirely possible for an all-round athlete to star in two and possibly three different games; today the inordinate length of all game seasons militates against the "all-rounder." Similarly, sports clubs like the Toronto Argonauts sponsored several team games during the athletic year and also fielded athletes in individual sports as well.

If team sports have been pivotal in Canada, why? What has determined the team games we play? Why has lacrosse, our earliest major team sport, all but withered away? Why has the Canadian brand of football retained its hold in the face of competition from English rugger and soccer and the later American football?

Sports compete with each other, not only for athletes, but for money, facilities and public attention as well. In recent years hockey and football have been ascendant in Canada and have siphoned off major shares of the sports dollar and the best athletes, too. Social factors also come into play: in the last thirty years, parents and social agencies have been convinced that team sports are valuable aids in keeping youngsters out of trouble. "Controlling juvenile delinquency," is the phrase that is used. As a result, minor league team sports have proliferated, teams have been sponsored by industry, commerce and communities. This interest, in turn, has provided a vast reservoir of youngsters (and parents), a reservoir from which future major league players and fans are recruited.

Choices about sport are affected as well by climate, facilities, the amount of available leisure time, the attitude of governmental and educational authorities, and the degree of affluence possessed by the particular community or region. Technology has been very important: refrigeration, electrification, air travel, and the electronic media have all had an impact on whether people choose team games or individual games, what games they choose, and the level at which they are able to participate.

Team games arrived from abroad or rose internally in Canada in the following sequence: cricket (1820s), lacrosse (1850s – of course, the Indians had been playing baggataway from time out of mind), rugby football (1850s), baseball (1860s), soccer (1870s), hockey (1870s), basketball (1900s), volleyball (1910s), and softball (1910s). If timing alone determined the success of a sport, then cricket would have won hands down, but in terms of active participation, spectator interest, community support and the crucial test – whether large numbers of youngsters play the game when they have the chance – cricket lost out. Here is how team games rank, in the world and in Canada, measured by a combination of active participants and spectator support:

RANK IN WORLD	RANK IN CANADA
1/ Soccer	1/ Ice hockey
2/ Basketball	2/ Softball
3/ Volleyball	3/ Football
4/ Field hockey	4/ Baseball
5/ Cricket	5/ Soccer
6/ Baseball	6/ Curling
7/ Rugby	7/ Lacrosse
8/ Football (Canada-US)	8/ Basketball
9/ Ice hockey	9/ Volleyball
10/ Water polo	10/ Field hockey
11/ Curling	11/ Cricket
12/ Bandy*	12/ Water polo
13/ Lacrosse (field)*	14/ Lacrosse (box)

* Neither field lacrosse nor bandy is much played today in Canada.

Cost can be a factor in determining which team games are played. Ice hockey, for example, requires a relatively high investment in equipment; soccer or basketball can be played quite adequately with little more than a ball and a patch of level ground.

Social critics have often pointed to violence – or the *possibility* of violence – as a factor affecting a game's popularity. The claim is difficult to assess. Professional hockey is already one of the most physical of sports; critics say that additional brawling degrades the game and drives the customers away. Still, some of the most popular (that is, well-supported) teams of recent years have also been the scrappiest. One thing is certain: the more violent a game, the more need there is for tough, uncompromising rules and the more need there is for the players to accord full authority to the referee. To evolve and enforce such rules is an achievement; to establish a national code for a team game is both an organizational feat and a measure of the game's popularity; to win through to international standards of play is a triumph.

If we apply some of these factors to a consideration of lacrosse we may learn why the country's first team sport has suffered a near-fatal decline in the last few years. To say, as many have, that lacrosse declined because of dirty play is like saying that the *Titanic* sank because she struck an iceberg; the explanation is too simple. Rough play was certainly a factor, but it was symptomatic of deeper problems that struck at the roots of the game.

In 1900 the game seemed immortal. In its Montreal home lacrosse had been strengthened as French-Canadian players and fans joined in from the 1880s on. In British Columbia it had become the dominant sport; in Manitoba it was doing nicely. Almost every community in Ontario, except the Southwestern towns where baseball reigned supreme, supported junior and intermediate clubs; the larger towns fielded senior teams. A league which was comprised of teams from Ottawa, Cornwall and *two* teams each from Montreal and Toronto was producing competition of highest calibre; attendance and gate receipts were high. Yet – although one would not have suspected it from the newspaper space the sport received – the base of the game was narrow. There was no adequate minor program for the game had made no inroads at the public and high school levels. More important, the game had not caught on with the colleges and universities, with the notable exception of Toronto. (In the United States, from the 1890s on, it was college play that saved the game.)

Nor, despite George Beers's missionary work, did lacrosse succeed in establishing itself as a truly national game. Though it was played enthusiastically in the Maritimes during the eighties and nineties, it never attained the strength or the quality to enable Maritime teams to challenge consistently for national ti-

28

Notman Photographic Archives, McCord Museum

Lacrosse was Canada's first team sport to gain acceptance on a broad basis. Adapted from the Indian game of baggataway during the 1850s it quickly became so popular that by 1900 it was considered by many to be immortal. Competitors were very well-conditioned, most playing the entire game without relief. Hugh Beckett *(left, top)* an outstanding player of the 1870s, is shown in characteristic garb of the time. Note the obvious lack of padding. Dr. George Beers (in front of goal, *left, bottom)* wrote the first recognized set of rules for the game and is generally credited as the "father of lacrosse." Lest one think that the white man completely took over the game, note the sartorial splendour of the Caughnawaga Indian team of 1876 *(above)* and an apparent lack of excess weight on any of the twelve players. The Montreal Lacrosse Club of 1867*(right)* displays more elegance with caps and buttoned tunics.

tles – or even to compete regularly with central Canadian teams. On the Prairies, before 1914, lacrosse did rather well, especially in Manitoba, but the distances inhibited intercity and interprovincial play. Only in British Columbia did the game take firm root. West Coast Indians played it with the same flash and verve as the Iroquois of Caughnawaga and St. Regis. On the Lower Mainland, lacrosse became *the* community game in New Westminister and Vancouver neighbourhoods; on Vancouver Island, Victoria bounced with lacrosse activity. British Columbia had what the Maritimes and the Prairies lacked: more concentrated communities, better grounds, better weather, a pioneering program to support boys' play in the playgrounds, and the economic base to provide good jobs for good players, to import stars from the East, and to undertake costly challenges to the best Eastern teams.

These structural and regional weaknesses made lacrosse vulnerable to seasonal competition from other sports and recreations. Baseball was a major rival. Early on, there was considerable resistance to baseball as a Yankee import; even so, it caught on in Southwestern Ontario. In 1882, Toronto joined the International League, a strong professional loop only slightly below the National League in classification. By 1900, the Americans had built an impressive structure of major and minor leagues, and the US colleges had taken to the game in a big way. As a result, American college students were available to play in Canadian community leagues during July and August, and helped to give baseball the lead over la-

crosse in many regions. The Canadian sporting press helped too; mesmerized by baseball's big-league glamour, and spoon-fed by the American wire services, sports editors and reporters gave major coverage to baseball at the expense of lacrosse.

In areas where there were large numbers of British immigrants, soccer rose to challenge lacrosse; later, softball proved more alluring for many. In lacrosse's heartland, the central provinces, the increasing popularity of the summer resort and the summer cottage drew off thousands who might have been watching or playing lacrosse to such recreations as swimming, boating, fishing and camping. As one manager of the twenties, Frank Selke Sr., has said, it was impossible to find the players for a Saturday afternoon's game: "They were up in Coboconk or somewhere with their families . . . there were no customers for lacrosse and not enough players."

What about violence? Did the game prove too rough for a younger generation of Canadians? It is undeniable that the game was rough. Many a Torontonian, for example, will remember "that brilliant general and deadly shot" of the Tecumsehs, Charlie Querrie; Querrie's face was as welted and seamed as a lumberjack's boot.

On the contrary, violence may have *drawn* customers. "If the people knew there was going to be trouble [to quote Frank Selke Sr. again] they'd swarm. They wanted to see it."

On the evidence of newspaper sports pages, it is clear that lacrosse was no rougher than, say, hockey or rugby football. It is also

Tecumseh Park—Game between Tecumsehs, and Stars of Syracuse.
COMPOSITION PHOTO BY EDY BROS., - - - - 280 DUNDAS STREET, LONDON, ONTARIO.
(COPYRIGHT APPLIED FOR.)

apparent that serious injury was *less* frequent than in the other games. Nevertheless, disapproving voices were being raised as early as the 1880s. In 1885, the *Canadian Sportsman* warned that "lacrosse is killing itself; it is too savage." Both it and the Montreal *Gazette* agreed that "the referee question" was crucial; the players were being allowed to get away with too much. Such criticism swelled in the 1890s and 1900s.

What it really signified was that lacrosse was growing weaker within itself. Poor refereeing, a failure to adjust rules to serious infractions in play, perpetual quarrelling over under-the-table professionalism, the use of "imports," player stealing and eligibility rules – all these were symptomatic of a deterioration in leadership. More and more, the men who had patronized lacrosse, and whose patronage had given the game its tone, were now deserting it for rugby football and hockey. Football, not lacrosse, drew support in the universities, while such leagues as the Ontario Hockey Association were being directed by the community leaders who had once been identified with lacrosse.

Who replaced these leaders? Too often, for the sport's own good, promoters and fast-buck entrepreneurs moved into the positions vacated by responsible leaders. W. A. Hewitt, from the vantage point of a long, productive life in sports, put it this way:

> Harry "Sports" Murton was . . . a great player and he once declared that the blow that killed lacrosse was delivered by its promoters. Its destruction began when business enterprises – railways, ferry companies, wealthy individuals – started spending large sums on the purchase and salaries of players . . . That discouraged local pride . . . enthusiasm waned . . . the game ceased to be a drawing card.

To compound lacrosse's problems, the professional league was out of balance. The two Toronto and two Montreal teams outclassed and outdrew the weaker Cornwall and Ottawa teams. In 1912, R. J. Fleming, a former mayor of Toronto, bought the Toronto's franchise and rationalized the league by getting Cornwall and Ottawa dropped. In the short run, this expedient paid off: attendance, interest, receipts all climbed. But the "solution" carried the seed of the league's destruction; competition was reduced to a two-city, four-team seesaw and not even the most loyal fan could bear *that* for long. Fleming and his brother promoters cut lacrosse off from two cities which had been traditional strongholds of the game and they failed to recognize that minor and junior competition was necessary to the health of the professional league.

With the first world war, the professional leagues disbanded and senior amateur play collapsed; only limited junior play con-

E·J·DOPP. Rover.

Charlie Querrie *(top)* **is remembered as "that brilliant general and deadly shot" of Toronto Tecumsehs. E.J. (Gene) Dopp, another fine player, was for years secretary-treasurer of the Canadian Amateur Lacrosse Association.**

31

tinued. By this time the missionary spirit that had carried the game to Britain and the Antipodes was long dissipated. At the end of the war, the only real bases for the game were the smaller towns and cities of Ontario, like Orillia and Brampton, and British Columbia's Lower Mainland. Baseball was stronger than ever; softball was coming on with vigour. In the high schools, now growing because boys were staying longer in the school system, rugby football and basketball, not lacrosse, were the favoured sports. Men like Gene Dopp, a fine lacrosse player who for years was secretary-treasurer of the Canadian Amateur Lacrosse Association, and stellar players and enthusiasts like Ted Reeve laboured for years to revive the game. But even Reeve was hard put, by the mid-twenties, to find material to fill his lacrosse column.

The *coup de grâce* was administered by a short-lived professional league playing *box* lacrosse rather than the field game Canadians had always known. As the name implies, box lacrosse is played in a circumscribed area surrounded by a "box" much like the boards of a hockey rink. Indeed, it was the notion that lacrosse could be moved indoors and fill hockey arenas during the summer months that led to the development of the game. Frank Selke Sr. was one of the several hockey promoters involved in the new league in the 1930-31 season:

> I was in it with Conn Smythe and the brand-new Maple Leaf Gardens [Selke has said]. We argued that lacrosse would keep the gardens going in the summertime . . . We thought it might spur interest if we got the US into it so [through contacts with New York promoters] we got a match between the Canadiens and the Leafs at Madison Square Garden. We filled the house . . . terrific game but there were some injuries . . . The Americans concluded it was too bloody. We weren't getting the crowds . . . [we] folded, so did the Leafs . . . lacrosse went back to the small towns.

It went back, unfortunately, as box lacrosse, a form of the sport played only in Canada, and cut off from the old Canadian game which is still played in the United States and Britain. There seems little chance now that lacrosse in Canada will ever again achieve its former level of popularity.

In 1974 the future of the Canadian Football League became a national political issue of the first rank. The controversy raged as to whether the CFL needed federal legislative protection from the intrusion of American football league franchises into Canada. As it happened, 1974 was the centennial year for Canadian football. A hundred years before, Canadian teams had engaged in their first intercollegiate game, their first interprovincial game, and their first international game. Marginal as the distinctiveness of Canadian football may seem today, the marvel is that anything uniquely Canadian survived at all.

Canadian football is the only successful professional team sport which is played *solely* in Canada.

The history of Canadian football is tortuous, its early period as obscure as its rules seem to have been. This is a contrast to English rugby which inspired it, to English soccer which competed for favour with it, and to American football which has been the strongest influence upon it. At home, these other three games have inspired an elaborate, analytical and critical literature whereas Canadian football sparked few articles and fewer books before the second world war.

Good fortune, as well as strong leadership and community pride, played a part in Canadian football's slow development and survival. For different reasons neither American college football nor American pro leagues were in a position to connect with the Canadian game in any permanent way during its formative stages. By the late 1950s when much of the Canadian public was being exposed to American football through television, a stable Canadian pro league was well in place, giving a seasonal focus to a mass Canadian interest which culminated in the annual Grey Cup match and bash. One feature of this Canadian professional enterprise was that roughly half the player supply was drawn from the United States where high schools and colleges steadily produced hundreds of fine players.

In its beginnings and until the 1920s Canadian football was a pastime for a relatively small, well-educated and comparatively wealthy group. It is unlikely anyone will ever reconstruct accurately the course of the game's rules and competition before the early 1890s. We know that varieties of both soccer and rugby were played in Canada before the basic forms of each were crystallized in England in the Football Association ("soccer") rules of 1863 and the Rugby Union ("rugger") rules of 1871. Despite the public school origins of both games, a class distinction between the two formed rapidly. H. E. Bates has claimed for soccer that since it alone is a purely kicking game, all other variations are bastard. An English sociologist observed in 1911 that "association football thirty or forty years ago was imposed on many schools by mothers. They demanded a game that was not 'rough,' something that in-

The history of Canadian football is tortuous but it is the only successful professional team sport which is played solely in Canada. Montreal was the early stronghold; the first Canadian Football Association formed in 1870 was dominated by Montrealers. Other centres produced good clubs, however, such as Ottawa in 1890 *(right, top)* and Kingston's Queen's College team of 1882.

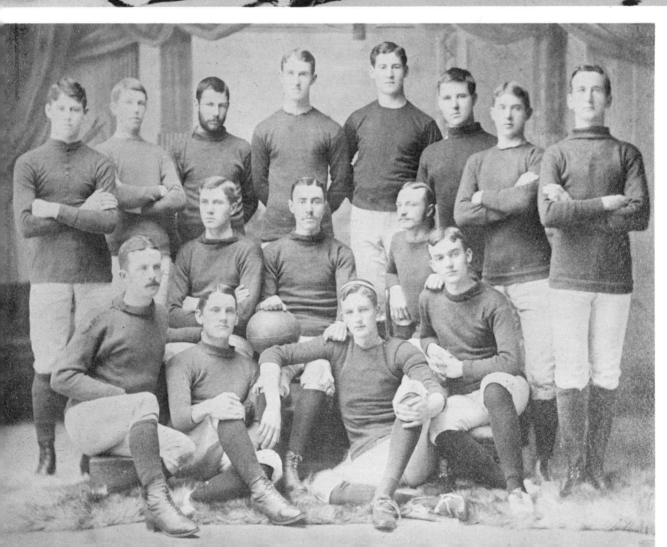

33

volved less tumbling on the ground, less dirtying and damaging to the clothes." It was this purer, more genteel game which won popularity with the English working classes, and became professionalized by 1885. Meanwhile the rougher, less formalized rugger became the game of the English upper and middle classes, perhaps because it was seen as a toughening process for duty in the services and building the empire.

Montreal was the stronghold of the rugby game in Canada. *Gazette* stories in 1867 indicate that a form of it was being played between the Montreal Football Club (founded in 1866) and teams of British army officers. The Canadian Football Association, formed in 1870, was dominated by Montrealers.

In Ontario, at first soccer more than held its own. The reminiscences of Sir William Mulock and James Loudon, both Toronto undergraduates in the 1860s, show that a formless kind of soccer permitting limited ball-handling was the vogue. Queen's was playing a similar game in the early 1870s, though the townspeople preferred rugger. The first Canadian intercollegiate football game was probably one held between Queen's and Varsity on 17 November 1874; Toronto won on two goals by David Forsyth.

It was Forsyth who carried soccer into Southwestern Ontario. In 1876 he went to Berlin (Kitchener) as a school master, and was so successful an organizer that within a few years every high school of any size west of Toronto was playing the game. In 1880 he took the lead in founding the Western Football Association, now the oldest continuing organization of its kind in Canada; later he led touring teams to the United States and Britain. To the Toronto *Globe,* such success was elixir; soccer – "Ladies can attend it!" – was much to be preferred to rugby's crudities. (The *Globe* obviously missed the report of a Berlin soccer game which featured fisticuffs between "Billy" King, later prime minister, and a player from a rival team.)

But rugby too was on the rise. From its base in Montreal, it spread slowly out to Ottawa, Hamilton and the Royal Military College in Kingston. In Toronto, a citadel of soccer, the Argonaut Rowing Club, formed in 1872, took up rugby the following year led by H. P. Glazebrook. Glazebrook's insistence kept rugby alive in the Queen City. Later the Argonauts were joined by a team from the Toronto Lacrosse Club, and then the game caught on at Varsity itself. By 1882 Queen's, probably through the influence of RMC, had been won over and by the end of the century had developed its peculiarly fanatical approach to the game. The Queen's *Journal* of 1900 told the student body that "every man must do his duty so that we may win the intercollegiate title," while Queen's women, who had claimed that they were receiving no benefits from their athletic fees, were told that their function was to support football.

Rugby had been helped to its crucial victory over soccer in Canadian universities by the fact that it could have playable grounds later in the fall than soccer; thus it better fitted the college year. Unlike soccer and lacrosse, rugby football did not have to compete seasonally with either rowing or baseball. Outside the universities many of the early football teams were started by rowing clubs, like the Argonauts, Montreal's Britannia Club, and the Ottawa Rowing Club. Rugby's rugged nature, the belief that it was excellent training for rowing, the fact that to play it excitingly demanded less immediate skill than soccer, all explain why the rowing clubs took up the game so keenly. This greatly broadened the base for the sport. Rowing clubs were very numerous in the late nineteenth century; as year-round associations with clubhouses, strong local support and a kind of internal "farm" system of age-class teams and crews, they were of vital importance in extending participation and interest in rugby football.

The most memorable game of 1874 was the famous international match between Harvard and McGill which Americans freely acknowledge to have been the origin of American football. On 14 May 1874 McGill played Harvard at Cambridge, Massachusetts, losing 3-0 in a game played with a round rubber ball according to soccer rules. The next day, McGill's "oval football of leather" was used, as well as "the rugby rules of the game." The two colleges played for three half-hour periods, with no scoring. "Harvard then took up the rugby game," said the *Harvard Graduates' Magazine* of 1905, "discarding its rubber ball and style of play. But the American mind, quick to take advantage where there is no penalty, has constantly modified the game. Thus Walter Camp of Yale developed interference; the rule said that the man when 'off-side' could not touch the ball or tackle an opponent; but he was not penalized for getting in the way of an opponent – and so he did get in the way under skilful coaching – and American football began."

What is generally forgotten is that Harvard continued to play McGill and other Montreal teams into the early 1880s, by which time "the American mind" had made a game too divergent for the Canadians to play. Indeed, Harvard paid a return visit to McGill in the autumn of 1874. Perhaps two thousand people saw McGill, "in red and black striped caps, jerseys and stockings, and white knickers," resume its rivalry with Harvard, "distinguished by their magenta handkerchiefs and jerseys. They wore old tweed trousers and neither side had any protective padding." The game lasted an hour and one half, Harvard winning by three touchdowns. "In response to the 'tiger' of the McGills," wrote the Boston *Advertiser,* "the Harvard 'rahs' were declared with a vim, and every stranger on the field seemed much astonished at the style of the cheer, many being disposed to think it a joke."

From 1874 on, Canadian football grew steadily, though not spectacularly, in playing strength and public support. By the turn of the century, big city high schools and numerous junior and intermediate athletic clubs in places as diverse as Peterborough, London and Petrolia had teams. The main spectator sports were still lacrosse, baseball and distance-running; soccer had slipped into obscurity. But rugby football, recruiting its leadership from university graduates, was proving more and more interesting to the business and professional classes. Canada produced no Walter Camp to direct the form of the game, though James Smellie, later registrar of the Supreme Court, P. D. Ross, later an Ottawa publisher, and Mike Fallon, a future Catholic bishop, all had an influence; so did such staunch backers as Principal Dawson of McGill, President Loudon of the University of Toronto, and (especially) Principal Grant of Queen's. A powerful national association was slow to emerge, explaining in part why the Maritimes and British Columbia were so long in giving up English rugger.

While the Canadian Rugby Union dates from 1882, its precursors, the Ontario and Quebec Rugby Football Unions, were the actual governing bodies until the Intercollegiate Union was formed in 1897. Not until 1891 was the CRU able to launch an annual series for the Canadian championship. In 1907 the birth of a new senior league, the Interprovincial Rugby Football Union (the so-called Big Four), marked the triumph of the idea that the best teams should play each other regularly and exclusively. Even so, the emergence of the Big Four showed the administrative immaturity of football. The new league was engineered by George Ballard, then president of both the ORFU and the Hamilton Tigers, with the collusion of the MAAA. The Big Four grouped the two strongest teams from each provincial union. Although it nearly wrecked the ORFU in establishing itself, the new league soon had the quality of play and the crowds to command broader public interest and support.

Canadian football rules in this period were as slow to take shape as was the organization of the sport. With some delay, and much reluctance, the Canadians tended to follow American innovations. For example, within two years of the initial Harvard-McGill match,

Sports Hall of Fame

Sports Hall of Fame

With university graduates supplying most of the leadership, Canadian football by the turn of the century had grown steadily in playing strength and public support. Two of the men who played influential roles later became very prominent in Ottawa: P.D. Ross *(top)* and J.F. Smellie, a star at both Osgoode Hall and Queen's.

35

the Americans had discarded the scrum, that shoving circle of players by which the ball was put into play, in favour of the snap back to the quarterback. This change guaranteed possession of the ball to one team and made possible the ordered and intricate development of offensive and defensive tactics.

In 1882 the Americans decided that the offensive team must gain fixed distances in several downs or lose the ball. This idea of "gaining yards" was not widely accepted in Canada until 1907, although the scrum in Canada had given way to a tussle for the ball between two trios of "scrimmagers" during the 1880s. These scrimmagers were flanked by seven wing-men who preoccupied themselves chiefly in wrestling with their opposite numbers, rather than engaging in set plays. Interference or "blocking" entered the American game from the start; the Canadians adopted a limited form of it in 1921, after many years of complaints in the sporting press that "the other team" was using it illegally. To simplify play, the Americans cut the size of teams to eleven from fifteen in 1880; Canadian football became a twelve-man game only in 1921, after years of switching from fifteen to fourteen and back again. In 1884 the Americans gave the touchdown a larger value than the field goal, putting the premium on running, not kicking; Canada made a similar move a decade later, although the retention of the single point for end-zone kicks and three downs rather than four kept punting more to the fore in the Canadian game.

Judging from action photography which began to appear in the daily press of the 1890s, the Canadian game was still a relatively formless one with much wrestling, mauling, dribbling, kicking and argumentation with the referees. Ottawa College, then an Irish-Catholic preserve, and Queen's were the powers of the time. Ottawa, with Mike Fallon as outstanding player and then coach, had many boarding students from the USA: their foreign "trickery" was much deplored in Toronto and Kingston. Queen's also created controversy, perhaps the most notable centring on the "immortal" Guy Curtis. Curtis played football for Queen's from 1886 until the intercollegiate union enforced eligibility rules in 1898; he then played hockey for the Tricolour until 1901.

Occasionally charges of professionalism were made but football was comparatively free of such controversy before the first world war, unlike lacrosse and hockey. In these years its leadership was so top-drawer – with Blakes, Masseys, Claxtons, Hendries and Robinsons galore – and its aim so obviously to beat the other fellows, rather than to make money, that it kept a purer name. Not that it didn't make money. Varsity began charging admissions in

1893; three years later a Queen's-Varsity match drew 5,000. Soon the colleges began to expand their facilities and to use football income to support other college sport.

Before 1914 a few individuals attempted to bring more order into the game, though not with conspicuous success. James Smellie, a star at Queen's and Osgoode Hall for a decade, tried in 1891 to reduce the number of players, to improve the officiating and to bring in alternate offensive and defensive play, but the only advance was to replace the non-playing captains as referee's assistant by an umpire and judges of play.

In 1899 Thrift Burnside, a slashing outside wing and ex-Varsity captain, once again proposed reforms to meet what the press was calling "the crisis in Canadian rugby." That crisis had been precipitated by a touring Irish rugger team, so expert that the *Globe* thought Canadians had "either to choose the American game or its nearest neighbour, or take up the English game." It was Queen's that held out against any rule changes whatever, but the Burnside rules were nevertheless adopted by private schools, the Toronto high school league, and the interfaculty league at

In 1909, Albert Henry George, the fourth Earl Grey *(above)*, with Lady Grey, donated the Earl Grey Cup as a trophy for the amateur rugby football championship of Canada. He never did see a Cup final for his forty-eight dollar investment

The Interprovincial Rugby Football Union, also known as the Big Four, was born in 1907, engineered by George Ballard, then president of Hamilton Tigers

the University of Toronto. Harry Griffith, longtime Ridley headmaster and the man who coached such Varsity players as Hugh Gall, Smirle Lawson and Billy Foulds to the first Grey Cup in 1909, gave the Burnside rules high marks. "The Burnside rules did not win popular favour but they were directly responsible for the insertion of the 'ten yards' rule, the improvement in scrimmage play, and the general opening of the game."

Along with Burnside, chief credit for ensuring that Canadian football would finally turn from the "flow" of rugger to the stop-and-start American pattern must go to Frank Shaughnessy, coach at McGill. Shaughnessy, a bluff man from Notre Dame, was named McGill coach in 1911. In the climate of that year's reciprocity election, he was regarded as an agent of American imperialism. Shaughnessy took full

advantage of the largely uncodified Canadian style of play. What had been a game of wrestling on the scrimmage line together with punting and dropkicking by backs playing deep became more ordered and planned. McGill teams concentrated its backs "on the run" as the ball was heeled back by the centre, and the run for the touchdown began to outshine the kicking game. Such tactics could only be met by bringing the backs on defense up closer to tackle the runners.

In 1921 a new and, eventually the most, vital dimension was added to Canadian football. Edmonton Eskimos came East to challenge for the Grey Cup, to be crushed by Argonauts with Batstone and Conacher running wild around the ends. Though the West failed repeatedly in its quest throughout the 1920s, it brought a new pressure to bear for change in the American direction. Unable to develop enough good Canadians, Western teams imported more and more Americans. In 1929 they adopted the forward pass, the Calgary Tigers bringing in the first American passer. The next

37

The first international football match was
played between Harvard and McGill in Cambridge, Massachusetts, in 1874. Later in the
year, the Harvard team came to Montreal for a
return match which the Americans won by
three touchdowns. The McGill team (in white
knickers) introduced the Americans to the oval
ball and this exchange of games is freely admitted by US historians as being the first, tentative
beginnings of American football. Canadian
football proceeded along its own course and
today is recognized as the only professional
sport played exclusively in Canada.

task was to convince the stodgy East that the pass opened up the game. Ted Reeve made a typical Eastern protest: "The forward pass has brought in so many complicated rules in the US that much of their best ball-carrying . . . is done by the referees." He thought the "punch of the attack" would be better improved by a ten-yard interference zone (that came in 1946, again after the West had pioneered it). Ironically, the Eastern clubs proved sharper at the passing game than the West when the forward pass was adopted in 1931.

It was Winnipeg's Grey Cup victory in 1935 that gave an enormous boost to football in the West, and to the development of the game nationally. That team, built around eight Americans, had a budget of $7,500, far short of the million-dollar plus budgets of today's CFL teams. The East countered in 1936 with a residence rule that effectively stopped the Western champions, the Regina Roughriders, from challenging for the cup. As Tony Allan wrote, this began an era of bad feelings, "and the bickering grew worse as East-West football rivalry increased. The prelude to every Grey Cup final for years was a committee-room battle over rules and player eligibility." The West's perseverance was to win for it most of the battles, as the two leagues moved into an interlocking schedule and the creation of the Canadian Football League with a Western and Eastern grouping for the eventual determination after playoffs of a Grey Cup champion.

Those who chose and classified members for the Canadian Football Hall of Fame in Hamilton divided the game's history into three periods: the first ran from 1874 to 1935 when the Blue Bombers first won the Grey Cup for the West; the second ran from 1936 to 1956 when the CFL was effectively created; the third period runs from 1957 forward. Probably 1920, 1948, and 1950 were more significant mileposts than 1935 or 1956. In 1920 the long-building pressure for rules reform broke through and the game took a shape still recognizable today. In 1948 the capture of the Grey Cup by Calgary electrified Toronto and suddenly Canada realized it had its own sports spectacle to cherish, analogous to the cup final in England or the

The Canadian Football Hall of Fame held its inaugural induction ceremonies in 1973 and seventy-three were honoured — twenty-four builders, forty-nine players. Among them were: Frank Shaughnessy *(top left),* **who became McGill coach in 1911 and helped bring order to a previously unorganized game; Hugh Gall** *(top right),* **one of the great kicking halfbacks of all time; Harry Batstone** *(bottom)* **Queen's triple-threat of the 1920s; and Smirle Lawson** *(opposite),* **Canadian football's original "Big Train" who starred with Varsity and Argos.**

40

Canada Wide Feature Service Ltd.

Football Hall of Fame

Football Hall of Fame

World Series in the us. In 1950 all pretence was dropped, inside and outside football in Canada, that there were any amateur elements left in Western and Big Four football; that same year a national television network was established by the CBC and the regular schedule and the playoffs, East and West, rapidly became a telecast staple of this network and of the CTV network as it took shape at the end of the sixties.

The first, grand induction ceremony for the Football Hall of Fame took place in mid-September 1973 when seventy-three members were honoured, twenty-four as "builders," forty-nine as players. The time range of the members ran from Seppi Du Moulin who played halfback for Hamilton Tigers in 1894 to Russ Jackson, the newest immortal and another Hamiltonian, who quarterbacked championship Ottawa clubs in the 1960s.

A dispassionate critic could argue that the first big cast of the Football Hall of Fame was light in two ways: Hardly any of the early zealots who kept a distinctive game alive between 1874 and 1914 were recognized and far too few of the many coaches, players and administrators of Canadian university teams made it. Of course, the hall was planned and aided largely by leaders of the CFL; thus the leaning of the football hall towards the pro league and its antecedents was understandable.

Nine of the twenty-four builders in the hall were administrators or coaches of teams in Western Canada. This total of nine builders from the West as against a mere trio of Western players – Eddie James, Paul Rowe, and Normie Kwong – seems too high. True, it was determined, aggressive management, successively in Regina (with Al Ritchie, Piffles Taylor, and Claire Warner), Winnipeg (Joe Ryan, Art Chipman, Bert Warwick and Frank Hannibal) and Edmonton (Moe Lieberman and Ken Montgomery) which brought the West up to par with the East in quality, largely by the recruitment of good American talent and genuinely community-based clubs. Of the sixteen Americans in the Canadian hall, eleven played on Prairie teams. It is somewhat misleading, however, that only five Americans who played for Eastern clubs are honoured. After 1948 the competition to recruit the best possible American players was wide open between the East and West. Before that the East had needed fewer Americans. Once the succession of great Argonaut teams faded in 1948, the imperative need for American coaching and top backfield talent, especially quarterbacks, dominated all Canadian football. Teddy Morris of those Argos was the last winning Canadian coach, and no subsequent Canadian team, even the Rough Riders with Jackson, Ron Stewart, Whit Tucker, etc., has had a cast of homegrown stars to match Joe

Krol, Royal Copeland, Steve Levantis, and their mates.

The football crisis of 1974 developed from plans of the World Football League to put a franchise into Toronto. The federal government warned the WFL to stay out of Canada and then introduced a bill in parliament which if enacted, would have made such an entry illegal. The bill as law would also have required the CFL teams to use gradually more and more Canadians and fewer Americans.

After the federal minister responsible for sport announced the barrier against American teams, a sporting and political uproar without precedent in Canada ensued. The proposed measure was welcomed as the salvation of Canadian professional football by most CFL executives and generally was seen more favourably in the West. In the East the proposal was seen as repressive, a dictatorial interference with free enterprise and with the individual's right to see what he wanted to see. Much of the sporting press comment was bitterly against the bill and it became clear that the sportswriters in Toronto and Montreal, in particular, were sure that the future destiny of our football, as with our hockey and baseball, was to be in North American professional competition.

During this uproar, the Toronto Argonauts team in the CFL was sold for $3.3 million by its most recent owner, John Bassett, to a large investment and trust syndicate. A hundred years before, H. P. Glazebrook had engineered the founding of the Argonaut Football Club. It, and the other clubs in Montreal, Ottawa and Hamilton had been built by the enthusiastic labours of hundreds of players, coaches and volunteer executives. None of them could have imagined that the fruits of their labour would bear such a cash value, nor that one man alone would reap the reward of them.

The origins of hockey are just as confused as those of football, and a good deal more controversial. In 1942 a Canadian Amateur Hockey Association committee headed by W. A. Hewitt decided that Kingston was the birthplace of the game. Its report, *The Origin of Hockey* in Canada, states:

Among the many fine players in the CFL is this group of six elevated to the Canadian Football Hall of Fame. Paul Rowe of Calgary (*opposite, top left*), Norm Kwong of Edmonton (*opposite, top middle*) and Eddie James of Winnipeg (*opposite, top right*) were great plunging backs. Teddy Morris (*opposite, middle left*) and Joe Krol (*opposite, bottom*) won lasting fame as football players with the Toronto Argos. Big No. 12 (*opposite, far right*) belonged to Russ Jackson of Ottawa who quarterbacked the Ottawa Rough Riders in the glory years of the early 1960s.

Football Hall of Fame

Football Hall of Fame

Sports Hall of Fame

The first hockey was played by the Royal Canadian Rifles, an imperial unit, stationed in Halifax and Kingston in 1855. It is quite possible that English troops stationed in Kingston from 1783 to 1855 played hockey as there is evidence in old papers, letters, and legend that the men and officers located with the imperial troops as early as the year 1783 were proficient skaters and participated in field hockey. It is more than likely that the pioneers played their field hockey in those early days on skates but that is not an established fact.

The slender evidence upon which Kingston's primacy is founded is contained in a diary of the 1850s kept by a Kingstonian who mentions groups of soldiers playing "shinny" on the harbour ice. We have turned up references to "shinty" on skates being played in Ottawa in 1852, and to "hockey" on the Halifax inner harbour in 1851 (this reference from a Boston paper of that year). But while we have no doubt that more such references could be found in the millions of words published by the British North American press before 1855, such evidence is really beside the point. (This is probably the place to explode a fantastic story told by an octogenarian Montrealer, John T. Knox, and published in the *Gazette* in February 1941. According to Knox, his father, Michael, had helped invent hockey in February 1837, and the first game had been played in Montreal between the Dorchesters and the Uptowns on "the last Saturday in February 1837." During that winter, the city's newspapers published many items about curling, sleighing and fencing – but not a single word about hockey.)

Shinny, shinty, hockey and bandy were all ancient ball-and-stick games played by many peoples – the Scots, Irish, French, and Dutch, among others – but the origins of these games are quite unknown. The word hockey itself is derived from the French *hoquet*, a shepherd's crook. Hanging in the Scottish National Gallery in Edinburgh is a painting titled "Winter Landscape" by the seventeenth-century Dutch artist, Hendrick Avercamp, in which a soberly clad group of Dutch gentlemen are pursuing a little white ball with curved sticks. There is evidence that both the New York Dutch and the New Englanders were playing something called hockey on ice in the colonial period. All these games, including that played by the Royal Canadian Rifles at the mouth of the Cataraqui in 1855, were essentially formless. They bear the same relation to modern ice hockey as does the confused melee of Indian baggataway to George Beers's consolidation of lacrosse.

To be considered an organized sport, rather than a folk game, hockey needed agreement on a standard field of play (the rink) and on equipment (pucks, sticks, and goals). Standard rules had to be accepted along with a means to enforce them. Teams and the structure of competition had to be defined, so that a winner and loser could be determined. Finally, there had to be a repetitive pattern of competition so that, even if changes occurred in the basic format, it would be possible to say that continuity existed.

In Montreal, and Montreal alone, were these conditions met. Montreal's case, in response to the CAHA report, was made by the late Professor E. M. Orlick of McGill, in an outraged communication to the *Gazette* on 27 November 1943. The evidence bears out his argument in every particular. Orlick claimed that the first true game of organized hockey was played in the Victoria Rink in 1875; that it had begun a couple of years earlier among a group of young men who were seeking a winter version of lacrosse; and that the leading spirit was James George Aylwin Creighton. Orlick's account came from Henry Joseph, then eighty-eight, the only survivor of the 1875 game. Joseph identified fourteen of the eighteen players in the original lineups.

Joseph stated that he and his friends began to experiment with ice hockey in 1873, playing "almost every day in the week and even on Sundays when we could bribe the caretaker of the Victoria Rink to let us in." He could not recall seeing hockey sticks before that time, nor anyone playing hurley or shinny on skates. He and his friends, who were members of the Victoria Rink, the Montreal Lacrosse Club and the Montreal Snow Shoe Club, had first tried to play lacrosse on skates but found it unsatisfactory. He declared that it was J. G. A. Creighton who suggested that they use shinny sticks and a ball and that to Creighton "should go the credit for the origin of ice hockey in Montreal." Since all the players played rugger as well, they decided to pattern their game after English rugby, including its key "onside" rule which lacrosse did not have.

What Joseph called "the first 'public' exhibition of the game of ice hockey" was announced in the *Gazette* of 3 March 1875:

> A game of hockey will be played at the Victoria Skating Rink this evening between two nines from among the members. Good fun may be expected, as some of the players are reputed to be exceedingly expert at the game. Some fears have been expressed on the part of the intending spectators that accidents were likely to occur through the ball flying about in a too lively manner, to the imminent danger of lookers-on, but we understand that the game will be

Controversy has long surrounded origins of ice hockey in Canada but some things have remained constant – essentials include ice, skates, a stick and some object to knock about. A replica of one of the original sticks is shown (*opposite, top*) while an actual game in action is illustrated below. Note the uniforms, the sticks serving as goalposts and spectators, all standing, along the sides.

QUEEN'S UNIVERSITY, KINGSTON, CHAMPIONS

played with a flat, circular piece of wood, thus preventing all danger of its leaving the surface of the ice.

The nine-man teams and the primitive puck are noteworthy. In its account of what it called a "novel contest," the *Gazette* observed that "the game of hockey, though much in vogue on the ice in New England and other parts of the United States, is not much known here." This refers to the kind of mass, undisciplined play on outdoor rinks or ponds that had probably been going on in North America for a long time. The *Gazette*'s reporter compared hockey to lacrosse, because it used flags to mark eight-foot goals. Captain Creighton's team won, 2 games to 1, a score that suggests that the lacrosse model was being used.

That the first game of organized hockey should have been played in Montreal is entirely natural. Montreal's Victoria Rink was the best such facility in the world; it is interesting to note that the dimensions of its ice surface, 200 by 85, are precisely those now used for hockey. More important, Montreal had a sizeable sporting élite, already experienced in athletic innovation, endlessly experimental and loaded with organizing ability. But Creighton, the leading member of the hockey group, was not a Montrealer. Born in Halifax in 1850 of a well-to-do family, and later a brilliant student at Dalhousie, he had worked as an engineering assistant to Sir Sanford Fleming during the survey and building of the Intercolonial Railway. In the 1870s he was active in construction projects in the Montreal area. It is quite possible that he had played as a youngster in bandy-like hockey on the big frozen spaces of the Dartmouth lakes or the Halifax harbour arms; when he arrived in Montreal he was already an outstanding skater, and served as figure-skating judge for the Victoria Rink in 1875-6.

In 1876 the *Gazette* again carried an account of a hockey match at Victoria Rink. This time one team represented the rink, while the other, captained again by Creighton, was from the Montreal Football Club and wore its red and black uniform. Again there were nine to a side, now specialized into four forwards, two halfbacks, two backs and a goalkeeper. Two umpires were used and their job was to enforce something the newspaper called "the 'Hockey Association' rules." It is clear that hockey tactics were beginning to develop, at least among the football-hockey players "whose defense and organization – the strong points of the football team – gave them a great advantage over their opponents."

In the 1920s J. G. A. Creighton wrote that he "had the honour to be captain of the first regular hockey club to be formed in Canada, which was at Montreal in 1877." That club was the Metropolitans, whose game with "eight gentlemen of St. James" (there is no explanation of the reduction in team size) was reported in the *Gazette* on 27 February 1877. To the two umpires had been added a referee; more important, however, was the printing in full of hockey's first rules. In part they read:

1/The game shall be commenced and renewed by a bully in the centre of the ground . . .

2/When a player hits the ball any one of the same side who at such moment of hitting is nearer the opponents' goal line is out of play and may not touch the ball himself, or in any way whatever prevent any other player from doing so until the ball has been played. A player must always be on his own side of the ball . . .

3/The ball may be stopped, but not carried or knocked on by any part of the body. No player shall raise his stick above his shoulder. Charging from behind, tripping, collaring, kicking or shinning shall not be allowed.

The bully, of course, was the primitive face-off; the term derives from rugger and is a word still used in field hockey. Both the bully and the onside rule (or "shinny on your own side"), vital to modern hockey, are strong supporting evidence for the view that organized hockey began in Montreal. As we have seen, most of the young men playing at the Victoria Rink in

Public Archives of Canada

By the early 1900s hockey had increased in popularity and women were playing quite as aggressively as men. Eva Ault models typical garb of the time.

46

these years were footballers as well, and seem to have carried over football terms and rules into their new game. Rugby players believed there was something unfair about forward passing, and revelled in the joy of putting the ball in play through the scrum or bully. But if Montreal hockey did indeed develop when a football-like game was moved from huge outdoor rinks onto a smaller indoor surface, the onside rule made poor sense. Only the inborn conservatism of rugby players would tolerate the incessant stoppages in play particularly in scrambles around the goals. Indeed, it was this feature which led to the first "blue line," a mere three feet in front of the goals. Gradually, from 1905 on, the Ontario Hockey Association pushed this line out to ten, twenty, then thirty feet, creating for each team a defensive zone in which defending players could freely pass and receive the puck. Had the rugby-derived onside rule not been breached, hockey would have been doomed to a somewhat static and highly individualistic game, with the premium on stick-handling. It took both hockey and football

Rideau Hall Rebels *(above)* **were a popular team of the 1890s in Ottawa. Two of its members were Arthur and William Stanley, sons of the governor-general, and it is believed it was their influence which prompted Lord Stanley to donate the cup which is today the premier prize among pro hockey teams.**

nearly sixty years to accept the opening up of the game through the forward pass.

Another claim made by the CAHA's report on the origins of hockey was that "the first organized league hockey was played at Kingston. . . The league comprised four clubs . . . That league operated in 1885-6."

It is quite true that several teams were formed in that year, but the Queen's *Journal* shows clearly how impromptu the matches were. Hockey in Kingston, in fact, looked to be at about the same stage the game had reached in Montreal some eight to ten years before. It is worth noting that one of the members of RMC's team, Edward Thornton Taylor, had played in the early games reported in the *Ga-*

47

zette; he and his brother Archie were active in the first McGill hockey club, organized in 1877. It is quite possible that Taylor, later a noted mountain climber and tiger hunter in India and RMC's commandant (1905-9), did the missionary work in establishing Montreal's form of ice hockey in Kingston. Moreover, the Montreal teams of the 1870s did not wither away – the Montreal Victorias, for example, had a continuous existence from the 1870s until just before the second world war.

Before we leave the origins of hockey, one further contribution by J. G. A. Creighton must be noted. After he took his law degree at McGill, he was appointed law clerk of the senate, a position he held until his death in 1930. He took his knowledge of hockey to Ottawa, and by 1888 was the mentor and senior member of a club called the Rideau Hall Rebels. The governor-general of the time was Lord Stanley of Preston; it was he who donated the Stanley Cup. His two sons, Arthur and William, became intensely fond of hockey, and their team, the Rebels, became a major attraction as an exhibition game opponent in Quebec and Ontario in 1889 and 1890. Other prominent members of the team were John Augustus Barron, a lawyer who was a Liberal MP for an Ontario riding, and Lieutenant-Colonel Henry Albert Ward, Conservative MP for Durham East, also a lawyer.

The influence Creighton had over these men cannot now be measured, but it must have been considerable. At any rate, Arthur Stanley, son of the governor-general, Barron (who acted as chairman), Ward, and J. F. Smellie from Queen's took the lead in founding the Ontario Hockey Association in 1890, in order to bring about province-wide play. Expansion into Ontario was just as fundamental to hockey's future as it had been for lacrosse; Montreal had no hinterland of satellite towns, and the French-speaking population was slow to take up the sports of the Anglos.

By the mid-1890s hockey had swept Southern Ontario with the same kind of broad age-class divisions and intense intercommunity rivalries that earlier had been typical of lacrosse. By this time, as Tait Mackenzie pointed out in an article written in 1893, the rules had developed considerably from the Montreal Hockey Association's first code. "Learned committees, composed of delegates from distant cities, have 'sat upon' rules and constitutions and by-laws and amendments and foot-notes." To this cause he assigned hockey's "wonderfully rapid progress in favour both with player and spectator," as well as to the covered rinks, now "found in every city and town throughout the Dominion."

The winter carnivals at Montreal, beginning in 1883, [Mackenzie wrote] gave the game its first great impetus, it gained rapidly in popular estimation and, to the visitors who thronged the city, the hockey matches in the Victoria Rink were soon among the chief attractions.

When Mackenzie wrote, the puck, "a cylinder of vulcanized rubber an inch thick and three inches in diameter," had been in use for about a decade, the goal mouth had been narrowed to six feet with a crossbar four feet off the ice, the size of the stick blade had been defined, and teams had been reduced to seven men. Positions had been named – goalkeeper, point, cover-point, and four forwards. "Forwards who play well together do a great deal of passing from one to another," he noted. "An opponent is sometimes eluded by making the puck strike the wooden curbing at the side of the rink, picking it up as it rebounds." Goal judges, still called umpires, were in place behind the goals, and the referee kept time and controlled play, having the power to rule off a player for fouling. The term "facing" was now in use as well as "bully"; there was provision for sudden-death overtime.

One of the dominant figures in the early days of the OHA was John Ross Robertson, publisher of the Toronto *Telegram* and the league's president from 1899 to 1905. Some of Robertson's presidential addresses provide a vivid picture of the state of hockey in this era. Obviously the league was already having trouble with towns that "imported" and paid stars from other centres. As Robertson said:

An open foe one may watch, but the pretended friend, the spurious amateur, the man who skates under false colours, the professional who treks in a disguise of hair dye and false whiskers is the curse of all true sport in this Dominion . . . He invades the railway train . . . he arrives on the platform of his destination. He ambles to the best hotel, calls the clerk by his Christian name, transmits a thirteenth-century autograph to the hotel register, gives the glad hand all round, has a vase of beer with friends, who, unexpectedly of course, drop in and next day, with his favourite brand, "The Pride of Havana," in the corner of his mouth, he walks the streets with all the airs of an old settler.

Noting the trouble caused when the Canadian Lacrosse Association and the Canadian Amateur Athletic Union had reinstated professionals, Robertson laid down the principle of amateurism without reinstatement. "We make no man a professional and no man an amateur. The man makes himself a professional, and the OHA should never unmake him."

Robertson had much to say about rough play and unruly conduct, by both players and spectators. Under his leadership the referee was empowered to "rule off the ice . . . a player who . . . has deliberately offended [by] . . . charging from behind, tripping, collaring, kicking, cross-checking or pushing." In 1904 there were four deaths from rough play in

Eastern Canada; these deaths occurred outside the OHA. Still Robertson warned that it was time to "call a halt to slashing and slugging, and insist upon clean hockey in Ontario, before we have to ask the coroner to visit our rinks." He deplored the brutality of teams in Orangeville and Smiths Falls, who roughed up their visitors on the ice and hazed them in the streets, and he had stern words for coal-throwing at Lindsay, bottle-tossing at Peterborough, and the mobbing of a team at the London railway station.

Clearly, hockey had moved well beyond its genteel origins, and was becoming a handful, even for the formidable Robertson. A man whose memory encloses the transition from that boisterous era to the beginnings of the modern period of professional dominance is Fred "Cyclone" Taylor. He was born in the village of Tara, Ontario, in 1885, when organized hockey did not exist in the province. In his nineties in Vancouver, he remains intelligent, perceptive and with an amazing recall of the early days. In the Tara of his boyhood, he

The Stanley Cup, oldest trophy in competition among professional athletes in North America, was first presented in 1892 by Lord Stanley, then governor-general of Canada. The original holders of hockey's most famous bauble were Montreal Amateur Athletic Association.

remembered "everybody was an all-rounder":

> We spent our summers playing baseball and lacrosse, and swimming. In the winter everything centred around the rink. If we weren't playing we'd go skating. There'd be band music and girls saying "Please take me around, Fred" or "Take me around again, Fred." The whole community took part in sport, either in playing or in support. There's just no truth in the picture of our towns as dreary places with everybody working long, long hours.

By the time Fred Taylor was seventeen, he was a promising junior player in Listowel, and began to encounter the seductions of the quasi-professionalism that John Ross Robertson was trying to stamp out. "As a junior," Taylor remembered, "you'd find a few dollars tucked in the toe of your shoe after a game. Once you had any kind of a name, visitors from many towns would drop by with offers to move and play elsewhere." Wherever he played, Cyclone Taylor was a star. By 1910 he had been drawn to Renfrew and the famous Millionaires, the fabulous team assembled by the O'Briens, and played with Lester and Frank Patrick for the first time.

Taylor admired the Patricks as innovators and "big thinkers":

> I wonder how many today know all the innovations they brought to hockey. They pioneered six-man hockey, dropping the rover. They brought in the forward pass and blue-lines. They and an old teammate of mine, Art Ross, really took the game to the US in 1926. They numbered players; they split the game into three periods; they started assists as a statistic.

The game Taylor played, so swiftly changing in the hands of the Patricks and others, was enough like our own for comparison to be made. It was rough, there was plenty of hitting, but no body checking was allowed within five feet of the boards. "Of course, there was more carrying of the puck and more passing than today. Possession of the puck was more important." In fact, the current Russian style strikes Taylor as similar to the old game. "You stickhandled and passed until you had a good shot." But, he thought, the great players of his day would hold their own today: stylish Joe Hall, Newsy Lalonde – "not so fast, but tough and cagey, so strong, always in the right place, a perfect sense of timing" – the speedy Joe Simpson, the slick Frank Fredericksen and many more.

Who is to deny Fred Taylor's judgments? He himself was thought of as the greatest player of his day – yet what of the deadly Joe Malone, who, in a brief season of twenty games with the 1917-18 Montreal Canadiens, potted forty-four goals, a pace today's Phil Esposito has never matched? As the era of Taylor and Malone was ending, the Ottawa valley produced a series of great stars – men like the stick-handling, poke-checking wizard Frank Nighbor of Pembroke, then two Ottawa boys, the heady Frank Boucher and that effervescent lightweight defenseman, Frank Michael "King" Clancy. There is no agreement among those who saw them as to which was the most outstanding – Clancy himself thought Howie Morenz the best player he ever saw.

In comparing players of different eras, statistics are meaningless. Each generation of players and fans carries mental images of the qualities of those performers who stood out, and there is no reconciling them. How difficult it is to persuade today's generation that modern masters like the indestructable Gordon Howe or the superbly gifted Bobby Orr had their counterparts in another day: To mention Eddie Shore is to draw blank looks. Goaltenders, one would think, would have more chance

Hockey Hall of Fame

Hockey Hall of Fame

John Ross Robertson (*top*) **was a dominant figure in early days of the Ontario Hockey Association and his iron-fisted approach helped remove much of the brutality of the game. He also donated a trophy** (*bottom*) **for Ontario championship competition.**

50

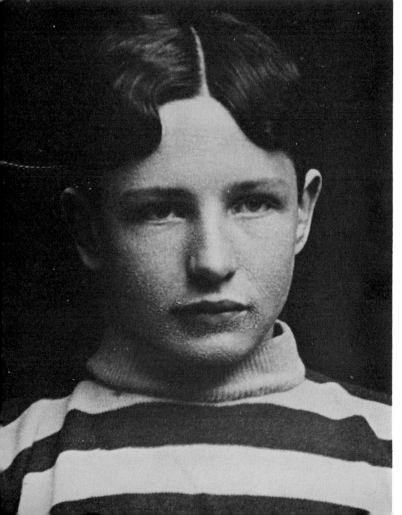

Four men whose names will always be synonymous with hockey are Fred (Cyclone) Taylor *(top left)*, Art Ross *(top right)*, Frank Patrick *(left)*, and his brother Lester *(above)*. Taylor was a brilliant player in every phase and at every position. Ross was an innovator, strategist, promoter and outstanding player. The Patricks played, coached, managed and were owners, and were innovators of six-man teams when they took professional hockey to the West Coast.

51

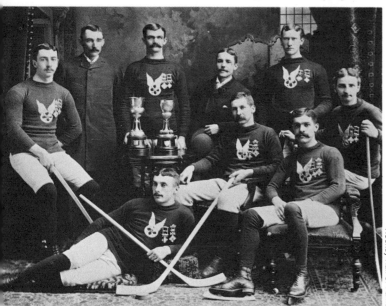

RENFREW 1909-10 HOCKEY TEAM

OTTAWA ALERTS, CANADIAN LADIES CHAMPIONS, 1923.

Famous, and infamous, teams have landmarked the history of hockey in Canada. *Far left top to bottom* is shown the Victoria professionals of 1911, managed by Lester Patrick; Eastern Canada's champion Montreal AAA team of 1889, a team that wore no padding or gloves; and the Simcoe team of 1899, winners of the Lacrosse Hockey League title under the presidency of John Ross Robertson who is seated in the middle. Second row *(top to bottom)* features a name long associated with Maritime hockey, the 1913 Sydney Millionaires; the Kenora Thistles of 1906-07, from the smallest community ever to produce a Stanley Cup champion; and one of Ottawa's famous Silver Seven teams, the 1905 Stanley Cup titlists. Third row *(top to bottom)* includes the 1897 team of Orillia, Ontario, a provincial power in its day; the famous Renfrew Millionaires of 1909-10 that included six future Hall of Famers but couldn't win the Stanley Cup; and Ottawa Alerts, Canadian ladies champions of 1923. *Above* is the Queen's University team, Kingston city champions in 1888, a team that included two doctors, two barristers and three others who later became men of note in the business world.

53

of living in memory simply because of their singularity. But aside from the trophy that bears his name, who today remembers George Vezina, or, for that matter, Clint Benedict, George Hainsworth, Frank Brimsek? Even Terry Sawchuk's reputation is beginning to fade.

One of the most remarkable facts of modern-day hockey is the wealth of French-Canadian talent. In most fans' minds, that fact is connected with the emergence of the electrifying Maurice Richard and his younger teammate, Jean Beliveau, whom many think of as almost the classic, complete hockey player. Yet long before these men, the Frenchmen flew: Didier Pitre, the Manthas, Aurel Joliat, "Pit" Lepine and many more.

Stars wax and wane, but as they do, their game has been changing greatly. There are two main threads in Canadian hockey development in the twentieth century: the spread of professional hockey into the North American urban market, and the up-building of amateur hockey to a regionalized federation tying almost every community in the country into local and national competition. The imperatives of the first were finally to destroy the second.

The Ontario Hockey Association became the model for other provincial and regional associations; from 1914 most of these associations were linked by the CAHA. This body was created largely through Western – especially Winnipeg – enthusiasm, though William Northey of Montreal was the convening chairman, and the first secretary was Norton Crow, a long-time official of the Amateur Athletic Union of Canada.

The CAHA converted the competition for the Allan Cup, the trophy for the senior amateur championship, from its awkward challenge format to a system of national playdowns. In 1919 it established the same pattern for juniors when the Memorial Cup was introduced. The years between 1920 and 1950 were splendid times for amateur hockey, whatever they might have been for society at large. There was always a chance that smaller towns – Kirkland Lake, Copper Cliff, Newmarket, Owen Sound, Kimberley, Moncton – could win a national championship, and right across the country there was a rich texture of regional competition.

At the same time, Canadian hockey was being carried to the world. With the Winnipeg Falcons in 1920, Canadian senior champions began to tutor European hockey through International Ice Hockey Federation "world" championships. Within a little more than three decades, the USSR, Sweden and Czechoslovakia first became competitive, then overpowered the CAHA-sponsored teams, by this time no longer drawing upon a huge pool of good talent. Senior

Hockey Hall of Fame

Hockey Hall of Fame

Joe Hall (top) died of the flu following the 1919 Stanley Cup final, the only year the cup didn't have a winner. Frank Boucher (bottom) was a master centre, one of the great play-makers of all time.

Hockey was first recognized at the Olympic and world championship level in 1920 at the seventh Olympiad held in Antwerp, Belgium. Canada's representative, ironically, was a team comprised of players who, all but one, were of Nordic or Icelandic extraction: the Winnipeg Falcons. Most notable graduate of this team was Frank Fredrickson (*fifth from left*) who later played in the National Hockey League and was elected to the Hockey Hall of Fame in 1958. Another man of distinction in the team picture is W.A. Hewitt, long-time secretary of the Canadian Amateur Hockey Association and the Canadian Olympic representative. He is standing in a business suit in the middle of the photograph. F.M. (King) Clancy (*left*) was a product of Ottawa who was to lead Toronto Maple Leafs to their first Stanley Cup victory in 1931-2. He also was elected to the Hockey Hall of Fame in 1958.

In the more than eighty years of competition for the Stanley Cup, it is hazardous to try to name some players as being more outstanding than others but few will dispute that Maurice (Rocket) Richard, *(above)* was in a class by himself. Named fourteen times to National Hockey League All-Star teams, he scored eighty-three winning goals during his NHL career and scored eighty-two goals in the playoffs, both records. Terry Sawchuk *(opposite, left)* as one of the greatest goalies in hockey history. He played more games (971) and recorded more shutouts (103) than any other goalie in the history of the NHL. Frank Nighbor *(opposite, top right)* was also known as the Pembroke Peach. A 60-minute centre with Ottawa for fourteen years, he was the mould for all great stick-handling centres of the future. George Vezina *(opposite, bottom right)* is one of the most renowned netminders of any era and his name has been perpetuated by the trophy presented annually to the goaltender of the team with the fewest goals scored against it in a National Hockey League season.

56

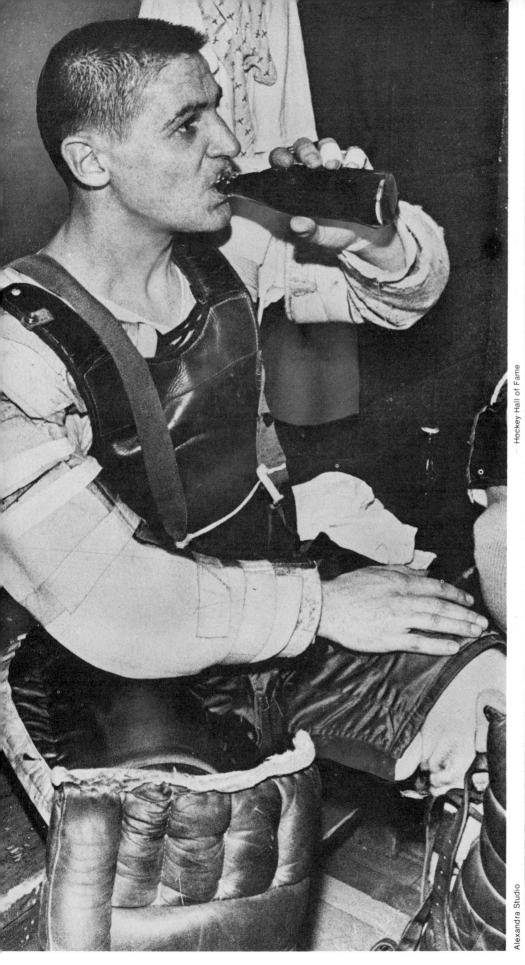

hockey, in fact, was beginning to die.

The National Hockey League's farm system, especially after 1945, had concentrated upon the development of junior players. This was done through the "c" form, giving the NHL clubs ownership of boy prodigies from the age of fifteen. The professionals concentrated the cream of the juniors in a few leagues, notably the OHA Major Junior League. The nurture of such talent was no longer left to the local community unless it happened, fortuitously, to be the site of a major junior enterprise. By 1967, when the NHL forsook its junior and minor farm system for an annual draft of graduating juniors, the major junior franchises had become so rewarding financially that there was no chance for a reversion to the old pattern in which dozens of communities took part. The midget draft and a weekly wage limit authorized by the CAHA reinforced the domination of age-class hockey by about a score of business enterprises.

The kind of national framework we had in amateur hockey, which drew us together as a people and pulled in communities and regions now unrepresented in the larger professional picture, was unique. American team games – baseball, basketball, football – never attained the level of competition for a US national amateur championship. Except in baseball, American professional entrepreneurs had no need to build their own farm systems. Their educational system, (unlike ours) provided the training and competition that annually produces its crop of recruits. From the beginnings of Canadian team sports one can discern the powerful, uncomplicated push of communities to put together the best possible club, first to defeat local rivals, then to win a Canadian championship. In hockey, professional and Junior A domination has snuffed out most such communal motivation. In place of the national amateur championships has come the extraordinary growth of minor hockey. Few healthy Canadian boys do not have the chance to play organized hockey, especially between the ages of eight and twelve. We now have large-scale tournaments for midget, bantam and pee-wee teams, supplemented during the summer by a profusion of hockey schools. The object is no longer the winning of national titles, but the identification of individual excellence, to be rewarded by the draft. Our national obsession, abetted by large-scale commercial advertising, and coupled with the enticement of well-paid careers, is a phenomenon virtually unmatched in any sport elsewhere in the world.

The consequences of this obsession are unfortunate in several ways. After the age of sixteen, when the best players have been creamed off, most Canadians cease to play hockey: the huge pyramid of minor hockey tapers to a miniature apex. Yet hundreds of boys

David Bier

Jean Beliveau *(above)* was to become a living legend. He scored 507 goals in an eighteen-year NHL career, an all-time record for a centre, but he was of a character that would have made him great and earned him respect everywhere, even if he had scored half that total. He played on ten Stanley Cup winners and was named ten times to NHL All-Star teams. Gordie Howe *(opposite)* trying to score on long-time friend Johnny Bower, was a man who never quit, a player of seemingly limitless ability and endurance. Often called "Mr. Elbows" by rivals, he could also have been called "the Most" as he established more records than any other NHL player, among them most seasons (25), most trophies as the NHL's most valuable player to his team (6), most NHL scoring championships (6), most career goals in regular season (786) and most selections to NHL All-Star teams (21).

who don't quite make the top might have shone in other individual or team sports had they not given themselves so totally to the pursuit of hockey. At the same time, our professionally oriented system does not necessarily produce the best possible hockey or hockey players. Its essential assumptions appear to be (a) that a worthwhile prospect can be recognized by age sixteen; (b) that skills and physique can best be developed through long schedules of games rather than by the kind of training which distinguishes between the individual and team aspects of hockey and then marries these elements tactically; (c) that hockey has little to learn from the techniques developed by other individual and team sports; and (d) that rough and intimidating play, including the specialized "policeman," is inseparable from the game.

What is now clear is that hockey is a world game in which Canadian supremacy has slipped; our narrow victory of four wins, three losses and one tie in the 1972 series with the USSR makes that embarrassingly apparent. (It is a spoilsport who would point out that on a total-goal basis, Canada *lost* the series 32-31.) At the moment it is difficult to see how the social and political disparities between Canada and, say, the Soviets can be managed to permit regular international competition. If the difficulties are overcome, it is almost certain that the professional structure of hockey in Canada will militate against Canada putting a team on the ice.

A craze for hockey swept Canada in the dying years of the nineteenth century. Here on a frozen slough of 1880 Saskatchewan, an impromptu game using primitive equipment was in progress.

Biographies

DONALD HENDERSON BAIN, 1876-1962

A man who spends some eighty-odd years of his life in the same community, who has wealth and who has been active in many fields, develops a reputation; he becomes a local character. That describes Dan Bain to a "T." By the mid-1890s he was a wonderful hockey player with speed and a reputation as a "policeman" on ice. At the same time he was the top cyclist in the West at the mile, and known as a formidable gymnast, roller skater, and figure skater. Salty in speech and strongly opinionated, Dan Bain was often too tough and individualistic for everybody's taste. As one veteran newspaperman put it: "He was determined to be the best at anything he turned his interests to, and that came through so strongly that he rather scared me."

The best he was – in many endeavours. It is hard to conceive that this country has produced many better all-round athletes. Dan Bain came from an earnest Scots-Canadian home where hard work and responsibility were stressed. He developed physical sturdiness in farm work and began his business career at fourteen years as a bookkeeper's apprentice in a firm of wholesale commission merchants in Winnipeg. In ten years he was a partner and by 1916 had bought out the business. He soon had one of the most successful wholesale firms in the country with branches in Canada's major cities.

The instances of great Canadian athletes who profitted not at all from their sporting ability are many, from Tom Longboat and George Young to Doug Hepburn. Bain proved that amateur sporting success was no barrier to economic success; indeed he used his wealth to further the cause of many sporting activities. For example, he became one of the best trap and skeet shooters in Canada and an enthusiast of wildfowl shooting. This led him into dog-breeding and to the acquisition of a large acreage of Manitoba marshlands. Eventually he owned the shoreline of Grant's Lake, perhaps the best geese lake in the Manitoba flyway, and turned this property over to Ducks Unlimited, another of his enthusiasms. He took up golf with great zest, and summer after summer he'd be on the course at 6 AM practising his stroke. He later helped bankroll several Manitoba golf courses whose creation he had advocated. An ardent figure skater, he gave an exhibition of waltzing in his late seventies with a partner a half-century younger. He had continued to skate and golf throughout the years although the combination of arthritis and an old hockey injury was painfully shortening one of his legs. He was the leading principal in establishing the old Winter Club in Winnipeg (now HMCS *Chippewa*) and after the second world war he helped organize the new Winter Club, a social and sporting club which still features figure skating.

Bain, Jack McCulloch and a player named Flett were the stars of the Winnipeg team which burst out of the West in 1893, "going East" to get a measure of how good Manitoba hockey was and what improvement was necessary. The team won nine of its eleven matches and won Winnipeg's adulation as well. In February 1896 the Winnipeg Victorias challenged the Montreal holders of the Stanley Cup. The Victorias won the game in the East and under the rules of the time, held the cup until the Montrealers were back West in December and took it back in another sudden-death game. Captain Bain scored in both games. As the *Free Press* described him: "Bain has the happy knack of always being just where he is wanted and does any amount of hard work. His speed at times was very effective." Montreal reports stressed his grace, speed and roughness.

Dan Bain retired from top-flight hockey, his first love, after his club won the Stanley Cup in 1901, but he retained an interest in it all his life; in later years he became more critical of the growing size of team rosters and the players' lack of stamina. After turning from hockey at the age of twenty-seven, Bain concentrated on shooting and on 15 August 1903 he won the Canadian trapshooting title at Toronto. He spent less time on lacrosse, baseball, gymnastics, rowing and bicycling, at all of which he had been ranked with the best in the province and fixed on golf and figure skating.

He was among the first automobile

enthusiasts in Western Canada and once he had bought a car he hated to sell it. At one time he owned thirteen cars, including a number of racy English sports models.

In 1887 when Dan Bain won his first medal, for the roller-skating championship of Manitoba in a three-mile race, he was thirteen years old. He was fifty-six in 1930 when he took his last figure-skating medal. He was a true all-rounder and when he was elected to the Hockey Hall of Fame in 1949, Dan Bain's first response to a reporter sent to interview him was: "It's goddamned near time."

NORMAN H. BAKER, 1923-

In late 1973 Norman Baker, back at work as a detective on the police force of the sprawling municipality of Saanich on Vancouver Island, after recovering from the double jeopardy of a disc operation and a stroke, was asked what reflections he had on his basketball career: "Basketball gave me wonderful opportunities – travel that was unusual at the time, and association with many fine people."

In the early forties Canadians recognized that Baker was a truly exceptional athlete, the best basketball player most of his countrymen had ever seen. At six-foot-two he was not overly tall for the game, wiry and tricky at about 165 pounds. In his mid-twenties he filled out to 200 pounds.

Voted in 1950 as the best Canadian basketballer of the half-century Baker knew his court skills were greater than those he had displayed on the lacrosse field, but he preferred lacrosse in one way – for its greater body contact. He has fond memories of his work as a forward on the New Westminster Adancas, Mann Cup winners in 1947 and finalists in 1948.

62

Norm Baker started in basketball with the Nanaimo Mosquitoes when he was ten. The game became his adolescent enthusiasm and he spent every minute he could at practice and scrimmaging. When fifteen, he was playing for a Nanaimo junior team that went to playoffs in Victoria. He was precocious enough to catch the eye of Dave Nicol, the brain behind the senior Victoria Dominoes. So at sixteen Norm became a regular on the Dominoes as they played through to take the Canadian senior basketball title, which they lost in 1941 and won back again in 1942.

At seventeen Norm joined the RCAF. The air force station at Pat Bay, BC, put together a wartime basketball club which took the Canadian championship in 1943 beating Windsor in the final, a series in which Norm set a record Canadian high to that time by scoring thirty-eight points in one game.

After his RCAF discharge Norm got an invitation to play with the Chicago Stags in the newly-formed Basketball Association of America, the forerunner of what has become the national pro basketball operation in the US.

Norm found the transition to pro play difficult at first, because he hadn't gone the normal route of college ball with its fine coaching and complex techniques and patterns. From Chicago he returned to play for the Vancouver Hornets in the Pacific Coast Basketball League. In two seasons in this league he dominated the scoring, in one year racking up 1,962 points in seventy games, a phenomenal score in those days. In 1948 he was picked up by the Portland team for post-season play in the pro world championships.

His repute was enough to draw the attention of Abe Saperstein, the promoter who made the Harlem Globetrotters world famous.

Norm remembers Abe Saperstein as "the finest man I've ever met." Baker was probably the first player ever to have a written contract with Saperstein, a step required before he could get a visa to live in the US. Saperstein was putting together his first overseas tour of the Globetrotters and Norm placed on the Stars of America club which played against the black marvels in a successful thirteen-week tour through Europe and North Africa. After the 1950 tour Norm returned to Victoria and married. After one last season with Boston he and his wife settled in Victoria and he turned to coaching lacrosse and basketball.

Norm believes that it's impossible to compare today's top basketball with that of the early fifties; the shooting today is "fantastic." The influx of taller men with speed and the emphasis on offense, leading to high scores, has changed the whole tempo and flow of play. There are fewer whistles now and many more jump shots. To him it's not a case of better or worse, just different, through the evolution in techniques and strategy. He'd enjoy it today just as much as he did in his prime.

LIONEL CONACHER, 1900-54

Lionel Conacher excelled in every sport he tried. When he was sixteen he won the Ontario 125-pound wrestling championship. Four years later, in his first competitive boxing bout, he won the Canadian light-heavyweight championship. He played for the Toronto Maple Leafs baseball team which won the Triple A championship in 1926, and for Toronto Maitlands when they won the Ontario Amateur Lacrosse League championship in 1922. He played professional hockey for the Pittsburgh Pirates, New York Americans, Montreal Maroons and Chicago Black Hawks. He was on winning Stanley Cup teams with Chicago in 1934 and Montreal in 1935, and in his eleven years with the NHL was considered one of the finest defensemen in the league. But of all the sports he played in his brilliant twenty-year career, football was his favourite. Playing for the Argos in the 1921 Grey Cup he scored three touchdowns. One of the foremost coaches in America, Carl Snavely of Cornell, said of Lionel: "He was probably the greatest athlete that I have ever coached in football or in any other form of athletics . . . I don't believe I have ever had a fullback who was a better runner in an open field, or who was a better punter, or who so fully possessed all of

Canada Wide Feature Service Ltd.

the qualities of speed, skill, dexterity, aggressiveness and self-control . . . "

Small wonder "the Big Train" was chosen Canada's all-round athlete of the half-century in 1950.

Lionel Conacher was indeed well endowed by nature. At six-foot-one and nearly 200 pounds of solid muscle, he had the height, weight, strength and stamina to be a great athlete. But the skills did not come easily. No one in his family before him had been an athlete. Remembering long afterwards the way he had encouraged his younger brother Charlie in what was to be a brilliant hockey career, Lionel said: "The family started out from scratch as far as athletic experience and heritage was concerned, and one has passed on inspiration and coaching to the other. It did not 'just happen.'"

Lionel grew up in the tough Davenport Road area in Toronto. His father was a teamster, and with ten children to raise, there was never enough money to go around. All Conacher children went, in turn, to Jesse Ketchum Public School and it was there they got their first taste of sports. The headmaster of the school realized that the best way to keep his pupils off the streets was to keep them occupied. He insisted that every youngster take part in some kind of organized sport at the school. By the time Lionel dropped out after the eighth grade (to help put food on the table) he had conceived a compelling desire to excel in all athletic activity. He had already realized that sports offered one of the best – perhaps the only – ways out of the poverty of his childhood.

He was twelve when he first played football in the Toronto City Rugby League. From there he went on to play middle wing for the Toronto Central Y when it won the Ontario championship in 1918, and in 1920 he was on the Toronto senior team in the semi-finals against Argos. At the same time he was a regular performer on the lacrosse field at Scarboro Beach, and on the baseball diamond at Hampden Park. Nor were his boxing skills overlooked; in 1920 he won the Canadian light-heavyweight championship, and boxed a three-round exhibition bout with the world heavyweight champion, Jack Dempsey, the following year.

64

Conacher joined the Argonaut rugby team in 1921 and for the next few seasons – until he turned to professional hockey – he delighted the fans with his sensational play. He was at the peak of his physical powers. In the days before the forward pass became part of the game, the emphasis was on kicking, running the ends, and evading tacklers. Conacher was famous for his phenomenal rushes down the gridiron and for his tremendous kicks. In 1922 he gained 120 yards against Ottawa in three downs; in a game against Montreal he gained a total of 227 yards. In the Grey Cup of 1921 Conacher was largely responsible for the Argo win over the Edmonton Eskimos by 23-0, when he scored fifteen points, an individual Grey Cup record which was not matched until Red Storey's three-touchdown performance for the Argos in the 1938 game with Winnipeg.

His physical endurance was often tested, since it was not unusual for him to compete in two championship matches on the same day. The story is told of a day in 1922 when he led the Toronto Hillcrest team to the Ontario baseball championship by hitting a triple in the final inning, then jumped into a car to drive across town to play for the Maitlands against Brampton in the Ontario lacrosse championship. When Conacher arrived Maitland was trailing 3-0. He scored four goals, assisted in another, and his team went on to win the championship by 5-3.

Conacher's superb physical skills were best suited to rugby and lacrosse. But in the 1920s there was little money to be made in these amateur sports so he turned his attention to hockey. This is how Conacher describes his start: "The average kid starts skating at the age of seven or younger. I laced on skates for the first time at the age of sixteen, and you'll never know the humiliation and utter weariness of the long hours which I spent on rinks with younger and much more skilled players before I won a post in junior circles." Conacher was as aggressive and determined when he played hockey as he was on the gridiron. But he was always awkward on the ice, and to compensate he became a brilliant tactician. Playing on defense, figuring all the angles, he developed a sliding method of stopping the puck, dropping on one knee with split-second timing. It was this technique that made sportswriter Ted Reeve dub him "the Travelling Netminder."

In the autumn of 1923 Conacher went to Bellefonte Academy near Pittsburgh and played football for the college. He also joined the Pittsburgh Yellow Jackets hockey club and was catapulted into pro hockey in 1925 when the entire team became the professional Pittsburgh Pirates in the expanding National Hockey League. He was traded to the Montreal Maroons, and from 1928 to 1930 had two good years with the club. Then he went into a slump. He was traded to the Chicago Black Hawks and made a great comeback in 1934 when he led his team to a Stanley Cup victory. The Maroons bought him back, and he responded by helping them take the cup in 1935. In his eleven years in the NHL as a defenseman, Conacher scored 80 goals and 105 assists. He gained a reputation as a tough player and to the end of his life he carried the scars to prove it. He had something like 600 stitches – 150 in his face and head alone – and his nose was broken eight times.

When Lionel Conacher retired from professional sport in 1937 he entered politics. He was elected as a Liberal MPP for Toronto Bracondale, in order to promote the idea of government aid to community parks in the poorer districts of the city. In 1949 he moved from the provincial to the federal scene, again representing his own area of Toronto, Trinity riding. He was always a backbencher, serving the needs of the people in his own riding above all else. His sister Nora ran his office in Toronto on Scollard Street, just a block down the street from where he was born, where all his constituents could bring their problems.

In May, 1954, Lionel Conacher drove from Toronto to Ottawa to take part in the annual softball game between MPS and members of the parliamentary press gallery. In the sixth inning he lifted a flyball into left field, raced to third base and suffered a heart attack. Within twenty minutes the greatest all-round athlete that Canada has produced was dead.

Aside from Lionel and Charlie, two other brothers, Roy and Bert, were excellent hockey players. The loss of an eye kept Bert from a sure-fire pro career. His twin, Roy, scored 226 NHL goals in eleven years. The other family twins, Nora and Kay, were outstanding softball players in an era when it was unusually competitive and high in quality. Sister Dorothy was a track star in the mid-twenties.

Two of Lionel's sons were good athletes, especially in university sports. Lionel Jr. was a fullback star for Western University. Brian was a tough-checking winger for Father Bauer's national team and author of *Hockey in Canada: The Way It Is*, a book which was highly critical of our hockey system and practices.

Thus, the sum of the Conacher contribution to Canadian sport is even greater than that of "the Big Train".

WILLIAM J. FITZGERALD, 1888-1926

Billy Fitzgerald was a flashing, darting lacrosse player whose ability to bring a crowd to its feet as he broke in to score brought him money and fame. He played for teams in St. Catharines, Toronto and Vancouver during the early part of the century. At the peak of his career, a Vancouver lacrosse promoter convinced him he should cross the country and play for a salary far above that which most Canadians could ever expect to earn. When his playing days ended, Billy Fitzgerald's love of the game kept him on as a coach and a referee.

A slim, agile young man, Billy Fitzgerald was born in St. Catharines in 1888 and grew up at a time when lacrosse fascinated thousands and when St. Catharines was developing into the home of some of the best teams in the country. He first played in a top-rated league at the age of nineteen when he joined the senior Athletic Lacrosse Club in that city. He was joining the best. The St. Catharines Athletics were to win the Globe Shield from 1905 until 1912; in the 1907 and 1908 seasons they were undefeated.

In 1909 Billy Fitzgerald turned professional with the Toronto Lacrosse Club. At twenty-one he was a star. He was a player who brought out thousands of fans eager to share the excitement he created. He was so exceptional that fifty years later Ted Reeve remembered him as "a lean, racing, crowd-lifting goal scorer who would come in from centre field like the wind, pick a pass out of the air for a flashing shot, or set up a play for one of his inside men with his sudden take-away burst of speed."

Lacrosse, in these pre-war years, was a big sport. Thousands organized their weekend around a lacrosse game. They would go to the park early, picnic beneath the trees, and listen to the band which performed before and after a game. It was a happy life in which the lacrosse player was idolized.

Given this atmosphere, Billy Fitzgerald was a hero sought out by both fans and promoters. Among those who wanted to hire him away from Toronto was Conn Jones of Vancouver. The cities on the British Columbia coast were burgeoning; one way to "get on the map" was to produce winning sports teams. To this end, they were willing to put up large sums of money to lure top players away from the hated Eastern Canadian teams. Vancouver had a further stimulus: the Salmonbellies from neighbouring New Westminster had been the top lacrosse team on the coast for several years and Vancouver chafed in its continual second-rate position. Conn Jones was determined to put together a team that would beat New Westminster and the world.

Jones paid Billy Fitzgerald $5,000 to go West and play for Vancouver. At that time, before inflation and before income taxes, $5,000 a year was a salary to dream of. Billy Fitzgerald accepted it and went to Vancouver where he joined other stars such as Newsy Lalonde. Conn Jones's investment paid off. The Vancouver team won the Minto Cup which then represented the professional lacrosse championship of the world.

After his year with Vancouver, Billy Fitzgerald returned East and played with the Toronto Lacrosse Club until the first world

war disrupted sports activities. He briefly went out to Vancouver to play again, but his real home remained in Ontario. After the war, Billy Fitzgerald helped organize the St. Catharines team in a semi-professional Ontario league which was put together in an attempt to revive interest in lacrosse. But it also helped end Billy Fitzgerald's playing days. With the revival of interest in the sport, the Ontario Amateur Lacrosse Association began to function and professional lacrosse died out. Since Billy Fitzgerald had played as a professional, he could not go back as an amateur.

However, Billy Fitzgerald turned to coaching and refereeing. The Toronto *Globe* in 1916 said he was considered "one of the brainiest players in the game and has the knack of imparting his knowledge to his candidates." This was written at the time that Hobart College in Geneva, New York, signed him as coach for a second consecutive year. Coaching jobs also took him to Swarthmore College and to West Point where he taught the fundamentals of lacrosse to future leaders of the United States army. Later his interest turned to helping younger players as a coach in St. Catharines. But he kept his connection with the older players by refereeing games played by teams in the senior group of the Ontario Amateur Lacrosse Association.

GEORGE GIBSON, 1880-1967

Most Canadians, even the professional sportswriters, tend to forget that at one time baseball was a major sport in this country and that Canadians in surprising numbers excelled at the professional level. The Sports Hall of Fame honours but one ball player – George (Mooney or Moon) Gibson. Yet catcher Gibson is symbolic of the spirit and skill that percolated out of Southwestern Ontario in the years between 1865 and the first world war.

The measure of Canada's achievement in baseball can be appreciated by the first sentence in George Gibson's obituary as carried by the Canadian Press in 1967: "Gibson was the only Canadian ever to manage a major league baseball team." Not so. Arthur Albert Irwin, a Toronto player born in 1858, had managed four major league teams: he was also credited with initiating the system of baseball scouting and with inventing the infielder's glove. Bill Watkins from Chatham managed four major league teams in the eighties and nineties.

Another Canadian, James Edward (Tip) O'Neill, born at Woodstock in 1858, over a ten-year career fashioned a reputation as an outfielder and hitter (.492 in 1887 with St. Louis), which was larger than that

with Pittsburgh; 1917-8 – played with New York Giants; 1919 – manager, Toronto, International League; 1920-2 – manager, Pittsburgh Pirates; 1923 – coach, Washington Senators; 1925 – coach, Chicago Cubs; 1926-30 – scout, Pittsburgh Pirates; 1931-3 – manager, Pittsburgh Pirates; 1934 – retired.

The peak of Gibson's playing career was the winning of the World Series of 1909 against Detroit and the famous Ty Cobb. Pitching usually makes the difference in the series. For Pittsburgh a freshman hurler, Babe Adams, took three surprising victories when the mainstays of the Buc pitching staff were hit hard. Adams had had a so-so season but under Gibson's shrewd handling, he became the star. The basepath terror of all time, Cobb, only stole one base on Gibson in the series.

Moon Gibson was a timely, not a devastating hitter; that is, he was a clutch performer, rather than a long-ball threat or a high average batter. His top average was .280 in 1914 when he only played forty-eight games, a far cry from the "every game" pace of 1909 when he set a record that stood for almost twenty years. He caught in all 150 games that his team played. He was most appreciated for his ability to hold runners on base and for offering a great target and smart pitch-calling to pitchers. In the dead ball era of baseball, rich in smart and aggressive players and managers from Cobb and Wagner to Conny Mack and John McGraw, Gibson exerted enough ability and judgment to win advancement to the managers' ranks. His problem in his two stints as Pirates' manager in the early twenties and thirties was not that his teams did badly, but rather that in each stretch Pittsburgh was expected to win the National League pennant because of its stars. Three second-place finishes in six seasons isn't bad; nor did a Gibson team finish in the second division.

At the tail-end of his playing career Gibson was hired by the great John McGraw of the Giants. "Little Napoleon" wanted Gibson as a backup catcher, and for his savvy. In 1917 the Giants lost the World Series to the White Sox, four games to two. But Gibson saw little action. When he turned to minor league managing in 1919 he had played in more than 1,200 games in fourteen seasons in the National League. Only three times in that period did a team which Gibson played for finish in the second division.

After retirement George Gibson went back to his farm, a few miles west of London, Ontario.

wrought by the tough, durable, combative Gibson two decades later. Irwin, O'Neill and a score of Canadians of the eighties and nineties are forgotten, but George Gibson is our baseball hall of famer, and he is a good one.

George Gibson was a blocky, powerful farm boy from near London, Ontario. Mike Rodden, a Canadian coach, referee and sportswriter, once wrote: "There is a legend concerning Gibson's entry into pro baseball. A scout heard there was a good amateur playing baseball in London. He went to look him over, saw Gibson in action and immediately offered him a contract. It later transpired that the good catcher referred to was not Gibson at all. However, Gibby made the grade from the start while the other receiver never got into professional company."

In a letter to the Sports Hall of Fame before his death, Gibson set out his career very tersely:

> 1904 – played with McClary's in the manufacturing league in London; joined Buffalo of International League late in season; 1905-1916 – played

WALTER KNOX, 1878-1951
If a magic computer could be programmed to assess all the athletes in the Canadian Sports

Hall of Fame it is likely the machine would come up with the name of Walter Knox as the best of them all, pound for pound, and Walter barely weighed 150 pounds at his heaviest. Knox was immensely versatile; as crafty, candid and roguish as any man ever to capture the imagination of Canadians.

When Walter Knox came on the national scene in 1900 as a track and field athlete that division of sport was in transition from a dubious amateurism, overlaid with professional running based on side bets, to a much better organized system of world-wide amateur competition, sparked by the Olympic Games revival and the enthusiasm for track and field which was rising in British and American universities.

Although Knox was born in Listowel, he grew up in Orillia, the premier sporting town for its size in Canada. He competed so often, in so many places, over so many years (from 1896 to 1933) that only he had a record of all his feats. He amassed a total of 359 firsts, 90 seconds, and 52 thirds in formal competitions. In one afternoon in 1907 he won five Canadian titles – the 100-yard dash, the broad jump, the pole vault, the shot put and the hammer throw. In those years Canada had world class and record holders in the persons of Ed Archibald, pole vaulter; Dr. Cal Bricker, broad jumper; and Bobby Kerr, the Olympic sprint champion of 1908. In one meet Knox beat all three at their specialty, while each was at the peak of his athletic ca-

reer. He held the Canadian titles at 9.6 seconds for the 100 yards, 22.8 seconds for the 220, 46 feet 5 inches for the shot, 12 feet 6 inches for the pole vault, 24 feet 2 inches for the running broad jump, 10 feet 7.5 inches for the standing broad jump, and 128 feet for the discus. In 1900-10 those marks would have put him near the top in any track meet.

In 1903 Walter became a college boy and attended Beloit College where Harry Gill was the successful track and field coach. While there Knox competed in many meets and won not only his share of victories, but also set records for some events. In this year he began to get the 16-pound shot regularly over the 40-foot mark; regularly cleared 11 feet and higher in the pole vault; and entered the ranks of consistent 10-second men for the 100 yards. The following year he competed under the colours of the University of Illinois and was a winner in most of his meets.

Making his first trip to the Pacific Coast in 1905, Walter took part in many athletic contests in which he was invariably the greatest point winner. He was the track and field sensation of the year. For the next couple of years Toronto was the chief Knox stamping ground. As a member of Central YMCA he established a lengthy string of records and performed with rare success in sprinting, jumping, vaulting, shot putting and other events. The years 1908 and 1909 were California years in the Knox travel system. In one race he defeated the great sprinter, Forrest Smithson, in the 50-yard dash, which Walter ran in 5.4 seconds.

On 25 July 1909, at the Golden Gate Stadium in San Francisco Walter won a 100-yard race in 9.6 seconds to equal the world's record. In 1911 the amazing Orillian first crossed the Atlantic and became a sports celebrity in Britain. On this trip he won fifty-seven firsts, twenty-three seconds, and thirty-one thirds. Returning to Canada, Walter was appointed coach of the Canadian Olympic team and went with the athletes to the games at Stockholm in 1912. While overseas with the Canadian team he competed in England and Scotland winning forty firsts, fifteen seconds and an equal number of thirds.

In June of 1913 Walter added the all-round professional championship of America to his achievements, defeating the United States holder, John A. MacDonald, in a matched contest at Hanlan's Point, Toronto.

Walter made another trip to Britain for the 1913 athletic season and repeated many of his successes of earlier trips. On 1 and 3 August 1914 Knox competed in a contest promoted by the *Sporting Chronicle* for the all-round championship of the world. His opponent was F. R. Cramb, the British champion, and the contest was held at Manchester. This was an eight-event match and the brilliant Orillian won six. He was appointed coach of the British Olympic team for the 1916 games that were to have been held in Berlin. When the war ended hope of a 1916 Olympic contest, Walter returned to Canada.

In 1920 he was again named coach of the Canadian Olympic team which competed in the international games at Antwerp. Later he was chief coach of the Ontario Athletic Commission for several years, developing schoolboy athletes.

Walter Knox left posterity an unpublished, partial autobiography which catches admirably the flavour of the man and his times:

> In my era, early in the century, a professional runner depended principally upon matched races for side bets, which varied from $25 to $200. To earn even those small wagers the winner first had to use all his wits to have his challenge accepted, then he had to watch for double-crossing and finally he had to have the ability to lick his opponent.

Why did Knox choose the vagabond life of the gambling athlete? For years he bounced from town to town, all over North America and Western Europe, often using aliases, making deals, outsmarting shysters, taking his lumps and risking his life and health with toughs and shakedown artists. Why did he not settle for orthodox recognition and a stable niche in a community and a profession like Ed Archibald or Cal Bricker?

Walter Knox sets the turning point of his life in 1908 when he was thirty. He'd been barnstorming in BC and Washington under various names. "I headed for the East and home but my brother Jack caught me in North Bay. Jack's eyes were shining and he bubbled so with enthusiasm that he could hardly talk. He insisted that I break my journey and go with him to Earlton, Ontario, where he was taking off timber from a grant given him by the government in recognition of his service in the Boer war.

"What could I do? I gathered a bush outfit and away we went. It wasn't so much the work on hand that had Jack steamed up. He had been in those parts long enough to catch the 'gold fever.' Strikes had been made further north that literally poured fortune after fortune from the ground."

Walter Knox had found his career, alongside and beyond athletics, as a promoter of mines and mining shares. It was one which suited him and he was to live comfortably, despite ups and downs, from it until his death in 1951 at seventy-three years of age.

Knox was caught up in the excitement of expansion and growth in the decade before the first world war. He was too individualistic and unorthodox to take the solid, legitimate chances for advancement and business success open to a great and clever athlete. Knox had enormous confidence in his track abilities and verbal gifts. He loved the excitement of gambling coups and sidebets. He revelled in acting the stupid farm boy who confronted the sharpies on the day of the race. His trail wandered from one mining camp to another, from one big track meet to another (sponsored by Caledonian societies, police and firemen's associations, or simply by some ambitious mayor or real estate promoter). He preferred to go as a mysterious unknown rather than as the well-known Walter Knox from Orillia.

The image of society and life which comes through Knox's tales is not the familiar one we have from our historians, intent on politics and staples and religion, nor is it the dour one of novelists like Frederick Philip Grove, or the nature-centred one of poets of the time like Lampman and Duncan Campbell Scott. Rather the image is one that must have triggered innumerable pulpit sermons and moralizing: a rowdy, lusty, frontier-like society, rife with schemes and dreams and very intent on sport. We must put Knox into the context of Louis Cyr and Sam Langford, the roving skaters like Jack McCulloch and Norval Baptie, Irish Tom Flanagan, the Toronto promoter, and his great protege, Tom Longboat, and the peregrinating hockey stars and main-chance seekers like the Patrick brothers, Cyclone Taylor and Art Ross. Runners, boxers, wrestlers, strongmen, hockey and lacrosse players, demon shortstops and longball hitters, literally hundreds of athletes, promoters and gamblers were on the move. The hotel and the saloon were important locales; so were mining towns and railway divisional points. Cobalt, Houghton, Gowganda, Blairmore, Medicine Hat, Slocan, Fernie, Vernon, Spokane, Sudbury, booming Vancouver, Frisco – you name the place with action and Walter Knox seems to have been there.

PATRICK JOSEPH LALLY, 1868-1956

The white man took over lacrosse from the Indians, but there is one area in which Indians have always been supreme – the making of lacrosse sticks. More than 97 percent of the world's supply of lacrosse sticks come from a small factory on Cornwall Island, Ontario, a plant that employs only Indians from the St. Regis reserve nearby. The man who built up the business and made it famous around the world was Joe Lally.

Lally was connected with lacrosse all his life as player, referee, international authority, and entrepreneur. Of Irish descent, he was born in Cornwall and spent most of his life there. For a lacrosse enthusiast, Cornwall was not a bad place to be at the turn of the century. The National Lacrosse Association, founded in 1867 with only six clubs, had grown to more than eighty within the year, and one of the most formidable teams in the association was fielded by Cornwall. The annual championship, started in 1885, was won by Cornwall in 1887 and 1888. The little town was proud of its team; most of the players worked long hours in the local factories with little time for practice, yet determination and hard work had gained them the championship.

A love of lacrosse was in the Lally family. Joe's older brother, Frank, founder of the stick manufacturing business in 1881, was a fine player, who played goal for the Montreal Shamrocks.

In the early years of the century the game continued to be popular, and the supremacy of the Eastern clubs was being suc-cessfully challenged by the enthusiastic teams on the West Coast. In 1925, therefore, the national association was reorganized to coordinate the various local associations, and to lay down a uniform code of rules. Joe Lally was instrumental in setting up the new Canadian Lacrosse Association, and remained connected with it for many years.

In 1930, to encourage the spread of the game, Lally established the Lally Perpetual Trophy, awarded annually to competing teams representing Canada and the United States. Lally is perhaps best remembered for his work as a referee. He earned a reputation for scrupulous fairness. On one occasion, two embattled teams from the West Coast imported Joe Lally as referee, since they knew they could rely on his impartiality. The story goes that Joe felt himself out of condition, so he practised running and skipping in the baggage compartment of the train taking him West. Certainly his performance on the field was much appreciated; the premier of British Columbia once nicknamed him "the Knight of the Whistle."

Lally's long-time association with lacrosse was recognized in 1945, when he was made an honorary member of the national association, and to the end of his life he retained his interest in the game and in the factory he and his brother had started.

EDOUARD LALONDE, 1887-1970

In an age of great players, Newsy Lalonde was a superstar. As a hockey player and on the lacrosse field, his fame was legendary, and it is difficult now to realize just what a sensational drawing card he was. He was in demand all over the country, and was the only player on teams that won both the Stanley Cup and the Minto Cup, the highest awards in hockey and lacrosse. In 1950 he was named Canada's outstanding lacrosse player of the half-century.

Lalonde once admitted that he preferred lacrosse, because "it's played in the summer, out of doors where you get lots of fresh air." He might have added that it also paid more money. Lalonde was one of the first professionals who was prepared to play for the club offering the most money.

Born of French-Canadian parents in Cornwall, Ontario, Lalonde first worked as reporter and printer for the weekly Cornwall *Freeholder*. It was there that he earned the nickname "Newsy" which stuck to him all his life. He started playing lacrosse for Cornwall at the age of sixteen, and stayed with the team for three summers. He played goal but on the memorable day that he stopped a shot and worked his way all down the field

to score the winning tally, Newsy decided his abilities were wasted in goal. From then on he preferred to play "home," the roving attacker.

Lalonde started travelling around the country, going wherever his talents were in greatest demand. In 1911 he found himself in Vancouver, playing lacrosse for Conn Jones, who offered him $6,500 to play sixteen games with the Vancouver club. It was the highest salary ever paid a lacrosse player – Newsy later worked it out at $7 for every minute he spent on the field. He returned East in 1912 to play for the Nationales, scoring a record sixty goals in twelve league games.

At the age of eighteen he broke into professional hockey, when Sault Ste. Marie of the old International League offered him $35 a week. After a long train trip he arrived thirty minutes before his first game; he stepped on the ice and scored two goals – a performance that so impressed his new owners that they increased his salary to $50.

Lalonde had played briefly with the Canadiens in 1910 when the club was formed by his teammate Jack Laviolette. In 1913 he returned to Montreal and remained with the Canadiens for ten years. He was at the peak of his career on the ice. Four times he led the league in scoring – in 1910, 1916, 1919 and again in 1921. He captained the team in 1916, the year the Canadiens won the league championship and beat Portland for the Stanley Cup. In 1919, with Lalonde as player-manager, the club again won the championship and went West to defend the Stanley Cup against Seattle. Newsy was the sensation of the series; in the second game it was Lalonde against the whole Seattle team, when he scored all the Canadien goals.

Lalonde was a born leader, and a tough player. He had a fierce temper, and would challenge anyone – not only opponents, but on occasion his own teammates or spectators. In the heyday of his scrappiness, cries of "get Lalonde" echoed around the rinks of the NHL. He was almost unbeatable. The great Lester Patrick, who knew him in those early days with the Canadiens, once said: "Lalonde had a wicked knee-high shot that was almost impossible to keep out of the goal. . . . The only way to stop him from scoring was to have three or four players – more if you could spare them – skate him to the side and picket him."

Lalonde's playing career with the Canadiens came to an end in 1922, when he was traded to the Saskatoon Sheiks in the Western Hockey League. He spent four years as player-manager with the team, developing fine young players and taking his team to the playoffs twice. Playing against Vancouver

in March 1925, he scored the last goal of his career – a total of 416 goals in regular league play.

Lalonde continued coaching, first for the New York Americans, and from 1932-34 with the Canadiens. He was not a great success; he had an acid tongue and no patience with his young players. For all the money he earned in his years in professional hockey, the most he made in a single season was probably the $5,000 the Ottawa Senators paid him for *not* coaching in the second year of his two-year contract; they had fired him after the first year.

Newsy Lalonde was a rabid supporter of the Canadiens to the end of his life. He was a familiar figure at the rinkside in Montreal, and sometimes on road trips as well, until his death in 1970, at the age of eighty-three.

JACK LAVIOLETTE, 1879-1960

Jack Laviolette was one of the finest all-round athletes to come out of French Canada. Equally at home on the ice, the lacrosse field or the motor racing track, he added colour and verve to the Canadian sports scene in the decades before the first world war.

Born in Belleville, Ontario, Jack moved with his family to Valleyfield, Quebec, in 1889. In his youth he played both hockey and lacrosse, as did many athletes of the era. Lacrosse was in the flood tide of its popularity. The summer season was all too short for some of its more enthusiastic players, who experimented with lacrosse on ice to prolong the season. The experiments were unsuccessful – and costly; a bouncing lacrosse ball indoors was no respecter of window panes. So

more and more athletes like Jack Laviolette turned to hockey for their winter sport.

Jack Laviolette started in amateur hockey in Montreal in 1899 as a member of the Overland junior team. Following a season with the CP Telegraphs, he joined the Nationales of the Federal League, and played for both their hockey and lacrosse teams. By the turn of the century the amateur status of many teams was being threatened increasingly by professionalism. Communities were intensely proud of local teams, and competition between clubs was fierce. The clubs, anxious to win championships and to cash in on gate receipts, hired outstanding players from all over Canada with handsome money offers. When the first professional hockey league, the International League, was formed in 1904, Laviolette was signed to play for the American Soo team. He stayed for four seasons, captaining the team in 1906. The league was disbanded in 1907 and Laviolette returned East, to play hockey for the Montreal Shamrocks and lacrosse for the Nationales. In 1910 he was a member of the lacrosse team that went West to play the New Westminster Salmonbellies for the Minto Cup. The Montreal club lost, but the playing of such French-Canadian stars as Laviolette, Pitre and Newsy Lalonde impressed the lacrosse-knowledgeable Westerners.

Laviolette was **exciting to watch**. He brought his infectious daredevil approach to everything he did, whether it was thrilling the crowds at a motorcycle race in Delormier Park, leading a spectacular dash towards the lacrosse goal, or rushing from one end of the ice to the other. Elmer Ferguson has given this picture of Laviolette in action: "He usually wore a toque in the cold rinks. Sometimes in the action this would be lost, and Laviolette would race along the ice with his long hair streaming out behind him. He had strong aquiline features, and a muscular body. He was a very good shot, a very clean player, who brought tremendous colour to the game."

In 1909, with the organization of the National Hockey Association, it was decided to form a French-Canadian team in Montreal, financed by the wealthy mineowner, Ambrose J. O'Brien. Laviolette was given the task of recruiting and managing the club. He was responsible, more than any other man, for the formation of the Canadiens, the oldest professional hockey club still in existence in Canada.

Laviolette was thirty-one when he joined the Canadiens, older than most of the others. But he could more than hold his own; his bursts of speed down the ice earned him the name of "The Speed Merchant." He played for five years on defense, then moved to the forward line in 1915 when Lalonde was out of action for most of the season. He enjoyed this position so much that when Lalonde returned the next year Laviolette stayed at left wing. The famous line of Pitre, Lalonde and Laviolette helped the Canadiens win their first Stanley Cup in 1916.

Laviolette's active career was cut short by a car accident in 1917, when he lost his left foot. Even then his connection with hockey did not end. When he was fitted with an artificial limb he became a referee. Those who watched him said he could skate better than most men with two legs.

NOEL MACDONALD, 1915-

When she was selected for admission to the Canadian Sports Hall of Fame, Noel MacDonald Robertson, the great centre of the Edmonton Grads basketball team, was "not altogether comfortable" at being singled out from the many outstanding players whom Percy Page had coached over a period of a quarter-century. As she said, "on the floor we were not individuals, we were a team." But there were very good reasons why she should have been chosen. It was not because she was stunningly beautiful, although she was. Nor was it simply because she was the

Grads' all-time high scorer with an average of 13.8 points per game. It was because in her skill, courage and selfless team-play she exemplified the qualities which made the Grads great.

Noel's father farmed near Mortlach, Saskatchewan, but like so many other wheat farmers of the drought-ridden twenties, was blown off his land and moved to Moose Jaw. Noel began school there but the family soon moved to Edmonton. Noel played basketball in public school, then for Westmount, Edmonton's smallest high school. During her final two years, Westmount defeated McDougall High, coached by Percy Page, for the city championship. Noel was a tall girl (she was five-foot-ten when she joined the Grads) and already a redoubtable centre; she was invited to join the Gradettes, the feeder team for the Grads. After a year and a half, she moved up to the senior team in 1933 and played until her retirement at the end of the 1939 schedule.

Like all coach Page's players, Noel was worked into the team's pattern gradually. She began as a substitute forward, but eventually replaced another great Grad star, Gladys Fry, at centre. Very fast for a tall woman, and with extraordinary reflexes, she became a pivotal part of the Edmonton machine. It was the period when the centre-jump still followed each basket, and the Grads developed a whole series of plays from Noel's success in controlling the tip. With Gladys Fry, she also controlled the backboards at either end of the court, and scored many of her points off rebounds. Never a set-shot artist, she was most effective on the move and around the key, with a quick snap shot almost impossible to check.

Noel MacDonald gave the Grads, and their fans, many memorable games. In one of them, as a frightened rookie, she was given the job of checking Alberta Williams, the us all-star centre of a team that was challenging the Grads for the Underwood Trophy. The American girl, an inch taller than Noel, was a prolific scorer, a hook-shot specialist who could drop them in with either hand. That night Noel gave the first indication of her brilliance, outscoring her check 20-4. On another occasion, in 1936, the formidable Eldorado Lion-Oilers were in town from Arkansas, again as challengers for the Underwood. They defeated the Grads 44-40 in the first game of the best-of-five series, and with seconds to go in the next, led 35-33. Noel, who had played without substitution, had scored 18 points but was in a state of near-exhaustion. Nevertheless, she won a jump, tipping the ball to a waiting Grad, and on the return pass sank the game-tieing shot

Blythe Studios

from outside the key. With time almost out, she got the next jump as well, and after one of those rapid-fire series of passes so typical of the Grads, got the ball back about twenty-five feet out and snapped a quick shot. The gun went as the winning basket trickled in; Noel collapsed and was carried to the dressing room. The Grads went on to sweep the

73

series in typical, freewheeling play.

In 1939 Noel MacDonald married Harry Robertson, then playing hockey for the Kimberley Dynamiters, and retired from the game. Until her husband's position with an oil company took the Robertsons abroad, Noel served on the executive of the Canadian Amateur Basketball Association and coached high school teams, in Estevan, Saskatchewan and Camrose, Alberta.

HOWARTH MORENZ, 1902-37

When Howie Morenz died in his thirty-fifth year, his tragically short life was seized intuitively by hockey people as symbolic of the game at its best. Morenz made pro hockey his whole life and the final weeks of his life, the nature of his death, seemed proof that his commitment may have been too complete.

Howarth Morenz was the youngest of six children in a closely knit family which moved from the village of Mitchell, Ontario to Stratford when he was thirteen. He brought to Stratford a small enthusiasm for school, a delight in music and an obsession with skating and hockey. His father worked in the Stratford railway shops and young Howie, a mischievous and impetuous personality, began to play in what we would today call minor hockey.

In his eighteenth and nineteenth years, Morenz became the star of the fine Stratford entry in the OHA junior competition. Some juniors received covert subsidization. There was, even then, a network of informants watching for likely prospects for hockey greatness. Many cities had sent emissaries to woo Howie Morenz and among them was Montreal. Although apprehensive about leaving his home in Stratford, Morenz became a pro, winning a place on the Canadiens and capturing the imagination of the Montreal fans in the fall of 1923. But at that time the National Hockey League was a far cry from the league as we know it today. The team schedule was twenty-four games, there were ten men on its roster and in the winning of the Stanley Cup in 1924 the Canadiens played only two-game play-offs, defeating challengers in Vancouver and Calgary.

By the time of Howie's death in 1937, the NHL schedule had increased to forty-eight games a team, rosters had grown to sixteen men and the play-offs were extended. Morenz's years with the Canadiens were successful for the man and for the team. Five times the league champions, the Canadiens won the Stanley Cup in 1924, 1930 and 1931. Morenz's career on that star-studded team was spectacular. In his fourteen years in pro hockey he scored 270 goals, earned 197 assists, for a total of 467 points. He was the league's leading scorer in 1927-8 and 1930-1 and winner of the Hart Trophy for most valuable player in 1928, 1931 and again in 1932.

But cold statistics give no idea of Morenz's greatness. King Clancy, fine player, referee and manager, said in 1968:

> One I can never forget, and neither can anyone else who ever saw him play, is Howie Morenz. He was in a class by himself, – the greatest player I ever saw. Morenz was the best in his day, the best I ever played against and the best I've ever seen since. Nobody could dig in and get moving as fast as he could; he could start on a dime and leave you a nickel change. And he could shoot a puck as hard as any player who ever performed in the NHL.

Morenz played with the Canadiens until 1934; then he was traded to Chicago. His great skills were allegedly tarnishing and the Montreal ownership excused itself by explaining that it did not want to see the adulation of the Canadien fans turn to sourness and hurt the sensitive Morenz. Chicago was a miserable experience for Morenz; from there he bumped to New York and more frustration. Then he was re-purchased by the Canadiens and came home to Montreal and a come-back.

Hugh MacLennan, the Montreal novelist, was a witness to the ending. He has written that:

> [Morenz was] the greatest all-round forward and the most beloved player the game has known. Morenz has been compared to Babe Ruth but he was much more like Walter Johnson; he had Johnson's rare combination of speed, power and gentleness and there was something in his style

that made everyone love him. I was in the Forum that January night in 1937 when his career ended. He had been playing marvellously that evening and the little smile on his lips showed that he was having a wonderful time. But once too often he charged into the corner relying on his ability to turn on a dime and come out with the puck. The point of his skate impaled itself in the boards. A defenseman, big Earl Siebert, accidentally crashed over the extended leg and broke it. Howie's head hit the ice with a sickening crack and he was carried out. Six weeks later, as a result of the brain injury, he died.

In hospital, Howie Morenz had been distraught at the prospect of a future without hockey and he fretted about his failure to provide security for his family. Canadians didn't appreciate that the grand career was over and the nation was stunned at his death, none more than the rush-section fans who in the thousands passed his bier at centre ice in the Forum.

Morenz has been seen as a naïve victim, a boy-man of innocence, broken by the pressures of big-time hockey as it jelled into a highly publicized and commercial mould through its American expansion. Certainly Morenz, more than any other player "sold" hockey to the fans of newly enfranchised teams in Boston, New York, Chicago and Detroit. The more recent feats of stars like Maurice Richard, Bobby Hull and Gordie Howe and the passage of time have tended to reduce the luminous reputation of the immortal Howie.

Perhaps Morenz's finest epitaph was offered a few years ago by Jim Coleman in a column recounting a chat with his son:

Who was Morenz? Don't they teach you anything at schools today? . . . Morenz was a dark-visaged, dashing knight. He was finely-tempered Toledo steel. When he picked up the puck, circled behind his own net and started for the opposing goal, he lifted you right out of your seat. His step was so light that he appeared to fly about two inches above the surface of the ice. . . . "Was he really as good as you say?" said the little boy. He was better . . . he could skate faster than Davey Keon, he could shoot as hard as Bobby Hull and he was as strong as Gordie Howe.

JAMES A NAISMITH, 1861-1939

In January of 1892 the Canadian inventor of basketball introduced the game to his students at the YMCA training college in Springfield, Massachusetts. Writing in *The Triangle*, the college publication, James Naismith said:

> We present to our readers a new game of ball . . . It fills the same place in the gymnasium that football does in the athletic field. Any number of men may play at it and each gets plenty of exercise; at the same time it calls for physical judgement, and co-ordination of every muscle, and gives all-round development. It can be played by teams from different Associations, and combines skill with courage and agility so that the better team wins.

A single man's creative genius had revoluntionized indoor sports; before the end of the nineteenth century his game, spreading like wildfire, had become international.

James Naismith was the second son of John and Margaret Naismith, who farmed in Lanark County two miles from Almonte, Ontario. His boyhood in this pioneer community was very like that depicted in Ralph Connor's Glengarry novels: hard work on the farm and in the bush, "manly" sports and pastimes, and the emphasis on education so prized in the powerful Scottish Presbyterian atmosphere in which James grew up. The young Naismiths were orphaned in 1870

75

when both their parents died of typhoid; they were taken in by an uncle, Peter Young. To help support the family, James withdrew from Almonte High School for three years. During that period he made up his mind about what he wanted to do in life. "I decided that the only real satisfaction that I would ever derive from life was to help my fellow beings. At that time the ministry was the way that one attempted to help his fellows."

After completing high school, Naismith went to McGill on a scholarship in 1883, took his BA in 1887 and graduated in theology in 1890. At the same time he developed into an outstanding athlete, playing centre for McGill's football team for six years and excelling at lacrosse, wrestling and gymnastics. He thought lacrosse "the best of all games," and in his last year at McGill he played for the Montreal Shamrocks. While studying theology, he acted as McGill's director of physical education as well, and it was at this point that he felt called to that special combination of Christian living and athletic endeavour that was the YMCA ideal.

As a result, Naismith went off to the training school in Springfield as a student, and shortly became one of its assistant directors of physical education, under the leadership of one of the outstanding American pioneers in the field of physical education, Dr. Luther Halsey Gulick. It was Gulick, in the fall of 1891, who assigned to Naismith the task of inventing some indoor game to fill the void between the football and baseball seasons.

The job was a formidable one. "All the stubbornness of my Scottish ancestry was aroused, all my pride of achievement urged me on," Naismith later wrote; clearly too, the analytical capacity he had acquired during his McGill years was stimulated. "My first generalization," he said, "was that all team games used a ball of some kind; therefore, any new game must have a ball." Games with small balls – cricket, baseball, lacrosse, tennis – required "intermediate equipment" and therefore special skills; he therefore decided on a large and light ball, a soccer ball. Since roughness in an indoor game was unacceptable, Naismith decided that rough physical contact of any kind would constitute a foul. Running with the ball would encourage tackling; therefore the ball could be advanced only by passing (dribbling was to come later). Some sort of goal was necessary, but what kind? "If the goal were horizontal instead of vertical," he said, "the players would be compelled to throw the ball in an arc; and force, which made for roughness, would be of no value. I would

place a box at either end of the floor and each time the ball entered the box it would count as a goal." But what if the defending players simply gathered about the goal, blocking all access to it? He realized that "if I placed the goal above the players' heads, this type of defence would be useless." The centre jump to start the game Naismith took from football, which was still using the sideline toss between opposing lines to begin play, but to eliminate roughness, he decided that the referee should throw the ball up between two players only. Although Naismith thought that any number could play his new game, he was clearly influenced by his favourite game of lacrosse in his view that "a goalkeeper, two guards, three centre men, two wings and a home man stationed in the above order from the goal" would be best.

The first game was played sometime in December 1891. Naismith scribbled out thirteen rules and explained them to the eighteen students in his class. Two nine-man teams were chosen (the captain of one was another McGill man, T. Duncan Patton of Montreal), and the building superintendent, asked to supply boxes, produced instead two half-bushel baskets, which were nailed to the gymnasium balcony. The game was an immediate success. The enthusiastic students suggested naming it "Naismith ball." "I laughed," said its inventor, "and told them that I thought that name would kill *any* game." One of the students put forward "basketball" as the name; obviously, the janitor should share the credit.

While the game he had invented was spreading rapidly, James Naismith went on to take a medical degree and then to become a professor of physical education at the University of Kansas. In 1936 he was guest of honour at the Olympic Games in Berlin, when for the first time, basketball was played as an Olympic sport by teams from thirty-three nations. The tribute this Canadian innovator received was well merited. He had created a fluid, exciting sport, easy to learn but capable of many levels of complexity and skill – wonderful to play and thrilling to watch. And the game had come from the values young James Naismith had absorbed from his Ontario upbringing. As he said in that epoch-making issue of *The Triangle,* "if men will not be gentlemanly in their play, it is our place to encourage them to games that may be played by gentlemen in a manly way, and show them that science is superior to brute force. . . . "

JOHN PERCY PAGE, 1877-1973
When, in 1950, Canada's best basketball team of the half-century was selected in a

press poll, the outcome was never in doubt. It *had* to be the Edmonton Grads – more properly, the Edmonton Commercial Graduates – a girls' team that compiled a unique winning record during its twenty-five years in existence. From 1915 to disbandment in 1940 the Grads played 522 games, won 502 and lost only 20 for an astonishing performance of 96.2 percent. At four Olympics – Paris in 1924, Amsterdam in 1928, Los Angeles in 1932 and Berlin in 1936 – the team won 27 consecutive games; although women's basketball was not an official event the Grads were considered world champions. At two points in their history they had consecutive winning streaks of 147 and 78. They won their first Canadian title in 1922 and never lost it thereafter. In 1923, against Cleveland, they won the first international series for the Underwood Challenge Trophy, and defended it successfully against all comers for seventeen years. The trophy was given to the club permanently when the Grads disbanded.

The one element of continuity in this astonishing record was a mild-mannered, self-effacing man named Percy Page, the team's coach. Page was born of Canadian parents in Rochester, NY, raised in Bronte, Ontario, was a gold medallist at Hamilton Collegiate, and graduated from Queen's University. He taught high school for two years in St. Thomas, Ontario; in 1912 he came West to introduce commercial classes at Edmonton's McDougall Commercial High School. In 1914 Page, a keen basketball player in his student days, took on the coaching of the girls' team at McDougall High.

The Grads were formed in 1915 with students and graduates of the high school as players. Throughout its life, the team was re- cruited from this source. Players came to Page through the McDougall "farm system." Page either coached or supervised these teams, and every player who finally wore the black and gold of the Grads had been assessed by him from her earliest playing days. Only twice were girls who had not been to McDougall High permitted to join the Grads; Gladys Fry and Mae Brown had been outstanding players on other Edmonton teams before coming to the Grads.

Undoubtedly the cohesion that derived from the recruiting system had something to do with the Grads' success. Page himself always gave credit to his girls. "They are champions," he said in 1923, "because they are the most whole-hearted, sport-loving girls that it would be possible to find; they have won because the spirit of the Prairie is born and bred in them." Many of the American teams the Grads met and vanquished were taller and huskier than the Edmonton girls, and had great individual stars; many of them were from the Prairies too.

It is clear that much of the Grads' success came from Percy Page himself. The Grads practised twice a week, except for the summer months. In twenty-five years, Page missed three practices: once to skip a city championship curling team, and twice while campaigning for a seat in the Alberta legislature. All this despite the fact that he was also coaching the two high school teams and became, in the course of time, the principal of the high school. One of his girls once said of him: "He's a perfect dear, but we don't have to do a thing he tells us unless we like." This was true only within limits. No Grad player drank or smoked; Page demanded from his team the same sacrifices he made himself. "You must play basketball, think

Alexandra Studio

basketball and dream basketball," he told his players. He was no tyrant, but the fact that he had been their school teacher as well as their coach, in a period when teachers still enjoyed unchallenged authority, clearly contributed to the great influence he established. For most of his career, the players called him "Mr. Page"; only in the last years did he acquire the affectionate title "Papa."

The basketball Page taught was simple. It was based above all upon physical conditioning. Many of the Grads' famous last-minute surges came when their opponents were too exhausted to cope further with the pace the Edmonton girls set. Page had no complex playbook. The Grads relied on a quick short-passing game, using simple weaves or grapevines to free a shooter around the key. And they had the shooters. In their last season's play their percentage from the floor was 38.6; they hit 57.1 percent in a game against the unfortunate Queen's University team during that season.

Though players changed as did opponents and game-styles, the Grads remained through the years a tightly-organized, beautifully conditioned and immensely proud team, always bearing the stamp of Percy Page. One night in 1925, in Guthrie, Oklahoma, while the Grads were defeating the state champion Red Birds for the Underwood Trophy, the inventor of basketball, who was teaching at the nearby University of Kansas, delivered his opinion of the Edmonton team: James Naismith thought it doubtful that any girls' team had ever equalled them "in all-round strategy, brilliance of play and doggedness of attack." There has been no reason to challenge Naismith's judgment.

Percy Page sat as a Conservative member of the Alberta house from 1952 to 1959, and from 1959 to 1966 was lieutenant-governor of the province.

ROBERT ALGER PORTER, 1913-
Bobby Porter came out of the Toronto east end and its playgrounds, the neighbourhood so affectionately chronicled by Ted Reeve. His dad, W. A. Porter, had been very active in sports, particularly as an executive of the Balmy Beach Canoe Club. There were times in the Beach's football fortunes when it was Mr. Porter's credit which kept the creditors from foreclosing.

Bobby was a squat 200-pounder who ran with such a wide stance that he often seemed to be ambling when he was really travelling. He was excellent at baseball, softball, football, hockey and lacrosse.

At Malvern Collegiate Bobby played both hockey and football, leading the school's

team to the city titles in 1929, 1930 and 1931. One of his hockey teammates, Jack Kent Cooke, was to go on to become one of the continent's promotional geniuses in baseball, hockey, basketball and football.

After high school, Bobby carried on in team games through all seasons of the year. He excited the interest of hockey and baseball scouts. He chose baseball and turned pro in 1936, going to the East Texas League. Shortly after he joined Toronto of the International League. In 1939 he was transferred to Syracuse and later to Springfield of the Eastern League. In 1941 he was sold to Washington of the American League but before spring training he broke his shoulder and his baseball career was cut short.

Later in 1941 the Balmy Beach Football Club signed Bobby but his right to play was challenged under the rule that as a professional in one sport he was ineligible for all amateur sport. The decision by the football league executive to keep him from playing set off a major uproar, prompting columnist Ralph Allen to describe it as the Big Fourflush league. Allen's point was that there was substantial evidence that the three other league teams were more worried about his threat against them on the field than about his tainted amateurism.

The Big Four packed up operations after 1941 for the war's duration and the Ontario Rugby Football Union carried on, its play dominated by the Hamilton Wildcats and a number of service teams. Bobby Porter played for the Beaches from 1942 through 1947, except for 1944 when he coached the Camp Borden RCAF team.

He also coached through most of the 1940s in the Little Big Four, the private college league of St. Andrew's, Upper Canada, Trinity, and Ridley. Throughout these years he was one of the leading hitters and

Sports Hall of Fame

fielders in the high quality Beaches Major Fastball League.

The Beaches, as a football club, was one of the last football evocations of neighbourhood spirit in a city becoming increasingly metropolitan. Undermanned, financed on a shoestring, the Beaches were the Cinderella club in the less glamorous ORFU while the Argonauts were considered the "class" team of the city.

Bobby Porter, cocky, an improviser, canny but prepared to take a risk, was almost the symbol of the Beaches, along with "Suzie" Turner, a huge, spirited lineman. The swan song of Porter as a football player came in the Eastern final of 1947, the underdog Beaches against the powerful Argos featuring Joe Krol, Royal Copeland and Billie Myers. The Argos won 22-12 (and then smashed Winnipeg, 35-0 in the Grey Cup). In their losing cause the Beaches and Porter were never more gallant. Porter had a brilliant day initiating the old "extension" run and quick-kicking adeptly with his left foot.

In 1951 Porter withdrew from the more bruising games and took up lawn bowling. "It takes skill and precision like any other sport," Porter told a reporter in 1970. "I played a lot of sports when I was younger but I wanted a sport I could keep playing."

In 1960 Bobby began a summer column titled "Kicking the Kat" for the now-defunct Toronto *Telegram*. He became a top-flight bowler and an articulate spokesman for the game.

FANNY ROSENFELD, 1903-69

Bobbie Rosenfeld – she was seldom called by her given name – was one of the leading figures of the golden age of women's sport in Canada. She came to this country as an infant in arms when her parents emigrated from Russia. As athlete and sports journalist, she had a forty-year career, and she remains the only woman all-rounder in the Hall of Fame.

The founding of the Toronto Ladies Athletic Club in 1920 was an important event in the history of female athletics in Canada. One of its founding members, Constance Hennessey, vividly remembered the young Bobbie. "She was not big, perhaps five-foot-five," she recalled. "She didn't look powerful but she was wiry and quick. Above all she was aggressive, very aggressive physically. No, I don't mean that she made a lot of noise or had a belligerent manner. She simply went after everything with full force. She was a fine hockey player. . . . She checked hard and she had a shot like a bullet. On the basketball court she drove with the ball if she had it, she drove after it if someone else

had it. She was just the complete athlete and I am certain she would have been good at any sport. Certainly, she was as good as one could see in track and field, hockey, basketball and softball."

Bobbie won her first trophy at a track meet in 1922 at Barrie, her home town. Forty-five years later Barrie held a testimonial dinner in her honour. Between those years, she amassed the record that brought her selection as best Canadian woman athlete of the century and entry to the Sports Hall of Fame.

She first drew the attention of Torontonians, including Elwood Hughes, influential manager of the Canadian National Exhibition, at a picnic in Beaverton. Bobbie was there with a girls' softball team. A small track meet was organized and someone prompted her to run in the 100-yard dash. She won, and was surprised to hear from Hughes that she had beaten the champion Canadian sprinter, Rosa Grosse. Later, after she moved to Toronto, she, Miss Grosse and Myrtle Cook became keen rivals. At one time Bobbie and Rosa shared the ladies' record for the 100 yards at 11 seconds flat.

Bobbie set three records in 1928 which lasted into the fifties: 18 feet—3 inches in the running broad jump; 120 feet in the discus; and 8 feet—1 inch in the standing broad jump. She played on several Ontario

reflected that her finest honour had been her choice as the best Canadian woman athlete, but the peak of her career had really been at the Amsterdam Olympics in 1928. She, Ethel Smith, Jane Bell and Myrtle Cook, were members of the gold medal relay team. She had taken the silver medal in the 100-yard dash, edged infinitesimally by an American runner in so tight a finish that many thought Bobbie had won.

The least of her accomplishments at Amsterdam said most about her as a person: she ran fifth in the 800 metres.

Here is how the late Alexandrine Gibb, manager of the first Canadian women's Olympic track team, described the fifth-place finish:

> Remember . . . Miss Rosenfeld was not trained for this distance . . . She was put in the 800 metres only to encourage Jean Thompson. Bobbie . . . on the stretch down the track came from ninth position to close behind seventeen-year-old Jeannie and when she saw the latter falter . . . coaxed the youngster to come on. When [Bobbie] came up from behind, she refused to go ahead of the youngster . . . let Jean finish fourth, taking a fifth for herself.

When arthritis struck Bobbie again in 1933, she had to give up active sports, and took instead a job with the Toronto *Globe* writing a column called "Sports Reel." Although a natural humourist, she was not a facile writer. She held her job by hard work, covering a wide range of sports from wrestling to horseracing and never writing solely for the distaff side. The essence of her personality should be familiar to a generation brought up on Jewish comedians, so adept at satirizing life by making wry fun of themselves. From her first emergence as an athletic marvel, she was described in the press as "refreshing" and "irreverent." From the start, Bobbie Rosenfeld balanced intense competitive fire with an instinctive comic sense; she lived out her pain-wracked life with the same flair she had when she first burst upon the sporting scene.

DAVID TURNER, 1903-

When Dave Turner was named in 1950 as Canada's outstanding soccer player of the half-century, many Canadians thought of soccer as a game played by European teams with names familiar mainly through football pools. Yet when Dave Turner was at the height of his fame in the 1920s and 1930s, soccer was intensely popular in Canada. Each city and province ran its own leagues and championships; rivalry was so keen that players were frequently suspended for fighting on the field – with spectators who often joined in the general fracas.

and Eastern Canadian basketball championship teams. She won the Toronto grass courts tennis championship in 1924. One great afternoon in 1925 the Patterson Athletic Club won the points title at the Ontario Ladies Track and Field Championship; she was the only entrant for the club. She took first in the discus; the 220; the 120-yard low hurdles, and the running broad jump; she was second in the 100-yard dash and the javelin. She coached the women's track team in the 1932 British Empire Games.

In 1929 she had her first bout with arthritis and spent eight months in bed and a year on crutches. But in 1931 she was back as the best slugger and pepperiest fielder in the leading softball league. And the following winter she was the top hockey player in women's competition in Ontario.

Bobbie liked hockey best of all her sporting activity. She'd learned it as a young girl on the corner lots, playing with boys. However, she recognized that track and field put athletes into the public eye more readily and kept them there. Reminiscing once, she

Dave Turner was a burly, solidly-built Scot whose powerful kicking and skilful use of his head made him one of the foremost players of his day. As inside left for the New Westminister Royals in the British Columbia league, he led his team to four Canadian championships in nine years.

Born in Edinburgh, Dave Turner came to Canada when he was eleven, and settled with his family in Edmonton. By the time he was fourteen he had developed into a keen soccer player. At one time he used to play for a Boy Scout team in the morning, a high school team in the early afternoon, and a senior team in the evening. And, surprisingly, he also managed to get himself an education; by the time he was sixteen he was through normal school and teaching in Camrose.

Dave stuck to teaching for three years. But in 1923 when he was nineteen, he and another soccer-playing friend, George

Graham, took off for Vancouver to make their names in football on the coast. The first team they tried was St. Andrews. Dave played with such gusto, however, that he kicked the ball right out of the field into a neighbouring lumber yard. He was not asked to play again. He and George worked their way over to Vancouver Island, where they had heard of a team called Cumberland United. Once again, their first outing with the club was not impressive. The surface of the field was hard-packed coal dust, and Dave recalls that the ball bounced as if it was hitting cement. The local paper reported their debut coolly: "The two new men on the Cumberland lineup gave a fair account of themselves and will no doubt improve when they get better acquainted."

Improve they did. The following week against Nanaimo, the dominion champions, Dave Turner kicked three goals and George Graham one; final score, 6-1. In the return match, Cumberland again beat Nanaimo 3-1, Turner scoring two of the goals. Indeed Cumberland did so well that year that it won the British Columbia title, defeating Alberta, and got as far as the semifinals of the Connaught Cup before being beaten by Winnipeg.

After the successful seasons with Cumberland, Turner returned to the mainland. St. Andrews now welcomed him back and he played for two years with them before turning to professional soccer in the United States. He played in the us pro circuit for one season before returning to Canada to play for the Toronto Ulster United. The following year he toured New Zealand with the Canadian All-Stars, and was persuaded by the New Westminster Royals to join their club and continue his studies in agriculture at the University of British Columbia.

Dave Turner stayed with the Royals for nine years, helping them to the Canadian championship in 1928, 1930, 1931, and 1936. He was a clean but aggressive player, described by sportswriters as "185 pounds of muscle and bone who would bull his way right over you."

Dave Turner's soccer career ended in 1937 when he returned to teaching. In 1944 he obtained his MA from the University of British Columbia and received an honorary doctorate from Cornell in 1946 for his work in conservation. He joined the British Columbia Department of Lands and Forests in 1947, and was appointed deputy minister of the Department of Recreation and Conservation in 1957, a post he held until his retirement in 1968.

CANADIAN
Illustrated News

Vol. XVIII.—No. 15.   MONTREAL, SATURDAY, OCTOBER 12, 1878.   { SINGLE COPIES, TEN CENTS.
} $4 PER YEAR IN ADVANCE.

Canada's first frontier was the Atlantic. Perhaps even before the time of Columbus, European fishermen were frequenting the banks and in the course of time a tough and hardy population of fishermen was established in Newfoundland, Nova Scotia and along the Fundy shore. As the Atlantic economy developed, the outport fishing fleets were soon supplemented by the maritime merchant marine, controlled by a prosperous mercantile class in the ports of Halifax, St. John's and Saint John, and supported by a large shipbuilding industry.

It is hardly surprising that this bustling maritime activity should spawn water sports. At the beginning of the nineteenth century, with the Royal Navy assisting, Canada's involvement in water games began.

In the circumstances, rowing was the people's sport and pleasure-sailing the sport of the wealthier. (Not all competitive sailing was for pleasure, though, and the working classes were deeply involved in the fishing fleet races, for example.) The oldest sporting event in Canada is undoubtedly the Newfoundland Regatta. On 6 August 1816 the *Royal Gazette and Newfoundland Advertiser* informed its readers that "a rowing match will take place on Monday next between two boats, on which considerable bets are depending – they are to start at half past one from alongside the prison ship." The races were managed by merchants and officers of the Royal Navy and the partici-

Edward (Ned) Hanlan was Canada's first national sporting hero. Known internationally as "the Boy in Blue," part of his prominence was due to the immense interest in rowing all over the English-speaking world but a good part of the adulation was due to his personal magnetism and style.

pants were fishermen. In the early years there were already signs that the regatta would ripen into the great folk festival it has since become. In 1827 the officer in command of the Royal Engineers complained to the governor that "with reluctance I have been obliged to give the workmen a half-holiday in consequence of a boat race they wish to attend." Over the next quarter-century there are only scattered references to the event in the press, apparently because its frolicsome nature kept "respectable" people away. Though Governor Sir Herbert Murray refused to attend in 1897 "because it was not patronized by the best people," it had by that time long been Newfoundland's great holiday. Beginning in the 1820s "the races" had shifted to "the pond," Quidi Vidi Lake.

The races are unique in a number of ways. They are open to all comers, though there are special races held for firemen, policemen, young people, civil servants and so on. The first race for women took place in 1855; Mary Brace, Jenny King, Lizzie Hanton, Crissie Squires, Jessie Needham and Ellen Walsh made up the pioneer winning crew. In the beginning gigs and whaleboats were used and when shells were adopted in the 1890s they were made to the whaleboat design, seating six with a cox.

The regatta has its special traditions, too. For example, there is the extraordinary career of the ageless cox, Levi "Shotty" Rogers, or the story of the Placentia Giants, who in 1866 walked nearly sixty miles to St. John's with their boat on their shoulders, won the grand challenge race, then walked home. In 1910, Lord Brassey, warden of the Cinque Ports, gave seven gold medals to be awarded to the crew breaking the record set in 1901 by the Outer Cove seven. The record is still unbeaten and the warden's medals have been passed down through three generations of the Higgins

T.STOCKHAM
SAIL MAKER

THE WORLD-FAMED PARIS CREW

STROKE	AFTER MID	FORWARD MID
Robert Fulton	Elijah Ross	Samuel

Canada's first victory in international athletic competition was won by four New Brunswick rowers from Saint John. Because of their astounding double victory in 1867 at the Paris Exposition, they became known forever as the Paris Crew. Their flesh-colored jerseys, dark cloth trousers, leather braces and bright pink caps were in stark contrast to their well-dressed rivals representing Europe's best oarsmen, but they won in both in-rigged boats and outrigger shells.

family, their custodians in perpetuity.

The tone at Halifax, with its more complex and wealthier society and a strong military and naval presence, was more refined. As early as 1826 a sailing regatta was held in Halifax harbour under the patronage of Rear-Admiral W. T. Lake. In attendance with Sir Howard and Lady Douglas were Major-General Sir John Keane and the Earl of Huntingdon. After the races it was reported "the amusements of the day were concluded by a dinner and ball on board HMS *Jupiter* . . . the arrangements are said to have been elegant."

Nova Scotians claim that their yacht club at Halifax is the oldest in North America. D. C. Harvey, Nova Scotia's historian, says: "The Royal Nova Scotia Yacht Squadron . . . was formed in December 1875, by separation from the Royal Halifax Yacht Club . . . which had been reorganized in March 1857 to continue the work of the Halifax Yacht Club of July 1837 . . . That date makes it seven years older than the first yacht club in the United States of America, and only twenty-five years younger than the first yacht club in Great Britain." There is no proof that the Halifax Yacht Club of 1837 had a continuous existence until 1857, but (except for members of the Royal Canadian Yacht Club of Toronto) the tradition harms no one and pleases Haligonians.

Under the auspices of the yacht club, fishermen's rowing races were encouraged at Halifax regattas. One of the club members, a physician, Dr. Arthur Charles Cogswell, raised a fund in the 1850s to support annual sculling races for the championship of the harbour "similar to those so popular on the River Thames" and donated the Cogswell belt – a glittering band of ornately worked silver, about three inches wide, on a blue velvet background – as the trophy. When George Brown, the Herring Cove fisherman who was soon to become one of the world's outstanding professional scullers, won permanent possession of the belt in 1868, "it was presented to him at a great public ceremony in the Legislative Council Chamber, attended by all the dignitaries of the province as well as by Sir John A. Macdonald . . . "

It was also the RHYC that introduced the aquatic carnival of 1871, intended to be a showpiece for the champion "Paris Crew" of Saint John, New Brunswick. The carnival attracted professional crews from England and the United States with the then enormous prize of $3,000. But though Nova Scotia and New Brunswick were to produce other strong scullers such as John O'Neill and the professional Wallace Ross, the Maritimes never produced the strong club base for rowing that was to grow up in other parts of the country.

The same was not true of yachting,

85

however. The Royal Nova Scotia Yacht Squadron has remained a vigorous organization, taking the lead in ocean racing (in 1905, with the Eastern Yacht Club of Marblehead, Massachusetts, the RNSYS inaugurated the Halifax-Marblehead races). It could draw upon both wealth and superb seamanship; one of its most notable members was W. J. Roué, who in the 1920s and 1930s designed many boats for the club as well as the classic *Bluenose.*

In central Canada aquatic sports developed for the most part along the vital chain of waterways that rises in Lake Superior and ends in the St. Lawrence. Along the St. Lawrence from Montreal west to Lake Ontario a whole series of communities – Cornwall, Prescott, Kingston, Belleville, Cobourg, Toronto, Hamilton and others – first looked to the river and lake as an economic resource and as a means of communication, but increasingly turned to it for recreation as well.

By the end of the 1830s Toronto's magnificent bay was becoming a hive of aquatic activity and the local press was making passing references to the "annual regatta." In the early years all classes joined in the events, though there were special rowing races for fishermen and for "gentlemen amateurs." Undoubtedly the regattas acted as a social solvent in a community which had been riven by deep social and political divisions only a few years before. "In bringing together in social measure the different members of the community," said the *Examiner* in 1843, the regatta "relaxes those frigid rules of etiquette which widely separate the different ranks. It dispels asperities of a political nature and establishes, at least for a time, a freedom of intercourse which it would be gratifying to observe at all times." The regattas were glorious holidays for a good part of the city's population. Spectators thronged the waterfront or bought places on a boat (made more pleasurable by the military bands they invariably carried) to watch the races close at hand; in 1869 the *Globe* fretfully reported "the huge steamers, *City of Toronto, Rochester* and *Norseman* were loaded to an almost frightful extent and the *Transit* and *Bouquet* puffed about, laden to their utmost capacity." Occasions like these were made for politicians. At the regatta of 1867, John A. Macdonald and several members of his cabinet put in an appearance.

Earlier, the regattas had been run by the yacht club; it was an exclusive sort of institution. "We know," said the Toronto *Leader* in 1853, "that disreputable ideas sometimes attach themselves to yacht clubs, but we believe that there is no ground whatever for entertaining any such feeling against the Toronto yacht club." How could there be? The list of its original members reads like an honour roll of the old Tory élite: Jonas Jones, George Draper, William Cayley, Samuel Sherwood, W. B. Jarvis, J. G. Spragge, George Duggan, Colonel Samuel Jarvis. It had been founded in 1852. In 1854 it acquired the right to use "Royal" in its title and became the RCYC. In time distinguished sailors such as Aemilius Jarvis, the Gooderham family, and Sir William Mulock made it and Toronto "the greatest yachting centre on the Great Lakes," according to the US magazine, *Sail and Sweep.* The Toronto *Star* of 1904 maintained that "Toronto could give any other city on the Great Lakes aces and spades and beat her out in the race for supremacy in any line of aquatic sport."

It was yachtsmen from Toronto (notably George Herrick Duggan and Aemilius Jarvis) who took the lead in organizing the Lake Yacht Racing Association, a body which flourishes today. The LYRA encompassed clubs around the Lake Ontario shore and it changed yachting from pleasure-cruising to competition by laying down regatta dates, setting sailing measurements, rules of classification, and inaugurating a series of trophies still competed for. Eighteen ninety-six was a great year for central Canadian yachtsmen. They finished well in LYRA competitions, and Duggan, now sailing for the Royal St. Lawrence Club of Montreal, took the Seawanhaka Cup from its New York City holders. Aemilius Jarvis, sailing the Scottish-designed and built *Canada,* defeated the Chicago yacht *Vencedor* off Toledo in Lake Erie. This victory, which inaugurated the Canada Cup series, was greeted exuberantly by the Canadian press. The *Mail and Empire* trumpeted:

> Canada by 26 seconds! An eagle with its feathers pulled is not in the humour for screeching. A bird without pride is a bird without voice. The Canadian Beaver has quietly accomplished its purpose. Canada by 26 seconds! The Maple Leaf rustles gladly in the brisk summer breeze. The hearts of the people are swelled with national pride. The Lion, with the talons of the eagle still marked on its back, looks on approvingly. Canada wins!

Canadians had won, said one yachting writer, "pretty nearly everything in sight, save the America's Cup." The America's Cup, the blue ribbon of international yachting, was not available to freshwater sailors. A Canadian had seen to that, just fifteen years before, in the second of the only two challenges Canada has ever made for this famous trophy. The key figure in both was Captain Alexander Cuthbert of Cobourg.

Scottish-born, Cuthbert's trade was shoemaking, but he educated himself as a designer, builder and sailer of yachts. In 1876 a Cobourg syndicate commissioned Cuthbert to build and race a yacht for the America's Cup. The challenge, delivered through the RCYC, was accepted by the New York Yacht Club. The Canadian challenger, the *Countess of Dufferin,* 107 feet overall and the largest yacht yet built on the Great Lakes, was Cuthbert's version of a Yankee schooner. The Americans scoffed at her. "There is nothing foreign about her," said the New York *World.* "Her shape is American, her rig is American, her blocks are Westerman patent of New York, her steering gear is of New York manufacture and from stem to stern, inside and out alow and aloft, she is simply a Yankee yacht built in Canada." She looked frowzy beside the sleek American defender, *Madeleine.* The *Countess's* hull was "as rough as a nutmeg grater" and her sails "set like a purser's shirt on a handspike." Her backers lacked the money to fit her properly and she was soundly beaten in two races. After the second she was seized by the sheriff to satisfy creditors but the resourceful Cuthbert, in the dark of night, slipped the *Countess* into the East River and fled for Canada.

In 1881 Cuthbert was back again, this time with *Atalanta,* a sixty-four foot sloop he had built. The challenge came from the Bay of Quinte Yacht Club, though it was funnelled to New York through the RCYC.

This Canadian challenge set off a series of misadventures which sorely tried the dignity of the New Yorkers. When *Atalanta* was finished, it was too late in the season to sail her by sea to New York; instead, Cuthbert took her down the Erie Canal from Oswego. Unfortunately, she was so broad she had to be hove on one side, and thus she was towed down the canal by mules. Again Cuthbert lacked the money to properly equip his boat and the Belleville yachtsmen who were supposed to crew never turned up. He hired American sailors on a day's notice and they lost him forty minutes in the first race; in the second, Cuthbert mistook the position of one of the turning buoys and was soundly beaten by *Mischief.* The Americans were scathing. The *Spirit of the Times* called the contest "a stupid comedy in which a tried and proved sloop, one of the fastest in the world . . . fully manned and magnificently handled, distanced a new yacht, hastily built, totally untried, miserably equipped . . . and bungled around the course by an alleged crew who would have been overmatched trying to handle a canal boat anchored in a fog." It was all too true. Though the *Atalanta,* and other Cuthbert-designed yachts, had long and successful careers on the lakes, the New York Yacht Club ensured that no more challenges would come from inland Canadians by ruling that future challenges must come from yacht clubs located on an arm of the sea.

Though there was a momentary disgruntlement, the America's Cup losses scarcely dented the Canadian psyche. In these years

Canadian sportsmen had something more important to cheer about; it was the great age of the Canadian oarsmen, Ned Hanlan in particular. Even before he won the world's professional championship in 1879, this magnetic athlete had Canada at his feet. The adulation Hanlan received was comparable to that accorded a modern professional superstar. But for his generation he symbolized more; he was a national hero, summing up in his career and personality the aspirations of Canadians. The son of a poor Irish-Canadian family whose father had squatted in a shanty at Mugg's Landing on Toronto Island, Hanlan defied social barriers, won international acclaim against the world's best and carried the whole thing off with the manly modesty his era prized. Some indication of the grip Hanlan had on the popular consciousness can be seen in the *Globe's* description of his match with Fred Plaisted, the leading American sculler, on Toronto Bay 15 May 1878:

> As each succeeding train disgorged its human freight, it seemed as if an exodus were taking place from all the surrounding counties . . . Many hundreds from across the line. At least 40,000 people saw or tried to see the race . . . No fewer than twenty steamers were afloat . . . crowded like beehives . . . Men were to be seen on the roofs of the elevators and all . . . warehouses along the route, the Great Western Railway stationhouse, the Court Street firehall and all the houses from whence a view could be had . . . Hanlan won as he liked.

Not everyone shared the enthusiasm. In 1881, when the Toronto city council discussed whether Hanlan should be exempted from city taxes

Public Archives of Canada

A beautiful ship that touched some deep responsive chord in all Canadians, the *Bluenose* one of the finest fishing vessels ever built was a last, lovely challenge to the mechanical conformity of progress. Captained by Angus Walters, Nova Scotians were to refer to her fondly as "Stormalong" and "Old Weatherleg."

for life, Goldwin Smith thundered in the *Bystander* against the world of professional athleticism. "It is not a question, as some would make out, between physical and intellectual worth, but between worth of any kind and that which is worthless . . . No part of the affair is more offensive than the suggestion that Canada is indebted to a professional oarsman for redemption from obscurity and contempt."

The brilliance of Hanlan's career (and the careers of other world-class professional oarsmen such as Wallace Ross, William O'Connor and Jake Gaudaur) has tended to obscure an important fact: It was a time of great individual effort but it was also the golden age of amateur rowing in Canada. Clubs proliferated along Lake Ontario, on Lake Simcoe, at Ottawa, Peterborough and Montreal. Clubs like the Toronto Argonauts (1872) and the less posh but equally distinguished working-class clubs like the Don, the Bayside, and the Hamilton Leanders, not only competed in the annual regattas of the Canadian Association of Amateur Oarsmen (1880) but took title after title from its American counterpart. Joe Laing of the Grand Trunk Club at Montreal took two American sculling championships in the early eighties; an Argo eight, led by the great all-rounder, Joe Wright, Sr., took the US Nationals in 1901; in 1904 Lou Scholes of the Don Rowing Club took the Diamond Sculls at Henley-on-Thames. And the gospel was carried to the West. George F. Galt, stroke for the Argo four that won the CAAO title in 1880-1, started the Winnipeg Rowing Club in 1883.

As rowing was reaching its boisterous peak in the 1880s, canoeing, a gentler sport, was just hitting its stride. Though canoeing had its athletic aspects, it was only part of the summer recreational movement which swept the middle classes of the cities and towns in the late nineteenth century. The Indian birchbark canoe, high in bow and stern, was the model for the graceful, cedar-ribbed basswood canoe developed by I. S. Stephenson and in use at Peterborough regattas in the 1850s. By the 1860s this canoe, variously called the Stephenson, Rice Lake or Peterborough, had begun to appear on lakes and rivers throughout central Canada. Inevitably, a whole series of clubs sprang up, beginning with the Point St. Charles Club of Montreal in 1875.

American canoeing, meanwhile, was taking quite another course. The US canoe was, in effect, a kayak, a decked canoe suitable for sailing and double-bladed paddling. This canoe, the Rob Roy, had been re-invented by a Scot, James MacGregor, who had been impressed by the Eskimo original. His books on canoe cruising in Europe and the Middle East popularized the little vessel in England. The Rob Roy was imported into the United States in 1868 and in 1871 the New York Canoe Club was formed. The two canoes, the Rob Roy and the Peterborough, were the originals of the present K and C (Canadian) Olympic classes.

The American Canoe Association was formed at Lake George in 1880 "to unite all amateur canoeists for the purposes of pleasure, health or exploration, by means of meetings for business, camping, paddling, sailing and racing." From the first, Canadians took part in the American annual gatherings, the most notable of which was at Stony Lake, near Peterborough, in 1883. The Canadians brought a brash competitive element to these affairs, typified by the embryo Winnipeg Canoe Club's pronouncement that "as we have proven our ability to defeat the world in hockey, we propose to follow up in canoeing." The Canadians dominated the early paddling competitions of the ACA and once they got the hang of the decked sailing canoes, began to win those races as well. From this point of view, the Americans must have been somewhat relieved when the Canadian Canoeing Association was organized in 1900 and began to hold its own national competitions.

The real point of canoeing, however, was not in its athleticism but in its significance as the expression of the yearnings of citified Canadians. The Toronto Canoe Club was highly regarded among the canoeing fraternity not because of its racing successes but by its "good fellowship in camp and the musical contributions of its trained chorus at the evening camp fires." For a couple of weeks each summer, the newly urbanized middle-class Canadian could play at being a sturdy son of the True North, "roughing it" with store-bought equipment and re-creating, in a more comfortable fashion, the heroic life of the voyageurs. Thus an enthusiastic writer in *Massey's Magazine* in 1896 speaks of the joys of changing from his neat grey business suit into flannels and tennis shoes, setting up his tent and "dealing out tin cups of ready-made cocktails." Canoeing led also to the recreational penetration of the Canadian Shield. The literature of the time is filled with the wonder of discovering the wild beauty of the Kawarthas, the Muskoka lakes or Georgian Bay in the silently gliding canoe. The canoeists' romance with the Shield answered to the same kinds of emotional needs evoked by the art of the Group of Seven. The sequel was the twentieth-century cottage movement.

The story of Canadian canoeing in modern times has been a disappointing one athletically. With the exception of Francis Amyot's brilliant win in the 1936 Olympics (canoeing events were not recognized before), Canadians have fallen badly behind the Europeans. In recent games, Canadians have failed to finish in the top six in any canoeing event.

The Canadian Canoeing Association was formed in 1900. Until that time Canadians paddled in American annual gatherings, often dominating competition.
Above, Ottawa's Canoe Club house at regatta time in 1894. *Below*, Rideau Canoe Club members racing.

Today, both as a sport and a recreation, canoeing is enjoying a renaissance in Canada, but whether the European lead in the Olympics can be overcome is problematical. It is daunting to consider that while there are thirty-five clubs and 5,000 competitive paddlers in Canada, the German city of Hamburg alone has fifty clubs and 50,000 competitors.

Rowing, too, has fallen on evil times. The dying burst of the great era of amateur rowing came with the Diamond Sculls victory of Joe Wright Jr. and Jack Guest in the 1920s.

89

The major exception has been the performance of British Columbia crews in the 1960s, and the pairs gold medal of Roger Jackson and George Hungerford in the 1964 Olympics. A long tradition of competition by the University of British Columbia and the Vancouver Rowing Club against fine American crews from the Pacific Coast, the solid support given rowing by the Vancouver community, and the inspired coaching of Frank Read brought hope of a Canadian rowing revival.

But the national base for the sport has been sadly eroded. The depression dealt a crippling blow to smaller, less prosperous clubs – shells are very expensive and there is no recreational intent in rowing – one does not take out a racing shell for a pleasure spin. Potential oarsmen have been drawn off into other summer sports and recreation – sailing, water skiing, power boating – less demanding physically and mentally than the arduous rowing grind. The club base has proven an insuperable obstacle to the development of a strong national organization, and so Canadian rowing lacks a logically integrated program to bring oarsmen along from high school and through university. High school rowing is concentrated mainly in the St. Catharines area (the site of the Royal Canadian Henley) and in some of the private schools; few universities have rowing programs. And no heroes, like the Hanlans and the Gaudaurs of old, have arisen to inspire a new generation of Canadian youth.

Sailing has a continuity with its nineteenth century past that few sports can equal, stemming from historic trophies and competitions, the conscious evolution of design, and the wealth that enabled most clubs to weather the depression. The lordly image has gone, replaced by the current boom in small boat sailing. But even that had its roots well in the past. Dinghy sailing was becoming popular soon after the turn of the century, following the design of the first twelve-footer by J. Wilton Morse, a Toronto banker. Walter Windeyer, the accomplished sailor who won a world title in the Dragon Class in 1959, was a product of the strong interest in dinghy sailing that developed on the Great Lakes in the earlier part of the century.

Smaller boats, a higher degree of general prosperity and revulsion against the gasoline engine has meant that today sailing is both accessible to, and more popular with a broader section of the population. In 1971 the Canadian Yachting Association estimated that the number of sailors in Canada had doubled in a decade to one million. In 1972 sailboat manufacturers reported a 300 percent jump in sales; and so popular has sailing become that in 1973 there were ten-year waiting lists for moorings at some Lake Ontario clubs.

The enormous expansion in recreational sailing has been accompanied by a degree of national organization and development that competitive sailing in Canada has never known before. Clearly the emergence of international one-design classes has been crucial: the design peculiarities of particular clubs and regions have yielded to emphasis upon such classes as International Dinghies, Finns, Dragons, Lightnings or Snipes. This has made it possible for the CYA (with substantial support from industry) to establish such events as the Canadian Olympic Training Regatta at Kingston, where sailors from all of Canada meet annually with some of the world's best international class sailors; to operate a national training program for junior sailors; and to offer sophisticated training seminars for racing sailors in such subjects as hydrodynamics, meteorology, navigation, racing rules, racing strategy and tactics.

Canadian swimming has been a twentieth century development. To nineteenth century man, water was a dangerous element, and swimming something of a foolhardy adventure, typified by the fate of Captain Matthew Webb, the conqueror of the English Channel, who perished spectacularly in 1883 while rashly attempting to swim the Niagara rapids. The drowning toll however, led to agitation for swimming baths to encourage personal safety. Though competitive swimming began as early as 1876 with the formation of the Montreal Swimming Club, there were still only two public pools in Canada in the 1890s – in Montreal and Toronto. The general state of swimming was summed up unconsciously in an 1895 survey which identified a Toronto youth named Bath as "certainly the best floater in Canada." Montreal's lead in competitive swimming was reflected in the exploits of George Hodgson and Frank McGill before the first world war, and by the initiative taken by Montrealers in forming the Canadian Amateur Swimming Association in 1909 and staging the first national championships in the same year.

But the real popularization of swimming was promoted through the mass teaching methods of the YMCA and the Royal Life Saving Society. In 1906 George Corsan of the Toronto Y toured North America demonstrating the first mass teaching techniques for beginners. A. L. Cochrane, the swimoing instructor at Upper Canada College for twenty-seven years, was tje Royal Life Saving Society's pioneer in Canada; he promoted the building of public pools, demonstrated lifesaving techniqugs, and was responsible for the rapid spread of RLSS branches throughout Canada before 1914. Ornamental swimming came directly out of the swimming skills required at the higher levels of the RLSS tests; Peggy Sellers won the first trophy for it in 1926. By the end of the 1960s the YMCA alone had seventy pools in Canada and 200,000 swimming members, was training 25,000 persons to swim every year, and was turning out hundreds of instructors, examiners and lifesavers annually.

Canadian swimming has had two peaks. One of them was in the extravagant era of marathon swimming, set off by George Young's Catalina swim in 1927. For years thereafter the CNE at Toronto made "the swim" one of its great attractions, as Young battled personal problems, public fickleness and such performers as Ernst Vierkotter and Gianni Gambi. The obsession with endurance carried over into the post-1945 years, with the exploits of the Gus Ryder-coached swimmers, Marilyn Bell and Cliff Lumsden.

But these individual feats obscured Canada's general backwardness in world-class swimming and diving. No Canadian has ever won an Olympic gold medal in either sport, and it was only in the late 1950s and early 1960s that Canada began to produce a crop of young world-class swimmers; the second peak period had begun. Although some of these new stars come from other parts of the country, British Columbia is the country's real aquatic leader. Ocean Falls, BC, is a case in point. This isolated company town, 350 miles north of Vancouver, got a community pool in 1928. The local mill, in an attempt to head off mounting social problems with the town's young people, built the pool, brought in first-rate instructors, got swimming linked to the school athletic program and opened the facility to the community all year long. By 1950, 95 percent of the children three years of age and older could swim, and under the instruction of coaches like Dan McGowan and George Gate, such fine swimmers as Allan and Sandy Gilchrist, Lenore Fisher and Ralph Hutton emerged.

The heartland of Canadian swimming is British Columbia's Lower Mainland, and Percy Norman was the key figure in its development. This big Vancouver butcher, who won the Point Atkinson-Kitsilano swim in 1929, was a magnetic, warm-hearted person with great organizational talent. He was the driving force behind the Vancouver Swimming Club; his enthusiastic persuasiveness won swimming a place in the athletic program of the Vancouver-area schools and won municipal support for the massive program of the Vancouver Parks Board. Norman was Canada's first swimming coach of international calibre, training such swimmers as Phyllis Dewar, and taking teams to the Olympics and the British Empire Games in the 1930s. From the enthusiasm and mass participation he generated there came the Lower Mainland's four Olympic-sized pools and great swimmers like Elaine Tanner.

FRANCIS AMYOT, 1904-62

For a country whose early history centred around the fur trader's canoe, Canada has been singularly unsuccessful in international canoeing. Our achievements in canoeing in the Olympics have been limited virtually to one person, Frank Amyot. He was six times Canadian singles champion and our only gold medallist in the 1936 Olympics in Berlin.

In the sports explosion after the first world war both recreational and competitive canoeing flourished again, almost regaining its glory of the late eighties and nineties when the Canadian canoe and the camping vogue had made it an activity which vied with bicycling for the public's enthusiasm.

Frank Amyot was a Viking-like figure: tall, handsome, blonde, and tanned. The physique and the water skills were acquired in countless hours spent on streams and lakes from early boyhood, and from a decade of serious training. As a teenager in Ottawa Frank Amyot wanted to be a sculler but couldn't afford the shell (about $250 at the time). So he built a canoe and never looked back to rowing again.

Frank's father, Dr. John A. Amyot, was Canada's first deputy-minister of health and pensions and an internationally-known pioneer in preventive medicine. All four sons were canoeists. At a Carleton Place meet in 1925 the four Amyots swept the board in the junior, intermediate and senior singles events. For Frank, as he admitted later, "canoeing was something of a religion." On his way to work Frank invariably stopped off at the Britannia Yacht Club and paddled around the widening of the Ottawa River known as Lake Deschenes.

His racing career began in 1923

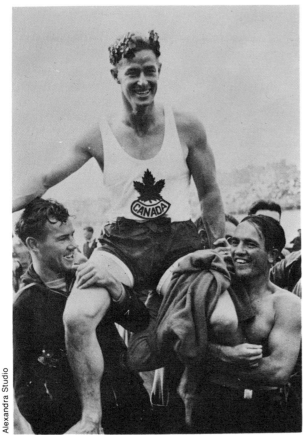

when he won the Canadian intermediate singles. Subsequently he went on to the senior competition, winning six times before his 1936 win at Berlin crowned him as world's champion.

Prior to that victory, most of his fellow citizens thought of him as a lifesaving hero. One Sunday in June 1933, he helped to rescue three men who were being swept towards the wild Deschenes Rapids. One of the three was Dave Sprague, an all-time Canadian football great. Paddlers in three pleasure canoes had spotted the men's predicament but it was Amyot, out practising in his singles canoe, who reached the men. "With the trio clinging to his canoe, merely hanging on until further help arrived, Amyot battled desperately upstream, literally from the brink of the rapids," one account read. "In the nick of time the other three canoes came up and, working quickly, each took a man aboard . . . Those who witnessed the rescue were emphatic that Amyot's speed in reaching the scene was largely responsible for the rescue."

In 1935 Amyot was appointed coach, manager and member of the Canadian Olympic paddling team but COA officials told him that no money would be available for the canoers' expenses. It took the generosity of Ottawa clubs and friends to get Amyot and three other members of the Canadian canoe team to Germany. Later Frank noted: "We were an orphan from start to finish, and we cut a pretty poor figure compared with small countries like Sweden and Denmark." But as fund-raiser, manager, coach and competitor, Amyot supplied the leadership that ensured Canadian representation.

Amyot was big for a paddler, almost six-foot-two and about 200 pounds. He had a competition canoe built to his size. In Berlin most of the craft were the rather unwieldy, decked kayaks, a much different boat from the lighter, smaller V-shaped, open canoes familiar to Amyot. Amyot felt that strategy held the key to victory:

> Personally, I always plan an important race and very often start out with all I've got. My stroke is a peculiar one, long and not as many strokes to the minute as the majority of paddlers. Even when I'm going all out, I seem to be putting out comparatively little effort and if I break in front, those behind seeing me get ahead with seeming ease tend to become a little discouraged. In a championship event the morale effect of this tactic is highly important.

As the flag dropped to signal the start of the Olympic race, Amyot pulled into the lead and after only 300 metres of the 1,000-metre race, led by several lengths. Within a hundred metres of the finish, Karlic of Czechoslovakia surprised Amyot with a spurt that left him a length behind. The Ottawan responded to the challenge to win by four lengths in the then record time of 5:32.1 minutes.

The triumphant return and reception of the only Canadian gold medallist led to some difficulties. At a testimonial dinner to Frank Amyot, the city of Ottawa and his admirers presented him with a purse of $1,000 which they had raised. This led to his suspension from amateur status by the Canadian Amateur Swimming Association. Although Frank did not plan to paddle competitively after the 1936 pinnacle, the ruling was aggravating and caused an uproar in the press. He had taken "a card" in the swimming association merely to help the local Plant Swimming Club as an official at its meets. The CASA was an independent body and its action regarding Amyot seemed petty; the Amateur Athletic Union of Canada had not been pleased about the purse but they had taken no action. The Canadian Canoeing Association was angry at the suspension and assured the Olympic champion that he was eligible for their meets.

Amyot continued to enjoy canoeing and sailing as recreations after his competitive retirement. He joined the Canadian navy during the second war and served as a lieutenant-commander. He died suddenly in Ottawa at fifty-seven years of age.

GEORGE ATHANS, JR., 1952-

Marry a man who has won a gold medal in springboard diving at the British Empire Games with a girl who was an all-round acquatic performer and one of the best synchronized swimmers in Canada, and the result for the Athans family of Kelowna, BC, – three sons, all water skiers – with the eldest, George, Jr., chosen for the Hall of Fame in 1974 at the age of twenty-one.

The British Columbia Sports Hall of Fame states of George Athans, Sr., that he is "considered Canada's all-time best male diver." The US Pacific Coast champion from 1938 to 1942, he later held the Canadian title for four straight years. He competed at the 1936 Olympics and won a gold and silver medal at the 1950 Empire Games in New Zealand. After his retirement he coached divers and his protégé, Irene McDonald, was the best of all Canadian women divers before the 1970s.

> My parents never pushed me in sport, [said the younger George.] Both of them were still active in the water when I was small and my summers centred on the lake. But my dad was not determined that I should follow him and both he and my mother have always made it clear that an education and an occupation were very important aims.

The younger George Athans first got into serious water skiing at the age of nine when he came under the tutelage of Fred Schuler, a German immigrant who had established a marina business at Kelowna. For the next four years whav tips and encouragement George got were largely from Schuler. At the age of thirteen he competed in his first Canadian national championships at Winnipeg, and after that most of his summer months were spent in Eastern Canada. At eighteen he moved from home in Kelowna to Montreal from where he has trained at Hudson and Sherbrooke in Quebec and attended Sir Georges Williams University as a student in the film arts.

George Athans considers himself essentially a self-taught athlete in his sport, although a number of people from his parents to Fred Schuler to Clint Ward of the Canadian Water Ski Association have supported, guided and advised him as he moved to world championship class. He holds the following Canadian records: junior boys' jump – 117 feet; men's jump – 164 feet; boys' figure skiing – 4,600 points; men's figure skiing – 5,200 points; men's slalom skiing – 37½ buoys.

George won his first overall Canadian championship in 1968 and repeated his win every year after that through 1973. He won the Western Hemisphere slalom title in 1968 in Colombia, its figure title in 1970, the overall world title in 1971 in Spain, and again in 1972 in San Francisco, and both the world overall and the world slalom crowns in 1973 at Bagota, Colombia.

George is a wiry athlete with 145 pounds on a five-foot-ten frame. While he has had some help from government in the form of a four-year scholarship, he has had the problems of a youth without wealth in a very costly sport. His boat and motor cost $10,000. Another $10,000 or so each year is needed to ensure facilities at the lake and to transport him and his equipment to competitions. Most of his revenue for these purposes comes from equipment endorsements. At the competitive level, as he says, water skiing tends to be

"classy" because it is expensive. On the other hand, the sport has steadily developed an enormous recreational base and is on the edge of big developments in Canada. George who was made a member of the Order of Canada in 1974 is especially proud that in the most recent world competition with forty nations competing, Canada has twice finished second.

It has been a dilemma for George and his younger brothers, Greg and Garry, because they excel at both water and snow skiing. All of them had enough potential to be asked to try out for the Canadian ski team and in the winter of 1973-4 George competed on the Canadian professional ski racing circuit. Although he thinks he could have been as successful on the slopes as on the lakes, George chose to concentrate on the summer game but it was not a preference based on greater pleasure or more honours. "I wanted to get an education and in snow skiing you have to be on the hills for the whole long winter. I can combine school and a professional career much better with water skiing."

MARILYN BELL, 1937-

The swimming feats of Marilyn Bell fit better into the myths of a national folklore than into the annals of sports and games. Above all it was her endurance and stamina – across Lake Ontario, the English Channel, the Straits of Juan de Fuca – which seemed so unbelievable in a slip of a girl. This "unbelievability" underlay her achievements and fantastic recognition. She was a victor against cruel distances rather than over competitors or time records.

Marilyn is now an American citizen, the mother of four children and wife of Joe Di Lascio of Willingboro, New Jersey. As modest as always, she makes this self-assessment: "Swimming taught me, particularly in the beginning, to plug along. I was never very fast. Whenever I raced I came in third or fourth, but I always kept at it."

Marilyn Bell's mentor was the great coach, Gus Ryder of the Toronto Lakeshore Swimming Club. He started coaching her in her early teens. After watching Marilyn swim, Ryder told his wife: "Marilyn has got a sort of deep well, a kind of reservoir. I bet that kid could swim forever if we asked her." Ryder felt that he had a half-dozen swimmers in the club who were physically more likely to have made the swim across the lake. "But it wasn't courage so much," Ryder said, "or even will or tenacity, as a kind of response, a natural generosity that kept her swimming – swimming on strongly long after

she'd lost track of time and place."

An impromptu, haphazard set of circumstances led to Marilyn's triumph over Lake Ontario. Certainly no one anticipated the size and emotion of the audience or foresaw the outcome.

Toronto's Canadian National Exhibition has long been noted – and notorious – for its marathon swims. It began when George Young came home to Toronto in 1927 after winning the famed Catalina swim. Endurance contests became part of the CNE's annual sports presentation. The 1954 event was planned around Florence Chadwick, a thirty-four-year-old from the US who was considered the world's best woman swimmer. If Lake Ontario could be swum Miss Chadwick was the person to do it – so ran the reasoning. The course was set from Youngstown, NY, to a landfall at the Ex grounds. Ten thousand dollars was to be the award for Chadwick's successful completion of the course.

Though they weren't invited to take part and no provision was made for them to share prize money if they were successful, two Toronto swimmers entered the race:

94

Winnie Roach Leuszler, twenty-eight, and sixteen-year-old Marilyn Bell. Neither Winnie nor Marilyn expected to race; each was determined to prove that if Lake Ontario could be conquered, it could be conquered by Canadian swimmers. The Toronto *Star* paid the expenses for both.

A minority of people knew that Mrs. Leuszler was a good strong swimmer but not in Chadwick's league; Marilyn's only publicity had come eight weeks before when she was the first woman to finish the twenty-five mile Atlantic City swim.

The CNE swim was an all-night affair; the sponsors hoped Chadwick would approach the Ex grounds in mid-afternoon. She walked into the chill waters of Lake Ontario off Youngstown at eleven PM on 8 September and was pulled out after twelve miles, sick and exhausted. Leuzler plunged in soon after, withdrew when she lost her boat in the dark, started again and made a brave twenty miles before she was defeated.

Shortly before midnight young Marilyn kissed her parents and slipped into the water. For several hours she sprinted and three miles from shore left Chadwick behind. By four AM she enjoyed a commanding lead, but the lake which had been calm turned choppy.

As Marilyn swam and the other two swimmers faltered, across the lake, Toronto, thirty-two air miles from Youngstown, was waking up unaware of the drama that would seize its collective throat by nightfall. The agents which created the excitement were the radio stations and especially the no-holds-barred competitive evening dailies, the *Star* and the *Telegram*.

By noon the Ex had a sensation on its hands; people began to flock to the waterfront; radio bulletins alerted the country. A tiny girl was still in the water; the world's greatest swimmer was out. In a few hours the hopes of literally millions came to focus on Marilyn and her faithful coach, Gus Ryder. Would she, could she make it?

The lake was cold. As the afternoon waned, the wind came up; the waves and currents began to force her west of the Ex landfall. Exhaustion flooded over her and she pleaded to be pulled out. Gus Ryder urged her on; a girlfriend joined her in the water.

At last, at 8:06 PM she touched the breakwater west of the Ex twenty-one hours later, after forty miles of swimming. The waterfront was jammed. Through the day offers of prizes and gifts poured in. The Ex itself announced she would get the $10,000 posted for Chadwick's swim.

While Toronto and Canada exploded in pride, doctors checked the girl and found her heart, pulse and respiration normal. She complained of sore eyes and rubbery legs, nothing else. She had actually gained a pound during the swim.

Cash, gifts and testimonials flooded in; some estimates placed the total value as high as fifty thousand dollars. In more than one way Marilyn was a lucky girl; her parents were unassuming people with their feet firmly planted on the ground. They refused to let the adulation and burgeoning offers of money affect their daughter. Marilyn continued in school and continued her swimming lessons with Gus Ryder. In 1955 she swam the English Channel from France to England in fourteen and one-half hours, the youngest to have made the passage. She collected $15,000 from the Toronto *Telegram* for that feat. In 1956, at eighteen, she conquered the Strait of Juan de Fuca on her second try, swimming the eighteen-mile stretch of tide-swept water in ten and one-half hours.

After that Marilyn Bell withdrew from the spotlight of marathon swimming, at eighteen loaded with honours and medals, the pet of her countrymen. She was not to face again the eels of Lake Ontario or the slimy jellyfish of the ocean. She went on with her education, married an American boy and became as unobtrusive as any other housewife and mother.

While the new generation of Canadians may only hear of Marilyn Bell through flashbacks, none of them can ever fully recreate the way her Ontario swim captured people's interest and affections. And when she stood revealed by fame in her youthful simplicity and quiet candour, Canada saw her as the archetype of the Canadian girl.

CAPTAIN ANGUS WALTERS & WILLIAM J. ROUE
THE BLUENOSE, 1921-1946

The *Bluenose* was a beautiful ship that touched some deep chord in all Canadians. Because she was beautiful? Partly. Because with her ten thousand square feet of sail filled, she showed her heels to every American schooner that challenged her title as queen of the fishing fleet? Certainly. But more. She was a proud and defiant symbol of the passage of another age, and of the tough Nova Scotian sailors who for generations had fished the banks in their little sailing ships. The technology of steel and steam had ended Nova Scotia's greatest age a half-century or more before; the *Bluenose,* the finest fishing schooner ever built, was a last, lovely challenge to the mechanical conformity of progress.

The *Bluenose* came out of a century and one-half of rivalry between the fishermen of Lunenburg, NS, and Gloucester, Massachusetts. Gloucester was the centre of the fresh-fish trade, and her men sailed light, fast vessels that, with refrigeration, could get out to the banks and back again with a saleable cargo. Lunenburg, Nova Scotia's oldest outport, settled soon after Halifax by "foreign Protestant" Germans and Huguenots, was in the salt-fish trade, so her ships were noted more for capacity than for speed. Nevertheless, Nova Scotians and New Englanders traditionally raced each other – to the banks, to a good fishing ground, for bait, or just to relieve the monotony.

In 1920 the owner of the Halifax *Herald*, W. H. Dennis, decided to formalize the custom and put up for competition among working fishing schooners the International Fisherman's Trophy, with a cash prize of $4,000 to the winner. That fall, *Esperanto*, out of Gloucester, defeated the Lunenburg schooner *Delawanna* in races off Halifax. It was then, as the dean of Canadian sailing ship historians, C. H. J. Snider, puts it, that "some good Halifax sports, joined with thrifty Lunenburgers and a few central Canada 'angels' – and behold there came out this *Bluenose*."

It wasn't quite that simple. The difference between *Bluenose* and her predecessors was that whereas Nova Scotian fishing vessels had traditionally been built from the whittled models of long-established builders, with rule-of-thumb modifications by those who sailed them, the new ship had a designer. He was William J. Roué of Halifax, a recent graduate of Nova Scotia Technical College. Roué was a sailing enthusiast and a member both of the Royal Nova Scotia Yacht Squadron and the Armdale Yacht Club who had followed his childhood hobby of modelling sailing vessels into adult life. Before tackling the *Bluenose* he had designed a number of successful yachts, including the *Zetes*, whose lines, enlarged, were to be those of the new challenger. Some features of Roué's design were controversial, especially the very low centre of gravity, the use of streamlining in the rudder, and the narrow, almost canoe-like stern. The senior partner of Smith and Rhuland, whose yards had seen a hundred or more schooners slip down the ways, was frankly scornful: "I don't think nothing of her. She is different from any vessel we ever built. We built her as close to the Roué lines as we knew how. If she's a success, he gets the praise. If she's a failure, he gets the blame." As launched on 26 March 1921, the *Bluenose* was 112 feet at the waterline (143 feet overall), with a 27-foot beam and a displacement of 285 tons.

Her captain and crew (she carried

thirty two for racing) were ready. The captain was Angus Walters of Lunenburg, who was part-owner of the $35,000 schooner. Of German and Scottish extraction, Walters had gone to sea at thirteen apprenticed to his skipper-father. Forty years old in 1921, he had a reputation as a tough and able master with a belligerent, colourful tongue.

Walters took *Bluenose* to sea for her obligatory spell on the fishing grounds. In October he brought her to Halifax to meet the other Nova Scotian challengers; in a series of races she defeated vessels from Lunenburg, Shelburne and La Have. Already she had proved herself strong on windward tacks; eventually Nova Scotians would refer to her affectionately as "Stormalong" and "Old Weatherleg." *Esperanto,* the American title-holder, had been lost off Sable Island in June; the American committee selected the fishing schooner *Elsie,* captained by Marty Welsh of Gloucester who had won aboard *Esperanto.* Over a forty-mile course, the *Bluenose* won two straight races and the International Fisherman's Trophy.

After a successful season on the banks, *Bluenose* sailed for Gloucester to defend her title against the newly built *Henry Ford,* Captain Thomas McManus at the helm. The first race was called off by the committee, but the two captains sailed anyway despite light winds; the *Henry Ford* won but the committee nullified the race. It took the American Secretary of the Navy, Josephus Daniels, to persuade the *Henry Ford's* crew to race again. Again in light winds, the American vessel won; then came the stiff breezes *Bluenose* preferred, and she won the

96

next two races to retain the cup.

In 1923, *Bluenose* faced her best challenger, *Columbia,* which the proud Gloucestermen had commissioned. In the first race, her captain, Ben Pine, forced the *Bluenose* onto the shoals near the mouth of Halifax harbour; *Bluenose's* main boom fouled the *Columbia's* rigging as Walters was beating for sea room. Though *Bluenose* won, the committee ruled that in future all buoys must be passed to seaward. *Bluenose* won the second race by nearly three minutes, but the committee ruled, on a protest from Pine, that she had passed one buoy to the inside. Walters, deeply incensed, since his craft had sailed as much water as the American, took the *Bluenose* home to Lunenburg, and the committee was forced to declare the whole event no contest.

This debacle ended the international series for some years. In the interim, *Bluenose* met and mastered a challenge from the man who had designed her. Roué, under commission from a Halifax syndicate, built the *Haligonian* to defeat his own creation. Angus Walters described the outcome:

> I knew what she was before they matched us. We'd met her outside in the fishing. – I'd watched her sail. "Don't talk race," I begged Roué. "Please, Mr. Roué, for your sake, don't talk race." "We've got to race," Roué said. "All right," I said. "I won't do a thing. No racing canvas. Nothing special. We'll just wash up and come as we are from the fishing." They took *Haligonian* up to Halifax and got all tuned up. We came in and they passed us coming up the harbour. On the wharf there were two fellows. "How do you feel about meeting the *Haligonian*?" they said. "Well," I said, "I don't make a practice of talking about my vessel before a race . . . but you and your partner bring a couple of boxes of good cigars down to meet us when we get in after tomorrow's race. I and my boys will have them half smoked before *Haligonian's* got a line ashore.

And that was how it went.

Bluenose's last rival was the *Gertrude L. Thebaud,* built in 1929 on commission from a Boston syndicate. Sir Thomas Lipton had donated a cup for fishing schooners, and the Bostonians were out to take the *Bluenose.* Off Gloucester, in 1930, she did just that, though Walters declared that "she didn't beat the *Bluenose,* she beat me," putting the loss down to his use of faulty racing sails and to bad tacking. The next year, off Halifax, the *Gertrude L.* was beaten decisively. The last match for the International Fisherman's Trophy featured the same two vessels, in 1938. Walters was reluctant to race, because he had installed engines in the *Bluenose* and her racing rim was altered. *Bluenose* won, three races to two, but it was a close-run thing. "How we ever beat her I don't know," said Walters. "We were so close

the water from our bow washed over *Thebaud's* deck."

As profits declined from fishing, the *Bluenose* became a losing venture. In 1939, Captain Walters bought her outright from the syndicate of owners, but with the coming of the war, she stood idle. In 1942 she was bought as a Caribbean freight carrier by the West Indies Trading Company of Tampa and Havana; she ended her days on a reef off Haiti in January 1946. In 1963, a replica was built and launched by Smith and Rhuland on commission from Oland Breweries of Halifax. But neither this replica nor *Bluenose's* representation on millions of ten-cent coins can substitute for the splendid original.

GEORGE BROWN, 1839-75

Halifax on 8 July 1875 was a city in mourning, with flags flying at half-mast from its buildings and from the ships and yachts in its harbour. At one of its cemeteries a Catholic priest, Father Abbott, spoke to a large crowd of mourners: "We are standing at the grave of a great man – of one who though of obscure birth has won a world-wide fame. He has done honour to this place and to his country." The man thus eulogized was not a statesman or a soldier, but a fisherman from the little nearby village of Herring Cove named George Brown, one of the first – and surely one of the least known – of Canada's outstanding athletes.

Herring Cove was a village of fishermen. From the time he could handle an oar, George Brown, like thousands of other hardy Nova Scotians, sought his livelihood from the waters of the Atlantic. Somehow, the young fisherman came to the attention of James Pryor, a well-to-do Halifax sportsman who had done much to encourage rowing in Nova Scotia. In 1863, at twenty-four, Brown with Pryor's backing competed for the Cogswell belt, emblematic of the Halifax single-sculls championship, but lost to George Lovett who has already won the three previous years. From 1864 to 1868, however, Brown won the competition and was awarded permanent possession of the trophy. Between races he went back to his nets, and made no effort to build upon his local reputation.

In 1871, a group of Halifax enthusiasts organized the Halifax Aquatic Carnival, attracting scullers from England and the United States. George Brown came from Herring Cove to be bow oar in a four James Pryor had assembled; in addition, Brown was entered in the singles. To the anger of Haligonians, the "Paris Crew" of New Brunswick withdrew at the last moment, and it was left to the untried Pryor crew to uphold Maritime pride. They did so brilliantly, finishing second to the crew from Scotland in a tight race, and showing their heels to first-class boats from England and the United States. The following day Brown rowed against Joseph Sadler, considered the world's professional champion. Over the five-mile course in Halifax harbour, Brown finished second to Sadler by four seconds.

Over the next year Sadler repeatedly ducked challenges from Brown for a match race; because of his reluctance, Nova Scotians convinced themselves that Brown was undoubtedly entitled to be called champion oarsman of the world. Meanwhile, Brown embarked on a short but extremely successful professional racing career. In July 1873 he defeated Robert Fulton of the Paris Crew for $1,000; in September, for $2,000 he won in Bedford Basin over the American John Biglin by 200 yards over a five-mile course. Then, on 8 July 1874 at Boston, he rowed the US singles champion, William Scharff, for $4,000 and the title. According to the New York *Herald,* the excitement engendered by this race was "unprecedented in the history of American aquatics;" pools were sold on it in Halifax, Saint John, Springfield, Boston, Pittsburgh and New York, and it was estimated that $250,000 was bet. Americans thought the race a contest of Scharff's "science and skill against strength" (Brown weighed only 154 pounds), and contrasted Scharff's "finished stroke" against the Nova

Scotian's "old-fashioned open hand fish stroke." Since Brown had the reputation of being "slow to take the water," the strategy in the American camp was to jump into a commanding lead immediately and then hold it. Through all the ballyhoo and confusion, Brown remained characteristically calm. He "stepped into his boat almost mechanically and adjusted his oars, without a word or a smile of recognition to his many friends about him . . . preserving to a marked degree the coolness and reserve which is peculiar to him." Scharff was never able to get more than half a length lead, and by the middle of the fourth mile, Brown had established a three-length gap, going on to win by six seconds. Despite his reserve, he must have smiled inwardly; he had bet his life's savings on himself.

Brown won one more race in his short career, defeating Evan Morris of the United States at Saint John on 24 September 1874. While training for the world championship race to which Joe Sadler had finally agreed, George Brown suffered the stroke that ended both his career and his life. Ned Hanlan was to reap the honours that might have come to Brown, but though almost forgotten in Canadian sports history he is remembered in Herring Cove where a monument stands to his memory.

PHYLLIS DEWAR, 1916-61

Dora Dewar Ellsworth remembers a mile swimming race at Watrous, Saskatchewan, when she was sixteen and her kid sister, Phyllis, was eleven. They swam side by side, well ahead of the other entrants until they were about fifty yards from the finish. "Phyl said to me, 'Let's sprint the rest of the way.' I agreed, but she got there 25 yards ahead of me . . . she liked to win."

Phyllis Dewar came out of Moose Jaw at eighteen to become the Canadian darling with a record-sweeping series of performances in the 1934 British Empire Games in London. Her story as a swimmer really began with her mother who grew up as a self-proclaimed tomboy in Kenora, Ontario, swimming off the town dock at Lake-of-the-Woods, developing into a strong, fearless swimmer. When she married a CPR conductor and moved with him to Vancouver, the young mother started her two girls swimming at English Bay. Phyllis could swim at four years of age and came along naturally, largely, said her sister, "by keeping up with mother."

When father Dewar got regular runs out of the CPR divisional point at Moose Jaw, the family settled there. Nearby was good swimming and an aquatic club which encouraged swimming, canoeing and rowing. Albert Tomlinson and Don McKay, pillars of the club, recognized Phyllis Dewar's talents as a swimmer. With their support, and encouraged by her father, she began to race competitively, sometimes in Regina and Winnipeg, and later at Banff. Often she competed against boys. Her time improved, although at first she was stronger in longer races than sprints.

By seventeen, she was the best girl swimmer on the Prairies and was aiming for the British Empire Games of 1934 by training in Vancouver. In the trials she got her 100-yard freestyle time down to 64 seconds and made the swimming team, along with two other exceptional swimmers, Phillis Haslam of Saskatoon, who had set the then world record in the 100-metre backstroke, and Irene Pirie of Toronto.

The Canadian swimmers, and especially Phyllis Dewar, dominated the games, taking eight titles, more than half those at stake. Phyllis Dewar got four, in the 100-yard and 400-yard freestyle, in the 300-yard medley relay and the 400-yard relay.

After London Phyllis decided to settle in Vancouver to take advantage of year-round swimming. And there she got what amounted to her first coaching. She was aiming for the 1936 Olympics in Germany. She made the team but made a poor showing in the Olympics, coming down with influenza. Next she aimed for the 1938 BEG in Australia. She made the team and, while she performed well in heats, she and the team won only one gold medal – the 440-yard freestyle relay in which she, Dorothy Lyon, Mary Baggaley and Dora Dobson posted a time of 4:48.3 minutes.

Sports Hall of Fame

By 1938 Phyllis was tired of the training necessary for a swimmer. She joined the WRENS early in the war and was stationed at Halifax where she met a young RCN lieutenant, Murray Lowery. They were married at Halifax. Murray was killed in a car accident in 1954, leaving Phyllis with four small children. She, herself, had lost all interest in swimming. Even when her youngsters were splashing along the shore she refused to go into the water. Her health began to fade and she died at the age of forty five.

"In some ways," her sister says, "all the stardom brought on by the London victories left Phyllis rather frightened . . . It was very hard for her – I guess for any kid – to live easily with it."

GEORGE HERRICK DUGGAN, 1862-1946

At his death George Herrick Duggan was not only the dean of Canadian yachting but was known as "the grand amateur of racing and cruising in America." Yachting has always been a sport chiefly indulged in by the well-to-do, and Duggan was no exception. He was born in Toronto, the son of a well-known Toronto lawyer. The family's summer home was Toronto Island, and as a boy Duggan learned sailing and boat building from a pioneer islander, William Armstrong. While a student of fifteen at Upper Canada College, he built his first boat; at eighteen he designed and built a thirty-two-foot yawl, *Escape*. That year he and some of his friends broke away from the Royal Canadian Yacht Club and founded the Toronto Yacht Club; four years later he and other young yachtsmen formed the Lake Yacht Racing Association, taking in every yacht club, Canadian and American, on the Lake Ontario shore, and giving form and order for the first time to lake racing.

Meanwhile, Duggan was beginning the career that was to reinforce (and make financially possible) his lifelong hobby. As a civil engineering student at the University of Toronto, he won the gold medal, and found time to captain the Varsity football team. After graduation in 1884, he was a construction engineer for three years with the CPR and then joined Dominion Bridge in Montreal, becoming its chief engineer within a few years. The skills that brought him to the top of his profession were now to make Canada a power in the field of international yachting.

In 1895 the Seawanhaka Corinthian Yacht Club of New York put up for international competition the Seawanhaka Cup, with the intention of providing a small-yacht alternative to the America's Cup. In the

first year of competition the New Yorkers defeated an English challenge. Because cup competition was limited to yachts fifteen to twenty-five feet under the waterline-sail area rule, it opened up an opportunity for the ingenious designer. In 1896 Duggan's club, the Royal St. Lawrence of Montreal, challenged for the cup and in preparation eighteen boats were built for its trials, including five designed by Duggan. One, the *Glencairn I* with Duggan himself as skipper, defeated the American yacht *El Heirie* at Oyster Bay – Duggan's first experience of salt-water sailing. *Glencairn's* design, with a shortened waterline length of only 12.25 feet, gave her 300 square feet of sail as against *El Heirie's* 240.

Glencairn* was a triumph not only for Duggan's design and sailing abilities, but also for Canadian workmanship, because by the rules of the competition, yachts had to be completely built from native materials. The builders were a Toronto shipyard; Ontario white pine and cedar went into her planking; the deck was British Columbia cedar; and the sails and fittings were manufactured in Montreal.

The 1896 victory inaugurated a remarkable series of successful defenses of the cup by the Royal St. Lawrence Club. Against challenges from New York, the White Bear Yacht Club of St. Paul, Minnesota, and in 1901 a yacht from England, Duggan-designed vessels defeated all comers on the home waters of Lake St. Louis. In all but the last victory, in 1904, Duggan himself was the skipper.

Part of the reason for this remarkable string of successes lay in the advantage of home waters; part, too, in Herrick Duggan's outstanding abilities as a sailor. He was described by his contemporaries as "absolutely fearless," a man who knew how to challenge wind and water to just short of disaster in order to get the utmost in speed from his craft. But most of all it was Duggan's creative originality as a designer, keeping at least one jump ahead of all rivals, and exploiting brilliantly the engineering possibilities opened up by the Seawanhaka Cup rules. The most remarkable of all his yachts was *Dominion,* designed for the challenge of 1898 from the Seawanhaka Corinthians. *Dominion's* floor was arched between the bilges, with the top of her central tunnel riding two and one-half feet out of the water. Officials of the New York club protested that *Dominion* was a catamaran, and that such double-hulled types were not permitted by cup rules. The St. Lawrence club stood firm, on the dubious ground that *Dominion* was a single-hulled vessel with two waterlines; *Dominion* then proceeded to defeat *Challenger* of New York in three of four races. Both clubs agreed not to use double waterlines again.

In 1889 the secretary of the White Bear Club of St. Paul pronounced that in Herrick Duggan "Canadians possessed a perfect treasure. He is without doubt the best designer of small boats in the world today." Before Duggan's sailing life was ended in a Laurentian automobile accident in 1946, he had designed and built the amazing total of 142 boats. He will always be remembered by Canadian sailors as perhaps the greatest figure in our yachting history.

JACOB GILL GAUDAUR, 1858-1937

Jake Gaudaur grew up in a locality that produced a remarkable galaxy of athletes in the late nineteenth century. Not only Gaudaur but Walter Knox, George Gray, Harry Gill and a large number of other athletes of only slightly lesser calibre came from the Orillia-

Coldwater area, a part of the country still thought of as the northland by Torontonians of the time.

Gaudaur had a most interesting ancestry. The story begins with Donal MacGuil, a British soldier who fled to the United States from Halifax in the 1790s after striking a superior officer. In process, MacGuil became Gill. Jacob Gill came to Upper Canada from his father's farm at Hadley, New York, during the war of 1812, took up the carpentry trade, married the daughter of one of Wellington's Scottish veterans, and settled down at Coldwater to raise a large family. Out of that family came an astonishing number of athletes. Jacob's grandson, Harry Gill, became the all-round track and field champion of North America in 1900 and later a leading track coach in the United States; George Gray, the great shot putter, was Jacob's great grandson (four of his brothers were also champion athletes).

Jacob's sixth child, Jennet, married Francis Gaudaur, whose father Antoine Godard, a Métis, was Orillia's first settler; their son, Jacob Gill Gaudaur, was thus of Scottish, French and Indian ancestry – all tough, hardy stocks. The Gaudaur house was right at the narrows between Lakes Couchiching and Simcoe, and from the time he could handle the oars young Jake's spare time was spent on the water. By the time he was seventeen, he was racing lapstreak skiffs, and he and his brother Frank, some ten years older, carried all before them at the regattas on Simcoe's Kempenfeldt Bay. It was at this point that Gaudaur's career first became entangled with that of Ned Hanlan.

Jake Gaudaur has often been considered as Hanlan's successor, and in a sense he was, since he held the world's professional championship after the Toronto sculler. Actually, however, Gaudaur was only three years younger than Hanlan and the two often raced. Gaudaur was the larger man; he stood six-foot-two and at his peak weighed 175 pounds. Hanlan, with his attention-getting personal style, his racing showmanship, his genius for publicity and his occasionally dubious associations, fascinated the rowing public even when long past his peak; Gaudaur won his place in public regard by dint of achievement over a very long athletic career. He was a retiring, almost self-effacing man; it was "like pulling teeth," a reporter once observed, to get him to talk about himself. He was an impressive-looking man, with a face that was "handsome and uncommon," sparing in speech, mild in manner, without the arrogance that so often overtakes the superior athlete, and of great personal dignity and integrity.

It was Ned Hanlan who engineered Gaudaur's first significant victory. In 1875 the favourite son of east-end Toronto was Hughie Wise. Wise's backers thought he was the man "to cut Hanlan's comb," but Hanlan refused to row in skiffs. Instead, he put Gaudaur – "tall and sinewy and a likely looking customer, but . . . unknown to fame," up against Wise, and backed the Orillian for $500. Gaudaur beat Wise easily on Lake Couchiching and was on his way.

Gaudaur took a long time to come out of Hanlan's shadow. His first significant race in a shell was at the Barrie regatta in August 1879, when he finished a strong third behind Hanlan and James Riley in their famous draw. During the early 1880s, while Hanlan was standing the rowing world on its ear before finally losing his title in Australia, "the star of the north" began to rise. A Toronto hotel-keeper backed Gaudaur (the chief expense, aside from shells, was constant training). As Gaudaur said in later life, professional rowing was not a particularly lucrative sport. There was and could be no gate money. Income came from stakes, and these were eaten up by expenses. Gaudaur trained hard. "I was always a great believer in hard work and plenty of sleep. While I was in training I did not smoke or drink except for an occasional pint of champagne which I found beneficial. When I was not rowing I was out in the bush carrying packs. An oarsman who rows three miles or five miles has to have stamina. If there is a weak spot in him it will soon be found out."

By 1886 Gaudaur, now rowing out of Creve Coeur Lake, near St. Louis, Missouri, was acknowledged to be one of the top half dozen oarsmen in North America. In the sports pages of these years, his name is to be found in accounts of races at Pullman,

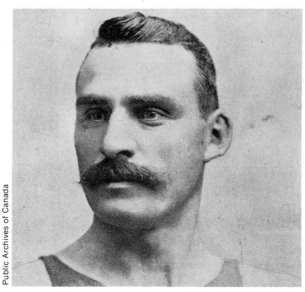

101

Illinois, New Orleans, Calais, Maine, Boston, White Bear Lake, Minnesota, Pittsburgh, Pleasure Island, NY, and many other racing hotbeds including Canadian waters. Even so, when he challenged Hanlan's conqueror, William Beach, for the world title, the Montreal *Gazette* considered that "Jake Gaudaur would do well to beat some good oarsmen here before issuing a challenge to row Beach for $5,000 and the championship." That was unfair; but it was true that Gaudaur had not established clear superiority over such oarsmen as the American John Teemer, Ned Hanlan or William O'Connor. Nevertheless, his race with Beach on the Thames has gone down in rowing history as perhaps the most thrilling single sculls contests ever held. The two men rowed themselves out (Gaudaur losing a lead when misdirected by his coach through the wrong span of one of the Thames bridges); both collapsed over their oars a few yards from the finish, the exhausted Beach stroking across the line a half-length in front of the Canadian.

As he approached and passed the age of thirty, Gaudaur seemed to hit his peak. In 1887, on Lake Calumet near Chicago, he met and cleanly defeated Ned Hanlan for $5,000 and the North American title. Hanlan was as slick as ever, and in fact rowed the course in record time, but during the last mile Gaudaur passed him "with machine-like precision" and won by four lengths. For the next decade or more Jake Gaudaur was virtually invincible. Repeatedly, from 1888 on, Gaudaur set new records nearly every time he rowed.

From 1892, it became clear that Jake Gaudaur was the world's best oarsman. In that year he defeated Charles Stephenson, the New Zealand champion, at Orillia. In 1893, against a magnificent field, including Hanlan, John Teemer, James Stanbury of Australia (the world's champion), and J. Peterson of San Francisco, he set a new world's record for three miles with a turn of 19:6 minutes at Austin, Texas. The next year, again at Austin, and with Hanlan and three top-ranking English oarsmen among his opponents, he set a new world mark of 19:1.5 minutes for the same distance. This time has never been bettered.

Jim Stanbury could not be lured into a race for the world championship until 1896, when, at the age of thirty-eight, Jake Gaudaur won an easy victory on the Thames. He was rapturously welcomed home. Toronto gave him a civic reception. At Orillia, he was brought to town from his home at the Narrows on board the steamer *Islay* escorted by six other steamboats. He was honoured with a gold watch and the mayor's salute for

"the white flower of a blameless life".

Despite such civic adulation, Gaudaur shortly moved to Rat Portage (now Kenora) on the Lake of the Woods. In 1898 he defended his world title against R. N. Johnson of Vancouver on Burrard Inlet. Unfortunately, some "wretched pieces of driftwood" knocked Johnson's shell out of the race; Gaudaur, who rowed the course and was entitled to the stakes, sportingly agreed to void the race, a gesture that won him admiration not only in Vancouver but throughout the rowing world. In the sequel, he defeated his much younger opponent easily.

Jake Gaudaur's last race was at Rat Portage on 7 September 1901 against George Towns of Newcastle, New South Wales. The Australian both in style and physique reminded many of Hanlan. He was twelve years Gaudaur's junior, six inches shorter and a good deal lighter. He won by a good four lengths, ending, in effect, the era of professional sculling in Canada. At the finish, Gaudaur went out like a champion. Rowing over to Towns, he took off his cap to him and said: "George, the best man won." As Towns said later, "I only wished that I had a cap on myself, that I might have taken it off to him."

In his epilogue to *Too Much College,* Stephen Leacock wrote of Gaudaur:

> Jake was a magnificent figure of a man; he stood nicely over six feet in his stocking feet. . . . He was broad in the shoulders, straight as a lathe, and till the time when he died, just short of eighty, he could pick up the twenty-pound anchor of his motor-boat and throw it round like a tack-hammer. . . . When Jake's championship days were over he came back to Canada and 'kept hotel' in Sudbury. . . . in the unregenerate days of the old bar thousands of people spent five cents on a drink just to say they had talked with Jake Gaudaur. . . . So Jake made his modest pile and then came back to our part of the country, the Lake Simcoe District, and set up at the Narrows, at the top end of the lake as a professional fisherman, taking out parties on the lake for bass fishing.

Jake's reputation is perpetuated by his son, an outstanding football player and commissioner of the Canadian Football League.

JOHN SCHOFIELD GUEST, 1906-
In their day, Jack Guest Sr. and Joe Wright Jr. were known as the rowing twins of Canada. Not only had they been born on the same day in 1906, but they both rose from the ranks of the sweepoars to become great single scullers, were both coached by Joe Wright Sr., rowed together as an outstanding pair, and climaxed their careers by winning the Diamond Sculls. There, however, the resemblance ends. Guest's career was rela-

tively brief, building rapidly to a pitch of perfection (matched only, perhaps, by the legendary Ned Hanlan) and ended right at that point.

Guest was born in Montreal, but grew up in Toronto where he went to school, at Morse Street Public School and Central High School of Commerce. Summer vacations were spent at the family cottage on Toronto Island. As a gangling youngster, he splashed doggedly around in the bay, showing no particular promise but much dedication. Serious rowing began with the fours and eights of the Don Rowing Club. While rowing eights in 1927, he showed the first flash of brilliance winning the junior and association singles at St. Catharines. Guest subsequently joined the Argonaut junior eights.

Now coached by Joe Wright Sr., he found himself in the shadow of young Joe. He was beaten by Wright in his first attempt for the Diamond Sculls in 1928, and it was natural, perhaps, that the senior Wright should select his son for the Olympic singles over the still relatively undeveloped Guest. The next year on the Thames it was the same story; Joe Wright Jr. stormed past him in the last few yards to eliminate him. It was small consolation that Guest beat Wright at the Canadian Henley.

It is hard to escape the conclusion that a certain tension developed between Guest and his home-town rival. At any rate,

Alexandra Studio

in 1929 Jack Guest left the Argonaut Rowing Club to return to the Don RC. He turned to a new coach, an experienced English waterman named Harry Arlett, and with his father's encouragement embarked on a twelve-month training program of unprecedented severity. With a singlemindedness now characteristic of the champion athlete but relatively unknown then, Guest put himself through a winter of gym workouts, including hours of back-breaking work daily on the rowing machine. With the ice off the bay, Arlett insisted that he concentrate not on sprints or time-tests but upon form and stamina. Infection from blistered hands almost put an end to training, but they healed quickly, and by early summer the pair went off to England to continue training on the Thames. Not until a couple of weeks before the Henley Regatta did Arlett allow Guest to open up; when he did, Guest must have felt a great surge of confidence because of the power he could now generate so smoothly.

By the opening heats of the singles, Guest had been brought to his physical peak, and his form had been honed to a flowing beauty that almost disguised the power. Joe Wright Jr., after winning his first two heats, was conquered by the German oarsman, Boetzelen; it was Boetzelen whom Jack Guest met in the finals. The race was almost an anti-climax. Guest, rowing effortlessly at 34 strokes per minute, kept pace with the German to the half-way mark, and then, increasing the beat, pulled away to one of the most one-sided victories in the history of the Diamond Sculls. Though no lengths were given, the margin was at least 200 yards.

Jack Guest was a popular winner. His easy, long stroke was beautiful to watch; the English sporting papers raved about it. As Ted Reeve wrote at the time, "The Henley crowd dotes on a good style, and when the big Canadian came down the course as if he were coasting they were ready to roll over and butter themselves." In the highest tribute ever paid to any Canadian sculler, Guy Nickalls, the great English rower who won five consecutive Diamond Sculls, wrote in his 1939 autobiography that Jack Guest was "the most perfect sculler I have ever seen."

And then, after an exuberant Toronto reception, Jack Guest retired. He never severed his connection with the old Don Rowing Club, acting as its president from 1938 to 1952. He also served as president of the Dominion Day Regatta Association for ten years, as president of the Canadian Association of Amateur Oarsmen in 1955-6, helped manage the Canadian team at the British Empire Games in 1962 and 1966, acted as a director of the Canadian Olympic Association, and in 1969 became the first Canadian elected to the governing body of world rowing, the International Rowing Federation.

EDWARD HANLAN, 1855-1908

As the Montreal *Gazette* said during his heyday, Ned Hanlan was not only "our first national sporting hero," but, as world rowing champion, he was really our first great international sporting figure. Part of Hanlan's amazing prominence was due to the immense interest in rowing all over the English-speaking world, with rowing regattas attracting huge crowds, heavy gambling and stimulating great public excitement. But a good part of the adulation Hanlan received was because of his own personal magnetism and style. He was a small man, only a little over five-foot-eight and never weighing more than 155 pounds in competition against far bigger men – although, as an American reporter remarked, "the more clothes he takes off, the bigger he gets." He was a strikingly handsome man, and set off his good looks with a distinctive rowing costume; as "the Boy in Blue" he was recognized in London, New York and Sydney, Australia. He had the drive and pride that makes a great competitor, but his personal modestly, coupled with a flair for the dramatic when racing, kept him in the public eye wherever he went, and won him a measure of acclaim no Canadian before his time had achieved, and few have since.

Hanlan was Toronto-born, on 12 July 1855. As a youngster he worked in his father's hotel on Toronto Island, and spent his off-hours fishing or rowing about the harbour on a makeshift shell he had built by

sharpening a two-inch plank at both ends and mounting a seat and outriggers on it. Between 1873 and 1876 the young Hanlan won a series of single-shell races that established him as the best sculler in Ontario, but he was completely unknown outside his own province. Then, in 1876 on the Schuylkill River at Philadelphia, the unheralded Canadian won the centennial single-sculls, defeating some of the best oarsmen on the continent. From that point, Hanlan's rise to the top of the world professional rowing was spectacular. In 1877 he defeated Wallace Ross of Saint John, New Brunswick, for the Canadian championship on Toronto Bay; then in a tough race in 1878 on the difficult waters of the Allegheny River near Pittsburgh, he defeated the outstanding American sculler, Evan "Eph" Morris for the United States title. These victories brought him many challenges; he took on all comers, with unvarying success, in races for large purses (and substantial side bets) throughout eastern United States and Canada.

By 1879 he was the undisputed master of rowing in North America, and was looking for new worlds to conquer. Backed financially by the Hanlan Club, a group of Toronto sportsmen formed shortly after Hanlan's Philadelphia victory, he decided to challenge the shrine of rowing itself. After defeating the trial horse John Hawdon on the Tyne on 8 May 1879, Hanlan took on William Elliott, the champion of England, for the championship and the Sportsman Challenge Cup. This race, over the three and a half mile Tyne course, was rowed before a crowd of tens of thousands; to the astonishment of the English, the colonial won by eleven lengths. The next year he returned to England to defend his title and the cup against the world professional champion, Edward A. Trickett of Australia, a giant oarsman who stood six-foot-four and outweighed Hanlan by at least fifty pounds. They rowed over the historic Thames championship course from Putney to Mortlake, a distance of 4 miles 440 yards. In many ways it was Hanlan's most astonishing victory. Stroking 35 to the minute to Trickett's 40, he had pulled into a two-length lead by the end of the first mile, and for the rest of the race toyed with Trickett, waving to the crowd, lying down in his boat, and pulling away whenever his opponent threatened. He won the race, and the world's championship, by three lengths, but the English papers, while lecturing him sternly on his clowning, agreed that the race was "a mere procession." As a reporter said, "I fully expected him to stand up in his boat and dance the Highland fling."

Hanlan's career as a world-class

athlete lasted an amazingly long time. He successfully defended his world crown six times, as well as winning scores of other races, before losing to William Beach, an Australian, on the Paramatta River in 1884. His last race for the title, again with Beach, was in Australia in 1887. Throughout his career, the international sporting press speculated on the secret of this bantam athlete's remarkable success. He has been credited with inventing, or at least first using, the sliding seat. He did neither, although he was clearly the first to master its use fully. What caught the knowledgeable English eye when he first rowed there was his stroke. "His style of sculling strikes us," said one journal, "as being remarkably easy and effective, and while his strokes are much above the average length, they are cleanly pulled through, and the six-inch blades come out of the water with a swish. He is very quick back again, and there is not the slightest rocking motion in his boat . . . The old folks at home do not know what to make out of Hanlan's stroke – it is long and slow." Hanlan himself described his stroke to the *Police Gazette:* "A full, long reach out over the toes, with both arms straight; a sharp, clean 'catch' of the water; a powerful, steady horizontal stroke, with an application of the whole force at the moment of immersion; a clean feather and a low, quick recover, shooting out at the moment of the finish." At least part of Hanlan's secret, however, lay in his racing tactics; few opponents until Beach were able to survive the scorching pace he set over the first few hundred yards.

Wherever Hanlan went, he received the kind of attention reserved later for film stars. Public receptions were held for him in London and in Madison Square Garden in New York. In Australia, as Hanlan said, "I met and was wined and dined by all of the nobility, state officials, and big guns of the country." After his Australian trip, he took a bemused reporter on a tour of his hotel room:

> This ring which has 4 half carat diamonds, and five large rubies was presented to Mrs. Hanlan by a wealthy squatter and sheep raiser near Sydney. Here's another ring with 20 good sized diamonds of the first water, and a large sapphire, given to me by the citizens of Sydney. This pearl studded bracelet is a present to Mrs. Hanlan from the Mercantile Rowing Club of Melbourne, and here's a horseshoe diamond pin and a pair of solitaire diamond sleeve buttons presented to me by the crew of the United States steamer *Iroquois.*

The world of professional rowing had its shady side because of the feverish betting that went on, and once or twice Hanlan was touched by scandal. In 1879, for example, on the morning of a race at Chautauqua, New York, the shell of his opponent, Charles Courtney, was found sawn in two. But his standing in Canada, and especially in his home town, was proof against any allegation. The spur he had given to the ordinary Canadian's sense of national pride was immense. When the United States press claimed him as a "pure, thoroughbreed American," he said, "there's no harm in them calling me an American but I am not an American in the sense they want to have it. I was born in Canada, and I am a Canadian, and I don't care what they say."

Hanlan died 4 January 1908 after winning more than 300 races, rowing competitively well into the 1890s and serving his city as alderman. In 1926 Toronto sportsmen erected a statue to his memory, looking out from the grounds of the Canadian National Exhibition over the waters where Ned Hanlan first learned to row.

GEORGE HODGSON, 1893-

Living in a country so plentifully endowed with lakes and rivers, Canadians have always been keen on water sports. It is surprising, then, to realize that Canada has had but one gold medal winner in Olympic swimming meets. Since 1912 when George Hodgson won two golds in Stockholm, Canada has not fielded another winner.

George was born into a sporting family. His father was one of five brothers, all of whom were fine amateur athletes, particularly in hockey and lacrosse. His father was a member of the famous lacrosse team taken to England by Dr. Beers in 1878 which played at Windsor Castle before Queen Victoria. The youngest brother, Archie, played for the Montreal Amateur Athletic Association hockey club and was on the team that won the first Stanley Cup championship in 1894. For more than thirty years the Hodgson brothers took part in annual curling and golf matches with the five Ross brothers who had been their youthful teammates and rivals at the MAAA.

At the beginning of the twentieth century swimming was not a particularly popular sport; those who were interested in swimming looked upon it as pleasurable exercise rather than a competitive sport. It was not until 1909 that the first public baths in Canada were opened in Toronto. The same year the Toronto school board included swimming in the public school curriculum. George was lucky to live in Montreal, where he was able to join the MAAA and swim in its pool while still at high school. He had little formal instruction; the family spent its summers in the Laurentians, and he kept up

105

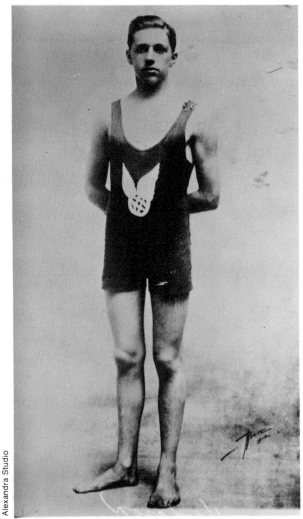

Alexandra Studio

training in the lakes.

Training for international competition was a much more haphazard affair at that time, and athletes were not under the tremendous pressures that have characterized more recent Olympics. George Hodgson describes his accomplishments with typical understatement: "Compared with swimmers of today, we were slow-poke second-raters. When I started there was only one pool in Montreal. Now competitive swimming is a very serious sport. Swimmers benefit from rigid coaching. In my time we swam for fun and coached ourselves. Why, at Stockholm the Canadian team actually didn't have an official coach."

Hodgson's spectacular wins at the Olympics were not his first successes in international swimming. In 1911 he had represented Canada at the Festival of Empire Games, held in London to celebrate the coronation of King George v and Queen Mary. The manager of the Canadian team, Norton Crowe, entered Hodgson in the one-mile race, but was disconcerted to discover a few days before the race that George had never swum the distance. Nevertheless, George won the race, beating the record holder, Sid Battersky of Great Britain, and Malcolm Champion of Australia.

Following this victory, Hodgson was the natural choice of the Olympic selection committee to represent Canada at Stockholm the following year. By 1912, international competition was growing. The Stockholm games, the fifth Olympiad of the modern series, was attended by twenty-eight nations. Hodgson won the gold medal in the 400-metre freestyle and the 1500-metre freestyle, setting world records for both events that lasted for twelve years until Johnny Weissmuller's performance in the Olympics of 1924. Hodgson's time over 1,000 metres was also a record, although this distance was not an official race in Olympic competition in 1912.

George Hodgson returned to Canada and attended McGill University. He served with the RAF in the first world war, and won the AFC in 1918. He represented Canada again in the 1920 games, but this time did not win any medals. He was beaten by an American, Norman Ross, in the 400- and 1500-metre events, although his times of 5:24 and 22:00.0 minutes respectively, set in 1912, remained unbeaten.

George Hodgson came back to Montreal, and gave up international swimming. He formed the brokerage firm of Hodgson, Robertson, Laing and Company in 1928. He has continued to swim for pleasure and has been an enthusiastic tennis player. His two sons have become keen swimmers and have competed in Canadian amateur championships.

GEORGE HUNGERFORD, 1944-
ROGER JACKSON, 1942-

It is no strange alchemy that creates a winning athletic combination out of diverse talents. Talents mesh through long hours of physical conditioning, drilling and training. At some stage in that process, if a team is to be created, an instinctive emotional bonding must occur as well. In the supremely disciplined sport of rowing, the object of training is to eliminate differences, to submerge the individual in the group, to build that two-, four- or eight- oared organism called a crew.

At least, that is the way it is supposed to happen. But on a windy afternoon at the Tokyo Olympics in 1964, two young men named George Hungerford and Roger Jackson added some new elements to the old gospel when they won a gold medal in the pairs for Canada.

The circuitous path that led the two to a half-share in the same shell began for

George Hungerford *(left)* **and Roger Jackson.**

Roger Jackson at the University of Western Ontario. During an all-round athletic career at Lawrence Park Collegiate in Toronto, the six-foot-five Jackson had never tried rowing; he took it up with a convert's enthusiasm when he went to Western. After graduation he went on to the University of Toronto for an MA, and under the coaching of Jack Russell of the Argonauts, he stroked the Varsity eight to the intercollegiate championship. In the spring of 1964 Jackson transferred to the University of British Columbia graduate school, hoping to earn a place on one of the UBC Olympic crews. He did not win a place on the UBC eight which qualified for the Olympics, while the UBC four, which he stroked, lost out to St. Catharines in the trials. He was selected for the UBC pairs with Wayne Pretty and the two settled in to train.

George Hungerford, a six-foot-four, 198-pounder from Vancouver, had already made the UBC eight. At Shawnigan Boys' School on Vancouver Island, an exclusive private school noted for its emphasis on sports in the British tradition, Hungerford had been a gifted all-round athlete. Like his father, a Vancouver businessman, George had a highly developed competitive spirit. When a dislocated shoulder prevented him from playing rugby, he took up rowing and excelled in it as he had in other sports.

It was during the summer training grind of 1964 that the shuffle began which brought Jackson and Hungerford together. George came down with mononucleosis and had to be dropped from the eight. His place was taken by Pretty and Jackson's year of work looked wasted, though he was still to go to Tokyo as a spare. So, too, was Hungerford. Six weeks before the games, with Hungerford still recovering from his debilitating illness, the two began to work out as a pair. Dave Galander assumed the task of coaching. Their routine never varied; early each morning they rowed for an hour and a half, then Jackson went off to classes and Hungerford to bed. After another two hours in the evening, the exhausted Hungerford would go back to bed until it was time for the morning stint. It was still doubtful that Hungerford had the strength to last 2,000 metres, but when they got to Tokyo, Jackson noticed that Hungerford was beginning to row with authority. "Then I knew we were going to be a pretty good pair," Jackson said. "We seemed to fit well together because we are about equal in strength."

When they won their heat (their first race together) with a time faster than the favoured Dutch and German pairs, they surprised many. Even so, the odds were against them. They had not worked long together; neither the Dutch nor the Germans had been pressed in their heats. For the race – 2,000 metres without coxswain – the Canadians were rowing a rudderless shell, and although they rowed so well together that they did not need to be constantly correcting their course, there were circumstances under which the lack of a rudder could be a disadvantage. And there was the still unanswered question of Hungerford's stamina under supreme pressure.

On the day of the race a headwind was blowing straight down the course. Here was an advantage for the Canadians: their power gave them an edge over the smaller men in the other boats.

The two rowed a carefully planned race, designed to keep them in contention and at the same time save Hungerford for the final pull. They began with a furious burst at 39 to 40 strokes a minute, then quickly settled back to a 34/35 stroke pace. This held them with their rivals, even though they seemed relaxed; the Dutch and Germans were doing 36/37 strokes a minute but their style was choppier and more abrupt than the long stroke of the Canadians. At 1,000 metres they were even with the Dutch and decided to give it a "big ten"; their spurt won them a three-length lead. As they drove for the finish, exhaustion almost overwhelmed Hungerford and the lack of a rudder almost cost them the race, since the still powerful Jackson was beginning to pull the boat around. Just hanging on, they won by half a length over the Dutch. Their power, skill and courage had won for Canada its first gold medal in the summer games since the UBC four had won at Melbourne in 1956.

FRANK MCGILL, 1893-

Frank McGill, an all-round athlete particularly noted for his feats in football and aquatic sports, was a latter-day member of that Montreal élite which transformed Canadian sport in the late nineteenth century. McGill University and the Montreal Amateur Athletic Association were the twin institutions that fostered his athletic career though he had already shown himself to be an outstanding athlete during his years at Montreal High School. McGill was also an example of that generation of Canadian athletes whose careers were shortened, distorted, or cut off altogether by the first world war.

Before the war, McGill played hockey for the Emeralds, the MAAA Juniors, Knox Church and Montreal High School, and starred for McGill. He won his first Canadian swimming championship at fifteen, and under the guidance of George Hodgson, the Canadian Olympic champion, went on to win eight more medals for national titles and records. On the track his specialty was shorter races but he also was dominion champion for the mile. He was on three MAAA Canadian championship teams in water polo, captaining one. (After the war, he captained two more MAAA titleholders in this sport.) In 1913 he was awarded the Sir Vincent Meredith Trophy as the best all-round

athlete at the Montreal Amateur Athletic Association.

McGill graduated from McGill University's School of Commerce in 1914, but got little chance to establish himself in business. In 1915 he joined the Royal Naval Air Service, and flew as a pilot for the remainder of the war.

After the war, McGill returned briefly to sport, playing senior hockey and water polo. While at McGill, he had been an outstanding football player, and during the 1919 and 1920 seasons, he captained and quarterbacked the MAAA Winged Wheelers in the Interprovincial Rugby Football Union (Big Four). The Winged Wheelers won the Big Four title in 1919, one of their most important victories being over the tough Hamilton team in the Tigers' home town. Legend has it that McGill, suspecting that the Tigers had broken his signal code (in those days, teams did without huddles and the quarterbacks barked set numbers) called out French signals. The Winged Wheelers, with a comprehension not usually ascribed to the Montreal English of that day, responded to such commands as *"Maintenant, Monsieur Moe (Herscovitch), emportera la balle à droite."* Over the years, the Hamilton behemoths have been maligned in many ways, but it is hard to believe that not one 1919 Tiger had been exposed to high-school French.

Frank McGill also made a contribution to Canadian sports as an executive and administrator. At various times he was a member of the athletic board of McGill, on the advisory committee of the Canadian Olympics Committee, a director and vice president of the MAAA, president of the Big Four, and a member of the Canadian Rugby Union rules committee that adopted the forward pass in 1929. In 1934 he organized No. 115 Auxiliary Squadron for the Royal Canadian Air Force, and during the second world war rose to the rank of air vice-marshal.

JOHN O'NEILL, 1877-1967

John O'Neill got his start in rowing when his father asked him to row across Ketch Harbour on an errand when he was seven years old. For all of that, he was a late bloomer. As a young man, he joined the Royal North West Mounted Police, and left the waters of his native Nova Scotia far behind. At the time of the South African war, he joined the Canadian Mounted Rifles and served with them in the Canadian Special Service Force that Laurier despatched to fight in one of Britain's unhappiest colonial wars.

O'Neill did not actually begin com-

petitive rowing until he was twenty-five, when, on his return from the Boer war, he joined the St. Mary's Rowing Club of Halifax. Within two years he had established himself as the best of the local scullers, winning the championship of Halifax harbour (as George Brown had done before him) in 1904. After a series of victories throughout the Maritimes, he was sent by his club to the Middle States regatta at Philadelphia in 1905, and won the singles prize there; at Springfield, Massachusetts, he did the same in 1907. In 1908 he duplicated Lou Scholes's feat of 1903, winning the US association singles.

His major achievement came in 1909, on the tricky waters of the Detroit River. He was not in the best of shape; his coach, Frank Greer, reported that he was seven pounds under his best weight of 158 pounds. In the finals of the senior quarter-mile event, he was decisively beaten, a result that did not augur well for his chances in the US national's chief event, the championship single sculls over a mile and one-quarter. That race was rowed on 9 August; back in Halifax, hundreds of people stood for hours outside newspaper offices waiting to see how their thirty-two year old champion would make out.

The race began easily for O'Neill. He got a good jump, and by the half-way mark appeared a certain winner. Then an oarsman of the New York Athletic Club put on a spurt and caught O'Neill just before the one-mile point, and from there on they sprinted to the finish line. O'Neill won by a fraction. The wire story from Detroit said that "so hard was the fight that O'Neill

dropped the oars the instant he reached the line and saw the flag fall. O'Neill looked the class of the race at the start, but at its finish it was merely a case of which would last."

It had been a long time since the glorious days of George Brown but Haligonians were fully aware of that tradition. One of the first things O'Neill did after his triumphant return was to make a pilgrimage to the Brown monument at Herring Cove. Before that, he was towed through the streets in a carriage drawn by his clubmates; all along the Northwest Arm bonfires flared and waves of civic rhetoric washed over him.

At 89, John O'Neill was still to be seen rowing about Halifax harbour or near his home at Ketch Harbour. "You rust very quickly if you stay in the house," he said.

CONRAD RILEY, 1875-1950

Conrad Stephenson Riley was eight years old when his family moved to Winnipeg, then in the middle of a boom that was pushing its population over 10,000. His father was a successful business pioneer on the Prairies in insurance and trust company enterprises, and although Con Riley spent his youth in the upper economic and social bracket of Winnipeg, a look back over his career proves that he was far from pampered. At sixteen years of age he left school after taking a course in typing and shorthand and went to work in a railway office. As Winnipeg grew into a metropolis, Con developed into a successful and prosperous citizen. Between his eleventh and twenty-first years he milked the family cow morning and night. While keen on all sports, Con Riley's favourites were curling, hockey, riding and shooting. His riding enthusiasm made him the best of the

early polo players in Manitoba and one of its crack trapshooters but gradually he put other sporting interests in the background after he joined the Winnipeg Rowing Club in 1892.

The Winnipeg Rowing Club was organized in 1883 and incorporated in 1886. Its founder was George F. Galt, a Torontonian who had been captain of the Argonaut Rowing Club. After spring ice jams demolished the first clubhouse in 1884, a magnificent new one was built on property donated by Donald Smith, later Lord Strathcona, at the junction of the Red and Assiniboine Rivers. The WRC quickly became the athletic and social centre for the young men in commerce of the fast-growing city. Under Galt's leadership, and later Con Riley's, the club took the lead in organizing the Minnesota and Winnipeg Rowing Association, which developed into the Northwestern International Rowing Association, sponsoring an annual regatta with crews from Kenora, the Canadian and American Lakeheads, Minneapolis and St. Paul, and occasionally from Regina.

In 1889 Con Riley first became interested in rowing during the local celebrations over the victory of a Winnipeg four in the "senior" event at the North American Amateur Oarsmen regatta at Pullman, Illinois. One of the defeated crews, to the Winnipeggers' delight, was the best Argonaut four, stroked by the immortal Joe Wright.

Con Riley was in his fifth season of rowing before he found his best niche – stroking a four! For technique and training methods he consciously modelled himself after George Galt. The Winnipeg Club only had professional coaches for two brief periods. The captain and vice-captain supervised most of the crewing, the training and the organization for regattas, home and away. In 1900, the year the club bought its first eight, Con Riley became vice-captain, a few years later the captain, then successively vice-president, president (1911) and honorary president (1929). Before he retired to the honorary post, Con Riley had spent (saving the war years when he fought in Europe) thirty-seven busy seasons as rower, coach and official for the WRC. Although he never rowed competitively after the war, his record as both stroke and captain in the period between 1900 and 1914 was magnificent, matched by only one other amateur oarsman, Argonaut's Joe Wright, Sr.

Almost every year Winnipeg oarsmen won races at the Canadian and North American championship regattas and on several occasions Riley-stroked fours and eights went to the mother regatta of rowing at Henley. Their greatest single triumph was in 1910 when they won the Stewards' Challenge

Cup in the fours. The regatta performance, however, which simply overwhelmed the rowing world of the day came in 1912 at Peoria, Illinois. A contingent of fourteen Winnipegers, led by Con Riley brought home seven trophies from the North American championships, including the eights, the fours, and the senior and intermediate doubles and singles. Every Winnipeg entry won its event.

Despite this long, intense involvement in almost every aspect of the Winnipeg Rowing Club's affairs, Con Riley played a role in business through general and fire insurance companies and as a senior director in Canada of the Hudson's Bay Company. He and his wife had six sons and two daughters and most of the boys were dedicated rowers. In his privately-published memoirs his rowing reminiscences have pride of place and space over all other aspects of his life. Clearly a mover and a doer, rather than a reflective man, Con Riley does make clear the inspiration he got from the attitude to sport of his model, George F. Galt. Once in the 1920s Galt had joined Riley in a veteran's four for some fun and exercise. "As we came down the river," wrote the younger man, "he shouted 'pick her up ten' which we did. He was then seventy." And Con Riley himself, in his last and seventy-fifth year, was still travelling, keeping in touch with business and old sporting associates.

LEVI ROGERS, 1887-1963
There is no sporting event in Canada quite like Regatta Day at St. John's, Newfoundland. Until the province entered Confederation in 1949, the Queen's Plate was the oldest annual sporting event in Canada; that honour now belongs to the regatta. Surviving records show that the regatta was held in August 1826, but these documents refer to the event as an annual one, so the regatta may be even older. Grey Cup Week grips many Canadians, but even this national spectacle cannot match the intense interest Newfoundlanders take in the regatta. It takes place each August on Quidi Vidi Lake at St. John's, the precise date fixed by a small committee, supposedly wise in the vagaries of Newfoundland weather. The whole province sits poised while the committee consults the omens each August morning. Once the decision is made the whole island is on holiday, and 35,000 to 40,000 people trek to "the pond" to see the races.

The regatta has always been open to all comers; it is a people's event in every sense. Traditional clubs like the Patricians mingle with crews from Walsh's Bakery or the outports, or crews from visiting ships.

110

The course is a mile and three-fifths; the shells are six-oared with coxswains.

The regatta, in sum, is dear to the hearts of Newfoundlanders. And for most of this century, when they thought of the races, they thought of Levi "Shotty" Rogers. (According to oldtimers, he got his nickname because "he travelled like a shot.") For an incredible fifty-eight years, five as an oarsman and fifty-three as a coxswain, Rogers participated in the regatta. A tiny man of five-foot-four who never weighed more than 120 pounds, Rogers coxed more than 300 crews to victory during his competitive career.

Shotty was always reluctant to select one crew as the best he ever steered, for obvious reasons. But on one occasion he suggested that the 1930 championship crew was perhaps the best. "They could have done the course in 9:08," he thought (the record of 9:13.8 minutes was set in 1901 by an Outer Cove crew). "With Tom Breen stroke and a crew of Pat Malone, Martin Roche, Ned Tilley, Dick Pittman and Pat O'Donnell they covered the first half of the pond, from the starting stakes to the turning buoys, in 4:08. But they got a notion to wave to the spectators on the return trip up the pond and coasted home in 9:31."

Not only was Shotty Rogers the most successful cox in the history of the regatta, he was also the premier rowing coach in Newfoundland. Weight distribution and rhythm keyed his approach to a crew. What he looked for in a potential oarsman was "a person around twenty-one years, not too fat, and having the guts, strength, knack and determination to pull an oar." He disclaimed "making" fine oarsmen; the love of rowing had to be there to begin with.

Sports Hall of Fame

"There's no halfway measures. Either a boy loves the grind or he doesn't. If he does he can become good, if not he has two strikes against him from the start."

Shotty Rogers steered his last crew to victory in 1962, at the age of seventy-five. When he and the William Summers Jr. crew won, he decided to retire. The next year, in regatta month, one of the most extraordinary competitors in the history of organized sport died at St. John's.

GUS RYDER, 1899-

Canada's Man of the Year in 1955 was not the usual public dignitary or politician (Lester Pearson was the runner-up) but a sportsman, Toronto swimming coach Gus Ryder. His most memorable achievement at that time had been his coaching of Marilyn Bell to her conquest of Lake Ontario in September 1954. But Ryder's contribution to Canadian sport has been immeasurable – all the more so since his dedication to the cause of swimming in Canada has been so constant and so unassuming.

Born in Toronto, Gus Ryder played a variety of sports in his youth. A husky, well-built five-foot-ten, he played defense on the Aura Lee junior hockey team and played football for the Excelsiors and the Toronto Argonaut intermediates. He spent four years rowing for Argos, and represented Canada against the US in handball, a sport that he continues to play today with enthusiasm. He was also an enthusiastic swimmer and took part in several across-the-bay races in Toronto.

Gus Ryder might have continued to develop into a great all-round athlete, had it not been for an incident in 1917, when he was eighteen. He was playing hockey on Grenadier Pond in Toronto's High Park when the ice gave way and two of his companions fell through. In rescuing the boys, Gus himself was trapped under the ice. He made a vow at that moment that if he got out, he would learn all he could about swimming and lifesaving and teach it.

He was to keep the vow – twelve years later. In 1930 he was offered a job as a lifeguard at New Toronto beach. Gus took it because "it seemed to me that most sports had all kinds of coaches but there didn't seem to be anybody showing youngsters the proper way to swim. I figured I could help."

Help he did. By the end of the summer his New Toronto Swim Club had 700 members. So many youngsters came from other lakeshore areas that the name was changed to the Lakeshore Swim Club. For the next twenty years the club operated from the New Toronto beach in the summer, and the West End YMCA and Humberside Collegiate pools in the winter. The club's string of successes was remarkable. Twice Lakeshore won the Royal Life Saving Society award, in competition with 110 clubs across Canada – not bad for a club without its own pool. It was not until 1952 that the club had a permanent home, when the New Toronto War Memorial pool was opened.

The club's most famous members were Cliff Lumsden and Marilyn Bell. Cliff started at the club when he was six, and Ryder coached him to become one of the outstanding marathon swimmers. He won the world title four times in five years. Marilyn Bell came to Gus in 1948, at the age of ten, and immediately showed great promise. In 1954 the Canadian National Exhibition offered $10,000 to the American swimmer Florence Chadwick if she could swim Lake Ontario; the CNE was obviously of the opinion that no Canadian could do it. Ryder thought otherwise, and started Marilyn on intensive training. On a September day the sixteen-year-old girl swam the forty miles from Youngstown, New York to Sunnyside, Toronto, in a gruelling twenty-two hours. Both Marilyn and her coach became famous overnight.

Before the excitement of that great Lake Ontario marathon, another event had taken place in Gus Ryder's life, which was to have far-reaching consequences. In 1948 two boys paralysed with polio were brought to him and he was asked if he could teach them to swim. He found they did extremely well, and in consequence the Palsy Crippled Chil-

Sports Hall of Fame

dren's Association asked for his help. And so started his association with handicapped children. Ryder calls this side of his work the real heart-beat of the club: "I'd rather work with crippled kids than coach an Olympic champion."

Over the years the handicapped have engaged more and more of his time and their achievements have given him his greatest pleasure. As he watches a crippled boy wheel his chair to the pool side, jump in and swim across, or a blind boy beat sighted youngsters, or a kid with one arm swim four miles, Gus Ryder has reason to be proud. Over the years he has taught thousands of youngsters the skills of swimming and lifesaving, and has brought new hope to the handicapped.

SAINT JOHN FOUR (PARIS CREW), 1867
"Among the strange looking people this regatta had brought together," wrote the correspondent of the Manchester *Guardian* from the Paris Exposition of 1867, "not the least strange were a certain crew of four sturdy New Brunswickers, who . . . had brought two homemade boats some thousands of miles to show the rest of the world how to row. With their flesh-coloured jerseys, dark cloth trousers, leather braces and bright pink caps, they were in striking contrast to their neat competitors." These strange looking people were four Saint John men, Robert Fulton, George Price, Elijah Ross and Samuel Hutton. Ross was a lighthouse keeper; the others were fishermen in the summer and ships' carpenters during the winter. Their presence in Paris, at a regatta which attracted the leading oarsmen of Europe, was the result of a remarkable community enterprise. As the New Brunswick *Reporter* of Fredericton put it, "Although to the great International Exposition we have sent no elaborate works of art, no specimen of ingenious handicraft, no sample of the products of mine or field, we have nevertheless sent to Paris such an 'exhibit' of our energy, our hardihood and pluck as shall render us famous among all the famed at that grand international tournament." Just to "give an additional security," however, the oarsmen were accompanied by Sheriff Harding of Saint John, for had not the provincial government subscribed $2,000 and the citizens of Saint John, another $4,000 to send them to sinful Paris?

Though the Saint John crew seemed quaint to sophisticated Europeans, they were no strangers to international competitions. Since the mid 1850s, crews from Saint John had enjoyed almost unbroken success against American rivals from New England and New

The Saint John Four was comprised of George Price *(top left)*, **Robert Fulton** *(top right)*, **Elijah Ross** *(lower left)* **and Samuel Hutton.**

York. Nevertheless they were rank outsiders in Paris. When they practised, English reporters scoffed at their rowing style "by no means in accordance with received ideas," since they pulled "almost entirely with the arms." Most ridiculous of all, they rowed without a coxswain, and would probably, through erratic steering, be a menace to all other crews.

The Saint John men were entered in two races. In the first, for heavy in-rigged boats, they were matched against crews from Boulogne, the Rowing Club des Régates Parisiennes (the Geslings), and two English crews, the Western Rowing Club and the Dolphin RC of Brighton. Here is an English description of the first Canadian athletic victory in international competition:

> The Canadians were supposed not to have a chance, and betting was strongly against them. They took the lead at a great pace, rowing some 46 or 47 strokes per minute, followed by the Geslings. A determined race ensued between the Canadians and the Geslings, in which the former always led, but the Geslings pressed them very hard right up to the buoy, where the Canadians came first . . . . Nearly all fouled at the buoy, including the Canadians, who, however, being without a coxswain and turning the boat themselves, were considerably benefited thereby, and passed round clear. Gesling drew up to the New Brunswick boat after the rounding, and for a time there

seemed a prospect of the Parisians rowing their opponents down, but all the opposing crews had yet to learn that the New Brunswickers could row any distance. More astonishing still was their victory in the race for four-oared outrigger shells. They were pitted against the great names in rowing: Oxford University, The London RC and the Leanders of London. Even though it was now realized that a skilled coxless crew had a decided advantage, their boat described as "a curious old-fashioned outrigger," looking like "a Chinese puzzle painted green . . . and curiously put together," outweighed the beautifully fashioned English shells by more than a hundred pounds. Yet they won by three lengths, with London second and Oxford third, and at the finish they were "plowing away, clear of the others, talking and laughing in the easiest manner possible."

Fulton, Ross, Price and Hutton (and the faithful Sheriff Harding), returned home 8 August to a Saint John wild with enthusiasm. The city itself was decked with bunting; the Saint John Brass Band, flocks of notables, and 7,000 people were there to cheer as the men were given the freedom of the city and $500 each (shattering forever the amateur status they had so studiously maintained in Paris).

The victory of the Paris crew (as they were hereafter always known), gave an enormous stimulus to rowing in Canada. The crew stayed together for several years after their 1867 triumph. In 1868, for example, they defeated the best American four, the Ward brothers of Cornwall, NY, on the Connecticut River at Springfield, and won numerous other races throughout North America. In 1870 at the Lachine regatta, they met their match in the Tyne crew stroked by James Renforth, single sculls champion of England. Their defeat was a disaster for their home town. "Saint John is dead," moaned a citizen. "The race will take quite $100,00 out of this place. Many have lost their all. Everyone here, except Sons of Temperance, seemed to get intoxicated." In a rematch on the Kennebecasis in 1871, watched by 20,000 people, with the Paris Crew pulling away, Renforth suffered a heart attack and died an hour later.

The Saint John Four, in winning at Paris just a month after Confederation, and in going on to further international victories, stirred national feelings in our new country in a way no politician could hope to achieve. The Toronto *Globe* summed up their distinction. "Perhaps nothing since Confederation has occurred which so thoroughly brings home to the broad mass of our people that our bold Maritime friends are now our fellow-countrymen in name and in fact. To be the first to uphold the strength, skill and pluck of our country's athletes in a downright, old-fashioned British contest is a distinction to be proud of."

LOUIS F. SCHOLES, 1880-1942

Down near the mouth of the Don River in Toronto the old Don Rowing Club, formed in 1878, was to be found. It wasn't the "class" club in the city (that title belonged to the Argonauts) but the club of the Irish and Catholic community. For many years it produced some of the doughtiest oarsmen, beginning with the redoubtable William O'Connor, at a time when Toronto was certainly one of the rowing capitals of the world. Not the least was Lou Scholes, a superb amateur oarsman who in his relatively short career brought high honours to his club and to his country.

Lou came from a sporting family. His father, John F. Scholes, who ran the Athlete Hotel on Yonge Street, had been an all-round athlete – an oarsman, track star, snowshoer, champion boxer. Lou's brother Jack was an outstanding amateur boxer, winning the Canadian featherweight and lightweight titles; in 1900 and 1901 he won the United States amateur championship in the featherweight class. The Scholes kids were brought up to fend for themselves. "I tried to bring them up good," their father told the Toronto *Globe*. "They were left motherless when they were in knickerbockers." According to his father, Lou was always a little wild, but "I told him to fight it out himself if he was right." Scholes Sr. encouraged the boys to go into athletics; he was an official of the Don Club, so Lou got his start there.

We know little of young Lou's early development as a rower, but in 1901 he was good enough to be sent to the US nationals at Philadelphia wearing the Don colours. There he won the US intermediate singles. Though he was marked as a promising rower, the big news for Toronto sports fans was the victory of the Argonauts in the heavy eights.

In 1902 Lou Scholes began to attract some attention in his own right. At the Harlem regatta in May he won the two premier senior sculls fixtures. Significantly, in the major event he defeated the reigning US amateur champion, C. S. Titus, through sheer drive and toughness. The same year both Titus and Scholes competed for the Diamond Sculls at Henley-on-Thames, but neither won.

Scholes was a conscientious and hard-working athlete. Preparing for another crack at the Diamond Sculls, he rolled up an impressive record in 1903. With his partner, Frank Smith, he won both the Canadian and American double sculls titles; in singles he won the Dominion Day regatta at Toronto, the Canadian Henley and then the National

Rowing Association of the USA title. By 1904 he was ready for Henley-on-Thames.

Lou breezed through his first two heats. But the third heat was crucial. Scholes rowed against F. S. Kelly from Trinity College, Cambridge, a classic stylist who was the darling of the British rowing public. Kelly, an Australian, had won the Diamond Sculls in 1902 and 1903. The sporting press was harsh with Lou. Despite the fact that Kelly also was from abroad, Scholes was invariably referred to as "a colonial visitor," or as a foreigner, and his "rough and ugly" style was contrasted with a man "reckoned the finest, if not the strongest sculler the regatta has seen." In line with all the predictions, Kelly jumped off to a good lead, having two lengths on Scholes after half a mile, but with a great spurt Lou caught him at the three-quarter mile mark, and simply wore him down. To prove that his victory was not the fluke the British papers alleged, Scholes went on to defeat A. H. Cloutte of the London Rowing Club. Characteristically, he came from behind to win by more than a length, and dumbfounded his detractors by doing it in the record time of 8:23.2 minutes.

Lou Scholes, the first Canadian to win the Diamond Sculls, was given a civic reception before an estimated 80,000 of his fellow Torontonians, including Ned Hanlan. "The frank, sunny, boyish smile of the champion, like a glint of sunshine, carried gladness to thousands of hearts that had known him only as a name," one paper gushed. The

Alexandra Studio

Diamond Sculls (for which the City of Toronto put up the $5,000 deposit gracelessly required by the Henley committee to guarantee their safe return to England) were proudly exhibited in the elder Scholes's hotel. The British press reported vindictively that "at times they get mixed up with the cigar boxes." As R. D. Burnell, the English historian of the Henley regatta, says, the treatment of Lou Scholes by the British press was "not very honourable," but it showed "the sensitive, and even belligerent feelings of the British public, at that time, as regards foreign and even Dominion sportsmen."

MARGARET SELLER, ca.1905-

When asked her year of birth for our record, Mrs. Seller wasn't coy. "A lot of people who know me would like to know that. They'll find out when I'm six feet under. Just say I'm a busy grandmother." She's been busy in sport, particularly anything to do with swimming, since the early 1920s. In 1974 she was working hard to get a synchronized swimming event held during the 1976 Olympics in her home town of Montreal. Since it couldn't be part of the official sports program, she was determined to get it into the "aquatic arts" roster of cultural activities associated with the Olympics.

In 1926 Florence Gale of the Montreal Amateur Athletic Association donated a cup, the Gale Trophy, for "fancy swimming." Mrs. Gale was an enthusiast about swimming and the work of the Royal Life Saving Society. The society's emphasis on scientific swimming strokes and "trick" techniques had been pushed by innovative Montrealers like Mrs. Gale, Mrs. C. Lockerby and Jimmie Rose, to the stage where they held a provincial competition in 1924 for the best demonstration of "the art of scientific and graceful swimming." This was the germ of what grew into "synchronized swimming." Mrs. Seller feels that international competition and recognition for this sport did not become fully accepted until 1949. In the twenty-five years of fighting to further this goal, technically and organizationally, Peg Seller has been its leading proponent.

Mrs. Seller notes that the name "synchronized swimming" originated in Chicago or Detroit and, although American swimmers were the first to swim in rhythm to music, it was in Montreal that the first elaborate routines were developed and where the first musical accompaniment was used.

In 1923 Peg held all Royal Life Saving Society awards; she won the Gale Trophy four years running; she had captained the national champion water polo team three times; she held the Canadian three-metre

diving title; in 1928 she won the provincial titles in the 100-yard dash, the javelin and the broad jump.

Peg married dentist Reg Seller in 1931 and spent the next five years in what economists call "family formation." In 1936 she returned to the sports scene as a diving judge for the Canadian Amateur Swimming Association. Since that date she has been a major force in the association's work at the local, national and international levels. She has concentrated both on improving standards of performance and judging in swimming and on promoting the acceptance of synchronized swimming. She says: "To have Canada recognize synchronized swimming is the culmination of my hopes."

Synchronized swimming is a blend of orthodox swimming strokes, innovative tricks and skilful, gliding movements. It has variously been described as "fancy swimming" and "water ballet." In establishing standards for judges, in outlining routines, in organizing meets, in getting trophies, in writing the rules, Mrs. Seller did it all. She wrote the first rule book in 1938. She became the first woman secretary of the *Fédération Internationale de Natation Amateur* in 1948 and in 1952 wrote the federation's rules governing international competition.

Subsequent to this successful international debut of the sport, Peg Seller collaborated with the fine American swimmer, Buelah Grundling, in writing a book on the coaching of the sport. Later, in 1963, this indomitable pair travelled across Europe seeking ways to get the sport on the Olympic list.

Meanwhile, Peg Seller kept up her own active athletic schedule. Aside from active curling, she once gave an exhibition of

115

synchronized swimming at the MAAA to a fast-paced Tchaikovsky concerto, this some thirty years after her first swimming competition. "Not bad," as she said at the time, "after twenty-five years at the sport."

Peg took a team to the Olympics in Helsinki in 1952 to demonstrate the sport; there was interest but not international recognition. Finally, at the Pan-American Games in 1955, the sport was admitted as an official, international competitive event. In Mexico City in 1968 the Canadian women swimmers won four of the six individual events.

Mrs. Seller remains as breezy, and outgoing as she was during her youth. Her associates speak highly of her and hold her in some awe because of her undiminished enthusiasm. A great athlete and a persistent, selfless advocate and builder, she is the embodiment of a great sportswoman.

MISS SUPERTEST I, II & III, 1954-61

Sixteen years after Gottlieb Daimler's first gasoline-driven boat chugged a few yards on the Seine at Paris, an English press magnate, Sir Alfred Harmsworth (later Lord Northcliffe) donated the trophy that became the highest prize for international powerboat racing. When the English boat *Napier* I defeated a French boat at Queenston, Ireland in 1903, to become the first Harmsworth winner, her average speed was 19.53 MPH. Before the first world war, boats from England won the trophy a further four times, as did American boats, while the French captured the trophy once. Through these years, improvements in engines and hull design brought the speed of *Maple Leaf* IV, England's victor in 1913, up to 57.45 MPH. After the war, the long American domination of the Harmsworth began. Garfield A. "Gar" Wood and his succession of *Miss Americas* swept the nine races held between 1920 and

1933, losing only one heat during the period. When the event resumed after the second world war, American boats and drivers continued their supremacy. *Slo-Mo-Shun* IV, driven by Ted Jones, established a new record of 95.623 MPH on the Detroit River in 1950.

By this time the Harmsworth race was an event for unlimited hydroplanes; that is, the boats themselves planed over the water rather than displaced it, and there was no limitation placed upon either power or design, except upon the use of devices to secure aerodynamic lift. So long had the United States held the trophy that it seemed unlikely that other countries would ever successfully challenge her wealth and engineering know-how, and was most unlikely that such a challenge would come from Canada. Yet so it happened.

The first Canadian to enter the Harmsworth picture was Harold Wilson, who drove his own *Miss Canada* V to defeat Stanley Dollar's *Skip-A-Long* in 1945. *Miss Canada,* renamed *Miss Supertest* I, was taken over by James G. Thompson in 1952, beginning the process that was to win the Harmsworth Trophy for Canada.

Jim Thompson, a native of London, Ontario, had been educated at Royal Roads Military College, the University of Toronto, and the University of Western Ontario. He became president of the London-based Supertest Petroleum Corporation. *Miss Supertest* II was the product of Thompson's designing genius, based upon his experience with Wilson's boat. In 1956, driven by Bill Braydon, she was defeated by William Waggoner's *Shanty* I, but even in defeat managed to win a heat. The following year

The Harmsworth Trophy, highest prize for international powerboat racing, was won in 1959, 1960 and 1961 by *Miss Supertest* III, designed by Jim Thompson of London, Ontario.

116

she established a new world's speed record of 184.54 MPH.

For Thompson, *Miss Supertest* II had been an experimental boat. He now turned his talents and his experience to the development of a craft to be known as *Miss Supertest* III. (The public was amused by the fact that the boat was built in a former chicken house on Thompson's farm, with a chief mechanic named Vic Leghorn and a driver, Bob Hayward, who was a former chicken farmer.) The boat was built in late 1958 and early 1959. When completed she was more than thirty feet in length, and weighed about three tons; her mahogany-coloured hull was set off with orange trim and a prominent white tail fin. Though externally similar to Thompson's previous design, *Miss Supertest* III was in fact, a completely new boat. The bottom hull was cherry plywood laminated with a thin sheath of magnesium for strength. Under power, the hull sat eight inches out of the water, riding on two sponsons protruding from the hull at the front and the hub of the propellor. At speeds of more than 100 MPH, this huge projectile had only one and one-half square feet in contact with the water. Stability (insofar as such a craft can achieve it) was obtained by knife-edge stabilizer on the hull, a keel-like fin that prevented skidding on turns. The rudder was offset to counter engine torque and to avoid the turbulence of the propeller. *Miss Supertest* III had a pluming rooster tail of some thirty-five feet in height caused by the water hurled back by the propeller blade which surfaced for half a revolution.

These design features were mated to an enormous power plant, a 2,000 HP Rolls-Royce Griffon. This engine was the last production piston type used by the Royal Air Force; it had powered the later marks of the Spitfire. Thompson modified the engine for his boat, but its chief feature was retained; a supercharger-impeller, revolving at speeds up to 40,000 RPM, pumped air into the cylinders and gave *Miss Supertest* III tremendous power.

The last element in the equation that brought the Harmsworth Trophy to Canada was R. D. "Bob" Hayward. A quiet man of thirty-one years, rather plump and redfaced, he looked like the Ontario farm boy he was, rather than a thrill-seeking driver of sophisticated hydroplanes. As a boy, he had raced outboards on the Thames; later, he drag-raced in a 1938 Chevrolet with a Buick engine. He joined the Thompson crew as a mechanic in 1957, but when allowed to drive *Miss Supertest* II in test runs he showed himself a cool, skilful driver. His first race was a heat of the Silver Cup at Detroit in 1957; in

1958 he drove *Miss Supertest* II to victory in the St. Clair International Boundary Trophy race.

At Sarnia, in June 1959, *Miss Supertest* III underwent her first water trials satisfactorily and then won the Detroit Memorial Race on 4 July. She was ready for the Harmsworth. The American defender was *Maverick*, owned by William Stead; the races were fifteen laps over a three-mile course on the Detroit River. The first race, won by Canada, was not a true test for either boat, as *Maverick* broke an engine part. The second heat, the American out-manoeuvred Hayward at the first corner and maintained a small lead throughout. On the third day, Hayward got away to a magnificent start and was never headed. For eleven laps the two boats, never far apart, roared around the course in spectacular tandem; then, on the twelfth lap, *Maverick* broke down. Hayward reduced speed but still set a new Harmsworth record of 104.098 MPH overall.

Bob Hayward and *Miss Supertest* III successfully defended the Harmsworth against US challengers at Picton, on the Bay of Quinte, in 1960 and 1961. In neither of these races was the supremacy of the Canadian boat and driver ever in doubt; the 1960 event saw a new record of 116.464 MPH established and both races were won in straight heats. Then, in September 1961, while racing *Miss Supertest* II in the Silver Cup at Detroit, Bob Hayward was killed. Jim Thompson retired from hydroplane competition: "With the untimely death of Bob Hayward, the members of our racing team would derive little satisfaction from further success."

ELAINE TANNER, 1951-

The cry, "Wa-a-y to go, Mighty Mouse" was first voiced by a Prince George, BC, swimming coach. The nickname and the cry were taken up by all Canada as it cheered the exploits of its own swimming champion, Elaine Tanner. And the little Vancouver girl's exploits were something to cheer about. At the age of fifteen she swept all before her at the British Commonwealth Games in 1966, winning four gold medals and three silver, which made her the greatest individual woman performer in the history of the games.

Elaine's sudden emergence as a record-breaking, world-ranking swimmer at the age of fifteen surprised and thrilled Canadians. Canada had not won an Olympic gold medal in swimming since George Hodgson's in 1912. Here at last was a chance for Canada to show the world the superiority of her new crop of young swimmers. The petite, five-foot-two school girl from West Vancouver

117

Cunningham

became the country's idol.

Elaine Tanner was a fine natural swimmer. Her coach, Howard Firby, called her a coach's dream, a girl who never questioned, never argued, just did. "She swims every event so well, the backstroke, the butterfly, the freestyle and the medley, that it honestly baffles me. She's a water-born creature . . . "

But in the fiercely competitive world of today, talent is not enough; to achieve international status, a swimmer's life must be dedicated to the sport. There must be constant practice, continual striving to clip seconds off your own, then off world records, a single-minded sense of purpose, and above all, a will to beat all competitors. All these qualities Elaine Tanner had.

Elaine's parents emigrated from England to Vancouver before she was born. When she was eight the family moved for six months to California, and she was persuaded, against her will, to take swimming lessons at the local country club. Her instructor was impressed with her ability, and she started winning prizes in children's races. When the family returned to Vancouver, Elaine joined the Dolphin Swim Club, and came under the aegis of Howard Firby, one of Canada's foremost swimming coaches. Firby had been coach to the 1964 Olympic team and had trained Margaret Stewart when she won two

world records and a gold medal in the butterfly at the 1962 Commonwealth Games at Perth. He recognized in Elaine even greater potential, and set about helping her become a world champion. Elaine's parents also supported her efforts. Her mother took a job to help pay for her training and travel expenses; her father used to get up at six o'clock to drive Elaine five miles to her swimming lesson before taking her to school. Two or three evenings a week the trips to the pool were repeated. It was an intensive training program for a school girl, but it paid off.

Elaine started racing in Canadian meets – and winning – when she was thirteen. In April 1966 she took the US championship in the 100-yard backstroke and butterfly. The following July at the BC championships in Vancouver she set a world record of 2:33.3 minutes for the 220-yard individual medley. These successes set the scene for her best-ever swimming meet – the British Commonwealth Games in Kingston, Jamaica, in August 1966. She won the 110-yard and 220-yard butterfly, the individual medley, and sparked the Canadian girls to a world-record victory in the 440-yard freestyle relay. As if this was not enough, she gained silver medals in the 110-yard and 220-yard backstroke and the 440-yard medley. In recalling the Commonwealth Games Elaine says: "The games were the most thrilling victories I've ever had . . . I was quite young and it was the first occasion the new Canadian flag had been flown at an international meet."

Canadians expressed their appreciation of Elaine's victories; she was named Canada's top athlete for 1966, the youngest ever to receive the recognition. Elaine meanwhile was back at the training grind, preparing for the Pan-American Games to be held in Winnipeg in August 1967; once again she came through with a tremendous performance taking two gold medals, three silver, and breaking two more world records.

All Canada was watching Elaine Tanner in 1968. To win a gold medal at the Olympic Games is the pinnacle of achievement for every amateur athlete, the moment that makes worthwhile the weary months of training and self-denial. Elaine trained hard, and went to Mexico full of confidence and determination to win. She carried with her the hopes – and expectations – of all Canadians. Reporting from Mexico the day before the swimming finals, a sports columnist wrote: "Elaine could win Canada's only gold medals of this Olympics. And that's quite a load to heap on the shoulders of a high school girl. But it's about time 'O Canada' was played here. And it's about time the Maple Leaf was raised . . . " It was too great a load for Elaine. She described her feelings afterwards: "Usually, before a race, you're concentrating on strategy, the other swimmers, the race. But at Mexico all I could think about was the twenty million people who were expecting me to win." Elaine gained two silver medals and one bronze.

The disappointed girl returned to Vancouver not to a tumultuous welcome of thousands and victory parades, but to a smattering of friends and supporters. She returned to school, and officially quit international competition a year later. After ten years of intensive international competition she was content to retire and leave the field to younger swimmers.

THE UBC FOUR, 1956

In November 1956 on Lake Wendouree, Australia, a four-oared crew without coxswain from the University of British Columbia and the Vancouver Rowing Club won an Olympic gold medal in its event. In so doing, the crew not only won the first gold in rowing ever obtained by Canada, but its victory signalled a decisive shift of Canadian rowing excellence from its traditional base in Toronto to the Pacific Coast. The four members of the crew were all British Columbia boys: Don Arnold, stroke, from Kelowna; Lorne Loomer, No. 2, from Nelson; Walter d'Hondt (a champion hammer thrower who at six-foot-four and 190 pounds was the biggest crewman) No. 3, from Vancouver; and Archie McKinnon, bow, from Cranbrook. Of the four, only Arnold had had any previous rowing experience. He was twenty-one; the other three were nineteen.

The man chiefly responsible for turning raw oarsmen into Olympic winners

1956 Olympic champion four-oared crew, all from the University of British Columbia, included (*from left*) stroke Don Arnold, Walter d'Hondt, Lorne Loomer and Archie McKinnon.

(the UBC eight won a silver, as well), and for much of British Columbia's surge to prominence was Frank Read, a Vancouver hotel manager and a former rower, who had taken over as coach for the Vancouver Rowing Club in 1950. His crews established a strong reputation in the annual regattas at Newport Beach, California, in the early fifties; then in 1954 a Read-coached eight stunned the rowing world by defeating England in the British Empire Games. The next year, at Henley-on-Thames, the same crew lost by a whisker to Penn in the finals after decisively beating the favoured Russians in the heats.

Of Read, Walter d'Hondt said: "He is fantastic the way he can inspire us. He makes us want to do anything for him." Frank Read put his sixteen-man rowing squad through a training program as rigorous as anything Canadian athletes had known. The men ate and slept at the VRC clubhouse, rowed every morning from five to six-thirty, worked as construction labourers during the day, rowed together for an hour and one-half in the evening, and were in bed by nine. On weekends, they went on thirty-five mile rows under the driving supervision of their coach. "Our early training," Read said with only small exaggeration, "is done in sixteen-man barges with a catwalk down the centre . . . . the coach can get his hands on a man and break his neck, if necessary." They trained on the "junk course" of Coal Harbour, with the constant hazard of driftwood, submerged logs and skittering small boats. The water was normally so rough that Read taught his crews to feather their blades until the last split second before the catch, creating a style so distinctive that everyone at the Olympics noticed.

Read crews had two hallmarks: maximum effort, maximum cohesion. Each crew member was taught to subject himself to the total rhythm of the group. "Now, let's get

119

the timing," Read would shout. "Everybody together. In and out together. Now feel it . . . sense it . . . in and out together . . . . forget about the power . . . let's get it smooth." Smoothness, once achieved, was harnessed to the great power generated by superbly conditioned, deeply motivated athletes. "All of us," Read observed, "have more courage and more capacity for understanding and developing than we ever call upon. By demanding the supreme effort from these boys, I believe they will discover these latent forces . . . "

The UBC four had originally been assembled as a spare crew for the eight. Despite an outstanding performance in the Olympic trials, they were almost deprived of a trip to the games, until the Canadian Olympic Committee relented, providing local financing could be found. From rowing enthusiasts as well as the VRC and the provincial government, $25,000 was raised to send both crews.

In the first heat of the 2,000-metre event, the UBC four defeated Germany, Austria and Denmark. Up to the halfway mark, Germany led, but then the Canadians took command, and with a great display of smoothness, power and the fine steering of Don Arnold, swept to victory by five lengths in 6:36.6, just six-tenths of a second off the world record. The semi-final was a walkover, the four winning by twelve lengths over France, with Russia and Poland trailing. In the final, Canada trailed the USA, France and Italy, but just after the 1,000-metre mark began to hit 36 strokes per minute and ran away with the race, with the US finishing second, five lengths back. Months of selfless commitment had climaxed in three smashing performances.

When Frank Read told a post-victory news conference that Arnold, Loomer, d'Hondt and McKinnon had been novices only a few months before, a French newspaperman exploded: "C'est impossible." As Read later remarked, in a most fitting testimony, "Of course, it *was* impossible. I think it was the most phenomenal effort ever made in international athletic competition. At least I don't know of any parallel."

WALTER WINDEYER, 1900-64

Walter Windeyer, who brought Canada its first world championship in the international Dragon Class in 1959, lived for sailing. It is true that he also played badminton, tennis and softball – chiefly to keep in shape for sailing. Given his tactical mastery at the helm, many of his friends believed it was no accident that he was also an active member

of the magicians' association.

Windeyer's enthusiasm for sailing came naturally. His father, Major W. F.N. Windeyer, was a Great Lakes skipper of note, especially successful with International 14-foot dinghies; as a member of the Royal Canadian Yacht Club, he won the Townsend Cup in this class in 1919, 1921, 1927 and 1938. The Windeyer family spent its summers on Ward's Island, and from an early age young Walter profited from his father's long experience in international racing and from the lore of other sailors. Walter won his first race at the age of twelve, and like his father became an expert dinghy sailor. In 1919 he won the Douglas Cup, the individual trophy long competed for between the Rochester and Toronto clubs, and for three years running in the late 1920s captured the Wilton Morse Trophy, named for the originator of the sailing dinghy. In 1936 he was a member of the Canadian team that won the Currie Cup in the International 14-foot Class at Lowestoft, England.

Windeyer's interest was not confined to smaller boats. Aemilius Jarvis, Toronto financier and longtime commodore of RCYC, was a family friend, and young Walter often served as helmsman on Jarvis's 12-metre yacht, *Metina*. As his reputation grew, he came more and more to be in demand as a skipper for RCYC boatowners. In 1932, for ex-

Walter Windeyer *(centre figure)*

ample, he was chosen as skipper for *Invader II*, an RCYC yacht designed and built to challenge for the Canada's Cup against *Conewago* of the Rochester Yacht Club. This trophy, the blue ribbon of freshwater sailing, had been monopolized by the United States since 1903 when *Irondequoit* defeated *Strathcona*. Brilliant sailing by Windeyer and his crew could not avert a defeat by the American boat and her skipper, Wilmot Castle, in three of four races. In the first race, Castle surprised the Canadians by using a "parachute" spinnaker. This huge billowing sail, more than twice *Conewago's* measured sail area, proved decisive over *Invader II*'s conventional spinnaker. This was the first appearance on the Great Lakes of the now familiar form of the spinnaker, but it had been pioneered in Sweden four years earlier. Windeyer managed to have a similar spinnaker rushed up from New York for the following races, but the Canadians never succeeded in overcoming *Conewago's* initial advantage.

Windeyer continued to sail *Invader II* with considerable success before and after the second world war. In the mid-1950s, however, he became interested in a new and smaller class of yacht, the Dragon Class. This beautiful and seaworthy type, measuring a little more than twenty-nine feet overall, had been developed in Sweden in the 1920s. It was designed to sail the stormy North Sea, but despite its sturdiness it was an exquisite racing machine. The royal yacht clubs of Sweden, Denmark and Norway formed a committee to control the class in 1929. The Dragon thus became a "one-design" class, each yacht conforming to standard dimensions. (Yet no two boats, of course, are ever identical.)

In 1936, the International Dragon Cup, or Dragon Gold Cup, was established as the world championship trophy. In 1948 the Dragon became an Olympic class. The Dragons came to Canada in 1950, and in 1954 the O'Keefe Trophy was put up to encourage the class on the Great Lakes. In 1958, after two years' experience with the type, Walter Windeyer won the trophy with *Corte*. This victory carried with it a trip to Europe in 1959 to compete for the Dragon Gold Cup. Deciding that *Corte* was not fast enough to handle the Europeans, Windeyer formed a syndicate to buy the Danish-built *Tip*, which had won the Gold Cup in 1957.

Windeyer, fifty-nine years old, had a young but experienced crew: Kenneth Bradfield of the RCYC and Sicotte Hamilton of the Royal St. Lawrence Yacht Club. Against them were arrayed forty-one Dragons from Denmark, Sweden, Norway, Germany, Britain, Italy, Holland, Russia and Bermuda. After three races *Tip* was fifth; a tenth-place finish in the fourth race moved her up to fourth. Windeyer realized that to defeat his chief rival, the Danish *Chok*, he would have to win the final race; as he later said, "Consistency is the big thing. You can't have a bad race. I'd hate to be lower than fifteenth in any race." Consistency had brought the Canadians to the edge of victory; now they had to go all out. In the event, it was an easy triumph. "We gained a safe berth at the start," Windeyer said, "and led the fleet from start to finish in 20- to 25-MPH winds."

Windeyer was the first non-European to win in the Dragon Class world championships, not only because he had a fine boat but also because he and his crew were first-class representatives of a Great Lakes sailing tradition that reached back more than a century.

When Windeyer returned from Europe he was given the usual civic reception, during which he had to accept that to Mayor Nathan Phillips he was "Mr. Wintermeyer." He reeled off three further victories with *Tip*: the O'Keefe Trophy, the *Telegram* Trophy, and the Olympic trials for the Dragon Class. In 1960 the slight, muscular veteran took *Tip* to Holland to defend the Gold Cup, before going on to the Rome Olympics. Before the fourth race, he suffered a mild heart attack; he insisted on taking the helm but at the end of the race he was rushed to hospital and the cup went by default, while a substitute sailed for Canada in the Olympics. Even so, Windeyer was back on Lake Ontario in 1961 to win the Duke of Edinburgh Trophy and permanent possession of the O'Keefe Trophy by winning it for the third time. He died of a heart attack in 1964.

JOSEPH WRIGHT, SR., 1864-1950
Joe Wright Sr. was one of the greatest natural athletes Canada ever produced, a man whose personality as competitor, coach and friend made an unforgettable impact upon everyone who came in contact with him. Joe Wright – "Mr. Joe" to the sporting community – started rowing just as Ned Hanlan was reaching his peak, and his life was synonymous with the development of rowing in Canada. He took part in so many sports, and did so well in all of them, that a mere list of his achievements would overflow this space. That list, moreover, would be incomplete, because Joe Wright was disarmingly casual about his accomplishments.

Although he reached greatest preeminence in rowing, Joe Wright made his mark in other sports as well. Blessed with a magnificent physique, great stamina and a fierce competitive spirit, he excelled in all, and revelled in challenges. A great pitcher during his college days, he pitched the University of Toronto to victories over Yale, Cornell and Harvard – in the same day. He was one of the first Canadians to run the 100-yard dash in ten seconds flat; he set Canadian records in the shot put and hammer throw; and he won championships in billiards. He was the Canadian amateur heavyweight wrestling champion, and at the age of thirty-five he won the Canadian heavyweight boxing championship, and fought exhibitions with such professionals as Bob Fitzsimmons, Jake Kilrain and Peter Jackson. For an astonishing eighteen seasons, for sixty minutes a game, he played football for Toronto Argonauts – and during his last season, when he was forty-three, his son George was also on the team.

Joe Wright's first love, however, was rowing. He started when he was thirteen, at the old Bayside Rowing Club in Toronto. Later, he joined the Toronto Rowing Club, and was captain for ten years; finally, he shifted to the Argonauts, and was associated with that club as oarsman, coach and executive for the rest of his life. No one has kept accurate account of the number of rowing championships he won; the estimates vary from 137 to 149. He rowed everything from single sculls to eights. He was a member of a winning crew for the first time at the age of sixteen; when he was twenty-two, he was part of a Toronto Rowing Club four that won the US nationals. Eights did not become popular in Canada until the 1890s; Joe Wright was a member of the Argonaut eight which lost the US nationals by a foot. He was also a member of the great Argo crew which in 1901 won the US nationals by defeating the Vespers of Philadelphia, a crew that had won the world championship in Paris the year

before. When Argonaut eights invaded England in 1899, 1902 and 1906, Joe was with them. The 1906 crew, with Wright as the forty-two year old stroke, won two heats handily, only to be beaten in the finals. As early as 1895, with Pat Mulqueen, he carried the colours of the Toronto Rowing Club to the first US nationals title to be won by a Canadian pair. Even earlier, in his first crack at single sculls, he won the US junior title in 1891, and in 1892 won the US intermediate crown. In 1895, having been defeated at the Royal Henley in pairs with his partner, J. J. Ryan, he tried for the Diamond Sculls and lost. Nothing daunted, he challenged for the Bedford Cup, rowed on the River Ouse, and won the first English amateur singles title to be taken by a Canadian.

Well before his career as an active oarsman ended (and it is hard to decide just when that was, since he won the Argonaut club championship at the age of fifty-one), Joe Wright had begun a new career as a superlatively successful coach. Not only the Argo crews that won dozens of Canadian and American titles bore the impress of his tough discipline and unrivalled knowledge, but every Olympic rowing team from the beginnings of Canadian involvement until 1936 was coached by him. Two of his protegés, Jack Guest Sr. and his own son, won the Diamond Sculls. Wright-coached eights won the Canadian Henley and the US nationals in 1905, 1907 and 1911; his intermediate eights did the same in 1905, 1906, and from 1909 to 1911. On one occasion he took eight Argo members, seven of whom had never sat in a shell, worked them for one winter on rowing machines, and took them to the Canadian and US titles.

It was this kind of record that brought Wright the coaching job at the Uni-

versity of Pennsylvania from 1916 to 1926. A purist on the Argonaut executive persuaded his fellow officers that Wright should be suspended since he was now a professional. Wright never answered the letter of suspension, but later, on a trip to Toronto he burst into an Argonaut executive meeting, pounded the table with a huge fist, and bellowed: "I'm not a professional. I'm merely professor of rowing at the University of Pennsylvania and don't let a damn one of you claim that is being a professional." The executive meekly agreed. The story illustrates something of the style and personality of this formidable man. Wright was said to be the only rowing coach in America who did not need a megaphone to instruct his crews. Yet for all his fire and bluster, he was at the same time deeply versed in his sport, and meticulous in its smallest detail.

After his career at Pennsylvania, which ended with two brilliantly successful years coaching the Penn AC, Joe Wright returned to Toronto. Like Ned Hanlan before him, he was a Toronto alderman for a time, but he reserved his greatest zest for sports. In 1950, two months after he died, he was selected as Canada's greatest oarsman of the half-century.

JOSEPH WRIGHT, JR., 1906-

One of the most heartbreaking moments in the history of Canadian sport occurred in the last few yards of the Diamond Sculls in 1927. Joe Wright Jr. of Toronto, matched against R.T. Lee of Worcester College, Oxford, after having fought his way through the heats, had his race won when he fouled an oar on a rope dangling from a boom, and while he struggled frantically to free it, Lee flashed by to victory. It was a bitter moment, a devastating climax to years of Spartan training, and it would have defeated any man.

That it did not defeat Joe Wright was a testimony to his courage and his commitment to his chosen sport. "Young Joe" was, of course, fortunate in his parentage. He had inherited his father's giant frame and toughness of spirit, and from childhood was trained by one of the best coaches in rowing history. Like his father, though not to the same phenomenal extent, he was an all-rounder in high school, excelling in field events, basketball and football. At eighteen, in his first year of rowing, he stroked both junior and senior Argonaut eights to championships at the Canadian Henley. In 1925 his father took him to the United States, where he was coaching Penn Athletic Club, and Joe sat No. 6 in the Penn crew that won the Middle States regatta that year. The

next year, under his father's tutelage, he became, with startling suddenness, a great sculler. Not only did he row in the Penn eight that spreadeagled its rivals in four regattas, including the nationals at Philadelphia but he won four singles events in classes from junior to senior, one of them in record time, and defeated the American quarter-mile star, Walter Hoover, at his specialty. Early in 1927 he won the senior singles at the American Henley, also in record time, and the US press began to boom him as a potential Diamond Sculls winner for his adopted country.

The Wrights – or more probably, Joe Wright Sr. – had other ideas. It was from Canada, with the backing of the Argonaut Rowing Club that "Young Joe's" unsuccessful assault on the Diamond Sculls took place. Joe returned home to sweep the board. At St. Catherines he won the senior singles and the quarter-mile dash; at the US nationals at Wyandotte, Michigan, he was unbeatable, setting records in the quarter-mile and the association singles, and winning the senior singles as well. The St. Catherines regatta was particularly notable for one of Joe's most remarkable feats; within one thirty-minute period he rowed and won against the US quarter-mile champion, *and* the US Pacific Coast champion in the one-mile 550-yard senior event.

In 1928, Wright was not to be denied the Diamond Sculls. On the way to the finals he defeated his fellow-Argonaut, Jack Guest,

Alexandra Studio

123

and Collett of England; in the final itself, in a driving finish, he edged his rival of that unhappy race a year before, R. T. Lee, and became the second Canadian (after Lou Scholes) to win the Diamond Sculls. He and Guest, with Joe Wright Sr., crossed the channel to Amsterdam to compete in the Olympics. The Henley had taken its toll, however; Joe could do no better than second to Collett, and was knocked out of the singles altogether in the semi-finals by Bobby Pierce of Australia. In the doubles, an event they were favoured to win, Wright and Guest had to settle for a silver, losing to McIlvaine and Costello of the US by five lengths.

Although winning the Diamonds in 1928 was the peak of Joe Wright's rowing career, he was by no means spent as a sculler. In 1929, in the finals of the Diamond Sculls, he lost by three feet to L. Gunther of Holland; in 1930 he won two heats in the Diamonds and, as usual, won the quarter-mile and the Singles championship at the Canadian Henley. He competed for the last time on the Canadian Olympic team in 1932 at Los Angeles.

Joe Wright Jr. was not, perhaps, the prettiest sculler in the world to watch. Although his 1928 victory was popular in England because of his mishap the previous year, the experts there criticised his bent arms when catching the water (accepted form dictated that the arms should be straight), and also the tremendous whip he gave the oars at the end of each stroke. Wright compensated for the somewhat jerky movement of his boat by the enormous power generated by long and heavily-muscled arms, by the fact that (along with Jack Guest) he used more inboard (the length of the oar from outrigger to end) than any other sculler in the world.

No account of Joe Wright's athletic career would be complete without mentioning his years with the Argonaut Football Club, an activity he carried on during and after his great sculling career. He played snapback (centre) and inside (guard), was on the 1933 Argonaut team that won the Grey Cup, and in 1970 was named to the Argonaut all-star team of the 1921-41 era. After his active days in sports ended, Wright was an executive of both the football and rowing clubs, and a president of the Eastern Football Conference.

GEORGE YOUNG, 1910-72

On 16 January 1927 there was one name on the lips of all North Americans – George Young, the seventeen-year-old kid from Toronto who was the first man to swim the Catalina Channel from Catalina Island to the California mainland. Newspapers across the continent carried the story under eight-column headlines; editorials compared Young to the heroes of ancient Greece. Toronto was beside itself with pride, and Prime Minister Mackenzie King sent a telegram assuring Young that all Canada was rejoicing in the honour he had brought his country.

One year later Young was being reviled as a quitter, a guy with no guts who folded up as soon as he was not winning. Never had an idolized hero been so quickly denigrated. Young's greatest triumph also became his greatest tragedy.

George Young was born in Toronto's east end. His mother, a widow, worked as a cleaning woman to support her family. George had his early swimming training from Johnny Walker, instructor at Toronto's West End YMCA. As a boy Young had won the Toronto cross-the-bay swim four times and the Montreal bridge-to-bridge swim three times; he was also Canadian champion for 220 yards. But no one gave him much chance to win the gruelling twenty-mile Catalina marathon. When George and his friend, Bill Hastings, decided to try for the $25,000 being offered by William Wrigley Jr. to the first swimmer to cross the channel, they could find no one to finance their trip. The two boys started out on Bill's battered motorcycle which got them as far as Arkansas before breaking down. They finished the trip to Los Angeles driving with a honeymoon couple arriving in early December 1926.

George Young didn't look like a champion; he was a diffident, solemn youth, barrel-chested and slow moving. He was overshadowed among the swimmers attracted by the race – champions, conquerors of the English Channel, some of the world's best distance swimmers. The challenge seemed beyond his experience. The only recorded crossing of the Catalina Channel had been by a fifteen-man relay team which had conquered the treacherous currents and tides in twenty-three hours.

The fifteenth day of January 1927, was cold and windy, when 103 of the world's best swimmers entered the water at noon. Once in the water, Young soon drew attention. He seemed to glide effortlessly through the water with powerful strokes. He settled into a steady rhythm of 44 strokes per minute, soon outdistancing most of the field. By late afternoon he had taken the lead but the worst was yet to come. With darkness, the water became bone-chillingly cold. Young had to force his way first through an oil slick, then through a patch of clinging kelp. Worst of all, having distanced his human competitors, he found himself accompanied

Alexandra Studio

in the black water by a shark, until it, too, turned back. One last obstacle remained – the ebb tide from the mainland shore. While thousands lined the shore with lighted beacons and shouted encouragements, a mile offshore Young battled for an hour until the tide passed. He eventually stepped ashore to a triumphal reception, having swum the channel in the truly incredible time of fifteen hours, forty-five minutes. His rival, Norman Ross of Chicago, declared George Young to be one of the greatest swimmers of all time.

In the water George was confident, sure of himself; on land it was a different story. He was an instant sensation – the sportswriters called him the "Catalina Kid" – and immediately he became the target for every shady promoter and get-rich-quick merchant in North America. The contest promoter, William Wrigley Jr., without consultation, put the $25,000 prize in a trust fund which George couldn't touch until he was twenty-nine. His mother had signed away forty percent of his earnings to the mysterious "Doc" O'Bryne, who later became his trainer. It was a story of sordid exploitation, which the naïve, unsophisticated boy from downtown Toronto could not withstand. During the months that followed, publicity appearances probably earned Young something like $26,000, apart from the prize, but he was still in debt when all the bills were in.

George Young came home to the big-gest reception Toronto had ever given; more than 150,000 people jammed the streets and marathon fever hit the town. The Canadian National Exhibition decided to cash in on the enthusiasm and staged its own marathon in Lake Ontario for a prize of $30,000. Young was the star attraction. Thousands lined the shore to cheer, waiting for him to repeat his victory. This time, though, George was not in condition, and the lake was frigid; after five miles, he had to be pulled from the race. The public vented its disappointment; Young was branded a quitter, a phony. He continued to compete in the annual CNE swims. In 1928 none of the 199 entries finished because of extremely cold water; Young was taken out after four hours. In both 1929 and 1930 he failed to complete the course, so that the cry, "George is out," became a sneer. By the time he won in 1931, nobody cared anymore.

George Young never made a comeback. The spirit had gone out of him, and with it the will to win. He had difficulty keeping a job during the depression and moved to Philadelphia where he worked on the Pennsylvania railway. When his second wife died in 1953 he moved to Niagara Falls, where he worked for the parks commission until his death of a heart attack in 1972. Young, more than anyone else, was responsible for the large crowds that came to watch the CNE swims; yet such is the fickleness of the public that he died a forgotten man.

125

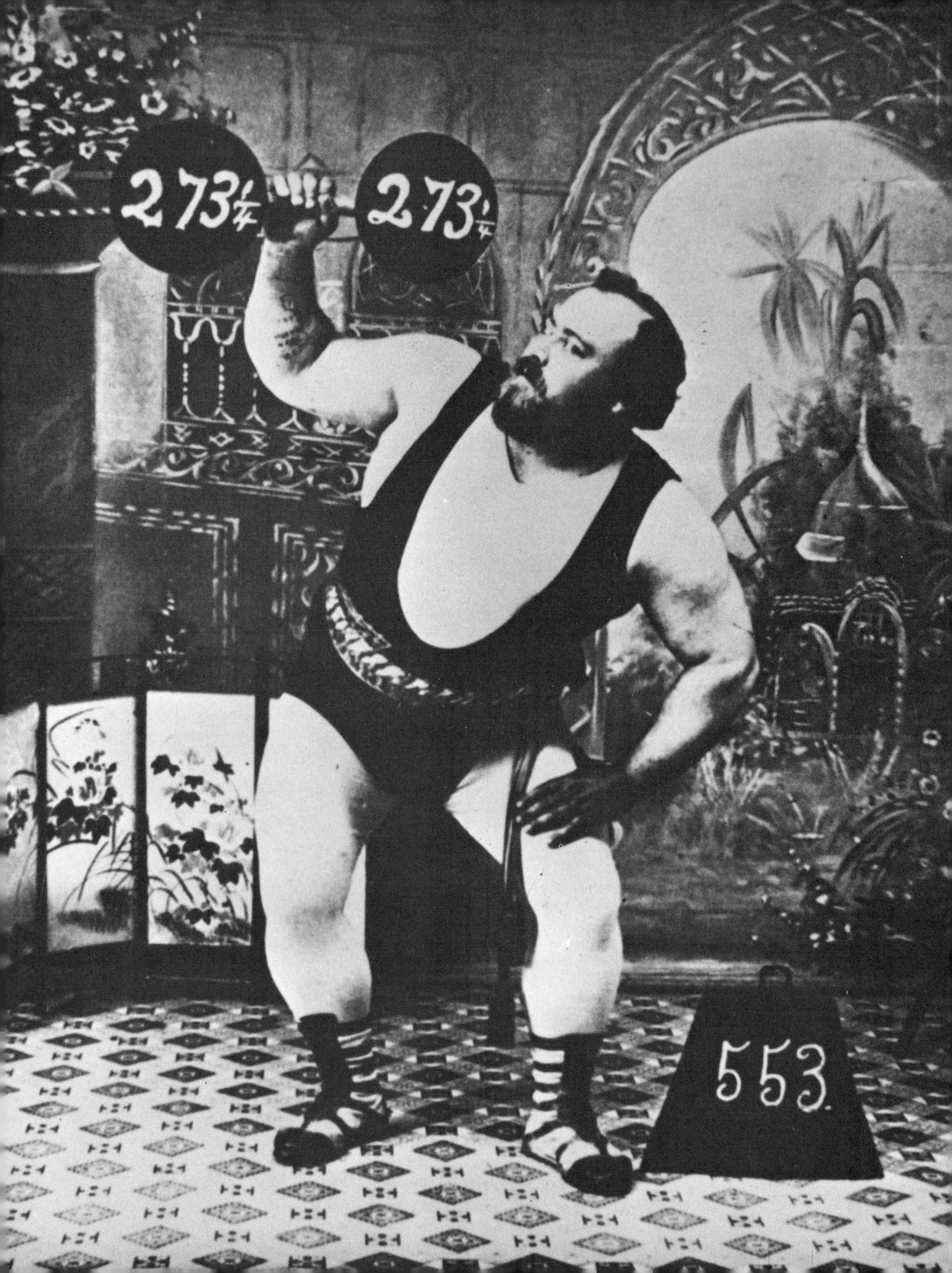
2 73¼
2 73¼
553.

Science & Strength

Chapter 5

For more than a century boxing has been severely and publicly criticized in Canada. Wrestling, too, would have suffered the same abuse had it not faded as a serious competitive professional sport in the nineteen twenties. Yet no amount of sermons, medical testimony, punitive legislation and belittling by sophisticates has erased the "gut" appeal of man-against-man in a boxing match. Major world fights still rouse Canadian fans even though almost all matches come to them via television.

The highly regularized modes of competition in weightlifting are widely practised in Canada today but hardly with a mass base of participants, although it is a field where Canada, through the Weider brothers of Montreal, has been in the forefront of equipment design and manufacture. Weightlifting has a long, honourable heritage back through Louis Cyr to the Cape Breton Giant to Joe Montferrand. Perhaps the irony of modern weightlifting is that its strength-building advantages, so long scorned because of alleged "muscle-bound" products, are now widely used as conditioning exercises for players of team games like hockey and football.

Boxing, wrestling and contests of strength have always been with us; even in primitive societies, dominance in the group is largely based on physical strength. The book of Genesis records Jacob's bout with an angel. Art objects from the civilizations of Greece and Rome illustrate the man-to-man grapplings that were so much a part of the athlete's training. We inherited both boxing and several

forms of wrestling from Britain, directly and via the United Empire Loyalists.

In the fur trade, on the frontier farm, and among the labourers on our docks, canals and railroads, respect (and often lionization) was automatic for the especially tough, strong man. At taverns, in logging and mining camps, and eventually in theatres and gymnasiums, grapples and bouts took place from the earliest days of settlement. Reports of the fights, often with scandalized comment, dot our daily papers from the 1850s on.

In assessing Canada's pugilistic record it is usual to begin with a trio of world-class boxers – George Nixon, Tommy Burns, and Sam Langford – who rose to fame in the United States just at the turn of the century; their stories are in our biographies. Here, we shall concentrate on the moral and legal problems of boxing in order to put the hall of fame nominees into the Canadian as well as the world contexts.

Jack Batten in his book, *Champions,* elaborated a few major themes. One was " . . . the often seamy, sometimes ludicrous, frequently picaresque, occasionally inspiring, more usually sordid story of boxing in Canada."

Another of Batten's themes was the pathos in Canada's long absorption in feats of brawn from Louis Cyr to the wrestlers like Whipper Billy Watson and Gene Kiniski with "their concocted routines that blended brutality, low comedy, and the grotesque," to the sad discovery of Doug Hepburn that despite the title of world's strongest man "muscle wasn't the answer."

Jack Batten emphasizes the tinsel and tawdriness, the exploitation and the frustration of simple, often stupid men in endeavours which are by their nature "flash" and rife with dishonesty and double-dealing.

Louis Cyr *(opposite)* **was a legend in his own time. He never backed down from a challenge and was never defeated. Once, in London, and before the prince of Wales, he lifted a weight of 551 pounds – with one finger.**

127

A reasonable man cannot deny that such themes seem preeminent in boxing and wrestling; but in them is the element of the sophisticates' "put-down" of many brave and honest athletes. There is occasionally a majesty, often an integrity, in the fighters and the strongmen which shines through the crowd's brute demands for blood and the shady promotional and managerial manipulations.

The Canadian flowering of modern boxing and wrestling came in a seemingly antagonistic social environment, at least if one takes parliamentary debate seriously. On 11 February 1881 there was debate in the House of Commons on a bill to amend the Criminal Code with "an act respecting prize fighting."

In moving the bill, the minister of justice said:

> This bill was suggested from occurrences which took place on our borders during the season just passed, of a very disgraceful character, in which a number of people from across the border sought to make the soil of Canada the battleground for a disgraceful, lewd prize fight. It was found that the law was defective in reference to the vindication of public morality and the peace of the people, and this bill was introduced to remedy that evil.

The bill was debated and passed; it became law and some phrases from it persist in the Criminal Code of the 1970s. With the bill's enactment Canada joined the US which at that date forbade prize fighting; it was the bans in various states which had made border points in Canada such popular locales for matches.

The most informed speaker in that 1881 debate was John Charlton, MP for Norfolk County, in whose riding the "disgraceful incident" had occurred.

> That prize fight [said Charlton] took place in Long Point, a wilderness, an uninhabited section of the county and the end of the point. It was necessary for the sheriff . . . to charter a steamer as the place was inaccessible in any other way. The sheriff . . . employed to assist him a portion of the 39th Battalion. They proceeded to Long Point and suppressed the fight . . . In doing so [the sheriff] incurred an expense of several hundred dollars which he has been left to pay out of his own pocket. The authorities of the dominion and of Ontario refused to pay that expense, claiming that the act did not come within their jurisdiction.

Long Point, Point Pelee, Port Ryerse, Fort Erie, Squirrel Island and many other border centres attracted prize fights. Armed with the powers of the Criminal Code of 1881, the sheriff of Norfolk County took to the waters again later that year and effectively blocked a much-touted battle between Frank White of New York and George Holden of England for the featherweight championship of America.

The biggest name in boxing at the time was John L. Sullivan. In the fall of 1881 rumours out of Buffalo had John L. fighting Irish Paddy Ryan somewhere in Canada near Fort Erie. The prospect roused good Canadians and the police forces. Sullivan had his fight with Ryan months later in Mississippi, and it occasioned all kinds of subterfuges to escape the law.

The first recognized American world heavyweight champion, John L. Sullivan stands at the end of the bare-knuckle era and at the beginning of highly organized and publicized world boxing under the Queensberry rules. But Sullivan was not a sudden, isolated figure. He symbolized the swing of boxing supremacy from Britain to America and the mass popularization of both boxing and wrestling. Suddenly boxers and wrestlers were not merely on the fringes of this rising ferment; they participated as athletes, trainers, promoters and fans well before the glory years of professional boxing which lasted until the beginning of the second world war. Forgotten now are the boxers and wrestlers of great talent from the earlier years: George Fulljames, Harry Gilmore and Jack Scholes of Toronto; Gus Lambert and George Lablanche of Quebec; John L. Dwyer from St. John's; Jack Munroe from Cape Breton; Tom Kelly of Saint John; and Duncan Ross, a vagabond from Turkey who wrestled largely in Canada. While New York, preeminently, and to a lesser degree London, Philadelphia, San Francisco, Boston and New Orleans became the major centres of the ring sports, drawing Canadian fighters to their auras and rewards, most of the best boxers and wrestlers fought in Canada – in Montreal, Toronto and Victoria, in particular. From the 1880s on, there were invariably a few Canadians in contention for world, American or British championships. For a brief period, between 1895 and the early 1920s, amateur boxing built itself into a national framework. From 1910 to the outstanding successes of Canadian amateur boxers at the Antwerp Olympics of 1920, Canadians can fairly claim to have had the best amateur boxers in the world.

But it was the first world war which wrapped the sanction of complete, even élitist, approval around boxing. At home and in France boxing bouts were seen both as entertainment and as the ideal means to prepare men for trench warfare. The science inherent in boxing and its worth as self-defense was much proclaimed. The universities and the YMCA took up the sport enthusiastically. It was "manly," invigorating, a test of courage and fitness.

Some interest had been fanned by the search for a "white hope" to regain the world heavyweight championship from Jack Johnson, in 1908 the first black to win the title.

The discrimination against Negroes, so strong after Johnson, was not limited to the

US. In 1913, the boxing committee of the Amateur Athletic Union of Canada announced that "no coloured boxer will be allowed to compete in the Canadian championships." The committee stated that "competition of whites and coloured men is not working out to the increased growth of the sport."

This Canadian prohibition seems to have been effective in amateur boxing into the early twenties. A similar ban in pro boxing in Britain lasted right into the 1930s. For example, Larry Gaines, the Toronto black heavyweight who fought with such distinction in British and European rings, won the British Empire championship but he was never able to contest the championship of the British Isles because he was black.

One of the most colourful and significant figures in Canadian boxing during the nineteen thirties and forties was Deacon Allen – manager, promoter and matchmaker. His friend, Jim Coleman, doesn't know exactly when the nickname "Deacon" took but its aptness was obvious. Deacon, dressed in dark suits and white shirts, his lips were pursed, he walked primly as though on a carpet of eggs.

John Finlay Allen was born in the early 1890s near Sacramento, California, the son of an Irish "boomer" or telegrapher. He moved to Alaska in 1917 and settled in Vanvouver the following year. He sponsored his first fight in Vancouver's old Dominion Hall on Pender Street in the early nineteen twenties, and was off on a career in and around boxing that stretched over forty-five years.

In the depression Deacon Allen was sponsor of various enterprises, including walkathons. Once he and the walkers were arrested in Winnipeg after the troupe's treasurer had absconded. Deacon and the gang got released from jail by insisting on medical treatment for one of the walkers who could throw an epileptic fit on command. For a time Deacon was assistant matchmaker to Jimmy Johnston, "the Boy Bandit," at Madison Square Garden.

In the mid-thirties Deacon went back to Vancouver and took up the managing of a ranking welterweight, Gordy Wallace. He brought Wallace to Toronto to fight and there became matchmaker for Toronto promoter, Jack Corcoran. In Toronto Deacon Allen settled as a general boxing entrepreneur, managing, sponsoring a gym, matchmaking, and promoting. He managed a varying stable of American and Canadian boxers; the last well-known Canadian boxer he managed was heavyweight George Chuvalo. Before that he'd managed Arthur King and Allan McFator. One of his clubs, the Toronto Amateur Athletic Club, sat cheek-by-jowl on Church Street with the palace of the Catholic archbishop of Toronto, James Cardinal McGuigan.

Deacon Allen died broke, slumping with a heart attack at the door of his apartment, aged seventy-two. His friends noted that he had the latest *Racing Form* in his pocket, a cold, cooked chicken in one arm, a bottle of wine in the other.

Deacon Allen had friends and contacts in every North American city where pro boxing took place. In his odd but effective way he gave sponsorship and continuity to Canadian pro boxing through the years of the nineteen thirties, forties and fifties when it had vitality. With his passing and the exit of men like Nat Fleischer, one senses twilight has come for "the game," at least in North America.

Like Allen, Nat Fleischer was only briefly a fighter, yet his influence on modern boxing and wrestling has been enormous. At an early age he went into sports journalism. When he died in 1972, Jim Proudfoot of the Toronto *Star* wrote: "More than any other sportswriter who ever lived, he was the universally accepted expert. . . . The information and opinions he provided in boxing were regarded as official."

A Jewish New Yorker, the indefatigable Fleischer, ruddy-faced, squat and friendly, ranged the world to watch bouts. He edited *Ring* magazine, a monthly which rated the contenders in each weight division of boxing. He wrote fifty-three books about boxers, wrestlers,

Alexandra Studio

Larry Gaines was a Toronto heavyweight who won the British Empire championship, but was never able to contest the championship of the British Isles because of a ban on black vs white matches.

129

and their lives. He founded the Boxing Hall of Fame and an associated museum of boxing, rich in records and relics of the game.

Fleischer helped bring order, continuity, and considerable reasonableness into both the promotional and competitive aspects of boxing; he formalized how championships should be declared, how often and against whom champions should defend their titles; he established rules for timing, referees, judging, and medical examinations.

In Western society where the irresistible urge in almost all sport is to find "No. 1," Nat Fleischer was a pacemaker with his rankings. While many critical sportswriters deplore aspects of boxing, they follow the great little New Yorker in viewing boxing as competitive and its champions as real champions.

It is to Nat Fleischer's credit that he helped end the colour bar in boxing through constant reiteration of the talent and quality of Negro boxers – including the wildly unpopular Jack Johnson. Today, when a television audience of 100 million plus has watched the Frazier-Forman title bout at Kingston, Jamaica, in 1974, it is hard for us to understand either Tommy Burns's invective against Jack Johnson or Johnson's refusal to fight Sam Langford because a good crowd would not come to see two blacks.

In his annual *Ring* encyclopedia, the Bible of the sport, Nat Fleischer provided his all-time ranking of world boxers in a "top ten" in each of the ten weights from flyweight to heavyweight. Five of the names are among those to be found in Canada's Sports Hall of Fame: heavyweight Sam Langford (ranked seventh); light heavyweight Jack Delaney (ninth); welterweight Jimmy McLarnin (tenth) and bantamweights George Dixon (first) and Johnny Coulon (seventh).

It is notable that Nat Fleischer and his magazine *Ring* gradually lost interest in wrestling; by the late 1920s boxing had pushed wrestling out of *Ring*.

By the mid-1920s wrestling had become entertainment, a kind of stage presentation. Consequently, the best performers were the best actors, not necessarily the best wrestlers. World champions bloomed all over, depending on the gall and reach of the promoter. Pro wrestling today is often brilliant, wild entertainment appealing to a broad common denominator. Its performers are often fine athletes but no one in sportswriting takes pro wrestling seriously as a competition.

By the late forties pro wrestling had begun to draw large crowds in Toronto and Montreal. Promoter Frank Tunney in Toronto had several Canadians who attracted a following, particularly Toronto's Whipper Billy Watson and Pat Flanagan. Maple Leaf Gardens

drew weekly crowds ranging from eight to fourteen thousand, and the spread of wrestling through TV exposure in the next few years was to enliven the circuits and the fans' interest throughout North America.

In most matches good is pitted against evil. Justice does not always triumph, but rematches will continue until right *does* prevail. Ethnic villains come and go; Germans, Japanese, and Russians have been postwar favourites as villains, just as Turks were in the 1920s.

In combat, a number of conventions must be upheld, at least in theory. When action comes to the ring borders and the ropes are touched, the wrestlers must break openly and begin anew. Strangleholds, eye-gouging, punching or the use of abrasive materials such as coins, peanuts or adhesive tape, are forbidden.

Less than half a match is spent at grips; basic wrestling holds on the mat are dull to watch. So there is a lot of action to supply variety – up and down, in and out of the ring. There are frequent appeals to the referee and much circling with gestures and grimaces.

There has been a pattern in the use of former boxing greats like Jack Dempsey, Jack Sharkey, Joe Walcott and Joe Louis as wrestling referees. Supposedly, they are impartial and able through the explosiveness of their fists to keep the villains in line. This myth is rooted in the knock-out punch. Supposedly it never leaves a man, even when he's into his sixties.

Football players with dropkick, tackle and elbow-smash techniques often gravitate to pro wrestling when they slow up on the field. A particularly cherished villain with wrestling fans in recent years has been Angelo Mosca, long-time tackle with the Hamilton Tiger Cats.

It is a continuing mortification for amateur wrestlers and their coaches that they should even share the identity of the word "wrestling" with the travesty that is pro wrestling. Devoted enthusiasts like Jim Trifunov have slowly been broadening the base and improving the calibre of amateur wrestling. Seven or eight Canadian amateurs, mostly in the lighter weights, are now ranked in the world class. If school wrestling is totalled in, the Canadian Wrestling Association estimates almost 300,000 Canadians per year wrestle under guidance or instruction. It is certainly clear that many more Canadian boys wrestle than box. In the annual world wrestling championship, held in the early seventies, the Canadian teams placed regularly in the top ten.

Perhaps boxing and wrestling will never be completely socially accepted in Canada. Certainly over the years they have been merely tolerated. The 1881 amendments to the Criminal Code were not changed substantially until 1933, and before that time all kinds of loopholes were resorted to in order to get around the law. Private club membership was used to evade the rules governing a "public" performance. With the disappearance of side bets, the economic base of pro boxing became "the gate" rather than "the stake." There was increasing sponsorship of both pro and amateur cards by policemen and firemen's associations.

A reformist movement emerged in Canada during the first world war. By this time, the acceptance of boxing, particularly amateur boxing, as a manly art was so high that even the most puritanical reformers did not campaign for its abolition. Instead, the reformers sought regulation and control.

In 1920 the Ontario government set up the Ontario Athletic Commission, whose object was " . . . to assist, promote and encourage amateur sport and recreation in schools, community centres and through associations of amateur sportsmen." Three sections provided for the licensing of promoters and fighters of all boxing and wrestling matches.

Essentially, the Ontario act of 1920 was the beginning of provincial involvement in both professional and amateur sport. Revenues for license fees and a tax on gate receipts at professional boxing and wrestling matches were used to sustain the commission and to provide funds for the support of amateur sport. Fifty years later the OAC is still dispensing funds on request to minor athletic organizations. Otherwise, its main role is licensing and supervising pro and amateur boxing and wrestling in Ontario. In 1973 there were some thirty-five amateur boxing clubs in Ontario. The previous year only 28 boxers had been licensed to fight professionally. This, in contrast, to the licensing of 280 wrestlers. License and tax revenues for the financial year 1972-3 brought the Ontario Athletic Commission only $16,664 from pro boxing.

The statistics of boxing in Canada in the 1970s are not impressive. There are estimated to be 250 or so pro boxers in the whole country of whom less than 40 fight with any regularity and only half-a-dozen make a reasonable income. Some 5,000 amateur boxers train with some regularity in a hundred or so clubs and gyms. In other words, there are more boys playing hockey in Regina or in Sudbury than are boxing in all of Canada.

What is clear from the boxing-wrestling story in Canada is that the puritanical and high-minded restraints found expression in law but small backing in practice. Every few years there is uproar somewhere and demands for abolition of boxing. Out of each such cycle boxing emerges and carries on, and if it is in a relatively parlous state today it is more because

of other attractions and alternatives for athletes and spectators.

Boxing and wrestling simply cannot undertake the fostering of mass participation and competition because there are too few clubs and their facilities cannot find a realistic economic base. Judo and karate, for example, have burgeoned through professionally organized studios and training centres. Team games like hockey, basketball, soccer and baseball, offer much better organization and infinitely more opportunities to take part, even in the low-income sections of metropolitan areas which used to be a great breeding grounds of ring aspirants.

Weightlifting and its associated training, on the other hand, is such a spectacular bodybuilder that eventually it attracted legions of followers. To any boy who caught the bug it seemed to offer the best means to a magnificent physique. There has always been an intellectual tendency to couple strength, muscle and size with stupidity. Further, there's little of grace or combativeness in weightlifting competition. Thus, from both inside and outside sport came a patronizing attitude toward weightlifters as ox-like and muscle-bound. Gradually, it got

Sports Hall of Fame

Etienne Desmarteau, a Montreal native, was Olympic champion in the hammer throw in 1904, tossing a 56-pound weight 34 feet, 4 inches.

131

In his annual *Ring* encyclopedia . . . the Bible of the sport of boxing, Nat Fleischer provided his all-time ranking of world boxers in a "top ten" in each of the ten weights from flyweight to heavyweight. Five of the names on this list are honoured members of Canada's Sports Hall of Fame, including: George Dixon *(opposite)*, described by Fleischer as "the greatest little fighter the black race has ever produced"; Sam Langford *(above)*, called the Boston Tar Baby; and three white fighters *(bottom, from left)*, Jack Delaney, Vancouver-born Jimmy McLarnin and bantamweight champion Johnny Coulon.

133

through to coaches that a "weight" program was intrinsic to developing strength and stamina for almost every energetic sport. Nancy Greene had a weight program; so do most competitive figure skaters and almost all top-flight football, soccer, hockey and basketball players.

If one man can be credited with creating modern competitive weightlifting in Canada it is probably Harvey Hill. He took the first weightlifting team to the London Olympics in 1948. It was the culmination of more than two decades of personal leadership, particularly in the province of Quebec. Anyone scanning the list of Canadian weightlifting records today in seven classes from bantamweight to heavyweight for the three basic competitions (the snatch, the two-hand press, and the two-hand clean-and-jerk) notes the overwhelming predominance of French-Canadian athletes.

In 1924 at the age of twenty-eight, Harvey Hill was the only English-speaking, competitive weightlifter in the province of Quebec. He trained and taught at the Southwestern YMCA in Montreal Verdun; at the Central Y, Charlie Walker taught weightlifting and barbell expertise while Lionel St. Jean trained scores of weightlifters at the Palestre Nationale, also in Montreal.

Harvey Hill formed the first regional weightlifting organization, the Quebec Amateur Weightlifting Association. Two of his athletes, Gerry Grattan and John Stuart, were the first Canadians to compete at the world championships in Philadelphia in 1947.

The regularization of weightlifting into the three basic competitions took place in Europe. The rules and the enthusiasm for formalized, matchable feats of strength were gradually taken up in Canada after the first war. French-Canadian strongmen with their tradition of spectacular feats slowly turned to the more orthodox system which permitted genuine determination of which man was strongest in a single weight class.

Since those world and Olympic entries of Canada in 1947 and 1948, the organization and structure of weightlifting efforts across Canada has fleshed in. Training and competition has made its way into clubs in most Canadian cities; by 1973 improving standard of performance by Canadian weightlifters placed them at or just below world class.

No weightlifting enthusiast would pretend that his sport has caught fire with Canadian fans or that it has widely expanding horizons for spectator interest. The satisfaction for the Harvey Hills and the Lionel St. Jeans is that their once-scorned or belittled endeavours have a strong, organized status. To a limited degree almost every good athlete today is a weightlifter and the weights' room is one of the busiest in almost every Canadian gym.

134

Biographies

ALBERT BELANGER, 1906-69
Ten thousand fans poured into the Coliseum at Toronto's Exhibition grounds on 19 December 1927 to see a local boy battle for the world flyweight title. At the age of twenty-one, Frenchy Belanger beat Ernie Jarvis in what has been described at the time as Toronto's most successful boxing bout.

The way to the top was not easy for Frenchy Belanger. The Cabbagetown in which he grew up was a depressed square mile of Toronto's east end, where street fights were common, and the little kid with the French-Canadian name was a natural target for neighbourhood bullies. A small, hard-muscled youth with slicked-down black hair and dark, intense eyes, Frenchy never backed away from a fight. Like many other fighters, the skills he picked up in the streets he turned to good account. As he later recalled: "I found you could do the same thing in a different place and get paid for it."

Belanger fought a few bouts under the auspices of the organized amateur groups in Toronto before he turned professional. Most of his career was centred on Toronto. He never became a main event man in New York. But for homegrown fans in Toronto, Frenchy was a crowd pleaser. With a wide, pugnacious stance, he waded in absorbing all kinds of punishment in return for getting close enough to inflict some of his own. His style led to many knockdowns and knockouts, and kept the crowds on their feet. His style eventually brought him to the attention of Dave Garrity, operator of what was then known as the Union Jack Athletic Club in Frenchy's Cabbagetown. Garrity became his manager, and this proved a lucky break for Belanger. In the next three years he only

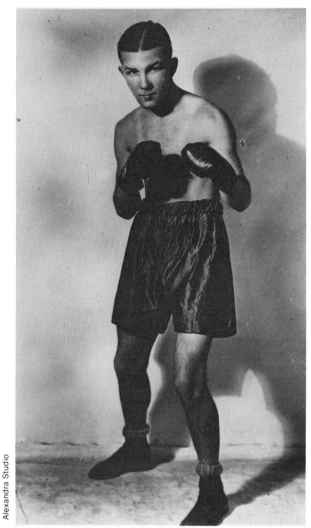

Alexandra Studio

lost one bout.

After a succession of victories in preliminary bouts Belanger was promoted to main events and in October 1927 took a decisive victory over Newsboy Brown, a leading contender for the flyweight division championship. In November he followed this up by a close win over Frank Genaro in New York, thereby earning the right to meet England's Ernie Jarvis in the title bout.

Belanger's victory over Jarvis at the Coliseum came on a unanimous decision after twelve rounds. It was a hard-fought match. Frenchy decked Jarvis in the first and third rounds, but was himself knocked down in the eleventh. But he came back to finish strongly and take the bout and the championship.

Belanger was not able to hold on to the title for long. Less than three months later, again at the Coliseum on 6 February 1928, Frank Genaro came back to win a decision after twelve rounds.

Belanger stayed in the ring for two more years, and fought with some success, including two tremendous bouts with Steve Rocco, another Toronto boy, for the Canadian flyweight title. Belanger lost the first in June 1928 and won the second in January 1929. He retired in 1930, after six years as a professional with sixty-one bouts to his credit – thirteen by knockouts, twenty-four decisions, seven draws and seventeen losses, only one by a knockout.

During his years as a top flyweight Belanger earned more than $90,000 but he spent freely to support his flamboyant life style. He was idolized in Toronto and he enjoyed playing the role of "The Champ." By 1934 money was running low, and he was back in Cabbagetown – a waiter in a beer parlour.

In 1962, at the age of fifty-six, Belanger suffered a severe stroke which left him paralyzed, but with the help of a friend, Murph Blandford, Belanger fought back. Blandford had worked in Belanger's dressing room the night he had won the flyweight championship, and he devoted himself to helping Frenchy regain his speech and his ability to walk. Blandford put up $700 to form a softball team – Belanger's Aces – to give the old boxer a new interest. Belanger spent his last years happily reminiscing about his former triumphs in the ring and talking about the future successes of his softball team.

EUGENE BROSSEAU, 1895-1968

The fans who saw Gene Brosseau fight were convinced he was the best boxer Canada had ever produced; when in 1917 he won the American amateur middleweight crown, a Boston boxing critic was prepared to go even further: "He can go back to Montreal . . . the most professional looking amateur that

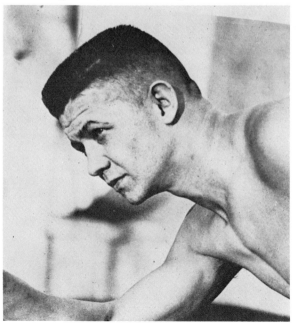

Sports Hall of Fame

ever donned a mitt."

Brosseau was born in Montreal and learned his trade in amateur competitions in that city. He earned a reputation as a thoughtful fighter with a talented left hand and a solid knockout punch; in 1915 he parlayed his experience to the Canadian amateur welterweight championship, winning decisions in two three-round fights in two days. He retained the title in a 1916 defense and in the same year took the American welterweight championship in Boston, winning one of four fights in a knockout, the other three by decisions.

Brosseau now moved up to the middleweight division and fought in Toronto and Montreal in addition to taking the middleweight title mentioned above. In 1917 in San Francisco, he fought a series of benefit exhibitions for the Red Cross and in two days added $12,500 to the society's funds by knocking out two opponents one day, a third the next.

During the first world war Brosseau trained as a pilot with the British airforce but the war ended before he was sent into action. After the war Gene turned professional and his success in the ring continued; in his first pro bout he knocked out George McKay in two rounds, a few months later defeated Red Allan in three, again by a knockout. Brosseau was rapidly establishing himself as one of the leading middleweight boxers in the world, and the future looked bright. Then, in November 1919, he met former champion George Chip in a punishing twelve-round bout in Portland, Maine. It was a no-decision fight that went the limit. Chip was a powerful boxer with a looping punch that repeatedly landed on the back of Brosseau's neck. After the fight Gene found his left arm was paralyzed.

Brosseau made a brave recovery and returned to the ring early in 1920, but his left hand was no longer the powerful instrument that other fighters had once feared. He was still capable of scoring knockouts over such fighters as Jack Holland, Young Ahearn, Jack Lunney, Young Fisher and Al McCoy, but he was beaten by the British boxer Jack Bloomfield, and knocked out by Mike McTigue, who was then on his way to the light-heavyweight title of the world. Gene endured a few more fights, then retired to a quiet job in the post office. As a professional boxer he had achieved the remarkable record of twenty-four wins in twenty-seven fights, seventeen by knockouts – in less than two and one-half years.

For awhile after retiring Brosseau retained some connection with the fight game, serving as instructor to Canada's

Olympic boxing team in 1924. In later life he was proud of the fact that he was the only Canadian ever to win two US amateur titles and that he had been selected to halls of fame as both a professional and an amateur boxer.

LOU BROUILLARD, 1911-

Lou Brouillard was a savage "south paw" slugger who leapt briefly into world ring prominence during the great depression. Competition was fierce. A boxer had to be tough to get to the top. Yet within three years Brouillard had won and lost world titles in both the welterweight and middleweight divisions. While he had little finesse, he was a body-puncher who could keep up a punishing attack, seemingly impervious to his opponent's blows.

Born in Quebec of French-Canadian parents, Brouillard moved with his family to Danielson, Connecticut, when he was three. He began his boxing career as an amateur in Worcester, Massachussets, when he was sixteen. After four successful years he turned professional, and in October 1931, at the age of twenty, he met Young Jack Thompson in Boston for the world welterweight championship. The fight went fifteen rounds and Brouillard won on points.

Brouillard did not hold his welterweight title for long. In January 1932, three months after he had won the title, he fought Jackie Fields in Chicago and was decisively

Sports Hall of Fame

beaten; by the sixth round Fields had passed Brouillard in points, and in the eighth opened a cut over Brouillard's right eye which impaired his vision. The fight went the full ten rounds but Brouillard was completely out-boxed.

The defeat did not discourage young Brouillard. He was strong, and determined, and he went on to win several more bouts as a welterweight, including an important ten-round decision from Jimmy McLarnin in August 1932. This was Brouillard's first fight in New York, and it drew a crowd of 15,000. The fans liked the sight of Brouillard who, according to one reporter, "battered and pounded McLarnin through ten rounds of primitive fighting to gain a decision that met with the undivided support of the on-lookers at Yankee Stadium." The New York *Times* called Brouillard "a savage customer" and attributed his win to "his rugged inexhaustible strength." Against such a concentrated attack McLarnin, with his careful boxing style and long-range defence, was powerless.

But Brouillard also lost some fights, which he attributed to his constant struggle to keep down to the 147-pound welterweight limit. When he moved into the middleweight division he was immediately successful. In August 1933, in New York, he beat Ben Jeby and gained recognition in New York as the middleweight champion. From the beginning of the bout it was obvious that Jeby was doomed. He took a terrible beating from Brouillard, who eventually knocked him out in the seventh round.

Two months later, in Boston, Brouillard was outpointed over fifteen rounds by Vince Dundee, a veteran fighter from Baltimore whose superior skills over Brouillard's savage rushes proved that strength and punching power were not enough.

Brouillard was unable to win back the title although he fought for it twice against Marcel Thil in Paris. He lost both bouts on fouls, and after the second disqualification the International Boxing Union barred Brouillard from fighting for one year, and suspended his manager for life. Although Brouillard was able to get a few more fights in the late thirties, his career was effectively ended. In 140 fights he had won 66 by knockouts and was knocked out himself only once. When the second world war started he joined the US Army. He settled in Hanson, Massachussets, after the war where he worked as a crane operator in a shipyard.

TOMMY BURNS, 1881-1955
Tommy Burns, Canada's only world heavyweight champion, was a pugnacious, stout-hearted man. Recent boxing historians agree that his reputation has been downplayed undeservedly. At five-foot-seven and weighing under 175 pounds, Burns was the shortest man to ever win the heavyweight crown. A fast mover and crisp puncher, he had both the killer instinct and a cocky, taunting attitude in the ring. His bitter tongue often psyched his rivals into rage and mistakes, and he never hesitated to take on ranking boxers bigger than himself. In a career of sixty fights he only lost four. In two years and nine months Burns defended his crown ten times, more than any other champion in a similar time span.

Burns was an all-round athlete who became a boxer by accident. He was the twelfth of thirteen children born to Frederick and Sofa Brusso (he changed his name when his choice of a career upset his mother) in a log cabin farmhouse near Hanover, Ontario. His parents were German Methodists and despite a strict upbringing young Tommy (his Christian name was Noah) loved to fight and eagerly joined in the schoolyard free-for-alls. He excelled in lacrosse, hockey and skating. One day while working on a passenger boat in Lake Erie he got into a fight with a burly second mate and trounced him. This episode made Noah begin to think seriously about boxing as a career. He jumped ship at Detroit and joined the Detroit Athletic Club where his training began in earnest.

For six months he didn't meet an opponent or put on the gloves; he skipped rope, he shadow boxed, he pounded the heavy bag – he trained. One night he and some friends had gone to see one Jack Cowan fight. Cowan

waved to the crowd from the ring apron, vaulted over the ropes and collapsed with a twisted ankle. Burns was pushed into the ring by his buddies to fight in Cowan's place. He went to work with gusto and knocked out his opponent in the fifth round. The year was 1900.

He now started fighting regularly and after five wins, all knockouts, he was middleweight champion of Michigan. One of his bouts, with Ben O'Grady, was so devastating that O'Grady was unconscious for three days and Burns and his seconds spent the night in jail for assault.

Tommy was steadily improving, but he still could not get a fight for the middleweight crown. In 1905 James Jeffries retired as world heavyweight champion and passed his title to Marvin Hart. Hart had to defend his new title and, looking over the field of contenders, decided that Tommy Burns would be an easy opponent. He underestimated the cocky young Canadian as he was to find out in the ring at Los Angeles in February 1906. Burns deliberately insulted Hart and taunted him into losing his temper. For round after round Hart chased Burns with wild rushes, while Burns kept pounding away, making every blow count. After the scheduled twenty rounds both boxers were still on their feet but Burns had won a resounding victory; the heavyweight title passed to a Canadian.

Burns was determined to prove that he deserved the crown despite his size; he embarked on a worldwide tour to defend it. In San Diego he met two challengers in one night – and knocked both out in the first round. He took on Jim Flynn, a solid puncher who outweighed Burns by thirty pounds. After a brutal fifteen rounds, Burns landed a shattering right that knocked Flynn to the canvas and ended the fight. At his first meeting with Philadelphian Jack O'Brien, light-heavyweight champion, the two men boxed to a draw, though reporters insisted that Burns had won on points. In the rematch a few months later Burns won easily. He finished his triumphal progress in the United States by knocking out the Australian Bill Squires at 2.28 of the first round.

Burns then went to Europe to look for challengers and gates. As the seventh Marquis of Queensberry later observed:

> Burns was prepared to tell anyone who would listen that he was in a class by himself. As champion he was arrogance itself during the preliminaries leading up to his fight with Gunner Moir, the best English heavyweight available at that time. . . . In view of his offensive conduct it is not strange that for once the National Sporting Club members permitted partisanship to sway them. It was not so much a case of plumping for Moir as it was a devout hope that the braggart and mannerless visitor should be taught a salutary lesson. Unhappily the Gunner was not equal to the task; Burns was too good for him, scoring a knockout in the tenth round.

The Canadian knocked out another Englishman, Jim Palmer, in four rounds, then disposed of the Irish champ, Jem Roche, in the first round. (This match remains the shortest heavyweight title defense on record.) Only his Irish-sounding name saved him from the wrath of the Dublin crowd. He moved to Paris for two knockout wins, one over Jewey Smith, the other over a former opponent, Bill Squires.

Then came the fateful trip to Australia, taken, some say, because the formidable Jack Johnson was headed for London to challenge him. After the long sea voyage Burns took on Squires for the third time. According to Burns's later account he carried Squires for thirteen rounds so the Australian would look good to the local fans. Jack Johnson had followed to Australia and was demanding a title match. Johnson was one of the great heavyweights of all times – some say the greatest. The Negro was a giant compared to Burns; he stood six feet tall and weighed 203 pounds. He had a tremendous reach, much experience and an almost impregnable defense. Burns was persuaded to meet Johnson for a guarantee of $30,000 – the first of the championship "golden gate" fights – and the bout was held in Sydney, appropriately enough on Boxing Day 1908.

Accounts of the fight vary. Johnson was not liked by the American boxing public. Black fighters were unpopular and Johnson's relationships with white women did nothing to improve his reputation. If Johnson was not a good boxer – the argument went – the man he defeated must be worse. Reports sent back from Australia were lurid and biased, one of the worst coming from the novelist Jack London. Sober second thought has admitted that Johnson was an exceptional champion, and no one needed be ashamed of losing to the first black heavyweight champion.

Burns himself admitted that he had "badly underrated Johnson's boxing skill, his tremendous strength and unquestionable cunning. The situation demanded that I move rapidly round the ring, boxing carefully, at all times. It actually was my only chance to cope with the larger man, but I had elected to tear into him and outfight him." The results were predictable – and disastrous. Burns tried to bore in on Johnson from the start of the first round, but was tied up by the bigger man. Near the end of the round Johnson delivered a tremendous right uppercut to the jaw and Burns dropped like a log for a count of five. The fight is described most graphically in Tommy's own words: "From the start of the second round it was simply the story of a small man who never gave ground gaming it out against a great fighter. The big fellow dealt out terrific punishment as the tussle progressed."

The punishment went on until the fourteenth round when police stopped the fight and Johnson was declared the winner. Burns retired for two years, then returned to the ring in 1910. Over the next ten years he had six scattered fights and quit forever when he was knocked out for the first time on 14 July 1920. He tried running a clothing store in Calgary, then a pub in England. Eventually he turned to religion and became an evangelist. He was on the evangelical trail when he died of a heart attack at the home of friends in Vancouver; he was seventy-three.

JACKIE CALLURA, 1917-

Jackie Callura was one of seven children born to Italian immigrant parents in the north end of Canada's steeltown, Hamilton. Jackie was small – at the peak of his featherweight career he never weighed in at more than 126 pounds – but he was tough. The family was desperately poor and Jackie early learned that ready fists were an adequate reply to the taunts of more affluent bullies. He helped his father carry home railway ties for firewood; he sold newspapers and battled older boys who tried to take his earnings. He grew up proud, cocky and would fight any boy who made fun of his size.

Jackie found that his fighting could also make him money. His aggressive spirit brought him to the attention of the men who ran Hamilton's informal bouts – the so-called "Friday-night smokers." Jackie had his first fight at the age of nine, a diminutive figure in outsized borrowed bathing trunks held up at the crotch with a large safety pin. One of the promoters was Hugh Lennox, a service station operator and ex-amateur fighter who had built a gym above his garage where Jackie got his first training.

Jackie soon built up a following in Hamilton. A good puncher, with strong arms, Hamilton fans loved the scrappy little guy who could take punishment and come back fighting, and they delighted in the local boy beating out-of-towners. The image of a poor boy fighting to feed his family added just the right touch of sentiment.

In 1931 Jackie won the Canadian amateur title in the featherweight class, which enabled him to represent Canada in the 1932 Olympics. In 1936 he turned profes-

sional in the featherweight division, but his career did not take off until Leo Bradley became his manager. Bradley had contacts in the fight business and got Jackie matches that moved him up the featherweight ranks. Under Bradley's direction Jackie became a more polished boxer. He was still aggressive and hard hitting, but he learned to defend himself against men who, though not as quick nor as strong, were skilful enough to get inside his guard and pile up points by pounding his body.

The highlight of his career came in January 1943 when he beat Jackie Wilson for the National Boxing Association featherweight championship in Providence, RI. The fight went the full fifteen rounds; Callura won nine rounds, Wilson five and one round was a draw. It could scarcely be called a stylish fight; three times the boxers tangled their feet and both fell to the floor. For all his new-found boxing skill, Jackie still showed the old free-wheeling whirlwind attack. Wilson managed to keep out of the way of Callura's flailing arms for the first eight rounds, but when Jackie landed a punishing left blow to the body, that clinched the fight. Wilson received $7,500 of the gate of $12,000, but Jackie got nothing; he had paid off his purse to get a crack at the championship. He expected to cash in on his title in the future.

But it was not to be. He successfully defended the title two months later in a re-

139

match with Wilson. Then, in August 1943, just seven months after winning the championship, he lost it when Phil Terranova knocked him out in the eighth round. Callura won a few more bouts but when he got a December rematch with Terranova he was knocked out in the sixth.

After that it was all downhill. In one hundred pro fights Jackie had won forty-three decisions and thirteen knockouts.

For a few years all went well. He was battered and scarred from his years in the ring, but he was still tough. He walked eight to ten miles a day and stayed in condition. He needed that toughness in 1951 when his wife died as a result of a botched abortion. Jackie had not even known she was pregnant. Jackie closed the Hamilton restaurant he had been running and went to work in a Buffalo steel mill.

JOHNNY COULON, 1889-1974

At the peak of his fame Johnny Coulon stood a smidgin less than five feet and never weighed more than 110 pounds. In 1910 he won the world bantamweight championship, a title he was to hold and defend for four years.

Coulon's parents were both born in New York but they married and had Johnny before they moved to Toronto. Canada was never to be Johnny's permanent home; in a career total of ninety-six fights only one – in Windsor, 1913 – was fought in Canada. Chicago was Johnny's base from 1905 when he turned professional until 1917 when he retired. In retirement he operated a Chicago gym and training school for young boxers that brought him almost as much fame as his boxing career had done.

Early in his career Coulon realized that his small size forced him into defenses other than strength: to survive he had to move fast, dodge punches and cultivate his inherent stamina. In the 1960's Johnny reminisced about his career:

> The only reason I've got all my marbles and don't walk around talking to myself is that before I turned pro I learned how to avoid the other fellow's blow. . . . Those boys today just don't know how to box. They just wade right in and slug and don't give a hoot if they get whacked four or five times to land one.

Along with his defenses, Coulon had cultivated his offense; he had developed a respectable punch and won many of his early bouts by knockouts. He was a thinking-man's boxer, prepared to feint at arm's length seeking an opening, before lashing out at his opponent. When the world bantamweight title became vacant in 1909, Coulon summoned all his offensive and defensive skills to beat out the

Sports Hall of Fame

other contenders.

The chief claimant was the English boxer, Jim Kendrick. Coulon met him twice within a space of three weeks, in February and March 1910. In the first match Coulon won a tenth-round decision. The second time he made no mistake in his bid for the championship; he knocked Kendrick out in the nineteenth.

In the next few years Coulon defended his title successfully against the top fighters in his weight. But his speed and his ability to avoid his opponent's blows had begun to slow. In 1913 he fought only three times, twice in 1914. It was in the last fight – 9 June 1914 – with Kid Williams of Baltimore that Johnny lost his title. He was decked by Williams in the third.

Following this defeat Coulon left the ring for two years. He made a brief moderately successful comeback in 1916 and then spent the years 1918-19 in the US army as a boxing instructor. At the end of the war he began to train young fighters. He was teaching every day, often accompanying his young fighters around the world for their matches, even at the age of seventy-three.

LOUIS CYR, 1863-1912

On 24 June 1885 the following advertisement appeared in the pages of the Montreal *Gazette*:

140

I hereby challenge any man in the world, bar no-one, to a heavy weightlifting contest, without harness, for any sum from $100 to $500 a side. Yours, Louis Cyr.

The naïve gall of such a challenge may amuse us today; before the first world war, however, the challenge of one strongman to all others aroused world-wide interest. In that age the exploits of the professional strongmen were followed as avidly as those of today's movie stars. In Canada it was mainly French Canadians – men from the farms and lumber camps of rural Quebec – who became famous at home and abroad for muscular endurance. Of these supermen, the hero of them all, the man once billed as the "strongest man who ever lived," was Louis Cyr.

Louis Cyr is *still* a legend in French Canada. His fame was earned before accurate records were kept. For example weight-lifting was not included in the Olympic Games until 1920, eight years after Cyr's death. In Cyr's day, man proved his superior strength by taking on all challengers. Strongmen travelled around the countryside in troupes or with circuses, presenting shows that were a curious mixture of conventional weightlifting and showbusiness tricks. Louis Cyr never backed down from a challenge, and he was never defeated. He was a colossus of a man. He inherited his physique from his mother, who stood six-foot-one and weighed 267 pounds. Louis was one of seventeen children, and the family was very poor. At the age of twelve Louis left school and went to work, first at various jobs and then as a lumberjack. Legend has it that once,

Canada Wide Feature Service Ltd.

when he was seventeen, he pulled a loaded farm wagon out of the mud by lifting it on his back. It was at this time that Louis determined to be a strongman and started training, using what crude equipment he could gather.

He was soon ready to leave the lumber camps and challenge some of the reigning strongmen. At that time David Michaud claimed to be the strongest man in Canada. Cyr challenged him to a test to see who could lift the heaviest stone. Cyr finally won by lifting a boulder weighing 480 pounds which Michaud had been unable to budge.

In 1885, at the age of twenty-two, Cyr joined the Montreal police force and found himself patrolling the tough Ste. Cunegonde district. The sight of his enormous uniformed figure is reported to have had a sobering effect on the young hooligans of the city but it also marked Cyr as an unmistakable target for Montreal's toughs. One day Louis broke up a street fight and carted off the two antagonists, one tucked under each arm. After he was attacked on the beat with an axe, Louis resigned from the force but word of his exploits had spread. Richard Fox, leading fight promoter in New York, heard of Cyr's feats, verified them, and signed Cyr on with the billing, "The Strongest Man in the World." He offered $5,000 to anyone who could match his strength. Cyr defeated all comers, among them some of the world's most renowned strongmen: Otto Ronaldo, the German champion; "Cyclops," the Polish strongman; and the Scandinavian champions Montgomery and Johnson.

Fox also sponsored Cyr on a twenty-three month tour of England; it was a triumph and Cyr became a household name in the Western world. The highlight was his performance on 19 January 1889, at the Royal Aquarium Theatre in London, before a capacity house of 5,000 and in the presence of the prince of Wales. The official report of his stunts on this occasion is impressive: he lifted a 551-pound weight with one finger, lifted 4,100 pounds on a platform stretched across his back, lifted 273 1/4 pounds with one hand to his shoulder and then above his head, and lifted to his shoulder with one hand a barrel of cement weighing 314 pounds.

The French-Canadian giant was a huge success with Londoners. They enjoyed his showmanship and liked his friendly and unassuming manner. He was fêted and lionized. At a luncheon in Cyr's honour the Marquis of Queensberry suggested that one of his driving horses should be hitched to each of Cyr's arms, and if Cyr could hold them to a standstill, he could take one of the horses

141

back to Canada. Cyr won the wager and for many years after drove the nobleman's horse about the streets of Montreal.

Cyr continued to tour the United States and Canada, giving exhibitions and challenging local champions. Undoubtedly one performance will remain in the record books as his best feat. In Boston in 1895 he lifted what is claimed to have been the greatest weight ever lifted by one man – 4,337 pounds. He accomplished the feat using the method for which he was most famous, the back lift. The load consisted of the combined weight of eighteen fat men standing on a platform.

Between tours, Louis Cyr made his home in Montreal where he operated a tavern on Notre Dame Street. He would amuse his customers by tossing around 300-pound beer kegs, or by lifting his 120-pound wife, Melina, on the palm of his hand. His prodigious appetite matched his size. For Louis, a good dinner included at least six pounds of meat. Unfortunately such overeating ruined his health and he died of Bright's disease at the early age of forty-nine. All Quebec mourned him, and Montreal gave him one of the biggest funerals in that city's history.

VICTOR DELAMARRE, 1888-1955

Delamarre was the last of the great French-Canadian strongmen. By the time of his death, the technological advances of Western society had rendered brute strength meaningless; survival was no longer dependent on the power of one's arms or back. French Canada's strongmen retreated into folklore.

But when Victor Delamarre was born in the rural Lac St. Jean region of Quebec, it was only one year after Louis Cyr had been the toast of London. Victor grew up in Quebec City and dreamed of emulating Cyr's feats, of bettering his record. A poor scholar, Victor often played hooky and spent most of his free time in the local gym; to Delamarre *père*, however, hanging out in the gym was only slightly better than hanging around a pool hall. In 1901 Victor was sent to the country to finish his schooling and to work on the farm and in the woods surrounding Hébertville. It was the perfect life to develop the youth's physique, but if the father had hoped it would alter the boy's dream, he was to be disappointed. Victor's ambition remained the same – to be the strongest man in the world.

Victor's uncle, Eugene Tremblay, had more sympathy for the youth's ambition. Himself a wrestler of considerable talent, he ran a tavern and gymnasium in Monteal, and when Victor visited him in 1908, the older man allowed Victor to work out with some

of the best French-Canadian athletes of the day and encouraged him to initiate a training program.

Victor realized that if his ambition was to be realized he would have to leave the woods and live in Montreal, the Mecca for the strongmen like Barre, Decaire and Cabana whom he wanted to contest.

So, like his hero Louis Cyr before him, Victor joined the Montreal police force. He was accepted into the force with some reluctance. At 154 pounds and only five-foot-six tall, he hardly seemed a likely candidate to keep law and order. But his looks belied his ability, and he was soon giving exhibitions of his prodigious strength. In 1914 he lifted 309 1/2 pounds with one hand, a feat which was officially recognized in 1930 as a world record.

Delamarre toured Canada and the New England states. A devout Roman Catholic, he billed himself as "the Man with no Master but God" and "the New Samson." After he had accomplished some particularly impressive feat, he would declare, "it was not I . . . it was the sacred heart." Delamarre performed countless exhibitions of strength; he challenged local strongmen, lifted enormous weights with one hand – once lifting 201 pounds with one *finger* – and lifted platforms on which sixty or more people stood, weighing as much as 7,000 pounds. In October 1928, he lifted thirty of Quebec City's finest, each policeman weighing at least 200

pounds of muscle and brawn.

Some of the feats Delamarre invented to show off his strength have a modern flavour. One such performance prompted this description: "Delamarre would do a backbend, a limousine loaded with people would drive up a ramp propped against his chest, pause for a few seconds, then drive down the other side. The ramp alone weighed 1,200 pounds. Then Delamarre would strap the vehicle – it weighed 2,260 pounds – to his back and climb a high ladder."

Victor Delamarre continued to give exhibitions of strength almost to the end of his life. But after the first world war, the skills of professional strongmen began to go out of fashion. It was the beginning of the depression and Delamarre was married, with a family of four boys and six girls. So in 1931 he became a professional wrestler. Until his retirement, he is reported to have had more than 1,500 bouts, meeting such wrestlers as Yvon Robert, Paul Lortie, Martin Levy, Zelis Amhara and George Zarinof.

Delamarre never weighed more than 165 pounds but he kept his phenomenal strength almost to the end. In 1951, for example, at the age of sixty-one, he undertook a successful tour, demonstrating his still considerable strength in towns and cities of New England and across Canada to Manitoba. The wrestler Yvon Robert said of him that for his size he was without doubt the strongest man in the world. After his death the town of Lac Bouchette, his home from 1903 to 1932, named its new recreation centre "Parc Victor Delamarre."

JACK DELANEY, 1900-48

Madison Square Garden is recognized as the Mecca of professional boxing in North America and when the new garden was built in 1925 (an even newer garden has since been built), one of the headliners chosen to christen the new headquarters was the great Canadian boxer, Jack Delaney. Delaney's real name was Oliva Chapdelaine but he sacrificed his Gallic inheritance in favour of the Irish name when he turned professional in 1919.

Delaney was an attractive boxer, tall, lithe, a thrower of fast punches. He'd earned a reputation as a knockout artist and came equipped with a deadly right hook. In a career total of eighty-six fights, he won seventy – forty-three by knockouts, twenty-seven on decisions.

And so, on the night of 11 December 1925, at the new Madison Square Garden, Delaney fought Paul Berlenbach, the rugged New York holder of the world light heavy-

Sports Hall of Fame

weight title. The two had met before, in March 1924, when Delaney had knocked Berlenbach out in the fourth round. Delaney was a worthy opponent, and the capacity crowd of 25,000 was treated to what one reporter called "a slashing, sensational bout." At the start Delaney took control; he knocked Berlenbach down in the fourth round and punched him groggy in the seventh. But with his title at stake, Berlenbach pulled himself together and came back in the last six rounds with a slashing, swinging attack that Delaney could not withstand. With a furious finish – Delaney took a short count in the twelfth – Berlenbach won the decision; but it had been a near thing.

In the following months Delaney had eleven bouts against other leading light heavyweights and won six of them by knockouts. The stage was set for a rematch with Berlenbach for the world title, and the pair met again on 16 July 1926. The fight was held at Ebbett's Field in Brooklyn before a crowd of 45,000 and it drew a gate of $475,000.

This time the tables were turned. It was Delaney who produced the "flashing, smashing finish that swept his foe before him throughout the last five rounds." Although he had crushed a thumb bone in the second round, Delaney never let up his attack. Berlenbach managed to stay on his feet, but in

143

at least three of the closing five rounds Delaney's right uppercuts to the body and left hooks to the jaw were punishing. A smashing blow to the stomach in the eleventh proved to be the turning point, and Delaney was quick to press his advantage home. With the crowd yelling for a knockout, Delaney nailed Berlenbach on the point of the jaw with a vicious right in the fourteenth. The champion sagged at the knees for a moment and grabbed for the ropes, then fell into a clinch to save himself from further punishment. Delaney took the fifteen-round decision to become the new world champion. It was a spectacular victory, with as courageous and skilful a finish as any boxer had exhibited in years. The crowd loved it and gave Delaney a tremendous ovation.

Delaney retained the championship for about a year but he was having trouble getting down to the 175-pound weight limit so he moved into the heavyweight division. But with the heavier boxers he was not so successful. In April 1928 he was knocked out in the first round by Jack Sharkey, and he knew his career was coming to an end. He fought one more bout and then retired and went into business. He was persuaded to make a brief comeback in 1932, and had three fights which he won by knockouts, but he soon gave up the game for good. He died of cancer in 1948.

GEORGE DIXON, 1870-1909
"The greatest little fighter the black race has ever produced." So wrote Nat Fleischer, the dean of boxing and its history, about George "Little Chocolate" Dixon. He also rated Dixon as the greatest bantamweight champion of all time. The little Nova Scotian's life had the stock tragic elements of rags to riches and glory, followed shortly by poverty and early death. He was the first black man to win a world boxing championship; in fact he held two, the bantamweight and the featherweight.

Dixon started in the game when he was sixteen in his home town of Halifax, knocking out Young Johnson in the third round. The next year he moved to Boston, in search of fame and fortune. His first fight there, in 1887 – a successful eight-round decision – brought him only fifty dollars, part of which his manager kept. But gradually the purses improved and soon Dixon was fighting often enough to put together respectable sums of money.

The little fighter's break came in 1890. At Washington Hall, in the heart of Boston, Dixon took on the prominent New Yorker, Cal McCarthy. Wearing two-ounce gloves, the two men fought an incredible sev-

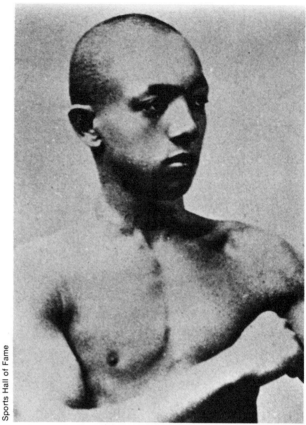

Sports Hall of Fame

enty rounds. After four hours and forty minutes they agreed to a draw. With a solid reputation behind him, Dixon went to England in June and knocked out Nunc Wallace in eighteen rounds to win the world bantamweight title and a $2,000 purse. He defended the title once, in Providence, RI, winning a forty-round decision against Johnny Murphy. For that bout he collected a $1,500 purse and $1,200 on a side bet – a not inconsiderable sum.

Dixon then moved into the heavier featherweight division. On 8 July 1891 he knocked out Australia's Abe Attell in five rounds to take the world title and the hefty purse of $4,250. Big fights and big purses, and short fights (more for the exercise than for the money) followed in rapid succession for the next six years.

Dixon's long string of successes ended in October 1897 when he lost the featherweight title to Solly Smith in a twenty-round bout in San Francisco. Dixon came back the following year to win the crown again in a battle with David Sullivan in New York. This time he held the title until January 1900, when Terrible Terry McGovern knocked him out in the eighth round.

Years later, Elmer Ferguson, the sportswriter, was to assess Dixon's stamina.

The short fights of today [Ferguson wrote] the ten- to twelve-rounders, would be mere workouts for

144

battlers of Dixon's era – and for Dixon himself. In 1899, in perhaps the most arduous year any fighter undertook, he fought three twenty-five rounders, three at twenty rounds, one at ten, three at six. In England in 1903 . . . he had three fights of twenty rounds each, three at fifteen, thirty-four in six, and one eight-session bout. A man of iron was little George Dixon.

George Dixon battled Abe Attell again to a twenty-round draw in October 1901, but was beaten by Attell after fifteen rounds when they met for the third time eight days later.

Gradually the fights got fewer and the losses more frequent. At his last fight in 1906, at the age of thirty-six, he still had enough stamina to last fifteen rounds. At his death, friends and followers rallied to save him from being buried in potter's field, the cemetery for paupers. They raised funds to send his body to Boston, where he was interred in Mount Hope Cemetery.

HORACE GWYNNE, 1913-

The 1932 Olympic Games in Los Angeles produced an unusual sports hero for Canada – a small, stubby, jockey-turned-boxer named Horace Gwynne. Lefty Gwynne (nobody ever called him Horace) won for Canada the gold medal in bantamweight boxing; the only other gold won that year was the high jump medal taken by Duncan McNaughton.

When he was thirteen Lefty started doing odd jobs around the old Woodbine race track in the east end of his hometown, Toronto. He was soon taken on as an exercise boy and eventually a jockey. "They used to have maiden jockey races," Lefty was to recall later, "and I rode in every one . . . Didn't win one." It was possibly his failure as a jockey that turned Lefty to the ring. In the twenties Toronto was a boxing town; crowds of fans jammed each bout and such men as Frenchy Belanger and Steve Rocco were local heroes. Lefty's slight, compact build made him a natural bantamweight and he started serious training at the Central Y. With each fight – in Canada and the US – he honed his inimitable style; by 1932 he had won a spot on the Canadian Olympic boxing team.

To capture the gold medal Gwynne had to win three bouts and his chances looked slim when he drew Vito Melis, the Italian champion, to fight in the first bout. The Italians had a strong team, and they had not yet had an Olympic defeat, until Lefty beat Melis in a decisive fight. He took all three rounds by a wide margin and once had Melis on the floor with a powerful right.

Gwynne's second fight was against José Villeneuve of the Philippines. Once again Lefty's solid punching and offensive tactics won him the decision.

In the final bout Gwynne met the European champion, Hans Ziglarski of Germany, a formidable opponent. With the gold medal within his grasp Lefty decided to box cautiously. Ziglarski, in typical European style, rushed at Gwynne in the first round, throwing overhand rights and wild lefts which the Canadian evaded. At every opportunity Gwynne moved in, with sizzling left hooks to the head and a cross-cutting right to the body. Gwynne won the first round handily.

In the second round Lefty had Ziglarski down for a count of two with a clean left to the head. Ziglarski managed to keep out of the way of most of Lefty's blows and hung on to the end of the round, but he was clearly outclassed. In the third round Ziglarski tried to keep Gwynne at long range, but when he was thrown coming out of a clinch, the fight was clearly over.

Lefty returned to Canada as a national hero and a celebrity in his hometown. But that didn't last. The depression hung heavy on Canada; there was little money to be made in amateur boxing. Lefty joined Jim Brady's boxing stable in Detroit and went to work in an automobile plant for seven dollars a day. As Lefty recalls, "I made so little on fights around Michigan that it didn't pay to take the time from work. Got a fight against Henry Hook . . . and we were guaranteed seventy-five bucks each. There wasn't that much in the house."

Sports Hall of Fame

145

In 1938 Lefty returned to the race track and worked for several jockeys. He quit the track in 1953, joined the Toronto recreation department and later became director of various community centres.

DOUG HEPBURN, 1926-

The world weightlifting championships were held in Stockholm in 1953. Europeans have always been keener for this sport than North Americans. Men from twenty nations took part before a packed stadium of five thousand fans. The underdog – and the crowd's favourite – was an unknown giant from Canada, Doug Hepburn. He had a withered leg and walked with a limp because of a sprained ankle. He was alone without a companion or a coach. His few friends in Vancouver had managed to scrape up only enough money to send him to Sweden. Yet against all these odds, Doug Hepburn came through to win the world heavyweight championship with a total lift of just over 1,030 pounds.

Back in Canada Hepburn was equally unknown, even in his home town of Vancouver. The city fathers set out to make up for such neglect at his home coming. Both city newspapers gave him banquets. In Toronto the *Star* voted him the Lou Marsh award as Canada's athlete of the year, and the Newsman's Club of BC elected him British Columbian of the Year. Mayor George Hume of Vancouver guaranteed him $150 a

month while he was in training for the British Commonwealth Games to be held in Vancouver the following year. To preserve his amateur status he was put on the city payroll as the mayor's personal bodyguard, though he was never called upon to perform any services in that capacity.

But Hepburn's moment of glory soon faded. Weightlifting had never really caught on in North America. Its practitioners were too often considered uncouth, overweight individuals, with plenty of brawn but little brain. In no time at all Hepburn sank back into the anonymity from which he had so suddenly sprung.

Doug Hepburn had never had an easy life. He was born with a clubfoot and crossed eyes. As a child he had operations to correct both conditions, but the doctors bungled the operation on his foot, leaving him with atrophied calf muscles and a permanently weak ankle. When he was five his parents were divorced and he lived for a time with his grandmother. His mother later remarried and Doug went back to live with her and his stepfather.

He hated school. His classmates ridiculed him for his scrawny appearance and physical deformities. Living the Charles Atlas "I was a 97-pound weakling" myth, he turned to weightlifting to gain strength and whip the school bullies. Every spare moment he lifted barbells. His school work suffered so he dropped out. He left home and got a job as a bouncer in a beer parlour.

He began to stuff himself at meals. "It seemed logical," he has said, "that if I wanted to get bigger I would have to eat everything I could get my hards on. . . . One day I gained seven pounds." His weight crept up from 145 to 255 pounds.

Lonely and self-taught, Hepburn at first knew nothing about competitive weightlifting. When, after several years, he found out about the sport, he set out to learn the three Olympic lifts: the press, the clean-and-jerk, and the snatch. He entered a competition in Vancouver, in which he pressed 300 pounds – a new Canadian record. The officials in Vancouver sent details of this lift to the weightlifting headquarters in Montreal, but the national officers would not accept it. Who was Doug Hepburn? No one had even heard of him; news of the lift sounded fishy.

Hepburn went to Los Angeles in 1949, where he won the US national open championship by beating John Davis with a press of 345 1/2 pounds. Still Canadians paid no attention; Hepburn was not invited to be a member of the team sent to the 1952 Olympics at Helsinki, and the gold medal in the heavyweight division there was won by

John Davis, the man Hepburn had defeated in California three years before. Finally, Hepburn's friends raised the money to send him to the Stockholm world championships in 1953 where his triumph justified their faith. But after the brief flurry of publicity Hepburn settled back into his old life, living alone in a cheap rooming-house, mixing with bums and drunks, and spending all his spare time at the gym or in a bar.

At the British Commonwealth Games in 1954 Hepburn did not disappoint his small following; he won the gold medal and established new games records, with lifts of: the press of 370 pounds; the snatch, 300 pounds; and for the clean-and-jerk, 370 pounds. This success, however, still did not bring him recognition as the world's strongest man; instead it marked the end of his career. Now that the games were over, the city dispensed with his job. No one raised the money to send him to a defense of his title in Germany and Doug couldn't afford the trip himself. He was persuaded to take up pro wrestling and hated every minute of it. After a year he quit with nothing but $800 and a new Cadillac to show for it. He opened a chain of gymnasia in the city but he was an ineffective businessman and they soon folded.

His drinking increased and he hit rock bottom. Finally he underwent treatment with LSD for his alcoholism at Vancouver's Hollywood Hospital. Slowly Doug Hepburn, one of the world's strongest men and a unique Canadian athlete, moved onto the long road of rehabilitation toward a life of dignity.

RICHARD HOWARD, 1928-
Kid Howard was a journeyman boxer, well ranked in the lightweight listings – he was once sixth on *Ring's* list – who held the Canadian lightweight crown for some time. But for fight fans with long memories, the question may arise: "Why Howard? Why Kid Howard in the Sports Hall of Fame when there are dozens of others his equal or better?"

Why not, for example, New Brunswick's Tom Kelly, a claimant to the featherweight title in the 1860s? Why not that marvel of longevity, Larry Gaines, who KO'd Max Schmeling in 1925, decisioned Primo Carnera in 1932, held the British Empire heavyweight title in the thirties, and fought a main bout with Tommy Farr in 1939? Why not one of the dozens of good Toronto boxers from Fulljames and Gilmore to Steve Rocco, Sammy Luftspring, Frankie Genovese, Baby Yack, Arthur King and George Chuvalo? Why not Frankie Battaglia from Winnipeg or Al Ford, Wilfie Greaves or Billy McGrandle

of Edmonton? Why not Montreal's Johnny Greco, Dave Castilloux or Armand Savoie? Why not Vancouver's welterweight, Billy Townsend or Vic Foley or Al Foreman or Yvon Durelle or Arthur Pelkey?

Why not, indeed?

The question reminds us that Canada has produced a plethora of good journeyman boxers, many of them now forgotten, but who, at the height of their ring careers, pushed this country into the mainstream of modern boxing. Surprisingly for their size, the Maritime provinces have produced more than their share of ring notables.

Recognition of Kid Howard in the Canadian Sports Hall of Fame is a nod to the Maritimes as a breeding ground of Canadian ring talent. His spirited willingness, his honesty and his ability to please a fight crowd, are symbols of all the brave, tough Maritime scrappers from Tom Kelly to Tiger Warrington, Al and Lenny Sparks and the Durelles. In his fifteen years in the ring, Kid Howard met most of the leading lightweights of his day; of 108 recorded fights he won 77, lost 26 and drew 5. He was never knocked out. In only four bouts did he fail to go the distance – once when he was knocked down three times in one round and three times on cuts.

Howard was born in Terrace Bay but he grew up in Halifax, and it was there he began his boxing career, turning professional in 1945. The Kid was short for his weight, and thus took most of his opponents' punches on his head. He had a great capacity for absorbing punishment, and for holding on with dogged determination.

His reputation bloomed in 1949 when he beat Kid Lantz to win the Maritime title. He became the Canadian lightweight champion in 1954, beating Armand Savoie, the pride of Quebec, in a Halifax bout. In the next few years he fought most of the top-ranking lightweights, including Kenny Lane, Orlando Zulueta, Ralph Dupas and Brian Kelly.

Kid Howard never did quite make it in the international league; however, he had a bout with the South African champion, Willie Towell, for the British Empire championship, which he lost on a close decision. He also had a fight in Montreal with the French champion, Ray Famechon, who was a leading contender for the world featherweight title; but again Howard lost.

After several successful years in the Canadian ring and in the United States, Howard's skills began to decline. He retired once, and then tried a comeback, because, like so many other fighters who return, he needed the money. Against advice from his friends, he took on a match with Tommy Tibbs, a young boxer from Boston whom he had once defeated and the outcome was sad. Kid Howard was outclassed by Tibbs, but he went out fighting, still on his feet to the last bell. Howard hung up his gloves for good.

SAM LANGFORD, 1880-1956

If Sam Langford had been born with a white skin it is entirely possible he would have become one of the great heavyweight champions of all time. Sam was born black and in a long ring career never got a shot at a title match.

In 1908 Jack Johnson had beaten the Canadian Tommy Burns for the world heavyweight crown. Prejudice ran high. The public and managers were looking for a "white hope" to take the title back from the cheeky, high-living Johnson. Langford was in his prime during Johnson's reign; the Canadian fighter was forced to travel the world looking for matches, usually against bigger men and for small purses.

Sam Langford was born in Weymouth, NS, the son of a part-time sailor, part-time logger. After a beating by his father, Sam ran away at twelve to Boston where he worked for several years in odd jobs. One day, while working in a   saloon owned by Mike Foley, Sam got into a fight. Mike was impressed with the boy's skill and told him he could make money in the amateur fight game.

Mike Foley got me some battered old tights [Sam later recalled] and a pair of gloves and in my first fight, there's me and a Scotch fellah. I knock him out and I get a watch that I can hock for thirty dollars. I fight a couple more times and then one day Mike says, "Sam, do you know a fellah named Joe Woodman?" I say no and Mike says this fellah's a druggist who's interested in fighters and he wants to see me. So I go, and Woodman says, "You got no business fightin' amateurs. I know where you can get some money." That's all I wanted to hear. I became a pro and Woodman became my manager.

It was 1902 and Langford started off as a lightweight at 132 pounds. He grew through the welterweight and middleweight divisions and, according to Woodman, his best fighting weight was 172 pounds – "at seventy-two he'd have eaten Joe Louis." His judgment of distance was uncanny. According to a Boston boxing writer, "he would glide out in a crouch and when his opponent led, he'd move just a fraction and let the blow graze his head. And he could hit like a terror with both hands." The Marquis of Queensberry, son of boxing's patron, said of Langford: "Excepting only Johnson, no heavyweight in the world could have stood up against the Boston Tar Baby in a finish fight. A freak was this amazing Negro – fourteen stone of whipcord muscle and bone under a jet black skin – a neck as big as another man's thigh, a chest like a barrel, arms so grotesquely long he could scratch his ankles without stooping – and he stood five-foot-four in his bare feet.

148

But it was his reach – eighty-four inches – that made him the devastating fighter that he unquestionably was; in a word – a human gorilla."

Langford had need of all the skill and cunning he could muster. Black athletes were not accepted. Few managers would put up a white boy against an opponent like Langford. When Georges Carpentier was lightweight champion he refused to meet Langford. The great middleweight champion, Stanley Ketchell, would not give Sam a title bout. Most of all Langford wanted a title bout with Jack Johnson; the two had met in 1906, before Johnson was heavyweight champion. Although Langford had taken a severe beating, he had weighed just 151 pounds to Johnson's 186. Johnson ducked Langford's attempts to corner him into another match. "On a good night Sam is just liable to beat me or make it close," Johnson said in 1914, "and what's the sense of that for the kind of money we'd draw."

In the main Langford had to fight other blacks. Invariably he got the worst of physical odds. He fought bouts with Sam McVey, who weighed 195 pounds, Joe Jeanette and Harry Wills, both over 200. All through his years in the ring his purses were small. He recalled a fight in New Orleans: "The bout drew seventy-five dollars and I got a fourth of that. Most of the time I got a couple of hundred dollars."

Langford didn't make huge sums of money in his twenty-three years in the ring; one estimate of $300,000 seems high. He enjoyed spending on fancy clothes and booze. In his adopted home town of Boston a black man could rise above the crowd; Boston had been a stronghold of the abolitionist movement. Langford lived there with more dignity and acceptance than he would have found in other parts of the US or Canada.

Eventually the physical punishment of his hundreds of fights and high living were too much for Langford. In June 1917 he took on a 215-pound Kansan named Fred Fulton; Langford weighed 181 and was out of shape. He took a terrible pounding. By the sixth round Fulton was swarming all over him, with blows to his eyes, nose, jaw and stomach. At the start of the seventh Langford signalled that he could not continue. His left eye was completely closed; he never regained its sight.

Langford carried on for a few more years, a husk of the man he'd been. He quit in 1923 and soon became totally blind. Alone, destitute, he dropped from sight into the dark world of a New York ghetto. He was found in 1945 by New York boxing writer Al Laney, who started a fund for the fighter.

Through Laney's actions, Langford was able to live out the rest of his years at a Boston rest home, reliving his fights for any sportswriter who cared to listen.

EARL MCCREADY, 1908-

Earl McCready always wanted to be a doctor but he never realized that ambition. His other youthful dream – to fight and beat the world's best wrestlers – *did* come true. In one glorious year – 1930 – McCready won every amateur wrestling championship in Canada, the United States and the British Commonwealth.

Although he was born in Lansdowne, Ontario, Earl was raised on a Saskatchewan farm. By the time he was fourteen he weighed 200 pounds and was as strong as the proverbial ox. But the youth didn't know how best to use his strength and on the farm there was no one to teach him. A magazine advertisement promising instruction on "How to Handle Big Men with Ease" caught his eye and he sent off for the mail-order instructions which had been prepared by two of the greatest of all wrestlers, Frank Gotch and "Farmer" Burns. Earl practised diligently and tried out holds on the men of the threshing teams which came to the farm. He started high school in Regina and signed on with the wrestling class at the YMCA under a former Saskatchewan wrestling cham-

Sports Hall of Fame

149

pion, Dan Matheson, as the team's coach.

In 1926, although completely inexperienced in competitive wrestling, McCready represented Regina at the Amateur Athletic Union meet at New Westminster, BC. He won the Canadian heavyweight championship by beating Charlie Strack of Oklahoma Agricultural and Mechanical College. The Oklahomans were impressed with McCready and persuaded him to wrestle for their school. McCready still hadn't forgotten his dream of medicine and figuring the Oklahoma offer might be his last chance at a college education, accepted. In four years at Oklahoma he won every intercollegiate match as well as successfully defending his Canadian heavyweight title. He was national US collegiate heavyweight champion in 1928, 1929 and 1930 and US national amateur champion in 1930. His record has never been equalled.

McCready was also a member of the unbeatable Canadian team at the 1930 British Empire Games in Hamilton, Ontario, and won the gold medal in the heavyweight division to complete Canada's clean sweep of seven gold medals in the wrestling events.

By that time he had gone as far as he could in the amateur field, so he turned pro in 1930, and began touring the world in search of opponents. He made thirteen trips to Australia and New Zealand, three to England, and a couple to South America. He was a contender for the heavyweight title, and met most of the famous champions of the day, including Strangler Lewis, Jim Browning and Dick Shikat. At the peak of his career in 1932 he met champion Jim Londos, the "Golden Greek," in New York, but was unable to defeat the master.

After twenty-five years as a professional McCready retired from wrestling and became a masseur. He had obtained his degree in physical education from Oklahoma in 1930 so it was natural that he should turn his attention to physical fitness in his adopted home, Seattle. In 1966 his left leg had to be amputated as a result of osteomyelitis, but that did not put an end to his active life. In no time he was fitted with an artificial leg, and opened a steam bath and massage parlour in his home. He still gives much of his time to advising and coaching young people, particularly members of the local high school's wrestling and football teams. He is understandably proud of the fact that he is the only Canadian to be elected to both the American and Canadian Sports Halls of Fame.

JIMMY MCLARNIN, 1907-

Canada's most successful fighter was a baby-faced Irishman from Vancouver named Jimmy McLarnin. During his thirteen years in the ring he twice won the welterweight title; and he probably met and defeated more champions or future champions than any other fighter. McLarnin earned something like one-half million dollars from his fights, and saved most of it; when he retired he had enough money to keep him comfortably for the rest of his life. McLarnin retired in 1936 – at the ripe old age of twenty-nine.

What was it about the scrappy little fighter that thrilled fans and made him one of the most popular boxers in New York during the depression? Perhaps the explanation lies in McLarnin's own philosophy: "A boxer must be made. He cannot be born. Even if he is born as strong as an elephant, as brave as a lion and as swift as a gazelle – and I wasn't – someone has to teach him to be a boxer. The learning has to come slow and hard and it's never finished."

McLarnin came to Canada from Ireland at the age of three, and the family moved to Vancouver when he was nine. There were twelve children in the McLarnin family, and while they were not poor, they seldom had much to spare. Jimmy recalled that his mother gave the children a strict Methodist upbringing that helped him in his career. "I never had to be told that wine, women and song could ruin a boxer because I already . . . believed that wine, women and song could ruin anyone."

Pop Foster was the man who guided McLarnin's early career and the boy was about thirteen when he first caught the older man's eye. Foster was a former boxer working at the time as a part-time stevedore; he saw championship material in McLarnin.

Pop Foster worked McLarnin hard. He taught the boy that the best defense against an opponent was speed – with the feet, the hands and the head: "If they can't hit you they can't hurt you." He taught McLarnin basic ring strategy: "Box a fighter and fight a boxer." And he taught him to develop his left hand to such effect that fourteen years later McLarnin won the welterweight championship in the first round in a fight in which he didn't throw a single punch with his right hand.

When McLarnin turned sixteen, he and Pop headed for San Francisco, which was reckoned a good fight town. It was not easy to get a fight for the youthful, baby-faced McLarnin, and they weathered some thin times. Eventually they arranged a bout in Oakland in which McLarnin, at 108 pounds, went three rounds with the 145-pound Jimmy Duffy. The local promoters were impressed and Jimmy started getting four-round preliminary fights, for $50 a bout

at first and $200 later.

In 1924 they went to Los Angeles and McLarnin began to get main events fighting tough opponents. In 1928 Pop Foster decided McLarnin was ready to conquer New York. On 24 February McLarnin fought Sid Terris at Madison Square Garden before a capacity crowd, and knocked him out in the first round. This fight established him as the Irish hero and set the pattern for McLarnin's future success in New York – the Irish boy matched against Jewish boy. Irish and Jewish fight fans followed the bouts avidly and packed the garden to see McLarnin take on a variety of Jewish opponents including Ruby Goldstein, Al Singer, Benny Leonard and Barney Ross.

Sammy Mandell was the reigning lightweight champion when the two met for a title bout in May 1928. McLarnin was completely outclassed and could barely find Mandell, let alone hit him. This defeat rankled and they met again for a rematch at Chicago in November 1929. This time McLarnin took the measure of his opponent. He worked inside on Mandell's body and slowed him down before he began pounding blows to Mandell's head. He was awarded the decision in ten rounds, but by 1929 McLarnin had outgrown the lightweight mdivision, and it was not a championship fight. As Pop said, "You licked the right fighter at the wrong time."

In 1930 McLarnin met Bill Petrolle at the garden. Petrolle was a bustling fighter who liked to work at close quarters; but for once Jimmy ignored Pop's advice and instead of boxing Petrolle he decided to try for a fast knockout. McLarnin broke his hand on Petrolle's head in the second round and although he kept pounding away, he took terrible punishment. Petrolle was awarded the victory after ten rounds. After a rest of six months McLarnin met Petrolle twice more, and these times made no mistake, beating him in New York in May and August of 1931.

With these successes to his credit, McLarnin got a championship match with welterweight holder, Young Corbett III. Corbett, a big, strong left-hander, came out in the first round pounding McLarnin's ribs with his left and throwing lefts to the head. But McLarnin had noticed from earlier fights that when Corbett threw his left he dropped his right a little, so McLarnin countered with a left to Corbett's chin. It worked; Corbett dropped to the floor for a count of nine. McLarnin knocked him down twice more and Corbett was counted out at 2:37 of the first round. After ten years as a professional fighter McLarnin had won his first world title.

He kept it for a year. In May 1934, before 65,000 fans in New York, he defended the title against Barney Ross, and lost on a split decision after a gruelling fifteen rounds that left McLarnin exhausted. He took on Ross in a rematch in September and in that fight McLarnin was awarded the decision, in what the Toronto *Globe* reporter described as "a close, desperate and punishing fight." In the third fight between the two men at the New York Polo Grounds in May 1935, Ross recaptured the title, in a decisive fifteen-round verdict. There were no knockdowns but the fight developed into a savage exchange of punches.

A year later McLarnin retired. After thirteen years in the ring he had achieved a record of sixty-three wins in seventy-seven professional fights. In 1950 Canada's sportswriters named him the nation's boxer of the half-century.

BERT SCHNEIDER, 1897-

Canada's boxing team in the 1920 Antwerp Olympics was a strong one – members came home with one bronze, two silver and one gold medals. Curiously, the Canadian gold medal was won by an American citizen, Bert Schneider.

Schneider was born in Cleveland. The family moved to Canada in 1906 when his father, a metallurgist, came to work for a Montreal steel plant. Young Bert attended the Commercial and Technical High School on Sherbrooke Street and it was there he got his first boxing lessons. Bert was slim in the legs but his arms and shoulders were well-muscled; he developed into a scrappy welterweight with a solid left. He was fast on his feet but preferred to trade punches rather than dance about feinting with an opponent.

When the war came in 1914, Schneider tried to enlist, but he was turned down because his father was German by birth and he himself had been born in the United States. After a few years in the merchant navy (and a short spell in an English jail as an alien) Schneider returned to Montreal and once more became involved in athletics. He later described how his boxing career began: "Some of the fellows joined the Casquette Club for boxing and I went along. There I got a lot of my training from Gene Brosseau, the classiest boxer around Montreal. When the Casquette Club broke up a few of us joined the boxing classes at the Montre-

Sports Hall of Fame

152

al AAA. I won the welter championship of the MAAA and boxing for them, went on to win the city championship and then the championship of Canada twice. I never lost a bout as an amateur."

Schneider had no thought of competing in the Olympics and was therefore amazed to read in the Montreal *Star* the headline, "Schneider for the Olympics." As an American he did not consider himself eligible to represent Canada, and he had not even realized that boxing was an Olympic event. There had been a revival of interest in boxing with the first world war. It had lost some of its unsavoury reputation and came to be looked upon as a manly sport. Canada reflected this change in attitude; the training and encouragement Schneider and his fellow medal winners had received at home brought them international success.

At the Olympics Schneider had four winning bouts in three days. Several years after the Olympic triumph he turned professional but he never went far in the tough welterweight division. He quit in 1928 to join the US border patrol. When he retired in 1960 he returned to Pierrefonds, Quebec, with his wife, a Montreal girl he had met years before on the skating rink of the old MAAA.

JAMES TRIFUNOV, 1903-
Wrestling has been Jimmy Trifunov's whole life, first as Canadian amateur champion ten times over and later as administrator and coach of Canada's Olympic teams. When amateur wrestling hit the peak of its popularity in Canada after the first world war, Trifunov represented Canada in the Olympics of 1924, 1928 and 1932, winning a bronze medal in 1928.

Trifunov came to Canada from his native Serbia as a boy of seven and settled with his family on the Prairies. His father died in 1913, leaving the family nearly destitute, and his mother, two brothers and his sister all went to work; Jimmy, the youngest, stayed at school, adding his bit to the family income by taking on a paper route for the Regina *Post*. Unable to afford a bike, he walked five miles every morning delivering his papers before setting out on the three-quarter mile hike to school. It was excellent training for his future athletic career.

Jimmy got into wrestling almost by accident. He remembers:

"I was going around with some boys who were interested in boxing and it was natural for me to box. I was not very good, but I kept on, until one day in the YMCA gymnasium I saw two boys wrestling . . . Wrestling seemed so much easier than boxing that in a

short while I quit boxing and took up wrestling."

He joined the forty-member wrestling club at the Y and began serious training, but as the club did not have a coach, Jimmy had to teach himself. During the summer months Y activities moved outdoors and Jimmy took up baseball and joined the harrier club. He played a good game of basketball and started a running program – two to five miles every morning, even in winter – that stayed with him for the rest of his career.

Despite its lack of coaching, the Regina wrestling club was successful; in 1923 Trifunov was a member of the team that went to Winnipeg and won four Canadian championships out of seven classes. Since he was only five-foot-five and weighed about 120 pounds, he competed in the bamtamweight division.

The following year Trifunov was surprised as well as honoured to be selected for Canada's team for the 1924 Paris Olympics. It could, however, be a rather expensive honour for amateur athletes in those days since they had to pay all their own expenses, and as Jimmy was nearly broke at the time, 132 of his colleagues at the Regina *Leader-Post,* where he was then employed, contributed a dollar each to send him on his way.

The next four years were successful ones for Trifunov. He won the Canadian amateur bantamweight championship in 1925, and defended the title against all challengers in 1926, 1927 and 1928. In 1926, in New Westminster, BC, he also won the featherweight championship. The decision of the Olympic committee selectors not to invite him to be a member of the 1928 team was, therefore, all the more disappointing considering his Canadian successes. But once again his friends in Regina – and the Saskatchewan government – came to his aid. Six hundred dollars was raised for his fare to the games in Amsterdam, where Jimmy competed and had the satisfaction of bringing home the bronze medal in the bantamweight division.

The British Empire Games were held in Hamilton, Ontario, in 1930, and it was a momentous year for Canadian amateur wrestling. Canadian wrestlers took gold medals in all divisions, an achievement they have not been able to duplicate since. Jimmy Trifunov was the bantamweight winner, having gained a decisive victory over Joe Reid of England. In the first round neither man had been able to secure a fall but the bout was given to Trifunov, who had clinched the match in the second round by pinning Reid to the mat with an armlock and crotch-hold after nine minutes.

Jimmy Trifunov has been in the newspaper business all his life, first with the Regina *Leader-Post,* and for the past thirty-six years with the Winnipeg *Free Press.* During his entire working life Jimmy has also been involved with amateur wrestling, but after a bout of ill health in 1931, he gradually retired from active wrestling. The help and encouragement that Trifunov once received as a competitor he now passes on to the younger generation as an administrator. He coached Canada's Olympic team in 1952, 1956 and 1960, and was manager of the team for the British Commonwealth Games of 1954 and 1970. He has been a member of the YMCA for more than fifty years and chairman of the physical education department committee for many years. He is president of the Manitoba Wrestling Association and vice-president of the Canadian Amateur Wrestling Association. Amateur wrestling in Canada is greatly in Jimmy Trifunov's debt.

153

Horses

Chapter 6

In the 1850s the iron horse came to Canada. The steam engine was to melt forever the "ice and apathy" which had gripped Canadians for generations – or so predicted the engineer T. C. Keefer. The scattered colonies of British North America were to be tied together with a ribbon of steel and move forward together towards the boundless future that seemed to await them.

The iron horse was to accomplish miracles but the miracle of the iron horse itself was accomplished by manpower and horsepower – plain, old-fashioned, flesh-and-blood horsepower. The work gangs that pushed the roadbed through the granite of the Canadian Shield, across the endless miles of Prairie grass, through the treacherous passes of the Rockies were powered by that other horse, the real one. Supplies and food came in by horse, and survey parties on horseback ranged in advance of the railhead. When the railway spanned the Western provinces the settlers came by the thousands; their first purchase on the site of their new homestead was invariably a horse, the real kind.

As late as 1921 with Henry Ford's invention bidding fair to overtake the iron horse in popularity, there were still three and one-half million horses in Canada; today there are a mere 385 thousand. For every Canadian who remains an appreciative judge of horseflesh there are thousands who think the horse's natural place is late-night westerns on TV.

Curiously, while the horse population dwindles, sports involving the horse draw more spectators, represent a higher capital investment, and cut across a broader spectrum of so-

ciety than any other sport. Horsey sports fall into two categories: equestrianism and everything else from the Queen's Plate to polo.

Modern equestrian competition has three elements: dressage, the ancient art of guiding a trained animal through a complicated series of schooled movements; jumping; and the three-day event which combines elements of dressage and jumping with a stern cross-country challenge. Only in recent years have Canadians begun to crack the long-standing dominance of European and other American nations.

Excellence in this sport comes from horsemanship, fine animals, skilled training, a high level of competition and the kind of social environment suitable for its nurture. Though the military has made its contribution, that environment in Canada has been largely within the class traditionally associated with the hunt. Most Canadians, to put it with restraint, have regarded the hunt as an unnecessarily complicated way of slaying the miserable and unoffending fox, but among our wealthy and leisured there have always been some attracted to this elaborate and ritualistic importation.

Nineteenth century newspapers treated the hunt with faithful obsequiousness. The Montreal *Gazette* always began its hunt stories with a list of the upper-crust notables in attendance, and the Montreal Hunt Club would be congratulated "on the increasing interest taken, not only by our wealthy residents, but by their sons." Hunt descriptions were unvaryingly rhapsodic – splendid turnouts of hounds, horses and "goodly arrays of pinks," sumptuous entertainment, stirring descriptions of the chase through the woodlots of uncomprehending farmers, with the bush magically transformed into "coverts," and then, the kill: "Miss Arnton receiving the brush, which was a splen-

When horses were the main mode of travel in Canada, sights such as the huntsman and the hounds were common. *Opposite* **the Montreal Hunt Club of 1891.**

did one, its late owner being a large dog fox; Mr. A. Galarneau took the pate." Every urban centre of any social pretension had its hunt club, and expatriate Englishmen brought the hunt even to the baldheaded Prairie. Near Rapid City, Manitoba, a Mr. Munn brought in eleven hounds from Moosomin and began hunting in 1887; later he bought the pack of a former lieutenant-governor of British Columbia, "hounds of the purest blood, being bred from such packs as the Badminton, Lord Lonsdale's and the duke of Bedford's." Meanwhile, down in southwestern Alberta, a tightly-knit society of English ranchers not only hunted, but in 1889 at Pincher's Creek, began to play polo.

Steeplechasing was the first offshoot from the hunt clubs; the earliest recorded race was at Toronto in 1843. Show jumping came later; by the late nineteenth century it was a feature of such large fairs as the Dominion and Industrial Exhibition, the ancestor of the CNE, and horsemen competed for the D'Alton McCarthy and Earl of Minto Cups. By the time of the first world war, a number of prominent riders and breeders had emerged; Sir Adam Beck, father of Ontario Hydro, was one. Master of the London Hunt Club for many years, he was a noted judge and rider, and loaned two of his mounts to Canada's first international equestrian team when it competed at London, England, in 1909.

At the end of the war, Sir Clifford Sifton, long a power in the Ottawa hunt, imported the French stallion Matelot along with several English brood mares, to improve the breed in Ontario. Further signs of interest in bettering the quality of horses were the formation of the Canadian Hunter and Light Horse Improvement Society (1926) and the beginnings of a stud book in the 1930s.

Competition was improving as well. In 1922 the Royal Agricultural Winter Fair launched its international horse show, and Canadian riders competed through the 1920s and 1930s against teams from the United States, Europe and Latin America. In the late thirties Harry Price, the founder of the Canadian Horse Show Association, became the driving force behind equestrianism; the Canadian Equestrian Association was established as a section of the CHSA.

The groundwork of the interwar years came to fruition after 1945. A national organization and excellent training by Major Anatol Pieregorodski, a Polish cavalryman who had been a member of his country's Olympic team in 1936, brought Canada its first medal, a bronze in the three-day event, at the 1956 Olympics. From that point on there has been a steady improvement in Canadian performances abroad. In 1960 W. Denis Whitaker was appointed chairman of the Canadian equestri-

an team, training and competition patterns were further regularized, and a somewhat less haphazard selection system established. The victory of the Canadian team at the Mexico City Olympics in 1968 may have astonished the international set, but it was the culmination of a steady improvement in Canadian equestrianism that had its roots deep in the nineteenth century. But despite the equestrian centres springing up near many Canadian cities, the sport remains one for the few. The expense of horses, upkeep, clothing, tack, instzuction and transportation are beyond most Canadians.

Horseracing has a much more complicated public image than equestrianism. It, too, has been the sport of the wealthy, it is drenched in tradition, it has historic and beautiful tracks, and in the Queen's Plate the oldest continuously run stakes race in North America. Yet it has its sordid side. Behind the upper-class veneer, the beautiful animals, the excitement, flash and colour of racing, there is the rich sub.culture of the backstretch; the trainers, the jockeys, the grooms, exercise boys and hot walkers, shading off to the hangers-on, the shills, the touts, the bookmakers and even shadier types looking constantly for an angle. Racing is about pounding hooves and improving the breed, but it is also about gambling and purses; Canadian racing history has to do both with the development of breeding and rac-

Canada's first equestrian medal in Olympic competition was a bronze in 1956, won by a team coached by Anatol Pieregorodski, a former star with the Polish cavalry and Olympic team.

156

The flailing hooves of flying horses have always created excitement among Canadians. *Above,* **a closely grouped collection of horses and riders take a steeplechase water jump in 1901.**

ing and with the unceasing search of the racing industry for respectability in the face of attacks upon it by moral reformers, governments and the betting public.

At the time of Confederation horseracing was already well-established, not only at Toronto's sandy Carleton track and Montreal's Blue Bonnets, but on far-away Beacon Hill at Victoria and on dozens of dusty little ovals throughout central Canada and the Maritimes. No one meeting or track dominated; indeed, when Barrie, Ontario, opened its one-mile track in 1872, it was thought "better than anything hitherto attempted in the province."

The history of the Queen's Plate and the Ontario Jockey Club reflects many of the themes that persist in Canadian horseracing; they are miniature vignettes of the history of Canadian racing. In the early years, the plate was shifted from track to track. Its first recognized winner was Don Juan, at Toronto's Carleton track in 1860. He was owned by the James White stable of Bronte and Milton; White horses won four of the first nine plates. The

1865 winner was a steed named Free Press Bob; on closer examination the judges identified him as a ringer who was in reality Limerick Boy, and disqualified him. The quality of early plate winners is suspect also: Trumpeter, who won the 1875 race at Woodstock, was eight years old and still a maiden.

Repeated scandals, a desire to give racing a better name and a wish to improve the breed lay behind the formation of the Ontario Jockey Club at a meeting at the Queen's Hotel in Toronto in August 1881. Its chairman was Colonel Casimir Gzowski, brilliant engineer, aide-de-camp to Queen Victoria and later to be knighted. The first directors were as overpoweringly respectable as their chairman. They included J. D. Dickson, descendant of a Niagara peninsula clan which had been part of the Family Compact and had pioneered racing in that area; William Hendrie from Hamilton, a cartage, banking and railroad millionaire; H. Quetton St. George of Toronto, descended from a French royalist emigré who had first come to Upper Canada during the French revolution; and T. C. Patteson, Eton and Oxford graduate who since coming to Canada in 1858 had played international cricket and through the benevolence of Sir John A. Macdonald had been successively assistant provincial secretary, edi-

157

tor of the Toronto *Mail,* and postmaster of Toronto. Gzowski's announced aim was "to lift horseracing out of the mire," and he was satisfied that "if the club was placed in the management of gentlemen of position, quite as attractive meetings might be held in Toronto as in the United States."

The OJC rented scenic Woodbine Park, east of Toronto, and held its first race meeting there in September 1881. Two years later Gzowski engineered the attendance at the Queen's Plate of the Governor-General the Marquis of Lorne and his wife, the Princess Louise, a social master stroke that fixed the running of the plate permanently at Toronto by royal fiat. Soon after, Canadian racing gained its first dominant figure. In 1891 a horse identified only as Terror Colt, after his sire, won the plate and was promptly re-named Victorious by his owner, Joseph E. Seagram of Waterloo. For ten of the next eleven years, Seagram horses won the plate.

The patriarch of Canada's foremost racing family at the turn of the century was Joseph E. Seagram, of Waterloo. Seagram horses won twenty Queen's Plates between 1891 and 1935.

Michael Burns Photography

Seagram bought his first racehorse the year Don Juan won the plate; he was able to buy more – many more – when, in 1883, he bought out the Waterloo distillery he had joined thirteen years before. He set out to enjoy his wealth as diligently as he had acquired it. Year after year he imported English thoroughbred yearlings and mares. By the turn of the century his stables housed a hundred or more horses under training, and his black and yellow silks were known on many North American tracks.

The Seagram family won twenty Queen's Plates between 1891 and 1935. No other stable has come close. T. C. Patteson, one of the best turf writers we have had, explained what the Seagram achievement meant. "The ordinary farmer has no real chance to have his horse broken, trained or ridden in a manner that will enable him to vie with such establishments as those of Mr. Seagram, Mr. Hendrie or Mr. Dyment. The days when Mr. James White of Bronte trained winners of the Queen's Plate in a forty-acre field as full of pine stumps as a man's hand is of fingers are gone." The advent of the millionaire-owner had changed the sport. "Racing and yachting are princely games," Patteson wrote, "and it is of no use for a lad to harbour a champagne thirst if he has only a lager beer pocketbook." Patteson knew that racing form was established by bloodlines (all thoroughbreds racing today are descended from the Byerly Turk, the Godolphin Arabian and the Darley Arabian; most trace their lineage back to Eclipse) and that crossbreeding with less pure American stock was to be avoided. In the costly lottery of racehorse breeding "the odds against Canada producing a crackerjack . . . are tremendous, but so were they against the production of a Hanlan." Even in the 1890s it cost the big breeders like Seagram about $1,000 per head to support their stables.

The glory of victory wasn't enough, however. Patteson knew that big breeders and owners, even if they were "banking and brewing barons with money to burn," had to have some rough balancing of the books, and that depended on purses and stud fees. High stud fees depended upon a winning record; purses depended upon track attendance and betting. Betting brought race track operators, even eminently respectable ones like the OJC, squarely up against the considerable capacity for moral outrage latent in the puritan Canadian soul. The characteristic Canadian, when lectured by moral authority on the evils of gambling, is apt to hang his head, glaze his eyes and shuffle his feet; organized goodness has always cowed him. But call gambling by any other name, or suggest that its purpose is supported officially or semi-officially by church or state, and the characteristic Canadian will use the milk money to support raffles, bingos, the Irish Sweepstake or the Olympic Lottery.

At the turn of the century, the fashion in which bookmakers operated at Canadian tracks was enough to make even the $2 bettor pause. They shortened the odds in their favour, ran their own horses under others' names, and fixed races by bribing jockeys and trainers. By 1906, racing had been banned in all but four states; in 1910 New York banned betting at the track. Bookies and crooked owners flooded into Canada. A Supreme Court decision had already forbidden bookies to operate booths at the track. When they were then prosecuted for taking bets on the run, the secretary of the Ontario Jockey Club virtuously declared to the court that "the club had no connection direct or indirect with the betting carried on nor was it aware that any bets were made on its grounds." In 1910, by one vote, parliament saved racing's skin by banning bookies. Betting, now administered directly by the tracks, became more honest with the introduction of pari-mutuel betting in 1912, followed by the automatic totalisator (first used on a North American track at Colwood Park, Victoria, in 1924) and the ticket-vending machine.

Jim Coleman's delightful *Hoofprint on My Heart* shows that such reforms touched only some of racing's seamiest problems. In the interwar period, stimulants were widely used (the trainers who used them were called "chemists" along shedrow); "animal painters" produced ringers; horses were charged with batteries. Trying to make ends meet on the leaky-roof circuit, horsemen would instruct their jockeys to "pull" their mounts; Coleman knew one jockey reputedly so strong he could stop an elephant going for a bale of hay. The depression, sharply reducing cash flow at the tracks, tended to heighten abuses, and Canadian racing hit a low point. R. S. McLaughlin, Harry Hatch and the Seagrams did most of their racing in the US.

Many of Coleman's stories deal with the bad old days of racing in the West. When famous jockeys like Johnny Longden and George Woolf began their careers, racing in their native Alberta was a matter of barnstorming from fair to fair. It was R. L. "Jim" Speers who began in the early twenties to organize what became a Prairie racing empire, stretching from Winnipeg to Calgary. A Toronto boy, he went West at eighteen, got his start in the grain and feed business in Saskatchewan, and eventually came to control tracks or meetings in Winnipeg, Regina, Saskatoon, Calgary and Edmonton. From his own breeding farm in Manitoba came many of the horses that raced on Western tracks; by the mid-thirties he had replaced R. S. McLaughlin as the country's largest breeder. After the second world war two wealthy Albertans, Max Bell and Frank McMahon, joined company with Johnny Longden in one of North America's most successful racing, breeding and training operations.

By this time much had been done to clean up racing, both by governments and racing operators. Saliva tests, film patrols, provincial racing commissions, and knowledgeable racing secretaries and stewards all helped. It was at this juncture that Canadian racing became an industry as well as a sport. The man who did it was E. P. Taylor, who found in racing the same kind of challenge to judgment and management skinl that he enjoyed in the world of finance.

Taylor bought his first thoroughbred in 1936. In 1973 the US Thoroughbred Racing Association named him its man of the year. Between 1960 and 1970, Taylor was annually the top race-winning breeder in North America. From his Windfields Farm stable, or from his National Stud Farm at Oshawa (formerly R. S. McLaughlin's Parkwood Stables) came fifteen Queen's Plate winners, and such magnificent horses as Northern Dancer, winner of the Kentucky Derby and the Preakness, Nijinsky, a wonder horse on European tracks, and many others. From 1953 to 1973, Taylor was president of the Ontario Jockey Club, and during these years rationalized horseracing by closing down several old tracks, and using their charters to concentrate racing days at a re-built Fort Erie and at the new Woodbine plant at Malton. With longer racing seasons, the crowds and handles rose, better horses were attracted by higher purses, and owners, breeders and government were happy. Since the OJC had also acquired a substantial interest in harness racing, off-track betting seemed the only cloud on the horizon.

Great though Taylor's contribution to thoroughbred racing was, there was one development he could not control: the amazing increase in public favour for harness racing in the 1960s. In Quebec, historic Blue Bonnets, cradle of thoroughbred racing, was losing out to Richelieu Raceway; Hervé Filion was licking J. Louis Levesque. Even in Ontario the "jugheads" seemed to be taking over. During the 1960s, while attendance at thoroughbred meetings remained fairly steady at a little less than two million a year, harness racing attendance rose from less than one million to about three million. In 1962, there were 196 thoroughbred racing days in the provincial calendar and 270 for standardbreds; by 1972 the figures were 197 and 1,055 respectively. The betting figures were even more extraordinary: in 1961, $89 million was wagered at the tracks on thoroughbreds, and a mere $15 million on trotters and pacers, but by 1971, while thoroughbred betting had risen to $115 million, harness racing recorded a staggering $177 million handle at the tracks.

This prodigious growth in harness racing and betting has taken place almost without public attention. No cries of outrage from the traditional enemy of gambling, the pulpit, have been heard. The battle between the good and the immoral seems all but ended; over the past generation social attitudes towards gambling have changed immeasurably, signalled by the legalization of lotteries. Only a religious revival of positively volcanic dimensions could reverse the movement of social mores sufficiently to menace once more the racing industry and the betting that sustains it. So long as the public thirst for wagering continues, the only danger to the industry would appear to be from illegal practices such as betting rings and fixing races.

The standardbred horse (recognized as a distinct breed in 1879) was the product of the breeding of thoroughbreds to the North American road horse; the strong pacers of French Canada contributed heavily to the breed. While the doings of equine aristocrats and their owners got the ink in the city press, most country fairgrounds, whether in the Maritimes, Quebec or Ontario in the nineteenth and earlier twentieth centuries, had an oval for the trots. In the winter, harness horses raced on the harbour ice at Charlottetown, on the St. Lawrence, or on Ashbridge's Bay at Toronto. It was a country sport and a poor man's game. But precisely because low costs made it possible for thousands of individual owner-drivers to engage in it, it was difficult to regulate, and gained an evil reputation. There were good reasons for "the prejudice that has existed against trotting tracks," as the Montreal *Gazette* observed in the 1870s.

For a long time the tendency was for Canadian harness-horse men to affiliate with stronger American organizations. In 1884, for example, a Canadian circuit of the US National Trotting Association was created, comprising centres in Ontario and Quebec. An American paper suggested that now the Canadians had eliminated "the predatory horde," Canadian tracks offered "a very desirable opening for many of our horsemen who fear their trotters will not have enough speed to cope with the many who flock to the June meetings at home."

Today's situation is that Maritime harness racing is regulated by the US Trotting Association, while the Canadian Trotting Association governs the rest of the country. And the worm has turned. Not only have the standardbreds conquered our cities, but Canadian-bred trotters and pacers, produced by such breeders as the mammoth empire of the Armstrong brothers at Brampton, and Canadian drivers like Hervé Filion, Keith Waples, Joe O'Brien and Dan McKinnon, have taken their place with the best south of the line.

162

Biographies

HERVÉ FILION, 1940-

The thoroughbred may still be the king of the racecourse. But standardbred racing has come a long way from the country fairs and rural surroundings of its humble origins. It is big business nowadays. And no one in Canada has made more out of the sport of harness racing than Hervé Filion.

Since he first won the championship in 1968 with an unprecedented 407 winners in one season, Filion has dominated harness racing in North America. In 1970 he drove 486 winners, and topped that in 1971 by driving 543. In 1972 his score was an amazing 605 wins, with a total of almost $2.5 million in purses. To date, Hervé Filion has driven more than 4,000 winners with total earnings of more than $10 million. That's not bad for a farm boy from Angers, Quebec, who started working at the tracks when he was thirteen.

There were eight boys in the Filion family of ten, and Hervé's father struggled to keep the family together. The boys, like their father, were crazy about horses but Hervé was less crazy about school – he preferred to spend his time in the barns grooming the horses. Of those early years Hervé has said: "I quit school in the fifth grade. Instead I went to school at the harness track. I watched Ken Waples drive a horse every chance I got. He taught me how to lift the sulky and put it in a hole without bothering the horse's head. I also saw how he rated his horse, and how he seemed to make it feel like it could win."

Filion learned Waple's lessons well, and has made the skills peculiarly his own. His incredible ability to move the sulky two feet sideways to fill a gap in the field has been dubbed the "Hervé hop." Filion drives every horse to win, and even with an indifferent animal, his driving skill can be worth a length or two in a mile race. As Filion puts it: "I use every tactic available. I'm not afraid to make a move at any time in a race. I ask my horse for everything he has. Horses will fool you sometimes, giving you more than you think they can. But the animal won't do that unless you give him a chance."

It is this determination to win, and a consuming love of harness racing that has brought Filion to the peak. But he has had his problems along the way. In the early years he was suspended on Canadian and US tracks nine times between 1957 and 1964 for various infractions. And in 1965, when he decided to invade the lucrative US circuits in a big way, he was handed a twelve-day suspension at Liberty Bell Park, Philadelphia, following a losing drive on a horse named Roy Abbe, for "insufficient effort." Looking at his previous record, the US Trotting Association decided this was one violation too many, so they revoked Filion's licence indefinitely. Filion was stunned; it could have meant the end of a career that had only barely started.

He went to Judge Milton Taylor, who had given him the original twelve-day suspension, and pleaded for another chance. Taylor was convinced and persuaded the USTA to restore his licence.

Filion made the most of his second chance. He moved to Brandywine racetrack in Delaware, and started to attract the fans' notice. His successes got him better horses; he was on his way up. Two years later, in 1967, he posted a total of 256 wins, the third best in North America. Then in 1968 he broke the world record with a total of 407 wins, easily topping the previous best of 386 held by West Germany's Eddie Freundt.

His progress since then has been marked with one long string of shattered records. By the end of 1972, he led all other North American drivers in wins for five consecutive seasons. He has been named driver of the year by the Harness Tracks of America each year since 1969, and was Canadian Harness Horseman of the Year in 1970. At the first world harness racing championship, held on North American tracks in 1970, Filion won with the final race of the seven-day meet, beating such strong challengers as

Alexandra Studio

Sholty and Dancer of the US, Kevin Newman of Australia and Eddie Freundt of West Germany. The following year Filion won the International Drivers' Invitational Stakes at Sydney, Australia.

In August 1970 Hervé Filion made harness racing history at Brandywine by driving five winners, each running the mile in less than two minutes.

Filion's greatest ambition is to own and drive a real champion. But he knows you can't buy a champion, you have to train and develop one. Filion now owns a thirty-five acre farm at Lachine near Montreal. And it is there, at Capital Hill Farms, that he is raising some of the best yearlings in the business. He is determined to make the name of Filion remembered in harness racing. And at the rate he is going, he just might do that.

JOHNNY LONGDEN, 1910-

Opinions may differ over which was the greatest American-born thoroughbred of all time. But no one will deny that Johnny Longden was one of the greatest jockeys in the history of racing. In a career stretching from 1927 to his retirement in 1966, Longden rode 6,032 winners, a record for the time. He was the first North American jockey to ride 4,000 winners, and in 1956 he rode winner No. 4,871, beating the record established by the famous English jockey, Sir Gordon Richards. When he retired at the age of fifty-six, Longden had won most of the highest honours of the racing world, including the Triple Crown in 1943 aboard Count Fleet.

Longden's greatness came not only from his determination and hard work but also from the tremendous rapport he had with his mounts – what he describes as "feel." "I can talk to a horse and he can talk to me – through my hands. I can tell exactly how my horse feels, how he is striding, how much stamina he has left – through my hands."

Longden's style of riding was unconventional, and perhaps not always elegant. One Australian commentator once said he looked like a frog on a log. He was also known as "the Pumper," from his habit of pumping his horse in close finishes. Longden's agent, Basil Smith, has explained Johnny's style:

> Longden has won more nose finishes than any other jock because of his pumping style in the stretch. He has very short legs. His riding style is more of a stand-up than a sitting crouch. He raises and lowers his body in rhythm with the horse's stride and at the finish he raises up, pumping his arms vigorously in order to get more out of a horse, hand riding his mount for that last effort.

Alexandra Studio

Johnny Longden was born in England but came with his family to Canada when he was two. They settled at Taber, in Southern Alberta, where his father worked in the coal mines. There were six children in the family and money was scarce. When Johnny was ten he became a summer cowboy, riding herd on neighbours' cows which wandered the unfenced Prairie. He left school at thirteen and went to work in the mines, digging coal from seven in the morning until four PM for one and one-quarter dollars a day. On weekends he attended local fairs; an Alberta horseman, Spud Murphy, hired Johnny to ride quazterhorses. Longden rode in the Roman races (one foot on the bare back of each of two horses), and in the summer of 1924 won fourteen races. The following spring he went to work at Spud Murphy's ranch, galloping horses for thirty-five dollars a month, room and board. He continued riding at local fairs, but in 1927 he decided to venture further afield and pay a visit to Salt Lake City. His family were devout Mormons and he wanted to visit the mother city of the faith; he also managed to time his arrival to coincide with the thoroughbred racing season. At the racing stables at Salt Lake City Johnny made the acquaintance of a big black gelding named Hugo K. Asher. The horse was a good racer but with an unfortunate dislike for carrying a jockey on his back, and therefore his owner was willing to give Johnny five dollars to ride him in the race. Johnny accepted, and won, his first victory in thoroughbred racing. From then on he knew racing was to be his life; he would never go back to the drudgery of the coal mines.

In the beginning it was hard. But in 1928 Longden met up with a trainer from the state of Washington named "Sleepy" Armstrong who was looking for a regular jockey. He took Longden on, and together they toured the Prairie circuit in Canada. Longden said that meeting Sleepy was the best thing that ever happened to him, that Sleepy taught him just about everything he knew about riding. One thing Longden learned was to get up early, a habit he has maintained all his life. All through his career he has been out at the track by 6:30 AM exercising his horses, learning their idiosyncracies; the knowledge stood him in good stead when he rode them in the afternoons.

From the Prairie circuit in summer, Longden moved to Mexico and California in the winter. Things began to improve; he won more races, and he got better mounts. By the end of the thirties he was winning some of the big races – the Brooklyn Handicap, the Champagne Stakes, the Louisiana Derby and the Arlington Handicap. But it was in 1942 that Longden met the horse that was to be the greatest mount he ever had, Count Fleet. The colt was then a two-year-old, strong, fast, but headstrong. Longden set about training him. No other jockey ever rode Count Fleet, in his morning workouts, or in his races – fifteen is a two-year-old and six when he was three. It was as a three-year-old in 1943 that Count Fleet showed his true worth, sweeping to victory in the Kentucky Derby, the Preakness and the Belmont Stakes, the coveted Triple Crown of racing.

The Kentucky Derby is probably the one race more than any other that a jockey wants to win. Yet Longden remembmrs the 1950 San Juan Capistrano Handicap as probably the most gruelling and most satisfying of his career. He was riding Noor against one of the finest of all American thoroughbreds, Citation. Citation was leading the field when Noor caught up with him at the half-mile post. For the last half-mile the two horses were going flat out, nose to nose, Noor getting under the wire a lip ahead of Citation in one of the most thrilling finishes in modern racing. The race set a new American record for the mile and three-quarters.

In his years of racing Longden has had his share of accidents. He has been thrown, kicked, rolled on by frightened horses. He has had a broken back (and won a race with two broken vertebrae), a broken collarbone, broken legs. Five times doctors told him his racing days were over, and each time he fought back. In 1955 it looked as if arthritis would force him to give up; but with the aid of expert medical advice and determination, Johnny Longden went on to have one of the best years of his whole career in 1956.

When Longden retired in 1966, he inevitably turned to training, and here also he has been successful. He is still out early at the stables, giving the horses their early morning workout, and bringing to this job all his years of experience and understanding.

DANIEL MACKINNON, 1876-1964

Dan MacKinnon first drove a sulky in 1890. He was still training and driving his pacers and trotters at the age of eighty-five, winning several races with his pacer Blue Skylark in 1962, his last season on the track. In a long and distinguished career, as soldier, fox farmer, businessman and sportsman, Colonel Dan was a familiar figure on all Maritime race tracks. He was the father of harness racing in the East, and made his native PEI truly "the Kentucky of Canada." It was fitting, therefore, that the first harness racer, and also the first Prince Edward Islander, to be elected to the Hall of Fame should have been Colonel Dan.

Dan MacKinnon was born in the village of Highland, a few miles from Charlottetown. He was orphaned at the age of ten and had no further formal schooling. He registered in a mail-order course in pharmacy and successfully wrote the Nova Scotia Pharmaceutical Society examinations; at twenty he became the first registered pharmacist in PEI.

Early in his life he became interested in sports. He played football, and was a champion runner, winning the Maritime title for the one mile in 1896, and retaining it in

165

1897 and 1898. In 1901 he joined the 4th Regiment Canadian Artillery. As a gunner he was a member of the Canadian team that won the Londonderry Cup at Petawawa in 1907, and he led the Canadian heavy artillery team that beat the British team in 1912. He was a crack rifle shot, and was a member of the PEI team at the Dominion Rifle Association meets on several occasions.

He went overseas in 1916 and served in Europe with the 36th Battery, CFA. He was awarded the DSO for outstanding service on the Somme, took part in the Canadian defense of Vimy Ridge, and entered Mons with his battery on the morning of 11 November 1918. For his gallantry at Passchendaele he was awarded the French Croix de Guerre.

Back in Canada after the war, he retired from active militia service in 1923, and was appointed aide-de-camp to the governor-general.

His commercial activities proliferated. He moved into the commercial fox farming business, and during the 1920s and 1930s became one of the world's foremost breeders. He ran a school of silver fox farming at Charlottetown, which attracted students from as far afield as Norway and Sweden. He owned the Charlottetown *Guardian* (the largest daily paper in the province) for more than twenty years, until he sold it in the late 1940s, and contributed a weekly column on harness racing called "Down the Back Stretch."

Harness racing became the consuming interest in Colonel Dan's life. It was an interest that had started in his youth, and he bought his first horse in 1890. In his long career he owned and trained seventy-eight horses, and campaigned them all over the Maritimes and the US. He started racing in 1912 and one of his best driving performances was in 1915 when, in a twelve-day period, he won fifteen heats of sixteen starts with his pacer Helen R. In 1931 at Charlottetown he scored a surprise victory with his pacer Volo Rico over Eula H., an American-owned horse that had been undefeated. His horse, The Yank, set a world record for ice racing at Mount Clemens, Michigan, in 1923. In the years 1936-8, Colonel Dan campaigned with his two trotters, Heatherbelle and Harvest Melody, and won consistently on Maritime tracks. Through the years he had victories with many of his horses – Our Peggy, Dick C., Colonel Aubrey and The British Soldier. Even in 1959, at the age of eighty-two, Colonel Dan was driving two horses regularly, the trotter Windy June and the pacer Stalag Hanover.

Colonel Dan's involvement with harness racing was not limited to training and driving, however. He did more than anyone else to promote the sport in the East. In 1930 he bought the Charlottetown Driving Park and before he sold out in 1947 he had built up the track to such an extent that harness horses came from all over the Maritimes and New England for his races. When he retired from active racing in 1962, he had devoted more than half a century to the sport.

R. S. MCLAUGHLIN, 1871-1972

Colonel Robert Samuel McLaughlin was one of Canada's foremost entrepreneurs, an industrial pioneer who, more than any other man, was responsible for the establishment and growth of a Canadian automobile industry. But although all his working life from the age of sixteen until his death in 1972 was devoted to making carriages and automobiles, he found time to become an enthusiastic sportsman. His excellent health and prodigious energy, which stayed with him to the end of his life, enabled him to develop his interests in a wide variety of sporting pursuits – cycling, yachting, fishing and horseracing.

Sam McLaughlin was born on 8 September 1871 at the village of Enniskillen, north of Oshawa. His father – known to his family as "the Governor" – was a farmer, whose talent as a woodcarver led him into the carriage-making business. He made his first cutter in 1867 for an ardent Orangeman, who insisted that the cutter come complete with a painting of King Billy crossing the Boyne. The business expanded slowly and in 1876 the family moved to larger premises in Oshawa.

At the age of sixteen Sam left school and was apprenticed in the business. In 1892 Sam and his younger brother, George, were

Alexandra Studio

taken into the business as partners, and within a few years Sam had become the chief designer. By 1899 he had created 143 different designs for carriages and cutters, all of which were being produced.

By the turn of the century, a new kind of vehicle was making its appearance on the roads around Oshawa – the automobile. It didn't take Sam long to convince his brother that these clumsy, spluttering contraptions were the machines of the future and that the McLaughlins should get into their manufacture on the ground floor. The governor remained unconvinced, but allowed Sam to travel around the United States investigating the various motor companies that were springing up. In 1907 the McLaughlin Motor Car Company was founded. The company signed a contract with the Buick company which would supply the engines and the McLaughlin company would design and make the car. Later on the cheaper Chevrolet was added to the line, and the fledgling Canadian automobile industry prospered. But in the North American market mass production was essential to keep costs down, and the smaller independent companies were being forced out of the market. In 1918, Colonel McLaughlin sold to General Motors, on the understanding that he and his brother would continue to manage the Canadian operations.

The merger brought expanded production and prosperity to the Oshawa plant. George retired in 1924, and at fifty-three, Colonel Sam himself decided it might be time to take life easier. In his youth he had been a keen cyclist, in the days of the old solid high-wheelers, often riding the sixty miles from Oshawa to Toronto and back in a day. But that was a bit too strenuous for a man in his fifties, and Sam McLaughlin turned to the other love of his youth, horses. The family had always owned horses, and Sam had been riding since he was a boy. He started to buy show horses – hunters, jumpers, saddle horses – and in 1926 entered his first show. For the next ten years McLaughlin horses competed at shows and fairs throughout Ontario, Quebec and the United States, with great success. One of his horses, Charlevoix, won more ribbons than any horse in Canada. In the thirties, he gradually changed from show horses to thoroughbred racers, and built up at Parkwood Stables a superb racing stable. He became a familiar figure at leading Canadian and American tracks and the McLaughlin colours were seen increasingly in the winner's enclosure. Three of his horses won the King's Plate – Horometer in 1934, Kingarvie in 1946, and Moldy in 1947.

In 1949, for the first time in his life,

Colonel McLaughlin suffered a serious illness, and was forced to slow down. He sold his racing stables to his fellow industrialist, E. P. Taylor. Parkwoods Stables have been renamed the National Stud Farm and are known the world over as a showplace of horses.

To the end of his life Colonel McLaughlin retained an interest in racing, and in many other forms of sport. He was an avid fisherman, and owned forty-five miles of salmon fishing on the Cap Chat River in Quebec. Among his many philanthropies was the donation of a summer camp, Camp Samac, to the Boy Scouts, and a $2 million planetarium at the University of Toronto.

NORTHERN DANCER, 1961-

When E. P. Taylor's Windfields Farm was located at Willowdale, north of Toronto, it attracted horsebuyers from around the world to its annual yearling sale. Every September Taylor auctioned off the colts (usually about sixty) born the previous year at his stud farm. Subject only to a minimum reserved bid, the colts were sold to the highest bidder. In 1962 forty-eight yearlings were offered and fourteen were sold. Of the lot, two colts carried the highest price – $25,000 apiece – but only one was sold. The second colt was returned to Taylor's barns to be trained and raced under his own colours. That stocky, bay colt, standing only fourteen-hands, two and one-half inches, was Northern Dancer, the most phenomenally successful thoroughbred in Canadian racing history.

Canada's preeminence in world thoroughbred breeding during the past few years is almost entirely due to one man – Edward Plunket Taylor. Racing in Canada was at a low ebb in the 1950s when he decided to put a large part of his considerable fortune into building up his stables and improving the standards of Canadian racing. Since then the 1,600-acre stud farm at Oshawa has become one of the most up-to-date in the world, second perhaps only to Taylor's own Windfields Farm, now located in Maryland. It was from horses bred and raised on his Canadian farms that E. P. Taylor became the first man ever to breed the winners of the Kentucky Derby, the Epsom Derby and the Irish Sweeps Derby. And the star thoroughbred of the Taylor stables, the most outstanding horse ever to come out of Canada, has been Northern Dancer.

Northern Dancer's sire, Nearctic, was also from the Taylor stables. He was a fine sprinter who set a Canadian record over six furlongs at Woodbine in 1958; but he seldom won at any distance of more than a mile and was a difficult horse to ride. How-

167

ever, in July 1958, Nearctic won the Michigan Mile at Detroit, breaking the course record, and winning more than $40,000 in the purse. A month later a bay filly, Natalma, daughter of Native Dancer, caught Taylor's eye, and $30,000 of his Michigan purse went to purchase her.

Natalma's career was something less than successful. She started in only seven races, won three of them, and earned only $16,000. In the spring of 1960, when she was a three-year-old and a week before she was to run in the Kentucky Oaks, she broke a bone in her knee. Her racing days were over and, young as she was, the decision was made to bring her home to Canada and breed her to Nearctic, then in his first year at stud. In May 1961 Natalma foaled her first colt, a small bay which would one day make racing history.

But Northern Dancer's future was not apparent in those early days. Joe Thomas, Taylor's racing manager, was disappointed in the colt: "He was so short and so damned chunky – and he had cracked heels."

So, for what in hindsight appears

E.P. Taylor poses with his outstanding thorough -bred, Northern Dancer, after winning the Queen's Plate in 1964. Bill Hartack is in the irons.

the bargain price of $25,000, Northern Dancer was passed over in the 1962 yearling sales, and was turned over to Horatio Luro, trainer for the American division of the Taylor stables. It was a happy decision. The charming Señor Luro learned much of his training methods on his father's ranch in Argentina. He was a good judge of a horse's potential, and he had the patience to give an animal time to develop. Northern Dancer was strong and bred for speed. Luro taught him discipline so that he could carry his speed over a mile and one-quarter. Under his guidance the Dancer developed into a game little horse with a tremendous will to win.

As a two-year-old, Northern Dancer's debut was delayed by cracked heels and it was not until August 1963 that he was entered for his first race at Fort Erie. He won easily by seven lengths; the staff at Windfields Farm were sufficiently impressed to enter him in the Summer Stakes, the richest

168

juvenile race at Fort Erie. The track was soft, but the Dancer led all the way, to win by more than a length.

With a string of five wins in seven starts behind him, Northern Dancer was shipped to New York in November. In his first race the colt immediately attracted attention from the New York racing experts by a brilliant win of eight lengths over Bupers, winner of the $140,000 Coronation Futurity. The next big race of the season was the Remsen Stakes, and the Dancer was entered for it – but not without some misgivings on Luro's part. He had noticed a quarter-crack on the inside left forefoot – if the crack spread it might mean the loss of a whole year's racing while the colt grew a new hoof. But the trainer decided to take a chance – the foot held, and Northern Dancer won the mile and one-eighth distance in the amazing time of 1:47.8 minutes.

If the colt was to go on racing early in 1964, his injury would have to be repaired. By good luck Luro heard of a blacksmith called Bill Bane in California, inventor of the "Bane patch." Bane was an expert at patching cracked hooves with his patented rubber composition. Taylor paid $1,000 to bring Bane to New York, where he spent the whole day repairing the Dancer's hoof. The patch held, and the colt was able to continue racing. In Luro's words, "that was probably the best $1,000 Mr. Taylor ever spent."

Northern Dancer now entered the most important year of his racing career – as a three-year-old all the top classics were open to him, races that were competed for by the cream of the world's thoroughbreds. He started 1964 with renewed health; he had developed a pugnacious personality and presented a picture of restless energy, waiting to explode into action. His first major success was in the $100,000 Flamingo Stakes, which he won by a decisive two lengths. Then followed the Florida Derby, which he won over a mile and one-eighth in the unimpressive time of 1:50.8 minutes. In both these races Northern Dancer had been ridden by the American champion jockey Bill Shoemaker who, though unimpressed with the colt's performance in the Florida Derby, agreed to ride him in the Kentucky Derby. But less than a month before the race, Shoemaker elected to ride Hill Rise in that race instead. Bill Hartack was immediately engaged to ride Northern Dancer, and on their first outing together they won the Blue Grass Stakes most convincingly.

The second day of May 1964 was a day Canadians will long remember, when Northern Dancer – their own plucky little horse, bred, raised and owned in Canada –

raced to a tremendous finish in the Kentucky Derby, beating Hill Rise, with Shoemaker up, by a neck, to win in the all-time record of two minutes flat.

Two weeks later came another triumph, when the Dancer won the Preakness easily by more than two lengths. Canadian hopes were high that he could take the Belmont Stakes, and become the first Canadian horse to win the coveted Triple Crown. It was not to be; the mile and one-half proved too much for him, and the colt finished a poor third behind Quadrangle and Roman Brother.

In spite of a hard season in the US, Taylor brought his horse back to Canada to compete in the Queen's Plate. Northern Dancer did not disappoint his millions of home fans; like the champion he was, he swept to a seven-length victory at Woodbine. It was to be his last race. He developed a bowed tendon later in the season, and Taylor decided to retire the colt to stud. In his short career Northern Dancer had fourteen wins, two seconds and two thirds with total winnings of $580 thousand.

Northern Dancer was named horse of the year in 1964, and elected to Canada's Sports Hall of Fame in 1965. But his success on the racetrack has been more than matched since by his success as a stud. Since he was retired to stud, demands for his services from American owners have been fantastic. The number of money-winning offspring from Northern Dancer is so great that in 1970 he was the leading sire in the world. The list is impressive: Northfield, Laurie's Dancer, True North, One for All, Minsky, and, of course, the magnificent Nijinsky.

Northern Dancer sired Nijinsky in his second year at stud, and such was his reputation even then that in 1968 Nijinsky sold at that year's highest price for a yearling – $84,000. Nijinsky's subsequent racing career in Europe was as brilliant as his sire's in North America, winning the Epsom Derby, the Irish Derby, the Two Thousand Guineas and the King George VI and Queen Elizabeth Stakes. When he retired to stud in 1970, he was syndicated for $5.44 million.

The demands to breed to Northern Dancer have continued to rise. In 1970 the horse was moved to Windfields Farm, Maryland, to be nearer the finest American mares. He, too, was syndicated, for $2.4 million. The members of the syndicate (whose share entitles them to breed one mare a year to Northern Dancer) include four Canadian horsemen, thus ensuring that some of the Dancer's future progeny will be Canadian, and continue to carry Canadian colours on racecourses around the world.

169

JOE O'BRIEN, 1917-

Prince Edward Island can properly be called the cradle of harness racing in Canada. Her stables, trainers and drivers have been among the finest in North America, and the Charlottetown track has become a magnet for harness racers in the Maritimes and the northeastern United States.

One of the top driver-trainers to come out of PEI has been Joe O'Brien, the second man in the history of harness racing to drive 2,000 winners. He has raced in the United States on the Grand Circuit since 1947, and in a career spanning more than twenty years, has won most of the big races: the Hambletonian twice, the Kentucky Futurity four times and the Hanover Filly nine times. In any given year, O'Brien has always won more than 20 percent of his races, and has won more than 120 races in two minutes or less.

Joe O'Brien comes of farming stock. His grandfather emigrated from Ireland and built up one of the best farms in PEI. Although he kept a stable of horses, he never raced. But Joe's father, as soon as he got a farm of his own, immediately built a half-mile track. Joe and his four older brothers, therefore, grew up with horses, and watched their father train them. Joe won his first race at the age of fourteen, and raced with his father and brothers on Maritime tracks until 1935. He then left the family and set up his own public stables in Nova Scotia. He started slowly with only two horses and earned but ten dollars a week for training

Michael Burns Photography

each horse. By 1938 he had picked up a few more horses when the war intervened. He enlisted in the army, only to be discharged because one leg was shorter than the other. The rest of the war O'Brien worked in a New Glasgow munitions factory, managing to find time on the side to train and race his horses. He was so successful on the tracks at this time that for five straight years, from 1943 to 1947, he led all the Maritime drivers in races won.

By the fall of 1947 Joe O'Brien was getting restless with the limited Maritime racing scene and decided to try his chances in the United States. At the Foxboro, Massachusetts, meetings that year he won forty-seven races and was the leading dash winner. His success brought him to the attention of the wealthy Californian racehorse owner, Sol Camp, who in 1952 persuaded O'Brien to give up his own stables and go and work exclusively for him. Over the next ten years Joe had the opportunity to select, train and drive some of the best trotters and pacers in the country – Scott Frost, Blaze Hanover, Little Rock, Diamond Hal, and Shadow Wave.

These years were the most successful of his career, and one of the finest trotters he ever drove was Scott Frost, the first horse in history to win the Hambletonian, the Yonkers Futurity and the Kentucky Futurity, the Triple Crown of harness racing.

Joe O'Brien is a skilful trainer, and a cool driver. His style has been described as old-fashioned, because he likes to hold back as long as possible and lie on the rail until the stretch, when he will come up with a burst of speed. His record of wins over the years is impressive, as is the money he has earned. In five of the six years 1954-9 he topped the list of money winners in the Grand Circuit. In 1966 he won ten races in one day, taking eight in the afternoon at the Illinois State Fair at Springfield, and going on to win another two in the evening at Chicago. In early 1974 O'Brien won the Old Glory Pace at Yonkers Raceway in New York and set a sizzling track record of 1:58.8 minutes for the mile event under lights. He drove the Canadian-owned Armbro Nesbit.

O'Brien competed in the Grand Circuit from May to December, and then retreated to his California farm; he would not race a good horse more than thirty times a year merely to pick up extra money. It was this training tenet that led to his break with Sol Camp; O'Brien established his own stables in the late 1960s. And it was then that he trained and drove the other outstanding horse of his career, the Canadian-owned Fresh Yankee. O'Brien had twenty victories with Fresh Yankee in 1970 alone, the same year the horse was named US trotter of the year, and US harness horse of the year.

Over the years Joe O'Brien has trained and raced many successful trotters and pacers, and he is nothing if not versatile. Perhaps the strangest race of his career took place in 1969, on a tour of France and Sweden, when he found himself in Lapland racing reindeer. Afterwards he remarked, "It's like driving a car on slippery ice. There's no bridle or halter and you can't steer them." Joe has certainly never had any trouble steering his trotters and pacers in North America, which accounts for his consistently successful performance on the tracks.

OLYMPIC GRAND PRIX JUMPING TEAM, 1968

It was the last day of the 1968 Olympics at Mexico City. There had been the usual avalanche of American and Russian medal winners; not a single Canadian had earned so much as a bronze in track and field, rowing, gymnastics or sailing. Had it not been for the silver medals of swimmers Elaine Tanner and Ralph Hutton, and a third-place finish by the girls' team in the 100-metre freestyle, Canada would have been shut out entirely. Even the Canadian Olympic team's *chef de mission*, Howard Radford of Montreal, had left for home the night before.

But 80,000 spectators jammed the Estadio Olimpico to watch the day-long final event, the Grand Prix jumping competition among the three-man teams of the premier equestrian nations of the world. The favoured teams were those of Britain, France, Germany and the United States. Although a West German publication had recently suggested that Canada might be a "dark-horse" entry, the Canadians, managed by Brigadier W. D. Whitaker of Toronto, had been hoping for no more than a fifth- or sixth-place finish. Whitaker optimistically revised that estimate to a bronze medal on the morning of the competition, but he knew that the Canadians were long shots; this was the first time in Olympic history that Canada had even entered the event.

The three members of the Canadian equestrian team were scarcely neophytes. They all came from the horsey belt to the north and north-west of Toronto; two of them conformed to the public's conception of the upper-class character of their sport. Tom Gayford, thirty-nine, and Jim Elder, thirty-four, were both private school products and graduates of the University of Toronto; Gayford was a Bay Street broker, Elder an executive in his family's firm. Both came from families whose interest in horses and the

Jim Elder of Toronto was thirty-four years old when he and his fellow equestrians won the Olympic gold medal. Elder rode The Immigrant.

hunt was of some duration. The third team member, Jim Day, was only twenty-one, an Oakville car salesman whose parents operated a horse breeding and training school near Thornhill. Gayford and Elder had been members of the gold-medal winning team at the 1959 Pan-American Games; Elder had been on the team which won a bronze medal at the 1956 Olympics in the rugged three-day event. All three had been members of the Canadian team which had made an excellent third-place showing at the 1967 Pan-American Games in Winnipeg; Day, in fact, had won the individual gold medal. The Immigrant, the horse Elder was to ride, had been purchased in Ireland. The other two were failed racehorses, bought for a few hundred each. Day's Canadian Club had been purchased as a pleasure horse; Big Dee, owned by Gayford's father, was bought at Fort Erie and trained first as a hunter.

Grand Prix jumping takes place over a course composed of some fourteen obstacles with seventeen jumps in all, one a fifteen-foot jump over water. The object is to com-

171

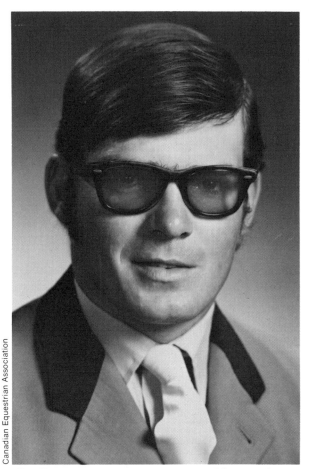

Jim Day was a twenty-one-year-old car sales-man when he helped cinch Canada's gold medal aboard his mount, Canadian Club.

plete the course within a prescribed time, taking as few penalty points as possible. Penalty points are assessed for such infractions as refusal to jump, fouling the barriers on jumping or exceeding the time limit. Each team member rides the course twice.

It was commonly agreed among the national teams that the Mexican course was not only difficult but unusually compact. As Gayford said, "it looked like a tough course, with the jumps coming up at you bang, bang, bang. Most courses we've been on have given a bit of room between jumps so you can manoeuvre and get ready. This was different." At the end of the first round of jumping Canada was second to Britain, mainly on the strength of an excellent ride by Elder that only David Broome of the British team had bettered. As the long, hot afternoon wore on, team after team was eliminated or encountered crippling disaster: the British, for example, were eliminated when Marian Coakes and her horse Stroller fell at the seventh jump and were unable to continue in time. Gradually it became apparent that the Canadian lead was unassailable; Jim Elder

and The Immigrant assured this with a solid round in their final ride. The Canadians won with an aggregate of 102¾ penalty points to 111 for France and 117¼ for West Germany.

Their victory was hailed with delight in Canada, even though there was little public understanding of the nature of the event; its total unexpectedness and timing took the sting from what had been a most disappointing performance by athletes far more heralded than the Ontario horsemen. To the international equestrian set, the Canadian victory was a shocker; there was much talk of fluke. The fact was, however, that Canada had arrived as an equestrian power, though the Canadian sporting public was uncomprehending. At the North American Grand Prix, held at the Canadian National Exhibition stadium in Toronto in June 1969, the Canadians swept the board. "Today we underlined and confirmed Mexico to all the sceptics," said Gayford. "After the Pan Am and the Olympics, this was only our third appearance in open stadium competition. They said the Mexico course might have favoured us because it was tight and what we have

Tom Gayford was an experienced equestrian at thirty-four years of age when the three-man team posted its Olympic victory. Gayford rode Big Dee.

been used to in indoor competition where there is less room between jumps. What do they say now?"

JAMES SPEERS, 1882-1955

Jim Speers used to say, "Every man who has acquired a bit of money should have a hobby and a worry – and he can have both, if he owns a racehorse." It was a shrewd assessment of his own career. Speers, dean of horseracing in the West, and Canada's leading thoroughbred breeder until his death in 1955, started to operate his first racecourse in 1922, and within three years had built three racecourses in Western Canada. But it was not enough to own tracks; breeders had to be persuaded to race at the meets. Jim Speers got into the thoroughbred breeding business himself; for years during the depression his stables were a constant drain on his finances. But he perservered, and in thirty years of racing bred some of the finest horses in the country, including Loyalist, the winner of the 1955 Canadian Derby. He was the first Canadian to win more than $1 million with his own horses in North America, and his horses won 1,338 races in twenty years.

Jim Speers was born in Elmbank, Ontario. His father was a blacksmith who operated a forge on the site of the present Toronto International Airport. Jim owned his first racehorse when he was nine, and started to work for his father when he left school. At eighteen he journeyed West. He stayed in Winnipeg for five years, then went to Old Battleford, Saskatchewan. Speers was ambitious, with all the instincts of a born gambler. He started dealing in cattle, and from there went into the feed and grain business in the small town of Wilkie, Saskatchewan. At that time, also, he started horse breeding, racing in competition against other local cattlemen. He heard of the oil boom in Alberta and went into the oil brokerage business in Calgary in 1914 – just as the boom was over.

It was in Calgary that same year that he got a contract to supply horses to the French government for the war on the Western front. That contract was to have far-reaching consequences for Jim Speers. While scouting for horses in Idaho in 1916, he was involved in a train crash which landed him in hospital for nine months, and left him with a permanent limp. His lawyer, R. B. Bennett, obtained damages of $38,000, and with this cash in his pocket, Speers returned to Canada.

His cattle business was thriving, and he decided to move back to Winnipeg in 1920. He was soon expanding his business again – this time he got seriously involved in horseracing. He leased River Park in 1922,

and staged two successful meets. Encouraged, he built his own track at Whittier Park, on the banks of the Red River at St. Boniface. The following year he built Polo Park in Winnipeg and shortly after Chinook Park, outside Calgary.

But racetracks were not enough – breeders had to be induced to send their horses to untried, far-away tracks up in Canada. Despite the popularity of Jim Speers, and the assistance of his many friends, the operation was on shaky ground. So Speers took another gamble and established his own racing stables at St. Boniface, to provide horses for his own tracks. As a money-making proposition it was a failure; the depression and the continuing Prairie drought meant money was scarce. Speers's finances were further depleted by a disastrous venture into the US racing circuit when he built a track in Butte, Montana, and held a meeting in 1929 which was a complete failure. He tried again in 1930, but the meeting lasted only four days.

Speers's big break came in 1933, when he bought the stallion Craigangover in Kentucky for $8,000. He came back to Canada with the stallion and twenty-eight brood mares. This was just the stimulus his farms needed, and from that time horses bred in the Manitoba stables produced winners in races all over North America.

Jim Speers was "Mr. Racing" in Western Canada; he founded and dominated the racing scene for more than thirty years. But his contribution has been to the sport in Canada as a whole. He introduced parimutuel betting in Canada at his Manitoba track in 1922, and pioneered the daily double in North America when he brought the system over from England in 1931. And it was

173

Speers who installed the first closed automatic starting gate on the continent at his Whittier Park track in 1939.

In his efforts to improve the quality of thoroughbred stock in Canada he established the Prairie Thoroughbreeders Association in 1925. In 1930 he started publication of the *Red Book of Canadian Racing*, the first accurate and comprehensive record of the sport in Canada. When he died in 1955 he had built up a formidable racing empire in the West, and had become Canada's leading thoroughbred breeder, a legacy that others would continue and build on.

KEITH GORDON WAPLES, 1923-

To the two-dollar bettor at the trotting tracks, the name of Keith Waples may not be familiar. But to the track professionals – and especially to the drivers – Waples is known as a driver of the highest calibre ranked with Filion, Haughton, Dancer and O'Brien. Hervé Filion said it all when he remarked, "The drivers' driver is Keith Waples. I've been studying him for years."

Keith was born and raised at Victoria Harbour on Georgian Bay, not far from the farm of a Penetanguishene foundry owner, J. T. Payette, who bred and raced standardbreds. During a race at Penetang, Payette put young Keith, then seven, on the lead pony. From that moment the youngster knew what he wanted to do. At the age of twelve he got his first taste of sulky racing, driving his father's Grey Ghost; he won three heats at a little track at Sundridge, Ontario.

In 1968 Keith passed the 2,000 victory milestone. His skill and experience were built up over many years, at a time when harness racing was not the popular sport it has become since the mid-fifties. He became master of his craft in the years when the farmers of Ontario maintained the breed and sustained the competition on dozens of small tracks scattered throughout rural Ontario.

On 21 July 1959 at the half-mile track of Montreal's Richelieu Park, Waples drove Mighty Dudley to Canada's first sub-two-minute mile. Not even the honour-laden Filion has matched Waples's record of 246 wins on Canadian tracks in 1967. At Blue Bonnets in 1972, driving Strike Out, he won the first $100,000 race to be held in Canada for either standardbred or thoroughbred. A month later he drove Strike Out to victory in standardbred racing's most prestigious event, the Little Brown Jug. Strike Out was the first wholly Canadian owned horse to win this classic. In January 1973 Waples had a great day at Toronto Greenwood, racking up five wins for his best performance on a pari-

Michael Burns Photography

mutuel track.

Keith Waples, with well more than 3,000 winning races to his credit, chooses to keep mainly to Ontario tracks, only occasionally taking horses to the major American races. In 1962 he had a year of racing in the United States with the Miron stables of Montreal. "It was awful," he later said. "I couldn't wait to get back to the farm. The constant travel, day in and day out, was too much for me. And now, no matter where I'm racing, I can usually get back to the ranch the next day."

The Waples ranch is at Durham, Ontario. Like most of the best harness drivers, Keith has been drawn into breeding and training while still pursuing his driving career. Waples's real forte is training. Here his infinite patience and relaxed handling of horses has paid off.

GEORGE WOOLF, 1910-46

When the American Jockey Hall of Fame was opened at Pimlico, Maryland, in 1955, three jockeys were elected – Earle Sande, Eddie Arcaro, and the Canadian-born George Woolf. In his nineteen years on the track before his tragic death in 1946 the little rider from the Southern Alberta ranch had come a long way.

Riding was in George Woolf's blood. Before settling down to farm life in the foothills around Cardston, his father had been a rodeo rider in Utah, and his mother had been a circus trick rider. George learned to ride bareback almost before he could walk; two brothers also became rodeo riders.

174

George owed his start in racing to Calgary horseman and owner Fred Johnson, who engaged Woolf to ride some of his horses on the Western Canadian tracks. (It was also Johnson who helped George's boyhood friend Johnny Longden gain experience on the same circuit. The boys went on to become two of the greatest jockeys in the history of American racing.)

After a brief fling on Canadian tracks, George was apprenticed to the US stables owned by Mr. and Mrs. Lemuel Whitehill. He began racing on American and Mexican tracks in 1928, riding his first winner at Tijuana. Early in his career he earned the nickname "the Iceman" for his coolness in the saddle. He became well known for his apparent unconcern until the last stages of a race, when he would come from behind to win by a nose. He knew how to judge his mount and could wait for the right moment to make a move.

His growing success made him sought after and he was offered the chance to ride some of the best American thoroughbreds. In 1936 he won the Preakness on Bold Venture. Two years later he rode Seabiscuit (in his opinion, the best mount he ever had) to victory over War Admiral in the great match race in the Pimlico Special. He won both the American Derby and the Hollywood Gold Cup three times straight. Towards the end of his career, in 1945, he won the Santa Anita Derby on a horse named Bymeabond. On that occasion he was riding against Johnny Longden, who cheerfully describes how George sneaked up past him on the rail to beat him at the post in the inimitable Woolf style. But George Woolf never rode a winner in the Kentucky Derby, and this was to be his greatest disappointment.

In 1942 and 1944 he was champion rider of the United States in the amount of money won. He was never champion jockey (the most winners in a year) mainly because he did not accept as many mounts as most others. Indeed, there was a time in the mid-1930s when he thought of retiring; he drove all the way from Mexico to Canada to sign on with the Royal Canadian Mounted Police. But he was rejected as too short. It was almost six months before he would return to the tracks.

George Woolf was a diabetic, and by the mid-1940s he was having difficulty getting his weight down. He had settled in Arcadia, California, and put his winnings into a restaurant. By 1946 he had decided to retire at the end of the season.

He was signed to ride Please Me at Santa Anita on 3 January. Johnny Longden was watching the race, and he has described

Alexandra Studio

the accident: "As the field of six horses swung into the clubhouse turn . . . Georgie had Please Me running well, winging along on the rail clear of all interference, when suddenly he seemed to stumble. The unexpectedness of the move threw Georgie off balance and he fell to the track on his head. I kept watching for him to get up but he just lay there." George Woolf never regained consciousness, and died the next day. In his nineteen years he had ridden such famous horses as Whirlaway, Seabiscuit, Alsab, Pavot and Challedon. He had won 721 races, been second 589 times and third 468 times, a truly outstanding record.

A life-sized bronze statue of the Iceman was erected to his memory on the Santa Anita course, and the George Woolf Memorial Award for the most sportsmanlike jockey was set up in his honour, an award won in 1951 by his old friend and fellow Canadian, Johnny Longden.

Shooting

Chapter 7

On 9 September 1881 a colourful crowd had assembled on the banks of the Rideau River in Ottawa.

> The concluding of the governor-general's match was witnessed by a large assemblage of the youth and beauty of Ottawa [an observer wrote in the local press]. The tasteful dresses of the ladies, the brilliant uniforms of the officers . . . the snow-white tents, the gay flags . . . formed a picture which was strikingly beautiful. The musical selections . . . were rendered by the Governor-General's Foot Guards . . .

The match, in fact, had been the most successful in the twelve-year history of the Dominion of Canada Rifle Association (DCRA). More than 300 militiamen from all parts of the country had come to compete for more than $5,000 in prizes, donated, in the main, by the federal government and banks. The match was the outward manifestation of the importance attached to rifle-shooting in the decades before the First World War. So important were the matches that those attending included the Governor-General, the General Officer Commanding the Militia, the Minister of militia and often, the prime minister himself. The press gave detailed coverage, not only to national contests like the one above, but to regimental competitions as well. Today's marksman, who competes almost in private, would find such publicity incomprehensible.

From its inception in 1869 until 1884, the DCRA president had been Casimir Gzowski, father of competitive rifle-shooting in Canada. Gzowski was born into an aristocratic Polish family in St. Petersburg, Russia, in 1813. While training as an army engineer, he had taken part in an anti-Czarist revolt in 1830 and was

Lady Macdonald prepares to fire the first shot of the Dominion Rifle Match Association at Ottawa's old ranges on the Rideau River.

exiled. After a stay in the United States, he came to Canada and embarked on a long, successful career as a construction entrepreneur; among other major enterprises, he built the Toronto-to-Sarnia section of the Grand Trunk Railway.

During the unsettled days of the American civil war and the disturbances associated with the Fenian raids, Gzowski and some vocal companions agitated for the formation of civilian rifle associations. The agitators believed that the war of 1812 had been won by the rifle-toting Canadian frontiersman – not by the British regulars – and, they argued, rifle associations would permit the citizenry "to arm for defensive purposes . . . " Not that much defense was needed against the "few miserable Fenians," but steps were certainly needed to protect the country against "that gigantic power from which alone we have anything to dread" – the United States. In addition, the agitators said, rifle clubs would encourage investment when foreign capital recognized the country as safe and, even further, the creation of rifle clubs would create "a great national pastime that would go far to blend in harmonious unity the diverse and . . . antagonistic elements . . . of these provinces. . . . "

Gzowski started small; he organized a Grand Trunk Rifle Brigade among the men who worked on his construction crews. Later, the Province of Ontario Rifle Association was formed, with Gzowski as its president.

In England in 1860 the National Rifle Association had been formed, and its annual matches became a magnet for the best marksmen of the British Empire. The first Canadian team to compete was sent over in 1871 by the Ontario association; from 1872 to the present, the DCRA has been the sponsoring body. In earlier years, much of the expense was borne by

177

Gzowski himself and he did things in style. "The reception tent of the Canadians [it was reported in 1874] is par excellence Oriental in grandeur. Heavy Wilton carpets, luxurious lounges, radiant mirrors, blue and gold damask hangings, massive epergnes, richly carved oaken sideboards, tempting easy chairs, and altogether such a mint of splendour and comfort that will render memorable . . . the name of Gzowski and the team of 1874."

These annual meets, first at Wimbledon and later at Bisley, were great imperial occasions, drawing marksmen from many corners of the British Empire. Bisley has remained the Mecca for Canadian riflemen, though all of the former imperial touches have long gone. Bisley's highest honour, the Queen's Prize, has been won by Canadians eleven times – T. H. Hayhurst was the first in 1895. Canadians have won the Kolapore Cup, a team prize, sixteen times since 1872. But it has been in the twentieth century that Canadian marksmen came into their own with such sharpshooters as the Boas, Desmond Burke and Gerry Ouellette.

Trapshooting has had a different kind of history in Canada; its traditions lie not in the military, but in the hunt, and its weapon is not the rifle but the shotgun. The sport started in England in the early nineteenth century, when live birds were released from traps. Later, glass globes were used as targets, and then, in the 1880s, the ingenious McCaskey clay pigeon, made of silt or rock powder and tar, was invented.

Exactly when Canadians began to compete in trapshooting is not clear. By 1890 there were some 150 gun clubs in the country, with more than 15,000 members. Well before then, however, in the 1870s and 1880s, the press carried frequent accounts of trapshooting competitions at such clubs as the Lachine Gun Club, the Toronto Gun Club, or the St. Hubert Club of Ottawa. The Canadian trapshooter turned to clay pigeons very slowly. In 1889-90 the House of Commons debated for two sessions a bill that would ban the use of pigeons, sparrows, and other live birds for trapshooting. The bill attracted the derision of rural members who attacked "the spurious sentimentality of certain officious humanitarians." In an absurd flight of oratory in which love of trapshooting was equated with love of country, one MP said that marksmen shooting captive birds catapulted from spring traps displayed "the taste for sport which every true Briton loves . . . There were pigeons shot in the Old Country by men of as kind hearts, aye, and as strong brain, and as truly loyal as are any in Canada today." A member from Western Ontario warned against discouraging "manly sports," which had a miraculous effect upon young men: "They drink less, they play cards less, they learn less evil habits . . . their morals are better, they have more manliness in every way."

Canadian trap and skeetshooters have long been content with clay pigeons. Their sport, like rifle and pistol shooting, has little spectator appeal, nor are its ardent followers necessarily huntsmen. From Walter Ewing to George Genereux, they tend, like the riflemen, to be quiet enthusiasts never much in the limelight nor expecting to be. Canada has never venerated the gun as the United States has. Our laws do not enshrine the right to bear arms, nor have we mythologized the gunfighter, the Indian killer or the gangster. Though hundreds of thousands of Canadians were trained in weaponry during two world wars, we have developed no gun lobby comparable to the US National Rifle Association.

The Dominion of Canada Rifle Matches were important events in the 1800s attended by notables from across Canada. Pictured here in the Ottawa match of 1896 are Lord Aberdeen with Colonel Gibson (seated, *far left*) and Sam Hughes (standing, *far right*).

Biographies

GILMOUR S. BOA, 1924-73

Gilmour Boa was a Toronto civil engineer who since 1949 had been recognized as one of the world's best in rifle shooting. Interest in the sport runs strong in the Boa family. Gil's father, James Sr., qualified for the Canadian Bisley team more times than any other person (except Lieutenant-Colonel Desmond Burke), won a number of Bisley prizes, and coached Canada's Bisley teams on a number of occasions. Both Gil's uncle and brother also qualified for the Bisley team, and three members of the family, including Gil, have won the Governor-General's Prize.

Gil Boa himself began competitive shooting at fourteen. Very often he competed against his father; for example, in 1948 he

Sports Hall of Fame

was second to his father for the Governor-General's Gold Medal. In 1949, as an officer cadet of the 48th Highlanders, he placed on the same Bisley team as his brother, Lieutenant James Boa, and in that year won the stock exchange event in the mannual Commonwealth shoot at Bisley. This early in his career he was earning a reputation as an extremely cool shot, a vital characteristic in a sport in which the slightest advance in pulse rate may destroy a good score. In 1951, again on the Bisley team, he won the competition for the King's Prize, a test which has been called "the most exacting test of marksmanship." Throughout the meet, Boa wore the jacket that his father had worn in winning the Governor-General's Prize in 1948; the rifle he used was the same his father had shot in competition for twenty years. "This is the best day we have ever had," Boa said after his victory. "It feels wonderful to have won the prize and I only wish father was on the team this year to see it."

For a Canadian rifleman, winning the King's Prize at Bisley is the acme of achievement. Boa has, however, won many other distinctions. He won a bronze medal at the Olympic Games at Melbourne in 1956, the year that Gerry Ouellette won a gold for Canada in the same event. He matched his father by winning the Governor-General's Prize in 1955. At the British Commonwealth Games at Kingston, Jamaica, in 1966 he won the gold medal in the smallbore rifle competition, with 587 out of a possible 600.

Perhaps his greatest day (aside from winning the King's Prize) came on 17 November 1954 at the thirty-sixth world shooting championships at Caracas, Venezuela. He won the world's smallbore carbine championship, called the "English match." It consists of thirty shots at 50 metres and thirty at 100 metres. At 50 metres Boa shot a perfect 300; so did Boris Pereberin of Russia. Their performance at 100 metres attracted a huge crowd, with spectators walking back and forth behind the two as they shot. Here Boa's winning experience told. He dropped only two points to set a new world's record of 598 for the competition; Pereberin finished at 595. The physical and mental control needed to achieve such results is prodigious; Boa says shooting is "more a religion than a sport."

DESMOND THOMAS BURKE, 1904-73

By any measure, Desmond Burke was a remarkable man whose achievement in his profession and in his recreation was of the highest order. Burke enjoyed the respect and admiration of his colleagues and his fellow riflemen for more than a generation. Profes-

179

sionally, his field was medicine. He graduated from Queen's in 1932 and during the 1930s made a number of important contributions to the literature of radiology. During the second world war he served with the Royal Canadian Army Medical Corps in Britain, Italy and northwest Europe. After the war Dr. Burke was chief radiologist at Sunnybrook Hospital and a member of the Faculty of Medicine at the University of Toronto. Later he was chief radiologist at Oakville Hospital.

This distinguished medical career was paralleled by his career as a rifleman. When a student at Ottawa's Lisgar Collegiate he took up shooting as a substitute for more active sports which an illness prevented him from playing. His father nurtured his technique through long hours spent in "dry" firing. A teacher allowed young Burke to use the collegiate's facilities and entrusted him with the training of the school cadet corps in musketry. This combination of circumstances, Burke wrote, "provided me with an experience that most beginners would not get in many years."

In 1924 Desmond Burke, as a member of the Canadian team and a private in the Governor-General's Foot Guard won the highest honour that Bisley offers: the King's Prize. Though ten other Canadians have won this prize between 1895 and the present, Desmond Burke, only nineteen at the time, remains the youngest ever. Before his career as a marksman ended, Burke accumulated more prizes and awards at Bisley than any Canadian in history. He won a place on

twenty-two Bisley teams, a record no Canadian has approached; he was able to accept twelve times. He was in the select circle of the King's Hundred seven times; won the gold cross for the grand aggregate twice; was runner-up for the King's Prize three times and for the grand aggregate once; in all he took fourteen firsts and eleven seconds during the years he competed in this premier event. And this is to make no mention of the innumerable prizes he won in Canadian events.

Desmond Burke was not only one of the world's best marksmen, he was also an innovative teacher. In 1932 he published *A Practical Rifleman's Guide*, and in 1970 there appeared *Canadian Bisley Shooting: An Art and a Science*, the fruit of his long experience. *Canadian Bisley Shooting* combines the most complex technical data about shooting with insights derived from Dr. Burke's medical knowledge and with a commonsensical wit that makes the book interesting even to the non-shooter.

Burke always regretted that the sport he loved so well should bear the stigma of war. As he pointed out, in more than a century of Bisley and DCRA shooting, there had never been a fatal accident in authorized competitions. The day would come, he hoped, when rifle shooting would be "never for war, never to cause suffering to wildlife, but only for sport."

WALTER H. EWING, ca 1880-?

Very little is known about the life of this pioneer Canadian trapshooter. He was a Montreal businessman, the representative of the Lackawanna Coal Company; that he belonged to a country club and lived in West-

180

mount indicates only that he belonged to that Montreal middle-class community which had led the way in so many Canadian sports.

The records of the Amateur Athletic Association of Canada show that Walter Ewing won a gold medal in trapshooting at the second Olympiad in Paris in 1900, but give no other details. The Montreal *Gazette* of 25 May 1906 informs us that "W. H. Ewing of Montreal scored the highest amateur score at the first annual meeting of the Canadian Indians yesterday, for which he will be awarded the Clarendon Cup." Presumably the Canadian Indians was a newly formed marksman's association, but all we know about its first meet, aside from Ewing's victory, is that he broke 189 birds out of 200, his nearest competitor scoring 183.

There can be no question that Ewing ranks as one of the best trapshooters in the history of the sport. He proved this at the fourth Olympiad in London in 1908 when for the second time he won the gold medal in trapshooting. The competition extended over three days, with Ewing leading from the start. His score was 72 out of possible 80; another Canadian, G. S. Beattie, was second. In the team competition, Canada lost out to Britain by two points. Following the games, trapshooters stayed over to compete for the Claybird International Challenge Shield, a team trophy, and the London *Times* Trophy, a handicap event for individuals. This time the Canadian team won, and Ewing placed first in the *Times* competition, despite the fact that his Olympic showing must have given him a difficult handicap.

GEORGE GENEREUX, 1935-

It is a curious phenomenon of Olympic Games that Canadian winners have frequently excelled in little-known sports. Few gold-medal winners have known much fame in Canada before their Olympic achievements. Such a one was Francis Amyot, the paddler who won an Olympic gold medal at the 1936 Berlin games. Canada had to wait until 1952 at Helsinki before another of our athletes won a gold medal, again in a little heralded sport, trapshooting. George Genereux was just seventeen when he won the clay pigeon event. No other Canadian had done that since Walter Ewing in 1908. Overnight the tall, good-looking youngster became a national sports hero. He was awarded the Lou Marsh Trophy as Canada's outstanding athlete, the youngest person ever to win.

Before his moment of glory at Helsinki, George Genereux was already well-known to the trapshooting fraternity, at least in the West. His father, Dr. A. G. Genereux,

Sports Hall of Fame

had first taught him to shoot, but George's subsequent development into an expert came through the instruction of Jimmy Girgulus, a well-established competitor in trapshooting events. Girgulus taught his young pupil the fundamentals.

After a year's shooting experience, George won his first competition at the age of thirteen, beating shots from Manitoba, Saskatchewan, Ontario, Minnesota and the two Dakotas for the Midwest International Handicap at Winnipeg. The same year and for the next two as well he won the Manitoba-Saskatchewan junior championship. A number of other victories followed, then came the big turning point in George's career. At Vandalia, Ohio, the site of the Grand American championships – the pinnacle for all North American trapshooters – Genereux won the North American junior championship. Genereux and his nearest competitor had tied at the end of 200 targets with 193 apiece. In the shootoff, George broke forty-nine of fifty birds, and became the first Canadian ever to win a Grand American title. After accumulating further honours at Vandalia, George returned to Saskatchewan to annex the provincial title, breaking 100 birds straight to win by two points.

George was selected for the Olympic team. Obviously, for a seventeen-year-old, the pressure was enormous. The event calls for instantaneous reflexes and great stamina.

The targets, saucer-like objects of limestone dust and tar, are hurled erratically from a trap sixteen yards in front of the shooter. The birds may dip, swerve, behave like a knuckleball, shoot high or low, and the wind may further complicate matters. George Genereux explained some of the hazards: "It gets to be quite a battle of nerves. A change in the wind, a fly on the gun barrel or a tricky opponent moving in the corner of your eye as you sight the bird, gets you jumpy. Or you may have a guy next to you who deliberately shoots in your echo . . . you get the idea you're holding everybody up and begin to rush. Then you notice you're chipping or splitting the birds instead of powdering them, which means you aren't centring your pattern on the target – just hitting it with a few pellets. That's when you start to blow."

In Europe, George didn't blow. As a preliminary to the Olympics, he took part in the thirty-fifth world shooting championships at Oslo. The title was won by Pablo Juan Grossi of Argentina, with 287 targets out of 300; Genereux tied for second at 286 with Knut Holmqvist of Sweden. At Helsinki and the Olympics, Holmqvist again finished second, but this time it was Genereux who won, defeating his Swedish rival 192 to 191.

GERALD R. OUELLETTE, 1934-

Gerry Ouellette doesn't look like a champion of anything. He is short, rather pudgy, with a pleasant, open face – until you notice the eyes. They are the eyes of one of the world's deadliest marksmen. If you happen to be a stamp collector, you will have seen those eyes sighting down the barrel of a rifle on a handsome, one-centavo triangular stamp of the Dominican Republic. Not even Canadian prime ministers get themselves on the stamps of other countries, but Gerry Ouellette, school teacher, tool designer and expert shot, did when he won the gold medal in smallbore shooting at the Olympic Games in Melbourne in 1956.

Ouellette was twenty-two when he established himself as one of the finest riflemen in the world at Melbourne. At thirteen as a student at W. D. Lowe Vocational High School in Windsor, he came under the influence of Major Wyn Jennings, a cadet instructor who encouraged Ouellette to take up shooting. For years Gerry's weapon was the .303 service rifle; with it, he won the junior and cadet service rifle championships of Canada in 1951 and the Lieutenant-Governor's Medal in 1952. By the time he qualified for the Olympic team, he was a veteran of several Bisley teams, and had won a number of other service rifle and smallbore competitions, including provincial, national, and American state awards.

Ouellette had only begun shooting smallbore rifles some four years before Melbourne, and was not regarded as a threat in the event. It was expected that the Russian, Anatolii Bogdanov, would be the man to beat; as it turned out, it was a teammate, Vassili Borissov, who gave the Canadian the closest run and finished only a point behind him. Ouellette was elated at his victory. "I ended way down on the list for the three-position shooting, and I think the ground position suits me best." (In three-position shooting each contestant fires from a stand-

GUARDS RIFLE TEAM
Presented to Major _____ in 1878 by the Members of the Team

ing, kneeling and prone position.) Ouellette used an American Winchester and his mark was a perfect 600×600, a feat never before accomplished. Unhappily, the Australian Olympic committee had erred by a few inches in converting the length of their range to the European metric measurement (50 metres), and Gerry Ouellette's score was not accepted as the world record it otherwise would have been.

Since that time, Gerry has remained one of the world's finest shots, and one of the most versatile. In 1957 he won the Canadian service pistol championship; with the service rifle he won the Bisley aggregate in 1959; and in smallbore rifle competition, also in 1959, he was Canadian sporting rifle champion and won a gold medal and several other awards at the Pan-American Games. At the annual Dominion of Canada Rifle Assocation competitions at the Connaught ranges near Ottawa, he has won the grand aggregate on more than one occasion, the most recent being in 1971. In 1971, also, he and his wife, a former member of the British Bisley team, qualified for the Canadian Bisley team, the first time a husband and wife have done so in a hundred years of Canadian competition in the event.

Canada has never venerated the gun as have some other countries, yet as early as 1868 there was a Dominion of Canada Rifle Association. Rifle shooting was a popular sport attracting large crowds. Canada sent its first team in 1871 to compete in England's National Rifle Association matches and a decade later marksmen were competing in this country for prize money in excess of $5,000. *Above*, members of the Guards Rifle Team of 1878, and trophies won; *below*, a DCRA meet at Ottawa in 1900.

Winter Sports

Chapter 8

Winter has doubtless much to do with the Canadian soul, and our winter sports presumably have some profound connection with that fact. The winter landscape is not so harsh as that braved by our pioneer ancestors – modern sports equipment has seen to that – but winter sports continue to support the Canadian's picture of himself as a hardy northerner. When they began, our forefathers, making a virtue of necessity, celebrated the bracing effects of our climate, and contrasted the sturdy northern people of Canada with the effete inhabitants of softer countries. Technology, however, soon brought winter indoors, and hockey, curling and figure skating were pursued in artificial environments, despite what such shelter would do to our hardy character. More recently better outdoor clothing, inventions like ski-tows and snowmobiles, and a new enthusiasm for fitness and the outdoors has brought renewed enjoyment of the winter landscape (but no marked decline in traffic to Florida and the Caribbean).

George Beers, that indefatigable sports booster, typified the defiant rapture of Canadians with their winter recreations when extolling the Montreal Winter Carnival in the English magazine, *The Century*, in 1886. The Canadians, he wrote, were "hardier and healthier than their cousins over the border":

> The historian who hopes to do justice to the development and idiosyncracies of the Canadian people will find it impossible to ignore the moulding influence of winter. . . . The Winter Carnival of Montreal has killed the superstition that our winter is inhospitable . . . It is possible to enjoy every hour here in a hundred ways in the open air of the coldest days, and

Six skaters, oblivious of cold, try out the ice of a frozen pond near Government House, Ottawa, in the 1880s.

to get more benefit than even mountain and seashore in summer can bestow . . . You cannot trace all through our winter one taint of the vulgar or brutal in our enjoyments; they are as pure as the snows.

The Montreal carnival, first staged in 1883, was one of the first organized attempts to beat winter at its own game. The first carnival lasted five days. It featured a bonspiel in two divisions, "iron" and "stone," which drew rinks from Ontario, the Maritimes and the United States. There were sleigh races, horseraces, tobogganning, a snowshoe meet and several night tramps by torchlight. Aside from recreational skating at four rinks, there were fancy- and figure-skating competitions. There was a hockey tournament and a fancy-dress masquerade on ice, a grand ball, and the storming of the huge ice palace on Dominion Square to the accompaniment of martial bands and fireworks.

The carnival put Canada "on the map" and, for a time, left the impression, especially in the United States and Britain, of a hardy nation of supermen. Montreal's enthusiasm for the extravaganza began to wane after the third, in 1885. It was wrong, Montreal businessmen began to realize, to promote their home as a city locked in ice and snow. As Montreal allowed the carnival to dwindle away, Quebec took up the idea and, today, Quebec City remains the only city with a major winter carnival as an annual event. (And even at Quebec, the sports aspect has been overshadowed by the artistic and convivial.)

Another reason for the decline of the Montreal carnival was the fact that tobogganing and snowshoeing, the sports which had provided most of the impetus for it, were already beginning to wane in popularity. This had important consequences, not only for the carnival but for two sports of the future. Some of the leaders in tobogganing and snowshoeing were to be drawn into skiing, very much to its benefit. But the abandonment of the elaborate toboggan installations in Montreal, and in other centres as well, meant that there was no evolution, as in Alpine Europe, from tobogganing into the sophisticated bobsled competition with its carefully designed and very expensive runs. Thus, when Canadian bobsled teams challenged in world competition in the late 1950s, they did so without the benefit of a single facility at home.

Yet, in scores of smaller centres across Canada, the spark that had launched the Montreal carnival was never extinguished. Indoor rinks began with the skating fad of the 1860s; they continued to be built until the first world war, much assisted by the spreading popularity of hockey and curling. The local arena became a genuine community centre, with bonspiels, ice carnivals (featuring not only local talent but also wandering troops of barrel jumpers and trick skaters) and hockey games. To an extent wholly unappreciated today, women were deeply involved in these activities; in hockey alone there were dozens of girls' clubs in Canada by 1914. The arena also made possible the mushroom growth of private figure-skating and speed-skating clubs.

In Canada, curling, figure skating and skiing have been distinguished, above all other sports, by able, often brilliant, executive and administrative leadership. Each has been consistent in keeping records, that is in having a feeling for the past, and in promoting publicity. The richness of the literature available on curling is unmatched by any other game, with the possible exception of golf. Both games, of course, were created, developed and carried to the ends of the earth by Scottish emigrants. The Scots have a keen respect for the past and the printed word. Thus, there is a surfeit of histories of curling, each of which owes much to the original mammoth work written by Dr. John Kerr and published in 1890. Kerr, and other curling historians, have provided an exhaustive analysis of every phase of the game from how to run a club meeting to the most minute dissection of the delivery of a stone.

Wherever the Scots went in Canada curling clubs sprang up. Each club looked back to the mother club, the Royal Caledonian Club, which had been formed in 1838. In 1896, George Bryce, skip of the Winnipeg Granite Club, attended the annual meeting in Scotland as a representative from Canada, in order to extend a personal invitation for Scottish clubs to send teams to Canada. The grand visit and tour came off in 1900. One consequence was that the homeland curlers realized that their offspring had surpassed them in skill and technique. Another outgrowth of the tour was Bryce's two-volume work, *The Scotsman in Canada*, in which he described the spread of curling as "the crowning success of the Scottish nationality in Western Canada."

There are several explanations for the almost disproportionate zeal for curling in the Prairie provinces, where coverage by the media and the sheer numbers of those who participate make it the premier game. The nature of Prairie farming, particularly after mechanization, gave considerable winter leisure to thousands. Once the automobile became common the potential for hundreds of curling clubs was enhanced. Of course, the long-established clubs in the Prairie cities were the pacemakers and the focus for the major bonspiels along the road to the Brier. The failure of hockey to establish a sound professional or senior competition in Prairie cities has been to the advantage of curling; so has the dearth of satisfactory slopes for ski facilities close to the main urban centres (except in western Alberta). Figure skating is not a real rival simply because its raw material tends to come from the younger age groups. Snowmobiling, though popular, does not seem to have challenged curling's place as an integral part of the Western way of life.

The game appears captivatingly simple. The object is obvious: to place and leave as many rocks of your foursome at or near the button, and to displace from the centre as many of your rival's rocks as possible. From the first rock the novice knows the object of the game. Of course, he soon learns it is far from a simple game in terms of skills. There are infinite varieties in strategy and tactics; there is room for participation by curlers of both sexes, any age, and all levels of skill. Nor has curling had any lasting problems with the professional versus amateur issue, the bane of so many other sports.

National championships for men and women, schoolboys and seniors, are held annually, with the interprovincial Brier competition for men, which began in 1927, as the model. By 1970 world championship competition on an annual basis had been established and American and Swedish curlers were genuine challengers to Canadian domination of the game.

When the figure skating department of the Canadian Amateur Skating Association was formed in 1913, it had 8 member clubs, almost all located in Montreal, Ottawa and Toronto. In 1937 there were only 12 clubs in Canada; by 1943 there were 39; by 1953, 105; by 1963, 246; and by 1974, more than 800. A prodigious latter-day growth had made Canada, in terms of its population, the leading figure-skating country in the world.

Unlike skiing, where the Canadian contribution was late and largely in organization, Canadians were inseparable from the rich, diverse history of figure skating, almost from the emergence in the 1860s of Jackson Haines, the American ballet master and "father" of the modern sport. Jackson Haines toured Eastern Canada, giving exhibitions of his colourful skating. From that time to the present remarkably few figure-skating stars have failed to skate before Canadian audiences, usually under the sponsorship of the Canadian clubs. After the initial entry into Olympic figure skating in 1924 by Ottawa's Melville Rogers, the Olympics, the annual North American championships, then the annual world championships, became the target for ambitious Canadian skaters. The summer schools multiplied, as did the tests, the judges and the coaches. Fine leaders such as Norman Gregory, Charles Cumming, Roger and Hugh Glynn, improved the capabilities of the Canadian Figure Skating Association beyond belief so that when substantial government grants became available in the early 1960s, only the Canadian Ski Association matched the figure skaters in taking quick, sound advantage of them.

Jackson Haines married the move-

A typical example of skating rinks of the nineteenth century is the one *(top)* at Saint John, NB. *Below,* an old Indian craftsman makes snowshoes for his family and tribe.

187

ments of the ballet to skating but, like a draftsman, the assumptions he worked from were in some ways mathematical. It was the English skaters in the mid-decades of the nineteenth century who formulated routines from the tracing of skates on ice. Imagine a large sheet of ice on a lake or fen, a pristine invitation to the skater. English enthusiasts soon noticed that the strokes of a skater's blades were incised like etchings on the surface. From this it was a short step to the tracing of certain numbers and conventional designs upon the ice and the learning of the body movements needed to make them. How could one tell whether a figure had been done well? Only through a close examination of the figure itself, both for cleanness of execution and for conformity to what soon became a rigidly established symmetrical formula. Here was the origin of compulsory figures and of modern judging techniques. Precision skating in mid-Victorian England was the enthusiasm of the country house set; the popularity of the sport was limited by the short and erratic skating season in Britain.

Recreational skating has been popular since time immemorial. But from the 1830s to the mid-1860s some sensational advances were made in skate and shoe design, largely by American and Canadian inventors. The products were mass-produced and had wide distribution and sale. Indoor rinks were built throughout the northern states and in Canada. In 1860 there wasn't a single good indoor rink in Canada; by 1870 there were a dozen, with Sherbrooke, Halifax, Saint John, Quebec City and Montreal leading the way. By 1875 skating in Canada had become subdivided into aspects variously called "fancy," "figure," "trick,"

Hockey is undoubtedly the No. 1 contemporary winter sport in Canada, but it wasn't always that way. In the late 1800s and early 1900s interest in winter sporting activities was widely diversified. Ice boating was popular in areas where there was sufficient stretches of ice to make a good run, as shown (top) in the photo of the group on Toronto Bay in 1887. Many rural residents were committed to bobsledding, to a point where they designed fancy machines and engaged in spirited competitions on the slopes. *Far left,* five rivals line up for a race down the slopes near Ste. Agathe. The more proficient on snowshoes also liked to race; some even went in for hurdling, as shown in a race between G. Moffatt and C. Lockerby at Montreal. Lockerby (dark sweater) won.

"stunt" and "speed" skating. From this time until about 1910 North American and European stars were making a living at skating, often, as in the cases of Norval Baptie and Jack McCulloch, as all-rounders contesting races, doing tricks or stunts, dancing and fancy skating and, more rarely, figure skating.

In European capitals Jackson Haines had found an enthusiastic reception for the flowing style of skating to music. There were three styles of figure skating in vogue until the first world war – the "English," the "international" or "continental" and the "North American," an adaptation of the English style with minor influences from the international style. It was this latter style which Canadians favoured. These early, regional styles explain why the history of the sport has included so much international misunderstanding. This constant problem was not solved until the 1970s when "free" skating, with its individualism, was finally given a weighting over the "school figures" in international competition.

George Meagher of Montreal was the most accomplished of the early Canadian figure skaters next to Rubenstein. Indeed, he was a younger rival during the late 1880s. He became a world-touring professional and an instructor of note after he won the unofficial world championship in 1891. He wrote *Lessons in Skating,* published in 1900, a most influential book which did much to popularize in Canada the greater flow and more relaxed postures of the international style.

After Meagher's day there was a long period in which Canadian skaters were in the shadow of the Europeans. But in the Minto and Toronto Skating Clubs in particular a steady improvement was underway in the 1920s and 1930s. The leaders in these clubs had identified three needs: better instruction based on standard tests; knowledgeable and consistent judges; and a range of activities to attract young skaters and the general public. The annual ice shows or carnivals of these clubs anticipated such familiar professional spectacles of today as the Ice Capades and Ice Follies. Toronto and Ottawa pioneered the marriage of the theatrical devices and methods of costuming, lighting, choreography, comedy routines and music to solo, pair and ensemble skating. By 1939, as a result, the best Canadian skaters were reaching toward the top of international excellence. By the end of the second world war, spurred on by Barbara Ann Scott's success, almost all the champion men and women skaters of Canada went on to professional careers in touring ice shows.

Until quite recently figure skating was the victim of one of Canadian sport's organizational curiosities. When the Canadian Amateur Skating Association was formed in 1886 it embraced both the figure skaters and the much more numerous speed skaters. The interests of the two groups diverged sharply and since the dominant element in the association favoured racing the figure skaters were thrown back on the resources of individual clubs. By the 1930s figure skating was winning the battle of the committee rooms for it had overtaken speed skating in popularity. Swiftly the figure skaters built a national administration and a cadre of excellent professional instructors far surpassing anything the speed skaters had developed. But such is the inflexibility of international sporting organizations that not until 1951 were the figure skaters able to free themselves from a group with a markedly different social and athletic constituency and gain separate representation in the International Skating Union.

In recent years speed skating has enjoyed a minor revival and Canadians are appearing again near the top of international championships. There has always been a tendency for good cyclists to be good skaters, as both sports demand powerful legs. Thus, the bicycle boom of the early 1970s may give a fillip to our speed skating. The essential problem of Canadian speed skating vis-à-vis world competition has been our relative lack of large outdoor skating facilities. The typical indoor ice arena is a limited training facility for speed skating. Again there are indications, pioneered in 1972 in Ottawa on the huge expanse of the Rideau Canal which the National Capital Commission maintains, that outdoor recreational skating in Canada may be coming back. When 50,000 or more skaters in one city take to the canal on many winter days, the prospects for a resurgence of speed skating seem good.

The acknowledged cradle of European skiing lies southwest of Oslo in Norway in the province of Telemark. The modern word "ski" comes from an old Norse word, *scidh,* a piece or billet of wood.

Both the snowshoe and the ski developed for the same reason – man in the north sought to enlarge the sole of his foot in order to get a better hold on the surface of soft snow. The snowshoe was a device of the North American Indian; the ski was not, almost certainly because it was not nearly so useful as the snowshoe in deep snow and bush thickets. Fridtjof Nansen's epic trek on skis across the barren ice shield of Greenland in 1888, one of the great travel sagas of all time, was largely responsible for popularizing the ski. Nansen's book, published in 1890, was the catalyst; thousands of Europeans swarmed to the hills on skis and set the stage for the genesis of the sport into Alpine events (downhill and slalom) as distinct from the Nordic which includes both

190

strenuous cross-country racing and jumping events. Almost coincidental with the explosive birth of skiing in the Alpine massif, Scandinavian immigrants, particularly Norwegians, were introducing the ski in dozens of places in North America, especially in mining and logging localities.

In February 1879 the weekly Canadian *Illustrated News* featured an account of a "Norwegian gentleman of Montreal" who was skiing on "patent Norwegian snowshoes" the 170 miles to Quebec City. The first ski jumps built on Mont Royal and at Ottawa were the work of Norwegians. Probably the first formal ski races and jumping in Canada took place near Rossland in British Columbia in 1897 and during the next decade all evidence confirms the leadership of Norwegian and Swedish migrants.

The National Ski Association of Western Canada was initiated in 1912 at Camrose, Alberta, and it is clear from the names of the founders – Engebretson, Iversen, Floen, Bolseng, Maland – that they were of Scandinavian stock. A lasting national organization was formed in 1920 and once again, as in so many other sports, Montrealers provided the spark in convening what became the Canadian Amateur Skiing Association. In the beginning cross-country skiing was predominant but once the ski slope with its tow was perfected, the speed thrills of downhill skiing were no longer countered by the drudgery of hill climbing.

Once again it was the Montreal skiers, especially the Red Birds Ski Club of McGill, who played a key role in developing competitive downhill racing. Not only did they discover the delights of St. Jovite, opening up the first major ski resort on Mont Tremblant, but their weekend meets with American universities popularized the slopes as an exciting social and athletic playground. Across the country both established and newly created clubs were attracting skiers and developing slopes, clubhouses, tows and jumps from Grouse Mountain, near Vancouver, to Winnipeg, the lakehead, Kingston, Huntsville, Gravenhurst and so on. In many places the original impetus had been Scandinavian, but when skiing boomed after 1945 the ethnic component was fractional and the hundreds of thousands of skiers of today know little about the Norwegian cradle or the feats of Fridtjof Nansen.

In spite of the phenomenal growth of skiing, neither Canadian nor the American competitors have enjoyed much success in international competition. The international ruling organization, Federation Internationale de Ski (FIS), is an unbelievably strong body even though for some years now it has, in effect, been directed by two men, a Swiss lawyer as president, and another official operating, without staff, in Stockholm. In 1974 it was estimated that 100 million people ski, one-tenth of them competitively. Obviously skiing ranks as the participation sport without parallel.

There are forty-eight member countries in FIS and half of them run races under international rules; there are one hundred races in the FIS annual list.

From its earliest years FIS paid lip service to amateurism – it wanted skiing retained as an Olympic event. But by the 1950s professionalism was so rampant as to be inescapable; manufacturers of equipment put racing skiers on year-round contracts. The FIS has been able to hold its ground against challenges from the IOC since it is now confident that the Olympics need skiing more than skiing needs the Olympics. Since 1970 the annual world championship skiing circuit has displayed enormous vitality; the quadrennial Olympic events have simply been incorporated into the skiing calendar as additional fixtures.

The competition for Olympic and FIS honours has been very significant to the sport in Canada. The CSA has conducted aggressive campaigns for funds and talent, especially for the very costly national team. The Canadian Ski Instructors Alliance (founded in 1938) listed more than 3,000 members on its 1974 roster. The Canadian Ski Patrol, "the Red Cross of the slopes," is active across the country wherever skiing is practised. Ski resorts, which started as a minor industry in the mLaurentians north of Montreal, have now blossomed into major enterprises all across the country. Ski clubs have mushroomed with the sport and today the largest club in the world with 14,000-plus members in 1974 is at Camp Fortune near Ottawa. With the membership of nearby clubs added, Ottawa probably has 50,000 to 60,000 skiers on the slopes each year. In recent years the sport of cross-country skiing has been revived with a vengeance: More than 100,000 pairs of Nordic skis were sold one recent winter in the Montreal-Ottawa region alone.

Our quartet of major winter sports – hockey, curling, figure skating and skiing – are all relatively expensive. Their base of participation is unusually broad, geographically and in numbers. Curling and skiing, in particular, attract both sexes strongly, and over a lengthy age range. A common witness in all four sports is simply sustained, organizational genius. In each we should recognize with some modest pride impressive abilities at improvising and innovating devices and institutions. We master our distances and harness our competitive zeal into the archetypal, Canadian framework – from local to regional to national to international.

MATT BALDWIN, 1927-

Matt Baldwin, the Edmonton skip who won the Brier in 1954, 1957 and 1958, has been trying ever since to win it again. Much of the sporting press has been cheering him on; Matt Baldwin is a big favourite with the press. Dick Beddoes, sports columnist with the Toronto *Globe and Mail,* has written that Baldwin is "refreshing in a sport where stodginess is not exactly unknown . . . He gave the game a ballet form; gliding low out of the hack in a fluid delivery that could carry him the length of the ice."

Another curling commentator, Doug Maxwell, says: "Some of Baldwin's appeal is simply his sandy handsomeness with a darned engaging smile. And he's colourful. At the first tournament of champions . . . the crowd was longing for some action. Bill Tracy slid the length of the ice after his rock, and as it popped the stone he was after, he wound up facing the wrong way. He'd drifted. The crowd loved it, so a demonstration was arranged. Four curlers were asked to slide the length of the ice. Each made a good delivery but Matt's was so perfect that he came like an arrow stem behind his rock – no drift – and in the middle of the slide he rubbed his nose, then put his hand right back on the handle. He was moving at exactly the same speed as his stone and directly behind it. . . . At the Brier in Victoria [1958] he came down with the flu; he looked and acted as though he was dying. He brought a chair to the rink and sat slumped in it . . . when it came time for his shot he would get up and make it. And they were great shots. Then in the Quebec Brier of 1971, the rink was hit by a power failure. . . . When the lights came back on all the stones of the Baldwin rink were on or

around the button. He'd put them there for the fun of it. . . . Baldwin was a wonderful contrast to the deadly serious Richardsons and the shy, unobtrusive Ron Northcott."

Many curling fans believe that Matt Baldwin is a stern skip and point to the many changes in his rink's personnel over the years. Baldwin expects the same attitude and perfection from his rink as he himself puts out. It is generally agreed that Baldwin is an original thinker; he is analytical, innovative and daring. He will experiment with strategy and the results sometimes trap him; often brilliant, he sometimes "psychs" himself out.

Matt Baldwin began his curling in Bradwell, Saskatchewan, a few miles from his birthplace at Blucher. It was 1941 and he was only fourteen. He was twenty-six years old in 1953 when he emerged as a star skip in the Edmonton city zone Consols competition, then went on to take his first northern Alberta title. He was beaten out in the provincial championship by the southern champions from Calgary. Next year he went all the way, winning the Brier in Edmonton.

The Brier record in 1954 was 9-1, the only loss being to Ross Tarlton's Ontario rink. On the way Baldwin beat the Garnet Campbell rink from Saskatchewan and the Jimmy Welsh rink from Manitoba. The daily

press accounts of the Brier stressed the fear-
some accuracy of the Baldwin four's shots.

At thirty, he was the youngest skip
to take the Brier. He mixed both the draw
and the knockout game. With his last rock,
Matt gave "a Winnipeg skid" down the ice
and the 3,000 spectators stood and cheered.

In 1955 Baldwin lost to his arch
Nemesis in Edmonton curling, Herb Olson.
In 1956 he stormed out of Alberta with a
new lineup in front of him but collapsed at
the Moncton Brier posting a mediocre 5-5 record.

In both 1957 and 1958 Baldwin went
all the way. Reporters agreed that it was his
personal skill and the nervy ability to come
through in the late ends with double-kill
shots that carried the rink. In 1957 at Kingston his Brier score was 10-0.

In 1958 Baldwin got out of Alberta
by defeating Herb Olson in a tight three-
game final. (This was to be Baldwin's last
conquest of Olson for a period of twelve
years.) His Brier record was 9-2, the losses to
Saskatchewan and Ontario. The week came
down to a playoff with Terry Braunstein's
Manitoba rink which he won 10-6. Braunstein led after two ends and the packed Victoria Rink was noisily behind the Winnipeg
kids. Baldwin fought back with superb, risky
shots. Two of his 1958 rink, Gordon Haynes
and Bill Price, had been with him in 1957;
Dr. Jack Geddes had replaced Art Klein-
meyer.

Baldwin's subsequent record has
been one of recurring failures to get out of
Alberta. Several times he seemed to have super rinks, only to fail in the last provincial
competition, several times at the hands of
skips like Hec Gervais, who had once played
for him. In 1972 and 1973, Matt Baldwin,
now "elderly" by curling's current emphasis
on youth, curled but not well enough to
make it into the provincial finals. He may
never make it back to the top of the Brier
and into the Silver Broom but he's registered
on curling the imprint of a strong, colourful
personality, and the memory of some of the
greatest shots ever dared.

NORVAL BAPTIE, 1879-1966

Speed skater, figure skater, barrel-jumping
ace, ice showman; there has never been a
figure in the skating world to match Norval
Baptie. For sixteen years, from 1894, his
speed over the ice was unbeatable. During
those years he held ten professional titles.
When he ran out of opponents, he turned to
fancy and trick skating and, in 1914, pioneered a brand new kind of entertainment,
the ice show. Even in old age, with both legs

amputated, he still gave skating lessons from
a wheelchair.

Norval Baptie was born of Irish
stock in the village of Bethany, Ontario, in
1879. A year later his family moved to Bath-
gate, North Dakota. Baptie first started skating at the age of ten, on skates borrowed
from his sister. He practised on the frozen
Prairie ponds and ditches, and sometimes
raced the Great Northern Railroad trains by
skating the frozen creeks alongside the
tracks.

At fourteen he became the North
Dakota speed champion, and two years later,
in 1894, he challenged the world champion,
Jack McCulloch, to a race in Winnipeg,
McCulloch's home town. Baptie won by a
comfortable margin; this was the start of his
record-breaking career. From then on, all
speed records fell before his flying blades. As
an amateur and later as a professional, he
remained in competition for more than a
quarter-century, winning close to 5,000 races

193

at distances that ranged from 220 yards to five miles.

Baptie turned to stunt and figure skating. He set records for the broad jump, for skating backwards, for jumping over barrels, and even for skating on stilts. He also took to exhibition skating, putting together one-man shows and barnstorming his way around the northern United States and Canada. In later years, looking back to these days before the first world war, he recalled fondly:

> The show consisted of seven acts. First, I would help the ticket taker at the gate. Then I would loosen up with an exhibition of speed-skating, just to get some of the 20 to 30 below zero weather out of my bones. . . . A fox chase usually followed, with as many as fifty local youngsters skating their heads off in an effort to catch me. I would then jump some barrels, and in some of those towns they had kids who were pretty handy at this and they wouldn't be satisfied until you upped the number to exceed their best efforts. This would be followed with an exhibition of figure or fancy skating, as it was then called. The finale usually consisted of a stilt-skating exhibition and mine were usually measured 26 inches, although most of those used by today's spectacular acts are only 14 inches high.

These shows were such a huge success that after the first world war, Baptie expanded them into the kind of ice shows still popular today. He performed in the shows as well, and he and his partner Gladys Lamb (who later became his wife) introduced many intricate manoeuvres and crowd-pleasing stunts into their acts. In the early 1930s he directed the first shows featuring Sonja Henie.

Baptie retired from active skating in 1938 and moved to Washington, DC, to become professional coach for the Washington Figure Skating Club. In 1954 his left leg was amputated because of complications associated with diabetes and in 1958 his right leg-was also removed. Confined to a wheelchair he continued to teach. He moved to Baltimore and coached there and in Washington almost until his death. In 1963 he and Sonja Henie were the first two skaters named to the US Ice Skating Hall of Fame.

LELA BROOKS, 1908-

Lela Brooks was born into a family of speed skaters; her parents – competitive racers both – encouraged Lela and her three brothers, and enrolled all four in the Old Orchard Skating Club in Toronto. (Lela was, in fact, the first female admitted to the club.)

A petite brunette at five-foot-two and weighing less than 120 pounds for most of her career, Lela Brooks was an intense competitor, at each race flashing away from the starting post to grab the lead, then never letting up. Those were the days before skaters competed only against a stop watch; then all entrants lined up together at the starting line. As Lela Brooks explained: "You had to break and get in front if you ever hoped to win."

This was a technique Lela mastered very early in her skating career. From the age of thirteen, when she started to compete, until she retired in 1935, she had held all the titles it was possible for a woman to win at speed skating – Ontario indoor and outdoor championships, all Canadian, the international championship and, finally, the world championship.

Lela was born in Toronto in 1908. Her earliest experiences on the ice were at about the age of five or six, when she started out in the backyard rink pushing a kitchen chair around.

In the period between the wars, there were few artificial rinks for skating and hockey, even in a city the size of Toronto. There were scores of municipally run outdoor rinks on corner lots and half a dozen private club rinks organized and supported by either speed or figure skating buffs.

Although Lela's father was a competitor, he did not push his young daughter. In fact it was Lela herself who decided to skate competitively. "It was in the last meet of the year in the spring that I was twelve," she recalls. "I entered myself and almost won, except that I fell. I decided that if it was that easy I would skate next year."

The next year, at the age of thirteen, she won the 440-yards and the one mile in the under-eighteen Ontario championships. It was a modest beginning, but as Lela said, "it was then that I decided I was pretty good. It wasn't conceit, just the confidence you need to be a champion."

In 1924, her first year of serious

competition, Lela entered the Ontario indoor competition and won the under-sixteen, under-eighteen and senior half-mile events to become provincial champion. In one day's competition at the meet she raced twelve times, a remarkable display of competitive stamina in a fifteen-year-old girl.

In 1925 Lela Brooks took three Canadian championships: the 220-yard dash, the 440-yard, and the under-eighteen 880. In the international competition at Pittsburgh she won the 220-yard, the 440-yard and one-mile events. Finally, in the same year, she won the Chicago silver skate derby against a field of more than 200 challengers. By year's end she had broken six world records and firmly established herself as one of the world's best speed skaters.

Early in 1926 Lela skated in the world championship events held that year in Saint John, NB. It was to be Canada's year. Her speed skaters swept the board in all seven categories. Inevitably the main focus of attention was upon the great Charles Gorman, who battled American and European challengers to take the men's title in the final race of the meet. Lela Brooks put on a splendid performance. She won three out of four of her races. Only in the 220 yards was she defeated when she fell. But she emerged as the overall winner, and the women's world titleholder.

The world championship was the high point of Lela Brooks's career, but she continued winning Canadian and North American championships wherever she competed over the next few years. She held several world records, including the half-mile indoor and outdoor, and the three-quarter-mile outdoor. In 1928, at the Mardi Gras festival in Detroit, she broke the world one-mile record, and her record of 1.26 minutes for the half-mile set at Pittsburgh in 1926 still stands.

In 1936 Lela Brooks married Russ Campbell and moved to Owen Sound. At the last moment she decided not to go to the Olympic Games that year, and her days of competitive skating were over.

Lela's record was astonishing but perhaps the most unusual aspect of her career is that at no time did she receive coaching; her training consisted of daily workouts at the Old Orchard rink and cycling in the off season. It was a small miracle of self discipline.

PETRA BURKA, 1947-

Petra Burka was born in Amsterdam the same year Barbara Ann Scott became the first Canadian girl to win the women's world

Sports Hall of Fame

figure-skating championship. Eighteen years later, Petra Burka repeated Barbara Ann Scott's triumph and brought the championship back to Canada which has been her adopted country since she was four.

Petra was an active child with a natural aptitude for skating. Her mother, Mrs. Ellen Burka, had been a Dutch skating champion, and became a skating teacher when the family emigrated to Canada in 1951. Petra was given her first pair of skates when she was six. Her mother recalls: "I took Petra to the open air rink on Eglinton Avenue [Toronto] and put her on the ice. She just walked away from me without fear and in a few minutes she was skating as if she had been doing it for years. No stumbling, no falling, no tears. Simply a natural skater."

Three times a week Petra studied with her mother, and improved rapidly. But at this time, skating was still for fun – no long hours at compulsory figures, no summer skating. When she was thirteen, Petra won the Toronto senior ladies' title. She also entered the Canadian junior competition that year, but finished last. Despite the loss, Mrs. Burka realized that her daughter had tremendous ability.

The Burkas, mother and daughter, began serious training. Petra accepted the long, arduous hours of repetitious skating that goes into the making of a champion. She was slightly taller than five-foot-one but at 135 pounds she was solidly built, and big boned. She developed into a strong athletic

195

skater, capable of executing difficult jumps and turns normally thought to be the prerogative of male skaters. In 1966 she became the first woman skater to perform in competition the difficult triple salchow.

In 1964 Petra took the Canadian championship from Wendy Griner. It was in 1964, also, that she ventured into international competition, winning a bronze medal at the winter Olympics at Innsbruck and third place in the world championships.

At that time, the reigning world champion was Sjoukje Dijkstra of Holland, one of the greatest of all world title holders. Petra Burka realized that the judges of world competitions were not impressed with spectacular leaps and brilliant athletic performances; they wanted to see graceful movements. She started to take ballet lessons, worked at improving her free skating, and put in hours on the compulsory figures which she had shunned in her early years.

In 1965, Petra Burka reaped the rewards; in the space of one month she retained the Canadian championship, won the North American title, and finally, with the retirement of Sjoukje Dijkstra, captured the coveted world title at Colorado Springs.

The public started to notice the little Canadian champion. In 1964 and 1965 the sportswriters voted her top female athlete, and Canadians were hoping for a gold medal at the 1968 Olympics.

First, Petra had to retain her world championship in 1966 against the challenge of us champion, Peggy Fleming. Before going to the world championship meet at Davos, Switzerland, Petra defended her Canadian championship. She won, but a thirteen-year-old girl, Karen Magnussen, captured the fancy of the crowd in free skating, and one of nine judges placed her ahead of Petra. The damage to Petra's reputation was more psychological than real, but she went to Davos with a strike against her, and managed to finish only third in the world championships.

Shortly after, Petra decided to give up amateur skating and join a professional ice show. She spent three years with the show, found it a lonely life, and left to return to Canada. But her connection with skating did not end completely. Under the auspices of the federal government and the Canadian Figure Skating Association, Petra has helped promote amateur skating in Canada and to organize skating clubs across the country. She is a sports consultant on the staff of Sports Canada in Ottawa. Along with Marion Lay, the former swimming champion, she fights for a broader acceptance by parents, especially mothers, of an active place in sports for their daughters.

Michael Burns Photography

ELIZABETH CLIFFORD, 1954-

The skiing career of Betsy Clifford has been unfolding in 1974. Thus, one cannot sum it up as ill-fated or comparable in human tragedy with that of the unfortunate swimmer, George Young. The impression remains, however, that rarely has any of our athletes in adolescence and youth had a harder time in finding a balance between high talent, intense competitive spirit, personal identity and the huge expectations of an interested Canadian public.

Too much was expected from Betsy Clifford by her countrymen, who were seeking a successor to Nancy Greene and determined to cast the Quebec youngster in that role. "Look, I'm not Nancy," Betsy once burst out at a press conference. "I don't ski like Nancy, I am just me. Nancy got her medal and did her thing; now I have my medal and I am doing my thing."

Betsy Clifford was born to ski, the daughter of skiers. Her home was literally at the foot of the slopes of Camp Fortune, Ottawa, the world's largest ski club. Her father, John Clifford, operated the tows on concession from the Ottawa Ski Club. Clifford had been the major force in the rapid development of skiing in the Ottawa region in the postwar years.

It was Betsy's mother who began teaching the girl to ski, at three. Mrs. Clifford, a graduate in physical and health education, had been a good athlete. Her husband was a Canadian ski champion in his own right, and he trained Betsy in racing techniques until she was about ten. From the age of six Betsy competed in meets; by fourteen she was a member of the national ski team at Grenoble and the youngest Olympic skier in history, an experience of which she said later: "I did terribly, but I learned a lot."

Betsy's talent and exceptional physical attributes have never been in doubt. When she reached her full size she was five-foot-five, and 130 pounds; a compact, sturdy girl with broad shoulders and powerful legs.

The achievements which brought Betsy into the Sports Hall of Fame were accomplished in the season of 1969-70. She has always preferred the slalom to the downhill and early that season in Europe her slalom times and placings were improving. Then on 14 February 1970, at the Val Gardena world championships, she won the giant slalom and became the youngest skier to ever win a world title.

The expectations were that the 1970-71 season would put her on the skiing pinnacle. Although she raced well on occasion, including a first in the giant slalom at an Austrian meet, it was evident that the mercurial youngster was having her problems. At one point she left the team and went home. On her return she said the condition was that she should not ski the downhill race. "I never mastered the technique and the times seem to get faster." The coach of the national team, who thought her talent "super," considered that her relative lack of success in the downhill events stemmed from "defensive" skiing. On the other hand, her father felt that "there is no reason why she shouldn't be the best in the world in the downhill. She lost confidence with no one talking her into it and psyching her up for a race."

The focal point of the 1971-72 season was the winter Olympics at Sapporo, Japan. The Olympics had been Betsy's goal since her experience at Grenoble. Then, while training with the national team in Switzerland, she was cruelly injured, breaking both heels. Her chances to compete at Sapporo were gone. It was at that low point, and only eighteen years old, that Betsy Clifford decided to retire.

Of course, she couldn't quit skiing and gradually in the early winter of the 1972-3 season she got back both her form and perspective. She began to triumph over the pain of the heels and entered local meets and then the Can-Am Trophy series. Ultimately, she won the women's division of the series and by the end of February there were headlines: "Betsy's back." As the national team moved through its early European phase in 1974, Betsy was near the top in world ratings.

FRANCES DAFOE, 1923- & NORRIS BOWDEN, 1919-

Frances Dafoe and Norris Bowden were the first pair of Canadian figure skaters to become world champions. In their wake followed many more. Dafoe and Bowden burst on the international scene in the early 1950s with a new style of skating. With superb artistry and precision, they executed a bewildering variety of lifts, jumps and triple turns, giving an excitement and originality to figure skating which the more conservative, stereotyped European routines had lacked. The audiences loved it. But in the complex, sometimes murky politics of international judging, the Canadians' style was often put down as "athletic." It was, perhaps, this athletic virtuosity that lost Bowden and Dafoe the world championship in 1953 and an Olympic gold medal in 1956. But in 1954 and 1955 they beat back intense European competition and partisan judging to become Canada's first pairs world champions.

There was about the team of Bowden and Dafoe a freshness, a close harmony, and an independence of spirit unique among competitive skaters. They invented all their own routines, and were always planning new and more spectacular ones. Frances designed all the costumes for their international competitions. They were fiercely competitive and determined to get to the top, yet their dedication never got out of hand. They both had other careers at the same time – Norrie as an insurance salesman and Fran as a fashion designer. They could say quite truthfully, "Skating is a hobby. We love every minute of it." And when they had achieved the highest honours in the amateur field, the world championship and a silver medal at the 1956 Olympics, they quit. Fran explained it: "There are only three roads open to you after you've won your amateur titles. Either you turn professional and travel from city to city with touring ice shows; you teach skat-

Sports Hall of Fame

197

ing; or you retire. We retired."

Both Norrie Bowden and Fran Dafoe were Toronto-born, and were members of the Toronto Skating Club. They were singles of outstanding ability, especially Norrie who at one time held almost every Canadian title available–champion in singles, pairs, dance, the waltz. First, his studies at the University of Toronto, then his insurance career, did not leave him the time to go farther in the exacting singles competitions. Fran had had to give up her thoughts of singles championships in 1948 and 1949 when she broke her ankles. Fran and Norrie decided to team up at the instigation of their coach, Sheldon Galbraith.

The man who had coached Barbara Ann Scott to world and Olympic championships, Galbraith has probably done more than anyone else to raise the standard of figure skating in Canada and to develop the Canadian winning style in international competition. He gave to Bowden and Dafoe the confidence and polished style that put them into world contention. Even more important, he prepared them for the fierce national rivalries and political jockeying for favours that have always been part and parcel of the European judging scene. Canadian officials were singularly inept at understanding this exasperating problem. They would not even admit that such favouritism between judges of different nationalities existed. Many times Canadian skaters would be at a disadvantage in international competition–no officials to support them, inadequate practice facilities, impossibly heavy exhibition schedules arranged for them by European skating associations. Sheldon Galbraith was aware of these pitfalls. Several times he was able to accompany Bowden and Dafoe as coach only because the skaters themselves and their families paid his expenses.

The partnership of Bowden and Dafoe was successful from the start. They had perfect timing, a smooth stride and an understanding between them both on and off the ice. In 1952, their first year of competition, they were Canadian pairs champions, and placed fourth in the world championships in Paris. In 1953 they took the North American championship and were edged into second place for the world title by a British pair.

They went to Oslo in 1954 fully prepared to take the title. They presented a beautifully integrated, musical routine which contained a spectacular new lift, in which Bowden tossed Fran to a sitting position on his right shoulder, then let her slide head-long down to the ice, ending in a mad spin. "We always like to think up some new

figures every year," Bowden told reporters at the time, "to let the judges know that we haven't gone stale." This time there could be no doubt of their superiority. They placed far ahead of the Swiss team of Sylvia and Michael Grandjean, to become Canada's first world pairs champions.

Bowden and Dafoe successfully defended their title the next year in Vienna. They turned in an even more brilliant performance. It was given in the teeth of a gale, with snow swirling and in below-zero temperatures. Afterwards Bowden said: "The snowstorm was so thick there were times when I couldn't even see Fran, but everything clicked marvelously."

There remained only the honour of winning a gold medal in the 1956 Olympics. Bowden and Dafoe had decided to retire at the end of the year; this was to be their chance to win. The victory was almost literally snatched from them by the Austrian pair of Schwartz and Oppeit by the slimmest of margins. The pair seemed to tire towards the end of their performance. Fran Dafoe lost her balance momentarily and faltered in her lift. She quickly recovered but the slight fluff undoubtedly lost them the gold medal.

When they returned to Canada they were highly critical of the attitude of the CFSA's attitude in support of the Canadian Olympic team. This led to their suspension by the association. Norrie's forthright comments did lead to an improvement in the CFSA. In recent years it rates with the best-organized skating associations in the world.

Both Bowden and Dafoe retired into private life without regrets, and watched with pleasure as, the following year, the world championship title they had vacated was won by another Canadian pair, Barbara Wagner and Bob Paul.

THE VICTOR EMERY BOBSLED TEAM, 1964

To the delight (and bafflement) of the sporting public, and to the embarrassment and confusion of the official and press representation at the 1964 Winter Olympics, four Canadians ascended the Innsbruck victory podium to accept gold medals for their completely unexpected victory in bobsledding. The sport had been dominated for years by Europeans, especially the Italians and Austrians. It had (seemingly) no roots whatever in Canada, and little in North America, since the only bobsled run was at Lake Placid, New York. Was the victory of the Canadians, who were referred to as "playboys" by the sportswriters at Innsbruck, a mere fluke? The answer lies in the nature of the sport,

Canada's victory in the world bobsled competition at St. Moritz in 1965 was achieved by this foursome. *From the left,* **Michael Young, Victor Emery, Gerald Presley and Peter Kirby.**

and the background and experience of the men who made up the Canadian team.

Bobsledding means riding a steel sled down an ice chute. Sled runs, usually about a mile long, curve and switch back throughout their length, although straight-aways give some infrequent relief. The runs are built up from foot-thick ice blocks; once the chute is formed, tons of water are poured down to create a glassy smooth track. One bobsledder has described the sensation of racing as similar to parachuting: "in those moments before the chute opens, you feel your face being squashed into peculiar shapes by an immense blast of cold air." Air currents buffet the body and the smashing bumps in the run slam through the steel frame to be felt in every bone; above everything else, there are powerful gravity forces of up to four G's compressing the sledders as they whip into curves at high speeds. The movements of the sled driver must be absolutely precise, and he must make them to the ac-companiment of a roar of sound that has been compared to a freight train on the loose. A tiny error of judgment, a momentary failure of nerve, the slightest false move, and the bobsled may smash into an ice wall, or somersault down the chute, or climb the rim and spin off to the waiting mountain-side.

Bobsledding, like automobile racing, is a dangerous and thrilling sport. Of 104 competitors in the 1963 world championships bobsled competition, 23 went to hospital; in the course of the winter games some half-dozen have died.

Bobsledding is also an expensive sport–doubly so for Canadians. The sleds cost $2,000 each; practice time at Lake Placid means great expense, and experience on European runs is essential–and costly. In Europe the sport is the diversion of wealthy men and of athletic gypsies; the four Canadians at Innsbruck were scarcely either. It all started when Victor Emery, a spectator at the Cortina Olympics in 1956, became fascinated by bobsledding and had infected his brother John with his own enthusiasm. Vic was a graduate of the University of Western Ontario and the Harvard Business School, a top sailor, skier, a pilot. His brother John, now a surgeon, had been an all-rounder at Trinity College School and Queen's University. By 1959 the brothers had assembled a like-minded group around them, having formed the Laurential Bobsledding Association in 1957. And after a certain amount of practice at Lake Placid, a four-man team entered the world championships at St. Moritz. Of sixteen teams entered, the Canadians finished thirteenth. Not an auspicious beginning but enough to hook all four.

Canadian bobsled teams entered every world championship between 1959 and the 1964 Olympics. They didn't win one event but they did draw together an experienced team. The Emery brothers remained the nucleus of the group; all members (there were two Canadian teams at Innsbruck) were young professional men like themselves, with a similar background in athletics. Douglas Anakin, one of those chosen to ride in the No. 1 sled, was a Queen's graduate and a high school teacher; he had been an intercollegiate wrestler, was an expert skier and a keen mountain climber. Both the Emerys were six-footers and big men; Anakin was only five-foot-seven and weighed 150 pounds. The other member was a Montrealer, Peter Kirby, a Dartmouth graduate in geology who had been Canadian junior alpine skiing champion in 1951, a member of the Canadian FIS team in 1954, and captain of the Dartmouth ski team in 1956.

Bobsledding is a sport that measures its winners and losers in hundredths of seconds, taking total time over four runs. The start is crucial, and is made by the whole team charging like sprinters from blocks, and leaping on the sled at the last possible moment. Tenths of seconds lost here cannot be made up once the downhill run starts. Prior to Innsbruck, the Canadians had been able to practice starts only as dry runs in the gymnasium and in their infrequent trips to Lake Placid. At Innsbruck, they had had four practice runs only; the Italians, Austrians and others had been training there for weeks.

On their first run, the Canadians, with Vic Emery as driver, Anakin as number two, John Emery in the third position and Kirby as brakeman, took a commanding lead with a record run for the course. They almost lost everything on the second run; an axle seized as they were about to start; they took off anyway because disqualification would have come from any delay. On the last of the thirteen hairpin turns, the sled began to fishtail. "I had a sickening feeling," Dr. Emery said, "as I knew we were losing time. As we went up the wall, we all leaned away from the incline and that got us out of it." They continued to hold their lead through their third run, and on the last run they went all out to record the fastest run of the day and nail down the only gold medal Canada won at the Innsbruck Olympics.

The other Canadians attributed their victory to the "competitiveness and psychological readiness" of their cool pilot, Vic Emery; he, however, gave the Italians, and especially Eugenio Monti, who finished third, the credit. From 1960 on, it was the Italians who advised the inexperienced Canadians;

"they taught us all we know," said Emery.

As proof that the 1964 victory was no fluke, a Canadian team retained the world four-man bobsled title at St. Moritz in 1965. On this occasion, Vic Emery and Peter Kirby were joined by two men much younger than themselves. Michael Young, a twenty-one-year old business administration student at the University of Western Ontario, had two years of bobsledding experience. The other, Gerald Presley of Arnprior, was a cadet at the Royal Military College of Canada, Kingston. The Canadians won three of the four runs in the championship, winning the title over an Italian team piloted by Nevio de Zordo by two full seconds. "It's always a relief to win the second time," said Emery. "You're not real champions unless you can do it a second time."

CHARLES GORMAN, 1897-1940
Charlie Gorman's successes in speed skating brought fame to his hometown of Saint John, NB, and earned him the title of "the fastest man in North America." He won the world speed championship in 1926 and the following year captured four more international titles. In the incredible 1927 season he made a clean sweep of every title available to him. He was a tenacious competitor with a consuming desire to be best; he never won an Olympic gold medal and he carried that disappointment with him to the grave.

Speed skating was already a popular sport in the Maritimes when Charlie Gorman was born; indeed, the first marathon race in

Sports Hall of Fame

the world had been held in Saint John in 1884. The winters provided plenty of opportunities for outdoor skating, and Charlie took to the blades when he was quite young. He served in Europe in the first world war and returned home with a shrapnel wound in his leg. But Charlie was nothing if not determined. He skated hard, kept fit, and entered all the local races. He had some success and steadily improved. But he was unable to sustain his speed to beat the more experienced skaters who came from all over North America to the meets. He soon realized that his short, rather choppy stride tired him out too quickly. So he set about changing his action to the long, sweeping stride that was to bring him victory.

Gorman's first big win was in 1924 when he won the US national amateur outdoor championship and went on, a few weeks later, to take the international title at Lake Placid, NY, with an all-out effort in the three-mile event. "The guy with the million-dollar legs" became a star attraction at skating meets but the bubble was to burst in 1925 when he lost both titles. Some observers thought Gorman had passed his peak but they ignored the Maritimer's dogged determination. In 1926 he fought back to the world championship and in the process defeated the 1924 Olympic gold medallist, the Finn, Clas Thunberg.

Then came the winter of 1927. Gorman began by winning the mid-Atlantic championship; next he tied for first place in the US outdoor national; at Quebec City he won the Canadian indoor title; he retained his own world championship, broke the world record for the one-sixth mile, and shaved a second off his own mark in the 440-yard event; finally he took the US national indoor title.

With this impressive season behind him, Gorman went to the 1928 Winter Olympics. In the 500-metre event he placed a disappointing seventh after another runner had fallen in front of him. The judges refused Gorman's plea for another heat and he left the games in protest.

Gorman died in 1940 but the record he set in the 220-yard indoor, the 440-yard indoor and outdoor, and the one-sixth mile still stand.

NANCY GREENE, 1944-

Nancy Greene was Canada's tiger of the ski slopes–a tough competitor who fought hard to win. She twice captured the women's world ski championship, and won a gold and a silver medal at the 1968 Olympics. She was adored by millions of Canadians, not just ski

buffs and sports fans, but also by people who never got closer to a ski slope than their TV set. She has been a valued ambassador for Canada throughout the world, and Canadians recognized her contribution by naming her woman of the year in 1968.

Nancy Greene says she can't remember not being able to ski. Like most folks in Rossland, BC, the Greene family–father, mother, and six children–spent their winters skiing down Red Mountain, and from the age of three Nancy went along too. From the start she showed natural ability. She was not interested in racing until she was picked for her high school ski team. When she was fifteen the Canadian junior championships were held at Rossland. This was her home ground; she knew every bump and ridge of Red Mountain and she was determined to compete for the championship. But she was not a member of Canada's ski team, and it was only when two members of the team had to drop out that officials let Nancy try the course. Her performance was impressive and within two years she was selected for the Canadian Olympic team.

From then on competitive skiing occupied nearly all of Nancy's life. With her fiercely competitive spirit she embarked on a decade of continual hard work to become the world's best at a sport she had begun for pleasure. In winter she had a daily regime of exercises and skiing; in summer there were more special exercises and ski trips to glaciers in Canada or the slopes of South America.

As a member of Canada's team at the 1960 Winter Olympics at Squaw Valley, Nancy finished twenty-second in the downhill race. But she continued to improve, and in the 1964 Olympics at Innsbruck, Austria, she was seventh in the downhill and fifteenth in the slalom.

Her big chance came in 1967, with the organization of the first World Cup competition. The sport at that time was dominated by the French skiers, and the idea was to introduce a little more interest and competitiveness into the sport. In World Cup competition a system of points are awarded, based on performances in nine meets in Europe and North America.

Nancy Greene emerged from the first three meets in Europe with an overall lead. But she missed the next three meets—she returned to Canada to fulfil a promise to promote races on Canadian slopes which she hoped would encourage the development of Canadian talent. When Nancy returned to World Cup contention in the last three meets in North America, she was behind two French girls, Marielle Goitschel and Annie Famose. Then Nancy revealed a trait which served her well throughout her competitive career—when things were toughest, she fought harder.

Nancy entered the final meet at Jackson Hole, Wyoming, twenty-one points behind Goitschel. She won both heats of the giant slalom—her best race—easily enough. In the women's slalom she flashed down the mountain through fifty-six gates for a first run of 46.16 seconds. This placed her second, with her chief rival, Goitschel, third. Before the second run, she was calm. "I never get nervous between runs. Now that I know what the ice is like I can run a little faster next time." And that is precisely what she did, making the run in 44.51 seconds, to beat Goitschel for the world title by seven-hundredths of a second.

In 1968 Nancy had a double objective—to retain her World Cup title, and to win an Olympic gold medal. The Olympics at Grenoble, France, came first. Nancy had sprained her ankle in previous competition, and there were fears that this might spoil her chances. These fears increased when she placed tenth in the downhill; she was badly beaten and discouraged. In the slalom, the second event, her first run was slow, but she came from behind with a tremendous second run to win the silver medal, losing to her old rival, Marielle Goitschel. That left only the grand slalom event. Nancy turned in a stunning performance, to capture the coveted gold medal. Afterwards she explained, "I attacked the course from the top to the bottom and I worked very hard all the way down. The course was in excellent shape and I had no time to make mistakes." Her performance showed why she was called "Tiger" – her margin of victory of four seconds over France's Annie Famose was the widest in recent Olympics. When it was over she beamed, "I feel great. It is the best race I've ever skied."

All that was left was to win the World Cup a second consecutive time. She did, in storybook fashion. She clinched her victory in the World Cup by winning a race on Red Mountain where she had learned to ski almost twenty years earlier. She entered the competition seemingly in an excellent position; but she nearly stopped the hearts of her hometown fans when she fell in an early race. Thus, once again she had to come back from near defeat to victory. The 1968 World Cup was her last skiing victory. The same year she was voted Canada's outstanding female athlete for the second year in a row.

Between these triumphs and her marriage in 1969 to Al Raine, Nancy served on the federal Task Force on Sport for Canadians with Harold Rea and Paul Des Ruisseaux. The recommendations of the trio have been largely put into effect by Ottawa.

Raine coached the national ski team from 1968 to 1973. After he resigned as coach, the couple plunged into the development of a new ski area called Brandywine, near BC's Whistler Mountain.

ANNE HEGGTVEIT, 1939-
On 26 February 1960 at the Winter Olympics in Squaw Valley, California, a twenty-one-year old Ottawa girl won a gold medal by taking the slalom with a combined time margin of 3.3 seconds over her nearest rival. Anne Heggtveit's victory went a long way towards dispelling the gloom that had settled over the Canadian camp when the United States had defeated the Canadian hockey team a few hours before. In describing her race, the Canadian Press reported that Anne had "flashed out of nowhere" to win. Nothing could be further from the truth. Her story is a kind of case history of the arduous and expensive process by which world skiing champions are made.

Anne's family included accomplished skiers on both sides. Her father Halvor, a bank employee, had been a Canadian cross-country champion; so had her uncle, Bruce

Canada Wide Feature Service Ltd.

Heggtveit. Another uncle, Bud Clark, had been a member of Canada's Olympic ski team in 1932 and 1936. Near at hand, during Anne's precocious skiing childhood, were first the baby slopes in Rockcliffe Park and then the hills and trails of Camp Fortune, that remarkable skiing incubator in the Gatineau Hills. Only a couple of hours away was the Laurentian skiing complex.

Halvor Heggtveit first took his daughter skiing strapped to his back. When she was two, however, she was put on her own skis. By the time she was five, Anne was forerunning slalom courses for the Ottawa Ski Club, an invaluable experience she later duplicated at Lake Placid. At seven, she launched her competitive career by winning the Gatineau zone senior ladies' slalom and combined at Wakefield, Quebec, doubtless a humiliating experience for the ladies but certainly confirmation of her father's belief that "the parents have the first chance to spot talent."

Under her father's coaching, and that of Ernie McCulloch at Mont Tremblant, Anne developed a high degree of technical excellence. By 1954, she had won almost every competition open to her in the Ottawa region, and had had her first taste of North American competition. That year she made her first international splash. At Oppdal, Norway, the fifteen-year old won the Holmenkollen giant slalom over a field of world-class skiers, the youngest person to win the event in the half-century since this famous meet had begun. Only the misfortune of a

broken leg sustained while practising in early 1955 prevented Anne from making her mark at the Cortina Olympics; as it was, she placed quite respectably though obviously not fully recovered.

Like Lucile Wheeler, with whom she had skied for many years, Anne was placed under the supervision of the Austrian coach, Pepi Salvenmoser, for advanced training in racing techniques. That final polishing paid off in 1959. At St. Moritz, in January 1959, Anne won the two-stage combined title in the white ribbon tournament. Two weeks later, at Garmisch-Partenkirchen, she won the even more prestigious Arlberg-Kandahar championship, the first non-European man or woman to do so.

Anne Heggtveit's Olympic victory, and the gold medals of the World Skiing Federation emblematic of world titles in slalom and Alpine combined, were no accident. Nineteen years of skiing, the most careful grooming, and personal qualities of determination, courage and concentration had gone into their production. After Anne had completed that dazzling, twisting second run down Papoose Mountain that brought her victory at Squaw Valley, she remarked that "I didn't play it safe today; I decided to go all out." But reckless daring was not really her forte. As she also said, "Concentration is the key. You can't win if you go too slow but you can also lose if you don't keep control. You have to think in terms of rhythm rather than stop-watches." She was full of praise for Salvenmoser. "Pepi developed my confidence in myself. I lost my nervousness in downhill racing because I felt he never told me I could do anything beyond my ability."

After her Olympic triumph, Anne Heggtveit retired from further competitive skiing, and was admitted to the Hall of Fame in the same year.

DONALD JACKSON, 1940-

Don Jackson is a quiet, self-effacing man. He is small – only five-foot-four and slightly built. But on the ice he is probably the finest skater Canada has ever produced. Sheldon Galbraith, the skating coach who has numbered Barbara Ann Scott, Barbara Wagner and Bob Paul among his students, has called Don Jackson "the greatest natural skater I have seen."

Jackson was born in Oshawa where he began skating lessons at nine. Even then he was a showman on ice and had announced to his parents his ambition to be a champion; his announcement wasn't taken seriously when he tried his first skating test five times before passing, his second four. By

the age of twelve he'd settled down into the disciplined routine necessary for the production of a champion. His family supported him in his ambitions, even though the financial burdens were considerable. His mother took a job, and over ten years contributed something like $30,000 to Don's training.

When the Oshawa rink burned down, Don was sent to Ottawa to train under Otto Gold at the Minto Club. He was an apt pupil, and in 1955, at the age of fourteen, he won the Canadian junior men's title.

Don Jackson spent the next three winters in New York training under the great coach, Pierre Brunet of the New York Skating Club. He trained with US women's champion Carol Heiss, and the experience he gained during these years started to pay off in international competition. In 1959 he captured the Canadian senior men's title and went on to win the North American championship in Toronto. In the world championships in Colorado Springs the same year he presented a strong challenge to the reigning American champion, Dave Jenkins. Jackson placed fourth in the compulsory figures, but his free-skating display was breathtaking. His delayed double salchow, where he stopped dead in mid-air before spinning twice, brought some cheering spectators to their feet. At the age of eighteen he gained second place, and it was obvious that this young man was a champion in the making.

In the 1960 Winter Olympics Jackson won a bronze medal; once again he placed second in the world championships. In 1961 he returned to Canada and came under the aegis of Sheldon Galbraith at the Toronto Skating Club. Galbraith's influence gave Don the extra polish that pushed him to the top. In 1962 he was in Prague to compete again for the world championship. The main challenger was Karol Divin of Czechoslovakia, silver medalist in the 1960 Olympics. After the compulsory figures Divin was 45.8 points ahead of Jackson, a seemingly impregnable lead. Jackson says: "I asked Mr. Galbraith if there was any way for me to win, and he said, 'There's room at the top.' So I went out and skated." And *how* he skated. Even veteran experts had seen nothing like it. Don progressed from one spectacular leap to another. He executed the first triple Lutz jump in the history of competitive skating; he followed with a triple salchow and three double axels, one of them with his arms folded across his chest. It was the first time the men's singles crown had been won by a Canadian.

Don Jackson never won an Olympic gold medal. Before the 1964 games he turned professional and joined an ice show. Don had always been very conscious of the sacrifices his family had made in order to make his success possible. He decided it was time to start to pay them back. But in 1969, now married and with a small son, he had had enough of travelling from city to city and living out of suitcases. So he quit the Ice Follies, in order to devote his time to coaching up and coming young Canadian skaters.

MARIA JELINEK, 1943-
OTTO JELINEK, 1940-
Maria and Otto Jelinek come from a prosperous, old Czech family; their father, Henry, was a thriving manufacturer of cork. Both Otto and Maria were born during the Nazi occupation of their country, when the nation and the Jelinek family lived in fear. Both parents were keen skaters, and they encouraged all five children in the sport. But only Otto and Maria showed any aptitude or enthusiasm. Their mother encouraged them and they practised assiduously, even through the turbulent postwar years of their country. By 1947 they were proficient enough to give their first public show, at Prague's Winter Stadium.

When the Communists nationalized the Jelinek cork business, the family decided to leave the country. With the aid of a friendly diplomat, and travelling with forged passports, they emigrated to Canada in 1951.

Henry Jelinek set about re-establishing himself in the cork business and after a few shaky years he prospered; there was again money for Otto and Maria to continue their skating lessons. They joined the Oakville Skating Club and came under the skilled coaching of Bruce Hyland. He understood the temperaments of his two young pupils – the fierce determination and almost devil-may-care drive for perfection in Otto, and the quieter but equally strong sense of dedication in his sister.

Their first success in national competition came in 1955, when Otto was fifteen and Maria twelve; they won the Canadian junior championship for pairs. A local reporter gave this lyrical description of the young couple: "On the ice they make a fascinating picture with their unaffected youthfulness. Otto is a most engaging boy, bright-faced and alert in body. His sister Maria, skating with her pig-tails merry-go-rounding gaily in her self-created breeze, is a vision right out of fairy-tale books." It is only fair to mention that the only other pair competing withdrew owing to injury. Nevertheless, they were on their way to the world championship.

At the time their competition was formidable. The pairs figure skating scene was dominated by the incomparable Canadian team of Barbara Wagner and Bob Paul. The Jelineks placed a surprising second to the Canadian couple in the North American championships in 1957, and third in the world championships in Paris the following year.

In 1960 Wagner and Paul were still the champions, and the best Otto and Maria could do was a fourth, both in the world championships and in the Winter Olympics at Squaw Valley. The Olympic result was disappointing. The two put on a dazzling display of double overhead axels, spins and Lutz lifts which should have earned them a bronze. Indeed the identical judges awarded the Jelineks a silver medal in the world championships held in Vancouver a short time later.

After the 1960 world championship, Barbara Wagner and Bob Paul retired, leaving the way clear for the Jelineks to move into the limelight. They lost no time, capturing the North American title in Philadelphia the same year. It was here that Otto's passion for perfection nearly led to disaster. In the practice session the day before they were due to perform, he insisted on rehearsing the reverse double Lutz lift just one more time. It was a lift they had performed many times before, but on this occasion Otto's skate caught in the ice and the pair fell heavily. Otto suffered concussion and needed three stitches to close his head wound; Maria had a deep gash in her thigh. Against medical advice, still stiff and shaken from their injuries they took to the ice the next day to give a stirring, near-perfect performance to win the title.

Sports Hall of Fame

The next stop was Prague, and the world championship but the meet was postponed for a year when the whole American team was killed in a plane crash.

The Jelineks had planned to retire after the 1961 world championship, but they decided to give it one more try and compete again the following year. And so it was that on 14 March 1962 Maria and Otto Jelinek became the world champions in their native city of Prague. It was a close victory; before 18,500 cheering fans, the brother and sister team beat the Russian challengers by 102.2 points to 102.0. Early in their performance Maria fell in a double axel jump, and it looked as if all chances of victory had gone. But they steadied themselves quickly and went on to give a brilliant display, including a daring new move, in which Maria went into a death spiral while Otto executed an axel jump – a manoeuvre now known as the Jelinek death spiral.

After Prague the Jelineks retired from amateur skating and spent two seasons with the Ice Capades. Later Maria went to the University of Michigan to study languages and Otto set himself up in the skate manufacturing business. Otto entered federal politics, as the Progressive Conservative MP for York Humber, winning this seat in the 1972 federal election. Maria has been managing a Toronto boutique.

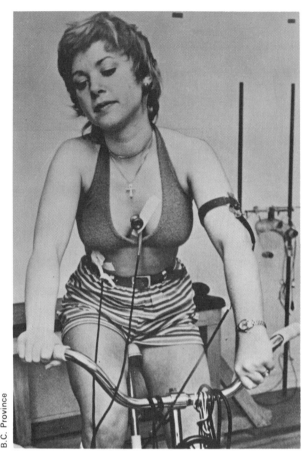

B.C. Province

KAREN MAGNUSSEN, 1952-

Karen Magnussen's first public appearance as a skater came when she was six and appeared in the role of a snowflake in a Vancouver winter carnival. In later years, under the coaching of Linda Branckmann, she was to become a world champion.

Karen first made the headlines in 1966, when she competed in the Canadian championships in Peterborough. A blonde reed of a girl at fourteen, she placed fourth. She showed such dazzling form, however, in her free skating that one judge scored her ahead of the reigning champion, Petra Burka. She was still a novice, though, and an unknown in international competition; in her first international meet at Vienna in 1967 she placed twelfth.

When Petra Burka retired, Karen took the Canadian title in 1968, only to lose it to Linda Carbonetto of Toronto the following year.

In the North American championships in 1969, Karen placed second to Janet Lynn of the US, a pert, vivacious skater just a few months Karen's junior, and like Karen, a crowd pleaser in her spectacular free skat-

ing programs. A few weeks later, the two girls were at Colorado Springs for a return match, this time in the world championships. But a few days before the championships Karen was suffering such pain in her legs that a doctor was called in. He diagnosed stress fractures in both legs; to Karen's bitter disappointment she had to watch the meet from the sidelines, in a wheelchair. "Even as I sat there I was planning for next year's competition. I never considered giving up – I always knew I'd be back."

Karen had her legs in casts for three months. Many people predicted that her skating career was over. That was not Karen's view, nor that of her family and coach. Within a few months she was back again on the ice, practising for all she was worth to make up for lost time. She made a startling comeback in 1970 to recapture her Canadian title, which she retained in 1971, 1972 and 1973.

In 1971 Karen competed against Janet Lynn again in the North American championships, and this time Karen became a prime contender for the world championships at Lyon a few weeks later.

Here, however, the challenge Karen Magnussen faced was of a different kind. International competition at that time still gave half the marks to compulsory figures, a

206

precise, demanding, yet unspectacular part of the figure skating art in which North American skaters have never been strong. The Austrian champion, Beatrix Schuba, while something less than inspiring in her free skating, was masterly in the uncanny precision she demonstrated in her compulsory figures. Schuba built up a commanding lead which Karen, with a below standard free skating performance, could not overtake. Karen had to be content with a bronze medal.

The story was repeated in 1972. The statuesque but unexciting Trixie Schuba won the gold medal at the Winter Olympics and retained her world championship, with Karen in second place, closely followed by the American girl, Janet Lynn.

But in 1973, two things combined to give Karen her chance: The reigning champion had retired, and the International Skating Association changed the marking system, giving the compulsory figures only 20 percent of the total, basic free skating exercises another 20 percent, and 60 percent to free skating. And so at the world championships at Bratislava, Czechoslovakia, it was Karen Magnussen all the way.

An English journalist, Clive James, in a short paragraph, described the Magnussen of 1973:

> In the compulsories Janet Lynn had mucked up her double jumps and left Karen Magnussen too far ahead to catch. With the competitive element eliminated, however, the spirit of the art was free to flourish and Magnussen turned in an absolute face-freezer – a display of dramatic power that ran like cold fury on silver rails, propelled by one continuous friction-free impulse from her eloquently stacked centre section.

Karen came home to a banquet chaired by Prime Minister Pierre Trudeau, and her hometown of Vancouver gave her an ecstatic welcome on her twenty-first birthday.

Later in 1973 Karen signed with the Ice Capades, in which she quickly became a major entertainer. In October 1973 Karen was invested by the governor-general with the Order of Canada; shortly after the Skating Institute of America named her ice skating queen of the year. She has found her own project to put something back into the amateur skating world; the Karen Magnussen Foundation was inaugurated in Vancouver to help young skaters. The fund is building with donations, and she both contributes to it and works to publicize it.

JACK MCCULLOCH, 1872-1918
Jack McCulloch was the first athlete from Manitoba to win world renown. He did so as a speed skater, though he was far more than that. As Tait Mackenzie wrote of him, "one can hardly call him a specialist, for besides speed skating, in which he is supreme, he is a good figure skater and hockey player; as an oarsman and canoeist he is noted, not to speak of gymnastics; while his fame as a cyclist, sprinter and jumper would be enough to make the reputation of most men."

Before McCulloch reached his peak as a speed skater, he had already made his mark as a Manitoba hockey pioneer. He helped form the province's first teams in 1889, and as a player with the Victorias, took part in the first regularly scheduled game in Manitoba on 20 December 1890. In 1893, wishing to gain experience against teams in the cradle of hockey, the Manitobans undertook an Eastern tour, playing in Toronto, Ottawa and Montreal. The outcome surprised both East and West. The Manitobans won nine victories in eleven games and outscored their opponents 76-36; Eastern newspapers stressed McCulloch's speed and grace, and the powerful play of Don Bain, another Sports Hall of Fame member.

Like Norval Baptie, Harley Davidson and other outstanding speed skaters, McCulloch was an accomplished cyclist, though not in the very highest class. In skating, however, he was a world-class performer.

McCulloch first won the Canadian speed skating title in 1893. The championship was determined by performance in four events at graduated distances from one fur-

Canada Wide Feature Service Ltd.

long to five miles; McCulloch won all four at Montreal. In 1896 McCulloch won the US nationals at St. Paul, Minnesota, by winning the quarter-mile and five-mile events; he also won the open mile and ten-mile races.

The world championships were held in Montreal in 1897; McCulloch's chief rival was the European champion, Alfred Nass of Norway. In the 1,500 metres the two men tied and had to repeat the race; in the 5,000 metres an official blunder nullified the race and it, too, had to be re-run. McCulloch won both and the world title.

In 1898, a year when gold fever was in the air, McCulloch turned professional. "He has left the athletic arena," said the Winnipeg *Free Press,* "and is endeavouring to fill his purse full enough to take him to the Klondike, from whence he hopes to bring back enough gold to keep his family in comfort." If McCulloch did make it to the Yukon, he must have found that hockey and skating were even more popular there than ladies known as Lou; what is certain is that for the next several years he barnstormed through the cities and towns of Canada and the northern states, giving exhibitions of speed, figure and trick skating, and occasionally racing other professionals for side bets.

After he retired from barnstorming, McCulloch settled in Winnipeg and went into business. As a skater, he had constantly experimented with varying types of blades, partly to compensate for his relatively short stride. Now he developed one of the first tube skates, and in partnership with a St. Paul businessman, manufactured the McCulloch skates which for many years remained the favourite of professional hockey players.

DONALD MCPHERSON, 1945-

Don McPherson was the first Canadian to win the Canadian, North American and world men's figure skating championships all in the same year. It was 1963 and by that time McPherson was a fourteen-year veteran of the figure skating world. Three months after the world title competition, McPherson retired – at age eighteen. He was the youngest male ever to win the world title.

Donald McPherson was born in Stratford, Ontario. At the age of four he started skating lessons, and entered his first competition when he was eight. Under the eye of coach Dennis Silverthorne, a former member of the English world skating team, Don progressed rapidly, starting to gain the attention of skating experts in 1959 when, at the age of fourteen, he won the Canadian men's junior championship. He entered international competition, a brilliant skater for

Sports Hall of Fame

his age, but always in the shadow of the reigning Canadian champion, Don Jackson. In the 1960 Winter Olympics Don McPherson was tenth, and later that year eighth in the world championship. In 1961 he only managed a fifth in the North American championships and was fourth at the world meet at Prague. In the Canadian senior title, he came second in 1960, 1961 and 1962, not capturing the championship until 1963, after Jackson had retired from amateur skating.

In many ways his career has been similar to Jackson's. He is an unassuming and serious young man off the ice – given to doing crossword puzzles before a big competition to steady his nerves – but when he is performing he has a brilliance and élan which sweeps all before him. Don McPherson is not strong on compulsory figures. This means that in international competitions he has always had to come from behind and put on a near-perfect display of free skating to remain in contention.

With Don Jackson's retirement in 1962, McPherson took over as the leading men's singles skater. As well as taking the Canadian championship easily, he went on to win the North American title. Then in 1963 came the supreme challenge, competing against the finest European skaters at the world championship meet in Cortina, Switzerland.

Conditions were bad for North American skaters, unused to Cortina's outdoor rink. To make matters worse, the weather was bitterly cold, and the ice hard and brittle. After the compulsory figures McPherson was thirty-eight points behind the leader, Schnelldorfer of West Germany. Early in his free-skating performance he fell while landing from a triple loop, but he went on to give a flawless display of spins, turns and leaps to win the title.

It did not take long for Don McPherson to turn to professional skating. It had been his intention to compete for Canada in the 1964 Olympics, but three months later he was offered a contract to appear in Holiday on Ice, touring Europe and the southern United States. After all the money contributed to his training by so many people over the previous ten years, Don wanted to pay them back and felt this was too good an opportunity to turn down. So, after only the briefest reigns as world champion, the eighteen-year-old skater left the exciting scene of international competitive sport.

RON NORTHCOTT, 1936-

During the nineteen fifties and sixties the curling championship of Canada was almost the private preserve of Prairie rinks. In the 1950s Matt Baldwin, the impeccable shot master from Edmonton, dominated the ice (with some competition from the Campbells of Saskatchewan). In the late fifties and early sixties, Regina sent the roaring Richardson rink to repeated victories (again, not without competition, this time from Hec Gervais of Alberta). The late 1960s belong to Ron Northcott's rink from Calgary. Northcott has changed the members of his rink several times during his career, but has had remarkable talent in leading each successive combination to victory.

Northcott's first taste of Brier championship play came in 1963, when he was third in Jimmy Shields's Alberta rink which lost to the Richardsons. The following year at Charlottetown he skipped his own rink, but could not upset the winning play of Lyall Dagg's British Columbia team. He won his first Brier in 1966 (this time Jimmy Shields was *his* third), but the next year was overwhelmed by Alfie Philips's brilliant Ontario rink. Northcott won again in 1968, this time with George Fink as his third. Then in 1969 the Alberta rink won again, its third victory in four years.

In the 1969 championship Northcott's rink was undefeated, winning all ten matches – the first rink to achieve this distinction since Matt Baldwin in 1958. In the final game, against Saskatchewan, it was touch and go right down to the final end. When Northcott came out of the hack to deliver his last rock, Saskatchewan had a rock on the four-foot ring and a guard rock out in front. With his long sliding delivery Northcott let his rock go. It slid past the guard, knocked out the Saskatchewan rock, and came to rest on the 12-foot ring to count one and win the Brier. It was a brilliant shot.

Ron Northcott is a tall, intense man who seems to play best under pressure. His large, black horn-rimmed glasses have earned him the nickname of "the Owl," and he has been described by columnist Dick Beddoes as "so lean that he looks like a curling broom with ears." On the ice, Northcott has superb control, and seems to be able to place a stone at will. If there is a crack big enough to get a stone past the guards, Northcott will find it. Yet he plays a flexible game. More often than not, he will ignore a

wide-open takeout and come up with a game-winning draw.

One of his greatest assets – and so essential for the modern skip – is his ability to read the ice. With a tricky surface, he has it figured out after two or three ends, and can play even the most temperamental ice with consummate skill.

Although Northcott's rink has changed over the years, his lead has most often been Fred Storey, one of the best sweepers in the game. Indeed, the sweeping of the whole team has been masterly, and one of the ingredients of its success.

For success has come to Ron Northcott not only in the Brier, but also in world competition. Like the Richardsons, Northcott has won the Scotch Cup on every occasion in which his rink has competed – and since the number of teams involved has steadily increased since the inception of the championship in 1959, the competition has become keener every year. But Northcott has continued the pattern of Canadian supremacy set by the Richardsons in the early 1960s when they scored their record-making four victories.

THE RICHARDSON RINK, 1959

In the Quebec City Brier of 1959 the rink from Saskatchewan was unknown, unheralded, untried – the underdogs. At the end of competition, though, Ernie Richardson's foursome was being described as one of the finest rinks to come out of the West. It was the youngest team to have won the Brier and the victory signalled the beginning of the most successful curling career in Canada.

To the residents of Saskatchewan, it was a heartening and well-deserved victory. The Richardsons were only the second rink to bring the Brier home to Saskatchewan, the curling capital of Canada, with more active curlers per capita than any other province. The first Brier had been won for Saskatchewan in 1955 by the Campbells, the four serious, unflappable, taciturn brothers from the village of Avonlea. The Richardsons, like the Campbells before them, were a tightly-knit family team from a small rural community. The game of curling in Saskatchewan has been part of the rural social life. In hundreds of small towns across the province, the curling rink is the social centre; it is not only a place to curl, but a place to criticize one's neighbours' curling style, to exchange gossip and, for the younger members, to meet girls. Indeed, curling is so much a part of the Saskatchewan way of life that when the Campbells won the Brier in 1955 it was considered only right that the four farm boys

from Avonlea should be honoured at a special session of the legislature.

The Richardsons – Ernie (born in 1931) and brother Garnet (usually known as Sam, 1933), and cousins Arnold (1928) and Wes (1930) – are in this Saskatchewan small-town tradition. They were all born around the village of Stoughton (population 200) where their paternal grandfather had settled before the first world war. Ernie quit school at seventeen to enlist in the RCAF. But after one year he decided that such a regimented life was not for him. So he bought himself out and joined his father in the housebuilding business. His younger brother Garnet followed him into the family firm. The third member of the team, Arnold, spent some time after leaving school helping his father (Ernie and Garnet's uncle) train and race harness horses, and did not take up curling seriously until 1953. The final member of the team, Wes, who played lead in the years 1959-63, also came late to the game, being more interested in baseball. He was for four years a top right-hander with the Regina Red Sox.

Ernie Richardson's curling career can be said to have officially started in 1944, when as a schoolboy substitute he competed in his first bonspiel in Stoughton. The natural ice on that occasion was so heavy that Ernie didn't get any of his rocks in the "house". In disgust he gave up the game – it was in his words a sport "for old men and muskrats." He was much more interested in football, but lost this opportunity to go further in the game when he quit school in grade 10. Any lingering hopes about playing professional football vanished for good in 1950 when he had a kneecap broken in three places in a car accident.

Ernie tried curling again in 1953, playing lead on a team skipped by his cousin Norman. Garnet and Arnold joined the rink, but the inexperienced team was not too successful – they lost 9 of the 18 games they played that year. When Norm was posted with the navy to Victoria the following year, Ernie took over as skip. By the time Wes joined the team in 1958 they were an experienced team on their way to the championship. But it had not been easy. In the beginning they only curled about 40 games a year (in comparison to the 200 or so most teams get in these days) and it was difficult to get enough time to practise. Ernie remembers those early days: "We used to work eleven, twelve hours a day in the good weather days. We worked our eight-hour shift at my dad's construction firm. Then we'd go out and work two or three hours building our

210

Canada's most famous and successful curling foursome, Regina's Richardson family, are shown, *from left:* **Ernie, Arnold, Garnet and Wes.**

own houses. Sam and I built three houses each that way. Then we built another one for my dad."

But in spite of that, in the 1958-9 season, on their way to qualifying for the Brier at Quebec City, they only lost three out of the forty-eight games they played.

After winning the Brier in 1959, the Richardsons entered the 1960 competition as favourites, and after a convincing victory, they were seen as "invincible." But competing in the Brier, where many of the Eastern teams are weak, is one thing; the fiercest battles for the Richardsons were fought at home in the provincial playoffs. In 1961 the Richardson rink was beaten in the South Saskatchewan playoffs by George Fink, each game being contested to the last rock of the final end. It was, according to Ernie, one of the toughest games he had ever played.

In 1962 they came back again to defeat the strong Alberta rink of Hec Gervais, the previous year's champions, and became the first rink in curling history to take three championships with the same personnel. Finally, they added an unprecedented fourth win in 1963 at Brandon, with Mel Perry taking over as lead that year when Wes developed a bad back.

Much has been written about the distinctive Richardson style of play that has made them so unbeatable, and certainly the game has been changed irrevocably since they appeared on the scene. Attention has been focused on their aggressive take-out play. In this open-style play the emphasis is on knocking out the opponent's rock; very little use is made of guard rocks, and the play results in many blank ends. To be successful at this type of game demands a mathematical precision and accuracy on the part of the whole team, and a cool calculating use of strategy by the skip. One of the chief strengths of the Richardsons has been their superb team work. Although they may not have put in so many hours on the ice as some of their opponents, they have thought about their game constantly. Ernie explains it in this way: "Three of us worked together and we'd go over everything and argue about shots. But we seldom disagreed on the ice because we usually had things worked out by then. You can't argue on the ice and win." All four are masters of every kind of shot. Both Garnet and Wes (second and lead respectively) are strong sweepers, so essential in modern curling; Arnold, as third, is not only a strong shot but has the calm temperament and high degree of communication with his skip that make him invaluable. But above all, it has been Ernie Richardson's ability as skip that has made the difference between victory and defeat in so many championship games. As well as his uncanny skill as a shot maker, he has a fine sense of strategy and a flair for confident and daring leadership. He rarely lets tension build up, and the Richardsons play a fast game. They

211

consider that some of the Eastern teams talk too much on the ice. As Garnet says, "The game's slow enough without wasting a lot of time talking out there."

In 1959, the year of their first Brier championship, the Scotch Cup, symbol of world supremacy, was inaugurated. The Richardsons travelled to Scotland to compete against Scotland and the United States, and to take on the home team at their own game in their own backyard. But the game the Richardsons brought back to Scotland was not the same game the Scots had exported more than two centuries earlier. In Scotland the game has now become the pastime of the well-to-do and today there are fewer than 300 rinks in all of Scotland. They still play the draw game, where knocking an opponent's rock out of the house is not considered to be quite in accord with the spirit of the game. The Richardsons proved the superiority of their style of play by a convincing win in 1959, which they repeated in 1960, against a younger and more aggressive Scottish team. Since then the Scotch Cup has been expanded to include other Western European nations. In each of the four Scotch Cup tests in which the Richardsons competed as Canadian champions, they won.

FRED J. ROBSON, 1879-1944

Fred Robson's prime coincided with the years when the sport of speed skating was in its heyday in Canada, the northern United States, Scandinavia and the Netherlands. Rinks all over Canada, and especially in the larger cities and towns, were given over to the sport, and competition was keen. Most clubs had their own speed-skating races, and cities sponsored championship events.

Fred Robson was described as a "flash on skates." As a sprinter he had no equal. A small man, weighing about 125 pounds, he excelled at the fast get-away, and would be off the mark like a shot. Even after twenty years of skating, Robson was still setting records and could beat many a younger skater over a short distance.

Fred Robson's father was a butcher who emigrated from England to Toronto before Fred was born. Fred lived all his life in Toronto and after he had left school went into the piano repair business in the city. In his youth he was an all-round athlete. With his slight build he became the cox for the Toronto Rowing Club. He was also a keen cyclist but gradually speed skating became his major interest.

Robson competed in his first skating race at the old Mutual Street Arena in Toronto when he was fifteen, wearing a pair of homemade skates; no record of his per-

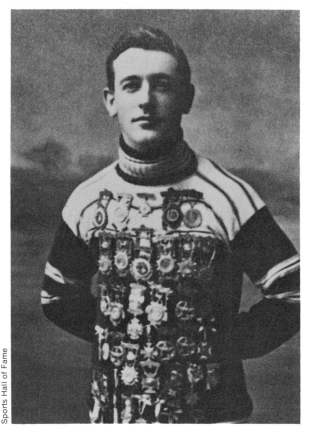

Sports Hall of Fame

formance exists. By 1897 he was Toronto junior champion, a title he held for eleven years. In 1897, also, he won the Ontario championship and retained that honour until 1902.

At nineteen he broke three world speed records and at twenty-two years broke world records for the 220- and 440-yard hurdles, and for the 60- and 75-yard dashes. At the peak of his career in the years 1899-1916, Robson held nine world records and shared the one-mile record of 2:41.2 minutes with Morris Wood of Philadelphia. When Fred set new world records for the 60- and 75-yard dashes in 1916, the records he broke were his own, set nine years earlier.

In 1915 Robson was elected president of the Toronto Speed Skating Club, an organization he had helped to found. He was still active in competitions for several years after this, despite repeated announcements of his imminent retirement. As a sportswriter in the *Globe* put it at the time: "The Toronto Flyer 'retires' every spring but when ice is available again the following winter he is found coaching the youngsters and finally goes to the mark as a competitor."

Robson did retire from active competition in 1919, however, and skated mainly in benefit performances during the 1920s. Even in exhibition and trick skating he won awards, holding the Canadian record for jumping eleven barrels and the record for the running high jump on skates of 4 feet 2 inches.

Fred Robson remained vitally interested in speed skating after his retirement. But by the 1930s, skating interest had swung strongly to figure skating, a competition in which Robson had never participated. He always remained an amateur, a fact of which he was extremely proud to the end of his life.

LOUIS RUBENSTEIN, 1861-1931

In comparative terms, there is no doubt that Canadians have done better in international figure-skating competition than in any other worldwide sporting activity in this century. Thus it is rather sad and regrettable that Louis Rubenstein of Montreal, the first recognized world champion in the sport, should be so completely forgotten now.

Yet from the early 1900s to his death in 1931, there was no more familiar figure at bicycle, track and field, automobile, canoeing and rowing meets than the portly, jolly alderman from Montreal. He was a true "builder" of sport in the sense that he organized and officiated at countless competitions, and in time, such activity, especially in connection with his beloved cycling, overlaid his early fame as a skater.

The Victoria Skating Club was formed in 1862, when the famous Victoria Rink was built. Just a year earlier Louis Rubenstein, Canada's first world champion figure skater, was born into an old established Jewish family in Montreal.

It is not known for sure how dancing on ice first got started. But the man who popularized the art in North America was a New York ballet master, Jackson Haines. He toured the United States and Canada to give exhibitions of his art. Haines also toured Europe and in the late 1870s, Louis Rubenstein went to Europe to learn the art of figure skating from the master himself.

The earliest mention of Rubenstein the skater is in an 1879 account of a "skating tournament" in the Montreal *Gazette*.

The account suggests that the competition was largely between Messrs. Periera and Barlow. Some of the phrases describing the figures are fascinating: "the inside edge, cross-roll backwards," "the pivot figures," "the double forward locomotive step," "the cross-cut figure." The total number of possible points was 400; the winner, Mr. Periera, got 351, Mr. Rubenstein, the third-place man, got only 300 points.

Here is how the paper described what was probably Louis Rubenstein's first public competition: "We would have liked to have referred more to Mr. Rubenstein's skating, he being but a beginner compared to his opponents. The form of his figures on the ice was very perfect in many cases, but the difficulty with which he attained the distinction was a bar to his taking the prize."

In the next few years Louis Rubenstein came on as a skater, developing power and grace, until by 1883 he was the star of the Victoria Club and the acknowledged champion of Canada. He retained this title until 1889 and was US amateur champion in 1885 and 1889.

In 1890 the first unofficial world championships were held in St. Petersburg, Russia. Louis Rubenstein represented Canada against some of the finest skaters from Germany, Finland, Sweden and Russia.

Rubenstein's reception in Russia was unpleasant. Anti-Semitism was never far below the surface in Czarist Russia. Rubenstein found himself followed wherever he went by the secret police. When he first arrived the police had ordered him to leave within twenty-four hours and only the intervention of the British ambassador saved him from prison or deportation. In spite of these unnerving experiences, Rubenstein's performance at the competition was superb. The competition consisted of three events; the execution of nine compulsory figures – the execution of five figures selected by the performer; and a ten-minute freestyle exhibition. Great emphasis was placed on accuracy, skating in place and the method of changing feet. Rubenstein displayed masterly control.

He could retrace a pattern on the ice three or four times without blurring the original outline, and executed all his figures with such grace and elegance that the judges were astounded. In spite of their hostility to foreigners, Rubenstein's performance left them no option but to award him the title.

Rubenstein was fêted in Europe after his victory. When he visited friends in Berlin, and took to the ice for a spin, he was immediately surrounded by admiring crowds, somewhat to his embarrassment. "It was a little bit uncomfortable, because unless skating in a match of some sort a fellow hates to put himself on exhibition. But then there was one thing gratifying. When people asked who we were, they discovered we were Canadians, and I don't think we lowered the reputation of the dominion as far as skating was concerned. The attention was flattering and, to tell the truth, I rather liked it."

Louis Rubenstein carried with him for the rest of his life this modesty, and a devotion to the cause of amateur sport in Canada. The highlight of his career had been that February day in St. Petersburg, but he became one of Canada's finest all-round sportsmen. Many people consider him the father of bowling in Canada. He was an enthusiastic cyclist, when the sport was still in its infancy, and held the presidency of the Canadian Wheelmen's Association for eighteen years. He joined his brothers in the family silver and nickel plating firm in Montreal but gave freely of his time for all kinds of amateur sports. In particular he was much in demand as a judge for ice-skating competitions (then, as now, a complicated and often unenviable task) and travelled all over Canada and the United States in this capacity.

In 1914 he was elected alderman in Montreal, and represented St. Louis ward until his death in 1931. The Rubenstein Baths were named in his honour. He was active in the affairs of his community until the end of his life. No city in the world has contributed more to sport than Montreal and no Montrealer has ever given more to sport than Louis Rubenstein.

ÉMILE ST. GODARD, 1905-1948

Émile St. Godard is the only dog-sled racer in the Sports Hall of Fame. The sport developed directly out of northern life. Like the canoe and the snowshoe, the dog team and sled provided transport long before the Europeans came to the continent. Until the aircraft and then the snowmobile revolutionized winter travel, the dog team was the basic means of transportation across the vast Arctic and Laurentian Shield country. To the earliest explorers, dog-sledding was a curiosity. Richard Hakluyt records in his *Voyages* (1577) that the natives of the Labrador coast "keepe certaine dogs not much unlike wolves, which they yoke to a sled." Europeans soon adapted themselves to the dog-team and sled; what had appeared novel was recognized as a vital necessity of the winter economy.

Oliver B. Smith, an American, is credited with inventing dog racing and dog derbies in 1919, but it is certain that as early as March 1915 The Pas was staging dog derbies. It is true that both in Alaska and New England, organized dog-sled races took place in the early 1920s, but by that time The Pas was holding the Northern Trappers' Festival, in which dogsled racing was the high point.

Expansion came to the small bush town of The Pas in the mid-twenties, as the Hudson Bay railroad pushed north. Well before that, in his early teens, Émile St. Godard had moved there with his parents. Once he saw a dog derby his one ambition was to put together his own team and win. Collecting and training a team, experimenting with various combinations of dogs, and building up his own endurance with much trail running occupied St. Godard for several years. During this time he won a considerable amount of prize money, most of it going back into the business of raising and training dogs.

Canada Wide Feature Service Ltd.

Most of Émile St. Godard's fame came from a series of contests with a well-known Alaska musher (by way of Norway) named Leonard Seppala. Seppala first attracted widespread attention for a mercy mission in 1925, when he and his team rushed diphtheria serum through the wilderness to the town of Nome. A match with the young St. Godard, who had won the annual 200-mile race at The Pas in 1925 and 1926, seemed a natural. St. Godard and his team, led by a half-huskie, half-greyhound named Toby, won handily on neutral ground at Quebec City.

In six successive years at Quebec the two great mushers raced each other, St. Godard winning four, Seppala two races. They met many other times – at The Pas, in Alaska, in Minnesota, and at Laconia and North Conway in New Hampshire, and the slim French Canadian won the majority of the prizes. Their last encounter was in 1932 when Seppala was fifty-four years old, and after defeat the Alaskan credited his rival with being "the best." In this race, a fifty-mile demonstration put on as part of the Winter Olympics at Lake Placid, NY, St. Godard led a field of twelve teams, including Canadians from Flin Flon, St. Jovite, Quebec and Ottawa.

At its peak, St. Godard's team raced 1,500 miles a season, a cruel demand upon animals, it might be thought. In fact, however, Émile's kindness and concern for his dogs was proverbial among the racing fraternity. It was displayed, for example, at a four-day race at Prince Albert in 1927, when the teams had to run a forty-mile lap each day. On the second day's lap, the weather had turned slush into sharp crystals and six of Émile's seven-dog team were hobbling as he came into the homestretch; the seventh was on the sleigh. Émile withdrew from the race. He said: "I am not going to bleed my dogs to win a prize. There is blood every yard of that course." When he decided that his lead dog Toby was no longer up to the racing grind, St. Godard retired.

The breeding and racing of the tough, intelligent and hard-working Siberian huskie and Alaskan Malemute is still popular. Despite the competition of snowmobile racing, young people are still drawn to sled-dog racing at winter carnivals in Quebec, The Pas, Yellowknife, Ottawa and a number of American towns. But no one over the years, despite great ingenuity in breeding and training, has ever matched the record of consistency in winning big races that Émile St. Godard displayed from 1925 to the mid-thirties.

Alexandra Studio

BARBARA ANN SCOTT, 1928-
When Barbara Ann Scott won the world figure skating championship in 1947, Canada fell in love with the blonde charmer from Ottawa. The next year she won the European, world and Olympic championships – within a six-week period – and the love affair bloomed into adulation. When she returned home she was met with mob scenes, autograph hunters, endless official dinners and receptions.

If ever an athlete had worked hard for such adulation it was Barbara Ann Scott. She had always wanted to be a skater, and her parents had given her her first pair of skates when she was seven. She joined the Ottawa Minto Skating Club and practised so diligently that within the year she had passed several skating tests. By the time she was ten she had passed all her tests with honours. At nine her skating was taking up so much time that she left school and continued her education with a private tutor. By 1939 Barbara Ann was ready to compete in national championships, and on her first try captured the Canadian junior title, at eleven the youngest skater ever to hold it. In 1941 she went after the senior championship, but was up against stiffer competition; in both 1941 and 1942 she was runner-up to Mary Rose Thacker of Winnipeg. The senior championship lapsed in 1943 because of the war, and Mary Rose Thacker turned professional, so that when the championships were held again in 1944, Barbara Ann Scott had no difficulty in gaining the title. She was to defend this title successfully in 1945 and 1946.

In 1941 Barbara Ann first entered international competition, placing sixth in the North American championships. Four years later she defeated the US champion, Gretchen Merrill, to take the title and make her, at sixteen, the youngest continental ice champion in history.

To achieve such heights in international competition takes not only talent and artistry, but also hard work and constant practice. International skating consists of two distinct tests – the compulsory figures and free skating. Barbara Ann excelled at both. But in order to perfect the compulsory figures, she would spend anything up to eight or nine hours a day at the rink. After her North American championship, her training began in earnest, with her sights set on the European and world titles. Skating occupied her time the year round, with practising at the Minto Club in the winter, and on the rink in the northern Ontario town of Schumacher in the summer months. When the test came, she was prepared.

In 1947 she went to Europe to compete for the first time in the world championships at Stockholm. There, skating against some of the finest champions Europe had to offer, eighteen-year-old Barbara Ann Scott became the new world champion. And for good measure, she took the European title in Davos, Switzerland.

Barbara Ann came back to Canada to a jubilant welcome, none more rapturous than in her home town of Ottawa. With well-meant enthusiasm the town presented her with a shiny new yellow convertible. But Barbara Ann still had one title to win – the Olympic gold medal – and to accept the gift might have damaged her amateur status, so back it had to go.

Without doubt 1948 was Barbara Ann's year. She retained both European and world titles and she dazzled the world at the Winter Olympics. Skating in Europe has always presented difficulties to North American skaters used to covered rinks, since all the competitions over there are held in outdoor rinks. At St. Moritz, the ice was bumpy, and a fall would lose vital points. With great coolness, Barbara Ann built up a big lead in the compulsory figures, and when it came to the free skating two days later, she put on a brilliant display of spins, leaps and spirals to emerge the winner. The crowds loved her, and mobbed her everywhere she went.

In Canada she became the celebrity of the year. Gifts were showered upon her, including the convertible from the citizens of Ottawa, this time painted in Barbara Ann's favourite colour, pale blue. Barbara Ann captured the hearts of the public not only for her exploits on the ice, but for her charm, friendliness and simple modesty.

With no more titles to win, she turned professional. Since that time she has travelled North America in ice shows. In 1955 she married Tommy King, whom she had met in the ice shows, and the couple now live in Chicago. Barbara has returned to Canada again and again, to help her old club, the Minto, in raising funds for skaters, coaching and facilities. She turned to riding as a sport and in her mid-forties is rated among the top equestrians in the United States.

FRANK STACK, 1906-
Jack Stack was a top-flight speedskater in Manitoba at the turn of the century when Jack McCulloch and Norval Baptie were international stars in the sport. His son Frank was born in Winnipeg on New Year's Day, 1906. Frank became such a steady performer and coach for so many years the Manitoba centennial committee in 1970 honoured him as "the speed skater of the century." Again, in 1973 the city of Winnipeg honoured the whole Stack family for their contribution to Winnipeg sport. Jack Stack had three other sons who distinguished themselves in a varie-

Sports Hall of Fame

216

ty of sports, including skating.

Frank's father started him in racing competition at the age of thirteen; so from 1919 to 1954 Frank took part in skating championships. He began in the era of mass start skating against other racers and concluded his career when the Olympic form of skating against time had become the norm. His father's emphasis was on developing stamina and an effortless style and rhythm. By his mid-twenties Frank Stack had become a powerful, tireless skater with quick acceleration, and titles began to flow his way.

He made his first great impression on Canadians with his capture of the senior men's title in 1931 at the North American indoor championships in Chicago. On a ten-lap track Frank set a world record for the five miles at 15:42.2 minutes which still stands. Later that year he won the United States national outdoor championship. In 1932 and 1938 he won the indoor title again and in the intervening years he was the runner-up. At this time he and another Canadian, Alex Hurd, were almost on par in ranking. Both were invited to Norway in 1934 to compete in four international meets at the distances of 500, 1,500, 3,000 and 5,000 metres. Frank placed well in all events at the meets and he won twice.

On seven occasions Frank Stack competed for the Canadian skating championship and he won six times, placing second in 1932. His last Canadian title was in 1954, his last year of competition. Frank had the honour of being chosen six times to represent his country at the Winter Olympics as a competitor or official.

The first Olympics Frank competed in were at Lake Placid in 1932. He placed fourth in the 500 and 1,500 metres, third in the 10,000 metres. In 1936 he was named to the Canadian team but a lack of funds and his inability to find training time forced him to decline the trip. The 1940 games were cancelled by the war but in 1948 Frank was back on the team and took sixth place in the 500 metres. In 1952 at the age of forty-six he placed eleventh in the 500 metres and acted as team coach. In 1960 he was manager-coach of the skating team which went to the Squaw Valley Olympics in California.

During his long career as skater and coach, Frank Stack was a member of the Winnipeg, Granada, and St. Johns clubs but more of his efforts, especially as a coach, went into the St. James Speed Skating Club. When the Canadian Speed Skating Association created the sport's own hall of fame in 1965, Frank Stack was one of the five charter members.

BARBARA WAGNER, 1938-
ROBERT PAUL, 1937-

The years since the second world war have been good years for Canada's figure skaters, and in no branch of the sport have they been more successful than in the pairs. The spotlight was occupied during the early 1950s by the team of Frances Dafoe and Norris Bowden. After their retirement in 1956 the incomparable duo of Barbara Wagner and Bob Paul emerged onto the scene. For sheer skill and gracefulness, they have not been equalled. They won the Olympic gold medal in 1960 – the first time Canada had captured the pairs event, bringing to an end thirty-six years of European domination.

Off the ice they seemed an incongruous pair – Bob Paul, a muscular, six-footer, and Barbara Wagner, a bubbling, petite blonde. Their partnership came about by accident. They were both members of the Toronto Skating Club, and had separately embarked on promising careers. In 1952 Barbara needed a partner for her dance test, and Bob volunteered. Their coach, Sheldon Galbraith, watched them together and recognized their potential. He realized that their different personalities complemented one another, and so, the most successful partnership in Canadian skating history was born.

Both Barbara and Paul are native Torontonians. Barbara did not start skating seriously until she was thirteen; Bob was

also a late starter; at the age of ten, while hospitalized with polio, he was given his first pair of skates. With discipline and hard work he became a gold medalist by the age of sixteen.

From its beginning the partnership was a success. Bob was shy; Barbara's vivacity helped draw him out. Bob's strong skating ability was an excellent stabilizer for Barbara's ebullience. Their first success came when they won the Canadian junior pairs championship in 1954. The following year they entered international competition, but could only manage fifth in the world championships at Vienna, although they were a creditable third a month later at the North American championships in Regina.

Then in 1956, after the Winter Olympics in which Wagner and Paul placed sixth, Frances Dafoe and Norris Bowden retired. From then on, every title fell to Barbara Wagner and Bob Paul. In the space of sixteen days during February 1957 they won the North American title in Rochester, the Canadian championship in Winnipeg, and the world championship at Colorado Springs. They retained supremacy by successfully defending all three titles in 1958, 1959 and 1960.

There was only one prize left to win – the supreme accolade of an Olympic gold medal. Barbara and Bob went to the Winter Olympics at Squaw Valley in 1960 determined to add this last award to their career. They put on a performance full of assurance and poise. Their brilliant display of leaps, spins, spirals and the breath-taking death spiral so impressed the judges that all seven awarded the pair the first.

But that was to be their last year in amateur skating. With no further prizes to win, Barbara Wagner and Bob Paul retired in their turn, to leave the way clear for the young brother and sister team of Otto and Maria Jelinek to follow in their steps. In 1960 Barbara and Bob turned professional, and spent two years with the Ice Capades before Barbara's marriage in 1964 dissolved the ice partnership.

KENNETH WATSON, 1904-

When Ken Watson skipped his championship Manitoba rink to victory in the Brier in 1949, he became the first man to win the coveted curling championship three times. It was a fitting victory, since Ken Watson has probably done more than anyone else to popularize the sport of curling, especially amongst youngsters, in the West.

The Brier – or, to give it its full title, Macdonald's Brier Tankard – is the most

Sports Hall of Fame

fiercely contested event in the Canadian curling calendar. Donated by the Macdonald Tobacco Company in 1927, the trophy was intended to stimulate and encourage friendly competition between the teams of Eastern and Western Canada. The championships have certainly succeeded in this aim. At the first competition at the Granite Club in Toronto, eight rinks competed – seven from Eastern Canada and one from the West – before a mere handful of spectators. Now every province is represented, and the games are played before crowds sometimes numbering more than 50,000. This interest is indicative of the growth of the sport, especially in the West, in the past fifty years. In the first Brier of 1927 there were some 90,000 curlers in all of Canada; today the figure is more than 400,000, including some 50,000 schoolboy curlers.

Second in importance to all serious curlers (and there are really no other kind – once bitten with the bug, the game becomes a life-long passion) is the annual Manitoba bonspiel, the world's largest curling tournament. This gathering of curling enthusiasts has a long history. The first curling club was formed in Winnipeg in 1876, soon to be followed by the Winnipeg Granite Club, founded in 1881. Clubs started to spring up in the surrounding towns of Emerson, Portage La Prairie, Brandon and Stonewall. In 1888 they got together to form a provincial association, and from that meeting came the famous Manitoba bonspiel, held annually at Winnipeg ever since. At first, it was attended mainly by local Manitoba teams, but with the coming of the railway, more and more rinks from the West started to attend. Railways gave cheap excursion rates, and as early as 1889, curlers were taking full advantage of this form of travel.

An account by James Hedley in the magazine *Outing* for that year gives a graphic description of a group of curlers en route to a bonspiel. "An express sleigh filled with curling stones and brooms drives up to the platform, a dozen men surround the sleigh, each grabs a pair of stones and a broom and makes for the baggage car. . . . Private sleighs and hacks begin to arrive. The methodical merchant has his curling stones slung in leather straps; a careful judge takes the handles off his and puts them into his bag, while the stones themselves are wrapped in paper and corded; a still more particular doctor carries his own box around with him, fitted with divisions, some say lined with cotton wool, which he watches like an immigrant his luggage; a devil-may-care lumberman dashes up to the doorway as the train moves off and, swinging himself on board, says: 'By George, boys, I came away without my curling stones! But it's all right, skip, old man, I know where I can borrow a pair as soon as we arrive'."

Curling has become much more expert since those far-off days, though it still remains the only major sport in Canada to be played almost entirely by amateurs, and with no professional organization. But the old enthusiasm is still there, and nowhere more so than at the Manitoba bonspiel.

It seems natural, then, that Ken Watson, born and bred in Manitoba, should take to curling early. He started curling at the age of fifteen, entered his first Manitoba bonspiel in 1923, and won his first trophy in 1926, at the age of twenty-one.

Ken Watson was a great strategist and innovator; it was he who developed the sliding delivery. At first his long slide out of the hack was unpopular, especially with the old-time curlers, and it often embroiled Watson in controversy. But it was popular with the increasing numbers of younger curlers who were being attracted to the game, and eventually it won acceptance, so that today the long sliding delivery is almost universally used by all rinks in Canada. Watson might also be said to be the first articulate and didactic exponent of scientific curling. He realized that curling is a deliberate game, where the time lapse between shots can build up terrific tension. It is here that Watson excelled, with his cool concentration and with his offensive play, right to the final rock. He was the supreme exponent of the draw game.

These talents soon brought Ken Watson and his Strathcona Club rink to the fore, not only in his native Manitoba, but in national curling competition as well. He skipped his rink to the Brier championships in 1936, 1942 and 1949, and at the same time won the Manitoba bonspiel with his rink in 1936, 1942, 1943 and 1949. He won the grand aggregate in the Manitoba bonspiel first in 1939, and went on to win it for six consecutive years from 1942-7.

For twenty years, from 1922 to 1942, Ken Watson taught school in Winnipeg and it was during those years that he encouraged curling among youngsters. In 1939 he founded the first provincial high school bonspiel in Manitoba, and he was instrumental in organizing school curling across the country. So successful was he in creating enthusiasm for his beloved sport, that his greatest problem was to keep a proper perspective in his pupils, so that curling did not supersede school work. When schoolboys take up curling, he once remarked, they have little time for anything else.

When he left teaching to manage his own business in Winnipeg in 1942, he became chairman of the Manitoba Curling Association junior committee, and from 1949-50 he was chairman of the Dominion Junior Curling Association Committee.

His teaching experience encouraged him to write on the sport, and for many years, starting in 1953, he was a frequent contributor to the sports columns of the Toronto *Telegram*. He also produced several books, and in 1950 he wrote his popular manual, *Ken Watson on Curling*, which has sold nearly 150,000 copies.

Ken Watson kept up his active involvement with the game until quite recently. And it was not until 1971 that he gave up curling after more than fifty years.

LUCILE WHEELER, 1935-

Skiing in Canada has had an extraordinary growth since 1945, and if any single person can be said to have put Canadian skiing on the map internationally it was Lucile Wheeler, a modest, determined young woman from St. Jovite, Quebec. Our sporting history could hardly have found a more appropriate person to accomplish so much, for Lucile's family had associations with the birth and popularization of skiing in Canada, and an indirect connection with the roots of Canadian organized sport.

Her grandparents ran a lodge in the rugged Laurentians around St. Jovite. In 1902, a forest fire wiped them out; they got by through taking in paying guests. Fortunate enough to attract the Montreal Snow Shoe Club, they soon found that "les tuques Bleues" proved a magnet for other Montrealers. As the Gray Rocks Inn, their establishment became the first of the many resort hotels which have converted the Laurentian region from a logging hinterland to one of the great winter and summer resort areas in North America. In 1933, Lucile's father Harry Wheeler, who had already developed Gray Rocks as a centre for skating, bobsledding, snowshoeing and his own favourite sport of dog-sled racing, brought in Ernst Wagner as the first ski professional in the area. Wagner's successor, the Austrian, Herman Gadner, had Lucile on skis at two. Convinced that she was a potential champion, he brought her along carefully, and when she was ten entered her in a downhill race at Mont Tremblant, where she finished seventh in a field of twenty-one of the best women skiers in Canada. At twelve, she was Canadian junior champion; by the time she was fourteen she competed as a member of the Canadian team at Aspen, Colorado.

After Gadner's death, Lucile was coached by three fine Canadian skiers, Johnny Fripp, Ernie McCulloch and Réal Charrette. In 1952, and for five winters thereafter, Lucile trained at Kitzbühel, Austria, under the tutelage of the master coach, Pepi Salvenmoser. Here she skied for five hours a day, wearing out eight pairs of skis a season, and keeping to rigid training rules. In the summer, it was back to St. Jovite to ride, swim, rock-climb and play golf and tennis.

During those demanding years, Lucile won recognition as Canada's best woman skier, but international success was denied her. By 1956, and the Winter Olympics at Cortina, Salvenmoser had trained her to a state of technical perfection; it remained to be seen whether she had the urge to win. After a disqualification in the slalom, she finished a creditable sixth in the giant slalom. In the downhill, however, she flashed to a third-place finish behind two Swiss girls; her bronze medal was the first Olympic medal ever won by a Canadian skier.

The Olympic showing convinced the Canadian skiing world that a Canadian star had been born. By 1958 the five-foot-four reddish-blonde girl from St. Jovite had reached her peak, and pointed for the FIS world championships at Bad Gastein, Austria. She was up against the cream: Carla Marchetti of Italy, Lotte Blattl of Austria, the Swiss Frieda Dänzer and other stars from France, Norway and the USA. On two successive days Lucile achieved a sensational sporting breakthrough for her country: in a superb exhibition of controlled skiing, she won the giant slalom, and then went on to win the downhill on the ferocious Graukogel run, over snow that all the skiers found soft and treacherous. In the latter race, speeding towards a turn at over sixty MPH, she later recounted that she lost the blue turn flag against "a huge dark wall of spectators," and was so concerned by the tenths of seconds she had dropped, that she almost lost her concentration on the final blinding straightaway. Had she not placed a poor fourteenth during the first day's slalom, Lucile would have won the combined title; as it was, she finished second overall to Frieda Dänzer.

220

After her 1958 victories, Lucile Wheeler retired from competitive skiing. She had brought home Canada's first two world championships; even more important, her great achievement was crucial in preparing other Canadians for the psychological test of international skiing. Canadian victories in the years to come were to owe much to her courage, skill and urge to win.

JEAN WILSON, 1910-1933

When Jean Wilson died at the age of twenty-three, her career as a speed skater had barely begun. Following Lela Brooks, the world champion of 1930, Jean Wilson swept all competition aside. She won four titles in two days' competition at Ottawa in 1932 and set a new Canadian record in one race.

Born in Glasgow, she had grown up in Toronto and did not start skating until she was fifteen. Her first awkward attempts brought jeers from her schoolmates but she persevered and within a year was a proficient skater. She joined the Toronto Speed Skating Club and came under the coaching of Harry Cody. He described Jean as "the strongest and most natural skater I ever handled and a tremendous asset to Canadian sport." Cody coached Jean from the time she started to enter competitions. His skill and encouragement, allied to her own courage and determination, were the secrets of her immediate success. That courage was shown in a dramatic way when Jean was fifteen. Single-handed, she rescued eight horses from the burning stables of George Coles Ltd., the confectionary firm where her father worked, making eight trips into the flaming barns to bring out a horse each time. Her bravery earned her the medal of the Society for the Prevention of Cruelty to Animals.

By the time she was eighteen, Cody felt Jean was ready for competition and a challenge to the reigning queen of speed skating, Lela Brooks. In 1931 she won a surprising victory over Lela in the quarter-mile dash and later the same year won the 400-yard dash and the one-mile race to become Toronto indoor champion.

With these victories to her credit, Jean went to Ottawa to contest the North American championships. The little fair-haired speedster from Toronto romped home in each of her races – the 220-yard dash, the quarter-mile, the half-mile and the three-quarter-mile events – to become continental champion.

In 1932 she went to the Winter Olympics at Lake Placid, NY. Women's speed skating events were scheduled on Olympic programs as exhibitions only from 1932 to 1956; no medals were awarded for the demonstration events. Nonetheless, Jean won the 500-metre event in the record time of 58 seconds, beating her two strong American rivals, Kit Klein and Elizabeth Dubois. In the heats for the 1,500 metres, Jean's time of 2:54.2 broke the existing world record; but in the final race, Kit Klein had her revenge and broke the tape just ahead of Jean. In her final race, the 1,000 metres, Jean fell, and had to be content with sixth place.

But Jean took her defeats with characteristic good humour and pluck. After the races, she had no regrets. "Falling before the tape will be done again and by others beside myself. The biggest thrill I had was in the 1,500-metre race, when Kit Klein and I raced for the finish to win. We didn't know who had touched the tape first and the officials finally gave it to her. After thinking it over I came to the conclusion that she did win it too."

Unfortunately, Jean was never to race again. On her return from Lake Placid, she was hospitalized suffering from a rare muscular disease accompanied by progressive fatigue and paralysis. She died, never able to take possession of a prize she had won – a trip to Japan.

The Toronto *Telegram* later donated the Jean Wilson Trophy to be given to the fastest indoor woman skater. It was perhaps fitting that the first winner of the trophy, in February 1934, was Jean Wilson's Olympic opponent, Kit Klein.

Sports Hall of Fame

221

Chapter 9

The golden age of Canadian track and field was in the years immediately preceding 1914. There was a long afterglow; some notable successes at the Olympic Games in the twenties and early thirties gave us an illusion of superiority. When, at the 1936 games, our runners, leapers and throwers became also-rans, an exaggerated feeling of national failure set in. Since then, the inadequacies which have kept us from the international front rank have been agonized over as if they signified a general Canadian inferiority in fitness and dedication.

Certainly early track and field was healthy enough. At the pioneer stage, no friendly gathering was complete without contests of strength, footraces and jumping. By the Confederation era, the annual picnics of policemen, firemen and religious organizations always included athletic events. Foremost among these early sports days were the Caledonian games. At the first gathering of the Montreal Caledonian Society in 1856, the events included such Scottish favourites as tossing the caber and putting the stone, as well as sprints, hurdles and high jumping.

From the middle of the century until the first world war, track and field was burdened with a bewildering variety of different events. Modern jumping, for instance, is limited to three events – the broad, the high and the triple jump (formerly called the hop, step and jump). But for Canadian athletes of a century ago there were a dozen variations in jumping; the same was true of hurdles and weight

The track career of Harry Jerome (*opposite*) was fraught with disappointment but he fought back from painful injuries to share a world record time in the 100 metres and silence his critics.

events. Once international competition between British and American athletes began, about 1880, a reduction in the variety of contests gradually took place. From the first, Americans took to the sprints, the English favoured the 440- and 880-yard events, and the Scots and Irish had a flair for field events. Similar patterns were found in Canada, but oddly enough, the smaller towns and villages tended to produce sprinters, while the city clubs, with better training facilities, emphasized the middle distances. Everywhere the quality of contestants and of training depended upon local leadership and traditions. Cities like Hamilton and Winnipeg, a middle-sized town like Orillia, and a small town like St. Mary's, produced a disproportionate number of good track and field performers before 1900.

Before track and field matured, it went through a circus phase. Pedestrianism or walking contests, for example, were the rage in the 1870s and 1880s, in every conceivable form. There were matches to see which competitor could walk farthest in 1,000 hours; there were six-day walks indoors and 500-mile walks outdoors; there were matches between fat men, men over fifty, one-legged men. Side bets were large and big crowds turned out to watch. The Montreal *Gazette* of 24 February 1879 gives us a glimpse of pedestrianism at its peak, in its report of a twenty-five mile race between Miss Warren of Philadelphia and Jessie Anderson of Montreal. The Canadian girl, decidedly the underdog in the betting, took an early lead:

Shortly after the sixteenth mile the American complained of the air of the place choking her, and in truth she had reason to feel it, as what with the wretched ventilation of the hall, the closeness caused by the crowd, and the amount of smoking and

223

Miss Warren fainted and was carried out at the twenty-first mile; the Canadian carried on to finish amidst great enthusiasm. The *Gazette* reproved the "unfeeling cads" who cheered when the American girl collapsed; they were "very properly hissed by the more respectable portion of the spectators." The occasion was typically rowdy. "It was but natural that the sympathy of the audience would be with the Canadian, but when that sympathy assumed the form of attempting to trip and standing in the path of the American, it was, to say the least, very disgraceful."

Similar to the pedestrians were the travelling sprinters, invariably professional, often shady, who under a variety of aliases worked the small towns. Walter Knox was such a gypsy athlete, knocking off favourite sons for side bets at distances from 40 yards to 300 yards. By the beginnings of the twentieth century long-distance running was replacing walking and sprinting as a magnet for spectators, sparked by the revival of the Olympics and its showpiece, the marathon. One of the most attractive winners in all Canadian sports history was little Billy Sherring, who, at a running weight of ninety-eight pounds, won the marathon in the unofficial Olympics of 1906. More characteristic of the time, however, was the great Indian runner, Tom Longboat, whose career was irreparably affected by the issue of professionalism, which clouded his participation in the 1908 Olympic Games.

It was the Olympic revival that brought to a head the professional-amateur debate. In Canada, that debate had been going on since the 1870s. At odds were clashing ideas of sport and the true sportsman. On the one hand there was the casual mixture of professional and amateur in all sorts of sport, from the Caledonian games to snowshoe meets, the zeal and practicality of townsmen who wanted the best players for their local team, no matter what the cost, and the ready generosity accorded by the community to great professional athletes like Ned Hanlan. On the other hand, there were those who took the view that a professional athlete took money for doing what better men did for the love of the game. This attitude had its roots in England. There, until the sports reforms in the public schools and universities, the best athletes had been professionals. When gentlemen entered sport, as they enthusiastically began to do by the middle of the nineteenth century, professionals were almost excluded. Social custom made it reprehensible for gentlemen to enter into competition with the labouring classes.

These exclusive conventions vaulted the Atlantic and embedded themselves in the codes governing sports in the universities and athletic clubs of major cities. Their strength was shown by the formation of the Canadian Amateur Athletic Union in 1884, dedicated to the ruthless enforcement of a standard of athletic purity uncontaminated by the dubious practices of touring athletes, professional promoters and the betting fraternity. The union's aim was "the promotion of athletics simply as a means of healthful recreation and innocent amusement, and the discouragement of everything calculated to upset our young men and tempt them from life's ordinary avocations and its more serious affairs into the unprofitable and ever disappointing field of professionalism." Though the CAAU dropped the English taboo against the "mechanic and labourer," its definition of an amateur was uncompromising. He was "one who has not competed in any competition for a staked bet or monies, private or public, or gate receipts, or competed with or against a professional for a prize."

The men who organized the CAAU had unquestionably given much to Canadian sport, but their outlook was that of a leisured and monied class. It was the same kind of men who from the start gained control of the International Olympic Committee and its self-perpetuating oligarchy. From the Olympic committee and the developing international federations in particular sports (who invariably drew their leaders from the same social level), there came the imposition, in Canada as elsewhere, of an amateur ideal at odds with the sporting customs of the country and their democratic and egalitarian flavour, and in conflict with the popular Canadian attitude that a good athlete who adorned a team and brought in the gate, deserved something in exchange. There was strong support in Canada for both views, but those holding the purist view tended to have both the social prestige and the economic clout to carry the day. It was easy for the Molsons, the Cassels, John Ross Robertson, Hugh Beck et, P. D. Ross or Sir Edward Beattie to be amateurs, it was easier still for them to find places of power and influence in Canadian athletic organizations. From their seeming victory stemmed the interminable wrangling over the amateur concept that has brought with it the ever-recurring cycle of suspensions, reinstatements and "shamateurism."

The amateur concept, as espoused by such men as Avery Brundage, quickly became confused with the "Olympic ideal." Yet what Baron de Coubertin had in mind when he inspired the founding of the modern Olympics in 1896 was an ideal of a different kind: the revival of the classic belief in the balance of mind and body.

Nevertheless, for Canadians, as for the athletes of most nations, the quadrennial

Olympic Games are the pinnacle of achievement. In recent years, though, there have been three other series of Games in which Canadian athletes compete. In order of establishment, these forums for athletic endeavour are the British Commonwealth Games (originally the British Empire Games), the Pan-American Games and the Canada Games.

Since their inception in 1930 at Hamilton, the British Empire and Commonwealth Games have been popular in Canada. Although the idea of the British Empire Games was first floated in the London *Times* in 1891, it took considerable initiative, especially by a Canadian, Mr. Bobbie Robinson of Hamilton, before the first games were held. The concept had been advanced by a trial run at the coronation of George v in 1911, when an interempire sports meeting brought together teams from Britain and the four dominions. In the 1920s the Canadians talked up the idea at the Olympic gatherings. The chief resistance was from British athletic leaders and the British public, who thought the British Empire Games might become an alternative to the Olympics. The other problem was financing. The costs of the Olympics had been difficult for many countries; who would put up the money for the empire games? Bobbie Robinson and the Hamiltonians worked out partial subsidization for many countries.

Hamilton's lead is instructive. Like Saskatoon and Winnipeg in the West, Hamilton was clearly the capital of track and field in the East from 1890 to the second world war. By the 1920s its strong, well-led clubs were producing star athletes and attracting hosts of aspiring youngsters. Industry in Hamilton was unusually interested in finding jobs for would-be athletes; Hamilton schools, primary and secondary, encouraged school sports programs, especially in track and field and rugby football. For four decades Hamilton had the best record of fostering and producing superior athletes. It was only right, therefore, that Canada should play host in 1930, to the first British Empire Games in Hamilton. (The fifth games in 1954, the year of the Landy-Bannister four-minute mile, were held in Vancouver.)

Until the Pan-American Games, the fifth in the series, were held in Winnipeg, they had excited little interest in Canada. The calibre of competition at the Pan-American Games, from their beginning in Argentina in 1951, tends to be higher than at the Commonwealth Games, largely because of the American presence. Canada sent its team to Mexico in 1955, entering contestants in six sports, with the girls' swimming team of Beth Whittall, Helen Stewart and Lenore Fisher winning four gold medals. The Pan-American organization is essentially an undertaking of the Olympic committees in each of the member countries; it is not a distinctive entity as is the British Commonwealth Games Federation. Canada's track and field performance was weak in 1959 at Cleveland, and it wasn't until the 1963 games in Brazil that more Canadian gold medals came with Nancy McCredie in the shot put and discus, Abbie Hoffman in the women's 880 metres, Alex Oakley in the 20,000-metre walk, and Don Bertoia in the men's 880 metres. The Winnipeg games were hugely successful and brightened by the best Canadian performance in any international competition, twelve gold medals, thirty-seven silver, forty-three bronze, with a solid second-place finish overall. The women track and field entrants continued to outshine the men at Winnipeg as they did again, four years later, at Cali, Colombia.

The conception of a quadrennial Canada Games as a national focus for the Olympic sports in an "off-year" was advanced by the Canadian Amateur Athletic Union in the mid-1920s. It was not until the late 1960s that a federal cabinet minister, John Munro, turned the concept into reality, filling in the four-year cycle of Olympics, Canada Games, Commonwealth Games and Pan-American games.

In 1969 the Canada Games were launched at Halifax, and repeated again in 1973 at Richmond and New Westminster, British Columbia. While track and field was only one of many sports at these games, as in the other three major games, it tended to get the most attention, although the swimmers have attracted more and more attention. In a sense, the Canada, Commonwealth and Pan-American Games are elimination series for the prestigous Olympic Games.

Dogged determination and perseverance were the characteristics of Bill Crothers who established himself as the world's premier half-miler and also as an anchor man in relays.

Sports Hall of Fame

225

It has become fashionable, especially for sportswriters, to bemoan Canada's dismal showing in the Olympic Games. Such breast beating reached a climax after the 1960 games at Rome when, for the third Olympics in a row, Canada did not win a single medal in track and field. The paucity of medals becomes even more apparent when the computerized totals of the US and USSR are flashed repeatedly on our TV screens. To add to our misery track stars from small countries such as Kenya, Jamaica, Taiwan and Finland walk away with honours. Although it doesn't cure the lack of medals, it helps to modify the embarassment to remember that Canada once had a time of track and field glory.

It is difficult to explain the sudden blossoming of Canadian athletes, especially the women, in the years after the first world war. The war played its part in breaking down social barriers and opening opportunities which women were quick to seize. Perhaps there was a national need to indulge in light, relatively carefree activities after four years of war's benumbing horror. Certainly by 1928 Canada had produced top-drawer athletes like Percy Williams, Ethel Catherwood, and the relay team of Florence Bell, Myrtle Cook, Bobbie Rosenfeld and Ethel Smith. They brought home from the Amsterdam Olympics a healthy collection of medals, a feat repeated at the 1932 Los Angeles games. But by the 1936 Berlin Olympics, Canada's track and field athletes had begun to fade. Since the games resumed in 1948 after a wartime hiatus, Canada's efforts have been less than outstanding, although individual stars like Bill Crothers and Bruce Kidd have saved national face.

If we are to hope for a resurgence of our fortunes in Montreal in 1976, perhaps it might be useful to assess our apparent failure in international competition. It might be worth examining our attitudes, so many of which we inherited from England. In *Modern Track and Field: Promotion, History, Methods,* J. K. Doherty notes that the English have idealized running as a recreation, that track stars are seen to have their greatest value in providing incentives to exercise and keep fit. This attitude supports a sporting code in which broad participation and social considerations count

The first thirty years of the twentieth century were glory years for Canadian track and field. **Ethel Catherwood** (*above*) won an Olympic gold medal in the high jump at Amsterdam in 1928. **Percy Williams** (*far right*) won both the 100- and 200-metre events at the same games. **Tom Longboat's** ribbons attest to his prowess and **Bill Sherring** is accompanied by Prince George of Greece, finishing winner of the marathon in the 1906 Olympic Games.

226

Alexandra Studio

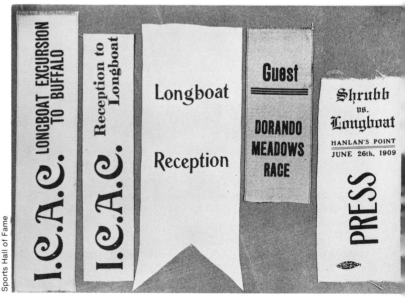

Sports Hall of Fame

for more than winning medals.

It is clear, Doherty says, that the English system of training is in marked contrast to the "never-ending and strenuous work of both the European and American systems." English training produces excellent results in middle distance races, particularly the 800 metres, but it is futile in the long runs. Obviously underwork "is effective at the shorter distances, where physiological factors are conceivably less vital. Apparently," says Doherty, "the English believe that genius in running is made up of 40 parts inspiration to 60 parts perspiration, whereas the American . . . system assumes the more common definition of only 10 percent inspiration and 90 percent perspiration."

Doherty argues, in essence, that inspiration, though important, is not enough, that it must be joined to an intensive program of strenuous physical training. Chris Brasher, once a fine middle-distance runner, had another view after the trauma of the Munich Games. "The utter fanatacism about the human body," he thought, "leads to the neglect of the mind, and thus to the negation of . . . completeness of life." Such fanaticism, spurred on by the ambitions of competing states, has led directly to the nationalistic and gladiatorial character of present-day Olympic competition.

Is this increased emphasis on intensive training and specialization the only road to excellence in international competition? In the past decade sportsmen have found reason to question the human dilemma posed by the pursuit, ever and always, of faster, higher, farther. From year to year new world records are established in running, jumping and throwing. In every event, the dedication to training and technique is a total commitment; specialization has become outrageous. One young man who hung around the gates to the Munich Olympic village for glimpses of the athletes, said: "By the second or third day of gawking I had come to know without asking, and despite sweatsuits and jackets, who were the sprinters, who were the jumpers, the wrestlers, the weightlifters, the boxers, the swimmers. Suddenly I thought, most of these contestants aren't athletes as I'd thought of athletes, but specialists with body types which suit specific events and which have been developed extremely by intense training."

Our view of the dilemma of excessive concentration in track and field athletics is not meant to denigrate either the dedication or the discipline which the runner and the jumper, and their coaches, must maintain. Aside from the loneliness and body punishment, athletes in these activities spend inordinate hours in repetitive training, with comparatively little competition and not much chance for the horseplay and the socializing so much a part of other sports. Those with major talent and ambition, like Bill Crothers and Abbie Hoffman, must know early in their careers that the high calibre of competition at the international zenith in their events, and the likelihood at any time of pulled muscles or strains, or even an inopportune cold, may turn their extraordinary personal endeavour into a poor showing and disappointment for those at home who have been rooting for them.

In track and field, as in modern swimming, diving and figure skating, the coach is a paramount factor, and almost always a necessary element for high performance and medals. Often a dominating father figure to the athlete, there is something guru-ish about the tie between coach and athlete.

The relative eclipse of Canadians in track and field in the past thirty years is not a reflection on the quality of our coaches but on the inadequate process for discerning talent, and the poor support facilities and resources that our coaches have had. There has also been the lack of recognition of their importance, not least in financial security, in a society where one's remuneration is synonymous with status and respect. The US and USSR, with their medal harvests, have systems which rate and recognize coaches, sustaining them with what an economist would recognize as production lines. Despite the fine records with small clubs by coaches such as Torontonians Fred Foot and the late Lloyd Percival, or Victorians Archie McKinnon and Bruce Humber, none of the Canadian coaches has had anything like the athletic factories of the typical track coach at a big American university. Former Canadians such as Harry Gill at Illinois or Lawson Robertson at Southern Cal long ago demonstrated what results could be achieved with an annual cadre of athletic scolarship holders, big fieldhouses, good tracks and a thorough, regular system of meets, bilateral, regional and national, in producing Olympic medal winners. Canada is lurching slowly, with belated government support, towards "national coaches," the creation of a paid coaching profession, and some concentration in both facilities and subsidies for the athlete with world-class potential.

The unprecedented audience among youth which Lloyd Percival's CBC radio Sports College attained in the years just before television came to Canada was proof of the possibilities among Canadian youngsters. But because track and field and the other non-team amateur sports have rarely been fostered in our schools, and because most of the country has such a short outdoor season, hundreds of "might-have-been" medallists at the Olympics and Commonwealth Games never get recognized.

228

JAMES BALL, 1903-

In 1933 when the Canadian Amateur Athletic Union named Jimmy Ball the finest track and field athlete in the country, sportswriter Ralph Allen wrote that no Canadian athlete "fashioned more notable achievements from such limited advantages." Ball's native Manitoba lacked the kind of constant competitiveness that any athlete needs to hone his talents. And, as Allen said, Ball spent six days of every week behind the counter of his drugstore while other athletes were training. "The slender kid from Dauphin became a great sprinter simply because he had everything it takes," Allen wrote.

Ball had a few advantages. He was born the son of athletes and his high school stressed sports. While taking his degree in pharmacology from the University of Manitoba he ran on the college track team. At twenty-two, Jimmy Ball won both the Manitoba and the Western Canadian individual intercollegiate titles. By 1927 he had proven himself one of Canada's best quarter-milers, winning the Canadian championship and also anchoring the winning mile relay team at the same meet.

But 1928 was his year. The Canadian track and field championships were held in conjunction with the Olympic trials in Hamilton. Ball won his first 400-metre heat in 51 seconds, with Gordon Dobbs, an Albertan from the University of Washington, finishing second. In the second heat, at the three-quarter mark, Ball was running in third place. He put on a burst of speed, passed the two front runners and set a new Canadian record of 49.4 seconds. Less than an hour later, in cruel heat, Ball lined up for his second run. On the last turn, after run-ning well back, Ball came charging to overhaul both his rivals and won in 48.6 seconds breaking the record he had set an hour before.

At the 1928 Amsterdam Olympics, seventy-eight runners from thirty-two countries competed in the 400 metres. All Canada's representatives won through their first heats, and three of them, Ball, Phil Edwards and Alex Wilson, qualified for the semi-finals with the field reduced to twelve. Wilson and Edwards failed to qualify, but Jimmy Ball won his way through to the final winning his heat in 48.6 seconds. It is quite possible that Ball's inexperience running on a track with staggered lanes cost him the final race. Drawn in the fifth lane, he almost immediately overtook the runner in the sixth lane and seemed to be running under wraps. In the turn home he found himself in fourth place, five yards behind the leader. In a blazing finish Ball all but caught the winner, electrifying the huge crowd with a driving spurt that left him inches back at the tape. The winner was timed in 47.8 seconds. Ball in 48 flat.

Ball was also a member of the excellent Canadian mile relay team that picked up a bronze. Before returning to Canada, Ball and other Canadians took part in a number of meets throughout Europe and Britain. At Hampden Park, Glasgow, Ball won his specialty, the quarter-mile; and in Dublin he was on the winning mile relay team, won the 400 metres and set a new Irish record in the 200 metres breaking the

229

one set by Bobby Kerr of Hamilton twenty years before.

During the years before the next Olympics, Ball continued to shine in many meets, establishing Canadian records in a number of events. He was a member of that remarkable Canadian medley relay team which defeated the best US runners at the Milrose Games in Madison Square Garden, New York, in 1932 – a team that also included Percy Williams, Alex Wilson and Phil Edwards. In 1932 he once again qualified for the Canadian Olympic team, and at Los Angeles again helped the mile relay team win a bronze medal. In the 400-metre semi-final Jimmy finished last. "They ran too fast," was all Ball would say when he left the track. It was Percy Williams who later disclosed that a painful carbuncle had destroyed Ball's chances.

CALVIN DAVID BRICKER, 1884-1963

Confidence is a quality that athletes prize; Cal Bricker, a world-class broad jumper for Canada in the pre-1914 era, had it in abundance. In those days, one of the joys of living in Toronto in summer was an excursion on a brightly-painted paddle wheeler to Hamilton or Port Dalhousie. Bricker and some of his friends from the University of Toronto had planned such a trip, but he failed to show up until the steamer had sounded its departure whistle. A frantic Bricker appeared, racing down the dock. A quick-witted policeman shoved the crowd aside and opened the gate. "By this time," Bricker recalled, "the boat was moving and the gangplank had been pulled in. . . . I took a chance and made a leap, landing on top of a sailor . . . " His friends thought he had leaped across twenty

Alexandra Studio

feet of water; they could have been right.

Cal Bricker was an excellent university athlete, winning the all-round championship at Toronto in 1905 and 1906, in the latter year taking six firsts. In the same two years he won the individual championship at the intercollegiate meet. His specialities were the running broadjump and the hop, step and jump; at the Olympic trials in Montreal in 1908 he won both events and set a record of 24 feet 1.5 inches in the running broad that was to stand for twenty-seven years. At the games in London, he was unable to equal this mark, but his leap of 23 feet 3 inches won him a bronze medal, and he was fourth in the hop, step and jump. Returning to university (he was a student in the faculty of dentistry), he continued his athletic career, and was again selected for Canada's team in 1912. In Stockholm, he bettered his performance of 1908 with a jump of 23 feet 7.75 inches, but had to be content with a second-place silver medal.

Following the 1912 Olympics, Dr. Bricker moved to Western Canada, setting up practice in Regina. He served in the dental corps overseas during the first war and was officer in charge of Canadian athletes for the games held in Paris in 1919 for all members of the allied forces still in Europe. It was Bricker, as ardent a nationalist as any member of the Canadian Corps, who was behind the "flag" incident. Rather than have the Canadian team carry the Union Jack, "there was a unanimous feeling that we wanted to emphasize that Canada was there. So we just adopted a flag – twelve feet long by six feet wide with a white background and a huge green maple leaf for the centre. This flag was carried at the head of the grand parade of Canadians by a tall officer from Toronto, and it received a standing ovation from the 35,000 people crowding that arena. Canada was there!"

Following the war, Bricker opened a practice in Grenfell, Saskatchewan, and remained there for the rest of his life.

ETHEL CATHERWOOD. ca, 1909-

The Toronto papers for 11 July 1928 carried photographs which present a grouping of a half-dozen girls in cloche hats and bobbed hair standing on the platform of a railway observation car. This was the most successful track and field team Canada ever sent abroad – the six young women who were to give Canada a triumph, 26-20 points, over US women in the unofficial standings at the Amsterdam Olympics.

One girl stands out – she is taller and seems more poised: Ethel Catherwood.

She was a high jumper of rare aptitude but she was also beautiful. Toronto sportswriters went into rhapsodies. One wrote:

> From the instant this tall, slim, graceful girl from the prairies tossed aside her long, flowing cloak of purple and made her first leap, the fans fell for her. A flower-like face of rare beauty above a long, slim body simply clad in pure white . . . she looked like a tall, strange lily – and was immediately christened by the crowd "The Saskatoon Lily."

Toronto did not let Ethel Catherwood return to the West (she had been born in Ontario). She became a member of the Parkdale Ladies Athletic Club, the enthusiasm of an unusual mining millionaire, Teddy Oke. Oke sent Ethel and her sister, Ginger, to business school and the girls went to work in Oke's brokerage offices, already largely staffed by a score of other girl athletes – swimmers, runners, softball players.

Oke hired Walter Knox to coach Ethel and the veteran all-rounder worked on her jumping technique; by the time of the Olympic trials she was regularly reaching the women's world record of 5 feet 3 inches.

The ninth Olympiad at Amsterdam in 1928 was Canada's peak year in the games. Percy Williams, of course, was that year's sensation with his double win in the sprints. But this was also the year in which women were given an official place in the program for the first time. The United States sent a team of twenty, and the Germans nineteen.

The women's high jump, held on the final day of the games, was the last event in which the Canadians had an entry. Ethel Catherwood had to face a field of twenty-three jumpers, including three Americans and the Dutch girl, Carolina Gisolf, the world record holder, now competing before a hometown crowd. The weather was cold and raw, and with the large field the jumpers had an obvious problem in maintaining both concentration and muscular flexibility. No one other than competitors was allowed on the field, so the Canadian girl, the only single entry, was left by herself. Fortunately, the Belgian team had received some assistance from the Canadians at an earlier stage in the games; after each jump Ethel was taken in hand by the Belgian jumpers, and wrapped in her red Hudson's Bay blanket.

With this warm encouragement, the Canadian girl soon showed herself to be one of the most graceful and superbly coordinated athletes at the games. With a leap of 5 feet 2.7 inches, Ethel Catherwood won an Olympic gold medal, and gave the Canadian women's team an overall victory.

At meetings of Olympic officials in Amsterdam a strong appeal led by several Canadian men had been forwarded to eliminate women's sport from future games. The chief argument, advanced by one of the Canadians, Dr. A. S. Lamb of McGill University, was that strenuous sport was physiologically and psychologically unsuitable for women. Such arguments didn't square with Ethel Catherwood. She and her teammates were perfect refutations of the argument.

The women's team returned to Canada and was received with adulation and buoyant enthusiasm. In 1929 Ethel and her sister moved to the United States; there is no record that she ever competed again as a jumper. She is now Mrs. Ethel Mitchell and lives in San Francisco.

CYRIL COAFFEE, 1897-1945

Cyril Coaffee's career is a reminder of how pitilessly short sporting memories are. Coaffee was a man driven by more than the normal determination to excel; he possessed a flaming competitive spirit. Some contemporaries thought of him as a loner, fighting to rise above a physical handicap. A Winnipegger who had grown up on the same north-end street recalled that "as a boy and a man he was moody and kind of single-tracked. Running and winning were all he really

wanted to do. You know, he had this crippled arm which he had to overcome. It gave him an odd stance as a runner, a far lean ahead. The legs would be spitting out behind and from start to finish he seemed to be lunging for the tape."

Coaffee's era was the early twenties, a period in Canadian sports history sandwiched between the days of the barnstormers like Longboat and Walter Knox and one of our peaks, the 1928 Olympics. The Canadian team for the Amsterdam Olympics – athletes like Williams, Catherwood, Ball, Peden, McCready, Rosenfeld – was the finest ever assembled. Coaffee, thirty-one and just past his prime, failed to make the team.

His competitive career began in 1915. Like many another north Winnipeg boy of that day, higher education (and therefore better coaching) was denied him, but he had great natural talent and enormous will to win. As a member of the Winnipeg North End Amateur Athletic Club, he made his mark in Manitoba meets. Competing at the Olympic trials at Montreal in 1920, he won the 100-metre final, in 11.2 seconds, but did not make the team. Winnipeg was indignant. But funds existed for a nine-man team only and Coaffee was number ten. Coach Walter Knox said the team would "take Coaffee if Winnipeg will raise the funds." Winnipeggers rallied round and Coaffee was sent to the Antwerp games. A third-place finish in his heat was, unfortunately, not enough to qualify for the semi-finals.

Two years later at the Canadian championship at Calgary in 1922, Coaffee ran the 100-yard dash in 9.6 seconds, equalling the world record. With four other sprinters Coaffee was entitled to call himself "the world's fastest human." As a Canadian record, Coaffee's 9.6 was to endure for more than a quarter-century.

Following this achievement, Coaffee was invited to run for the Illinois Athletic Club out of Chicago, and for the next few years it was his athletic base. In 1923 and 1924 he took part in meets all over the United States, and occasionally abroad. In 1924 he came back to Canada to qualify for the Olympics, and went to Paris as captain of the Canadian team. There is no explanation of his failure at the games. It is something of a mystery, because he seems to have been at his peak. At the Olympic trials, he had equalled the Olympic record of 10.8 seconds for 100 metres, and after the games, competing against many of the world's best sprinters in a series of meets in Britain, he ran up an astonishing number of victories at the 100- and 200-yard distances.

Cyril Coaffee's swan song was the Olympic trials in Hamilton in 1928. Running with a pulled muscle in his leg, he had qualified for the finals with desperate finishing spurts in each of his heats. In the finals, all attention focused on the new sensation from British Columbia, Percy Williams. A reporter from the Hamilton *Spectator* noted a sadder side to the story. "But as Williams's victory marked the rise of a new sprinting star, it spelled tragedy for a man who has been the greatest runner in Canada for a decade, and who has twice represented Canada overseas. As Williams trotted off the track amid the ear-splitting cheers of 5,000 people, Cyril Coaffee, joint holder of the world's record for 100 yards, limped off the course alone and forgotten."

GÉRARD CÔTÉ, 1913-

If Gérard Côté were asked what ingredients were necessary to make a successful long distance runner, he would probably say natural talent, good coaching, plus a training program that was carefully planned and rigorously followed. It was this combination that enabled him to win the Boston Marathon four times. The marathon was Côté's forte, but he loved other sports and played them all well. He once entered and won a roller derby. He played baseball and hockey. In 1958, he set a record of 46 minutes for snowshoeing in the eight-mile event at St. Paul, Minnesota.

Gérard Côté was one of eleven children. Born in the Quebec village of St. Barnabé in 1913 he moved at four years with the family to St. Hyacinthe and it was there that his interest in sports was awakened. He began to run to strengthen his legs for boxing – he'd become a fan of Joe Louis and Henry Armstrong. But Côté soon realized that running, not boxing, was his strongest sport; he could run and keep running without seeming to tire.

He entered five- and ten-mile races, but did not do well – he lacked that all-important burst of speed to accompany his endless endurance. For help, he sought out Pete Gavuzzi, a Liverpool-born Italian who knew all the tricks of the running trade. Gavuzzi watched Côté's style, his carriage, balance and action, and then showed him how to carry his body slightly forward, how to increase his speed suddenly and how to rate himself. He taught him to train for a combination of endurance and speed. Among the many pointers Gavuzzi put into Côté's head was: "Better three hours slow than two hours fast." This became the basis of the routine that prepared him for victory at Boston.

Under Gavuzzi's direction Côté initiated a rigorous training schedule. He ran three days of one week, four the next. He mixed marathon distances with shorter sprints.

He made his first try at the Boston classic in 1936. Accompanied by trainers, friends, and advisers, he arrived in Boston and prepared for the race with enthusiasm. He worked too hard; two days before the

Canada Wide Feature Service Ltd.

race, he ran the whole route and had nothing left for the big day.

In 1940 he arrived in Boston by bus, alone, and with seventeen dollars in his pocket. Côté did not touch a running shoe for three days before the race. He arrived at the mark fresh and relaxed.

At the halfway mark, his "flip-flop snowshoe stride" had put him in fifth place and it did not appear that he was much in contention. He pressed on, however, and by the twenty-first mile, he passed three of the four front runners including Tarzan Brown, the runner who had set the record the previous year. Côté set his sights on the leader, John Kelley, and passed him at mile twenty-two. He pressed on alone. At one spot, automobiles clogged the road so he had to dash onto the sidewalk and work his way through the crowd that lined the course. By the time he reached the finish, he had broken Brown's "unbeatable" record by twenty-three seconds, finishing the distance in 2:28:28 hours.

In 1942 Côté won again by the narrow margin of one minute, thirty-five seconds over his nearest rival, the great US distance man, John Kelley. In 1943 Côté and Kelley battled it out again; in the last three miles they tested each other in sprints, first Côté taking the lead, then Kelley. Kelley would find a reserve of strength and would pull away by a few yards, but Côté would fight back and regain the lost yardage. They were shoulder to shoulder as they raced through Kenmore Square, a mile from home, while the throngs of people that lined the streets cheered them on. Suddenly the strain was too much for Kelley. He faltered just enough to give Côté a five-yard lead. The Canadian beat him to the finish by just twelve and three-fifths seconds.

In 1948, Gérard Côté won his fourth and last Boston marathon. Again, he was engaged in a neck-and-neck struggle that lasted for some twenty-three miles, but this time it was with Ted Vogel, another American. Once the duel threatened to break out in fisticuffs. Vogel became incensed by what he considered to be unfair tactics, as Côté crisscrossed in front of him. Yet, with three miles left in the race, Côté pulled away and crossed the finish fourteen seconds out in front.

Other victories to his credit were his three successes in the United States Amateur Athletic Union marathon. Throughout his career he entered in 264 races, finishing first in 112 of them. He won seconds or thirds in another 82. Perhaps the greatest disappointment of his career was his seventeenth-place finish in the 1948 Olympic marathon. There, cramped leg muscles considerably hurt his performance.

ERIC COY, 1914-

Not long ago Eric Coy was asked what had kept him in amateur athletics for so long, when track and field performers receive little public attention and certainly no more tangible rewards. "I didn't do it to become a hero," he replied. "There was a progression. I was a comparatively poor boy who liked to run. It was natural to test myself against others. Then I found there were city championships, so I went after them; then there were provincial meets, and when in time I was good enough to win there, there was the national meet. With victory there came the chance for making a British Empire Games team. The Olympics were even bigger and there were the standards to shoot at if one was to get there, so I went on to meet those standards."

Such single-minded devotion to athletic excellence brought results. From 1935 to 1954 Eric Coy was Canada's outstanding athlete in field events. His first Canadian championship, in the javelin, came in Winnipeg in 1935; in 1938, in Saskatoon, he became national champion not only in the javelin but in the discus and shot put as well. This performance won him a berth on Canada's British Empire Games team the same year, and at the games in Australia he won a gold medal in the discus and a silver in the shot put. (He was named Canada's outstanding athlete that year by the Canadian Amateur Athletic Union.)

This progression through level after level of excellence began in Charleswood, then a suburb of Winnipeg. Eric Coy began as a sprinter, though at six feet and 190 pounds he was hardly the conventional model. When he found that ten seconds flat in the 100 yards wasn't good enough to win he turned his attention to the field events. Training was something Coy did in his spare time, because from the age of sixteen he worked for Manitoba Telephone. Many of his ideas on proper form came from reading magazines although for several summers before the second world war he took his vacation at the University of Minnesota, where the track coach let him work out with the university track and field team.

During the thirties Eric Coy was one of the continent's great snowshoers. From 1933 to 1941 (except for 1938, when he was in Australia), he won the snowshoe sprint titles at the North American championships. Though most of the competitors came from French Canada and New England, Winnipeg had a half-dozen clubs. Coy competed for the Wanderers. Though he enjoyed the competition for itself, he regarded it as a component of his track and field training program.

Sports Hall of Fame

During the war Coy served in the RCAF as an instructor, having won his wings as a pilot navigator. He was posted to Eastern Air Command where Group Captain Dave Harding had collected many athletes; Coy found himself pushed into football. Coy became a lineman on Lew Hayman's fine RCAF Hurricanes, and at the end of the war was approached by both Hamilton and Montreal to play for them. He decided on Montreal, but after only one Big Four game, the pull of Winnipeg proved too strong, and he returned to his job at Manitoba Telephone and to his concentration on track and field.

By this time Eric Coy was well into his thirties, but his days of achievement were by no means over. Once again he won Canadian titles in the discus and shot put, and won a place on our 1948 Olympics team (his second Olympics berth: he had been selected for the 1940 team but the games were cancelled). In both 1950 and 1954 he was a member of Canada's British Empire Games team. Since retiring from competition, he has continued to be active in the organization and coaching of track and field, wrestling and hockey.

WILLIAM CROTHERS, 1940-

Bill Crothers didn't look like the popular image of a modern sports hero. Tall, angular, studious-looking, with thick horn-rimmed glasses that he wore even when running, this is the man who in the sixties was acknowledged as one of the best middle-distance runners in the world, the man who brought

234

home Canada's only medal in track at the 1964 Olympics, a silver medal for the 800 metres.

Crothers was the star of track meets all over the world, winning in distances of 660 yards to one mile. His fans remember the glorious half mile Crothers ran at Varsity Stadium in Toronto on 10 June 1965 against the great New Zealander, Peter Snell. At that time Snell was world champion in both half mile and the mile. Crothers had raced him on four occasions, and each time had had to be content with second place. As recently as a month before, Snell had beaten Crothers in Los Angeles by a mere four yards in the 1,000 yards. This time, at Varsity Stadium, Crothers's strategy was masterly. He doggedly stayed on Snell's heels even though the New Zealander tried to get away from him in the back stretch. Boxed in by two other runners, Crothers slid between them sideways, dipping one shoulder as he passed, and was after Snell in a flash to take up his position again just behind his shoulder. And there Crothers stayed right up to the final 50 yards, when he poured on the speed and breasted the tape first, to the roars of 20,000 home fans. And just to prove that it was no fluke, Crothers beat Snell again in Oslo the following month.

The Varsity crowd that cheered Bill Crothers on were his hometown rooters, and Bill was their star. Born in Markham in 1940, Bill received all his academic and athletic training in Toronto. A graduate in pharmacy from the University of Toronto, in 1963 Bill went back to Markham to work at the local pharmacy, which he now owns.

Bill Crothers's track career started in 1960 when he joined the East York Track Club and came under the influence of coach Fred Foot. Bill was a coach's dream athlete – powerful, possessing a reserve of speed for the final dash, and with what seemed an infinite capacity for hard work. The East York Club was – and still is – composed of enthusiastic amateurs. At the time Bill joined, their most famous star was the seventeen-year-old Bruce Kidd, who was creating a sensation on the tracks of North America in the two- and three-mile events. East York also developed a crack relay team, with Crothers as anchor man, and soon the club was achieving for itself an enviable reputation in United States track meets.

By 1962 Crothers was winning consistently in the 440 yards and the half mile, and was reckoned to be a man to watch in the future. At the Milrose Games in New York, he won the half mile in the then record time of 1:50 minutes. He won the 1,000 yards at the Boston AAA meet, and followed that by a 500-yard win at Winnipeg in a record 56.9 seconds. Crothers continued to beat all the European and US middle-distance runners. By the end of 1963 he held championships for the 660 and 880 yards in Canada, Britain and the US, and was considered a leading contender for the 800 metres in the 1964 Olympics.

At Tokyo, Crothers had to face Peter Snell, holder of the world record for the one mile, half-mile and 800 metres. Crothers ran the fastest 800 metres of his career, in 1:45.6 minutes, breaking the world record. But it wasn't fast enough; Snell took the gold medal with a time of 1:45.1 and Crothers placed second.

Then came 1965, the year of Snell's defeat and the confirmation of Crothers's place as the world's number one half-miler. He was at the height of his powers. He had outgrown his tendency to stay too far back at the beginning of a race and allow himself to get boxed in by other runners. His timing was uncanny and his ability to summon up a final burst of speed made him almost unbeatable.

This was to be the high point of his career. His performance at the Commonwealth Games in Jamaica was disappointing, and at the Pan-Am Games in 1967 he had to settle for a second. Bill Crothers never made it back into world contention.

There were two reasons for Crothers's decline. He was suffering from the occupational hazard of runners – pulled muscles and sore ankles. At Jamaica his Achilles tendons were inflamed and his ankles so sore

Graphic Artists

that he could hardly walk when he got up in the mornings. Although he trained for the 1968 Olympics, a few weeks before the team left for Mexico he had to be operated on for torn tendons and could not recuperate in time.

The second reason was not Crothers's physical condition, but rather his mental attitude. He believes passionately in the cause of amateur athletics. He has spent many hours and a great deal of his own money promoting and participating in meets in this country and in sponsoring Canadian teams on trips to compete in European meets. In his fund-raising efforts he and his teammates at East York would compete as often as possible on the indoor-track circuit in an effort to raise money to provide more competition between young Canadian athletes. These activities became more important to Crothers than his own training program to defend his silver medal. Instead of an intense training regime Bill spent his time writing letters, making speeches and running in as many indoor races as possible to underwrite his meets. As he says, "You can't convince kids to train if they aren't going to compete." Teammate Bruce Kidd has nicknamed him "the Crusader," and Crothers would probably be proud of this description.

ETIENNE DESMARTEAU, 1877-1905

Etienne Desmarteau, the first Canadian to win an Olympic gold medal, is commemorated in Montreal by a park bearing his name; appropriately enough, some of the events of 1976 Olympics will be held in Desmarteau park.

Etienne, at six-foot-one and 225 pounds was the smallest of five brothers. One brother, Zacharie, was, like Etienne, a Montreal policeman, and the two teamed together in field and weight events to make the Montreal police formidable in the several police games held annually in cities such as Toronto, New York, Montreal and Boston.

Etienne had joined the force in 1901 after working in the CPR foundry. He was assigned to No. 5 station, under Captain Frank Loye. Loye had emigrated from Ireland to Montreal in the early 1880s after service in the Royal Irish Constabulary and had been responsible for introducing tournaments of strength in the city after the Irish police model. The French Canadians had an affinity for this form of athletics and Loye recruited onto the force a number of strong men, including Desmarteau. In the much-publicized tugs-of-war of the period the Montreal force, depending on the huskies of No. 5 station, had a great reputation.

The Olympics at St. Louis in 1904 drew athletes from only eight countries. However, there was a swarm of American entries which raised the total of competitors to 1,300. The bulk of the small Canadian team, including Desmarteau, came from Montreal, and were sponsored by the MAAA. Desmarteau's specialty was throwing the fifty-six-pound weight, an event dropped from the Olympic contests after 1920. No record remains of Desmarteau's throw at St. Louis but before the Olympics he had set world records of 15 feet 9 inches for height and 36 feet 6.5 inches in distance. Desmarteau's first-place gold was the only track and field first not won by Americans.

While we know little about the personal details of Desmarteau's early life or his training methods it is clear from obituaries that he was much beloved for his modesty and good humour. The recorder of the Montreal municipal court – "un juge Anglais" as *la Presse* pointed out – opened court the day after Desmarteau's shocking death from typhoid with a request that all present stand

Alexandra Studio

while he delivered an address in honour of the deceased – "brave as a lion . . . devoted to duty . . . a calm, equable temperament . . . an honour to his comrades in the force."

It is hard to put Desmarteau's achievements and his potential into present-day terms but it is a good guess that if he had been born twenty or thirty years later he could have become a world class performer in the shot put and the hammer throw.

For his compatriots, Desmarteau had a special place. His victory at St. Louis had been not just a personal achievement but a collective one; *la Patrie* headlined its story "Cette victoire honore les canadiens-français."His loss was, therefore, a special tragedy.

EDOUARD FABRE, 1885-1939

Edouard Fabre was eulogized as "the greatest runner of our time" by an obituary writer. Years later, reflecting on Fabre's remarkable career, the sportswriter Elmer Ferguson also came to the conclusion that the French-Canadian runner was better than Tom Longboat, Bill Sherring or Johnny Miles. "His feats were legion; his life a legend," Ferguson wrote.

Fabre was eight years old when he was orphaned. He was placed in an orphanage in the St. Henri district of Montreal but was desperately lonely and unhappy. One night he fled from the home and wandered across the Victoria bridge. At daylight he was exhausted and crawled under some bushes to sleep. He had bumbled onto the reserve of the Caughnawaga Iroquois. The Indian who found the lad brought him home and the family welcomed him. There Fabre stayed, grew up, became a construction labourer, and caught the fervour for distance running which had always distinguished this band of Iroquois.

Edouard Fabre was dark-visaged and handsome, more heavily muscled than most marathon runners. The demands of his trade and his indefatigible training explain his physique. He had a gargantuan appetite. Elmer Ferguson interviewed him in the mid-thirties. At a rest break during a race Ferguson found him in a tent. "He was reclining in a long chair, with both hands he held a large apple pie from which he was taking enormous bites. Beside him was a quart of beer from which he took the occasional hearty draught. 'I eat anything,' said Fabre, adding with a grin, 'I felt like a piece of pie.' "

In his thirty-year running career Fabre ran 315 races and collected hundreds

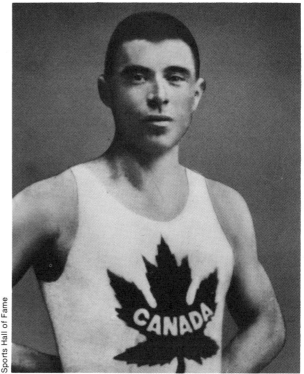

of trophies and medals. In his professional races he was not above eye-popping novelties. In one twenty-four hour event he was matched against a horse to see which could run furthest. Fabre won.

His determination was phenomenal, particularly if we remember that he reached manhood in a family and community with little in the way of economic and educational advantages. In 1905, when twenty-one, he scraped together enough money to take him to Greece and back, in order to run in an Athens marathon.

Distance races proliferated like rabbits after the famous Dorando marathon at the London Olympics of 1908. Cities, newspapers, magazines and athletic clubs sponsored road races galore and all over the world would-be marathoners popped up like mushrooms. Three Montreal papers, the *Herald,* the *Star* and *la Patrie* sponsored annual road races, many of which Fabre won. He trekked around the continent competing. He ran at the 1912 Olympics in Sweden for Canada.

The most famous annual race in North America was and is the Boston marathon. Fabre first entered it in 1911 and won it in 1915 on his fifth attempt. The race day was inordinately hot, eighty-four degrees, and more than a third of the starters dropped out. Fabre, running for the Richmond Athletic Club of Montreal, stayed well back in the pack and the leaders were four miles from home when he began to run them down. He swept home with a margin of more than two and one-half minutes in the time of 2:31:41 hours.

Elmer Ferguson considered that the Fabre "feat of feats" came in 1930 when he was almost forty years of age. A snowshoe marathon was run over six days between Quebec and Montreal. The finish was in the Montreal Forum where snow had been banked around the rim of the ice surface. The rink was jammed on the bitter night of 6 February when, to an enormous roar, Fabre, the leader and winner, raced through the doors on his snowshoes and ran the final mile. Frost had put a great beard of ice on his chin and he looked like a giant snowman. His time for the 200 miles was 34:46:24 hours. His nearest rival was three hours behind. Fabre had averaged just under six miles an hour.

GEORGE HENRY GOULDING, 1885-1966
Competitive walkers are among the most dedicated of all athletes, not merely because of the severe physical and technical demands of their chosen sport, but also because their efforts, especially in the modern era, either go largely unnoticed amid the more showy and crowd-pleasing events or invite amusement. It is true that there is something ludicrous about distance walking races: several score walkers, enormously intent, hats bobbing, bottoms rolling, elbows swinging in that peculiar, stiff-legged heel-and-toe gait that is the mark of the "bunion derby." It is a valid, and taxing sport for all of that, and in the early years of this century, when walking was vastly more popular, a Canadian named George Goulding was one of the world's best.

As a youngster in England, George was a fine gymnast and a good long-distance runner. After coming over to Canada in 1904, he ran at Central YMCA in Toronto and practised with the walkers as well. He fell so easily into a walker's racing stride that the physical director persuaded him to concentrate on this sport. In 1908 he was picked for our Olympic team both as a marathon runner and for the one-mile walking event. In the marathon (which the great Tom Longboat failed to finish) Goulding was nineteenth; he won his heat in the walk and finished fourth in the final. It was the last time that George Goulding was defeated in a non-handicap walking race. During his career he was to win more than 300 races at distances from one to forty miles.

Chosen once more for the 1912 Olympics at Stockholm, Goulding was not to be denied. This time he entered the 10,000-metre race, took the lead and won by eighty yards in a record time of 46:28.4 minutes.

Sports Hall of Fame

The greatest fear of any walker is that he will be disqualified for running; the merest alteration of gait may result in summary ejection by a judge. According to Goulding, the judges at Stockholm made everyone nervous. "They lay down on the grass, and at times they held up a newspaper to cover the walker's body from view, leaving only the feet visible. Then they got in behind or in front of the walkers." Goulding became convinced the judges were after him. "One of them said something in Swedish which I didn't understand, but when I turned toward him I saw a broad grin on his face and concluded he must have said something nice." His time might have been even better, he thought, had it not been for fear of the judges; during the last mile he slowed down to avoid disqualification. "Besides, in the first heat, I had rubbed the skin off my toes, while wearing almost new shoes; and in the final my feet were really torturing. However, in winning, I soon forgot the pain and remembered only the pleasure."

George Goulding was given a civic

reception in Toronto, after a triumphal progress down Yonge Street, reflecting, said the *Globe* "the spontaneous desire of the citizens" to honour him. But even before winning at Stockholm, Torontonians knew they had a prodigy in their midst. Ernest Webb, the British and European champion, had been brought over as early as 1910 to race Goulding in a series of match events; Goulding won all of the contests. On two occasions before 1912, Goulding had set world marks for the mile, including a time of 6:25.8 minutes, established at the Eaton games at Hanlan's Point in 1911. During his career he engaged in many stunt races, winning over ten miles at Guelph against a man driving a horse and buggy, for example, and defeating an American four-man relay team single-handedly in a four-mile walk at New York. In a walk of one hour around the Varsity oval at Toronto he covered eight and one-quarter miles, and in 1916 at the Rutgers University games at New Brunswick, NJ, he set a record for seven miles of 50:40 minutes.

It was also in 1916 that the American AAU questioned his amateur standing because he had become a physical director at Toronto Central YMCA. The *Globe's* testimony to him at that time bears repeating. "To have had Goulding adjudged a professional would have meant the loss of a man who without question is one of the greatest athletes in the world. He has a style that is as near perfection as perfection may be approached; he has more speed than any competitive walker on record; he has more records of merit to his credit than any walker in track annals. Goulding, more than any other man, has helped the maintenance of at least a passing interest in amateur walking . . . He is regarded as a marvel with his graceful smooth style – a style that has enabled the lithe Canadian to eclipse record after record and has placed him perhaps on a higher plane than any other world's champion."

GEORGE R. GRAY, 1865-1933

The shot put has never been as glamorous an event as the more spectacular sprints or the pole vault. However, it has always been popular at the Caledonian games, both in Scotland and everywhere in North America where the doughty Scots have settled. So it was that in 1885 at the Canadian Amateur Athletic Association meet in Toronto the shot put attracted considerable attention. The best from North America and Europe had come to compete. There was Lambrecht, the world record holder; Owen Hal, the English champion; and the famous Irishman, W.

J. M. Barry, a giant of six-foot-four and 250 pounds, who held the European record of forty-one feet.

Into this contest of champions there arrived a slight, twenty-year-old lad from Coldwater, Ontario. George Gray's first throw – 41:5.5 feet – was to be the winner. Barry and the other giants couldn't match the stripling's toss. George was immediately acclaimed as world champion and wonder boy because of the quality of the competition. So, in his first formal track meet and with his first toss, George Gray became the world's best. It was a position he was to hold for seventeen years.

George Gray came of sturdy, Scots pioneer stock. His ancestors had settled in the Penetanguishine area of Ontario soon after the war of 1812. His eldest brother, John, twice won the two-oared rowing championship of America; two other brothers were prominent in field events and fine hockey players. The famous rower Jake Gaudaur was his cousin, as was Harry Gill, the great all-round athlete and track coach. Coldwater was a small village of some 500 souls when George was growing up. After he left high school George went to work in the lumber camps in winter; in the summers he helped in his father's drygoods store and the lumber yard which had developed alongside the store.

In the evenings the young men of the village used to compete and train with each other in various events – running, jumping, throwing and vaulting. George showed an early aptitude for putting the shot. On his own he developed a style of

delivery that would shortly become the standard for decades.

After his sensational win in Toronto in 1885, George Gray started to travel to meets in New York, then the focus of track and field events in North America. At first he competed under the auspices of the Toronto Athletic Club. It soon became apparent, however, that neither the Toronto club nor any other organization in Canada were able to pay George's travel expenses. Yet without such financial support – the only aid officials would allow an athlete to accept and still retain his amateur status – George Gray knew he could not afford to travel from rural Coldwater to the track meets around the world. So in 1886 he accepted an invitation to become a member of the New York Athletic Club, the most powerful and affluent sporting club in the world. The club paid his expenses, and from 1887 on he competed everywhere under its banner. In that year he brought the world record for the shot put to his new club with a mark of 43 feet eleven inches breaking Lambrecht's record. From then until 1902 he held the record, breaking it often.

Canadians were justly proud of George Gray's achievements in meets all over the world. In 1898, a writer in the *Montreal Star* paid this tribute:

> For thirteen years he has met the best men in the world and has never been defeated . . . Thirteen years without an equal. Think of it! And he continues to improve, for this year, on August 1st, at Ottawa, he improved upon his own world's record by adding no less than 15 inches to it, the mark now being 48 feet, 3 inches . . . At Ottawa on the same day he threw the 14-pound shot 52 feet, 10 inches, adding 10 inches to the previous world's record held by himself . . . He measures 49 inches around the chest and has an astonishing expansion of 11 inches . . . He is neatly-built and as light on his feet as a dainty little maid . . . Early in his career he found out that to indulge in any other sport interfered with his shot putting, so he gave up everything else and concentrated on his favorite pastime. To be a real champion a man must be a specialist.

George continued to live at Coldwater with his mother and unmarried sisters during most of his competitive years, running the lumber business and what we today would call "contract logging" in the winters. He trained largely at home, commuting to New York and other cities a few days before meets. In his earlier years he competed in the broad and high jumps, the dashes and the 440 yards, the hammer throws and the discus. By the time of his retirement, he had 188 medals and trophies for first-place victories in the shot put.

Despite the lionization of the great metropolis and what must have been the

temptation of many offers of work and discreet subsidization, George Gray stuck to his roots and his career in his home region. In 1902 he joined the Spanish River Pulp and Paper Company. In 1903 he became woods manager for the company and a director. There could have been few tougher or more demanding jobs. He was to be logging manager for more than twenty years, responsible for the annual "cut" and its transport to the mills. He became involved in a host of power, paper and merchandising enterprises as shareholder, director and executive. He moved to Sault Ste. Marie; there he married in 1911 and eventually became director of Abitibi Power and Paper Company; the successor to Spanish River, and in charge of the Soo region operations.

In the Soo he was active in community affairs, particularly as a proponent of the Navy League of Canada. He was generous with his time, advice and money for community causes.

HARRY JEROME, 1940-

The 100-metre race is an event of flashing speed; fractional seconds separate the winner and losers. So it was in the Olympic Games

Sports Hall of Fame

of 1968 at Mexico City when the American sprinter, Jimmy Hines, won the 100 metres, setting a world record of 9.9 seconds. A mere two-tenths of a second behind but in seventh place and unnoticed by the crowds was Canada's top sprinter, Harry Jerome. For the man who had been the joint holder of the world record in both the 100 yards and the 100 metres, it was a sad end to his competitive career. But the 100 metres is a race for young men and at twenty-eight Jerome knew it was time to quit. After Mexico City he said: "Now I'm going to get involved in amateur sport in another way. I'd like to get involved with kids."

Perhaps some of the youngsters he is now inspiring will have it easier to the top than Harry Jerome. Born in Prince Albert, Saskatchewan, the son of a Pullman coach attendant on the CNR, he moved with his family to Vancouver when he was twelve. His teachers at North Vancouver High encouraged him to run and he joined the local track club, the Optimist Striders. His success was immediate. When he was eighteen he broke Percy Williams's thirty-one-year-old record in the 220 yards and the following year ran the 100 yards in what was then the phenomenal time of 9.5 seconds. Harry was offered an athletic scholarship at the University of Oregon. It was an offer that Harry accepted as perhaps the only way of getting a higher education and continuing his athletic training at the same time – an opportunity not available in Canada. Under the expert coaching of Bill Bowerman, Jerome was on his way. At a meet in Saskatoon in 1959, at the age of nineteen, he ran the 100 metres in 10 seconds flat. The time was later confirmed as a world record, which he shared with the German runner, Armin Harry, and which stood until the 1968 Olympics.

As a member of the Canadian team to the Rome Olympics of 1960 Jerome's performance was disappointing. He pulled a muscle in the semi-final heat of the 100 metres and did not qualify for the final. At the British Commonwealth Games in Perth, Australia, in 1962, the story was repeated; Jerome had to drop out of the final for the 100 metres when he ruptured a muscle in his left thigh, and some observers were writing him off as a flop.

Jerome fought back. Often moody and withdrawn before a race, sensitive to any discrimination because he is black, he seemed to the press sharp-tongued and arrogant. When the injury at Perth sidelined him for nearly a year, many of his detractors expected he would never run again.

But Jerome made an incredible comeback, going to the 1964 Olympics in Tokyo and taking the bronze medal in the 100 metres. Even more amazing, for a man of his age, was his performance in Edmonton in 1966 when he ran the 100-yard dash in 9.1 seconds. He was unmistakably in the world class again. This world record, which he shared with US sprinter Bob Hayes and others, stood until early 1974. Further vindication came in the British Commonwealth Games in 1966, when he won his first gold medal in a photo-finish with Tom Robinson of the Bahamas.

In the meantime Harry Jerome had become a physical education teacher at Templeton Secondary School in Vancouver. His own experiences at international meets had convinced him of the need to provide better training and facilities to our youngsters if Canada was to compete successfully with other countries which had the advantage of superior training programs and public support. It was only natural, therefore, that after his retirement in 1968, Harry Jerome should become an activist in promoting track and field to youngsters in high schools. Under the aegis of the federal Fitness and Amateur Sports Directorate he set up cross-country sports clinics. Nicknamed "Harry Jerome and His Road Company," six of Canada's top athletes led by Jerome travelled more than 11,000 miles, giving demonstrations and holding coaching clinics at high schools across the country. As a member of Sports Canada, Jerome continues to devote his talents to encouraging young people in sport.

ROBERT KERR, 1882-1963

Bobby Kerr's long-standing prominence in local, provincial and national sports organizations as organizer, official and one-man driving force tended to obscure an early career as one of the finest sprinters in Canadian track history. His family came out to Kemptville, Ontario, from Ireland when Bobby was a child, and after a little more than a year in Eastern Ontario moved to Hamilton. Today, Bobby would undoubtedly have won an athletic scholarship for his great natural ability made him a winner from the time he began to run. Instead, he went to work while still in his teens and as he said at the age of seventy-eight, "I just made the best of it, training after work – and that was the age of the twelve-hour day."

Not until Kerr was in his twentieth year did he achieve prominence, winning the 100-, 440- and 880-yard races at the Hamilton Coronation Games in 1902. Further victories in 1903 and 1904, including wins in the 100- and 200-yard events at the Canadian YMCA championships brought him entry in

Alexandra Studio

the St. Louis Olympics as a member of the small unofficial Canadian team. His $75 expense money came out of his own savings. He made the trip in a day coach and slept on the floor at a St. Louis friend's house. He won his heat in the 100-yards before being eliminated by the eventual winner, Archie Hahn.

Over the next few years Kerr competed wherever he could in Canada though most of his running was in Ontario or in American border towns. By 1907 it had become clear that he was the best runner at his distance in the country. In that year he not only won the Canadian title in both the 100 and 200 yards, but he took forty-one first places in all, set a new Canadian record of 9.4 seconds for the 100 yards, and established new meet records virtually everywhere he competed. His big year, 1908, began auspiciously with a new Canadian record for 50 yards in February, further victories at London, Ontario, and then a sweep of the sprint events at the Ontario and then the Canadian championships. At the Olympic Games in London, he won a gold medal in the 200

metres, and finished third in the 100 metres. This great athletic achievement, in events which had been and were to be dominated by American sprinters, was to be exceeded only by Percy Williams in 1928.

Before his Olympic triumph, Kerr competed in the British athletic championships at Stamford Bridge, and not only won the 100- and 220-yards events against the English, South African, Irish and Swedish champions, but was awarded the Harvey Gold Cup as the outstanding athlete at the meet. He returned in 1909 to defend these laurels at Dublin, winning both events once more and being acclaimed as an "Irish" champion.

Bobby Kerr continued to compete until 1912, when he was once again selected as a member of Canada's team for the Olympic Games in Stockholm. He turned down this opportunity, feeling that at thirty he was past his prime. During his competitive career, he had won close to 400 awards and trophies, set six Canadian records, and impressed all who had come in contact with him in terms not only of physical ability but for his personal qualities. In 1908, when the blonde Irish-Canadian flashed to victory at the Olympics, a Toronto writer said of him: "You feel that you are in the presence, not of an athlete merely, but of a man of strong character and of sound sense. He is an athlete after Earl Roberts's own heart, a boy clean of life, absolutely honest, modest and retiring, and he is a true Christian boy in the deepest and most significant meaning of that much ill-used word." These qualities were displayed in his later life, as an officer overseas with the 164th Battalion, CEF, as an official of various Hamilton athletic organizations, of the CAAU, the Canadian Olympic Association, and as a driving force behind the British Empire Games, held in Hamilton in 1930.

BRUCE KIDD, 1943-

Few athletes have burst on the sports scene as suddenly as Bruce Kidd. On 15 January 1961 newspapers in Canada and the United States headlined this unknown seventeen-year-old who had won the two-mile indoor race in Boston, breaking the US record. The feat was all the more remarkable in that the men he beat were all seasoned athletes, ten years his senior and more, at a distance considered too tough for youngsters.

This was the beginning of a brief but spectacular career as a long-distance runner. In the five years from 1961 to 1965, Bruce Kidd proved to be one of Canada's most able ambassadors of sport. He revived Canada's standing in world track events which had fallen sadly from the era of the great Percy Williams. This modest young man, with his loping stride and arm-thrashing style of running, spearheaded the re-entry of Canadian track stars into the US indoor circuit where they out-duelled some of the world's foremost athletes. Off the track, Kidd's outspoken views on Canadian sport and his political activist's approach on behalf of a better deal for Canadian athletes have done much to publicize the need for both public and governmental support, if Canada is to compete successfully at an international level.

Bruce was always popular with the fans who admired his pluck and stamina. They were proud of his successes as an eighteen-year-old in the gruelling six-mile and three-mile races. But there were those who shook their heads and declared that coach Fred Foot was pushing the boy too hard, that he would be burnt out within a year. They need not have worried. Bruce came of hardy stock. His pioneer grandfather had built his own sod hut on his half section of land on the Prairies at the age of twelve, and had lived there alone for weeks on end in the depths of winter. Bruce himself, in his last year at high school, put in a day which would make the average school boy wilt. Every weekday he arose at 5:30 to deliver his papers, then study from 7 to 7:45 before breakfast. After school he studied for another

forty-five minutes then hopped a streetcar to the track to work out with coach Fred Foot for a couple of hours. Back home he would do another hour's homework and be in bed by 9:30. It was a discipline of his own making, a routine to remain an honours student and at the same time develop his skill and power as a long-distance runner.

Like Bill Crothers, Kidd was a product of the East York Track Club and coach Fred Foot. He joined the club in the summer of 1958. A year later he had set a new Canadian record for the two miles and had run the three miles in 14:26 minutes. His win attracted the attention of a number of American universities, including Princeton and Harvard, but Bruce opted for the University of Toronto.

Following his famous two-mile win in Boston in 1961, Kidd was news wherever he ran. By 1962 he was making plenty of headlines in the sports columns all over the continent. There was the June 1962 meet at Compton, California, where he beat veteran Olympic champion, New Zealander Murray Halberg, in the 5,000 metres in the record US time of 13:43.8. There was the return match a few weeks later and this time Halberg beat Kidd, but Bruce had raced – and won – the six-mile race the day before. Finally, there was the triumphal showing at the Commonwealth Games in Perth, Australia, where Kidd captured the gold medal for the six-mile race and two days later came third in the three-mile event. With all these victories to his credit, it was not surprising that he should be awarded the Lou Marsh Trophy for 1961, and was named outstanding athlete of the year in Canada in both 1962 and 1963.

The following year Kidd was still the wonder boy of the long-distance circuit, but already he was bothered by sore feet and swollen tendons. He trained enthusiastically for the 1964 Olympics in Tokyo, and made the team easily. But Canadian fans were sad when Bruce limped in twenty-sixth in the 10,000 metres and had to scratch from the 5,000. They realized, as did Bruce himself, that his phenomenal career was coming to an end. In 1965 he had an operation on his ankles but his old power and will to win never returned. On graduation from university he spent a year in India, teaching English and physical education. In 1967, in spite of inflamed tendons he came to Toronto to take part in the *Telegram*-Maple Leaf Gardens track meet – an annual event which he himself had been instrumental in re-starting in 1963 after a lapse of twenty-seven years. He ran – and came last; but the fans, loyal to the end, loved him for his courage.

243

Kidd has continued to make the headlines in sport – though he may not be quite so loved by sports administrators and promoters of professional sports, who have often felt the full force of his criticisms. Always forthright, sometimes tactless, Bruce uses every opportunity to rouse public concern over the plight of amateur sport and the deleterious effects of pro sport on young athletes. He is an active member of the NDP and contested the Beaches riding of Toronto in the 1971 provincial election. He is also the author, with John Macfarlane, of an exposé of pro hockey in Canada entitled *The Death of Hockey*.

TOM LONGBOAT, 1887-1949

> Tommy practised running for two years on the reservation. He run every morning. He run every night. He run down to the Long House and get beaten. He came back and run some more. Soon he run five miles easy in twenty-three and a half minutes. Next time we have five mile race here, Tommy win by nearly quarter of mile.

So, after his victory in the Boston marathon, did an Onandaga mother describe, through an interpreter, the beginning of her son's rocket rise to fame. For all but a few athletes, the glory they win during their active careers evaporates swiftly after their playing days are over. Nothing is more fickle, less historical, than the mind of the sporting public. Tom Longboat, who dropped from the public eye almost as quickly as he had become the centre of attention, was to taste this bitter pill to the full.

The five-mile race the lanky young Onandaga had won was the annual 24 May race at the Caledon Fair, on the edge of the reserve. After this victory another Six Nations runner, Bill Davis, coached Longboat for the Hamilton round-the-bay race of 1906. Young Tom took something of a ribbing at the start of that race: he was wearing a droopy cotton bathing suit and cheap sneakers; his running style seemed slow and awkward, with his arms held oddly and his feet kicking sideways in a strange way. In fact, Longboat's stride was over six feet in length. After testing the favourite and front-runner, the experienced English marathoner John Marsh, for some time, the Indian "cut loose and left Marsh as if he had been standing," according to the Hamilton *Herald*, the sponsor of the race – and won by a full three minutes.

Importuned by get-rich-quick artists who could see he was a gold mine, Longboat was persuaded to join West End YMCA in Toronto, was given a room there and set to train for the 1907 Boston marathon, for which the Y had entered him. In the autumn of 1906, already well-tuned, he won the CNE-sponsored "marathon," a 15-mile event, with a field of 62 runners. The following April, against snow, rain, slush, the tough hills of the old course and 125 other entrants, Tom Longboat won the Boston marathon in the record time of 2:24:24 hours, a record not broken until the course was made easier. On his return to Toronto, Longboat was given an extraordinary reception. Huge crowds at Union Station, a torchlight parade to City Hall, a gold medal and flattering words from the mayor, the adulation of women: it was a heady brew for a youngster just a few months off the reserve who had suddenly become Canada's first national sports hero since Ned Hanlan.

Tom had neither the judgment nor the emotional balance to handle his new situation. Kicking against the strict training rules, he was suspended from the YMCA when found drinking whiskey and smoking. Two sharp Toronto Irishmen, Tom Flanagan and Jim O'Rourke, who together owned the Grand Central Hotel and had just formed the Irish-Canadian Athletic Club, moved in and dangled before Longboat the prospect of an Olympic gold medal in 1908 and a fortune beyond it. Tom joined the club and put his career into the hands of the promoter-trainer Flanagan. He trained, Flanagan-style, and that was good enough in 1907 to repeat in the Caledon and Ward marathons, win a twelve-mile race at the Soo and a fifteen-mile race at Montreal. Probably Flanagan and O'Rourke were cashing in on Tom with heavy betting. At any rate, Longboat was declared a professional by the US Amateur Athletic Union in November 1907, its president asserting that he "has been a professional from the time he began his athletic career. He has always been in the hands of a manager . . . he is taken from town to town . . . with bands and carriages and silk hats. . . . He ran all kinds of races at country fairs for money."

Whether Tom was a professional at this stage was not questioned by the Canadian press or public. The explosion of anti-American sentiment generated by this issue rivalled that in the reciprocity election just four years later. Yet the London *Sporting Life*, perhaps the most influential sports newspaper of the time, carried a letter from a Toronto man who pointed out that Longboat had no visible means of support, that he was living rent-free at the Grand Central Hotel, and that at best he was a "stall-fed amateur." Longboat was hurriedly installed by the Irish-Canadian AC as proprietor of a King Street cigar store to keep his amateur

standing inviolate; he is supposed to have smoked up most of the stock.

Somehow Longboat squeaked by the Olympic committee and was declared eligible for the London games. But the young Indian was not to repeat Billy Sherring's victory of 1906. From the start of the marathon at Windsor Castle, Longboat took the lead and set a pace almost as scorching as the English weather on that day. By the ninth mile, however, he had fallen back to fourth. Inside the stadium at Shepherd's Bush an incredible finish-line drama was occurring when well-meaning officials automatically disqualified the fainting Dorando Pietri by helping him across the line, thereby giving the race to Johnny Hayes of the US. Outside the stadium Tom Longboat had slowed down, then stopped altogether after nineteen miles. So high had expectations been that immediately there were rumours that he had been doped,

or that Flanagan and his cronies had won $100,000 on his defeat. Flanagan blamed it on the heat. More likely, Longboat was inadequately trained and had run a tactically impossible race.

It is ironic that the exciting Olympic marathon created an immense, if relatively short-lived, market for professional long distance running. Dorando Pietri and Hayes turned pro, and ran a rematch before a sellout crowd at Madison Square Garden in New York; Dorando won. Alfie Shrubb, a professional before the games and a superb middle-distance runner, was already clamouring for a race with Longboat; so were the New York promoters. Longboat ran a number of races as an amateur after his Olympic failure, with uniform success, including his third straight victory in the Ward marathon over a field of 153 runners. Once more a hot property, Longboat turned professional and was matched against Dorando Pietri of Italy for a share of the gate receipts by Flanagan; the race was run in Madison Square Garden on 15 December 1908. Longboat won when Dorando collapsed with half a mile to go. Two weeks later Longboat married Lauretta Maracle, and was given a wedding reception on the stage of Massey Hall in Toronto.

On 5 February 1909, there began one of the most famous rivalries in the history of sport, when Longboat and Alfie Shrubb ran "the race of the century" before 12,000 spectators at Madison Square Garden, a crowd that included Indian chiefs in full regalia and a uniformed Mountie whom Flanagan had secured for the occasion. By the fifteenth mile Shrubb was nearly two-thirds of a mile in the lead; from this point on the Indian's steady inexorable pace gradually ate into the tiring Englishman's margin. During the twenty-fourth mile Tom finally spurted past him; Shrubb thereupon collapsed and Longboat coasted home.

Longboat was at the peak of his fame and generally regarded as the world's best distance runner. He was shocked when Flanagan sold his contract to an American promoter for $2,000. "He sold me just like a racehorse," said Longboat, but Flanagan had his reasons. Having done very well out of the Indian, he saw the time had come to sell his meal-ticket. According to Flanagan, Longboat "refused to train properly and just generally went prima donna on me". At the age of twenty-one, Tom was beginning his downhill slide. Within a few months he had been sold again for $700. Despite a series of thrilling races with Shrubb and a brilliant race on Toronto Island in 1912 in which Tom set a new record for fifteen miles, a fatal pattern had appeared; in 1911 he received a suspended sentence for drunkenness in Toronto and rumours of his drinking bouts were rife.

Longboat served overseas during the first war; he was falsely reported killed and his wife remarried. On his return to Canada he drifted from job to job, his winnings long gone, winding up as a helper on a Toronto garbage wagon in 1927. He died back on the Six Nations Reserve in 1949, a victim of his own talents, the rapaciousness of promoters, the short-lived worship of the public, and his vulnerability to the corruptions of white society.

DUNCAN A. McNAUGHTON, 1910-

Since the first modern Olympiad in Athens in 1896, the high jump had been dominated by athletes from the United States. In 1932, at Los Angeles, there seemed little reason to doubt that an American would once more win the event. George Spitz, the world record holder at 6 feet 8.5 inches, led the American team, and its other members were also highly rated.

The Canadian competitor, Duncan McNaughton, was born in Cornwall, Ontario, but grew up in Vancouver where he was a notable high school athlete. In basketball, he was both captain and coach of the team that won the provincial championship in 1929. In the same year, he won the individual championship at both the annual track meet of the Vancouver high schools and at the first British Columbia high school Olympiad. In 1930 he enrolled at the University of Southern California in geology, and until his graduation in 1933 was a member of the university track team.

McNaughton was to win a gold medal for Canada in what still remains one of the hardest-fought high jump competitions in Olympic history. According to Henry Roxborough if McNaughton had not been "living in California, and thus available without expense, he would never have been added to our team." Perhaps team officials had been influenced by McNaughton's disqualification for an illegal jumping technique when he was a member of the Canadian contingent at the 1930 British Empire Games. Since that time, under coaching at Southern Cal and with particular help from his teammate, Bob Van Osdel, he had changed his style to the conventional western roll. With Van Osdel's help, McNaughton made the USC team and finally won the California state championship, setting a new state intercollegiate record with his winning jump. A year after the Olympics, at the national US intercollegiate championships at Chicago, McNaughton proved himself once again by winning the high jump.

Alexandra Studio

At Los Angeles there were twenty competitors in the field. Spitz went out at 6 feet 4 inches. As the bar inched up towards 6 feet 6 inches, only four remained – Van Osdel and McNaughton among them. Only Van Osdel and the Canadian cleared 6 feet 6 inches. They had been jumping for three hours, but another hour of gruelling competition lay ahead of them. Neither could clear 6 feet 7 inches; both the American and the slight, dark-haired Canadian were tiring visibly. It was at this point that the two approached the judges with the suggestion that first place be split between them. The officials rejected the offer and the two resumed jumping and both failed to clear 6 feet 6.5 inches. Finally, with the bar lowered once again to 6 feet 6 inches, McNaughton cleared it on the first try, and won the medal when Van Osdel was unable to leap it in three jumps. Duncan McNaughton, a man who secured his place on his country's team by the back door, must have felt a sense of pride and personal vindication. Canada won no other golds in track and field; McNaughton and boxer Horace "Lefty" Gwynne were our only gold medallists in 1932.

When his athletic days were over, Duncan McNaughton went on to a distinguished career in geology. He worked for the Canadian Geological Survey in the late thirties, joined the RCAF in 1941, and while a pilot with No. 405 (Pathfinder) Squadron, won the DFC with bar. After the war, he took

246

his PhD. in geology at USC, and after a stint as assistant professor there, was employed by various US oil companies until he set up his own petroleum consultancy firm in Dallas, Texas.

JOHNNY MILES, 1905-

The marathons of both the ancient and the modern Olympics were and are the supreme test of athletic training and endurance. Almost as prestigious is the annual Boston marthon which, each spring, attracts more entries from more countries than any other annual sporting event.

Thus it was expected that the 1926 Boston marathon would be a struggle between Albin Stenroos of Finland, the 1924 Olympic champion, and Clarence DeMar, the American master of the Boston course. However, an apple-cheeked, twenty-one year old, Johnny Miles of Sydney Mines, Nova Scotia, stole the prize from the favourites while slashing nearly five minutes off the course record. Even more astonishing, the young Canadian was a comparative newcomer to marathon competition.

Young Miles had entered his first road races in 1922 but it was not until 1925 that he gained much notice in Canada by

beating a fast field of middle-distance runners in the five-mile event at the national track championships. He proved himself further the same year by winning the Halifax *Herald and Evening Mail* modified marathon, covering the ten miles in a crisp 53:48.5 minutes.

Johnny received inspiration and training from his father, a PT instructor in two wars and an amateur boxer of renown in Britain. The older Miles had emigrated to Cape Breton to work in the coal mines after the first world war. In his eleventh year Johnny himself went into the mines, but when he began to show promise as a runner his father felt a healthier job was required and Johnny worked "on the surface" as a teamster.

The training system worked out by father and son was based on running ten miles almost every day, with occasional days on which Johnny would run only two miles all out. Every six weeks he would run the marathon distance of more than twenty-six miles, aiming at a steady pace of six minutes a mile.

Even as a teenager Johnny was eager to tackle the Boston marathon, but his father held him back until 1926. In January that year he began to point in earnest for Boston, slogging along the cold streets of Sydney Mines. In April he hopped the CN express for twenty-six miles and then ran home over the rugged island hills, often ankle-deep in snow and slush. His time was two hours and forty-one minutes. "I knew after that workout," said Johnny, "that I'd win at Boston."

The victory in Boston was followed by a string of twenty triumphs at various distances; then for some inexplicable reason Johnny Miles fell into a slump that lasted for more than two years.

Johnny returned to Boston in 1927 to defend his title and had to drop out at the five-mile mark. He had climbed on the running board of a passing car and, according to his dad, "he didn't realize what he was doing until some minutes after boarding the car."

A public controversy raged at once over the young runner's action. He was barraged with criticism. Explanations of badly blistered feet were dismissed with the folk wisdom that such were the occupational hazards of all distance runners. His father felt that he had lost his confidence. "He was worried and anxious before each race. He doesn't realize it but he was always under a severe mental strain, and an athlete's mind must be free of worry if he is going to win any sporting event."

Johnny believed that he had plenty

247

of races left in him and dismissed rumours that "he was all washed up." Still, the experience of the 1927 race continued to haunt him.

The 1929 Boston marathon was crucial to his own view of himself as a runner. Early in the race he found himself dueling with Whitey Michelson. They exchanged the lead over the first ten miles, then Johnny pulled away. He had a substantial lead going into the last few miles but two rivals were coming fast and he was fading. He had just enough left to hit the tape first in a record time of 2:33:8 hours. He had made his comeback. He had erased publicly and in his own mind the discouragements of the past two years.

Hamilton, where Johnny and his family had moved, held a civic banquet on his return. Johnny had taken a job with a manufacturing firm and for seven years after the second world war, had headed a large factory operation in France. He retired from competition in 1933.

THE OLYMPIC 400-METRE RELAY TEAM, 1928

One of the most glittering performances by Canadian athletes was the victory of the Canadian women's 400-metre relay team at the 1928 Olympics at Amsterdam. For two of the team's members in particular, the gold medal was sweet vindication for what had happened in the 100-metre event.

Canada had placed three sprinters among the six finalists for the 100 metres. Jane Bell, running with a tendon injury, had won her first heat but had been eliminated in the semi-finals. Our best hope was Myrtle Cook, well known in later years to readers of the Montreal *Star* as Myrtle Cook McGowan, sports editor and columnist. Myrtle was an all-rounder, outclassed only by Bobbie Rosenfeld in the history of women's athletics in Canada. She was a champion – or played on championship teams – in tennis, ice hockey, basketball, canoeing, bowling and cycling. As a sprinter, she cut a swath through track meets in Europe, the United States and Canada from 1925 to 1930, and in the Canadian Olympic trials at Halifax in 1928, she set a new world record in the 100 metres. In the Olympic 100-metre final she suffered a cruel disappointment, being disqualified for two false starts. This left Bobbie

Canada's Olympic-winning 400-metre team of 1928 was comprised of Jane Bell, Myrtle Cook, Ethel Smith and Fannie (Bobbie) Rosenfeld. The team broke its own record of the previous day by a full second.

Rosenfeld, Ethel Smith, one German and one American runner. In the race, Rosenfeld and the American girl breasted the tape simultaneously – the judges were split but on decision awarded the medal to the US. Rosenfeld took the silver medal, Smith the bronze.

In the preliminary heat of the 400-metre relay, the four Canadians won easily and set a new Olympic mark of 49.4 seconds. The following day they were pitted against teams from the United States, Germany, France, Holland and Italy. On the first leg a determined Bobbie Rosenfeld established a lead of about a yard when she made her pass to Ethel Smith; by the time Ethel had swept down the back stretch she had slightly increased it. Jane Bell, ailing and perhaps the weakest member of the team, ran the race of her life; when she came into the straightaway and made a perfect pass to Myrtle Cook the Canadian led by three yards. The last leg was Myrtle Cook's and, if anything, the Canadian margin at the finish had been further extended. In winning their gold medal the four Toronto girls broke their own record of the previous day by a full second.

WILLIAM J. SHERRING, 1877-1964

In 1906, after the failure of the first three Olympiads of 1896, 1900 and 1904 to attract satisfactory international recognition, a special Olympiad was held at Athens itself to infuse new life into the movement that had revived the games. Naturally the feature of the 1906 games was the marathon race of 26 miles, 385 yards, run between the site of the battle of Marathon and Athens – if not perhaps over precisely the same course run by that unknown runner who brought the good news of the Greek victory over the Persians in 490 BC. The United States and Britain had especially large teams at the games but many countries were represented. In the marathon alone sixty-seven runners started.

Canada's "team" at Athens was composed of three Toronto athletes and Billy Sherring, who represented the St. Patrick's Athletic Club of Hamilton. The money to send Sherring had been raised by the club and included the proceeds of a winning bet on a racehorse named Cicely by the bartender of the Commercial Hotel. Sherring, a railway brakeman, threw in his savings as well, and when he got to Greece took a job as a railway station porter to support himself while training.

Although Sherring was completely unknown internationally, he was an experienced distance runner. As a boy he had run perpetually – "it seemed more natural to me than walking." By the time he was sixteen, he was winning races at Ontario fairs.

At twenty he finished third in Hamilton's round-the-bay race (a race of slightly more than nineteen miles that today is the oldest annually run distance race in North America). He won the Hamilton race in 1899 and again in 1903; in 1900 he finished second in the famous Boston marathon.

At three o'clock of a blistering hot 1 May 1906 the tiny Canadian (he weighed only 112 pounds) lined up with the other contestants at Marathon to be sent off over the hilly course. Sherring did not take the lead until the race was more than two and one-half hours old. According to an account of the time, when Sherring "had gained a good lead, he took a little walk for air storage for the supreme effort which he well knew must come shortly. When he perceived the enemy approaching, he resumed his running and when they relapsed into pedestrianism, he did likewise." Billy Sherring passed the time with "salutes to the people and pleasantries," until he got close to the great new Olympic stadium, where more than 60,000 Greeks awaited hopefully for a countryman to claim the olive wreath. Instead, they got William J. Sherring of Hamilton, Ontario – now weighing 98 pounds; in the triumphant words of the Toronto *Globe,* "The first man to make the round of the stadium, the crowning stage of the race, was the wearer of the maple leaf."

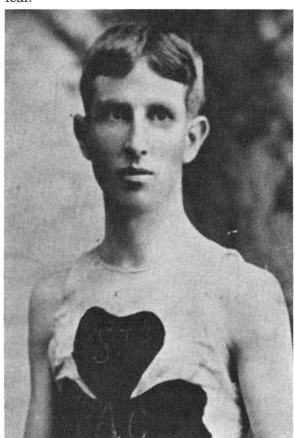

Well, not quite. Actually Billy was wearing an enormous shamrock, symbolic of St. Pat's AC, a curious floppy hat, along with a very large grin; he ran around the stadium accompanied by a large uniformed gentleman who applauded him as he ran. It was Prince George of Greece; the photograph of the prince and Billy Sherring running together to the finish line is one of the most unforgettable in all Olympic history. Billy had run his race in the record time of 2:51:23.6 hours, a feat that won him a host of friends in his home city for the rest of his long life. So, for the Toronto *Globe*, the significance of his Athens victory was that "here in the greatest historical arena of the world, a young Canadian triumphed over the chosen athletes of almost every civilized country."

HILDA STRIKE, 1910-

Canada's record at the Olympic Games of 1928 and 1932 in women's track and field events was impressive; 1928 was the first year that women were allowed to enter the previously all-male preserve of track and field. Canadian girls went to Amsterdam and came back with gold medals in the high jump and 400-metre relay, and one silver. In 1932 at Los Angeles the heroine for Canada was a petite sprinter from Montreal, Hilda Strike, who earned two silver medals for her performance in the 100 metres and the 400-metre relay.

Hilda was born in Montreal. Her father had played professional hockey and had been the leading scorer for the Calumets of Michigan in 1904-5, the year the team won the World International League champion-

ship. Hilda took part in high school swimming, skating, badminton, basketball – every sporting activity that was available. She was also a fine softball player, and when she was nineteen her talents attracted the attention of Myrtle Cook, sports columnist of the Montreal *Star*. Myrtle had been on the Canadian team at the 1928 Olympics, and had won a gold medal in the 400-metre relay. She recognized Hilda's potential as a great sprinter, and encouraged her to train. Hilda joined the Canadian Ladies Athletic Club, and began practising assiduously.

In the years from 1929 to 1932 Hilda competed in meets all over North America, winning a total of fifteen cups and thirty medals. She was five-foot-four and weighed about 105 pounds, small for a sprinter. Hilda made up for her lack of height and the longer stride which so many of her taller, more rangy competitors possessed by her amazing starting speed.

Her greatest success came in May 1932 at the provincial women's track and field championships in Montreal, when she ran the 100 metres in 12.2 seconds, equalling the 1928 Olympic record. After her excellent showing at the Olympic trials in Hamilton in July, she was selected as one of the nine girls to represent Canada in the track and field events at the Los Angeles games.

Hilda Strike put up a tremendous performance for Canada, against the most formidable opposition. Her chief opponent was the world record holder, Stanislawa Walasiewiczowna of Poland (named Stella Walsh by sportswriters who were defeated by the intricacies of the Polish language), in the 100 metres. Hilda was the smallest of the six finalists. Hilda streaked out to a brilliant start and led the field until the last yard, when the tall Polish girl caught up and breasted the tape ahead of Hilda. But so close was the finish that both girls were awarded the identical time of 11.9 seconds, a new Olympic record.

The second silver medal Hilda won was in the 400-metre relay, and here the result must have been a bitter disappointment to the Canadian girls. Hilda anchored the team, which was ahead right up to the last baton pass. But as Mary Frizzell handed off to Hilda something happened, and Hilda had to almost stop dead before she got the baton. Canada finished second behind the American team but once again the judges ruled a dead heat of 47 seconds although they awarded the gold medal to the US girls.

Hilda met Stella Walsh once again when the Polish girl came to compete at the Canadian National Exhibition in 1932. Again

Stella won, but once again Hilda had the satisfaction of pushing her to yet another world record in the 100 metres. That same year Hilda was named woman athlete of the year, and Montreal's most popular athlete.

In 1933 Hilda joined forces with her friend Myrtle Cook to form her own track club, the Mercury Athletic Club, where Hilda coached young runners. She still competed and in 1934 became the provincial champion in the 60 and 100 yards. She represented Canada in the British Empire Games in London in 1934 and once again won silver medals in the 100-yard and 110-yard relay. With her marriage in 1935 to Fred Sisson, Hilda retired from active competition, although her interest in running, and in coaching youngsters continued.

EARL THOMSON, 1895-

In 1920 the Olympic Games, held for the first time since 1912, were awarded to the city of Antwerp in war-ravaged Belgium. The United States, newly recognized as a world power, and anxious to establish its supremacy in international athletics, was assembling a strong team. One of the most promising prospective members of that team was a high hurdler from California named Earl Thomson, a world record holder and twice US intercollegiate champion. Thomson stunned American – and Canadian – Olympic officials when he pointed out that, by Olympic rules, he was ineligible to represent the United

States, having been born on a farm at Birch Hills, Saskatchewan, near Prince Albert. In 1903 the Thomsons had moved to California, settling in Long Beach. At high school, Earl played baseball and football and "did a little swimming," but hurdling was his sport. In his first year at the University of Southern California, he set a world mark of 14.8 seconds for the 110-yard high hurdles, only to have it broken by a teammate, Bob Simpson, a week later. Transferring in 1916 to the East and Dartmouth College, Earl scarcely had time to make his presence felt on the track team before he decided to enlist as an observer-trainee in the Royal Flying Corps. While at the training station at Beamsville, Ontario, he took part in the RFC track meet held in Toronto. Beamsville RFC won, largely because Thomson took five firsts, a second, six cups and a gold medal (he didn't get back to Toronto to pick up his trophies until 1948).

Thomson graduated and was commissioned as an observer in September 1918, too late to be shipped overseas. Instead, he zeturned to Dartmouth College and in the spring of 1919 set a new world's record for the 110-yard high hurdles of 14.4 seconds in winning at the IC4A meet at Philadelphia. He repeated his IC4A victories in the high hurdles in 1920 and 1921, and also won the low hurdles in the latter year.

After Thomson's disclosure that he was to compete in the Olympics as a Canadian, he went to Montreal for the Olympic trials, and qualified for the broad jump as well as for the high hurdles. His only competition in his specialty at Antwerp came from two Americans. In the hurdles, the three ran abreast for almost fifty metres; then Thomson took a narrow lead and held it for the remainder of the race, setting the new Olympic record time of 14.8 seconds.

Although Earl Thomson's outstanding career as a world-class hurdler owed little to Canadian experience or training, his associations with Canada both as a child and in that remarkable company of Canadian airmen during the first world war certainly entitled Canadians to feel some sense of pride in his accomplishment at Antwerp, particularly since he ran under the maple leaf and won his gold medal as a member of the Canadian team. After the Olympics, Thomson returned to Dartmouth, graduated in 1922 and was assistant track coach there for a time. He was track coach at the University of Western Virginia for a year, assistant coach at Yale until 1927, and then served as track coach at the United States Naval Academy, Annapolis, Maryland, for more than a quarter of a century.

251

Canada Wide Feature Service Ltd.

PERCY WILLIAMS, 1908-

One of the most dramatic sports photographs ever taken was that of Percy Williams winning the 100 metres at the 1928 Olympics: arms flung wide, head back and hair flying, mouth opened wide, chest thrusting for the tape. This frozen moment of the athlete's agony has been reprinted many times since the event, but as often as not it has been confused with another – that of Williams completing the double by winning the 200 metres. The reason for the confusion, apart from simple ignorance, is plain if one looks at the two pictures. Williams's attitude of supreme and ultimate endeavour is identical in both. It has usually been interpreted as *the* example of an athlete's raw will to push himself almost beyond human limits to win for Canada. No doubt it was. But it was also the outcome of meticulous training, the perfectly executed technique of a sprinter striving for all-important inches. Percy Williams at the tape was in a state, not of emotional and physical abandon, but of superb moral and athletic discipline.

If ever there was an unlikely and unwilling hero in Canadian sports history, it was surely Percy Williams. He was frail, even delicate, the result of a bout of rheumatic fever as a child which, the doctors had said, left him with a damaged heart. He was small – at the peak of his athletic career he weighed only 125 pounds. And he had no burning ambition to be a runner. He did a little half-hearted running in high school which amounted to a few weeks of work in the spring and a last-minute effort on sports day.

So it might have continued if one day in the summer of 1926 Percy had not accepted a challenge to run against Wally Scott, Vancouver's sprint champion. Scott's coach was Bob Granger, who watched with amazement as Percy ran his boy to a dead heat. He later described his first impression of young Percy. "I think he violated every known principle in the running game. He ran with his arms glued to his sides. It actually made me tired to watch him." From that moment Granger took Percy under his wing. Even in 1926 he was proclaiming to anyone who would listen that here was the winner of the 100 metres at the next Olympics.

Granger was a fanatic about sport. He was in his thirties when he met Williams and his own athletic days were over, though in his youth he had excelled at rugby and swimming and had been a fair track man. From then on he had devoted all his time, energy and money to developing school boy athletes. Training techniques fascinated him and no detail in the conditioning and developing of athletes, especially sprinters, escaped his notice. Now, all this energy and dedication would be concentrated on Williams. And victory at the Olympics.

Percy himself was less than enthusiastic. He had to give up swimming because Granger said it affected his speed. Not only was Granger always at him to put in more time on the track, but there were the proper techniques to be learned, particularly starts and correct arm movements.

Nowadays Granger's methods sound quaint, almost ludicrous. Where athletes now put themselves through ever more gruelling training regimens, Granger believed in conserving the boy's energy. (At the 1928 Olympics, just before the final of the 200 metres, when all the other finalists were going through their various warming-up exercises, Williams was lying in his dressing room buried under a pile of blankets. This was Granger's way of warming him up without sacrificing precious energy.) Granger went to any lengths to keep Williams protected. On a cold day, before a race, he would rub his body with cocoanut butter and dress him in three or four track suits and sweaters to prevent loss of valuable body heat. He got groups of his boys to demonstrate starts and arm motions, while Percy watched – again to save his strength. Later he would practise for hours in front of a mirror.

Gradually Williams's style began to improve. Granger entered him in the local meets, and every win increased his pressure

252

on the boy until Percy became as obsessed as Granger with the Olympics. By the spring of 1928 Williams was clocking some remarkable times for a schoolboy. When the BC Olympic trials took place in June he tied the Olympic record of 10.6 seconds for the 100 metres. Yet he was still unknown when he went East a few weeks later for the Canadian Olympic trials in Hamilton. There, against a field of experienced runners including the great Cyril Coaffee, Williams won both the 100 and 200 metres. A new Canadian star had appeared.

Williams was on his way to Amsterdam, and the greatest athletic contest in the world. But Granger was not with him; the Olympic committee paid the expenses of the competitors, but there was no money for coaches. In Vancouver, Williams's friends and his mother raised a few hundred dollars. Granger crossed the Atlantic on a freighter and arrived at Williams's hotel in Amsterdam three days after the team.

The heats for the 100 metres started on 29 June. Williams won his first heat easily, but in the second race he had to do his fastest time in the games, 10.6 seconds, to qualify for the semi-finals. The next day, in the semi-final, Williams made a bad start but recovered to come second. And so to the final. The line-up was impressive. Besides Bob McAllister of the US there was Jack London from Britain; Frank Wykoff, an eighteen-year-old Californian schoolboy who had tied the Olympic record four times and who was the favourite; George Lammers of Germany; and Wilfred Legg of South Africa. The skinny twenty-year-old from Canada was the decided underdog. Williams shot away from a perfect start into the lead, with the rest at his heels. He stayed out in front, in spite of challenges from London and Wykoff, and hung on to win by a yard. The crowd went wild.

But there was no time to savour his win. The next day the 200-metre heats started. Here Williams had to battle with a new, fresh group of athletes, men who were more experienced and had faster times than he. Granger had spent a lifetime studying the techniques of other great runners. He knew that the men Williams had to beat were the Californian, Charles Borah, his teammate, the veteran Charles Paddock and Helmut Koernig, Germany's finest runner. Once again Williams won his first heat easily. But the draw for the second heat pitted him against both Borah and Koernig – and only two could qualify. Granger sized up the situation and gave Williams his instructions: don't go to win; run to beat whoever is running second. When the race started Koernig took the lead with Borah on his heels. Williams was running third; at the halfway mark he tried to increase his speed and momentarily faltered. But with 60 metres still to go, he shifted into high gear and passed Borah in the last two yards.

By the time of the final, and the chance of a double victory, the pressure was enormous. Once again Granger's psychology came to the fore. He marked Koernig as the one to watch. He told Williams the German needed to be in front. If Williams could stick with him and come out of the curve level, he could win the race. Williams ran neck-and-neck with Koernig up to the final fifty metres. Then again he shifted into his driving finish and won by a yard. The whole stadium rose to applaud the slim, unassuming boy who had come from nowhere to beat the established athletes of the world, the first Canadian ever to win the double in two of the most prestigious events of the Olympics.

How had Percy Williams done it? He said himself that he owed everything to Granger; his first words on winning the 100-metres had been "Won't Granger be pleased?" But that is only part of the story. Charlie Paddock had the opportunity to watch him at close hand, both in the stands and on the track. He quickly saw the secret of Williams's power. "Williams commences a race as a pull runner (his leg action is in front of him and his knees coming up high). In the closing metres of a race he is not a pull runner at all, but distinctly a driver. In years of running and watching runners, I have never seen a sprinter who could employ two methods in a single race."

Williams came home to a tumultuous reception as he and his mother travelled across the country. In Vancouver the crowds were ecstatic. Percy was given a sports car and the faithful Granger was presented with a purse of $500. It was a great homecoming for the schoolboy who had hardly been known a few weeks before.

For the next two years Williams lived up to his reputation. But at the British Empire Games in Hamilton in 1930 he pulled a muscle in his left thigh in the final of the 100 yards. He struggled to finish – he actually won the race in spite of extreme pain – but his leg was never right again. He went to the 1932 Olympics but was eliminated in the semi-final of the 200 metres.

Back in Vancouver, Williams dropped out of competitive sport and devoted himself to business. Perhaps it was a relief. Interviewed in 1954 he remembered: "Oh, I was so glad to get out of it all."

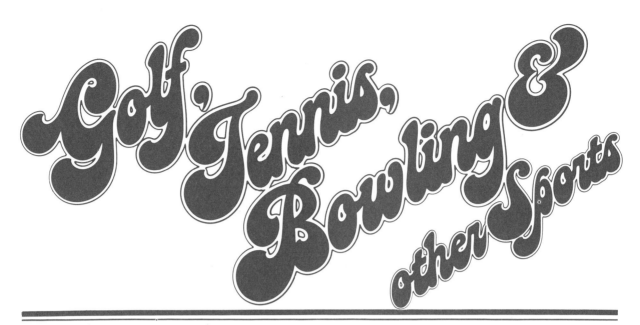

Golf, Tennis, Bowling & other Sports

Chapter 10

The sports grouped in this chapter have three things in common:

1/They are played with an instrument – a racket, a cue, a bowling ball – or a mechanical device like the bicycle.

2/While team games (hockey, baseball, lacrosse) also employ extensions of the human arm the games discussed here do not lend themselves to team play except in a restricted sense.

3/The third aspect they share is that in none of them have Canadians consistently excelled.

Only in golf have we produced a significant number of players of international calibre. Bowling is played world wide but most Canadians play local variants, like Thomas F. Ryan's five-pin game, that have no international acceptance. Graydon Robinson has been one of the few Canadians to excel in ten-pin, played by millions in the United States and elsewhere, but by relatively few in Canada. Snooker, billiards and allied table games, despite aristocratic pedigrees, have been exploited in a cheap, commercial way in Canada. George Chenier, a fine player who would have found acclaim in the respectable club atmosphere of Britain, spent his career here trying, unavailingly, to give his game "class."

Tennis and cycling are current fads, but it remains to be seen whether there will be a permanent increase in participation, and

Today's tennis players wear minimum covering but back in 1909 a casual game between friends was an occasion for wearing one's finery.

whether recreational interest will be translated into new levels of competitive excellence. The tennis craze is partially the result of the publicity given by the media to world professional tennis, familiarizing millions with the superlative play of Rod Laver, Billie Jean King and even Bobby Riggs. Perhaps out of the new popularity of the game, new players will develop who will surpass the best achievements of Jack Wright, Dorothy Walton, Bob Bedard or Lorne Main. Canadian tennis has never had a mass base like that in California, for obvious reasons. When Laver was asked how Canadians could improve their tennis he said: "Leave the country." Great tennis comes with good coaching in year-round outdoor play against strong competition.

The modern game of tennis dates from 1873. (An earlier form of indoor or real tennis had been popular in the courts and cloisters of the Middle Ages.) An English gentleman, tired of endless rounds of croquet, devised what he called "sphairistike," the name of an ancient Greek ball game. When some of his converts began calling the game "sticky," he revived his original term, lawn tennis. In 1877 the first all-England tournament was held at Wimbledon; among its twenty-two competitors few had ever played the game before. With extraordinary rapidity the game vaulted the Atlantic. In 1879 the Montreal Lawn Tennis Club held *its* first tournament; by 1881 some of its members were "old hands at the game."

Tennis spread rapidly. Part of the reason for its instant popularity was the fact that ladies could play it with decorum – as early as 1883 a Toronto club was holding mixed doubles matches. A year after the Canadian Lawn Tennis Association was formed, the first ladies' championships were held in 1891. In 1895 a tennis buff wrote that "there is an astonishing lot of lawn tennis played in Canada if one takes the trouble to look into it; nearly every city and town has its club, and villages too." Still, tennis was the game of the few. Good courts were costly, and tennis club memberships in the cities came high: one Toronto club charged an entrance fee of $25 plus annual dues. Public courts were well in the future; Edmonton and Calgary were to pioneer them nearly a generation later.

Tennis was saddled with a socially exclusive image which only today it is shaking off, and right from the start it fell well behind British and American standards of play. "I confess I never really considered the possibilities of lawn tennis until I went to the United States and saw the intense earnestness with which the game is played and encouraged there," wrote a Canadian in 1895. "We in Canada are not in it . . . we pat the ball; our strokes do not inspire confidence . . . man for man, we cannot approach our brethren across the border. They can chase us all over the lot." This gap, so early observed, has never closed.

Badminton is a racket sport in which Canadians have fared rather better. This ancient game was brought to England by army officers; it was launched at the Duke of Bedford's country house, Badminton, in 1873. Apparently it reached Canada in the 1890s; the oldest club of record is the Ladies' Montreal Tennis and Badminton Club, founded in 1907. The game found an immediate home in garrison armouries and school gyms, and was played there and outdoors as a pleasant recreation. In 1925 the Canadian Badminton Association sponsored a demonstration tour by leading British exponents that seems to have helped in the popularizing process. A second sponsored tour by the Britons in 1930 disclosed, however, that Jack Purcell, a Guelph native playing out of Toronto, was too much for the visitors to handle. As amateur and professional this remarkable athlete was almost invincible in the 1930s – but there was a long distance between Purcell and the next best Canadian player. After the second world war, badminton languished somewhat; there was a five-year period in which national competition disappeared. Players like Marjory Shedd, Jamie Paulson, and Yves Pare have demonstrated in recent years that we can play effectively at the international level, and that (since there is no climatic handicap) we may yet take our place as a world badminton power.

The cycling boom has been created by an ecology-minded generation in revolt against the smelly wastefulness of the internal combustion engine, and by commuters seeking to outflank traffic congestion at the urban core. The revival has political clout: who would have be-

lieved a decade ago that the National Capital Commission could close its popular parkway system to cars on weekend mornings so that cyclists could have the roads all to themselves, with not a peep from the motorists? The Canadian Cycling Association, the direct descendant of the original Canadian Wheelmen's Association of 1882, professes to believe that mass recreational cycling, plus the Montreal Olympics, may reawaken interest in racing in this country. There is quite a leap, however, from Sunday morning pedalling to the fierce rivalries of the velodrome.

The first cycling rage in Canada certainly included racing. The velocipede, known derisively as the "bone shaker," was invented in France in 1863. Its low gear ratio prompted James Starley, a Coventry engineer, to design the high wheeler, otherwise known as the "penny farthing" for its large front and small back wheels. It was this cantankerous vehicle which reached North America in the 1870s; the Montreal and Boston cycle clubs were the first on the continent. Difficult though it was to ride, the high wheeler was a transportation breakthrough. Riding it consumed less energy than walking, and increased a man's speed through his own muscle power by a factor of three to four. Almost immediately touring clubs sprang up, and each club elected a good roads committee to pressure local governments. The high wheeler was an expensive machine, and its use was confined to the relatively prosperous. By the 1880s, both north and south of the border, long lines of "wheelmen" garbed in club uniforms, had become a common sight on rural roads. In 1883 the American magazine *Outing* published a blow-by-blow account, in two parts, of "The Great Canadian Bicycle Tour," undertaken by gentlemen cyclists of Chicago, Louisville, Detroit and points east. The entire trip, raved the club president, "was one continuous frolic of four hundred miles through a strange and lovely country." Despite the frolic, it was a non-alcoholic jaunt and "no profane, vulgar or discourteous language was heard from the lips of any member of the party, except one who left before the tour was finished."

The party's guide through the strange new world of Southwestern Ontario was Dr. Percy E. Doolittle. Doolittle was an Aylmer, Ontario boy and Trinity College graduate who typified the exuberance, and the earnestness, of early Canadian cycling. As a lad, he built his first bicycle entirely of wood, working from an engraving in a magazine. He rode this contrap-

Economic situations of the times often dictate modes of conveyance. In 1885, cycles were all the rage, not just the regular two-wheeler but more exotic contraptions such as the one.
(opposite)

256

tion the fifty miles from Aylmer to Strathroy in a day. Doolittle was a champion racer and one of the founders of the Canadian Wheelmen's Association.

Technological development brought the happy age of the high wheelers to a close as abruptly as it had begun. Already, in the 1870s, the tubular frame, ball bearings and the chain-and-sprocket drive had been developed. Then, in 1885, J. V. Starley (nephew of the high wheeler's inventor) brought out the Rover safety bicycle. With its diamond frame and equal-sized wheels, it is, in fact, the modern bike. All that was needed to finish off the high wheeler was the invention of pneumatic tires in 1888 by John Boyd Dunlop, a Scottish veterinarian.

The safety bike set off quite startling changes in social patterns, attitudes and behaviour. Though it was expensive at first, when it was mass-produced in the 1890s it came within the reach of many thousands of city dwellers to whom it was not only a cheap method of transportation but a liberator; the poor man's reply to the horse and carriage. The older cycling generation viewed the departure of the high wheeler with some regret. The clubbish exclusiveness was gone, Doolittle wrote in 1896; the bicycle now was "the carriage alike of the patrician and the peasant."

Peasants were bad enough, but the safety bicycle, especially with the dropped frame and coaster brakes, brought legions of women to the sport. Gone were the days of the jolly masculine tours; "now our sisters and friends, with well-filled baskets" tagged along. Doolittle, on balance, welcomed this change: The girl of yesteryear, who played the piano, danced, and played a languid game of tennis was replaced by "the healthier new woman of today," when pedalling furiously after her, men "realize in her our equal." Young women, clad in the "rational dress" of Amelia Jenks Bloomer, scandalized old ladies of both sexes who wrote the newspapers; but the women revelled in their new freedom. Grace Denison summed it up in *Massey's Magazine* in 1896 when she wrote that "only some six or seven years ago there were no lady cyclists in Canada. Can you fancy it, my sisters? In one short demi-decade we have learned a new enthusiasm, gone through the battle of the bloomer, taken into our lives a new pleasure, the like of which we never before experienced or even in our dreams imagined."

The second wave of the cycling craze sparked a whole new growth of popular racing clubs, with names like the Hamilton Crescents, the Excelsiors, the Athenaeums and the Canadian Express. All across the country, but especially in Ontario, they competed in road races and on trotting ovals, sometimes for rather gaudy prizes. In 1895 at Waterloo, On-

tario, the winner of the premier event took home a thoroughbred horse, donated by the Joseph E. Seagram stables. One of the most notable of the new generation of racers was Toronto's Harley Davidson, later to move into motorcycle racing and manufacturing. Before its last running in 1926, Toronto's Dunlop Trophy race, begun in 1894, had become the oldest cycling event on the continent.

In the end, this first cycling craze burnt itself out. The automobile was partly responsible. Percy Doolittle, for example, drifted away from cycling to become the founder of the Ontario Motor League, and from 1920 to 1933, the president of the Canadian Automobile Association. Bicycle technology had helped prepare the way for the automobile. The first Fords used bicycle chains and wheels; many of the early car manufacturers, like Olds, Leland, Hillman and Morris, had started out as bicycle makers. Vancouver's W.J. "Torchy" Peden, the six-day racer of the 1930s, emerged at a time when scarcely an ember remained of the first great Canadian bicycle boom.

To a degree, golf is an exception among the sports we have been dealing with. Certainly it has been affected by some common Canadian problems: short season, high costs, restricted participation (until recent years) and absence of competition of the highest quality. Yet there is something about golf that makes it different from other sports; the standard generalizations do not apply so neatly.

The game got off to an early and ambitious start in Canada. In December, 1824, the Montreal *Gazette* carried this notice: "To Scotsmen. A few of the true sons of Scotia, eager to perpetuate the remembrance of her customs, have fixed upon 25 December and 1 January for going to the Priests' farm, to play golf. Such of their countrymen as choose to join them will meet them before ten o'clock AM at D. McArthur's inn, Hay Market." It may be that a blizzard, or some other consideration, kept them at McArthur's tavern, but these pioneers left no permanent heritage. The first North American golf club was that of Montreal, founded in 1873 with Alexander Dennistoun, a member of the Royal and Ancient, as its first president; the first interclub match on the continent was played between Montreal and Quebec in 1876; and the first of that great army of British professionals who were to bring the game to the new world was brought over by the Montreal club in the person of W.F. Davis of Hoylake.

By the turn of the century the Royal Canadian Golf Association had 33 member

The Capital City Bicycle Club of Ottawa was a long-established organization. *Above,* **several club members in competition;** *below,* **newspaper items of interest in the 1927 Ottawa** *Journal.*

258

C.C.M. INTRODUCES NEW RACING MODEL

Double Sprockets and Hand Brakes Are Features.

An entirely new type of racing bicycle has been brought out by the Canada Cycle & Motor Company to fill both general utility and sport purposes. This model has light tires with inner tubes that are easy to repair; comfortable racing handlebars; free rear wheel; front and rear caliper hand brakes; light saddle; quick detachable axle wing nuts; two rear-wheel sprockets for different gears when a change is desired on the road; and sufficient frame clearance so that mudguards may be used in stormy weather.

Incidentally, the price of the

CYCLING IS TWICE AS EASY AS WALKING

And It Is Also Three Times As Fast.

Medical authorities frequently advise people of all ages to do more walking. Hiking gives beneficial exercise.

Going a step further, however, it is a fact that bicycle riding is just as good for a human being as walking and the beauty of it is that a cyclist can go much farther into the country with less effort.

An old slogan points out that "cycling is twice as easy as walking and three times as fast."

With a bicycle, a person can enjoy new scenery and reach objectives that would be impossible in a moderate walk.

Why not try a bicycle for health,

clubs, most with flourishing women's divisions. George Lyon had appeared as Canada's first golfer of international repute; shortly, both open and professional championship competitions were to begin. A quarter-century later, there were 380 clubs in Canada with a total capital invested of $100 million; Ada Mackenzie had begun her long reign as Canada's premier woman golfer, and Sandy Somerville was honing the skills that brought him the US amateur title.

Did these fine golfers, and their post-1945 counterparts like Stan Leonard, Al Balding, Marlene Stewart Streit, George Knudson and Nick Weslock, emerge despite the handicap of Canadian conditions, or does golfing excellence have somewhat less to do with such conditions than we have customarily argued? Certainly there are many countries with kinder climates than our own, and a long golfing tradition, which cannot boast players of this calibre. There are a number of factors mitigating the effect of climatic and other drawbacks. One is that all-season courses south of the border have always been available for Canadians who had the money. Rough grind though it is, the American pro tour has been an accessible training school. Right from the start of Canadian golfing, professional teaching of a good standard has been available. But perhaps the central point about golf is that it is the most individual of all games. The golfer is pitted against the course and against himself. He has to perform the most delicate operations, with inadequate instruments, in circumstances of great tension when the will crumbles and the nerves scream. Excellence in golf is not just the mastery of golf's strange skills, but the conquest of fear. Our best golfers may have been penalized by the Canadian environment, but that environment may well have had a good deal to do with the unusual moral and psychological resources they all brought to the game.

From the time of George Lyon at the turn of the century, to the present day, Canada has produced fine golfers. The first North American golf club was founded in Montreal in 1873 and the first interclub match was played in 1876 between Montreal and Quebec. By 1900, the Royal Canadian Golf Association had thirty-three member clubs, most with flourishing women's sections. *Top,* **the Royal Montreal Golf Club of 1882; note the garb of the members and particularly the fact that all are wearing the "Sherlock Holmes" deer stalker's hat.** *Bottom, from left,* **are three of the finest golfers this country has ever produced: stylish Sandy Somerville of London, Ontario; Gary Cowan of Kitchener, Ontario, who along with Somerville has won the US amateur; and Ada Mackenzie of Toronto, queen of the links for many years.**

260

Public Archives of Canada

Alexandra Studio

Michael Burns Photography

Biographies

AL BALDING, 1924-

During the impressionable years of childhood, Al Balding lived across the street from the Islington golf course in west-end Toronto. From the age of eight he was caddying and playing the course when he could. At twelve he left school, worked for a couple of seasons on lake boats and moved from job to job; in depression years it was discouragingly difficult to find steady employment. During the second world war, Balding served as a gunner at Caen and in northwest Europe. At war's end he landed work making tires for a rubber company but burned his back severely in an industrial accident and was forced to quit. Driving a beer truck for a living, Balding played golf as often as he could and came to the attention of Jack Littler, the pro at Toronto Oakdale. He hired Balding as a pro-shop assistant.

In 1952 Balding spent ten weeks on the pro tour; his expenses were paid by an acquaintance and Balding conserved what little money he had by sleeping in his car. He won nothing on the tour but the experience was valuable. Later the same year he won his first tournament, defeating Stan Horne two and one for the Millar Trophy, emblematic of the Canadian professional match play championship.

In 1953, 1954 and 1955 Balding was back on the tour and drew a blank each year. Then, in December 1955 he won the Mayfair Open at Florida defeating the best of the US professional ranks. Balding won with four rounds of 69, 66, 66 and 68 over a relatively short course that gave him ample opportunity to demonstrate his superb irons play.

After the breakthrough Balding became a consistent if unspectacular golfer and in 1957 won the Miami Beach Open, the West Palm Beach Open and the Havana Invitational. In 1963 he won the Mexico Open. Then, in 1965, disaster struck; he was hospitalized with an operation for his back which had never healed properly after his accident. For two years ill health dogged him. By 1967 he was back in winning form and tied with George Knudson as best Canadian in the Canadian Open and won the World Cup with brilliant rounds of 68, 72, 67 and 67 at the Olgiata course in Rome. With Knudson as partner he won the team title for Canada.

GEORGE CHENIER, 1908-70

As North American snooker champion, George Chenier spent most of his professional career attempting to give to snooker the respectability it lacked. Although Joseph Dion of Montreal won the billiard championship of North America as early as 1867, the cue game was not an early success in Canada except in the largest cities. Despite its royal origins, the game of billiards and its off-shoots like snooker never managed, in Canada, to escape the stigma attached to "billiard parlours," smoky, low-ceilinged rooms patronized by raffish idlers.

As early as 1867, a Toronto billiards equipment manufacturer tried to change the game's image by advertising its "sanitary advantages." Billiards, he said, could bring social prestige, good health and a well-adjusted marriage, as well as being miraculously effective in the treatment of tuberculosis, pulmonary complaints, depression and yellow jaundice. It "expands the chest, which gives grace and elegance to the form, and affords even the illiterate mind a practical basis for the appreciation of mathematical and geometrical truth."

Young George Chenier absorbed the mathematical and geometrical truths of pool in the halls of his native Ottawa and Hull. Though small and seemingly frail (he had a certain resemblance to the jockey, Eddie Arcaro), he was a tough youngster who at first took more interest in hockey than snooker. While a member of the Royal Canadian Air Force in the 1920s, he played for the team at Camp Borden, and after leaving the service played commercial league hockey in Detroit. It was in Detroit that Chenier acquired the phenomenal expertise that made him a genuine master both of snooker and pocket billiards. "I've been through the mill," he told Dick Beddoes of the Toronto *Globe and Mail* the year he died, "but mostly I wanted the best players. Most I ever played for was $1,500 a game, against Jimmy Moore, the American champion [in 1947 at Amarillo, Texas]. We locked the doors so nobody could get out, or the cops in."

It was in 1947 that Chenier was acknowledged as North American snooker champion, after a tour of Canada and the United States in which he took on all comers. He was to hold the championship until his death. Twice he just failed to win the world championship, finishing second to Fred Davis of England in the 1950 tournament, and being defeated once again by Davis in 1958. In tournament play he had runs of 100 or more at least 400 times; in pocket billiards he twice scored a perfect 150 (going through a rack of fifteen balls ten times), once against world champion Irving Crane.

Chenier played in countless rooms all over the world and at one time or another owned billiard establishments in Montreal, Victoria and Vancouver. His later years were spent in giving exhibitions as the touring employee of an equipment manufacturer. Through it all he continued to play his exact-

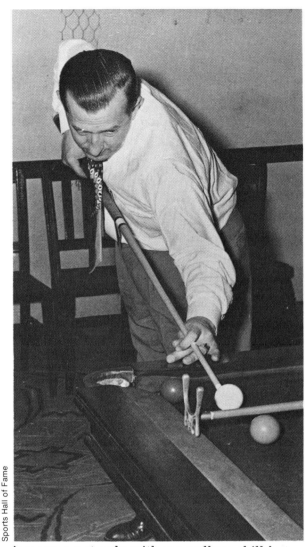

Sports Hall of Fame

ing game not only with marvellous skill but with immense dignity and courage. In 1966 he suffered a stroke that paralyzed his left side and allowed only restricted use of his left arm. Yet he remained a superb strategist at the table, even though he could no longer count on spectacular shooting. In two successful defenses of his North American title, in 1968 and in 1970 (a few months before his death) he controlled the play by "out-safing" his much younger opponents, forcing them to give him shots. "Snooker is the most scientific game in the world", he once said. "It requires skill, courage, patience, stamina. It teaches any man to look ahead – beyond the move he is making – to other moves that lie ahead."

GARY COWAN, 1938-

In an age when professional golf dominates the sport pages, when its great names acquire fortunes and celebrity status, the case of Gary Cowan continues to puzzle observers. Why has this great amateur not turned professional?

263

It was not that Cowan was born to affluence; Gary's father was a Kitchener, Ontario, policeman; he himself transferred to business school after completing Grade 10, and only in recent years has he begun to make his mark.

Gary was about ten when he began caddying at the Rockway club, and attracted the attention of the club professional, Lloyd Tucker, a man who has been responsible for the early training of a number of excellent golfers. Under Tucker's tutelage Cowan became something of a prodigy, winning the Ontario juvenile championship at fourteen, reaching the quarter-finals of the Ontario amateur when he was fifteen, and winning the Ontario and Canadian junior titles in 1956. At the age of nineteen, as a member Canada's America Cup team, he defeated in match play both the reigning US amateur champion, Hillman Robbins, and the 1955-6 champion, Harvey Ward, thus earning seven of the nineteen points Canada won in the competition.

Other triumphs followed, the most notable of which were the Canadian amateur title in 1961, the winning of medallist honours at the world amateur in Japan in 1962, and tieing with Deane Beman for low amateur in the Masters at Augusta in 1964. In 1966, Gary Cowan became the second Canadian to win the US amateur, defeating Beman in a play-off. On that occasion, Cowan expressed the hope that his victory "convinces Canadian golfers the Americans can be beaten". As it happened, *Sports Illustrated,* a well-known US publication, wrote of the tournament in terms of how Beman lost, rather than how Cowan won it.

Cowan's successes in national and international play continued. He won the Ontario Open with a record-tieing 204 in 1968, and again in 1971. In 1970, at Pinehurst, NC, he won the most important US amateur tournament after the national amateur, the North-South, defeating Dale Morey five and four in the final. In his match against Morey, he birdied five of the first ten holes; Morey said, "it was scary . . . like playing Nicklaus, Palmer and Player combined".

Then, in September 1971, Cowan cemented the view many students of the game have of him as perhaps the world's finest amateur by winning once more the US amateur, this time at Wilmington, Delaware. He won in spectacular fashion. One stroke ahead of young Eddie Pearce of Wake Forest University at the eighteenth tee, Cowan put his drive in the rough, 135 yards from the pin. With a nine iron, he hit a solid shot which bounced across the green into the cup for an eagle two and the championship. Cowan met with the press and asked if anyone was from *Sports Illustrated.* When the reporter acknowledged his affiliation, Cowan recounted for the entire crowd the magazine's gaffe of 1966.

From time to time, Cowan declares that he would like to give the pro tour a whirl – as an amateur. Become a pro full-time? He told one reporter: "I was playing in Sweden last fall. Jack Nicklaus was there, on one of those five-countries-in-five-day deals. If your goal is money and a star image, okay. But how much money can you use? Realistically?"

GEORGE KNUDSON, 1937-

George Knudson's approach to golf is that of the perfectionist. From the time he began to play in Winnipeg at the age of thirteen, he has been insatiably curious about every aspect of the game. Working in the pro shop at the St. Charles Club, he learned what there was to know about the building of a golf club and about the mechanics of a golf swing. His deep commitment to golf, his emotional intensity, and the relentless pressure of competition have occasionally been too much for him; as a result, he competes only in carefully selected tournaments.

Despite disappointments and periods of erratic play, Knudson has compiled the best record ever put together by a Canadian in professional golf. His first tour victory (three years after he turned professional in 1958 and won the McNaughton-Brooks Bursary three years in a row) was in 1961 at

Coral Gables; in 1962 he won the Maracaibo and Puerto Rico Opens; the Portland and Panama Opens in 1963; the Caracas and Fresno Opens in 1964; the World Cup individual title in Tokyo in 1966; the Greater New Orleans Open in 1967; the Phoenix and Tucson Opens in 1968; and the Robinson Open and the Wills Masters tournament in Melbourne in 1969. In addition, he teamed with Al Balding to win the World Cup title in Italy in 1968, won the Canadian PGA on three occasions, and the Millar Trophy in 1965. These impressive victories tell only part of the story. Despite his restricted tournament schedule, Knudson has generally been in the upper echelon of money winners, and has done particularly well in the US Masters, especially in 1969 when he finished second by a stroke to George Archer.

From tee to green, Knudson's game is superb. This judgment is borne out by computer analysis of performance during the 1968 tour. Only one player, Jack Nicklaus, was more consistent than Knudson in reaching the green. Putting has been his weakness; he lost the Masters because Archer took seventeen fewer putts. In that tournament, off the tee and on the fairways, there was literally no one in Knudson's league.

Knudson has never been one of the peacocks of the tour. Dressed in muted colours, shutting himself off from the galleries, he has played the game as an artist and as a perfectionist. He has always been frank about himself and his ups and downs. "[Ben]

Hogan never played up to a gallery," he once said. "They applaud scores. They applaud leaders. But they don't know to appreciate a good golf shot. They clap and yell like hell for a shot that might have been the worst the golfer hit all day."

In his pursuit of golfing perfection, George Knudson has been the first prominent professional, with the possible exception of Gary Player, to lay heavy emphasis upon all-round physical fitness. In 1967 he put himself in the hands of Lloyd Percival, and since then has devoted a significant part of his golfing year to physical training and conditioning. Even if George Knudson is denied one of the major championships he wishes to win, his natural ability, his deep knowledge of the game, and above all, his great determination have already made him Canada's finest professional golfer.

STANLEY LEONARD, 1915-
By 1955 Stan Leonard of Vancouver's Marine Drive Club had an enviable reputation: he had won the BC amateur twice and in the 1935 Canadian amateur stayed neck-and-neck with the great Sandy Somerville to the thirty-seventh hole; he had been leading Canadian in the Canadian Open five times (and repeated four times again in 1955-61); he won the CPGA five times (and three times more); he had won the BC Open five times,

265

the Alberta Open nine times and the Saskatchewan Open twice. All before 1955.

In 1955, after thirteen years as a club pro, Leonard at forty decided to chance the professional tour. He wanted to prove, he said, "that I was as good as I thought I could be." His characteristic long drive was shorter than in his prime but it was straighter, too. He could manoeuvre the ball and think at least one shot in advance. "Tournament golf," he said, "is a psychological and emotional exercise more than a physical one."

That Leonard's cool assessment was correct is shown by his tournament record. In 1957 he became the second Canadian professional golfer to win a major US tourney when he took the Greensboro Open by three strokes over Mike Souchak, the long-driving former Duke University football star. In sixty tournaments over the three years from 1955 to 1958, Leonard was out of the money only twice. Two of his finest performances occurred in Augusta, at the Masters. In 1958, when Arnold Palmer won with 284, Leonard was just two strokes back, with rounds of 72, 70, 73 and 71. In 1959 he led the first round of the Masters with a 69, took the lead again after the third round only to finish fourth, three strokes behind Art Wall. He got his revenge against Wall in 1960 in the Western Open. Trailing Wall by six strokes going into the final round, Stan fired a 68 while Wall carded a 74; Leonard won the playoff.

In Canada Cup play, in which two professionals from each competing country play four rounds for individual and team titles, Leonard participated with consistent distinction. Eight times a member of the Canadian team, he won the individual title against the world's best in Montreal in 1954 and again in Melbourne in 1959.

Perhaps the victory Leonard found most satisfying (as well as most lucrative) was his win in the Tournament of Champions at Las Vegas in 1958. In the first three rounds, he shot 69, 69, 69, and continued his sub-par play into the final round. Nevertheless, when he and his playing partner, Bill Casper, approached the seventeenth tee, they found themselves tied, with no one else having a chance to win. Casper's two-iron off the tee hit one of the two ponds on the fairway; Leonard played safely with a three-wood. His par, and Casper's double-bogey six, gave Stan a two-stroke edge going into the final hole. The eighteenth fairway had a lake on the right; the left was lined by a gallery of thousands. His drive, glancing off some spectators, fell to the fairway in good position. Leonard won the tournament by a single stroke with a new record of 275. It was worth $10,000 in silver dollars plus another

$10,000 from the grateful gambler who had "bought" Stan Leonard in the Calcutta pool.

By the early sixties, Leonard was easing off the tour, and by 1971 confessed that at fifty-six he had become a weekend golfer. "Nerves and age," he said, a notable concession for a man who had become one of the leaders in his profession at an age when most golfers are over the hill.

GEORGE S. LYON, 1858-1938

By the time he was thirty-eight, George Lyon of Toronto was an accomplished athlete. He had played football and soccer; at age eighteen he had set a Canadian record in the pole vault; he played second base for a team in the Toronto commercial league, was an excellent curler and lawn bowler; he was nationally known as a cricket batsman.

He had never played golf.

Then, in 1896 a friend dared him to hit a golf ball; Lyon took one swipe and was hooked for life. He won the Canadian amateur eight times from 1898 to 1914; in fifteen tournaments for the Canadian senior championship between 1918 and 1932 he won the title ten times and placed second four times, once at the age of seventy-four. He won a gold medal in the Olympics.

With the extraordinary adaptability of the great all-round athlete, Lyon soon mastered golf. In 1897 he went through to the semi-finals of the Canadian amateur; in 1898, at the Toronto Golf Club, he over-

whelmed the unfortunate G. H. F. Pattison of Hamilton twelve and eleven. From the start, Lyon's stance aroused criticism. To anyone who saw him play for the first time, his swing was a haphazard, if ruthless, swipe at the ball. Breaking every adage, Lyon was the soul of aggression, walloping his drives and his iron shots with enormous glee and enthusiasm. The secret of his style was that he had carried over into golf the finished form of an outstanding cricketer, making minimum concessions to the game. That outlandish form, plus a buoyant competitive temperament, made him a first-class match play golfer in short order.

Certain flaws remained in Lyon's game. His putting, for example, was inconsistent. "Mr. Lyon was very weak on the greens," wrote the Toronto *Globe* of his loss to J. P. Taylor in the amateur final of 1904.

The great feature of Lyon's game was his power off the tee and with his long irons. His spectacular hitting, more than any other single factor, led to his greatest single achievement in golf. In 1904, at the St. Louis Olympics, golf was part of the program. Eighty-seven golfers played the qualifying round, Lyon finishing seventh among the thirty-two qualifiers. For the rest of the tournament, Lyon played matches against international opponents. After defeating F. C. Newton of Seattle in the semi-final, he played H. Chandler Egan of Chicago, the us amateur champion, for the gold medal, and won. On his way to this first international triumph for a Canadian golfer, Lyon had made some remarkable shots. He had driven the 276-yard first green four times during his matches; on the eighth hole, against Newton, his drive, pin-high, was 327 yards. The St. Louis *Globe-Democrat* put Lyon's victory down to his "iron nerves", and to "his preponderating wisdom, born of longer experience" (a perfectly natural, if amusing assumption to make of a forty-six-year-old man).

George Lyon was a great builder as well as great exponent of golf. Throughout his life, whether as the veteran captain of his home course, the Lambton in Toronto, or in the countless matches he played, he tried to broaden participation in the sport.

ADA MACKENZIE, 1892-1973

Ada Mackenzie's career is testimony to the virtue of golf as a game for all seasons of life; in 1914 she won the Toronto Golf Club championship; fifty-seven years later in her eightieth year she finished sixth in the Canadian senior women's tournament at Ottawa. Not only was Ada Mackenzie the best Canadian woman golfer before Marlene Stew-

art Streit, but her pioneer activities on behalf of women's golf, her encouragement of young golfers (and her unerring eye for talent), her indomitable competitive spirit, her business success, and above all, her warm and good-humoured personality have made her, for many Canadians, the very personification of golf.

It all began before the first world war, when Ada's father took her on the handlebars of his bicycle to the Highlands Club (now Mississauga) where she learned the game. She was about ten at the time. At Havergal she shone in sports, was captain of the school ice hockey and basketball teams, and winner of the school's tennis championship. But it was always golf to which she returned. During the war women were encouraged to take jobs to free men for military service. Young Miss Mackenzie worked in the head office of a bank, an experience that later stood her in good stead. The year after the war ended she won her first major golfing title, the Canadian Women's Open.

There is no better way to form an appreciation of Ada Mackenzie's standing in Canadian golfing history since that first victory than to list her record. To begin with, she won the Toronto and district ladies tournament eleven times between 1924 and 1961, and the Ontario Open nine times between 1922 and 1950. She won the Bermuda ladies twice, and was runner-up as often. She was

267

medallist in the us women's in 1927 and went to the semi-finals on two other occasions. She won the Canadian Open five times, in 1919, 1925, 1926, 1933 and 1935, and was finalist twice. The Canadian Closed fell to her five times as well, in 1926, 1927, 1929, 1931 and 1935, and on three other occasions she was finalist. She won the Canadian seniors championship nine times since 1955, and in 1963 won the us North-South seniors title by nine strokes over her nearest competitor, shooting rounds of 79, 76 and 80. As recently as 1970 she was a member of the Ontario team that defeated New York for the Ada Mackenzie Challenge Cup; moreover, paired with Kay Helleur, she won her match.

Aside from her brilliant and extraordinarily long competitive record, Miss Mac-kenzie made a number of outstanding contributions to the game of golf, and particularly to the place of women in it. One of these was the Ladies Golf Club of Toronto. During a golfing vacation in England, in 1920 she
noted that the game was easily accessible to women, in contrast to the Canadian situation. "It occurred to me," she said, "that a [ladies'] club would give our girls a better chance . . . clubs for golf and tennis do not encourage women." On her own, she went hunting for a site. "As it was essential for a good golf course to have water on it, I followed various rivers along their course, the Humber, the Etobicoke, and the Don, keeping in mind that easy accessibility . . . was necessary." The site she found was near Thornhill, north of Toronto. She signed an option to buy, organized a bond issue to raise the purchase price, issued membership shares, and in 1924 launched the Ladies Golf and Tennis Club of Toronto, then (and perhaps still) the only course in the world exclusively for women (although men are permitted to play at certain times).

Ada Mackenzie's encouragement of junior players was one of her constant interests. As early as 1928 she had inaugurated the Ontario junior championship, which has been played ever since at the Toronto Ladies'. In addition, she donated the trophy for provincial junior teams at the time and place of the Canadian Women's Open. But no matter how willing she was to encourage young players, she never lost the urge to compete with them as well.

At her first open victory at the Montreal Beaconsfield course in 1919, she learned the value of concentration. Playing an approach shot, she lifted her head to look at the gallery packed around the hole, and topped her shot. She never forgot the advice she then received from an experienced play-er: "If you must regard the gallery, Miss Mackenzie, regard them as cabbages. It helps amazingly." Concentration, competitive fire, mastery of her clubs, and above all, a sense of inner relaxation, accounted for Ada Mackenzie's remarkable career. "Easy golf," she said in 1965, "I just make my mind a blank and swing easy."

WILBERT MARTEL, 1887-1958
In the Maritimes Marty Martel was "king of the candlepins". He pioneered the sport, and by his enthusiasm and skill, did much to raise it to the popularity and respectability it now enjoys.

Conditions in the game of bowling in Marty's day were a great deal different from the bowling alleys of today. The pins were slim and tough to knock down – they had to be squarely hit or they didn't fall. There were no automatic pinsetters, and the felled pins were left on the alley – they were known as "deadwood." Marty Martel could play this deadwood in masterly fashion, and he was a master of every shot. A short, stocky man, Marty hardly looked the figure of a champion. His competitive spirit never left him, and he was still taking part in tournaments in his seventies. He was renowned for his smooth swing and his short steps to the line and he passed on his skills to many other bowlers in competition all over Eastern Canada and the northeastern United States.

A native of Cape Breton, Martel arrived in Halifax in his youth and went into business as a bowling alley proprietor. With his bowling partner Jack Conn, he operated the Conn-Martel lanes for many years; when

Sports Hall of Fame

268

the building burned down, he started up again at the Imperial lanes.

For many years Martel held the world's record for a single string – 213. Putting his next two highest strings with the 213 gives a total of 496 for three strings, which is probably still the greatest total ever bowled. And Marty was a consistent bowler; he topped the magic number of 400 for three consecutive strings on at least twenty-five occasions.

Martel had great powers of concentration and body coordination. But most of all he had determination. Once he took part in a Maritime-East Maine tournament with a broken left arm; once he dropped a window on his bowling hand on the eve of a week-long tournament, but played all through the week to finish with the best overall average.

Marty Martel spent his life in bowling – as owner, player and promoter. But he was also a hockey sponsor, helping to found the Wolverines, a hockey team that later went on to win the Allan Cup for the first and only time for Nova Scotia.

RAY MITCHELL, 1931-

Like many other Canadians, Ray Mitchell started bowling in the boom years of the 1960s, when alleys were springing up all over North America, leagues proliferated in towns and plants across the country, and interest was stimulated by TV coverage and international competitions. Ten-pin bowling began to replace five-pin in popularity, and the game became an important part of the Canadian social scene.

For most people it has remained only a pleasant recreation. But for Ray Mitchell it has become a serious sport, demanding stamina, intense concentration and a mathematical precision. These qualities have propelled Ray to the top. He started ten-pin bowling years ago; in 1972 he emerged as the regional, national and world champion.

Born in Alberta, Ray returned with his parents to their native England during the depression. During his years in the UK Ray participated enthusiastically in a wide variety of sports, winning several regional championships in boxing and swimming.

On his father's death in 1951 the family came back to Canada and settled in Toronto. Ray joined Bell Canada, and started bowling five-pins in the Bell men's league. He also kept up his interest in other sports, playing minor hockey, boxing at the Y, and developing an enthusiasm for and some considerable skill in badminton.

Then Mitchell started ten-pin bowling. "I took a shine to the game after getting

Sports Hall of Fame

into it as a social thing in 1961. But the recreational aspect soon went. I attack it now as a sport. It's a rigorous, challenging and demanding game . . . I do not feel that I have a natural ability . . . I have to work at it. I have studied, read, queried, copied, experimented, and have achieved whatever proficiency I have by hard work and effort."

Mitchell's "hard work and effort" soon started to pay off. He entered into local and regional competitions, both on five-man teams and as an individual bowler. His scores increased, and so did the championships he won. In the 1967-8 season he was Southern Ontario singles champion and placed third in the Canadian finals. He was also a member of a Scarborough league championship team, and on another team that established a new Canadian three-game, five-man team record score of 3,385.

In 1972 Mitchell was Southeastern Ontario champion, and went on to capture the Canadian title.

Then in November of that year he went to Hamburg, Germany, to compete against bowlers from thirty-eight countries in the world championship. It took four gruelling days and fifty-nine games to establish Ray Mitchell as the world's master ten-pin bowler, an honour Canada had achieved only once before, in 1969, when Graydon "Blondie" Robinson had taken the title at Tokyo. Mitchell described the tournament as the toughest he had ever been in. "It was so gruelling that I realized I had to conserve energy for the end. All the other players seemed to go flat out from the start. Their

269

averages dropped as the competition continued, while mine grew. My game plan was simply to make each cut. I didn't care about leading."

The strategy worked, especially in the finals, when Mitchell eliminated Maranan of the Philippines in the three-game match. The games were played under extreme pressures. Mitchell found it hard to concentrate. "The crowd was lined three deep on each side of the alley and there was a camera on each side three inches from my arms and another six inches from my rear." However, Mitchell retained his cool, calculating game, and beat Maranan by a score of 550 to 532.

Mitchell failed to retain his title in Singapore in 1973 although he bowled very well until the late stages of the tournament.

WILLIAM JOHN PEDEN, 1906-

At the finish of a fifteen-mile road race sponsored by the Victoria *Colonist,* a sportswriter noted that "a flame-haired youth led the pack like a torch." So, in 1926, Torchy Peden got his nickname. In the 1930s it became a household word, and Peden remains the most famous cyclist Canada has produced.

Torchy was one of six children, a

gangling youth with "no more muscular control than a day-old colt" when he left school at the age of fifteen to work in his father's grain and feed business. Encouraged by his parents to participate in sport to build himself up, he played rugger, swam (winning high placings in the breast stroke in the Canadian championships) and tried track and field. But cycling proved to be his sport. Pointing himself towards the 1928 Olympic team, he spent the winter in a logging camp, and when the snow melted pedalled twenty-five miles per day on a blacktop logging road. Out of the bush, he swept four major West Coast races and was invited East for the Olympic trials, held at the velodrome in Toronto. By this time Peden was six-foot-two and weighed nearly 220 pounds; his size was causing problems with the twenty-one pound racing bike. A Toronto race manager, William MacMorton, helped Peden solve the weight problem by shortening the bicycle's wheelbase and by adjusting the rake or bend of the fork. Torchy then won the Canadian championships at one and five miles, and qualified for the Olympic team.

At Amsterdam two punctures in the 103-mile time trial cost him any hope of a high placing. "I decided to stay in Europe," he later wrote, "to prove to myself and friends at home that I could ride with the best of the world." In a three-month tour, he won races at Warsaw, Paris, London and Glasgow, and had the satisfaction of defeating Frank Southall of England, who had finished second in the Olympic 103-mile race, while setting a new English record of 1:03:39 hours for twenty-five miles. Then, after a winter in Victoria, Peden made a clean sweep of the Canadian indoor championships at Montreal in June 1929, setting national records in four events from the half-mile to five miles.

At this point Peden decided to turn professional, which meant the crazy circus of six-day racing. The six-day races got their start in 1891 in Madison Square Garden, riders competing as individuals on high wheelers. By 1899, the safety bicycle and two-man team racing had come in, pioneered by Ed "On-the-Spot" Spooner, a publicity man for a cycle firm. The sport did not come to Canada until 1912, when a six-day race with twelve teams from France, New Zealand, the US and Canada was held at Toronto's Arena Gardens. By the time Peden turned professional, there were two circuits in North America, one centring on New York and the other based in Montreal and operated by Willie Spencer, a former Canadian rider. Both New York and Montreal usually held two races a year until the sport began to flag late in the

1930s; other cities normally ran only one a year.

The atmosphere in which Peden now found himself was a strange one. The centre of attention was the steeply banked, pine-board track, usually ten laps to a mile. Since racing went on continuously from Sunday night (one minute after midnight in most Canadian cities) to the following Saturday midnight, the area within the oval was cluttered with double bunks, tables for quick snacks, and a tangle of extra bikes and equipment. The steady hum of the cycles picked up several times a day in frenzied sprints for which special money prizes were offered; points picked up in the sprints were also used to break ties if laps were even at the end of six days. At such moments the spectators were jolted out of their usual somnolent state into wild enthusiasm; normally, however, they sat mesmerized by the spinning ribbon of cyclists, by their own bootleg liquor or by the steady thump of hired jazz bands.

During Peden's era, the stars were such men as Reggie MacNamara, the Australian ironman who was just beginning to fade when Torchy came on the scene; Piet van Kempen of Holland, whose victory record Peden was to break; and the great German pair, Gustav Killian and Heinz Vopel. Peden had many partners, but among the most notable were two dazzling French Canadians, Henri LePage and Jules Audy, and Peden's brother, Doug. Torchy did not win a race until matched with LePage at the Montreal Forum in April 1931; his first victory at Madison Square Garden was in March 1932 with MacNamara. Once started on the victory trail, Peden proved hard to stop; of his first forty-eight races, he won twenty-four. By that time he had been recognized as the greatest individual star in this extraordinary sport.

He was a crowd pleaser, a huge, spectacular rider who loved to play to the gallery and clown with the fans in the dull periods, but he was not precisely popular with his fellow riders. His favourite tactic was to take advantage of the exhaustion following sprints by churning out of the pack to pick up a lap on the field. The "jam" he set off would bring off-duty partners tumbling from their bunks to the track in order to relieve their partners. Crowds loved it, and it paid off in victories. From his first race in 1929 to his last in Chicago in 1948 (with time out for service with the RCAF during the second world war), Peden took part in 148 races, and won 38 of them, a record that stood until 1965 when broken by Rik van Steenbergen of Belgium.

JACK PURCELL, 1904-

A lanky, lithe and loose athlete, Jack Purcell had a wide repertoire of badminton strokes to go with great stamina and a magnetic court presence. Paul Gallico, the literary giant of the sporting world, bracketed him with Dempsey, Bobby Jones, Bill Tilden, Ruth and Weissmuller in the constellation of superstars. Nearer home, Ted Reeve in the Toronto *Telegram* called him "the smooth Purcell."

While badminton has ancient antecedents in battledore and shuttlecock, its modern form was born in India under the British raj. Army officers sought a game somewhat like rackets and tennis which would better suit the facilities and the Indian climate. The officers brought the game home. The duke of Bedford gave it a name – after his country home – and patronage. In the 1890s it came into vogue in England, not least because it translated more readily than tennis into an indoor game. By 1900 championships for England were established which, in effect, were world championships.

Like every other sport of the British, badminton was brought to Canada by immigrants. It was taken up by sporting organizations with gymnasiums or halls, especially churches. By the end of the first great war badminton was fairly well-established in

Alexandra Studio

271

most of the major cities and towns. It became a broadly popular game across Canada in the twenties and thirties. In 1921, the Canadian Badminton Association had been formed.

Jack Purcell was born in Guelph. Among the family friends were the Drews; young George Drew, the future premier of Ontario and leader of the federal Progressive Conservative party, introduced Jack Purcell to badminton. In 1923 Drew, then mayor of Guelph, and Purcell went to Ottawa to represent Guelph in the Canadian championships. Jack overslept and didn't appear when their opening match was called. Drew got the blame in Guelph for the forfeiture because he was a notorious party-goer at the time. In fact, Drew arrived for the match in evening dress but ready to play.

Over the next five years Purcell won every title in Ontario, taking the men's singles five times in a row, and the mixed doubles for four consecutive years. In 1929, he won the Canadian singles championship. The following year he reached the peak of his amateur career when he not only retained his title but also went on to defeat, on successive nights, the four best British players who were on tour in Canada.

Early in 1931 Purcell travelled to England and, partnered by K. C. Livingstone, won the Surrey doubles. Three days later he competed in the all-England championship and advanced to the semi-finals. There he was defeated by T. P. Dick, the international champion for the past six years. Although Purcell made no excuses for his defeat, the ocean voyage had prevented him from reaching his top form. For four days, Purcell had lain in his berth. He arrived in England ten pounds under his normal weight.

He returned home to find that the Canadian Badminton Association's executive had changed. His amateur status was being questioned. The difficulty arose over his connection with Spalding's and over some newspaper articles which he had written to promote the game. Purcell was forced to turn professional. It was a disappointment because he had wanted one more try at the all-England title.

In 1933, partly as a commercial manoeuvre, he claimed the professional badminton championship of the world. He had a fair claim to the title. In a series of round robin matches, involving the best players from England, Canada and the United States, in Montreal, Toronto and Winnipeg, Purcell had beaten them all. After this he never lost a match that had his crown riding upon it.

Badminton was set back by the second world war and the short supply of rack-ets and birds. Purcell retired, undefeated, to work with Red Foster in radio advertising until 1942. By 1942 he was in Toronto's financial circles, where he can still be found. After injuring his eye while playing "a little fun game" in 1958, Purcell was forced to give up badminton permanently.

In 1950 the sportswriters of Canada chose Jack Purcell as the outstanding Canadian athlete of the half-century in the miscellaneous division of sports ahead of Barbara Ann Scott, Ken Watson and Johnny Longden.

GRAYDON ROBINSON, 1928-

In 1969 when a forty-one-year-old sheet-metal worker from the Toronto suburb of Weston won the world championship bowling title, few Canadians knew such an honour existed. It did – it was first up for competition in 1965 – and the crown was firmly settled on the unassuming head of "Blondie" Robinson.

Graydon Robinson bowled his first game in a four-lane alley in Port Colborne where, as a youngster, he had a job as a pin-setter. When he went to Tokyo for the 1969 championship he had been bowling ten pins for seven years, having drifted into the game when he found that he was not good enough to beat the best in the purely Canadian five-pin game. Among the men with whom he had bowled for years, Robinson was thought of as a streak bowler, rising to his peak when behind. Blondie didn't disagree; he said repeatedly that "I bowl better when I'm

272

down. I don't know how to go about protecting a lead."

That was the pattern he established in the tough road he followed to the title. His rivals, like himself, were all amateurs – but the bowling world is rather more straightforward about what constitutes an amateur than are certain other sports. An amateur in bowling is simply one who draws less than half his income from the sport. In the Toronto qualifying round, Robinson was the eighth and last to qualify. He won his regional six-game round by a single pin. At the Canadian final in Montreal, where the eight regional champions met, he took the fourth and last qualifying spot after the first round. True to form, he won his quarter-final by throwing strikes in his last two frames, won the semi-finals after being down fifty-four pins after three frames, and beat Bert Manarin of Vancouver by three pins in the final.

Streak bowling, however, would not have won at Tokyo. The competitors had to play thirty-six games, the top six to engage in final eliminations. Robinson, bowling with great consistency, finished second overall. The leader was Ut Lenevat, a twenty-seven-year-old businessman from Bangkok, Thailand. In the two-game final, Lenevat, a slim lefthander, took a big lead by winning the first game 215 to 166. Then Blondie Robinson, the terror of the Applewood Bowl, got hot. He finished with a flourish, bowling four consecutive strikes in the last three frames to defeat his rival by 379 to 373.

When Blondie Robinson returned to Toronto, to be given the kind of instant celebrity the media confer on a newsmaker, he took his sudden fame with a common sense and proportion that nonplussed the press and delighted the public. "I'll be back at work Monday morning," he said; "Tokyo was different than what I'm used to."

THOMAS F. RYAN, 1872-1961

Bowling is one of our greatest participation sports, and most Canadians who bowl play the five-pin game. This uniquely Canadian sport was invented in 1909 by a Toronto bowling alley proprietor, Thomas Ryan.

Tommy Ryan, during the course of his long life, was many other things as well. He was born in the baseball hot-bed of Guelph, and when he came to Toronto at eighteen and got a job as an invoice clerk, he soon made a name for himself as one of the best pitchers in the Toronto area. Clerking proved a dull life for the gregarious Ryan, and he took advantage of his many friendships in the Toronto sporting fraternity to open a billiard academy, then a bowling alley. From these successful operations he

moved into the hotel business, and when prohibition made his hotel unprofitable, he turned to the antique and auctioneering business. From the early 1920s until his death he ran the Ryan Art Galleries from the old Massey family home on Jarvis Street. Along the way, he organized baseball clubs, promoted boxing, owned a stable of racehorses, and in 1950 headed the campaign which returned Sunday sports to Toronto after an absence of eighty-five years.

In 1895 the American Bowling Congress had been formed in New York, and laid down the rules for ten-pin bowling. The game was almost immediately popular, and the ABC held the first national championship at Chicago in 1901. In 1905 Tommy Ryan introduced the first ten-pin bowling alley in Canada constructed according to ABC regulations. It was a toney establishment, with potted palms, a string orchestra and admittance by membership only. His aim was to attract the carriage trade, and he did. The benchers of Osgoode Hall, Sir John Eaton and other prominent Toronto worthies turned out to test muscles they hadn't used in years. Soon Ryan began to get complaints that the sixteen-pound ball was too heavy. Wanting to hold on to his custom trade, and noting at the same time that the heavy ball was doing a lot of damage to his fine new alleys, Ryan began to experiment with games using smaller pins, like duckpins and candlepins. The duckpin game, invented in 1900 by two famous baseball men, John McGraw and Wilbert Robinson, was played with a smaller ball and cut-down ten pins. Ryan's invention of five pins in 1908 or 1909 (the date is not certain) was an adaptation of duckpins. "I

273

had my daddy . . . whittle down five pins with a lathe and I figured out a scoring system," Ryan later recalled. The key to his new game was the four pin: no score counted unless it was knocked down. Among Ryan's tired business and professional clientele, the game quickly caught on. When it was found that the ball occasionally rolled between the pins, Ryan applied the finishing touch to the sport he had invented by fitting a rubber collar around each pin.

Five-pin bowling has since become an enormously popular sport and recreation in Canada. But like Naismith, the inventor of basketball, Tommy Ryan made no income from his creation except what he got from his own customers. In later life he genially explained his failure to patent the game: "I was the biggest sucker in the world but I had a racing stable at the time, I was managing some fighters, I had a bowling alley and I was hustling so much with all those irons and more in the fire that – well, I forgot."

MARJORY SHEDD, 1926-

It is pointless to deny that women have a rougher road in sports than do men. So strong does the prejudice against women remain, that many girls of high athletic potential never have their worth recognized during the crucial early years. Marjory Shedd was fortunate; she had a sports-minded father and three older brothers who were keen athletes. The family lived across from High Park in Toronto's west end, and Marjory, "a regular tomboy," played hockey, softball and touch rugby there with the boys. Like thousands of other Toronto families, the Shedds owned a summer cottage, but theirs, on Lake Simcoe, was unusual: it had a badminton court.

At high school Marjory was active in virtually every sport open to girls. She made her first mark in basketball as a defensive star on the Carltonettes when they won the Canadian junior championship in 1945. In 1950, she led Toronto Montgomery Maids to the national senior title. By the middle fifties, Marjory had given up basketball for the relatively more sedate sport of volleyball, but did not stop winning championships. The University of Toronto team she played for won five national titles; as one of the most devastating spikers in the country she was a natural choice for Canada's volleyball team at the Pan-American Games in Winnipeg in 1967.

It was as a badminton player, however, that Marjory Shedd reached the heights. She did not take up the game seriously until 1949. In 1950 she joined the Carlton Club, for many years a centre of first-class badminton in Toronto. Thereafter her rise was swift. After reaching the finals of the Canadian singles in 1951 and 1952, she took the title in 1953, and from then until her last singles championship in 1963 she took national honours six more times. As a doubles player, she has been just as successful, winning four mixed and eleven ladies titles between 1954 and 1969. She failed to match Dorothy Walton's victory in the all-England, though she won through to the semi-finals; but she has represented Canada six times on the Uber Cup team (the badminton equivalent of the Davis Cup) more than any other Canadian.

Like Dorothy Walton, Marjory Shedd is a great all-round athlete who brought to her chosen sport the strength, speed and stamina to excel at the demanding singles game. She herself considered that her left-handedness contributed to her success; certainly it gave her real advantages in both singles and doubles play, and added an element of unexpectedness to her powerful overhead game. Always noted for racket control and quickness, she also made full use of her five-foot-eight height at the net and in protecting the back court.

As a member of the department of athletics and physical education at the University of Toronto, Marjory Shedd continues to teach and coach young athletes in the sports to which she brought great distinction.

Sports Hall of Fame

She was inducted into the Sports Hall of Fame in 1970.

C. ROSS SOMERVILLE, 1903-

Golf in Canada during the 1920s and 1930s was still a gentleman's game. Canadian golfers, including the redoubtable George S. Lyon and Ada Mackenzie, had made little impact upon the public consciousness, and golfing remained largely a pastime of the prosperous and the well-placed.

C. Ross Somerville certainly belonged to the London, Ontario, establishment. His father, a well-known businessman, had once been mayor of the city. He sent his boy to Ridley College and to the University of Toronto. During his years of schooling, "Sandy" was an all-rounder, establishing records as a batsman in cricket at Ridley as well as being an outstanding track and field performer. At Varsity, he played halfback (once drop-kicking six field goals in one game) and hockey.

His first love was golf, however. His father used to take a winter vacation at Pinehurst, North Carolina, and from the age of five Sandy was batting old golf balls up and down the course. His first go at the Canadian amateur was a disaster; he did not qualify, and could not bring himself to turn in a card. In 1924 and 1925 he went to the finals, only to be defeated; but in 1926, at the Kanawaki course, he defeated C. C. Fraser of Toronto to become Canadian amateur champion for the first time. Over the next decade and more he repeatedly proved himself Canada's finest amateur golfer. He took the title again in 1928, 1930, 1931, 1935, and 1937. On three of these occasions he defeated American amateurs in the finals, including a lopsided victory over J. W. Platt of Philadelphia on Sandy's home course, London Hunt, in 1930. On two other occasions he lost out to Americans in the finals – in 1934 to Albert Campbell of Seattle (the defending champion), and in 1938 to Ted Adams of Columbia, Mississippi.

The man who put together this record was called by the New York *Times* "that unruffled golfer with nerves of steel and almost flawless skill." The lean Somerville, with his long, dour face, probably inspired jitters in his opponents. In fact, Somerville was a most modest and self-deprecating man, who applied the same intelligence and logic to golf that he employed as an insurance executive, and who was always ready to learn.

The goal of Sandy Somerville's constant drive for self-improvement was the American amateur. In the years before 1932, he entered it seven times. On only three oc-

Alexandra Studio

casions did he get past the qualifying rounds; on each of these he was knocked out early in match play. Throughout the spring and summer of 1932, he used the larger (but lighter) American ball to prepare himself for yet another run at the title; that he had not yet mastered it was shown in the Canadian amateur at Lambton when he was eliminated in the semi-final, observers noting that he was spraying his tee shots. Nevertheless, he was medallist in the district qualifying rounds for the American amateur at Cleveland, topping a good field by three strokes.

The US amateur was held in September at the Five Farms course at Baltimore. Two rounds of medal play reduced the field to the best thirty-two; Somerville at 150 was eight strokes off the pace of young John Fischer, the US college champion, but qualified for match play nonetheless. Match play was something at which the intelligent and consistent Somerville excelled; he defeated his first two opponents with relative ease. In the quarter-finals, thirty-six-hole matches began, and Somerville hit his peak, disposing of Bill Blaney of Boston and in his morning round setting a course record of 68. Though consistently outdriven in the semi-final, he defeated Jesse "Siege Gun" Guilford, and entered the final against twenty-two-year-old Johnny Goodman, the conqueror of the great Francis Ouimet in the other semi-final match.

In the morning round, the two were

even after the first nine; in the second, the lead changed hands until the eighteenth hole, when Somerville sank a fifty-foot putt and went, unsmilingly, one up. At the beginning of the second eighteen, Goodman got hot, winning four of the first nine holes to Somerville's one, to go two up. A bogey by Goodman on the tenth, and a steady par from Sandy, cut the margin. Then came the big shot. On the eleventh, Somerville hooked his drive into the rough, and found his line partly blocked by a tree. Instead of playing safe, he smashed a two-iron past the tree pin-high to the green, and fifteen feet from the cup. Unnerved, Goodman took a bogey and they were all square. Somerville than won two of the next five holes, and when they halved the seventeenth, he had won, two up and one to play.

Although Somerville was not to repeat his victory in the US amateur, he continued to dominate Canadian amateur golf for the rest of the thirties, and after war service, came back to win or share the Canadian senior title in four tournaments from 1960 to 1966. It was fitting that in 1950 he should have been chosen Canada's greatest golfer of the half-century. No man did more to awaken broad Canadian interest in golf than Sandy Somerville.

MARLENE STEWART STREIT, 1934-

In one of the early rounds of the Ontario ladies amateur in 1951, Canada's greatest woman golfer, Ada Mackenzie, found herself drawn against a tiny youngster from Fonthill named Marlene Stewart. Miss Mackenzie had been medallist in the qualifying round, and was thinking ahead to yet another Ontario championship. She never forgot what happened: "It was the only time in my life that I have ever been six holes down after playing six holes . . . that unbelievable child was four under fours for six holes. Just feature it; she played the first six holes in twenty strokes." When Ada won four of the next seven holes, she expected her inexperienced opponent to fold; instead, Marlene canned a pressure putt on the fourteenth, and went on to win the match, and the tournament.

The victory, won by Marlene at the age of seventeen, was to be the first of many. She had begun to play only three years before at the Lookout Point Club near her home town of Fonthill, Ontario. Under the tutelage of professional Gordon McInnes she worked tirelessly to develop her game, displaying the complete absorption that is the characteristic mark of most championship athletes. Despite her diminutive size, she was a long hitter from the start.

Marlene Stewart soon proved herself

Sports Hall of Fame

to be that extremely rare golfer, the consistently fine performer, exhibiting not only physical but mental control in a thoroughly integrated game. Perhaps the four years she spent at Rollins College in Florida taking a business degree, and playing golf against the best twelve months a year, gave her tournament toughness, but one suspects that those qualities of emotional stability and concentration were there from the start. In 1951 again, Marlene was one up at the thirty-fifth hole on Grace Lenczyk, the US and world amateur champion, in the final of the Canadian ladies' championship played that year at Laval-sur-le-lac, Montreal. She lay fifteen feet above the cup, needing to hole her putt to keep her lead. Twice, as she addressed the ball, her concentration was broken by a photographer; twice he was shooed away by officials, a circumstance sufficient to fluster any golfer. Then Marlene stepped up and sank the putt.

There can be little doubt that for a good part of her career Marlene Stewart Streit has been the world's best woman amateur golfer. Not only has she dominated the Canadian golfing scene – she has won seven Ontario titles, nine Canadian ladies' closed titles, and eight Canadian open titles. In international competition she has had the finest record of any Canadian amateur golfer, male or female. In 1953 at the age of nineteen she won the British title. In 1956, at Indianapolis, she won the US national, and in the same year won the North-South and the US intercollegiate crowns, as well as the

Canadian open and closed and the Totem Pole tournament. During that amazing string, she won thirty-four straight matches – not even Walter Hagen or Bobby Jones came close to such a record. In 1963, at the Royal Sydney course, she defeated Ruth Porter of Britain eight and seven to win the Australian women's golf championship and become the first woman to win the amateur championships of Canada, the United States, Britain and Australia.

In 1965 Mickey Wright, one of the greatest of women professionals, said of Marlene after playing a match with her, "I can't understand why she didn't go pro. She's a fantastic player. She'd have made a great one." Marlene's answer was simple. "Living out of a suitcase with no real home, it's not my idea of a very feminine life." The year after she graduated from Rollins College she married a Toronto stockbroker, J. Douglas Streit.

DOROTHY MCKENZIE WALTON, 1909-

Many Canadians who know nothing of her athletic career will recognize Dorothy Walton as one of the most effective and constructive public figures of the post-1945 years. As one of the organizers of the Canadian Association of Consumers, and later as its president, Mrs. Walton became the scourge of erring manufacturers, advertisers and retailers long before the Ralph Nader phenomenon. In this and many other organizations, she showed herself to be a forceful and responsible leader of important causes.

The daughter of Edmund McKenzie, a well-to-do merchant in Swift Current, Saskatchewan, Dorothy was an outstanding student at high school and at the University of Saskatchewan. She took a degree in economics, and went on to become private secretary to a provincial cabinet minister and to take her master's degree. Her marriage to William Walton in 1932, and a move to Toronto, brought a temporary halt to a promising public career. Parallel to these activities, however, was her emergence as one of the West's great athletes. In high school, she was an all-rounder, winning individual championships in track and field and tennis, and being a member of provincial teams holding titles in basketball and hockey. Her record at university cannot be adequately summarized, except to say that from 1926 to 1930 she was a member of fourteen intercollegiate teams in tennis, track and field, swimming, field hockey and basketball, and won individual championships in diving, discus, javelin, high jump, broad jump and the 220. In racket sports she was superlative, winning some fifty-four local, provincial and Western

Alexandra Studio

Canadian tennis titles between 1924 and 1931, and several badminton titles besides. Small wonder that she became the first woman to win her university's major athletic award for outstanding athletic achievement.

Despite her record, this Western Canadian girl was unknown in Eastern tennis and badminton circles, and was to remain so for two years after her move to Toronto. When she did resume competition, in 1934, badminton had become her major sport, and in that year she went to the singles finals in both the Toronto and Canadian tournaments. She won her first important victories the next year, taking the Toronto and Ontario titles. From 1936 to 1940, she dominated Canadian women's badminton, winning sixty-four singles and doubles championships in that span, including the Canadian, Ontario and New England Open titles. Tennis was not forgotten, however; Dorothy Walton emerged as one of the finest doubles players in the country, and during her splurge of badminton successes she was never ranked below sixth among Canada's women tennis players.

In 1939-40 Mrs. Walton so completely outclassed her North American competition in badminton that she made a clean sweep of every major singles title, seven in all, without the loss of a game. In addition, she won eight ladies and mixed doubles titles in badminton, and six more in tennis, during the same period.

The culmination of her career came in 1939, when she challenged for the all-England singles title, the equivalent of the world's amateur championship. To accustom herself to new competitors and to another style of play, she first entered – and won – the Surrey tournament. In the all-England, she swept all before her. In the semi-finals she met the defending champion, Miss D. M. S. Young, defeating her 8-11, 11-7, 11-0; then, on 11 March 1939 she defeated Miss D. Doveton of Bath in straight sets, 11-4, 11-5, to become the only Canadian ever to win the all-England championship. Mrs. Walton achieved No. 1 world ranking because of a rare combination of abilities. Her strength, speed and agility gave her the court coverage so vital in singles. The intelligence and deception of her play, especially at the net and in the production of beautifully placed, tantalizingly soft drop shots, enabled her to seize and hold the psychological edge that gives mastery in any sport.

In 1940, just as the war cut off her athletic career at its peak, Dorothy Walton was awarded the Rose Bowl as Canada's outstanding female athlete. She was runner-up for the Lou Marsh Trophy in the same year; that she never won it can only be attributed to the relative lack of publicity accorded to the sport in which she excelled, for this Saskatchewan girl must be numbered among the most superlative athletes so far to emerge in Canada.

NICK WESLOCK, 1918-

Ontario has produced two great amateur male golfers since the end of the second world war, Gary Cowan and Nick Weslock. Cowan has had greater success internationally, but more often than not he has found the slick shotmaker from Burlington too hard to handle at home. Weslock, now in his fifties, seems to get better with age. He has mellowed as well; in his younger days he was regarded as a somewhat prickly and contentious player. Born Nick Wisnock, he changed his name to Weslock early in his playing career, but retained his pride in his Polish ancestry. He once attributed his success to "Kielbassa and cabbage rolls – my Polish

Sports Hall of Fame

power food. When we were kids my mother would give us lots of Kielbassa . . . good but we couldn't go to school for three days because of the garlic."

Nick Weslock's record puts him among the all-time great Canadian golfers. He has won the Canadian amateur a record four times, the Ontario Open seven times (nothing gives him more pleasure than defeating the professionals), and the Ontario amateur eight times. Since he turned fifty he has won the Ontario seniors title three times. On nineteen occasions he has been low amateur in the Canadian Open, and nearly won it in 1947 at Scarborough, finishing third, two strokes behind Bobby Locke who won it at fourteen under par. Nick has represented Canada many times on World Cup, America Cup and commonwealth teams; he has been a member of the Ontario Willingdon Cup team a phenomenal twenty-one times.

In 1968 it appeared that Weslock's career was at an end. A gall bladder ailment had nearly taken his life, and he had undergone a hernia operation. On returning to golf, overweight and lacking his usual confidence, he had seemed a shadow of the golfer he once was. A program of physical conditioning and a rigid diet launched him on a remarkable series of tournament successes in 1969 and 1970, during which time he won the Ontario amateur twice, the Ontario seniors twice, and the Ontario Open in 1969. His 1969 open finish was dazzling. He went eagle-par-birdie on the last three holes, dropping a final twenty-two-foot putt for his one-stroke victory. His pro victim, Phil Giroux, said, "I

278

didn't know Superman was playing here this week."

Weslock, an industrial design engineer, has always had a thoroughly intelligent approach to the game, not only in his grasp of the importance of psychological one-upmanship, but in his analysis of shotmaking. For years he has kept a little book of nuggets of golfing wisdom he has picked up from the players with whom he has played. In 1957 Jackie Burke told him not to allow the butt of the putter handle to pass the clubhead on the through stroke; it went into the book. In 1960, at St. George's, Art Wall observed that if the left thumb is placed on the side of the grip, putter head rolling would be stopped. That went in too. "You can't play this game just on natural swing ability," Weslock once said. "You've got to think about it and put everything in place." During tournaments he shoots film of the best pros and has accumulated nearly 7,000 feet of edited film which has allowed him to analyse the swing patterns. To Weslock, the most important clubs in his bag are the wedge and the putter, and he practises endlessly with both. Watching Nick Weslock use a pitching wedge close to the green is to see a master at work; for twenty years he has been one of the best in the game at wedge shots.

JACK WRIGHT, 1903-49

Although Canadians have been playing tennis for well more than a century now, no

Sports Hall of Fame

Canadian has ever dominated the centre court at Wimbledon, or been among the top seeds at Forest Hills. Names like Vines, Tilden, Perry, Budge, Gonzales, Hoad, Laver and Rosewall have become familiar enough, but it is unlikely that more than a small minority of Canadians could name the members of any Canadian Davis Cup team. The game, after all, not only has climate to contend against in Canada, but also the fact that it has never been a majority sport, and lacks the kind of mass participation it finds in Australia and the United States.

Nevertheless, there have been a number of excellent Canadian tennis players, and one of the best was Jack Wright. Born in British Columbia, a province in which tennis is more popular than other parts of the country, Wright came into his own while a medical student at McGill University in Montreal. From 1923 to 1933, he was a member of Canada's Davis Cup team, playing in zone matches against the United States, Japan and Cuba. In 1927, 1929 and 1931 he won the Canadian championship.

Dr. Wright was both an intelligent player and an acute judge of the state of tennis in Canada. He was well aware of the disadvantages Canadians had to overcome in order to be competitive in international tennis. As he once said, the delicate question of money was part of the problem. "No tennis player, in Canada or elsewhere, can aspire to the heights, especially in international competition, unless he is able to forget the time and expense involved in constant travel, south in the winter, north in the summer, continuous day-by-day practice, and constant attention to one's physical well-being." Wright was fortunate enough to have the money to take an occasional swing through the American south, there encountering the kind of stiff competition needed to sharpen his game. His greatest day came in Montreal in 1927, when, in a singles match in a Davis Cup series against Japan, he defeated Tacheichi Harada in straight sets, 6-3, 6-3, 8-6. Harada was regarded at the time as the world's third ranked player, behind the American pair of "Big Bill" Tilden and William Johnson.

After his tennis career ended, Dr. Wright practised medicine in Vancouver, and was a medical officer during the second world war with the Canadian Army overseas. Though he was never quite able to duplicate his sensational victory over Harada, that feat and his dominance of the Canadian game for so many years won him selection as Canada's outstanding tennis player of the half-century in the 1950 press poll. He became a member of the Sports Hall of Fame in 1955.

279

The Builders

Chapter 11

Any parent who has ever rounded up and delivered a peewee hockey team to a distant rink, anyone who has ever stepped behind the plate as an umpire at a playground softball game, or anyone who has ever volunteered to publicize a sporting event in the local media knows something about the organizational difficulties and the uncertainties of sports administration.

A remarkable amount of work and planning goes into sport, usually by unpaid volunteers. If teams are to play, if matches are to have accepted outcomes, if championships are to be decided, if crowds are to be drawn, if gate receipts are to be substantial and to be honestly handled, then uncounted hundreds of people have to do the spade work. Yet few of us ever ponder about those who create and run the huge rambling structure of Canadian sport; usually our attention is focused on a narrower field of view – the game, the victory, the loss, the athlete. It is for these reasons, then, that Canada's Sports Hall of Fame pays tribute to the "builders" of sports.

Rarely does the builder, in a field so swiftly changing as sport, succeed in constructing for the ages. Sport is subject to stresses from within that constantly press upon its structures, its rules and its patterns of play. The jealousies of clubs, the ambitions of promoters, the waywardness of athletes, the ingenuity of coaches, the fickleness of the public and the importunities of the press present challenges that frequently prove too much even for the ablest sports administrator, the most carefully devised constitution, or the most flexible code of rules. But this is not all. Sports is immediately

Alfie Shrubb, the great English runner who later emigrated to Canada, shown with some of his immense collection of awards.

sensitive to social, economic and cultural changes over which its leaders can have no control. Urban growth, new waves of immigration, changing mores, fluctuating real estate prices, downturns in the business cycle – these and other broad movements can make the most decisive impact on the fragile edifice of play. The normal condition of the world of sport is one of conflict teetering on the brink of chaos, a toy world at war with itself, and those who struggle to bring to it the blessings of order and stability earn much merit – but they build upon sand. And, final irony, very often one man's builder is another's wrecker. It all depends on where one stands.

Any year, any season since the 1870s would show similar patterns. Quite at random (though they are typical enough) the autumn months of 1907, as seen through the sporting press, are selected to show the kinds of vagaries, tiny tempests and preoccupations that unendingly affect Canadian sport.

Violence, as always, was in the news. In September a touring Canadian lacrosse team departed from Australia with mixed reviews from the local press; their skill was admired but they were "too rough." Later that month there was a full-fledged riot at the last game of the lacrosse season in Montreal, with spectators pouring from the stands and players and fans alike being subdued by squads of police. Here was a sport in disarray. Sport finance, a perennial subject, cropped up repeatedly. For example, the Tecumsehs of Toronto reported a seasonal profit of $7,000; someone had done his job. Promoters, quick to sense new directions in public taste, were much in evidence. Thus Alfie Shrubb, the great English runner, made his first Toronto appearance in a professional track meet before packed stands at

281

Hanlan's Point; someone had guessed right. The Toronto *Star*, for reasons best known to itself, sponsored a ten-mile walking race for ladies in which eighty-four started; here was the Marilyn Bell formula at a primitive stage. What would a season be without complaints about refereeing? In October the Ottawa Rough Riders obliged, threatening not to play again unless incompetent officials were removed. The real problem, however, was the unsatisfactory state of football's rules.

The formation of a new football league, the interprovincial (the Big Four) was the biggest news of these months. To describe what occurred as a rationalization of an unsatisfactory competitive and financial situation would be accurate but misleading; the actual course of events was complicated, messy and often ludicrous. The four clubs with the best players and the largest gate receipts came together, but the secession of the Hamilton Tigers and the Toronto Argonauts from the ORFU, and the Ottawa Rough Riders and the Montreal Winged Wheelers from the QRFU, weakened those leagues drastically. George Ballard, president of the Hamilton Tigers, was the driving force behind the new league; in that sense, he was certainly a builder. Since Ballard was president of the ORFU when he assumed the same office with the new league, he was also a wrecker. J. B. Hay, the next president of the ORFU, said of Ballard that he "displayed a narrow club spirit . . . he held presidencies of both organizations at the same time."

Whether Ballard was a traitor or a statesman was not the only issue raised by the creation of the Big Four. At stake as well was the relationship of the league to the Canadian Amateur Athletic Union and the thorny question of amateur status. Montreal had a number of players who had competed in professional hockey and lacrosse, notably Ernie Russell, a star with the Montreal Wanderers hockey club. Both the CAAU and the Argonaut Rowing Club, the parent of the football team, took a purist view of such matters. Frenzied negotiations, aimed at securing the reinstatement of the compromised players through affidavits recanting their sullied past and avowing their intention faithfully to observe the amateur code in future, broke down in a welter of confusion and misunderstanding. The CAAU quite naturally refused to swallow the affidavits, the Argonaut Rowing Club was seized by a collective crisis of conscience, while the Hamilton club forthrightly declared that "the Tigers would play with Montreal and Ottawa without any amateur rule and the CAAU could go hang and the Argos with it." The climax came with a peculiar game between Montreal and Toronto, in which, to the bafflement of the fans and the bemusement

Ernie Russell, a member of the Hockey Hall of Fame, once scored three goals a game in five consecutive games. He also starred at football.

of the press, the Argos changed their name to the "Toronto's" in the hope that this transparent dodge would placate both the CAAU and the rowing club. The CAAU promptly disqualified every player on the field as having been irreparably contaminated by Russell and his fellow delinquents, while the rowing club disavowed all connection with its own football team. A few days later the rowing club changed its mind, withdrew from the CAAU, and the Big Four was on its way.

Scarcely had the uproar died away when the sports world was shaken by a new convulsion. The American AAU suspended Tom Longboat on suspicion of professionalism. Shortly thereafter Hugh Graham, the owner of the Montreal *Star*, made a well-meaning but deeply confused attempt to straighten things out by offering Longboat $2,000 if he would adhere to the amateur code. Longboat, cheerfully entering into the spirit of the thing, was quoted as telling Graham: "I know how you feel. You want Canada's name kept good. I feel the same. I will do my best. Five years from today I will send you a little bill for $2,000. I will buy a nice little wigwam for my best girl."

So we leave 1907, just as the CAAU suspended all fifty-six runners who had competed in Longboat's last race and with Canadian

282

sport well launched upon yet another stormy sea. The kinds of problems and issues raised in those few weeks have never really disappeared. They have simply re-emerged in an infinity of new guises, and as they do, sports administrators have to cope with them.

What kind of men have the administrators been? What particular roles have they played in developing and sustaining sports in Canada? There are the rare few who originate or crystallize games or competitions, men like George Beers, James Naismith and James Creighton, or a woman like Peg Seller. There are the organizers and officials of clubs, leagues, and federations; that is, the executives and administrators of sport like Billie Hewitt, Clarence Campbell and Jake Gaudaur. There are the legions of coaches, managers, trainers and scouts. There are the referees, umpires, judges and stewards who arbitrate the events and enforce the rules of competition. There are the reporters, editors, publishers, authors, artists, photographers and broadcasters who interpret sport for readers and listeners. There are the educators who teach physical education or engage in research into such subjects as physiology and sports medicine. There are the inventors of equipment and innovators in facilities and equipment. There are the patrons and the grand sponsors who lend their names and prestige to sporting endeavours; in recent years they have become more institutional and corporate rather than individual. There are the politicians, civil servants, government appointees, and the lobbyists who shape, develop, institute and direct programs and regulations

A Rhodes Scholar who chose to make hockey his career, Clarence Campbell, once a referee, later became president of the National Hockey League.

W.A. Hewitt was secretary of the OHA for fifty-eight years, treasurer of the Canadian AHA for thirty-eight years and helped form football's Big Four.

through government involvement in sport. Finally, there are the "pitch men"; the promoters, publicists, owners, agents, lawyers and salesmen who deal in franchises, financing, events, contracts, and the remuneration of players and athletes.

The two longest-lasting themes in Canadian sport are intertwined: the perpetual tussle along the frontier between the amateur and the professional, and the question of where or for whom the athlete should perform. The pursuit of excellence and the urge to win are always at work in sport. The fine athlete may surface anywhere but usually his or her talents are spotted quickly and coveted. But it takes time, training and coaching to nurture that talent. Who will pay for the time and support such concentration on skill? Is a job or even a sinecure enough?

To lure a star or to recruit a potential one from a distant place for a team or club requires some incentives. Should the athlete be free to move where he wills? What obligation does he owe to the community or club which

283

"Jake" Gaudaur, Jr., Commissioner of the Canadian Football League, with Mrs. Gaudaur Sr. at the unveiling of a plaque commemorating his father.

first fostered him? If a form of control or ownership is necessary to keep a balance in competition and stability in leagues, how is it to be exerted on the athlete? Even more difficult, how are those who lure an athlete away to be disciplined? If thousands of people are ready to pay to see an athlete who should get the money or how much should the athlete get?

A third theme will endure as long as men and women contest in sport. Where are the neutral, impartial, honest, capable people who will referee and umpire? It is rarely the nature of sportsmen to abide meekly by the rules or to hold a static interpretation of them. What are the ideal rules? What rule changes are made urgent by strategic or tactical or equipment innovations? Different interpretations of rules develop in different places. When competition brings the two interpretations together feuds erupt. Their settlement has occupied thousands of committee meetings and reams of correspondence over the years. Ancillary issues bloom. What is the "legal" stick for hockey or lacrosse? Are the age groupings in a competition reasonable? Is a certain piece of equipment safe? What agreements exist in the area of money for officials and expenses?

A distinguishing characteristic of sportsmen through the generations has been a distaste for the critical opinions of outsiders. With it goes a dearly held axiom: Sportsmen must run their own affairs. Sportsmen repel the interventions of outsiders, particularly of governments and legislatures. Not only do they tend to scorn outside opinion, they have little time for the views of spokesmen from sports other than their own. Thus "general purpose" sporting bodies such as amateur athletic unions and sports federations are normally in difficulties with one or another of their dissident parts. Sportsmen are sceptical enough of each other within their sports, let alone the stranger. The "snowbankers," men who come up from the corner lots, rarely trust even the most benign intruder. While there is an implicit cachet to those with an outstanding athletic record who become administrators and coaches, there is a bent towards irreverence for authority, particularly national authority. At the local and club level there is usually the conviction that the higher the office of the administrator the less he understands the realities of sport or "where it really is."

Several generations of sportswriters have worked up an enormous scepticism for those jeeringly called "the badgers." The badgers are the men who organize, officiate, and control amateur organizations. Still, in spite of the hostility from the ranks of sportsmen and indifference from the wider public, the builders have bestowed uncounted benefits upon Canadian sport. When we look at the roles played by some of these builders it is clear that many men and women have filled several roles – sometimes almost all – as in the case of Lester

A player, coach, manager and owner, Lester Patrick was one of hockey's real immortals, identified with all facets of the game.

Noted for bulldog perseverance, Conn Smythe is remembered for constructing Maple Leaf Gardens and building championship teams.

Patrick or Lloyd Percival or Conn Smythe.

It would be impossible to list the many people, most of them now forgotten, who have significantly contributed in time, energy, money and leadership to the cause of Canadian sport. Quite arbitrarily, we have selected three men, none of them in the Sports Hall of Fame, whose careers illustrate the varying role of the builder in relation to changing times.

Erastus Wiman was a man of the gilded nineteenth century with something of its flamboyant and piratical character, and the kind of vision and opportunism needed in a period when most of the options were still open. Teddy Oke flourished in the 1920s; a promoter in the great age of sports promoters. Yet he retained the moral earnestness of another time, and in his strong belief in women's role in sport he was a true pioneer. Melville Rogers played his part in the modern period of complex sports bureaucracies and of increasing government interest and intervention in sport. The very model of the quiet, constructive administrator, his controlled zeal swayed committees and opened politicians' doors.

Wiman was born near Toronto in 1834; he died seventy years later in New York. For more than thirty years, from 1865 to the late nineties, he was Horatio Alger to many Canadians. Wiman went from business success at home to become a major figure in the turbulent railway age of the United States where he hobnobbed with the likes of "robber baron" Jay Gould and fought with the Vanderbilt interests for the control of lands and railways.

From his base in New York and using his control of a telegraph system in Canada and the northern US, Wiman intervened dramatically in two federal elections in Canada (1887 and 1891) as an advocate of commercial union between the US and Canada. He was the adversary who drove Sir John A. Macdonald to wrap himself in the Union Jack in his last successful campaign and cry: "A British subject I was born; a British subject I shall die."

At the age of twelve Wiman became, as he claimed, "the first newsboy" in Toronto. His stand was in front of the classiest Toronto hotel of the early 1850s. His business grew into the first Toronto news shop, then into a news agency, then into a mercantile agency. He was hired as a reporter for the *Globe*, and was promoted to commercial editor. Then he went into the "commercial agency" and credit-rating business. Eventually he became a partner in what is now the firm of Dun and Bradstreet.

At one time Wiman controlled the properties of what is now the International Nickel operation at Sudbury. He held patents on many ore-extraction and milling processes. He challenged the CPR on numerous occasions, especially in relation to the telegraph. He was a prolific writer, an inveterate traveller, and booster for Canada. A relative, a one-time Canadian minister, the Honourable William McDougall, once told Prime Minister Sir John A. Macdonald that Wiman in New York was worth more to Canada "than five plenipotentiaries."

What had all of Wiman's activities to do with sport? Wiman was more than an enthusiast for games and fitness; he was a missionary, patron and drum-beater for Canadian sport of all kinds. He spent large sums to support Canadian teams. He underwrote trips of Canadian lacrosse teams to the United States and England. He brought Canadian cricket, lacrosse, rugby football, hockey and soccer teams to New York. He used his telegraph lines and his connections with the press to tout Canadian sports. He sponsored and paid for the first public baths in Toronto. He helped make the Montreal winter carnivals of the mid-1880s a success by sending trainloads of American visitors, including some of the leading journalists, to Quebec. He organized and was first president of the original Canadian Club in New York in 1885. He paid for the services of several Canadians who organized lacrosse in New York, Boston, and Baltimore. He got control of Staten Island and its ferries during his battles with the Vanderbilts; on the island he built the most modern sporting grounds and the lushest athletic club in the world. He brought to the us Buffalo Bill's Wild West Show, circuses, and sponsored innumerable matches in many sports, often featuring Canadian teams. He bought the New York Metropolitans, a baseball club in the American Association, and got noisily involved for several years in player disputes and ownership quarrels in big league baseball.

Whenever a Canadian talent in sport emerged, Wiman seemed to have a part as a booster or sponsor, whether it was a rower, a marksman, a jockey, a horse breeder, a runner or a team that wanted to tackle an American club.

In those days the telegraph companies provided the news coverage that has been handled in this century by what we call the "wire services." Wiman's communications system owned 40,000 miles of wire and 1,700 offices in five provinces and two states. He used this sprawling empire in the cause of Canadian sport, and sporting items became part of the regular news carried by his companies. Wiman put Canadian sports news into the American press; he encouraged local Wiman papers to cover sports events in other communities; and, most notably, his enthusiastic advocacy of Canadian sporting enterprises and his status among his high-powered American friends gave to Canadian athletes a cocky confidence in their own excellence. Wiman represented, in an extroverted swaggering fashion, a golden age in our sporting history when as a nation, we were convinced of our world-class quality.

As have other wheeler-dealers before and since, Erastus Wiman over-extended himself. His last few years were spent in and out of bankruptcy, in and out of courts. From being the best-known and most-publicized Canadian abroad, he dropped out of sight. From newsboy to multi-millionaire to bust.

Like Erastus Wiman, Teddy Oke was a self-made wealthy man, until the 1929 crash and the depression almost wiped out his fortune.

Born at Uxbridge, Ontario, in 1886, Oke was the captain and star centre of his town's entry in the OHA junior series of 1901-2. He was as good at baseball and lacrosse as he was at hockey. At seventeen he quit school and headed into Northern Ontairo to seek his fortune. A summer in Sault Ste. Marie sparked his interest in mining and he moved to the Cobalt mining camp, where for several years he prospected and staked claims, financing himself by playing hockey and baseball for ten to fifteen dollars a game. His reputation as a hockey player grew and by 1910 he was able to command a fair salary as a pro, playing variously for clubs in Toronto and Halifax. He was the star of the Toronto Tecumsehs, then of the

Toronto Blueshirts who took the Stanley Cup in 1914. He joined the sportsmen's battalion during the war and was commissioned as lieutenant, but severe illness in 1917 brought his discharge. His strength was no longer up to professional hockey so he got a job in a brokerage firm in Toronto and quickly branched off on his own as a broker of mining stocks, using money from claims he'd staked near Haileybury before the war. In 1922 he bought a seat on the mining exchange and became an overnight mining millionaire with branch offices of his brokerage firm around Ontario. No sooner was Oke in the money than he turned to spending a lot of it in sport. He had a simple credo:

> I believe a nation's welfare depends on sound bodies and a clean life. Athletics demands these qualities . . . Therefore, I am trying to help the athlete. . . . It can therefore, be no great wonder . . . that during my period of prosperity, I endeavour to provide more pleasant conditions for the young athlete of today.

The first major outlet for his spending was professional hockey. For several years he financed and practically owned all the teams and the players' contracts in the ill-fated Canadian Professional League. Then he bankrolled the International Hockey League with franchises in Toronto, London, Hamilton, Buffalo and Syracuse. Although these leagues had some excellent players who went on to become stars in the NHL, they never achieved great success at the gate, particularly in Toronto. One night when Oke's Toronto club had played at home to almost empty seats, he had a bugler play the "Last Post" after the game.

Thereafter, he fixed his sporting interests on basketball, lacrosse, swimming, and track and field. He tried to put together a basketball team which could defeat the invincible Edmonton Grads – and almost pulled it off. His "dream" athlete was the lovely Ethel Catherwood. He had planned a huge sports palace for women, to be built at Hampstead Park in Toronto, but he shelved the plans after Ethel Catherwood disappeared into the United States and never returned. After his death, some sportswriters said this had been the greatest disappointment of his life.

Teddy Oke outfitted his girls' teams and subsidized extensive travel for them. He paid school fees for girls who wanted to go to business college. He found jobs for scores of girl athletes. He lavished expensive perfume, clothes, and magnificent facilities on his girls of the Parkdale Ladies' Athletic Club. He sponsored a host of great athletes, including George Young and a score or so of girl swimmers. He sponsored lacrosse teams in Kitchener and a baseball team in London. He maintained a training camp at Port Credit for swimmers. He backed speedboat racers. He underwrote the

286

early speed skating career of Lela Brooks, paying for her travels to meets in the United States. For several years in the late 1920s, he equipped literally dozens of teams in hockey, baseball and lacrosse, from kids' clubs to seniors.

Teddy Oke abominated drinking and smoking. He disbanded a girls' softball team, a group he himself had trained and coached, when he caught some of the girls smoking. Strongwilled and abrupt, he never appreciated that too much subsidization for a comparative few played havoc with stable competition. The amounts of money he sunk into sport can only be guessed at today but an appraisal of estimates made in his heyday suggests that Canadian sport has never had a more lavish benefactor. Shortly before his death at fifty-one he was in straitened circumstances and down to one sponsorship, a girls' softball team. In the eulogies and obituaries, commentators emphasized his golden year of 1928 when so much of his enthusiasm and money went into the most successful Olympic team Canada ever sent abroad. Teddy Oke gilded a period in sport. While much of what he did was ephemeral he was the first prominent person to promote the participation of Canadian women in sport. Their record internationally, has been better than that of Canadian males ever since.

If Wiman and Oke represent flamboyance and generous spending on Canadian sport, Melville Rogers was the epitome of the solid, durable builder to whom sportsmen in general and figure skaters in particular owe a huge and largely unacknowledged debt. An Ottawa lawyer, Rogers died in 1973 at the age of seventy-four.

Rogers was the best overall skater in Canada during the 1920s, a champion at singles, doubles and in the fours. He was the first male Canadian figure skater to compete in the Olympics (1924), paying his own way. In all he won eighteen senior national and international championships. Later he became one of the world's outstanding skating judges. He was the "core" skater at Ottawa's Minto Club for two decades; when his competition days ended he moved into coaching and judging. One of the first to spot Barbara Ann Scott's potential, he was one of her early coaches. The Canadian figure skating organization realized that to sustain the enormous interest generated by the Scott triumphs, more and better judging had a priority, even over coaching; Rogers was named chairman of the judges' committee of the CFSA. Systematically and thoroughly, schools and courses for judges were developed through the 1950s.

Probably Rogers's finest achievement was as a lobbyist. He was what parliamentarians call "a great committeeman." Friendly, firm, patient, persistent, unafraid of detail, unabashed by rebuffs, Melville Rogers plugged away at one theme for more than twenty years. He wanted government involvement as a backer and sponsor of amateur sport. Rogers began to sell to his contacts across Canada the idea of pressuring politicians and civil servants to aid sport. His natural focus was on the federal government in Ottawa, where he lived. In 1949, Paul Martin, then minister of national health and welfare, had indicated clearly that he considered that "jurisdiction in the sports field was provincial and municipal." In 1953 the ineffective federal legislation for physical fitness was quietly withdrawn. It seemed that aside from occasional special grants to Olympic and Commonwealth Games teams, the federal government was not going to have anything to do with sport. However, with the formation of the Canadian Sports Advisory Council in 1949, Melville Rogers became the council's man in Ottawa. From 1951 until 1959 he marshalled every force and argument he could to persuade the federal government to change its mind about its responsibilities towards amateur sport. His campaign got an enormous shot in the arm when Prince Philip visited Canada in 1959. Rogers had sent the prince his material on the need for a fitness and sports program through a distinguished British friend made years before in skating circles. The friend, Sir Frederick Browning, took the case to Prince Philip and got an enthusiastic response. The prince's speech, given to the Canadian Medical Association, on the subject of physical fitness, made an enormous impact in Canada, not least on Prime Minister John Diefenbaker.

Although the Rogers's approach emphasized physical fitness, he saw amateur sport participation as one vehicle to a greater national fitness. In essence, he was convinced that once spending programs were enabled by legislation, sport would find its place in the grants and subsidy structure. He was right. Soon the active politicians were taking up the cause. When the National Fitness and Amateur Sport Act was passed in 1961 with a statutory ceiling of $5 million in annual spending there was much quiet satisfaction for Rogers. He was a member of the first National Advisory Council and the president of the new Canadian Sports Federation, the successor to the Canadian Sports Advisory Council.

Now that they are in place, such institutions and events as the National Sports Administration Centre, the Canada Games and the Coaching Association of Canada would seem to have been inevitable. Perhaps so, but Melville Rogers, more than any other person, broke the trail.

Biographies

GEORGE ANDERSON, 1890-

In August 1972 twenty young soccer players left Winnipeg for a month-long European tour, to play against junior teams in Holland, England and Wales. The instigator, organizer and tour manager of this ambitious project was George Anderson, at eighty-two years of age still a vital force in the promotion of the sport to which he has dedicated more than sixty years of his life.

The trip with the high-spirited fourteen-year-olds epitomizes two of the most important facets of George Anderson's work as a soccer administrator for more than half a century – his encouragement of junior soccer, and his genius for organizing tours. He has probably done more than any man in Canada to raise the standard of Canadian soccer and to promote it abroad, both by taking Canadian teams to Europe, and by introducing to Canada some of the world's finest players.

George Anderson was born in Aberdeenshire, emigrated to Canada when he was eighteen and after two years in Souris, Manitoba, settled in Winnipeg in 1911. During those early years he played soccer for Britannia in the Winnipeg and District League and for the Winnipeg *Free Press* in the Printers League. When war was declared in 1914, George was running a small weekly newspaper in Melville, Saskatchewan. He enlisted and went overseas in 1915. Twice wounded in France, he was posted in 1918 to the Canadian army printing department in England. On his demobilization in 1919, George returned to Winnipeg and joined Veterans Press Limited; he remained with the company as a compositor for thirty-seven years.

George Anderson's involvement with soccer administration in Manitoba started immediately after his return from the war. He set about organizing and promoting junior soccer in the province. By 1924 he was managing the Caledonian junior, juvenile and midget soccer teams in the Manitoba junior league. He was secretary of the Manitoba junior soccer association, and at the outbreak of the second world war, he was also on the executive of the senior association.

During the war years, the Dominion of Canada Football Association (DCFA) suspended all activities. Never a very lusty association, its reactivation after the war was mainly due to the initiative and enthusiasm of George Anderson. After its reorganization in 1946, he was the moving force behind the association, and served as its secretary-treasurer for eighteen years until his retirement in 1968.

It was during these years that George Anderson's talent for organizing tours proved invaluable. For many years tours of Canada by foreign teams provided the association with its only source of revenue. The Canadian public was able to see such internationally famous teams as Tottenham Hotspur, West Bromwich Albion and Sheffield United. His greatest coup in international tours came in 1956, when he arranged for a tour of Canada by the Russian soccer team, Moscow Lokomotiv, the first Russian team of any kind to visit Canada.

The tour was a tremendous success, although not without its tense and hilarious moments. George Anderson vividly remembers the first game the Russians played: "The

Sports Hall of Fame

first game was in Montreal and everyone was very nervous. We had arranged that the Canadian beauty queen for 1956, who was a Montreal lady, would kick off. The field was muddy and she came on beautifully dressed with high-heeled shoes. When she kicked the ball her shoe went with it, and there she was standing in the mud minus a shoe. However, the Soviet captain saved the day; he went up to her and presented her with a bouquet and kissed her. The crowd gave him a big hand so that tension relaxed and from then on the tour went off without a hitch."

This success was followed in 1960 by a return tour of Russia by a Canadian team. The tour went very well, but the Canadians had to leave behind the money they earned. It took George Anderson four years but with true Scottish thrift and tenacity, he eventually got the money transferred from Russia to Canada.

The DCFA entered a team in the world football cup for the first time in 1957. George Anderson had a hand in the selection of the team and arranged the tour. Canada beat the United States, but lost to Mexico in the qualifying round played in Mexico City. The association tried again in international competition when they entered a team in the 1968 Olympics. But once again the results were disappointing. The two qualifying games against Cuba were played in Edmonton, and Canada lost one game and drew the other, and was eliminated from further competition.

George Anderson has been Canada's ambassador abroad in the world of international soccer. He has represented Canada at the 100th anniversary of the Football Association in London in 1963, and was Canadian delegate to the FIFA in 1966. He has been a great believer in international competition, and has spent a lifetime working for the development of Canadian soccer at the professional level.

DAVID BAUER, 1925-

Father David Bauer was the planner and mover behind one of the finest dreams in Canadian sports – an ongoing national hockey team for international competition. The dream was never fully realized. In working towards it, Father Bauer enlisted the emotions of the country in the face of much discouragement and the deep, effective antagonism of the professional hockey interests of North America.

From the Winter Olympics of 1964 to the collapse of the world hockey championship tournament set for Montreal and Winnipeg in the late winter of 1970, the Bau-

Alexandra Studio

er plan unfolded in an atmosphere of hope and frustration. It might be described as the lost, last chance to recapture a national focus for our national game.

David Bauer was born into a large and athletic family. His older brother Bob was on the great Schmidt-Bauer-Dumart line of the Boston Bruins. One of his sisters, Rita, was an excellent hockey player – graceful, tricky, a good stickhandler. David played football and hockey at St. Michael's College in Toronto during the early war years. Then he was a leftwinger on the 1943 Memorial Cup champions of Oshawa. He took vows as a member of the Basilians and turned to teaching and coaching at his alma mater.

Recently he recalled the turning point in his attitude to hockey:

In a sense the founding of the national team dates back to when I was about fifteen years of age. It was then that my father told me that I would be a professional hockey player only after I got an education. During those years he also impressed upon me that one day I would have to account to God for the talents He had given me. My father viewed hockey as a means for the development of my personality, contributing to the growth of the physical and emotional side of my life within the framework of formal education. I could see something in that, but I also saw hockey as a commercial enterprise, a way of making a good living. The strong pull exerted by the image-makers, even then, had so powerful an influence on me that I knowingly opted out of school work in order to defeat the goals of my father. He was willing to compromise. He sent me to St. Michael's College where both sport and formal education were pursued with vigour and excellence. At the age of sixteen I attended the training camp of the Boston Bruins at Hershey. At the end of the camp I was invited to join the Boston Olympics, one of Boston's farm teams. . . . But something had also started to happen within me. I knew now that I could play in the NHL but I had been disillusioned

289

by what I had seen at the camp. I saw there an empty life. Seeing it somehow made me aware that I was looking for something more, a life in which I could fulfill goals beyond myself, goals of world peace which had begun to occupy my mind more and more.

Professional hockey is a business, nothing more, nothing less . . . the only real interest that the NHL has in the several hundred thousand Canadian boys playing hockey is that the best of them be available. . . . I have no quarrel with this. . . . The only thing I have ever quarrelled with is the excessive influence exercised by the NHL over amateur hockey. As the president of the NHL, Mr. Clarence Campbell, has said, the NHL has no interest in the general welfare of the players in amateur sport. But the whole point of any amateur sport should be the welfare of the participants. Amateur sport should not be a business.

At St. Michael's, the Basilians faced the problems of junior hockey. Father Bauer's brother, Bob, had played on the school team which won the Memorial Cup in 1935. That team played thirty-five games overall. In the early forties David Bauer's teams played only a few more games. But in 1961 the Memorial Cup champions he coached played ninety-eight games on the way to the title. After that victory, St. Michael's decided to pack up major calibre junior hockey. As Father Bauer puts it: "How could a boy, unless he was very exceptional, hope to carry a course of study while doing this?" After seven years of successful coaching in the best junior league, Father Bauer was transferred by his superiors to St. Mark's College and the University of British Columbia. There, he coached the UBC team.

Meantime, throughout the 1950s the Canadian teams for Olympic and world tournament competitions were being pushed out of top ranking, particularly by the Russians. The Swedes and Czechs were also coming on quickly. The Olympic team from Canada in both 1956 and 1960 had been from Kitchener – the Flying Dutchmen – and two Bauer brothers, Ray and Bob, had been closely associated with the teams as manager and coach.

Ray Bauer put the pressure on brother David to do something about getting a better calibre of Canadian representation. Father Bauer was becoming increasingly concerned that amateur hockey, national aspirations, and formal education be combined and harmonized through the example of a national team. These views coincided with a determination of the CAHA to upgrade Canada's quality at international tournaments.

The national team concept got underway with the organization of the team for the 1964 Olympics. It was based in Vancouver and had mostly university students as players. The team did not win the Olympics title but it played well and demonstrated a marvellous sportsmanship. The organizers of the games made the unique gesture of awarding an individual gold medal to Father Bauer at the end of the tournament for his exemplary leadership under great strain, particularly the restraint he displayed when he was struck in the face by a broken stick thrown by a Swedish player.

After 1964, the CAHA, Father Bauer, and a group in the West, including the late Max Bell, Father Athol Murray, Mervyn "Red" Dutton, and James Richardson, set up a permanent national team in Winnipeg. A large-surface rink was built at Ravenscourt school. The slow job of recruiting players began, the objective to get boys who wanted to combine education with the opportunity to play a disciplined, highly-coached style of hockey. The results were good on every count, even though it was disappointing each year at the world tournament to find the Russians almost unbeatable.

In Europe and in Western Canada "Father Dave" became a symbol of Canadian sportsmanship and idealism. His advice and counsel became much appreciated in Ottawa as the federal government became more and more involved in sponsoring and encouraging amateur sport.

When the national team was dismantled in 1970 after the refusal of the European teams to play under the terms agreed to regarding the eligibility of players for the Canadian team, Father Bauer could count many successes despite the lack of championships. With never more than the smallest, most grudging cooperation from pro hockey, his concept had allowed dozens of young men the chance to play hockey, gain an education, as well as represent Canada.

Father Bauer is still at St. Mark's, counselling and teaching. He has aided hockey developments in Japan and in Austria. He has played a large part in shaping the work of Hockey Canada in coaching techniques. While he didn't break the grip of pro hockey, he did create an honourable alternative and heightened the national awareness about the value of hockey as something larger than dollars and jobs.

GEORGE DUTHIE, 1902-68

When George Duthie died in Toronto at the age of sixty-six, he had spent thirty-five years as manager of the sports department at the Canadian National Exhibition. To him, more than to any other individual, goes the credit for building up the highly successful sports program of the CNE. Under his auspices the marathon swims became a popular attraction. A quiet, unassuming Scot, George Duthie's contribution to the promotion of

290

Canadian sports has been incalculable. In the words of one of his friends, Clarence James: "George had a flair for organization, the memory of an elephant, the kindest of hearts, and devotion to sports and his job."

George Duthie came to Canada from his native Scotland at an early age, and was soon active in sport. He joined the boys' department of the Toronto West End YMCA and became a member of the junior leaders' corps; he also managed the junior basketball team. This was the start of a lifetime's involvement with management and public relations at the YMCA. He was on the board of directors at the Etobicoke Y at the time of his death.

In 1931 he was elected as alderman to the Toronto city council, but he resigned in 1933 to take up the post of sports director at the CNE. From that time he worked indefatigably for the cause of sport in Canada. He achieved a reputation for getting things done quietly and efficiently.

Water sports had been a highlight of the Ex ever since George Young's spectacular conquest of the Catalina Straits in 1927 had prompted the CNE to stage its own marathon swim across Lake Ontario in the summer of the same year. By the 1930s, motorboat racing was also becoming increasingly popular and George Duthie was one of the men responsible for forming the Canadian Boating Federation, the governing body for motorboat racing in Canada. Growing interest in this sport led to the introduction of water skiing, and George Duthie was responsible for stag-

ing the 1953 world water ski championships as part of the CNE sports program. The event gave particular pleasure to Duthie; his own daughter, Carol Ann, won the junior championship at this event.

During the second world war Duthie served in the Royal Canadian Air Force, rising to the rank of squadron leader. Here again his talents for organization were put to good use. He formed interservice leagues in basketball, boxing, wrestling, football and hockey, and organized the No. 1 Training Command track and field championships, the biggest one-day meet ever held in Canada. He was awarded the MBE in 1948 for his work during the war as liaison officer between Canada and the United States on the victory loan programs.

After the war Duthie returned to the CNE. Although increasingly crippled with arthritis during his later years, he continued his work with great energy. He travelled across Canada on behalf of the Canadian Olympic training program and served on many committees of the Amateur Athletic Union of Canada. Both he and his daughter Carol Ann were elected to the CAAU's Hall of Fame, the only father and daughter team to be members. In 1967 he was appointed to the National Advisory Council on Fitness and Amateur Sport, and served until his death the following year.

J. W. HAMILTON, 1886-

Most hockey fans associate Saskatoon with the great Gordie Howe; Howe is certainly the

291

finest product of an excellent city system of hockey. But hockey in Saskatoon did not start with Howe. In 1918, long before Howe was born, a young lumberman named Jack Hamilton was busy organizing the construction of a 3,500-seat ice rink for the city.

That is only one example of the enthusiams and energy Jack Hamilton has brought to the cause of sport in the West. As organizer and executive, he has been associated with almost every sporting activity in Saskatchewan – athletics, hockey, football, baseball, shooting, aquatics.

Jack Hamilton first became interested in athletics when he was a young man in Ontario. Born of Scottish parents, he was educated at Caledonia, Ontario, and taught school for several years. With the instinct for hard work and the love of physical exercise so typical of his countrymen, Jack began to make his way in both the world of business and sport. He went to Saskatoon in 1909 to teach school; in 1911 he took a summer job with a lumber company. He left teaching, and forty-six years later he retired as managing director of the lumber company.

His involvement in sports started as soon as he arrived in Saskatchewan, and he established himself as an organizer and leader in the community. In the early 1920s he coached the Regina Vics hockey club. He later became president of the club, and was president of the Saskatchewan Amateur Hockey Association for 1925, 1926 and 1927. Jack Hamilton's contribution to amateur hockey was recognized in 1930, when he was elected president of the Canadian Amateur Hockey Association.

Simultaneously with his interest in hockey, Jack Hamilton became involved in football administration. From 1923 to 1927 he was secretary of the Regina Roughriders and in 1928 president of the Western Interprovincial Rugby Football Union (now the Western conference of the CFL).

His first love, athletics, was not forgotten during these active years, even during the hardships of the depression. He served as president of the Saskatchewan branch of the CAAU, and in 1937 was elected president of the national organization. In the same year his work for athletics was recognized by the award of the King George VI coronation medal.

Jack Hamilton has been, in a very literal sense, a builder in Canadian sport, recognizing early in his career the need for adequate sporting facilities in the community. He has used his enormous prestige and influence in Saskatoon and the province as a prominent businessman to raise funds for such facilities. He had been responsible for providing a hockey rink for Saskatoon back in 1918. In 1937 he headed the Queen City Gardens Company which raised funds to instal artificial ice in the Regina hockey rink, and continued to operate the arena for the next eleven years. Then he turned his building talents to Moose Jaw, organizing a fund-raising drive that provided a 3,500-seat rink for that city.

Both his adopted province and the country have recognized the contribution Jack Hamilton has made to sport in the West. In 1955 Saskatchewan presented him with an engraved gold ring in tribute of his fifty years in sport leadership, and in 1967 he was awarded the Canadian Centennial Medal.

CHARLES E. E. MAYER, 1901-71
Some called him "Uncle Charles" because he possessed the avuncular benevolence of Prime Minister "Uncle Louis" St. Laurent. To others he was "Trois Etoiles," or "Three Stars" Mayer not just because he chose the three stars for each game of the Montreal Canadiens' broadcast, but because on one memorable occasion, Charles Mayer awarded all three stars to Maurice Richard when Richard scored five goals against the Maple Leafs in a Stanley Cup game.

When Charles Mayer was honoured by selection to the Sports Hall of Fame

Sports Hall of Fame

292

shortly before his death, he was delighted and proud. In a way, his delight was less significant than the obvious pleasure of the Quebec press and broadcasting personnel. The last few years of Charles Mayer's life coincided with the rise of French-Canadian nationalism. The movement had strong elements of exclusiveness and often harsh criticism of anything continental or broadly Canadian. There was even a brief advocacy that the Montreal Canadiens be taken over by the Quebec government. There was a tendency among some French-Canadian journalists to pinpoint "vendus," sell-outs to the Anglos. As one of Mayer's colleagues said after his death: "I know no better indication of his position in the affections of French Canadians than the unanimous approval when he was named to the Sports Hall of Fame . . . in Toronto of all places."

For English-speaking Canadians who had little chance to appreciate Charles Mayer, he was, in Quebec, an amalgam of Ted Reeve and Billie Hewitt, with a dash of Foster Hewitt tossed in. He was a sportswriter and editor in the newspaper field, a radio and TV commentator, a sports official and for a time, a sporting man in politics. Every French Canadian interested in sport since the 1930s knew Charles Mayer, had read him or listened to him. What distinguished his work, aside from warmth and decency, was his penchant for records and statistics and his feel for the grand artists in sport – men such as Richard, Beliveau, and Gérard Côté. While his interests were broad, he was especially knowledgeable in hockey, baseball, boxing and horseracing. He caught the Olympic vision early in his career and, if one wanted to single out one man who first espoused and persisted with the idea of Montreal playing host to the Olympics, it was Charles Mayer – as early as 1950. He spearheaded an almost-successful attempt in the late fifties to get Montreal into the American baseball league.

In civic life he was for years publicity chairman for Federated Fund Charities, president and director of the St. Laurent Alumni Association, parish warden, councillor of Montreal from 1954 to 1960. He represented the mayor and council of Montreal at Jacques Cartier's 400th anniversary in France in 1956. He was for three years, a member of the National Council for Fitness and Amateur Sports.

In hockey, for many years he was French-language publicist for the NHL and in charge of the league's minor officials. He wrote the best-selling book (116,500 copies), *L'Epopée des Canadiens (1956)*. Of course, he was the founder of the "Hot Stove League"

on the French radio and TV stations. From 1943 to 1965 he was the commentator and analyst in French for the World Series. For six years he was vice-president of the Montreal Athletic Commission. He was president of the Canadian Boxing Federation in 1955 and 1956, later vice-president of the World Boxing Association, and, at his death, honorary president of both the Canadian and world boxing organizations. He was a boxing judge at Olympic and other world events.

In horseracing he held all positions at tracks in Montreal up to steward. He had graduated from the officials' course of the New York Jockey Club. For some years prior to his death he was director of information at Blue Bonnets and Richelieu racetracks.

He was an active supporter of amateur sport, making a steady contribution as governor and officer to the Palestre Nationale, for many decades the single, most important amateur sports club in Quebec.

The marvel was that Charles Mayer did so much, for so long, so competently, and with a warm humanity that left friends and admirers everywhere. His lifetime in sport coincided with the rise of French-Canadian interest in sport and pursuit of it. For various social and economic reasons organized sport, both amateur and professional, developed much more slowly in Quebec than elsewhere in Canada. In recent decades the interest has been growing and no single man did more to build this in a humane and thorough way than Charles Mayer.

ATHOL MURRAY, 1892-

The little village of Wilcox, Saskatchewan, is an unlikely site for a college; and the early 1930s, in the depths of the depression, was hardly a promising time to start one. But the man who began it all, Father Athol Murray, is a most unusual man. Now in his eighties, Père, as he is known to everybody, is the founder and guiding inspiration, the tough, irascible and beloved boss of one of the most famous colleges in all of Canada.

Notre Dame College is probably the only one in Canada that was founded to educate a baseball team. Yet that's how it all began. Ordained in 1918, Père was appointed chancellor to Archbishop Mathieu of the Regina diocese in 1923. He immediately organized a boys' athletic club, the Regina Argos, and the boys gained an enviable reputation locally in hockey, football, and baseball. When the archbishop died in 1927, Father Murray was offered a parish in Ontario where he had been born. Instead, he asked to go to the vacant parish of Wilcox, forty miles south of Regina. Some of his Argos decided

to go with him; they were attached to Père, and they wanted to keep the team together under him, since its reputation was so good that it was frequently scouted by the big-league teams.

The boys moved in with Père, doing the household chores, working at odd jobs, and playing baseball. Father Murray decided that his boys could do with a little book learning and more than encouraged them to dip into his extensive classical library. He persuaded the Sisters of St. Louis, who ran a girls' school in Wilcox, to give a high school course to his Argos. When they graduated he himself took over the teaching; and so it was in 1933 that the now-famous College of Notre Dame was founded, and affiliated to the University of Ottawa, as a degree-granting college.

The choice of the name, Notre Dame, was significant. The Canadian college was patterned on the ideals of Knute Rockne, the athletic director of Notre Dame, Indiana. Like Rockne, Père trains his boys in both character and body-building; he believes in clean, hard aggressive living, thinking, working and playing. "Sport helps enormously," says Père. "The individual comes out so fast. And the student who watches from the sidelines can't help but become part of it vicariously."

Under Père's inspiration, the little ramshackle collection of buildings among dirt streets and scrubgrass on the windswept Prairie gained an athletic and scholastic reputation second to none. His boys, the Hounds of Notre Dame, have made up some of the toughest teams in the country. Frank Germann, once a student and later a teacher at Notre Dame, recalls the early days: "We'd play anyone, anywhere and, with Père egging us on, we generally won. We travelled up to 8,000 miles a season, through bitter cold and choking dust, in the boxed-in back of a truck called 'the dog-house.' We often slept in it, and Père, hatless and shirt-sleeved in summer, swathed in buffalo coat and aviator's leather helmet in winter, always took the hardest bed himself."

The success of Père's methods are clearly illustrated by the numbers of his students who have achieved fame in the National Hockey League and in other hockey leagues from coast to coast; such men as the Metz brothers, Nick and Don, Jackie McLeod, Garth Boesch and Gus Kyle, to mention a few.

Over the years Père has been a friend and inspiration to his boys. Many of them remember him as Frank Germann does, "Roaring with laughter, eyes darting with excitement, sipping Scotch from an unwashed glass, his inevitable cigarette dripping ashes down his paunch, he demonstrates the ancient art of conversation day and night. He reigns in a tiny office as richly assorted as he is: walls lined with pictures of family, churchmen, Jimmy Durante; desk littered with mail, books, cheese, crackers, his troublesome upper plate." Though he has never been much of an athlete himself, this is the man who has contributed a great deal to the training of young athletes; few men have done so much for so many young players and for the game of hockey in Canada.

HARRY ISAAC PRICE, 1896-

In his late seventies, Harry Price, tall, lean and vigorous, looks as though he can go on forever. He is an advertisement for a busy, turbulent life and a cause for disbelief when one learns that he was invalided home towards the end of the first world war with tuberculosis after three years of active service as an officer in the 75th Battalion.

Harry Price's father, Isaac, was a rower who won the single sculls at the first Canadian Henley regatta, held in London, Ontario. Harry was intensely interested in sport as a youth, initially as a runner, then as a rower. He was a member of the Irish Amateur Athletic Association in Toronto, then noted for its great runner Tom Longboat and for the coaching and administrative leadership of Tom Flanagan, later manager and coach of heavyweight champion, Jack Johnson.

Harry Price joined the Canadian Expeditionary Force as a private in 1914 and lung injuries suffered at the front brought on his ill-health. On his recovery he went to work as a vocational director for the dominion government. In 1923 he was appointed to the Ontario Athletic Commission. The commission had been formed three years earlier to support amateur sport and to bring order and probity into boxing and wrestling which, at the time, were both popular and much criticized.

Harry Price was made vice-chairman of the commission and given boxing as a particular responsibility. His work in this field dovetailed with reforms being carried out by the boxing commissioner in New York, the famous William Muldoon, once world heavyweight wrestling champion. An agreement was worked out to have complementary rules for bouts and examination of boxers and managers in both jurisdictions.

It was as vice-chairman of the OAC that Price became involved with the Canadian National Exhibition which, in the 1920s, sponsored much more sport than it does today, particularly in track and field. After George Young's victory in the Catalina swim the Ex turned to the promotion of professional marathon swimming. As the officer of the agency responsible for pro sport, Price refereed the great swims for several years. He was given the office of chairman for the athletic committee of the CNE.

While Price could not compete actively in sport he turned to horses and riding in the twenties, riding for pleasure and buying show horses. He became chairman of the Canadian zone of the American Horse Show Association, a group committed to popularizing horse shows and standardizing rules for competition. He founded the Canadian Horse

Alexandra Studio

Show Association and chaired the Canadian equestrian team which competed in the US, Cuba, Mexico, and Europe in 1939.

In a determined effort to get backing for the costly equestrian teams Price approached provincial and federal governments through the CNE and the Royal Winter Fair organizations. The three levels of government were prevailed upon to support the creation at the Exhibition grounds of the horse palace, at the time a much-admired facility. In this period he worked with such equestrian enthusiasts as William Cleland, a great horseman, Gordon Perry, later president of the Winter Fair, and Colonel Ron Marshall, later president of the CNE.

Harry Price was an active member of the Toronto Hunt Club, serving terms as president. He owned a horse, Brownie, which took more show prizes than any other Canadian horse in the 1930s.

His experience with the OAC and equestrianism had convinced Price that one great failure in Canadian sport was the lack of honour and remembrance given great athletes. He brought this gap to the attention of the CNE board. Out of his efforts and those of like-minded enthusiasts at the CNE, came Canada's Sports Hall of Fame. When it was apparent that the Hockey Hall of Fame to be developed at Kingston was not making headway he worked with Clarence Campbell, president of the NHL and Frank Selke, one of hockey's grand old men, to bring the hockey shrine to the Ex grounds in a close association with the Sports Hall of Fame. Selke gives credit to Price's leadership in creating the joint operation which has distinguished the centre located behind the main stadium at the Ex.

For his work with the OAC, in boxing and in equestrianism, there was substantial reason to consider Harry Price entitled to membership in the builder category of the Sports Hall of Fame. He has done much more. He has had a long (and controversial) association with the Progressive Conservative party as treasurer in Ontario and as confidant of former Premier Leslie Frost. Through these associations he pushed the cause of sport, including personal encouragement to the Diefenbaker government for the policy that led in 1960 to the National Fitness and Amateur Sports Act and the commitment of $5 million a year from the federal treasury for the promotion of amateur sports and fitness. In the late 1950s Harry Price chaired an Ontario enquiry on physical fitness which led to some Ontario initiatives in the sports field. He has always believed that the provincial governments should integrate the many activities of its departments which involve sport.

Diefenbaker appointed Harry Price to the advisory board of Expo '67. He resigned from this role in November 1964, having divined that Mayor Drapeau of Montreal intended to make "Man and His World" into an annual event, not just a grand, one-shot exposition. As a long-time director of the Ex in Toronto he felt he should state his insight publicly and declare that the Ex was ready to compete.

Price has been director of many companies, a businessman in insurance and securities. In 1959 his home city honoured him, along with dignitaries like Lady Eaton, painter A. Y. Jackson, and the Right Honourable Arthur Meighen, with the Toronto Civic Merit Award. At one time he was president of the Don Rowing Club, once a provincial member of parliament for York West, and, of course, a founding member and first chairman of the Canadian Sports Hall of Fame.

AL RITCHIE, 1890-1966

The supreme day in Canadian sport comes late each year in November when the winning team of the Western football conference of the CFL meets the winning team from the East in the Grey Cup. It is often forgotten that the West did not take part in a Grey Cup game until 1921 – and then not with conspicuous success; the Edmonton Eskimos lost to the Toronto Argonauts by a score of 23-0. It was to be another fourteen years before the Winnipeg Blue Bombers won the cup for the West for the first time. If the Grey Cup is the national extravaganza, its vitality was largely created by the challenges from the West. It was the Westerners who led the way in so many changes and innovations in the game. The man who was the pivot in development of football in the West was Al Ritchie, coach and manager of the Regina (later the Saskatchewan) Roughriders, the most improbable of football clubs.

Ritchie's devotion to football is legendary, especially in his home town of Regina. A full-time employee of the customs office, Ritchie gave all his spare time and energies to developing and coaching local teams. As well as the Roughriders in the senior league, he was responsible for the formation of two junior teams, the Pats, in both hockey and football. He coached the Pats to the junior national football championship in 1928, and his hockey team won the Memorial Cup in 1925 and again in 1930. He is the only man in Canadian sports history to coach national champions in both sports.

Al Ritchie's early years were spent in Ontario, where his father was a school teacher. His interest in sport came from his father, who was a fine baseball player. Al played both baseball and rugby football in Midland, Ontario, before moving to Regina with his family in 1911. In Regina he joined the local football team, and came under the spell of coach Fred Ritter, a young player from Princeton. Ritchie caught football fever. Years later he recalled Ritter's influence: "I was exposed for the first time to a dedicated human dynamo – a man who breathed, slept, and ate football. He was our coach, our quarterback – our religion. I was the first man out to practice, the last to leave – I absorbed it all."

Al Ritchie absorbed a great deal from Ritter, which he himself was to put into practice later. But the first world war intervened, and Ritchie served in Europe with the artillery. On his return to Regina in 1919, he immediately started his involvement with the promotion of the sports he loved, an activity which was to last to the end of his life. It was in 1919 that he was instrumental in organizing an amateur hockey league in Saskatchewan, with teams from Regina, Saskatoon and Moose Jaw. At the same time he became manager of his old football club, in those days called the Regina Rugby Club, later christened – by Ritchie – the Roughriders. The Roughriders' success in the Western conference was tremendous, winning nine consecutive championships, and dominating the conference for years.

But the greatest prize, the Grey Cup, always eluded Regina. The first time Ritchie took the Roughriders to the East in 1923, they met Queen's in the final and were resoundingly beaten, 54-0. They tried again in 1928, to be beaten 28-0 by the Hamilton Ticats. The great dream was nearly realized in 1930, when the Roughriders met Balmy Beach for the Grey Cup. But in the last quarter Ted Reeve, almost single-handed, put Balmy Beach ahead to win by a score of 10-6.

Such defeats would discourage a lesser man, but not Al Ritchie. This is how he felt about those games: "I firmly believe one of the big contributing factors in building the great football structure we enjoy in Canada today was those early East-West games for the Grey Cup, despite the fact we absorbed some bad beatings. It kept the principle of declaring a national champion alive. It gave us an opportunity of studying Eastern tactics. Above all, it drew us closer together. It developed an East-West friendship which has obtained throughout the years – something which is of immeasur-

296

able value."

Also of immeasurable value to the game of Canadian football has been Al Ritchie's crusade for rule changes. He and his colleagues in the Western league were the moving spirits in initiating changes that are now an accepted part of today's game. The Western Canada Union adopted a rule reducing the number of players from fourteen to twelve in 1920, the first organization to do so. In the West they were using three yards interference when the East was still using one; they were using ten yards blocking when the East was still using five. They introduced the forward pass in 1929, two years before the East incorporated it into its rules. Finally, and of immense importance to the continued vitality of the game today, the Western Union led the way in importing experienced players from the United States to improve the quality of its teams. Both Regina and Winnipeg gained from the influx of new blood, even though such imports were not acceptable to the Canadian Rugby Union until after the second world war.

In all these innovations Al Ritchie played an active part. Although his coaching days were over by 1936, he continued to take a keen interest in both football and hockey, and at the time of his death he was still a scout for the New York Rangers hockey club.

FRANK J. SHAUGHNESSY, JR., 1911 –
His place of birth Roanoke, Virginia, had one important consequence for the younger Frank Shaughnessy. It gave him dual citizenship and so opened up an opportunity for him to represent the US at the 1936 Olym-

pics. But there was more significance to Roanoke than that.

Frank's famous father and namesake was probably the best-known American immigrant to Canada before 1914. His first visits were as a summer baseball player who otherwise studied and starred at football at Notre Dame. In Ottawa the college boy met the daughter of one Michael Quinn and married her. The new Mrs. Shaughnessy didn't care for the climate of the south, particularly that of Virginia. Although her second son, Frank, was born there while her husband managed the Roanoke baseball team she wanted to return to Canada, and when both Ottawa and McGill offered her husband positions as a football coach her wishes were met. From 1912 into the 1920s "Shag" Shaughnessy as coach of McGill became the most important single influence on the methods and tactics of Canadian football. Mrs. Shaughnessy went on to produce a family of eight boys and a girl over a span which saw a Shaughnessy on the Loyola football or hockey team every year for a quarter century.

Shaughnessy Sr. was a marvellous man. A dedicated, inspiring coach, he also had a great sense of public responsibility. He was known and cherished for his warm personality; his contributions to Montreal, his adopted city and to Canadian football and baseball were immense, especially as president of the International League.

Although Frank Jr., did not become an all-American end like his father nor the most respected football coach of an era, he was a good athlete at both football and hockey. He played defense for the last of the great amateur senior teams, the Montreal Victorias, and he was a solid member of the Loyola and McGill football teams. But his outstanding contribution to sport came in administration.

After graduation he went to work for Bell Telephone in Montreal. He remained with that firm as an executive until 1973 when he retired and moved to COJO to handle accreditation for the '76 Olympics. Aside from an interlude as a captain in the artillery fighting in northwest Europe in the second world war, Frank Shaughnessy Jr., has always had a hand in some phase of sports organization. He worked up from the club, to the regional, and then to the national level in both golf and skiing. He served as secretary to the famed MAAA. He organized national ski meets and golf tournaments. Above all, he served as *chef de mission* of five Canadian Winter Olympic teams from 1956 in Italy to 1972 in Japan. Kenny Farmer and Sydney Dawes of the Canadian Olympic As-

297

sociation had known Frank through hockey and McGill associations. They were aware of his contribution to the Laurentian zone ski committee and his work in organizing and raising funds for the ski team Canada sent to the world championships in 1954 held in Sweden. Once persuaded into Olympic work, Frank Shaughnessy has been unable to leave. The list of committees and responsibilities he has borne grew until what had been voluntary and part-time became a full-time career.

WILLIAM SIMPSON, 1894-1974

Bill Simpson has had a lifetime devotion to soccer. As player, coach, promoter and administrator for more than sixty years, he has done more than anybody else to foster and encourage the game in Canada, a country that has long been considered a distant outpost in world soccer. An imported game, soccer has drawn its support from immigrant groups, proud of their ethnic links and naturally carrying with them into their adopted homeland much of their intense partisanship.

Bill Simpson came to realize that the future of the game in Canada depended on its Canadianization, on a development from the grass roots of native clubs with names that would have a strong North American association. He has always had this objective in view in the many years he has been associated with the administration of the game – as secretary-treasurer of the Ontario Soccer Association for fifteen years, president of the Toronto and District Association for sixteen years, and as president of the Canadian Soccer Football Association.

Bill Simpson was born in Paisley, Scotland, and very early developed a love for soccer. At that time his greatest ambition was to play for Glasgow Rangers, and he was a very unwilling immigrant when his parents decided to come to Canada in 1911. In Canada, Bill was apprenticed as a plumber, and eventually became a foreman for Consumers' Gas. He played football on the company team, and later was persuaded by George Imlach (Punch Imlach's father), at that time manager of Toronto Fraserburg, to play for his team.

Bill developed into a talented inside forward, and soon moved up into senior soccer to play for Davenport Albion and, later, for the Toronto Scottish, who won the league championship in 1919.

When Bill Simpson's playing career was over in 1931, he naturally moved into administration. Perhaps his most valuable work on behalf of soccer in Canada came during his reign as president of the Canadian

Sports Hall of Fame

Soccer Football Association. He set standards of conduct and administered the rules firmly, without fear or favour. Even more important for the development of the game, he launched a five-year program of coaching and clinics across the country to encourage youngsters in the game and improve standards of play.

Bill Simpson also worked tirelessly – and it must be admitted, sometimes fruitlessly – to promote Canadian participation on the international soccer scene. He was mainly responsible for Canada's entry in the Pan-American Games in Winnipeg in 1967. That same year he ran the professional soccer tournament at Expo, whgn teams from England, Russia, West Germany, Austria, Belgium and Mexico played before large, enthusiastic crowds in Montreal.

Bill Simpson's biggest ambition was to see Canada compete in a world series. It was, therefore, a great disappointment to him when Canada was narrowly defeated in the qualifying heats for the world series in 1970, held in Mexico.

But soccer continues to thrive and grow in popularity in Canada. When Bill Simpson was elected to the Sports Hall of Fame in 1968 it was a fitting recognition to his contribution towards that growth.

EDWARD PLUNKET TAYLOR, 1900-

The successes in 1964 of his colt, Northern Dancer, were probably most influential in creating a popular image for E. P. Taylor. Before then, despite his good works in racing and elsewhere, he was the very symbol in Canada of tycoon and "bloated capitalist." Later, there was a steady, broad appreciation of Taylor clearly associated with the international honours he was bringing to Canada. When the Thoroughbred Racing Association elected him as "man of the year" in 1973 and honoured him at a magnificent award banquet in Florida there was wide approval in Canada.

E. P. Taylor was born into an Ottawa banker's family and after graduating in engineering from McGill he joined an investment firm at home. He was in his twenties when he assumed a directorship in a small Ottawa brewery, Bradings, and began reorganizing, consolidating and merging companies, a process usually attended with much controversy. There were thirty-six breweries in Ontario when E. P. Taylor began. He was to acquire more than two-thirds of them, close most, and markedly reduce the number of brands. From his base in Bradings he went on to organize Canadian Breweries Limited and Argus Corporation, the first great Canadian holding company to excite the criticism of Canadian socialists. Over a seven-year period court actions undertaken by the federal government under the Combines Investigation Act moved slowly, with much public attention, to an acquittal for Canadian Breweries and E. P. Taylor. As Barbara Moon noted in *Maclean's*, ". . . . the accompanying publicity and comment left 'Taylor' and 'monopolist' linked in the public mind."

Michael Burns Photography

There were at least two clear and simple ironies in this image of E. P. Taylor. The first was that despite his substantial income and holdings he was far from the wealthiest of all Canadians even though his name was the Canadian parallel to America's Rockefeller in the minds of his countrymen. The second was that his nature or personality was quite at odds with the conception of a scheming, hoarding, harsh capitalist. Like so many horsemen, he is a straightforward, direct man without "side" and pretensions. Perhaps the British racing world saw him more justly as "Eddie" Taylor, the aggressive unsophisticate who was headed on a simple straight-line course towards establishing the best breeding stables in the world.

E. P. Taylor carried out the same kind of consolidation in Ontario racing as he did in brewing. He was elected president of the Ontario Jockey Club in 1973 and during his presidency of twenty years he oversaw the closing of five small and largely dilapidated tracks and the refurbishing of several others, plus the building of new Woodbine racetrack, one of the finest facilities in the world. His rationalization of tracks and race meets extended into harness racing in the three tracks and seasonal meets at Greenwood, Mohawk and Garden City raceways. The quality of the surroundings and the services of OJC tracks became top-flight and the steady improvement in the calibre of horses, trainers, jockeys and purses were all largely consequences of Taylor's standards and determination.

But the aspect of racing in which he himself has the greatest pride is in breeding. In 1970 he was the world's leading breeder of thoroughbreds. From 1960 through 1969 the horses bred at his Windfields Farm won more North American races than those of any other breeder. He is in second place in North America in breeding stakes winners and nine of his horses have been selected Canadian Horse of the Year, and fifteen have won the Queen's Plate. He saw his first great breeding objective met in 1964 when Northern Dancer won the Kentucky Derby, his second when Nijinsky II won the Epsom Derby in 1970. But for all the fascination of victories and acclaim on famous foreign tracks and races, E. P. Taylor probably cherished most the occasions when his horses won the Queen's Plate and he accepted the guineas from the Queen's own hands. Although posterity in Canadian sport is both short and fickle, the scale of Taylor's contribution has been so large over so many years we are sure our children's children will know of him as an exceptional Canadian.

299

The journalism of sports in Canada is slightly more than a century old. Until the advent of film and radio it was confined solely to newspapers and magazines. It has never been a very self-critical journalism nor has it had much outside criticism.

In its beginnings sporting journalism was rather genteel and more concerned with the nature of sport than with those who played it. Only very slowly did sportswriting change, both in style and content. Although early writers aimed for their local public, sporting copy has always had a high degree of uniformity. The telegraph companies, then the wire services, quickly became major suppliers of sports news to the press. Moreover, Canadian sportswriters have always borrowed freely from each other, partly because so many of them know each other and read each other's material.

The colonial press – both French and English – carried sporting items from the start. The first sport to develop regular and thorough coverage was horseracing. By 1841 there was a North American racing annual carrying reports on "all races" in the United States and Canada. Weights, purses, riders, distances, times and wagering provided the bulk of the data but breeding and bloodlines were also featured. The sales and purchases, particularly the importation of sires and dams with good racing lineage, were well followed. The consistent gambling interest, so high in Britain, ran almost as strongly in North America. Of course, horses also represented what today we

In March 1923, Foster Hewitt aired one of the first hockey radio broadcasts ever, from Toronto's Mutual Street Arena. More than fifty years later he still brings the game's excitement to Canadian listeners.

would call an important industry.

Sailing, rowing, and rifle shooting – all functional activities – were the other early sports regularly noted in the pre-confederation papers and journals, along with cricket.

It was not until the 1870s that the post of "sporting editor" emerged in the daily press of Montreal and Toronto. By the 1890s, coincident with the newspaper reproduction of photographs, most dailies were carrying a solid sports page rather than mere "sporting columns" or "sporting items." Publishers of the dailies were coming to realize – partly from the large sales of special sporting magazines – that sports coverage was a magnet for readers. Since the early 1920s the format of the sports pages has not varied greatly, though the modern daily has more pages and features regular columnists of opinion.

Throughout the history of sporting journalism in Canada there has been a close relationship between those who write about sport and those who administer, promote, officiate and coach in sports. Such journalists of different eras as Billie Hewitt, Lou Marsh, Mike Rodden, Francis Nelson, Charlie Good, Doug Peden, Baz O'Meara, Trent Frayne and Jim Coleman were themselves active in sport in one way or another. In recent times, radio and television have given both print journalists and ex-athletes turned journalists many new opportunities for added income and recognition by a broader audience.

It used to be that the sports pages reflected the seasons, but the extension of competitive seasons, especially in professional sports, has blurred this former emphasis. In this, Canada reflects American trends, but unlike American sports pages, those in Canada have never given much more than local promi-

301

nence to school and university competition. Like their counterparts everywhere, Canadian sports pages have always been concerned with records and statistics, beginning with horse-racing and marksmanship, then with cricket, baseball and such later sports as hockey and football. Since the early 1900s, sports photographs, drawings and cartoons have been a staple of the sports pages. The wire service distribution of pictures, nationally and internationally established by 1950, regularized this feature in all but the smallest dailies.

While Canadian sporting journalism has flourished in the press, the same cannot be said of its health in book and magazine form. As early as the 1830s, Canadians began to publish pamphlets about various sports, but the earliest Canadian book devoted wholly to sport, George Beers's book on lacrosse, was not published until 1869. Not many of the surprisingly few Canadian sports books published since have been as good, particularly in terms of instructions for play. The history of periodicals of sports in Canada is a dispiriting record of failure, from the collapse of *Town and Country* in 1881 and the demise of *Athletic Life* in 1892 to the failure of *Sports Canada* in 1970. High distribution costs, inadequate advertising revenue and a shortage of run-in capital have hurt sports periodicals just as they have the Canadian periodical press generally. Another factor has been the penetration of the Canadian market by the slopover of American publications. The trend started in the nineteenth century with the *Police Gazette* and continues today with a number of sports publications such as *Sports Illustrated*. In 1954 when Time Incorporated began the slick weekly, *Sports Illustrated*, the Canadian circulation was 28,000. In 1973 the circulation had grown to 55,000.

It is clear that from the beginning newspapers have been generous in providing space for bulletin board items – the agenda of sports, as it were. Whatever the disproportion allotted to professional sports, it remains true that almost any sporting organization can get its pending activities into print, and if it takes the trouble, secure some notice of their outcome. It is also clear that sporting journalism in Canada has been venturesome in its use of photographers, artists and cartoonists. The early record of the Notman firm in Montreal and its licensees elsewhere was magnificent. Between 1890 and 1905 the Toronto *Globe* gave a lead in photo reproduction not only to other Canadian dailies but also to British and American newspapers. The high period for cartoons and line drawings was in the 1920s and 1930s.

One of the major shifts in the character of Canadian sportswriting has been in the manner of reporting games and matches. Until the 1920s the game itself was the thing. Reporters saw a match as a totality, with a beginning, middle and end, and attempted to convey its essence in terms of tempo, tactics and style. Gradually this form of reporting began to give way to the glorification of individual players or the coaching mastermind. With this change came the "dressing room gambit" with pre- and post-game comments right from the horse's mouth.

Long before reporters could assume that their readers probably had already seen the game on television, it was becoming difficult to find a straightforward account of what actually happened. Tied to this development has been the growth of feature material on athletes and coaches – the "insider" or personality cult fetish. It often seems that unless there is a personality "angle" there is no story. Such an emphasis went hand-in-hand with the rise, from the 1920s, of interest in autobiographical material from athletes. Starting as well-flogged and widely distributed syndicate features, such material has tended to diminish on the sports pages while it has become a flood from the book publishers.

Instructional or "how-to" stories got underway at the turn of the century; a later development was to run such stories, usually syndicated under the byline of some recognized sports figure. In Canada, golf, tennis, badminton, curling and swimming – essentially middle-class activities – were given early prominence in this fashion. More recently, skiing and hockey have taken over.

The most notable recent change in the sports pages has been the growing amount of social, economic and political analysis of sport. This is partly the result of American influence, particularly the struggle by blacks against racial barriers, but it also reflects the scramble by professional athletes for a larger share of the profits. Sport has become the happy hunting ground of the lawyer and the player's agent, and, much more obviously, a capitalist enterprise. At the same time, the intervention of governments at all levels, from subsidization of facilities to support for athletes and organizations engaging in international competition, has forced the Canadian sportswriter, often reluctantly, to depart from what Dick Beddoes has called his "toy universe."

One element of our sports pages goes back to the earliest traditions of sportswriting in Canada. Stories on outdoor recreation have to do, of course, with the first meaning of the word "sport": riding, hunting, fishing, a man and his friends in the great outdoors. It was almost obligatory for early British travellers to include in their books some description of Canadian field sports; George Head's *Forest*

Scenes and Incidents in the Wilds of North America (1829) is typical of the genre. Canadian sports journalism has always been concerned with such subjects, although it was not until the 1920s that they were to be found mainly on the sports pages of the newspaper. Today such columns are generally complemented by advertising placed in juxtaposition to them, whether it has to do with recreational resorts, powerboats and snowmobiles, or outdoor sporting goods. If many Canadian sportwriters have been closely associated with sports promoters, outdoor recreational writers have frequently been linked with sporting goods manufacturers and distributors, or have been handmaidens to the tourist industry.

Of course, the presence of the entrepreneur on the margin of the sporting scene – and not always on the margin – can be detected in sporting journalism from its beginnings in Canada. For the most part, the sporting press has gone along, willingly enough, whether it was a matter of promoting the Montreal winter carnival in the 1880s as a generator of tourist revenue, or the more recent activities of liquor, beer and tobacco interests in supporting such events as the Canadian Brier and the Grey Cup. Close association with sporting events continues to be important to business enterprises in terms of winning society's approval. For sports journalism the benefits range from the uncomplicated approval of support for sport to such considerations as advertising revenues and opportunities for sports reporters in the public relations field.

When Canadian sports journalism began, the reporter's biggest task was to provide local coverage. That duty has been consistently adhered to, although later developments have overshadowed local sport in the big-city dailies. National and North American coverage came together in the late 1870s, with the help of the telegraph. In the past twenty years, there has been a rapid growth of North American (read US) material in Canadian sports pages, and it has diminished both national and local coverage. American radio and television, reaching easily into most parts of populated Canada, has built an audience for American sporting events, and our press reflects the fact. Before 1914, much British sporting news was found in English-Canadian newspapers, but it has been receding steadily since the early 1920s. European and international coverage generally has never been strong in the Canadian press, although the post-1945 European immigration has led many dailies to publish items such as the European soccer scores. For the most part, however, international coverage of this type is restricted to the international autoracing circuits and to the Olympics.

What sports get the most coverage, and in what ways? A 1970 study, *Sports in the Daily Press in Canada*, compiled for the federal government, examined thirty dailies for three mid-year months of 1969. Five sports – baseball, horseracing, golf, football and hockey – were allotted about two-thirds of the space and comprised about two-thirds of all the items. (Sports coverage itself got 15 percent of newspaper space, ahead of politics and government with 12.7 percent and foreign affairs with 4.4 percent, but behind a category called "human interest" which included comics, crosswords, assorted advice columns and astrology.) Local and regional stories got more than 30 percent of total sports coverage. More than half of the stories came from the staffs of the publishing papers; smaller city dailies, however, tended to depend more heavily on wire service stories.

This study reached some predictable conclusions. Just about 65 percent of the sports stories were about professional sport. While it

When Canadian women began to make their mark athletically in the 1920s most major newspapers hired female ex-athletes as reporters. Myrtle Cook was one of the best in both fields.

Alexandra Studio

303

was found that seven of ten stories originated in Canada (the bulk of the others originating in the US), this figure was misleading, since much of the material classified as Canadian had to do with the "Canadian content" of American professional sport, whether horseracing, baseball, golf or hockey.

Most predictable of all was the fact that 87 percent of the stories were about male activities. That has always been so. When Canadian women began to make their mark athletically in the 1920s, most major newspapers hired female sports reporters, usually ex-athletes like Bobbie Rosenfeld, Myrtle Cook and Phyllis Griffiths. There was more coverage of women's sport from 1925 to 1939 than there is today – a striking anomaly, particularly in view of the fact that, ever since the dramatic display of the women's track team at the Amsterdam Olympics in 1928, Canadian women have always done better than men in international sport.

As the federal study verified, amateur sport comes off very poorly in the press (and there is no reason to think that it does any better on TV and radio, which receive sports news from the same wire services). Most amateur sports coverage deals with schools and universities, and occasionally a major track meet, but the newspaper space allotted does not begin to compare with that given the five major professional sports. In both column inches and frequency of items, thoroughbred- and harness-racing alone get far more coverage annually than school and university sport. The reason for this is understandable. The volume of American and professional sports material, with accompanying running statistics and daily feature stories, which pours from the wire services is immense. It is not only easier to use such material, but it is highly likely that both sports staffs and their readers prefer it. If a Canadian athlete wishes to achieve national recognition, he had best compete in a professional sport with an American and international context. Except for "builders" the chances of a Canadian athlete entering the Sports Hall of Fame on the basis of purely Canadian achievements are slight.

Apparently it is just about as difficult for a Canadian sportswriter to obtain entry. There are only two in the hall of fame, Ted Reeve and Elmer Ferguson (and no one would quarrel with their recognition), but everyone interested in sports has his favourite. One suspects that if a group of editors were asked to compile an anthology of the best Canadian sportswriting in English from the millions of words that have been written, they would pick (in addition to articles by Reeve and Ferguson) a good number of selections from Ralph Allen

and Jim Coleman among the moderns and some from George Beers and Tait Mackenzie from the early period. Scott Young in the *Globe and Mail* once wrote about honours paid to sportswriters: "A writer lives only through what he has written. Even that in most lives is fleeting." Young went on to say:

> A former *Star* sports editor, Lou Marsh, is honoured annually with an award and a dinner. The award is okay, but the dinner is painful; full of people who have trouble remembering who Lou Marsh was. The city sends an alderman, the NHL an owner (never Conn Smythe, who deplored Lou Marsh), and even the *Star* itself tends to send a representation that is more token than real. Maybe it's better to die only once, instead of once a year.

Scott Young's observation is given added point by the fact that Lou Marsh was a significant figure in the history of Canadian sporting journalism. He began with the *Star* as a fourteen-year-old copyboy, in 1893. When he died in 1936 he had been the *Star's* sports editor for six years. In the intervening years, as an athlete, official, promoter and writer, he had been involved with many sports. Big, strong, smart and brash, Marsh had been a fair sprinter, a good lineman with the Argonauts, a very good swimmer, an accomplished sailor and iceboater, and a first-class baseball player and boxer. He was a product of Tom Flanagan's St. Patrick's Athletic Club. As a sportswriter, Marsh flourished under the general editorship of Billie Hewitt; it was Marsh's drive that made the *Star,* for its time, Canada's most aggressive daily in sports coverage. His column, "Pick and Shovel," with its highly personal criticism, was the first of a new type. His flair was for liveliness and argument, not fine writing. Yet he could be inventive with language – for example, the word "seaflea" was coined by him. He was well known throughout the province as a hockey referee of the battling type. "The only way to stop a mob rush is to go after the first man and down him with a fast wallop," Marsh once said.

Now this vital man lives on only in the memories of senior members of his craft such as veteran Michael J. Rodden, born at Mattawa, Ontario, in 1891. Mike Rodden's memory is still phenomenal. Football has been his chief love, as player and coach, but he was a good hockey player, a tough hockey referee, a sportswriter, sports editor and columnist. He wrote his first story for the Toronto *Globe* in 1918 and still produced the occasional column for the Kingston *Whig Standard* in 1973. From 1920 through the early 1930s he was the most successful and most combative football coach in the country, coaching the Parkdale Canoe Club, the Argonauts, the Hamilton Tiger Cats and several other teams.

A member of both the Hockey Hall of Fame and Football Hall of Fame, Mike Rodden was also a referee, sportswriter, editor and columnist in the Toronto *Globe* and Kingston *Whig Standard*.

Mike Rodden is also a student of sportswriting history, and his judgments should not be challenged lightly. In his view, the first well-organized sports page in a North American newspaper was established by W. G. H. Good in the *Globe* in 1883. Comparison of the Canadian dailies on microfilm bears out this judgment; the *Globe* was well ahead of Montreal, Ottawa and other Toronto papers. By the early 1900s, however, the *Globe* had plenty of competition from the *Herald* and the *Star* in Montreal, and the *Star,* the *Telegram* and the *Mail* in Toronto. In Rodden's view, the best Canadian sportswriter is none of those we have named, but Francis Nelson, the *Globe* 's sports editor before 1914. His style was spare but his judgments were authoritative – he knew thoroughly the sports he wrote about – and he never offered an opinion without supporting it.

Yet there must be other Francis Nelsons this brief survey omits – journalists from Quebec and the Maritimes admired by their readers and ignored by metropolitan audiences. No survey, however, could pass over the flowering of a remarkably able group of writers in depression Winnipeg. If Jim Coleman, Ralph Allen, Trent Frayne, and Scott Young were subtracted from recent Canadian sportswriting, a large hole would be left, and a good deal of excellent wit would have gone unrecorded. And these men were only the most notable among a talented group. The late Johnny Buss of the Winnipeg *Tribune* established a standard of coverage for curling that is still maintained by his own newspaper as well as the *Free Press* and other Prairie papers. Herb Manning who died in his early forties after joining the Vancouver *Sun* was another polished writer. Tony Allan and Vince Leah were two others who

gave the *Tribune* one of the least parochial and most exciting sports pages in Canadian journalistic history. Why Winnipeg produced so much talent at one time (as it did in many other fields) is problematical. The city was certainly a football and hockey hotbed and it was the curling capital of Canada. But it was and remains the least insular of Canadian cities, looking east and west as well as south.

Although there are plenty of colourful and argumentative sportwriters around today, a good deal of richness has departed from the field. Today there are only a hundred-odd dailies in the country, and most of our large cities have only one or two papers. In the 1920s there were many more dailies, more sports pages, and much more variety in sports reporting, while competition between newspapers in the promotion of various sports and sporting events was at a peak. In Toronto, Montreal, Winnipeg, Vancouver, Hamilton and many other cities every paper had its annual favourite for promotion and sponsorship – road races, marathons, speed-skating tournaments, regattas, lacrosse trophies, bowling, and softball tournaments, bonspiels. Since 1945 this partisanship has tapered off, partly because there are fewer papers, partly because of the mesmerizing effect of professional sport on big-city audiences.

To some degree, the radio and televi-

Ace Foley, sports editor emeritus of the Halifax *Herald,* still contributes columns to the paper while serving on the selection committee of the Sports Hall of Fame.

Another polished sportswriter who came out of Winnipeg was Herb Manning. He died in his early forties after joining the Vancouver *Sun*.

sion networks have filled this gap. In fact, the impact of the electronic media upon sports journalism and upon sport in general has been immense. Both radio and television provide what newspapers cannot – "you-are-there" sensation. When this is joined to the capacity to serve an audience of millions, it is scarcely surprising that the electronic media far surpass print journalism in creating huge numbers of sports fans and in providing millions of athletic youngsters with new sporting heroes and heroines.

The hunger of the sports enthusiast for immediacy did, of course, predate radio and television. When professional hockey playoffs had their beginnings before the first world war, crowds that gathered in front of newspaper offices across Canada would stand, stamping their feet in the cold, waiting to get the first wire reports of results. W. A. Hewitt, in his autobiography, *Down the Stretch,* described a successful enterprise of his from the same period. It was, in effect, a huge outdoor baseball scoreboard, fed by wire reports, which enabled Toronto crowds to follow World Series games as they took place.

It was Hewitt's son, Foster, who pioneered sports broadcasting in Canada and whose broadcasts focused and intensified national interest in hockey. (The first hockey broadcast was by Norman Albert on 8 February 1923, when he described for listeners to CFCA, the Toronto *Star*'s station, the last period of a game between North Toronto and Midland.) On 22 March 1923, nineteen-year-old Foster Hewitt gave his first play-by-play broadcast; by the end of the decade, his broadcasts had become a

regular feature over the new network facilities. "He shoots. He scores!" became the Hewitt trademark, but a more significant phrase was the equally familiar, "Hello hockey fans in Canada and the United States." The driving tenor voice and descriptive phrases of Foster Hewitt made NHL hockey a Saturday-night obsession from sea to sea. The broadcasts were the product of a unique triumvirate, which foresaw the vital role that radio could play in making fans for the newly opened Maple Leaf Gardens: Conn Smythe, the colourful entrepreneur who daringly built the gardens in the hard years of 1930-1; Billie Hewitt, sports editor of the *Star,* secretary of the Ontario Hockey Association; and Smythe's long-time friend and associate; and Foster himself, by this time the leader of sports broadcasting at CFCA.

The jury is still out on what the long-term impact of television will be upon sport. This unchained monster raises both hope and apprehension in the hearts of sports promoters and administrators. "Television has made a substantial contribution to the development of spectator interest in Canadian football to its current all-time high level, but could inadvertently be its instrument of doom in the 1970s," Jake Gaudaur, the CFL commissioner remarked in 1970.

A few consequences are clear. If sport has a short memory, television has amnesia. Since every event is a promotion, the usual sports hyperbole about the "greatest game" or the "greatest series" is magnified time and time again. All is flux, perspectives evaporate, heroes are made and unmade overnight. Even as the latest superlative event unfolds before

Foster Hewitt pioneered sports broadcasting in Canada, focusing national interest on hockey.

our eyes, the practitioners of television journalism are beating the drums through superimposed graphics and voice-overs for the new crest yet to come.

Television is a fickle bride, mating well with some sports, awkwardly with others. Baseball has too broad a scope for its peering eye; the concentration upon pitcher and batter distorts the game's traditional symmetries. Football is transformed, as for the first time spectators are brought right into the complex and violent warfare on the field. The speed, fluidity, glitter and clash of hockey are matchlessly caught by the camera. Television has raised the Canadian consciousness of hockey to a level unparalleled by any other interest that binds or divides us as a people, as the extraordinary magnetism of the Team Canada-USSR series of 1972 demonstrated. A kind of pinnacle of national consciousness was reached; being a nation, in Canadian terms, may not only consist of doing things together but watching hockey together.

Television's appetite is insatiable. If the trite detective or western series is exhausted in a season, so also the scientific marvel of space flight jades its audience after a time. Television has found perhaps its most lucrative market in sport. Yet what will be the consequences of so much televised sport upon sport's most vital level, participation on the local scene? Television shows us sport played superbly in a dimension almost larger than life. How far will such experience erode our capacity to play or to enjoy sports spontaneously and unself consciously in our own communities?

Surely, more than ever before, there is a need for sporting journalism with some sense of proportion, a saving wit, and a vision of sport that embraces more than the latest electronic promotion. Back in 1934, an American city editor, Stanley Walker, divided sportswriters into two groups, and a few years ago columnist John Crosby commented on these types, "the Gee Whizz crowd" and "the Aw Nuts group":

> The Gee Whizz school was started by Grantland Rice, the first educated American sportswriter, which is to say he finished school. Any sporting contest, no matter how picayune, reminded Grantland Rice of the Spartans at Thermopylae. . . . The Aw Nuts school of sportswriting was founded by Ring Lardner, who thought most athletes belonged in schools for retarded children; most sports promoters, he thought, belonged in jail.

Canada certainly has not lacked the healthy sceptics of the Aw Nuts school. Lou Marsh and Andy Lytle (first of the Vancouver *Sun* then successor to Marsh at the *Star*) were classic debunkers, though they had a considerable admiration for the exceptional performer. Among the moderns, Dick Beddoes of the *Globe and Mail* is certainly a leader of the sandbaggers'

Winnepeg Tribune

Vince Leah, Winnipeg *Tribune* sportswriter, devoted much of his time to the organization and promotion of neighbourhood sport for kids.

chorus. "We're aware of a grave world beyond the playpen of the sports department," he has written; and John Robertson of the Montreal *Star*, Ted Blackman of the Montreal *Gazette*, Jim Taylor of the Vancouver *Sun*, and Jack Matheson of the Winnipeg *Tribune* are all columnists who share his irreverence. All these writers delight in challenging managerial and promotional authority in major sports to an extent undreamed of in earlier, less blunt eras.

In a special way, men like Ted Reeve, Vince Leah, Scotty Melville, Bill Westwick, Baz O'Meara, Charlie Good and Ace Foley made positive contributions to Canadian sporting journalism over the years. All of them instinctively recognized the bond between winners and losers, between the greats at the gardens and the kids on the corner lots. Roger Kahn, one of the ablest of American sportswriters, has written that "clearly sports is significant . . . It is a theater of truth and it holds up a mirror to society and humanity." Not many Canadian sportwriters would feel comfortable with such a statement, although oddly enough, the idea would have been most acceptable to our gentlemen-sportswriters of the late nineteenth century. Yet in the recent surge of book publishing there are favourable auguries, as in Jim Coleman's evocative *Hoofbeats on My Heart*, in Jack Batten's *Champions* and even in the muckraking approach of Bruce Kidd and John Macfarlane's *The Death of Hockey* and Laverne Barnes's *The Plastic Orgasm*. The bars of the playpen are dropping, and Canadian sports, now part of the mainstream of Canadian life, must face appreciation and assessment not only on their own terms but also in the broadest social, cultural and political sense.

Biographies

favour in his heart, Elmer had ambitions in the wider world, and in 1910 he made his way, first to Boston, then to Montreal. He left the *Transcript* after achieving a first for the Maritimes, a full page of sports daily.

After a brief stint on a church paper, the Montreal *Daily Witness,* Elmer switched to the *Herald,* because the *Witness*'s publisher frowned on any coverage of pro sport. Elmer went through a number of posts at the *Herald* – telegraph editor, city editor, news editor, drama critic – until he succeeded Frank Calder as sports editor in 1913. Frank went on to become the first president of the National Hockey League.

Elmer remained as sports editor of the *Herald* for thirty-nine years, and then carried on as a sports columnist until the *Herald* died in 1957, whereupon he moved his column, "The Gist and Jest of It," over to the *Star* where he continued until his death.

In the early twenties he was the first secretary of the newly founded athletic commission and held the post for more than twenty years. He was invariably a judge or steward at the Montreal racetracks. When the NHL went international in the mid-1920s, Elmer was the league's first publicity man.

In reading over some of the millions of words Elmer wrote for the *Herald* and the

ELMER W. FERGUSON, 1885-1972

History and perspective in Canadian sports journalism have come largely from a few of its practitioners with good memories and story-telling gifts. Perish the idea that Elmer Ferguson was one who belaboured the past, even towards the end of his sixty-two years of sportswriting: he helped give unity and texture to Canadian sport because he had literally seen them all.

Born in Prince Edward Island, young Fergy moved with his family to Moncton, NB when he was a baby. He began selling newspapers in the streets at six years of age, and later he became a newsie on the Intercolonial Railway. He was persuaded to take a business course in typing and shorthand by the owner of the Moncton *Transcript* and after completing it, he became a railway clerk. He didn't like the job and hired on as a copyboy at the *Transcript* in 1902 at the age of seventeen for three dollars a week. Although he began as a sportswriter, he worked his way up through city editor to news editor in eight years. He was athletically inclined and a fair sprinter, but a crippled arm, injured in a diving accident, inhibited top-flight achievement. However, he competed up to the age of twenty-three and had printed evidence and a gold medal to show that he had run the 100-yard dash in ten seconds flat on Labour Day 1908 at Springhill, NS.

At Moncton he began what would become part of his life for decades – working outside his newspaper duties as a sports official, serving as secretary for hockey and baseball leagues in New Brunswick.

Although the Maritimes never lost

Sports Hall of Fame

Star, several distinguishing qualities emerge. His interests were so broad he could offer his readers variety, and his style was vivid but simple. He was clearly more interested in personalities than techniques or strategy. He crammed an enormous number of names and opinions into his columns, and a reader of his was generally in touch with the sports and entertainment world of Montreal and New York – indeed of North America. His gossip was benign, humorous, and wry, but never malicious. He rarely feuded with anyone in his columns, as did Lou Marsh and Andy Lytle of the Toronto *Star,* nor was he a gee-whizzer. Honours from his peers and from sporting organizations came to him thick and fast.

Elmer Ferguson was a strong advocate of Sports Halls of Fame, and he brought to both the Canadian Sports Hall of Fame and the Hockey Hall of Fame the perception of his achievements over half a century.

"Strictly from a sentimental viewpoint," he wrote when the Canada Sports Hall of Fame asked him to join its selection board, "the hall of fame is a most valuable asset to Canada, its athletes and those who follow the athletic fortunes of our country."

It seems bootless to write further in appreciation of Elmer Ferguson as a man and as a symbolic figure in sport and sports journalism when Jim Coleman put it all so well in his column in the Toronto *Sun,* on 28 April, 1972:

> One of the secrets of Elmer Ferguson's longevity was his pleasant cynicism. Fergy, who died Wednesday in Montreal at the age of eighty-seven, made a career of watching the sporting scene from the sideline. Amused, tolerant, but seldom permitting himself to become deeply involved emotionally. . . . He had outlived most of his contemporaries. Accordingly, there are few persons left who can appraise his literary talents accurately. When he was at the height of his middle-aged writing production, Fergy was a sports columnist in the same class with Damon Runyan, Westbrook Pegler and Henry McLemore.
>
> His audience was small in those days because he presided over the sports desk at the Montreal *Herald,* which had a circulation of 50,000. Nevertheless, in journalistic circles he enjoyed an international reputation as a witty, exceptionally skillful writer and he was a very, very funny man.
>
> Apart from Montrealers, the only Canadians who will remember Elmer Ferguson are those who are at least in their late thirties or early forties. They will remember him for his contributions to the old Hot Stove League on the Saturday night hockey broadcast, a weekly show which became obsolete when national network television emerged.
>
> Fergy's sardonic comment and his encyclopedic knowledge of hockey lore rescued those Hot Stove League shows from banality. He was at his best if he had taken a few belts of the sturdy stuff before he went on the air; the judicious use of rye

whiskey lubricated Elmer's voice and his imagination.

> Elmer Ferguson lived with tremendous zest. After his first wife died in 1934, he became a man-about-town, who kept hours which appalled his younger and fresher colleagues. He seldom quit his ringside table until the last cabaret in town had closed down for the night. . . . there wasn't the slightest tinge of hypocrisy in Elmer Ferguson's makeup. Accordingly, he will arise from his grave to protest if his obituary writers depict him as a saintly old gentleman, remembered chiefly for his good works.
>
> Fergy was the last of an 'old breed' of sports editors; hardy realists who expected to receive cash tributes from importunate sports promoters . . . Mind you, I am writing of an era when 'payola' was a sorry fact of journalistic life. . . . In Montreal newspaper apocrypha there is a legend that Fergy gave his *Herald* salary to the chauffeur of his personal Cadillac limousine.
>
> Thus Elmer Ferguson never deluded himself with the thought that pro sport is as important as religion or motherhood. He admired individual athletes; he lived in amiable co-existence with sports promoters, but his attitude towards them was far short of reverence.
>
> Basically, Elmer Ferguson was a very kind man; always he was particularly generous in his encouragement of younger people who laboriously were climbing the ladder of journalism.

EDWARD H. REEVE, 1902-

In November 1930, the day after the annual Grey Cup game the following ditty appeared above Ted Reeve's daily sports column in the Toronto *Telegram*:

> When I was young and in my prime
> I used to block kicks all the time,
> But now that I am old and grey
> I only block them once a day.

In his typically modest, self-mocking tone the Old Groaner told his readers of his own key block in the Grey Cup game.

Balmy Beach, the Toronto team that Reeve had helped establish, was meeting the Regina Roughriders in the final game of the 1930 season. Reeve, with a shoulder injury from an earlier game, sat out three quarters of the game on the bench. In the final quarter, Regina seemed to be moving towards the winning score when Reeve took to the field. On the third down he barged through the line and blocked the Regina punt; Balmy Beach recovered and went on to win the game 10-6. Reeve was the hero of the hour and his jubilant teammates carried him shoulder-high from the field. It was to be his last big football game.

Lionel Conacher once described Ted Reeve as a man who "had all the requisites of a great athlete, except a body strong enough to carry out the things his mind wanted to do." Certainly in his years as a competitor playing football and lacrosse, Reeve had more than his share of accidents and broken bones. The list includes two skull

Jimmy Longfellow's Beaches team. Ted Reeve still remembers the thrill of those games:

> Thus it was we first watched bug-eyed one summer day on that wide green field when the flags were flying over the white grandstand; the band played from the awninged clubhouse and 17,000 fans poured in by the old open streetcars to see the unit we still recall as the most sensational of them all, the Nationals – "home" of Lalonde, Boulaine, Lamoureaux, Daredevil Gauthier and Didre Pitre . . . There was a verve, a dash and a sensational swing to their play as stirring as a bugle call.

Ted started to play for the Beaches, and this got him started in the writing business. Jimmy Longfellow asked him to write publicity releases for the papers, which led first to a lacrosse column in the *Star Weekly* and then to a daily column for the *Telegram* during the lacrosse season.

Ted Reeve was soon well known on the lacrosse and football fields. He began his football career with the St. Aidan juniors and then moved up to play for the Argonauts. In 1924 he organized the Balmy Beach club, and remained with them as player, coach and ardent supporter. The team won the Ontario Rugby Football Union title in 1927, and the Grey Cup in 1927 and 1930.

But lacrosse was the game that gave Reeve the greatest pleasure. Bill Beatty invited him to join the Brampton Excelsiors, and Reeve played for them for four years. Three times he played for teams that won the Mann Cup – for Oshawa in 1928, and for Brampton in 1926 and 1930. Ted Reeve remembers that 1926 championship game against Weston as his most satisfying day as an athlete. Here is his description of that day, written more than twenty years later:

> A great crowd that had come driving in from all over the countryside that Saturday had broken loose in a ferocious free-for-all in the first quarter. A six-goal lead won in Brampton had been almost swept away by a tremendous and sustained drive of the entire Weston team that brought them four straight tallies. Then the Excelsiors broke out for two counters – and proceeded to hang on grimly through the wildest, hardest-hitting everything-goes sport struggle we have ever seen or ever been in.
>
> There comes one spot in the career of every athlete when he senses "This is it. This is the best we will ever be in, this is as good as we will ever be." One such an afternoon as that when you are young and hefty can be worth a score of seasons sitting and watching someone else do it.

The time came when Reeve had to let someone else do it, but the next best thing to being in the thick of the action was to coach others. In the 1930s he coached the Balmy Beach team, then coached the Queen's University team of Kingston, Ontario, to three

fractures, a broken leg, a broken nose, several broken fingers, and an arthritic condition that has become increasingly painful with the years. Nothing has kept Ted Reeve down. When his playing days were over he turned with phenomenal success to coaching. And since 1928, when he first started to write the daily column, "Sporting Extras," for the *Telegram,* he has been delighting sports fans across Canada with his unique brand of humour, knowledge and nostalgia.

Ted Reeve is a Torontonian through and through. He was born in the Beaches district where his mother ran a bookstore, and it was while working there in his youth that Ted had his first contact with great literature. He read everything including the *Encyclopedia Britannica,* and it was from this early reading that the inimitable Reeve style developed. Dickens was one of his favourite authors and in Reeve's opinion "the best reporter I have ever read, even if his plots were awful."

Watching field lacrosse was also part of his youthful experience. Nearby Scarborough Beach stadium was the home of intercollegiate championships.

Back in Toronto in 1928 "Full-time out of work . . . also limping," Reeve went to see C. O. Knowles. The managing editor of the *Telegram,* Knowles was looking for a columnist in response to the tough competition provided by caustic Lou Marsh in the rival Toronto *Star.* The same week, the *Tely* put Phyllis Griffiths, a reporter and good athlete, on as its first women's sports columnist, a match-up with Alexandrine Gibb, the dean of women sportswriters at the *Star.*

There have been few more respected Canadian newspapermen in his time than the late J. V. McAree, the erudite columnist for decades with the old Toronto *Mail* and later with the *Globe and Mail.* On 13 September 1939, in his "Fourth Column" McAree wrote:

> Many of our own readers . . . are aware of a very striking feature of one of the afternoon newspapers. We have in mind Sporting Extras, by Mr. Ted Reeve in the *Telegram.* It is in our opinion the wittiest commentary upon current sports published not only in this city but on this continent. There are not many Canadians in any field who can be rated with or above the best Americans . . . Ted Reeve is almost unfailingly critical, informative and humorous. He not only writes with a most incisive wit, but his wit is employed to describe and illuminate something. He is not merely clowning, he is describing something that has happened so that he can be read for improvement by one with no sense of humour and for amusement by one having no particular interest in sport. . . .
>
> Among others he knows Dickens and Thackeray and Shakespeare, which probably makes him unique among sportswriters and also explains why he differed from most of them in having the writing man's interest in and respect for words.

In 1931 Ted Reeve married a Manitoba girl, Alvern Florence Donaldson. She was a superb athlete in her own right – a .300 plus hitter in top-flight softball, a high-scoring basketball player, and as Constance Hennessy remembers, "simply a beautiful hockey player, as good as Bobbie Rosenfeld and lovelier to watch."

When the second world war came Ted was nearly forty, but was eventually accepted. In 1941 Conn Smythe formed his sportsman's battery – the 30th Light Anti-Aircraft. Reeve joined and served as a gunner in Europe for three years. He fractured his elbow during the fighting around Caen in 1944 and was invalided home.

Back in Toronto after the war, Reeve resumed his daily column with the *Telegram,* and rapidly became one of Toronto's best-known newspapermen. George McCullagh, owner of the *Globe and Mail,* bought the *Telegram* for $3.6 million. As he later commented about the price: "That was a hell of a lot of money, but it was worth it – just to get Ted Reeve."

With unshakeable faith in athletes, Reeve often seems isolated from the larger affairs of the world but Ted Reeve as columnist has never been isolated from the grander themes and values of life beyond sport. Several qualities of his work are constant beacons – friendliness, fair play, generosity, and affection for kids, dogs and cats, his hometown, his neighbourhood, his rivals on the field and in the papers. Several attributes made him more than just a beloved Toronto institution. In football, in particular, and to a lesser degree through lacrosse, rowing and hockey, he has been the personal cement binding sportswriters, athletes, coaches and managers together in a long fellowship.

There's a plum-pudding richness to Reeve columns. Verses and jingles abound. He mocked himself and got good satirical advantage from some of his pseudonymous characterizations of himself – "The Squire of Squawg Hollow," "Moaner McGuffy," "Alice Snippersnapper," and "Nutsy Fagan." Each year his Christmas Eve story is a delight for adults that children can share. He has never flagged in his admiration for British values, and like Conn Smythe, his commanding officer during the war, he campaigned for retention of the Red Ensign.

The late J. P. Fitzgerald, *Tely* sports editor, wrote on Ted's return from the war in 1945 to a mob welcome ranging from the mayor to Reeve buddies of the Offshore Yacht Club (that is, the Beaches): "Perhaps no athlete or sportsman in this city ever had a following like Ted Reeve, and certainly no sportswriter had or has."

Another *Tely* colleague, the late Frank Tumpane, captured another quality of Reeve's: "I don't believe he was ever afraid of anybody, either in the physical or moral sense."

If Ted Reeve seems in retrospect almost everyone's ideal as both athlete and sportswriter, a sceptic may wonder whether the richness of his personality and work have blinded us to flaws. They seem hard to find. Perhaps as a writer he has had too much faith in the good intentions of both the athletes and sport promoters and so has enhanced an element of exclusiveness in the camaraderie of sport. He's conservatively minded and devoted to old traditions and nostalgia but that's a trait, not a fault. Memories, as we've said before, are short-lived in sport. For many, it's today's hero, tomorrow's game. Ted Reeve bridged and tied together the times and people of Canadian sport over decades with his carefully crafted prose and his gift of anecdote and analysis.

312

The Future

Chapter 13

Sports, for many people, is what fills a disproportionate amount of space in their daily newspaper and a correspondingly large chunk of time in their weekend TV schedule. Most of this coverage of sports in space, time and emphasis is professional sports, the big leagues, the crucial game, the scoring records, the wisdom – or its lack – displayed by the coach, manager or owner.

In the past twenty years, and with an almost frightening tempo in the last five years, pro sports have expanded in all directions. Sports once considered the amateurs' domain in North America (tennis, soccer and skiing, for example) are now dominated by professionals. Sports careers with salaries in the six-figure bracket attract thousands of youngsters. Given the dominance of professional sports and the relentless rhythm of their seasons, it is impossible to project the future of Canadian sports in other than a professional context.

Before anyone can consult the crystal ball, he must realize that there has been, in the years since the end of the second world war, a fundamental change in the pattern of Canadian sports development. Sports and recreation are increasingly entering the realm of public – that is, governmental – policy.

In part, this increasing emphasis is the result of a growing awareness of the part sport plays in shaping our distinctiveness as Canadians. Much of our history has been uneventful; this nation was *not* forged in a colonial war and was *not* tested by a civil war. Our historians have tried to fill this void with the cult of the great individual (Sir John A. Macdonald), or by recounting an economic epic **The architect's models for the buildings planned for the 1976 Olympic Games in Montreal graphically represent Canada's sports future.** *Above,* **Olympic Park.** *Below,* **Olympic Village.**

(building the CPR). But sport is one of the few dimensions of our life in which genuinely national folk heroes have been created and whose careers touch the mind of the people. The athletes represented in the Sports Hall of Fame have come from virtually every ethnic strand in our makeup, and their exploits, even dimly remembered, have bound us together.

All of these athletes have functioned within a web of relationships largely unexplored by historians and as a result the place of sport in Canadian life has been almost unacknowledged. The creativity of politicians in constructing the institutions to hold together a vast country, and their ingenuity in making them work; the daring involved in linking our spaces; the statesmanship implicit in the recognition that serious regional and social disparities have to be corrected – all these have been marked and celebrated. But the same creativity, ingenuity and daring has marked our sporting history, with incalculable consequences in creating a sense of ourselves as Canadians. We have reached a stage in our history when the vitality of our volunteer sports organizations is no longer adequate to meet the new demands made upon it.

When John Munro, health minister in the federal cabinet, announced in 1969 that, "We as a government accept responsibility for fostering sport, increasing its level of participation and improving its excellence," he heralded a period (we are still in it) of increased federal support for a sustained and diverse attack on the problems of sport and recreation in Canada. This commitment is probably the most significant intervention in sport in this century. It threatens or promises – depending on one's point of view – to affect profoundly both the texture and content of Canada's sporting program, just as it may influence the health of

Canadian society.

There were precedents for such governmental intervention. Sports bodies have always wished for and sometimes demanded the endorsement of government to cloak them with legitimacy or to endow them with emotional or financial support. What is unique in our current situation is the scale and impact of the initiative.

Sport previously enjoyed assistance from government as a privilege; now, the administrators of sports expect it as a matter of need and of right. The fact of government support has never been in doubt since 1969, but now it is certain that the level of financial aid will increase and that fewer qualms will be felt about it by politicians, bureaucrats and athletes.

Another minister of health, Marc Lalonde, pointed out in March 1973:

> I don't think it's necessary any longer to justify our being involved in sports and fitness, any more than we have to justify federal government's purpose – in sports and fitness as in everything else – which is to help all Canadians to enjoy richer, fuller and more satisfying lives.

Early in 1974 Lalonde proved that his policy was not all wind and no action; he introduced legislation in the House of Commons to prevent teams associated with the new World Football League playing in Canada. The Toronto Northmen – the first and only Canadian

Federal health minister, Marc Lalonde, early in 1974, introduced legislation that would have banned the World Football League from operating in Canada.

franchise in the WFL – subsequently pulled up stakes and moved to Memphis, Tennessee, where the team operated as the Southmen.

Lalonde's view – and he was surely speaking and acting for the government – puts sports right into the centre of public policy. But underlying this commitment is a problem that has not yet been fully faced: Who is to provide the direction for sport and recreation in Canada?

Hitherto, the prime source of direction has been outside government. In the nineteenth and early twentieth centuries, the social élite – members of the military, educational institutions, and the business community – guided sport as patrons and by setting the rules of play. The "upper crust" established clubs, competitions, and administrative structure, financed its progress and, in some degree, determined the level and conditions of mass involvement. The ethos of the age dictated that private enterprise, volunteer leadership, and relatively exclusive clubs should be the original driving forces.

The first sporting facilities such as pools, arenas, stadia, and sporting grounds were built or laid out as much for private profit as for public enjoyment. The role of governments was small. Municipalities were prodded to establish and maintain a minimum of public recreational facilities such as playgrounds, swimming beaches and docks, particularly in the interwar period. No one became upset if towns and cities organized teams, aided existing clubs with land or money, or encouraged such activities as fairs and sporting meets. Public leaders, from the governor-general down to local aldermen, were expected to lend their patronage to sporting activities in forms all the way from personal participation in prize-giving to administration. Out of the office of the governor-general there erupted in the Victorian period a collection of cups, medals and other awards with an exuberant profusion that was never to be repeated.

The federal government's direct role, on the other hand, was marginal. Early on, sports leaders were sceptical if not genuinely hostile to governmental influence above the municipal level. Aside from believing that public money and officialdom had no right to be in sport, sportsmen feared that government intervention would undermine their positions and destroy the volunteer gentility and self-willed endeavour which gave sport its special virtue.

To sportsmen, their field was not suffering from a diminished capacity to manage its own affairs. On the government side, there was a matching tendency for politicians to avoid any commitment or undertaking which might offend the national, provincial and local regulatory bodies of sport. The constitutional divisions of powers seemed to leave sport to the provinces and sports administration was fragmented. Budget priorities never placed national sports or recreation very high. Government intervened only in special circumstances. For instance, as early as the 1860s the federal government encouraged rifle matches and jaunts of marksmen abroad through grants, but this was justified as a defense measure, not as an encouragement to sport.

When the modern Olympic Games settled into a quadrennial pattern after the first world war, Ottawa accepted a small responsibility as a partial bankroller for Canadian teams. It had also endorsed a range of physical activities through the militia programs and the network of armouries, and it administered the endowment of the Strathcona Trust through the high schools. It encouraged the breeding of racehorses through the department of agriculture and punished both aberrant forms of sport like cock-fighting, and dangerous and brutal pastimes such as boxing and wrestling through the Criminal Code. Gambling and "fixes" were similarly restrained or outlawed.

But before the second world war no overall program for amateur sport development or a concern for recreation as an integral part of a national physical fitness plan had occurred. Meanwhile, music and the plastic arts were getting increasing support with the justification that these were intrinsic to culture; that sport, too, might be an aspect of culture was a European, not a Canadian, idea.

The provinces, too, eschewed a significant role, believing that their expenditures in education constituted a sufficient contribution to physical education. Early on, such activities – generally drill and gymnastics – found a niche in the public schools as an integral, though often begrudged, part of education.

By and large, Canadian high schools never took up the most broadly popular team games, such as cricket, lacrosse, baseball and hockey. In a limited way, rugby football and basketball were welcomed and sponsored with varying enthusiasm. But only in a few places at odd times did either game spill over from the high schools to mass neighbourhood and community participation. Soccer has always been the natural team game, spring and fall, for elementary schools, but neither its popularity nor continuity has been impressive.

Municipalities, with few exceptions, were indifferent to the needs of mass participation in sport. Sport lost or outgrew the leadership of the social élite in the interwar years and our national bodies and clubs were unable to cope with the scale and accelerating quality of international competition. Governments were slow to fill what quickly became a void – and an embarrassing one – in Canadian life.

Even so, the increase in leisure time and the intensification of national and international competition in amateur sport through the British Empire-Commonwealth Games, and later the Pan-Am Games, coincided with a halting movement towards a larger federal role. Grave misgivings about their autonomy notwithstanding, sports organizations needed money. It became increasingly clear that sports bodies in Canada were chronically amateurish in the worst sense of the word. Funding was the pry by which the federal and provincial authorities could influence the course of sport and recreation.

Starting with community-oriented programs such as fairs and exhibitions, governmental functions expanded slowly to include the provision of parks, arenas, canoe routes, hiking trails and boating facilities.

Jarred by the discovery that many volunteers for the military during the second world war were medically unfit, the federal government introduced the National Physical Fitness Act (1943) to encourage and finance, on a shared cost basis, provincial plans for fitness programs. But executive powers, official zealousness, and extensive funding were lacking. With victory, what official interest there was disappeared and the act was repealed in 1955 with politicians generally agreeing it had been a not very worrisome failure.

Seven years later came the federal Fitness and Amateur Sport Act. In the absence of alternate power structures, amateur sport's failings in quality competition had become clearly critical. The international performance of Canadians was dismal. National sporting bodies blamed a lack of funding, facilities and coaching. Not enough people cared.

The universities decried the absence of a strong provincial input, particularly for producing physical education teachers. The provinces rebuffed such comment by pointing to the increasing drain of education on public coffers. Sports editors railed about our steadily deteriorating international image in sport, and a scant few parliamentarians pressed for immediate action by Ottawa.

But the federal response was unambitious, limited largely to improving the level of sport for national and international competition. The emphasis was still on funding the initiatives of others and, as the Task Force Report on Sport recognized in 1969, the Fitness and Amateur Sport Act never lived up to the expectations of those who lobbied for it or those who framed it.

The task force itself, however, provided the drive for a substantial and central role for the federal government in sport. Most of its recommendations were acted upon by the Trudeau government, with John Munro vigor-

Former health minister, John Munro, was an outspoken defender of the Trudeau government's active encouragement of sports programs and physical fitness.

ously pushing and defending them, although in truth, defense was needed more for details, not for the thrust. Consquently, we have the federal government, post-1970, taking the responsibility for developing both sport and fitness. Ever-increasing amounts of money have been allocated. Departments of government as diverse as Indian affairs, DREE, the secretary of state through Opportunities for Youth and Local Initiative Program, as well as health and welfare, have become involved in sports and recreation. A complex administrative structure has been created and housed in Ottawa. The National Sport and Recreation Centre, Inc. is a corporation at arm's length from the federal government but financed by it. The corporation provides backing for an executive officer for each national sporting federation, a technical director for most, plus office, accounting, telephone, telex, reproduction, mailing, and public information services. The same support lies behind the Coaching Association of Canada and its research and training services.

It is reasonable to believe that this larger federal role, and the responses it has elicited from the provincial governments, is the most significant trend in contemporary sport. It is harder to divine its consequences or prophesy how some of the tensions and anomalies will be resolved. Its significance will be felt in quality and in the degree of mass participation.

One brute fact is that under the Fitness and Amateur Sports Act of 1962, annual spending of $5 million was authorized, yet this ceiling was never approached until 1969; in the mid-70s federal spending on sport is projected at more than $20 million annually.

Before John Munro became the minister responsible for sport in the federal government in 1968, there were no Canada Games, winter or summer, and no provincial games. There was no regular, national athletic scholarship and no bursary program. There were fewer than twenty full-time amateur sports executives and administrators in all of Canada before 1968. By 1973 there were several hundred.

"Game Plan '76" is the federally supported initiative to provide a better quality Canadian team for the Olympics in Montreal. It's a complex undertaking, involving the National Centre for Sport and Recreation, all the federations whose activities are on the Olympic program, the Canadian Olympic Association and the Olympic Trust.

The tensions, the potential dissension, the jealousies and the public niggling are many and real. The federal government as benefactor of sport is welcome; but the federal government as director of sport is another matter. The government sees itself as advisory rather than creative and direction-oriented. In 1973 Lou Lefaive, then the head of Sports Canada Corporation, said:

> Government sports administrators can't be more than a catalyst. The sports governing bodies are the ones really responsible in this country, and we are here to give them as much support and help as we can, whether it's money, or guidance, technical help, or whatever.

This is clearly unsatisfactory. It is not a sufficient response to the "serious difficulty" the task force saw as the lot of Canadian athletes.

The 1976 Olympics give a special urgency to questions about the level and nature of the government role in sport. A shoddy performance, in either the administration of the event or in the quality of Canadian athletic prowess, would seriously undermine the commitment that has been made. Sport and recreation under federal aegis, whatever their detractors may say, have achieved a fair momentum. An Olympic fiasco could lay waste the program so far established, deflate the enthusiasm of the administrators and, worst of all, wipe out the political support so far received.

Why the government? Have we simply fallen into the current habit of looking to it when other institutions should be our reliance in assuaging the ills or shortfalls in sport? The answers are obvious. No other in-

As the result of a task force report on sports in 1969, the government set up the National Sport and Recreational Centre to coordinate activities. Lou E. Lefaive is president.

stitutions can provide the expertise, draw on international experience, provide the crucial funding, and coordinate what should be a serious national effort at upgrading a deteriorating situation. However difficult it may be to equate the improvement of recreational and sporting standards with "peace, order and good government," the weakness of other bodies makes a strong governmental presence imperative.

Private sports bodies, such as the National Hockey League, the Canadian Football League, the Canadian Olympic Association, the Canadian Amateur Sports Federation, have shown themselves either unwilling to take any major responsibility, or to be without the authority or the resources to reach down to the community levels where the basic athletic endeavour takes place. In spite of vigorous attempts at upgrading our national bodies, they remain strongly influenced by a nickel-and-dime state of mind which, without direction, will retard sporting progress.

The universities, despite some giant strides in improving their facilities and programs, have failed at the provincial level to obtain the backing for expansionist designs. Too élitist and historically never identified with mass education in the fashion of American state universities, our universities have limited themselves largely to the production of health and physical education personnel and the fostering of rather insulated interuniversi-

ty competition. This is not to underrate some excellent intramural programs in our universities. But our universities, like our secondary and public schools, have been peripheral, rather than central, to our sports activity. Although the YMCA and YMHA, the Boy Scouts, the Girl Guides, the CYO and other youth organizations had a formative role in extending mass recreation, they are incapable, even if they saw it as their mandate, to muster the national initiative required to put sport at other than the professional level on a sound basis. No other organization or body can pretend to bring together the combination of factors required to sustain or to stimulate a creative and balanced national sports program which extends opportunities throughout the country. It is easy to see, therefore, why the federal government has already shouldered the responsibility for the championship-level athlete in such forums as the Canada and Arctic Games, and in support for a variety of Olympic programs.

Potentially crippling problems remain. Can the federal bureaucracy avoid administering creativity into oblivion? Amateur sports leaders, most of them conscious of the prerogative that comes from democratic election through their bodies, remain ambivalent about getting too close to governments or about devolving their authority to those they hire. Professionals are just as loathe to invite federal intervention in their autonomy and take the line that government regulation and control has no place in sport.

The challenge is to rationalize a diversity of individual efforts, to replace the unpaid volunteer with the professional in the administration, coordination and leadership of sports without extinguishing the volunteer's enthusiasm. The role of government at all levels is bound to expand and the techniques of influence, from funding to tax policy, will become more sophisticated and pervasive.

But why, it may well be asked, should sport be taken seriously either by governments or by the public at large? Surely more pressing matters confront society, whether they have to do with internal problems or those affecting our relations with the rest of the world? The short answer is that we have no quarrel with most of the traditional priorities of our politics; it is not intended here to argue that sport should be given a disproportionate place in our public life, in our national values, or in the structures of our educational system. But there is more to the question than this. Sport and recreation retain their eternal elements of joyful spontaneity and healthful exercise; but in today's overwhelmingly urban culture, they have come as well to be vital necessities, providing escape valves from the pressures of city life and its anonymities. Much of the criticism of sport and

317

W. Harold Rea, chairman of the board of
directors, Canada's Sports Hall of Fame, is the
man primarily responsible for the publication
of this book honouring the hall's athletes.

recreation is founded upon ideas deriving from
a simpler stage in our social development, upon
the confusion of the iniquities of giant commer-
cialized sport (which is more properly an aspect
of the world of business and finance) with the
less complicated world of play and recreation,
and upon simple ignorance of the importance of
physical activity to the well-balanced life.

Consider the views of the great
Canadian economist, Harold Innis, in his
Changing Concepts of Time. Innis represents
the very best in our intellectual tradition and
at the same time its one-sided, life-denying aspect. To this Western Ontario farm boy turned
intellectual and seer, sport and games were
matters of absolute futility and insignificance.
"The utter waste of thought and print in such
interests is a form of insanity which is worse
than a drug habit, as it implies a hopeless atro-

phy of the mind to interests which would help
it or develop it."

That a form of life was possible in
which full scope could be given to the development of all our faculties, physical as well as
mental, seems to have been beyond the
imaginative resources of Innis and the impov-
erished view of life and culture for which he
spoke. His mordant asceticism contrasts sharply with the breadth of the American philoso-
pher, George Santayana:

> Economic hatred of waste, become a passion, perse-
> cutes play, sport, ceremony and all the spontaneous
> homage that life pays to its own gracefulness and
> generosity. Such hatred assimilates play to vice,
> gambols to gambling, jollity to drunkenness, love to
> folly and religion to ignorant fear. . . . The econo-
> mists should remember that life itself is play, and
> utterly needless for making the planets go round the
> sun. It is only the free exuberance of forms springing
> up for no reason on the earth's surface that sets their
> hard duties on industry, commerce and morality,
> because exuberance is dangerous to itself.

In 1913, a Presbyterian minister named John
MacDougall, in *Rural Life in Canada,* celebrated the social and moral roles of play in a
manner that time has not withered. For him,
play and sports were great human needs; it was
not simply a question of athletics, or of amusement, but of the enrichment of life in childhood
and its refreshment in later years. Distressed
at the aridity and isolation of life in rural areas,
and at the mindless spectatorism of the urban
sports hippodrome, he wished to make freely
available to Canadians the "self-control, self-
reliance, self-denial" that derived from free
play:

> Play is one of the most ethical of human activities.
> In other activities we are largely controlled from
> without. In play we are most free. Play is spontane-
> ous; therefore self-expressive, and thus ethical. But
> it has also another great meaning. It is in play that
> the instinctive aversion of one individual to another
> is most fully overcome and the social spirit is fos-
> tered. It is when individuals come together with
> pleasure in mind that they merge so as to become a
> society, a community.

Today's government involvement in sports and
recreation is a recognition by politicians that
such activities have public significance. To the
politician, sport is chiefly about national prestige, though he may also see it as a cohesive
force cutting across our local passions. Recreation, for the politician, has to do with the fiscal,
medical and occupational advantages of creating a healthy population. More and more people, including politicians, are coming to see
that our present form of civilization has taken
us far from the natural environment from
which it sprang, at heavy cost not only to that
environment but to the human beings whom
civilization is organized to serve. Society at
large cannot go back to nature in which physi-

cal challenge and recreation were a normal and natural part of daily life.

Still, sport and games, the essence of which is freedom and spontaneity, seem to consort poorly with government intervention. Sports nationalism can spell élitism; public recreational programs can spell regimentation and bureaucratic empire-building. Clearly we need to provide the amenities and the opportunities, not only for our best athletes, but also for the population at large. Just as clearly, our historic forms of sports organizations are incapable of the task, whether for the people of the cities or for the inhabitants of regions of Canada for whom facilities for sport and recreation have never been available. Whether governments can meet the need, yet not kill the spirit, is the question. The need remains.

Where do these directions leave the parents of youth, the communities in which they are growing up, the so-called "private sector" of the economy, and the intangible but wonderful part so often played by the enthusiast for a sport who gives without expectation of any reward for his time and thought?

Around almost every member of our hall of fame can be found parents, teachers, coaches, clubs, communities, companies and an administering structure, which, in combination, provided the chances, the encouragement, the techniques or the competition to these exceptional athletes. None of these components to success is outmoded by the growing role of governments in sport.

While government support and initiative are to affect profoundly the future of sport, the role of the media is likely to remain minor, and at worst, rather negative. The chief reason why the media's role will only be mildly influential is because its attitude, like its sharply separated position in the papers and in the radio and TV schedules, is narrow, rather than comprehensive. Its leaders and pacesetters have always been committed to the pros, and the enormously colourful attractions of the continental – perhaps the more honest word is American – professional operations with their huge audiences of fans. Dick Beddoes of the *Globe and Mail,* at the Senate hearings on the mass media, labelled sports "the play-pen world," a world outside the serious and important aspects of real life. Many of his colleagues resent this attitude, but in fact demonstrate the truth of his observation by their utter rejection of any connection between sport and the wider concerns of our national life, and by the jealous resentment with which they regard the outsider who dares to challenge their sheltered fantasy world.

Sports reporters and columnists are usually ill-informed about, if not uninterested in, amateur and local sport. Lacking a unifying focus, and usually concerned with a limited, short-range perspective, the sport journalist has not influenced nor is he likely to affect the future course of sports development. Instead he will be there with the features, the adulation, and the boosting when the heroes and heroines emerge into remunerative professional glory and international stardom.

We are perhaps edging out of the radio-television age of sport. The mass audience, deeply fragmented by channel choices, is over-supplied. Hockey, in particular, like baseball before it in the US, has suffered from media overkill and the over-extension of so-called top teams and leagues. There are indications that more leisure does not necessarily mean more passivity but rather an increase in individual activities. It seems likely that media presentations of sports will slowly adjust to this trend. Networks face ever-increasing competition to satisfy their diverse audiences. The entry, or perhaps the re-entry, of women into sport, the burgeoning of national and international competition, and a more realistic attitude may in time lever the media into dealing with sports more interpretatively and critically and less as elements in a separate, unique world.

Whatever the input of federal and provincial participation, governments will never be able to dominate the complex of forces and motives which bring people into the practice and play of sports, nor to institute a new millenium in sports organization and administration. Certainly, the trend towards fitness for all through participation in organized, competitive sport should have a long and increasingly stronger run.

Canada has had an impressive sports history with many unique facets. The greatness of it only becomes apparent when we cease making invidious comparisons with what our larger neighbour and other older nations with longer, more stable traditions have done and are doing.

It is pointless to regret that our sport did not develop along the lines of the European emphasis on the sports club with its implicit assumption that sport is intrinsically cultural, or the American way with its placement of much sport within the high school and college contexts. Without the kind of top-level fostering given by the socialist states of Eastern Europe and Asia, Canadian sportsmen and athletes, almost spontaneously and from the very beginnings more than a century ago, have built organizational and competitive structures which led to national competition of one community against another, one region against another, East against West. No other nation has done anything like it quite as well. This has been done despite our space, our limited numbers and, until recently, our lack of affluence.

319

SPORTING HALLS OF FAME

Gerald Redmond, a professor of Physical Education at the University of Alberta, believes that the term "hall of fame" originated with the institution in 1901 of the Hall of Fame of Great Americans. In the late 1920s the U.S. National Ski Association proposed a ski hall of fame although a building for such a hall was not completed until 1954. In 1939 the Baseball Hall of Fame was dedicated at Cooperstown, N.Y. and the sporting fraternities in the United States and Canada turned to the creation of such halls with earnest enthusiasm.

Professor Redmond and Dr. Guy Lewis have written a book on such shrines. It was published in 1974 by the most prolific of sports publishers, A. S. Barnes of New York, and is titled *Sporting Heritage: A Guide to Halls of Fame, Special Collections and Museums in the United States and Canada.*

In 1943 the Canadian Amateur Hockey Association and National Hockey League approved the establishment of a Hockey Hall of Fame in Kingston, Ontario. Canada's Sports Hall of Fame was founded at the Canadian National Exhibition in Toronto in 1955. Although "The International Hockey Hall of Fame" was incorporated just after the end of the second world war and was to be built at Kingston, the slow progress in raising funds and obtaining a building resulted in the prior creation, side by side with Canada's Sports Hall at the CNE, of the National Hockey Hall of Fame. The Canadian Lacrosse Hall of Fame was established at New Westminster in 1965 where it is housed in the municipal buildings. The Canadian Football Hall of Fame was established in 1963 and housed in Hamilton in 1972.

We list those people inducted up to the date of printing in the three Halls of Fame honouring great players and builders in the major Canadian team games of hockey, football and lacrosse. By design these sports are hardly represented in Canada's Sports Hall of Fame. We have used the data supplied to us by those in charge of the halls.

THE HOCKEY HALL OF FAME
Toronto, Ontario

Alphabetical listing of members by category

Players	Year of Induction
Abel, S. G. "Sid"	1969
Adams, John J. "Jack"	1959
Apps, C. J. S. "Syl"	1961
Bain, Donald	1945
Baker, Hobart "Hobey"	1945
Barry, Martin "Marty"	1965
Beliveau, Jean A.	1972
Benedict, Clint "Benny"	1965
Bentley, D. W. "Doug"	1964
Bentley, Max	1966
Blake, Hector "Toe"	1966
Boon, Richard "Dickie"	1952
Bouchard, Emile "Butch"	1966
Boucher, Frank	1958
Boucher, George "Buck"	1960
Bowie, Russell	1945
Brimsek, Frank	1966
Broadbent, H. L. "Punch"	1962
Broda, Walter "Turk"	1967
Burch, William "Billy"	1974
Cameron, H. H. "Harry"	1962
Clancy, Francis "King"	1958
Clapper, Aubrey "Dit"	1947
Cleghorn, Sprague	1958
Colville, Neil	1967
Conacher, Charles	1961
Connell, Alex	1958

Cook, William "Bill"	1952
Coulter, Art	1974
Cowley, W. M. "Bill"	1968
Crawford, Samuel R. "Rusty"	1962
Darragh, John P. "Jack"	1962
Davidson, Allan "Scotty"	1950
Day, Clarence "Hap"	1961
Denneny, Cyril "Cy"	1959
Drinkwater, Charles G.	1950
Dunderdale, Thomas	1974
Durnan, William "Bill"	1964
Dutton, Mervyn "Red"	1958
Dye, Cecil H. "Babe"	1970
Farrell, Arthur	1965
Foyston, Frank	1958
Fredrickson, Frank	1958
Gadsby, W. A. "Bill"	1970
Gardiner, Charles "Chuck"	1945
Gardiner, Herbert	1958
Gardner, James H. "Jimmy"	1962
Geoffrion, Bernard "Boom Boom"	1972
Gerard, Edward "Eddie"	1945
Gilmour, H. L. "Billy"	1962
Goodfellow, E. R. "Ebbie"	1963
Goheen, F. X. "Moose"	1952
Grant, Michael "Mike"	1950
Green, Wilfred "Shorty"	1962
Griffis, Silas "Si"	1950
Hall, Joseph "Joe"	1961
Hainsworth, George	1961
Harvey, Douglas N.	1973
Hay, George	1958
Hern, W. M. "Riley"	1962

Hextall, Bryan	1969	Stewart, John "Black Jack"	1964
Holmes, Harry "Hap"	1972	Stewart, Nelson	1962
Hooper, C. T. "Tom"	1962	Stuart, Bruce	1961
Horner, G. R. "Red"	1965	Stuart, William "Hod"	1945
Howe, Gordon	1972	Taylor, Fred "Cyclone"	1947
Howe, S. H. "Syd"	1965	Thompson, Cecil "Tiny"	1959
Hutton, John B. "Bouse"	1962	Trihey, H. J.	1930
Hyland, Harry	1962	Vezina, Georges	1945
Irvin, J. D. "Dick"	1958	Walsh, Martin	1962
Jackson, H. "Busher"	1971	Walker, J. J. "Jack"	1960
Johnson, Ernest "Moose"	1952	Watson, Harry E.	1962
Johnson, I. W. "Ching"	1958	Weiland, R. C. "Cooney"	1971
Johnson, T. C. "Tom"	1970	Westwick, Harry	1962
Joliat, Aurel	1947	Whitcroft, Fred	1962
Keats, Gordon "Duke"	1958	Wilson, Gordon "Phat"	1962
Kelly, Leonard "Red"	1969	Worters, Roy	1969
Kennedy, Theodore "Teeder"	1966		
Lach, Elmer James	1966		

Referees	Year of Induction
Chadwick, William "Bill"	1964
Elliott, Chaucer	1961
Hewitson, R. W. "Bobby"	1963
Ion, Fred J. "Mickey"	1961
Rodden, Michael J.	1962
Smeaton, J. Cooper	1961
Storey, Roy "Red"	1967
Udvari, Frank	1973

Lalonde, Edouard "Newsy"	1950
Laviolette, J. B. "Jack"	1962
Lehman, Hugh	1958
LeSueur, Percy	1961
Lindsay, R. B. T. "Ted"	1966
MacKay, Duncan "Mickey"	1952
Mantha, Sylvio	1960
Malone, Joseph	1950
Marshall, John "Jack"	1965
Maxwell, Fred "Steamer"	1962
McGee, Frank	1945
McGimsie, W. G. "Billy"	1962
McNamara, George	1958
Moore, R. W. "Dickie"	1974
Moran, Patrick "Paddy"	1958
Morenz, H. W. "Howie"	1945
Mosienko, William "Billy"	1965
Nighbor, Frank	1947
Noble, Reginald	1962
Oliver, Harold "Harry"	1967
Patrick, Lester	1947
Phillips, Thomas "Tom"	1945
Pitre, Didier "Pit"	1962
Pratt, Walter "Babe"	1966
Primeau, A. J. "Joe"	1963
Pulford, Harvey	1945
Rankin, Frank	1961
Rayner, C. E. "Chuck"	1973
Reardon, Kenneth "Ken"	1966
Richard, Maurice "The Rocket"	1961
Richardson, George	1950
Roberts, Gordon	1971
Ross, Arthur H.	1945
Russel, Blair	1965
Russell, Ernie	1965
Ruttan, J. D. "Jack"	1962
Sawchuk, T. G. "Terry"	1971
Scanlan, Fred	1965
Schmidt, M. C. "Milt"	1961
Schriner, Dave "Sweeney"	1962
Seibert, Earl Walter	1963
Seibert, Oliver	1961
Shore, Edward William	1947
Siebert, Albert "Babe"	1964
Simpson, H. J. "Bullet Joe"	1962
Smith, Alfred "Alf"	1962
Smith, Reginald "Hooley"	1972
Smith, Thomas J.	1973
Stanley, Russell "Barney"	1962

Builders	Year of Induction
Lord Stanley of Preston G. C. B.	1945
Adams, Charles F.	1960
Adams, Weston W.	1972
Ahearn, Thomas Franklin	1962
Allan, Sir Montagu	1945
Brown, George V.	1961
Brown, Walter	1962
Calder, Frank	1947
Campbell, Angus D.	1964
Campbell, Clarence S.	1966
Dandurand, Leo V. J.	1963
Dilio, Frank	1964
Dudley, George S.	1958
Dunn, James A.	1968
Gorman, Thomas P.	1963
Hay, Charles	1974
Hendy, James C. V.	1968
Hewitt, Foster	1965
Hewitt, William A.	1947
Hume, Fred	1962
Ivan, Thomas N.	1974
Kilpatrick, Gen. John Reed	1960
Leader, G. Alfred	1969
LeBel, Robert	1970
Lockhart, Thomas F.	1965
Loicq, Paul	1961
McLaughlin, Maj. Frederic	1963
Molson, Sen. Hartland de M.	1973
Nelson, Francis	1947
Norris, Bruce A.	1969
Norris, James	1958
Norris, James D.	1962
Northey, William M.	1947
O'Brien, J. Ambrose	1962
Patrick, Frank	1958
Pickard, Allan W.	1958
Raymond, Sen. Donat	1958

Robertson, John Ross	1947
Robinson, Claude C.	1947
Selke, Frank J.	1960
Smith, Frank D.	1962
Smythe, Conn	1958
Sutherland, Capt. James T.	1947
Tarasov, Anatoli	1974
Turner, Lloyd	1958
Voss, Carl P.	1974
Waghorne, Fred	1961
Wirtz, Arthur W.	1971

THE FOOTBALL HALL OF FAME
Hamilton, Ontario

Alphabetical listing of members by category

Players	Year of Induction
Batstone, Harry	1963
Beach, Ormond	1963
Box, Albert "Ab"	1965
Breen, Joseph	1963
Bright, Johnny	1970
Casey, Tom	1964
Conacher, Lionel	1963
Cox, Ernie	1963
Craig, Ross B.	1964
Cronin, Carl	1967
Cutler, Wes	1968
Dixon, George	1974
Eliowitz, Abe	1963
Emerson, Eddie	1963
Etcheverry, Sam	1969
Faloney, Bernie	1974
Fear, A. H. "Cap"	1967
Ferraro, John	1966
Gall, Hugh	1963
Golab, Tony	1964
Griffing, Dean	1965
Hanson, Fritz	1963
Isbister, Robert (Sr.)	1965
Jackson, Russ	1973
Jacobs, Jack	1963
James, Eddie	1963
Kabat, Greg	1966
Krol, Joe	1963
Kwong, Normie	1969
Lawson, Smirle	1963
Leadlay, Frank "Pep"	1963
Lear, Les	1974
Lewis, Leo	1973
McGill, Frank	1965
Molson, Percy	1963
Morris, Ted	1964
Parker, Jackie	1971
Patterson, Hal	1971
Perry, Gordon	1970
Perry, Norm	1963
Quilty, S. P. "Silver"	1966
Rebholz, Russ	1963
Reeve, Ted	1963
Rowe, Paul	1965
Ruby, Martin	1974
Russel, Jeff	1963

Simpson, Ben L.	1963
Sprague, David S.	1963
Stevenson, Art	1969
Stirling, Hugh "Bummer"	1966
Timmis, Brian	1963
Tubman, Joe	1968
Welsh, H. "Huck"	1964

Builders	Year of Induction
Back, Leonard	1971
Bailey, Harold	1965
Brown, D. Wes	1963
Chipman, Arthur U.	1969
Currie, Andy	1974
Davies, Dr. Andrew P.	1969
DeGruchy, John	1963
Du Moulin, Septimus "Seppi"	1963
Foulds, William Crean	1963
Grey, Earl	1963
Griffith, Harry C.	1963
Halter, G. Sydney	1966
Hannibal, Frank J.	1963
Hughes, Billy	1974
Lieberman, M. I. "Moe"	1973
McCaffrey, J. P.	1967
McCann, Dave	1966
Montgomery, Ken G.	1970
Newton, Jack	1964
Ritchie, Alvin J.	1963
Rodden, Michael J.	1964
Ryan, Joseph	1968
Shaughnessy, Frank "Shag"	1963
Stukus, Annis	1974
Taylor, N. J. "Piffles"	1963
Warner, Clair J.	1965
Warwick, A. H. "Bert"	1964

LACROSSE HALL OF FAME
New Westminster, B.C.

Alphabetical listing of members by category

Players (Field Lacrosse)	Year of Induction
Allen, Angus J. "Bones"	1966
Bain, Frank "Piper"	1968
Barnett, Pete	1967
Beatty, Stewart	1967
Brennan, Paddy	1966
Brown, Blyth	1971
Clarke, Bun	1965
Conacher, Lionel	1965
Coulter, Bill	1967
Crookall, John "Dot"	1965
Davis, A. G. "Dutch"	1970
DeGray, Kelley	1968
Ewing, William "Buck"	1973
Feeney, George W.	1969
Feeney, Patrick	1966
Felker, Neil	1972
Fitzgerald, William J.	1965
Gibbons, David W.	1965
Gifford, Hugh W.	1969
Gifford, James	1965
Gifford, Tom "Sharkey"	1966

Godfrey, Harry	1970
Gunn, James	1972
Harshaw, Norman	1965
Hoobin, Henry	1965
Kalls, George	1965
Kendall, Gerald	1969
Lalonde, Edouard "Newsy"	1965
Large, Bert	1967
Longfellow, Edward	1965
McArthur, William	1965
McDonald, Angus D.	1968
Marshall, David "Bunk"	1967
Matheson, George	1965
Murray, Ernie	1965
Murton, "Sport"	1966
Peele, Clarence "Biscuits"	1965
Pickering, Harry	1965
Powers, Eddie (Sr.)	1967
Querrie, Charles	1965
Reeve, Edward "Ted"	1965
Rennie, George	1965
Spring, Clifford "Doughy"	1965
Sproule, George	1965
Stoddart, Haddie	1967
Storme, Thure	1971
Sullivan, Ed	1971
Thom, Gordon	1966
Thompson, George	1971
Turnbull, Leonard	1971
Vernon, John D.	1971
Wood, John W.	1967

Players (Box Lacrosse)	Year of Induction
Anthony, William	1965
Baker, Henry	1965
Baker, Ray	1967
Black, Clayton "Blackie"	1968
Bradbury, Ted	1969
Browning, Archie	1971
Bryant, Albert L.	1973
Carter, Harry	1971
Cavallin, John	1966
Cavallin, Roy "Fritzie"	1970
Cheever, Joe	1967
Dale, John	1967
Davidson, Charles	1967
Davy, Alfred	1965
Dickinson, William	1965
Douglas, James	1965
Downey, G. E. "Ed"	1966
Favell, Doug	1966
Ferguson, Arnold C.	1969
Fitzgerald, Jerry	1973
Fitzgerald, William K.	1970
Gair, Gordon	1969
Gimple, Gordon W.	1973
Hildebrand, Ike	1972
Isaacs, Bill	1965
Lee, Robert N.	1966
Lee, Walt	1967
McDonald, Blain	1970
McDonald, Wilfred "Bucko"	1971
McMahon, J. A. "Wandy"	1966
MacPhail, Don	1973
Madsen, Carl "Gus"	1965
Matheson, Don	1968

Morphett, Bill	1965
Morton, Roy	1968
Mulis, Bill	1972
Northrup, Jack	1972
Powless, Ross	1969
Sepka, Cliff	1973
Severson, Fred "Whitey"	1970
White, Eric "Rusty"	1965
Whittaker, Bill	1967
Wilkes, Bill	1965
Wilson, Bill	1965
Wipper, Harry R.	1971
Wootton, Lloyd	1965

Builders	Year of Induction
Anderson, Charles "Chick"	1973
Barnes, Edwin E.	1967
Bayley, Ed	1966
Beers, Dr. George W.	1965
Bishop, Jim	1969
Blair, Edward S.	1969
Brown, Albert "Ab"	1967
Calder, William G.	1971
Chisholm, Colin J.	1972
Conradi, Fred	1971
Dafoe, Dr. W. A.	1965
Damian, Brother	1968
Davis, Ivan "Turk"	1968
Dickinson, R. Lester	1971
Dopp, E. J. "Gene"	1965
Ferguson, Arnold C.	1969
Fletcher, Doug	1968
Friend, George	1972
Gair, Norman	1966
Gatecliff, Jack	1973
Gilmore, Les	1969
Gordon, Thomas	1969
Grauer, Carl	1970
Grauer, Rudy	1965
Hume, Fred	1965
Jacobs, Fred	1967
Jones, Con	1965
Kelly, M. E. F. "Mike"	1965
Kelly, Russell T.	1967
Lally, Joe	1965
Landon, Edwin	1972
McConaghy, Jim	1965
McDermott, Ed	1966
McDonald, Jack	1965
McKenzie, Dan	1965
McKenzie, Merv	1966
McLeod, J. C. "Jim"	1970
Maitland, Pat	1965
Miller, Douglas	1973
Murphy, Jim	1965
Nicholson, Leo	1967
Paul, Andy	1966
Peart, Clarence "Biscuits"	1970
Perrett, Dr. T. S.	1972
Phillips, R. H. "Pop"	1973
Rowan, Charles "Chuck"	1966
Smith, Leonard	1967
Spring, Gordon "Grumpy"	1966
Stimers, Rex	1971
Swanson, Oscar	1968
Waghorne, Fred C.	1965

BIBLIOGRAPHY

General Reading and Chapter I Genesis

Note: Entries marked "H" are especially useful for history; those marked "E" are exceptionally good reading.

Associated Press. *The Associated Press Sports Almanac, 1974* (an annual). New York: Dell, 1974.

EH Batten, Jack. *Champions: Great Figures in Canadian Sport.* Toronto: New Press, 1971.

EH Betts, John R. *America's Sporting Heritage: 1850-1950.* Reading, Mass.: Addison-Wesley, 1974.

EH ———. "Organized Sport in Industrial America". Ph.D. Dissertation, Faculty of Political Science, Columbia University, New York, 1951.

H ———. "The Technological Revolution and the Rise of Sport, 1850-1900". *Mississippi Valley Historical Review* 40 (1953): 231-56.

Blakeley, Phyllis R. *Glimpses of Halifax.* Halifax: The Public Archives of Nova Scotia, 1949.

H *Book of Sport, The.* 2 vols. New York: J. F. Taylor, 1901-04.

Bovill, Edward W. *English Country Life, 1780-1830.* Oxford: Oxford University Press, 1962.

Boyle, R. H. *Sport: Mirror of American Life.* Boston: Little, Brown and Co., 1963.

EH Brailsford, Dennis. *Sport and Society: Elizabeth to Anne.* Toronto: University of Toronto Press, 1963.

Brander, Michael. *A Dictionary of Sporting Terms.* London: Adam and Charles, 1968.

H Bull, William Perkins. *From Rattlesnake Hunt to Hockey.* Toronto: George J. McLeod, 1934.

Cosentino, Frank, and Howell, Maxwell L. *A History of Physical Education in Canada.* Toronto: General Publishing, 1971.

Cozens, Frederick W., and Stumpf, Florence. *Sports in American Life.* New York: W. B. Saunders, 1954.

Desjardins, Maurice. *Les surhommes du sport.* Montreal: Les Editions de l'Homme, 1973.

H Douville, Raymond, and Casanova, Jacques. *Daily Life in Early Canada.* London: Allen & Unwin, 1968.

Dulles, Foster Rhea. *America Learns to Play: A History of Popular Recreation, 1607-1940.* New York: D. Appleton-Century Co., 1940.

———. *A History of Recreation.* 2nd ed. New York: Appleton-Century-Crofts, Inc., 1965.

Dunning, Eric. *Sport: Readings from a Sociological Perspective.* Toronto: University of Toronto Press, 1972.

EH Frayne, Trent, and Gzowski, Peter. *Great Canadian Sport Stories.* Toronto: Canadian Centennial Publishing Company, 1965.

H Gard, Anson A. *The Hub and the Spokes, or, the Capital and its Environs.* Ottawa: Emerson Press, 1904.

Gardiner, E. Norman. *Athletics of the Ancient World.* Oxford: Clarendon Press, 1930.

Gillet, Bernard. *Histoire du sport.* Paris: Presses Universitaires de France, 1949.

H Guillet, Edwin C. *Early Life in Upper Canada.* Toronto: Ontario Publishing Co., 1933.

H Haley, Bruce E. "Sports and the Victorian World." *Western Humanities Review* XXII, No.2, Spring 1968.

H Hall, Ann. "Women's Sport in Canada Prior to

1914". Proceedings of the 1st Canadian Symposium on the history of sport and physical education, Edmonton, 1970.

H Harris, H. A. *Greek Athletes and Athletics.* London: Hutchinson, 1964.

———. *Sports in Greece and Rome.* London: Hutchinson, 1972.

EH Henderson, Robert W. *Ball, Bat and Bishop.* New York: Rockport Press, 1947.

———. *Early American Sport: A Checklist of Books by American and Foreign Authors Published in America Prior to 1860, Including Sporting Sons.* 2nd ed., revised and enlarged. New York: A. S. Barnes, 1953.

Holme, Anthea and Massie, Peter. *Children's Play: A Study of Needs and Opportunities.* New York: Humanities Press, 1970.

H Howell, Nancy and Maxwell. *Sports and Games in Canadian Life – 1700 to the Present.* Toronto: Macmillan Co. of Canada, 1969.

H Howison, John. *Sketches of Upper Canada.* Edinburgh: Oliver & Boyd, 1821.

E Huizinga, Johan. *Homo Ludens: A Study of the Play Element in Culture.* Boston: Beacon Press, 1955.

Jusserland, J. J. *Les sports et jeux d'exercice dans l'ancienne France.* 2nd ed. Paris: Plan-Nourret et Cie., 1901.

Kenyon, Gerald S., and Lay, John W., Jr. *Sport, Culture and Society – Reader on the Sociology of Sport.* New York: Macmillan, 1969.

Laurence, Henry Bockton. *Sketches of Canadian Sports and Pastimes.* London: Thomas McLean, 1870.

Lennard, Reginald, Ed. *Englishmen, at Work and Play: Some Phases of English Leisure, 1558-1714, by Members of Wadham College.* Oxford: Clarendon House, 1931.

H Lussier, Irenee. *Catholic Education and French Canada.* Toronto: W. J. Gage, 1962.

McBride, Peter. *Philosophy of Sport.* London: Heath, Cranston, 1932.

McIntosh, Peter C. *Sport in Society.* London: C. A. Watts & Co., 1963.

Mackie, Albert. *Scottish Pageantry.* London: Hutchinson, 1967.

Malcolmson, R. W. *Popular Recreations in English Society 1700-1850.* Cambridge: Cambridge University Press, 1973.

Menke, Frank G. *The Encyclopedia of Sports.* 4th rev. ed. New York: A. S. Barnes, 1969.

H Miller, Ivan, Ed. *Hamilton Centennial Sports Review.* Hamilton, Ont.: Centennial Sports Committee, 1967.

EH Paxson, Frederick L. "The rise of sport". *Mississippi Valley Historical Reviews* (1917).

Quinpool, John. *First Things in Acadia.* Halifax: First Things Publishers, 1936.

H Reed, T. A. *The Blue and White: A Record of Fifty Years of Athletic Endeavour at the University of Toronto.* Toronto: University of Toronto Press, 1944.

Revell, D. "Checklist of Current and Recent Publications on Canadian Sport". *Ontario Library Review* 48, February 1964.

H Roxborough, Henry. *Great Days in Canadian Sport.* Toronto: Ryerson, 1957.

———. *One Hundred – Not Out: The Story of Nineteenth-Century Canadian Sport.* Toronto: Ryerson, 1966.

Schulte, John, D. D. "Duty and Pleasure". *Canadian Monthly* 2, August 1877.

Steiner, Jesse. *Americans at Play: Recent Trends in Recreation and Leisure Time Activities.* New York: McGraw-Hill, 1933.

Stern, Theodore. *The Rubber-Ball Games of the*

Americas. New York: J. J. Augustin, 1950.

H Strutt, Joseph. *The Sports and Pastimes of the People of England.* London: Chatto and Windus, 1876.

Talbot, Edward Allen. *Five Years' Residence in the Canadas, including a tour through part of the United States of America in the year 1823.* New York: Johnson Reprint Corp., 1968.

Talmadge, T. De Witt. *Sports that Kill.* New York: Harper Bros., 1875.

Tennyson, Sir Charles. "They Taught the World to Play". *Victorian Studies* II (1958-9).

Van Vliet, Murray, ed. *Physical Education in Canada.* Toronto: Prentice-Hall, 1965.

Weiss, Paul. *Sport, a Philosophic Inquiry.* Carbondale, Ill.: Southern Illinois University Press, 1969.

Chapter 2 Montreal

An immense amount of printed material is available on Montreal generally and on sport in Montreal. McGill University Library, the Montreal Amateur Athletic Association and the Canadian Olympic Association have good collections of sports books, pamphlets and records. The Montreal Star library has much material. The most useful single history was Kathleen Jenkins's *Montreal; Island City of the Saint Lawrence,* published by Doubleday at Garden City, New York, in 1966. It includes a fine general bibliography.

H Becket, H. W. *The Montreal Snow Shoe Club . . . 1840 to the Present Time.* Montreal: Becket Bros., 1882.

H ———. *Saddle, Sled and Snowshoe.* Toronto: William Briggs, 1897.

E Beers, W. George. *Over the Snow or the Montreal Carnival.* Montreal: W. Drysdale, 1883.

H Canadian Wheelmen's Association. *Our City and our sports.* Souvenir official programme of the 12th annual meet, Montreal, July 1894. Montreal: Montreal Bicycle Club, 1894.

Collard, Edgar A. *Canadian Yesterdays.* Toronto: Longmans, Green, 1955.

H ———. *Montreal Yesterdays.* Toronto: Longmans, 1963.

H Cooper, John Irwin. *History of the Montreal Hunt, 1862-1953.* Montreal: Montreal Hunt, 1953.

Gibbon, John Murray. *Our Old Montreal.* Toronto: McClelland and Stewart, 1947.

H Jenkins, Kathleen. *Montreal; Island City of the St. Lawrence.* New York: Doubleday, 1966.

Montreal Amateur Athletic Association. *Souvenir of the New Club House.* Montreal: M.A.A.A., 1905.

Rexford, Elson Irving, Gammell, I., and McBain, A. R. *The history of the High School of Montreal.* Montreal: Old Boys' Association, 1951.

Chapter 3 Team Sports

There have been more books published on hockey and Canadian football than on all other sports. Most of them are straight biographies such as Jim Hunt's *Bobby Hull* (Toronto: Ryerson, 1966) or Andy O'Brien's *The Jacques Plante Story* (Toronto: McGraw-Hill Ryerson, 1972), but publishing of how-to-play books on hockey and football has also multiplied. We have listed only those books which are useful for historical purposes. In passing, we note that baseball is the team game that has drawn the most American authors and publishers. Only a few of the hundreds of baseball books touch on the game in Canada.

H Allan, Tony. *Football Today and Yesterday.* Winnipeg: Harlequin Books, 1962.

———. *Grey Cup Cavalcade.* Winnipeg: Harlequin

Books, 1959.

E ———. *Grey Cup or Bust.* Winnipeg: Stoval-Advocate Press, 1954.

H Altham, H. S., and Swanton, E. W. *A History of Cricket.* 2nd ed. London: Allen & Unwin Ltd., 1938.

E Batten, Jack. *The Inside Story of Conn Smythe's Hockey Dynasty.* Toronto: Pagurian Press Ltd., 1969.

H Beers, W. George. *The Game of Lacrosse.* Montreal: M. Longmore and Company, 1860.

EH ———. *Lacrosse: The National Game of Canada.* Montreal: Dawson Bros., 1869.

E Boucher, Frank, and Frayne, Trent. *When the Rangers Were Young.* Toronto: Dodd, Mead, 1973.

Bowen, Ronald. *North America in International Cricket.* Eastbourne, England, published by author, 1960.

H Boyd, Denny. *History of Hockey in B.C.: From the Denman Arena to the Pacific Coliseum.* Vancouver: Canuck Pub. Ltd., 1970.

Bryce's Canadian Baseball Guide for 1876. London, Ont., 1876.

EH Camp, Walter. *American Football.* New York: Harper and Bros., 1891.

Canada. National Advisory Council on Fitness and Amateur Sport. *Report on Amateur Hockey in Canada by the Study Committee on Hockey.* Ottawa: Dept. of National Health & Welfare, 1967.

Canadian Amateur Hockey Association. *Origin of Hockey in Canada.* Report submitted to the C.A.H.A. annual meeting, Toronto, April 1942.

Coleman, Charles L. *The Trail of the Stanley Cup.* 2 vols. Sherbrooke, Quebec: National Hockey League, 1966.

Conacher, Brian. *Hockey in Canada: The Way It Is!* Toronto: Gateway Press, 1970.

H Cosentino, Frank. *Canadian Football – The Grey Cup Years.* Toronto: Musson Book Company, 1969.

EH Currie, Gordon. *100 Years of Canadian Football: The Dramatic History of Canadian Football and the Story of the Canadian Football League.* Winnipeg: Greywood Publishing Ltd., 1968.

Da Grosa, John, ed. *A Complete Bibliography of Football.* Philadelphia: American Football Institute, 1935.

Drewe, George. *Cricket throughout the Empire.* Privately printed, Edmonton, 1926.

H Farrell, Arthur. *Hockey: Canada's Royal Winter Game: Handbook Containing a Short History of the Birth and Development, Its Rules, Hints on Training and Scientific Plays, with Sketches and Photography of Leading Teams, and Opinions of Expert Players.* Montreal: C. R. Corneil, 1899.

Fitkin, Edward. *The Gashouse Gang of Hockey.* Toronto: Baxter, 1951.

H Hall, John E., and McCulloch, R. O. *Sixty Years of Canadian Cricket, 1834-1894.* Toronto: Bryant Publishing Co., 1895.

H Herring, Donald Grant. *Four Years of Football.* New York: Carlyle House, 1940.

Hewitt, Foster. *Down the Ice.* Toronto, S. J. Reginald Saunders, 1935.

———. *Hockey Night in Canada.* Toronto: Ryerson, 1953.

Kidd, Bruce, and MacFarlane, John. *The Death of Hockey.* Toronto: New Press, 1972.

H Leah, Vince. *100 Years of Hockey in Manitoba.* Winnipeg: Manitoba Hockey Players' Foundation, 1970.

Lillywhite, Fred. *The English Cricketers' Trip to Canada and the United States.* London: F. Lillywhite, Kent and Company, 1860.

McAllister, Ron. *Football Stars, Today and Yesterday*. Toronto: McClelland and Stewart, 1950.

E McCabe, Eddie. *Profile of a Pro: The Story of Russ Jackson*. Toronto: Prentice-Hall, 1969.

McFarland, J. *Basketball at St. Francis Xavier University*. Antigonish, N.S.: St. Francis Xavier University Press, 1960.

E McFarlane, Brian. *Clancy: The King's Story as Told to Brian McFarlane*. Toronto: McGraw-Hill, 1968.

H ———. *Everything You've Always Wanted to Know about Hockey*. Don Mills, Ont.: Greywood Publishing, 1971.

———. *50 Years of Hockey: An Intimate History of the National Hockey League*. Toronto: Pagurian Press, 1969.

McNaught, W. K. *Lacrosse*. Toronto: Robert Marshall, 1873.

EH ———. *Lacrosse and How to Play It*. Toronto: Rose-Belford Publishing Co., 1880.

H Magoun, Francis. *History of Football from the Beginnings to 1871*. Bochum-Langendreer: Verlag, Heinrich Poppinghaus, 1938.

H Marder, John I. *The International Series: The Story of the United States and Canada at Cricket*. London: Kay & Ward, 1968.

H Naismith, James. *Basketball: Its Origins and Development*. New York: Association Press, 1941.

E O'Brien, Andy. *Fire-wagon Hockey: The Story of the Montreal Canadiens*. Toronto: Ryerson, 1967.

Padwe, Sandy. *Basketball's Hall of Fame*. Englewoods Cliffs, N.J.: Prentice-Hall, 1970.

Patton, B. M. *Ice-Hockey*. London: George Routledge & Sons, 1936.

E Percival, Lloyd. *The Hockey Handbook*. Rev. ed. New York: A. S. Barnes, 1961.

Proudfoot, Jim. *Pro Hockey '73-'74* (an annual). Richmond Hill: Simon & Schuster of Canada, Ltd., 1973.

E Reeve, Ted. *Grandstand Quarterback*. Toronto: Longmans, Green, 1955.

EH Roche, William V., ed. *The Hockey Book*. Toronto: McClelland and Stewart, 1953.

Roxborough, Henry. *The Stanley Cup Story*. 3rd ed. Toronto: Ryerson, 1966.

St. Catharine's Cricket Club. *The Canadian cricketer's guide containing full directions for playing the noble and manly game of cricket . . . by members of the St. Catharine's C.C.* St. Catharine's, Ont.: Constitutional Office, 1858.

Skrien, Dave, and Beddoes, Dick. *Countdown to Grey Cup*. Toronto: McClelland and Stewart, 1965.

Styer, Robert A. *The Encyclopedia of Hockey*. New York: A. S. Barnes, 1970.

EH Sullivan, Jack. *The Grey Cup Story: The Dramatic History of Football's Most Coveted Award*. Don Mills, Ont.: Greywood Publishing, 1971.

Tarasov, Anatoli. *Road to Olympus*. Toronto: Griffin House, 1969.

H Weyand, Alexander, and Roberts, Milton R. *The Lacrosse Story*. Baltimore: H. and A. Herman, 1965.

H Wheelwright, J. T. "A Football Game Thirty Years Ago." *Harvard Graduates Magazine* 13 (1905-6).

H Whiting, Colin F. *Cricket in Eastern Canada*. Montreal: Colmur Co'y., 1963.

E Young, Scott. *Hockey Is a Battle: Punch Imlach's Own Story*. Toronto: Macmillan Co. of Canada, 1969.

E ——— *The Leafs I Knew*. Toronto: Ryerson, 1966.

Chapter 4 Water Sports

Both canoeing and rowing were very well covered in the magazines before the first world war. Swimming has never had the same attention.

H Backman, Brian and Phil. *Bluenose*. Toronto: McClelland and Stewart, 1965.

H Berridge, Mavis. "The development of the Red Cross Water Safety Service and the Royal Life-Saving Society in Canada". Unpublished M. Sc. thesis. Madison: University of Wisconsin, 1966.

H Cleaver, Hylton. *A History of Rowing*. London: Herbert Jenkins, 1957.

Gibbon, John Murray. *The Romance of the Canadian Canoe*. Toronto: Ryerson, 1951.

H Grant, L. F. *History of the Lake Yacht Racing Association, 1884-1962*. Don Mills, Ont.: Lake Yacht Racing Association, 1962.

H Harding, William E., Comp. *Edward Hanlan, America's Champion Oarsman, with History and Portrait* (pamphlet). Toronto, n.d.

Henning, Harold, ed. *Rules and Laws Governing Swimming, Diving, Water Polo and Synchronized Swimming, 1969-1972*. Ann Arbor, Mich.: Braun-Brumfield, 1969.

H Hunter, Robert S. *Rowing in Canada since 1848*. Hamilton, Ont.: Davis-Lisson, Ltd., 1933.

McAllister, Ronald. *Swim to Glory: The Story of Marilyn Bell and the Lakeshore Swimming Club*. Toronto: McClelland and Stewart, 1954.

H Montreal Swimming Club. *Golden Jubilee Year, 1876-1925*. Montreal, 1925.

H O'Brien, H. *Historical Sketch of the Argonaut Rowing Club*. Toronto: Scott Printers, 1912.

H *The Ottawa Rowing Club Yearbook, 1900*. Including a section by Edward Hanlan. Ottawa: Federal Press, 1900.

H Riley, Con. *C.S. Riley*. (a privately published autobiography). Winnipeg, 1960.

Royal Life Saving Society, Ontario Branch. *Fifty Years of Progress with the R.L.S.S., 1908-1958*. Annual report, 1958.

H Snider, C. J. *Annals of the Royal Canadian Yacht Club, 1852-1937*. Toronto: Rous and Mann Press, 1937.

H Stone, Herbert L., Taylor, William H., and Robinson, William W. *The America's Cup Races*. New York: W. W. Norton, 1970.

Ziner, Feenie. *Bluenose, Queen of the Grand Banks*. Philadelphia: Chilton Book Co., 1970.

Chapter 5 Science & Strength

Aside from a few books published in French about strongmen such as Cyr and Victor Delamarre, there is an absence of Canadian monographs on these sports. However, the world literature on boxing and wrestling is varied and often of high calibre, particularly for the 19th century.

H Cox, William D. *Boxing in Art and Literature*. New York: Reynal & Hitchcock, 1935.

Britt, Jimmy et al. *La boxe; Anglais et Française, par les champions du ring*. Paris: Pierre Lafitte, 1911.

Desbiens, Raymond. *Victor Delamarre, "Superman du Quebec"*. Montreal: Les Editions La Press, 1973.

EH Fleischer, Nat. *John L. Sullivan: Champion of Champions*. New York: G. P. Putman's Sons, 1951.

H ———, comp. *The 1969 Ring Boxing Encyclopedia and Record Book*. New York: The Ring Back Shop, 1969.

E Johnson, Jack. *Jack Johnson Is a Dandy: An Autobiography*. Toronto: New American Library of Canada, 1970.

H Massicote, Edouard Z. *Athlètes Canadien-Français: Recueil des exploits de force, d'endurance, d'agilité, des athlètes et des sportsmen de notre race, de puis le XVIII siecle*. Montreal: Editions Beauchemin, 1900.

H Mongins, M. *La légende de Louis Cyr*. Montreal:

Editions Beauchemin, 1958.

Monpetit, A. N. *Nos hommes forts.* Quebec: C. Darveau, 1884.

Orban, William A. R. *Report to the Boxing Committee of the National Advisory Council for Fitness and Amateur Sport.* Mimeographed. June 14, 1968.

E Queensberry, Francis, 10th Marquis. *The Sporting Queensberrys.* London: Hutchinson, 1942.

E Strong, L. A. G. *Shake Hands and Come Out Fighting.* London: Chapman & Hall, 1938.

Weider, Ben. *Les hommes forts du Quebec.* Montreal: Editions du Jour, 1973.

———. *Louis Cyr: l'homme le plus fort du monde.* Montreal: Editions Beauchemin, 1958.

Chapter 6 Horses

Both the Ontario Jockey Club and the Canadian Trotting Association have kept good records of activities in their respective fields, and articles of some distinction on breeding, racing, the hunt and equestrianism have been appearing in Canadian magazines for over a century.

Beckwith, Brainerd K. *The Longden Legend.* New York: A. S. Barnes, 1973.

H Canada. House of Commons. *Special Committee on Race Track Gambling: Evidence taken . . . Relating to Race Track Gambling.* Ottawa: King's Printer, 1912.

H Canada. Royal Commission in Racing Inquiry. *Report of J. G. Rutherford, Commissioner.* Ottawa: King's Printer, 1920.

HE Coleman, Jim. *Hoofprints on My Heart.* Toronto: McClelland and Stewart, 1971.

Dodds, E. King. *Canadian Turf Recollections.* Toronto: Dodds Publication, 1909.

E Frayne, Trent. *Northern Dancer and Friends.* Don Mills, Ont.: Longmans Canada Limited, 1969.

H ———. *The Queen's Plate.* Toronto: McClelland and Stewart, 1971.

Guay, Donald. "Problemes de l'integration du sport dans la societe Canadienne, 1830-1865: Le cas des courses de chevaux." *Canadian Journal of History of Sport and Physical Education IV* (Dec. 1973) no. 2.

Hanson, Christelot. *Canadian Entry.* Toronto: Clarke, Irwin, 1966.

H *Lovers of the Horse: Brief Sketches of Men and Women of the Dominion Devoted to the Noblest of Animals.* Toronto: Hunter, Rose, 1909.

Luxton, Eleanor G. *History of Polo in Western Canada.* Unpublished paper. Calgary: Glenbow Institute, n.d.

MacEwan, Grant. *Hoofprints and Hitching Posts.* Saskatoon: Modern Press, 1964.

H Ontario. *Task Force Report on Off-Track Betting.* Toronto: Queen's Printer, 1972.

H Patteson, Thomas C. "The Ontario Jockey Club". *Dominion Illustrated,* July 1893.

———. "Race horses and their uses". A series of 12 articles in *Toronto News,* March and April 1905.

H Proctor, Frank. *Under Six Sovereigns: Fox Hunting in Canada.* 2nd ed. Toronto: Macmillan Co. of Canada, 1955.

H ———. *Fox-hunting in Canada and Some Men Who Made It.* Toronto: Macmillan Co. of Canada, 1929.

Ravenhill, F. G. *Horse Breeding in Canada* (pamphlet). Ottawa, 1887.

H Summerhays, Reginald S., comp. *Encyclopaedia for Horsemen.* Rev. ed. London: Frederick Warne, 1962.

Watson, W. P. *The Royal: A History of the Royal Agricultural Winter Fair.* Toronto: McClelland and Stewart, 1968.

H Valliere, D., ed. *100 Years of Racing: Canadian Horse Centennial Issue.* Rexdale, Ont.: Rexdale Publications, 1967.

Chapter 7 Shooting

The annual reports and records of the Dominion of Canada Rifle Association are the longest-running and the largest and fullest of any sporting organization in Canada.

H Boa, J. "Thirty years in the D.C.R.A., 1920-1950". *Canadian Marksman,* 1951.

H Burke, Desmond T. *Canadian Bisley Shooting: An Art and a Science.* Oakville: Desmond T. Burke, 1970.

Fauteux, Aegidius. *Le duel au Canada.* Montreal: Déom, 1934.

Hartman, Barney. *Hartman on Skeet.* Toronto: McClelland and Stewart, 1967.

Chapter 8 Winter Sports

The national organizations of the three major winter sports, figure-skating, skiing and curling, have all been assiduous in documenting their records and publishing programmes and reports.

Alpine Club of Canada. *Canadian Alpine Journal I* (1907).

E Batten, Jack. *Nancy Greene: An Autobiography, with Jack Batten.* Don Mills, Ont.: General Pub., 1968.

H Brown, Nigel. *Ice-skating: A History.* London: Nicholas Kaye, 1959.

H Creelman, W. A. *Curling, Past and Present.* Toronto: McClelland and Stewart, 1950.

H Douglas, H. P. *My Skiing Years.* Montreal: Whitcombe and Gilmour, 1951.

H Drummond, T., ed. *The Ski-runner in Canada.* Montreal Ski Club, 1912.

Jelinek, Henry, Jr., and Pinchot, Ann. *On Thin Ice.* Englewood Cliffs, N.J.: Prentice-Hall, 1966.

H Kerr, John. *Curling in Canada and the United States.* Edinburgh; C. A. Morton, 1904.

H ———. *History of Curling.* Edinburgh: David Douglas, 1909.

H Lunn, Sir Arthur A. *A History of Skiing.* London: Oxford University Press, 1927.

McCulloch, Ernie. *Ski the Champion Way.* New York: Harper & Row, 1967.

McLennan, Bob. *The Canadian Ski Scene, with Hillgrading.* Toronto: McClelland & Stewart, 1970.

E Maxwell, Douglas, ed. *Curling: An Authoritative Handbook of the Techniques and Strategy of the Ancient Game of Curling, as Described by Mr. Ernie Richardson and Miss Joyce McKee.* Toronto: Thos. Allen, 1962.

H Meagher, George. *Lessons in Skating.* New York: Dodd, Mead, 1900.

H *The Montreal Curling Club, 1807 – 1907.* A pamphlet published by the Club, Montreal, 1907.

E Ondaatje, Christopher, and Currie, Gordon. *Olympic Victory: The Story behind the Canadian Bob-sled Club's Incredible Victory at the 1964 Winter Olympic Games.* Toronto: Pagurian Press, 1967.

O'Rear, John and Frankie. *The Mont Tremblant Story: Including Skiing the Mont Tremblant Way.* New York: A. S. Barnes, 1954.

Rubenstein, Louis. *Skating in Canada.* London: Wyman & Sons, 1888.

Scott, Barbara Ann. *Skate with Me.* Garden City, N.Y.: Doubleday, 1950.

Sherman, Paddy. *Cloudwalkers: Six Climbs on Major Canadian Peaks.* Toronto: Macmillan Co. of Canada, 1965.

Stephenson, Lois and Richard. *A History and Annotated Bibliography of Skating Costumes.* Menden, Conn.: Bayberry Hill Press, 1970.

H Stevenson, John A. *Curling in Ontario, 1846 – 1946.* Toronto: Ontario Curling Association, 1950.

Watson, Ken. *Curling To Win.* Winnipeg: Stovel-Advocate Press, 1955.

E ———. *Ken Watson on Curling.* Toronto: Copp Clark, 1950.

Chapter 9 Track & Field

The three organizations which sponsor Canadian teams in the Olympics, the Pan-American Games and the Commonwealth Games are all active on a continuing basis and generally publish, either in periodicals or in "report" form, accounts or summaries of the membership and performances of Canadian teams (e.g., "Canada Competes at the Olympic Games, 1952", Montreal C.A.O., 1953). This is one of the best sources for material on track and field. Otherwise, articles over the years in general Canadian magazines such as *Maclean's* are the main means of tracing our best in track and field. Of course, there have been dozens of books published in Britain and the United States about the Olympics.

H Doherty, John K. *Modern Track and Field.* 2nd ed. Englewood Cliffs, N.J.: Prentice-Hall, 1963.

Hewitt, Foster. *Along Olympic Road.* Toronto: Ryerson, 1951.

E Kieran, John, and Daley, Arthur. *The Story of the Olympic Games, 776 B.C. to 1964.* Philadelphia: Lippincott, 1965.

Larouche, Jean-Claude. *Alexis le trotteur.* Montreal: Editions du Jour, 1971.

H Quercetani, Roberto L. *A World History of Track and Field Athletics, 1864 – 1964.* London: Oxford University Press, 1964.

H Redmond, Gerald. *The Caledonian Games in Nineteenth-Century America.* Cranbury, N.J.: Fairleigh Dickinson University Press, 1971.

H Roxborough, Henry. *Canada at the Olympics.* Toronto: Ryerson, 1963.

Chapter 10 Bowling, Golf, Tennis

It is easy to trace early history of golf, tennis, and badminton clubs through articles in periodicals. Few of the sports in this chapter, however, have been subjects for Canadian authors and publishers.

H Browning, Robert H. K. *A History of Golf: The Royal and Ancient Game.* New York: Dutton, 1955.

Coates, Len. *Challenge! The Story of Canadian Road Racing.* Sherbrooke: Progressive Publications, 1970.

H Denison, Merrill. *C.C.M.: The Story of the First Fifty Years.* Weston, Ont.: Canada Cycle & Motor Co., Ltd., 1946.

Grant, Doug. *Badminton: The Introductory Textbook to the Game.* Montreal: Graphic Pub. Co., 1950.

EH Potter, E. C., Jr. *Kings of the Court: The Story of Lawn Tennis.* New York: A. S. Barnes, 1963.

Sports Illustrated. *Book of Badminton.* Philadelphia: Sports Illustrated, 1967.

Whitman, Malcolm D. *Tennis Origins and Mysteries.* Detroit: Singing Tree, 1969.

Chapter 11 The Builders

H Bedecki, Tom. *An examination of the amateur code of Canada.* Unpublished manuscript. Ottawa: Dept. of National Health and Welfare, 1968.

H Barrette, Rosaire. *Leo Dandurand, Sportsman.* Ottawa: Le Droit, 1952.

H Crocker, John Howard. *Amateur Sports and Games in Canada.* Mimeographed pamphlet, prepared by the Amateur Athletic Union of Canada, 1953.

Hewitson, Robert E., ed. *Canada's Sports Hall of Fame.* Pamphlet. Toronto: C.N.E., 1967.

EH Hewitt, William A. *Down the Stretch.* Toronto: Ryerson, 1958.

Hussey, C. E. W. *Tait Mackenzie, a Sculptor of Youth.* Philadelphia: Lippincott, 1930.

E Kirshenbaum, J. "Bats and Busts, Size 15 Sneakers and a Dead Bird." *Sports Illustrated,* June 28, 1971, pp. 62-74.

H Lewis, Guy, and Redmond, Gerald. *Sporting Heritage: A Guide to Halls of Fame, Special Collections and Museums in the United States and Canada.* New York: A. S. Barnes, 1974.

EH Ross, Phillip Dansken. *Retrospects of a Newspaper Person.* Toronto: Oxford University Press, 1931.

EH Selke, Frank J., Sr., and Green, H. Gordon. *Behind the Cheering.* Toronto: McClelland & Stewart, 1962.

Chapter 12 Sports Journalism

Despite the billions of words produced by Canadian writers for sports pages and sports broadcasts, to our knowledge there are no substantial monographs or any substantial articles dealing specifically with the Canadian journalistic scene.

E Betts, John R. "Sporting journalism in Nineteenth-century America." *American Quarterly* (1953).

Foley, Ace. *The First Fifty Years: The Life and Times of a Sports Writer.* Windsor, N.S.: Lancelot Press, 1970.

Moscowitz, Jason. "A study of interaction between sports media personnel and amateur sports organizations." A mimeographed, unpublished study prepared for the Coaching Association of Canada, 1973.

Scanlon, T. Joseph. "Sports in the daily press of Canada". A mimeographed, unpublished study prepared for Sport Canada, Ottawa, 1970.

Turofsky, Louis J. *Photographs of Canadian Sports Events.* Toronto: Ryerson, 1966.

———. *Sports Seen: Fifty Years of Camera Work by Lou and Nat Turofsky, with Commentary by Ted Reeve.* Toronto: Ryerson, 1960.

E Woodward, Stanley. *Sports Page: The Story behind Newspaper Sportswriting.* New York: Simon & Schuster, 1949.

Chapter 13 The Future

Canada. *Report of the Task Force on Sports for Canadians.* Chairman, W. Harold Rea; members, Nancy Greene, and Paul Des Ruisseaux. Ottawa: Queen's Printer, 1969.

H Percival, Lloyd. *An Evaluation; Historical Background and Present Status of Sports and Fitness Standards in Canada; Analysis of Present Program; Available and Suggested Amendments and Additions.* Presented by Lloyd Percival, Fitness Institute, Toronto, to Hon. John C. Munro, Sept. 1st, 1970. Privately produced, mimeographed.

Percival, Lloyd, technical ed., and Taylor, J. W., ed. Proceedings of the International symposium on the art and science of coaching, October 1 – 5, 1971, held at the Fitness Institute, Toronto, under auspices of The Coaching Association of Canada and the Canadian Olympic Association, 3 vols.

H West, Tom. *Fitness, Sports and the Federal Government.* Unpublished study prepared for Sport Canada, Ottawa 1973.

INDEX

(† refers to Halls of Fame Membership Lists, pp. 320-323.)

(Numbers in bold type refer to biographies; numbers in italic type refer to photograph captions.)

Balding individual champion as Canada wins Wor

Tommy Burns
Only Canuck to Win World Heavy Title

Tommy Burns, only Canadian to wear the world heavyweight boxing crown, died yesterday in hospital at Vancouver. He was 74 and, at his death, was pursuing

Jim Jeffries, who had retired as world titlist the preceding year, refereed the bout. Hart stopped Root in 12 rounds and Jeffries presented him with the title. Hart's right to the

BOBBY KERR, ONCE WOR
TRACKMAN, AND HAS NEV.

This city of champions, the home of leaders in every conceivable line of athletics so many years,

and in 1901 Canadian c. to represen Olympic ga

His was

THE ROYAL GAZETTE, MONE

Former Sprint King Boasts
Great Career in Athletics

First Of Billiards Experts Arrives

CANADIAN SNOOKER CHAMP EAGERLY AWAITING DAVIS

Thinks Meeting Will Stimulate Billiards, Snooker Generally

Having recently made five century breaks in snooker to raise his total to 165, George H. Chenier, Canadian snooker champion and unofficial North American snooker champion, arrived by Trans-Canada Air Lines yesterday afternoon at Kindley Field, and will start practising for his exhibition matches with Joe Davis, world's champion, who is due to arrive in the Colony today.

Interviewed last night at the Eagle's Nest Hotel, where he is staying, Mr. Chenier told The Royal Gazette that his matches with Joe Davis would do snooker and billiards "a lot of good throughout the world."

"This tour," he said, "is going to cause a lot of talk in North America. In the United States, they love snooker and it is coming along well. It is a short game and has variety in it. It is going to be the game within two years. Our meeting might stir up quite a lot of interest in world tournaments."

He was full of extravagance in his praise of the Bermuda Amateur Billiards Association for arranging this exhibition. In Can-

The man has done a lot for himself and for the game. There is no doubt in my mind but that the man is a p and I've r

"You mi "that I playing Jo or another, I always him either or in Nor the condit so I took and agreed I am lool matches, a and billia who hibition ga cans are in

Rookie is most excited at Beliveau's 500th goal

The 22-year-old rookie who set up Jean Beliveau's 500th National Hockey League goal was more excited about the historic

ard, and Bobby Hull of Chicago Black Hawks are the other players to have reached the plateau.

Mahovlich and Norm Ull-

stopped a penalty shot by Minnesota's Jude Drouin.

North Stars were awarded the shot by referee Dave Newell after defenceman

into the clear for the second of his three goals at 6:10 of the final period. He scored his third less than five minutes later and Ken Hodge

Price 50c

Greenwood and Garden City Raceway Past Performances

Racing *Daily* Form

VOL. XLII. No. 273   654321T   TORONTO, ONTARIO, SATURDAY, NOVEMBER 14, 1964   50 CENTS EVERYWHER

Price 50c

Happy

By JACK MARKS
"It's gotta be great, the hell else could I f came the high-pitched of Al Balding, the Markland Wood golf pro nad just blistered Rome giata golf course with his and consecutive five-unde 57.
"That makes all three

SPORTS

KAREN SAVES CANADA FROM DOGHO